MODERNISM
1890–1930

Malcolm Bradbury was born in 1932 and has studied and taught at various universities in England and the United States. Since 1970 he has been Professor of American Studies at the University of East Anglia. A regular contributor to many magazines, he has been active as a literary critic. His publications include the novels *Eating People is Wrong* (1959), *Stepping Westward* (1965) and *The History Man* (1975) which received the Royal Society of Literature Award; a collection of short stories *Who Do You Think You Are?* (1976); and, in addition to critical essays, he has edited (with E. Mottram) *The Penguin Companion to Literature, Volume 3* (1971), *The Novel Today* (1977) and *Pudd'nhead Wilson* by Mark Twain for the Penguin English Library.

James McFarlane was born in 1920, and between 1947 and 1963 he taught at the Universities of Durham and Newcastle-upon-Tyne. Since 1964 he has been Professor of European Literature at the University of East Anglia in Norwich, and has served both as Dean of the School of European Studies and as the University's Pro-Vice-Chancellor. His special interests lie in the field of Comparative and European (particularly Scandinavian) literature and in the theory of translation. He has published several books on Ibsen and on Scandinavian literature, is General Editor of *The Oxford Ibsen*, and is editor of the journal *Scandinavica*. In 1975 he was awarded the Commander's Cross of the Order of St Olav for services to Norwegian culture; in 1977 he was elected to a Fellowship of the Norwegian Academy.

MODERNISM

1890 – 1930

EDITED BY
MALCOLM BRADBURY
AND
JAMES McFARLANE

PENGUIN BOOKS

Penguin Books Ltd, Harmondsworth, Middlesex, England
Penguin Books, 625 Madison Avenue, New York, New York 10022, U.S.A.
Penguin Books Australia Ltd, Ringwood, Victoria, Australia
Penguin Books Canada Ltd, 2801 John Street, Markham, Ontario, Canada L3R 1B4
Penguin Books (N.Z.) Ltd, 182–190 Wairau Road, Auckland 10, New Zealand

—

First published 1976
Reprinted 1978, 1981

—

Copyright © Penguin Books, 1976
All rights reserved

Made and printed in Great Britain by
Hazell Watson & Viney Ltd,
Aylesbury, Bucks
Set in Monotype Bembo

Contents

Notes on Contributors   9
Preface   13

PART ONE

1. *The Name and Nature of Modernism*
   (Malcolm Bradbury and James McFarlane)   19

2. *The Cultural and Intellectual Climate of Modernism*   57
   The Double Image (Alan Bullock)   58
   The Mind of Modernism (James McFarlane)   71

3. *A Geography of Modernism*   95
   The Cities of Modernism (Malcolm Bradbury)   96
   Berlin and the Rise of Modernism 1886–96
      (James McFarlane)   105
   Vienna and Prague 1890–1928 (Franz Kuna)   120
   Modernism in Russia 1893–1917 (Eugene Lampert)   134
   Chicago and New York: Two Versions of
      American Modernism (Eric Homberger)   151
   Revolt, Conservatism and Reaction in Paris
      1905–25 (Eric Cahm)   162
   London 1890–1920 (Malcolm Bradbury)   172

4. *Literary Movements*   191
   Movements, Magazines and Manifestos: The
      Succession from Naturalism (Malcolm Bradbury
      and James McFarlane)   192
   Symbolism, Decadence and Impressionism
      (Clive Scott)   206
   Imagism and Vorticism (Natan Zach)   228

Contents

Italian Futurism (Judy Rawson)   243

Russian Futurism (G. M. Hyde)   259

German Expressionism (Richard Sheppard)   274

Dada and Surrealism (Robert Short)   292

PART TWO

5. *The Lyric Poetry of Modernism*   311

    The Modernist Lyric (Graham Hough)   312

    The Crisis of Language (Richard Sheppard)   323

    The Poetry of the City (G. M. Hyde)   337

    The Prose Poem and Free Verse (Clive Scott)   349

    Poems and Fictions: Stevens, Rilke, Valéry
      (Ellman Crasnow)   369

    German Expressionist Poetry (Richard Sheppard)   383

6. *The Modernist Novel*   393

    The Introverted Novel (John Fletcher and
      Malcolm Bradbury)   394

    The Theme of Consciousness: Thomas Mann
      (J. P. Stern)   416

    Svevo, Joyce and Modernist Time
      (Michael Hollington)   430

    The Janus-faced Novel: Conrad, Musil,
      Kafka, Mann (Franz Kuna)   443

    The Symbolist Novel: Huysmans to Malraux
      (Melvin J. Friedman)   453

    The City of Russian Modernist Fiction
      (Donald Fanger)   467

    The Language of Modernist Fiction:
      Metaphor and Metonymy (David Lodge)   481

7. *Modernist Drama*   497

    Modernist Drama: Origins and Patterns
      (John Fletcher and James McFarlane)   499

    Intimate Theatre: Maeterlinck to Strindberg
      (James McFarlane)   514

Contents

Modernist Drama: Wedekind to Brecht
(Martin Esslin)   527

Neo-modernist Drama: Yeats and Pirandello
(James McFarlane)   561

Chronology of Events   571
Brief Biographies   613
Bibliography   641
Index   665

Notes on Contributors

MALCOLM BRADBURY is Professor of American Studies at the University of East Anglia. His publications include *The Social Context of Modern English Literature* (1971) and *Possibilities: Essays on the State of the Novel* (1973). He is also himself the author of three novels.

JAMES MCFARLANE is Professor of European Literature at the University of East Anglia. He is General Editor of *The Oxford Ibsen* (8 vols., 1960ff), and editor of *Scandinavica: An International Journal of Scandinavian Studies*; his publications include *Ibsen and the Temper of Norwegian Literature* (1960) and other works of literary criticism.

*

ALAN BULLOCK is Master of St Catherine's College, Oxford. His publications include *Hitler: A Study in Tyranny* (1952, revised 1964), *The Liberal Tradition* (1956), *The Life and Times of Ernest Bevin* (1960ff), and he is Joint General Editor of *The Oxford History of Modern Europe*. He was knighted in 1972, and made a life peer in 1976.

ERIC CAHM has since 1973 been Head of the School of Languages and Area Studies at Portsmouth Polytechnic. He is a specialist in pre-1914 French political and cultural history; his previous publications include *Péguy et le nationalisme français* (1972) and *Politics and Society in Contemporary France 1789–1971* (1972).

ELLMAN CRASNOW is a lecturer in English and American Literature in the School of English and American Studies, University of East Anglia.

MARTIN ESSLIN has been Head of B.B.C. Radio Drama since 1963. His books include *Brecht – A Choice of Evils* (1959), *The Theatre of the Absurd* (1962), *Brief Chronicles – Essays on Modern Theatre* (1970) and *Pinter – A Study of his Plays* (1970); he has edited an anthology on *The*

Genius of the German Theatre (1968) and a volume of critical essays on *Samuel Beckett* (1965).

DONALD FANGER is Professor of Slavic and Comparative Literature at Harvard University. The author of *Dostoevsky and Romantic Realism* and numerous articles on nineteenth- and twentieth-century literature, Russian, English and French, he is currently completing a book on Nikolai Gogol.

JOHN FLETCHER is Professor of Comparative Literature in the School of European Studies, University of East Anglia, and specializes in the theory of fiction and in the aesthetics of drama, cinema and television; he is probably best known for his work on Samuel Beckett. His most recent book was *Claude Simon and Fiction Now* (1975).

MELVIN J. FRIEDMAN is Professor of Comparative Literature and English at the University of Wisconsin–Milwaukee. A former editor of *Comparative Literature Studies* and *Wisconsin Studies in Contemporary Literature*, he is the author or editor of some dozen books, the most recent of which are *William Styron* (1974) and *Samuel Beckett Now* (2nd edition 1975). In 1972 he was a Visiting Senior Fellow at the University of East Anglia, and in 1976 Fulbright Senior Lecturer at the University of Antwerp.

MICHAEL HOLLINGTON is a lecturer in Comparative Literature in the University of East Anglia.

ERIC HOMBERGER studied at the Universities of California (Berkeley), Chicago and Cambridge and is now a lecturer in American Literature at the University of East Anglia. His publications include *A Chronological Checklist of the Periodical Publications of Sylvia Plath* (1970), *The Cambridge Mind* (ed. 1972) and *Ezra Pound: The Critical Heritage* (ed. 1972); *The Art of the Real*, a study of English and American poetry since 1939, will be published in 1976.

GRAHAM HOUGH was until his recent retirement Professor of English at the University of Cambridge. Among his many publications are *The Last Romantics* (1949), *The Dark Sun* (1957), *Image and Experience* (1960), *An Essay on Criticism* (1966) and *Style and Stylistics* (1969).

Notes on Contributors

G. M. HYDE has since 1969 been Lecturer in Comparative Literature at the University of East Anglia, where he was appointed after studying at the Universities of Cambridge and Essex. His publications include a translation of Mayakovsky's *How Are Verses Made?* (1974) and several articles; his book on Nabokov is to appear in 1976.

FRANZ KUNA is Reader in German in the School of European Studies in the University of East Anglia. His publications include *T. S. Eliot: Die Dramen* (2nd revised edition 1972) and *Kafka* (1974).

EUGENE LAMPERT, Lic-ès-lettres, D.Phil, F.R.S.L., is Professor and Head of the Department of Russian Studies, University of Keele. His special field of study is nineteenth- and early twentieth-century Russian intellectual history. His publications, which are mainly in this field, include *N. Berdyaev and the New Middle Ages, Studies in Rebellion,* and *Sons against Fathers.*

DAVID LODGE is Professor of Modern English Literature at the University of Birmingham. His publications include *Language of Fiction* (1966), *The Novelist at the Crossroads* (1971) and several novels, of which the most recent is *Changing Places* (1975). He edited George Eliot's *Scenes of Clerical Life* for the Penguin English Library, and *Twentieth-Century Literary Criticism: A Reader* (1973).

JUDY RAWSON is Senior Lecturer in Italian and Chairman of the Italian Department at the University of Warwick. Her publications include a translation of Machiavelli's *History of Florence*, and an edition of Ignazio Silone's novel *Fontamara.*

CLIVE SCOTT is a lecturer in the School of European Studies in the University of East Anglia.

RICHARD SHEPPARD is a lecturer in the School of European Studies in the University of East Anglia. His publications include *On Kafka's Castle* (1973); a book on *Dada* is in preparation.

ROBERT SHORT is Senior Lecturer in the School of European Studies at the University of East Anglia, and teaches modern European history.

He is co-author (with Roger Cardinal) of *Surrealism: Permanent Revelation* (1970) and has written a number of articles on various aspects of Surrealism. His main area of research interest lies in the politics of the *avant-garde* and of French intellectuals between the wars.

J. P. STERN is Professor of German and Head of Department at University College London, author of *Ernst Jünger: a Writer of Our Time* (1952); *Re-Interpretations: Seven Studies in Nineteenth-century German Literature* (1964); *Thomas Mann* (1967); *Idylls and Realities: Studies in Nineteenth-century German Literature* (1971); *On Realism* (1972); *Hitler: The Führer and the People* (1975).

NATAN ZACH is Senior Lecturer in Modern Comparative Studies in the Department of Comparative Literature, University of Haifa. Having studied philosophy at the Hebrew University of Jerusalem, he obtained his doctorate at Essex on the subject of 'Imagism: The Poetic of Hardness'. A leading Israeli poet and critic, his publications include *The Concept of Time in Bergson and Modern Poetry* (1967).

Preface

THIS is not, nor in the nature of things could it ever satisfactorily be, a comprehensive survey, a tidily finished account. To suppose that one could open up for composed inspection – like some fully excavated monument, trimly grassed and paved, confidently signposted, labelled and docketed – the kind of site that Modernism represents is to misunderstand the very nature of the phenomenon. However much it may have come to seem in the last twenty or thirty years that the great twentieth-century Modernist movement in literature is over, become historical, and that we have now moved into a different aesthetic, a new historical milieu, we nevertheless find ourselves constantly reminded that Modernism is in many of its features still very much *our* literature, still holds the kind of novelty that startles and disturbs, is still contentious, difficult to remain detached from, hard to talk about. That this literature remains perplexing, that we of today are in significant ways still of it, and that the critical arguments about it are still not yet out of the formative stage, was very much in our minds as we planned this book.

Unlike some other volumes in this series, the text has been written by many contributors (including a number of our colleagues who cooperate in teaching in this area at the University of East Anglia). In the interests of cohesiveness and continuity of style, the text has been here and there considerably revised by the editors. This pluralistic method is itself elegantly consistent with the relativism and perspectivism of Modernism; our intent was that various very different modes of approach to the topic, different central issues in its consideration, should be visible. We have therefore instructed ourselves and encouraged our contributors to execute a series of trenchings, boreholings, cross-sectionings through and across and into an area of which the proper demarcation remains in dispute. In the end we have concentrated on the years between 1890 and 1930 (for reasons argued in the body of the book); we have ranged not only across the continental European

13

literatures but also into English and American, for one of the defining features of Modernism has been the breaking down of traditional national frontiers in matters of literary and cultural concern. Our editorial task we have then seen as collating and ordering – not without numerous queries back – reports which were essentially heterogeneous in both scope and purpose, with the aim of composing not a survey, not a meticulously balanced and comprehensive inventory in which the separate entries were controlled and metered and sized to some 'handbook' notion of the relative importance of individual writers, but rather a stimulating anthology of distinct but mutually reinforcing accounts. This has meant that there are writers of great importance (one thinks, for example, of Bérnard Shaw, Stefan George, Sigrid Undset) who in a quantitative sense are significantly under-represented here, though the Brief Biographies and the Bibliography at the end of the volume are designed, among other purposes, to make clear what has inevitably had to be cut from so complex a topic in a book of this size. Finally, the pieces in this book raise questions about the nature of critical analysis itself, and of the kinds of analysis to which Modernism itself might be thought susceptible; for in many respects Modernism was itself a critical movement with deep implications for, and powerful influences upon, the problems of contemporary criticism. Moreover, the records themselves, though extensive, are not always particularly well collated, and we wished to establish much by way of background: to look at the ideas, the milieux, the groupings, the social tensions out of which Modernism emerged, as well as at the texts themselves. Hence the basic format of our book offers in its first part an extensive guide to these matters before contemplating the works themselves. The geographical, ideological, generic, national and thematic incisions made by our contributors will, it is hoped, lay bare those layers of Modernist achievement to which the reader's enquiring mind will find the essential relations.

There were technical problems about the dating of works. Sometimes (as with Freud's *Die Traumdeutung*) the date on the title page was not the actual year of publication; sometimes (as with Sorel's *Réflexions sur la violence*) a work was first published as a series of articles, or (as with Wedekind's drama *Der Marquis von Keith*) given periodical publication, prior to appearing in book form; sometimes the date of a play's first performance was a better guide to its historical

Preface

significance than its year of publication. Occasionally the complications are compound: Brecht's *Im Dickicht der Städte* underwent modification in the course of performance in 1923 and 1924 to both its title and its text before its final publication in 1927. And so on. Nor was it always the case that every contributor's purpose was best served by arbitrary adherence to some common date. Although, then, we have tried to eliminate from the body of our text what might at first sight have looked like merely careless inconsistency, it has to be admitted that it was not always possible to achieve *total* truth in a single simple date or even in a summary phrase.

As well as thanking all our collaborators for their patience and forbearance, for their ready and generous response to our editorial promptings during the relatively long period of the volume's growth, we would at the same time like to single out one or two names for particular mention: Enid Self, Jeannie Scriven and Carol Long for their skilled secretarial assistance; Diane DeBell for selflessly taking on much of the onerous task of collating the notes and preparing the Bibliography; Robin Young for his contributions to the Chronology of Events and the Brief Biographies; Dr Carla Lathe for preparing the index; and Professor John Fletcher, whose initiatives not merely as an orthodox contributor but also as one who has helped influentially to give editorial shape to the book have been invaluable. Michael Mason of the B.B.C., producer of a series of radio talks some of which have been drawn upon here, gave great help. James McFarlane is also glad to acknowledge the generous award of a Leverhulme European Faculty Fellowship for the year 1972–3 which materially facilitated the writing and editing of this volume.

University of East Anglia

Norwich

February 1974

M. S. B.

J. W. MCF.

PART ONE

ONE

The Name and Nature of Modernism

MALCOLM BRADBURY AND JAMES MCFARLANE

'Unlike dates, periods are not facts. They are retrospective conceptions that we form about past events,
useful to focus discussion, but very often leading historical thought astray.'

G. M. Trevelyan

I

CULTURAL seismology – the attempt to record the shifts and displace-
ments of sensibility that regularly occur in the history of art and literature and thought – habitually distinguishes three separate orders of
magnitude. At one end of the scale are those tremors of fashion that
seem to come and go in rhythm with the changing generations, the
decade being the right unit for measuring the curves that run from
first shock to peak activity and on to the dying rumbles of derivative
Epigonentum. To a second order of magnitude belong those larger dis-
placements whose effects go deeper and last longer, forming those
extended periods of style and sensibility which are usefully measured
in centuries. This leaves a third category for those overwhelming
dislocations, those cataclysmic upheavals of culture, those fundamental
convulsions of the creative human spirit that seem to topple even the
most solid and substantial of our beliefs and assumptions, leave great
areas of the past in ruins (noble ruins, we tell ourselves for reassurance), question an entire civilization or culture, and stimulate frenzied
rebuilding. That the twentieth century brought us a new art is undeniable, and it is the purpose of this volume to explore some of its
crucial manifestations. But we have also increasingly come to believe

that this new art comes from, or is, an upheaval of the third and cataclysmic order.

This view is not surprising; one of the features of the age we are talking about is that it is remarkably historicist, disposed to apocalyptic, crisis-centred views of history. So familiar is the view that it needs only brief exemplification. Herbert Read, for instance, writing in 1933, puts the point succinctly:

> There have been revolutions in the history of art before today. There is a revolution with every new generation, and periodically, every century or so, we get a wider or deeper change of sensibility which is recognized as a period – the Trecento, the Quattro Cento, the Baroque, the Rococo, the Romantic, the Impressionist and so on. But I do think we can already discern a difference in kind in the contemporary revolution: it is not so much a revolution, which implies a turning over, even a turning back, but rather a break-up, a devolution, some would say a dissolution. Its character is catastrophic.

Contemplating the impact first of Gauguin and Van Gogh, then of Picasso, Read claimed that 'we are now concerned, not with a logical development of the art of painting in Europe, not even with a development for which there is any historical parallel, but with an abrupt break with all tradition . . . The aim of five centuries of European effort is openly abandoned.'¹ The late C. S. Lewis constructed his inaugural lecture at Cambridge in 1954, *De Descriptione Temporum*, on a similar notion. In his view, the greatest of all divisions in the entire history of western man – greater than that which divides Antiquity from the Dark Ages, or the Dark from the Middle Ages – is that separating the present from the age of Jane Austen and Walter Scott. In politics, religion, social values, art and literature, a chasm lies between:

> I do not think that any previous age produced work which was, in its own time, as shatteringly and bewilderingly new as that of the Cubists, the Dadaists, the Surrealists, and Picasso has been in ours. And I am quite sure this is true . . . of poetry . . . I do not see how anyone can doubt that modern poetry is not only a greater novelty than any other 'new poetry' but new in a new way, almost in a new dimension.²

Latterly there have been attempts to locate the Great Divide even more precisely: the French critic Roland Barthes identifies it with the pluralization of world-views deriving from the evolution of new classes and communications and puts it at mid-century: 'Around 1850 ... classical writing therefore disintegrated, and the whole of literature, from Flaubert to the present day, became the problematics of language.'[3]

As a general article of belief – before the fretful details are reached and the character and causes analysed – the idea of a Great Divide between past and present, art before and art now, has drawn much allegiance. But it is also a fact that about the nature of the modern situation, and the consequences for that situation on the form and character of art, there is less than unanimity. '*Il faut être absolument moderne*' ('It is necessary to be absolutely modern'): Rimbaud's exhortation has a particular appeal to our temper, but it is subject to many interpretations. And the stylistic plurality of twentieth-century art – a plurality so great that André Malraux speaks, in *Les voix du silence* (*The Voices of Silence*), of the 'imaginary museum' of stylistic heterodoxy that marks our age – reminds us how variously it has been interpreted, by writers and artists themselves, and of course by the critics and commentators. There is an abundance of accounts of the condition of modern art, and a wealth of explanation of its character and causes. Most of these views are apocalyptic; though one is that our art is not totally divorced from tradition and humanism, and that there is nothing especially singular and novel about our art and situation at all. In the present state of artistic and critical opinion – a highly fluid state marked by sharp differences of view – then perhaps the most any account can offer is a personal or at least partial version of an overwhelmingly complex phenonemon, an individual selection from the infinity of detail, which may in time compost down with other views into that sifted and resolved thing, a critical concept.

But if about the phenomenon there is much variety and conflict of opinion, there is, alas, growing agreement about its name. Clearly the world of criticism has settled for some variant or collocation of the word 'modern' to identify the arts of its time, or if not all of them, then some part of them. So the Modern Movement; the Modern Tradition; the Modern Age; the Modern Century; the Modern Temper; Modernism; or – to all appearances a Germanic neologism, though presumably by analogy with labels like the Renaissance and the Enlightenment – simply The Modern, *tout court*. One's regret at the choice is not only that it predetermines the nature of our view of modern literature; it also comes from the inappropriateness of applying so semantically mobile and indeed febrile a term to a historical phenomenon we now wish to root in time. Modernity, in normal usage, is something that progresses in company with and at the speed of the years, like the bow-wave of a ship; last year's modern is not this year's. Apt as it is to the sensibility of the age to prefer such terms, to insist on the association with time and history, matters have now reached the point where we wish to fix and stabilize the modern. When an extra-historical dimension is admitted, when – following G. S. Fraser or the editors of *The Modern Tradition*[4] – one claims as 'modern' Catullus (but not Virgil), Villon (but not Ronsard), Donne (but not Spenser), Clough (but not Tennyson), and when one does the same for one's own time (Conrad, but not Galsworthy), the semantic instability of the term becomes obvious. Modernity is a crucial word for us, but it is tied up with definitions of our situation which are subject to change. The notion of the 'modern' undergoes semantic shift much faster than similar terms of comparable function, like 'romantic' or 'neo-classical'; indeed, as Lionel Trilling says, it can swing round in meaning until it is facing in the opposite direction.[5] We use the term historically to locate a distinct stylistic phase which is ceasing or has ceased (hence the current circulation of counters like Proto-Modernism, Palaeo-Modernism, Neo-Modernism and Post-Modernism). We also use it to sum up a permanent modern-ising state of affairs and the state of mind and view of man it engenders – that 'type of consciousness frequent in the modern world, obsessed by a compulsion to keep up, reduced to despair by the steadily increasing speed of the total movement'.[6] Yet the word retains its force because of its association with a characteristic contemporary feeling: the historicist feeling that we live in totally novel times, that contemporary history is the source of our significance, that we are derivatives not of the past but of the surrounding and enfolding environment or scenario, that modernity is a new consciousness, a fresh condition of the human mind – a condition which modern art has explored, felt through, sometimes reacted against.

The name, then, is clear; the nature of the movement or movements – the where, when, why and what of it – is much less so. And equally unclear is the status of the stylistic claim we are making. We have noted that few ages have been more multiple, more promiscuous in artistic style; to distil from the multiplicity an overall style or mannerism is a difficult, perhaps even an impossible, task. We can describe eighteenth-century literature in western countries as 'Neo-Classical', nineteenth-century literature in even more countries as 'Romantic'; though the labels paper over innumerable cracks, we can suggest a general drift in most of the significant arts among most of the significant artists we are dealing with in those periods. A. O. Lovejoy has pointed out that we use the term 'romanticism' to mean not only a wide variety of different things but a wide variety of contradictory things.[7] So we do; and the quest for definition is now raging again. But Romanticism has a recognizable general meaning and serves as a broad stylistic description of a whole era. What, though, is so striking about the modern period is that there is no word we can use in quite that same way. Modernism has been used, from time to time, analogously to Romanticism, to suggest the general temper of the twentieth-century arts; it has equally been appropriated by those who wish to distinguish and isolate *one* current at one particular time . . . a powerful movement, certainly, and an international one, reaching, like Romanticism, through the western cultures. It has been urged that Modernism is our inevitable art – as Gertrude Stein put it, the only 'composition' appropriate to the new composition in which we live, the new dispositions of space and time. But it has also been seen as a form of late bourgeois aestheticism, especially by Marxist critics like Lukács who see the characteristic, the truly self-realizing modern art as a species of Realism.[8] The term has been used to cover a wide variety of movements subversive of the realist or the romantic impulse and disposed towards abstraction (Impressionism, Post-Impressionism, Expressionism, Cubism, Futurism, Symbolism, Imagism, Vorticism, Dadaism, Surrealism); but even these are not, as we shall see, all movements of one kind, and some are radical reactions against others. In some nations Modernism has seemed central to the evolution of the literary and artistic tradition; in others it has seemed simply to visit and then go away again. Modernism does indeed exist; acknowledgement can no longer sensibly be withheld; the movements and experiments of modern writers have come right to the forefront of artistic attention. But on what scale, at what time, and with what character?

2

When we speak of the style of an age, we can mean two very different things. We can mean that 'general form of the forms of thought', of which Alfred North Whitehead spoke, which affects all a period's writing and is 'so translucent . . . that only by extreme effort can we become aware of it'.[9] But we can also mean a conscious mannerism, elected by some writers and artists though not by all, which expresses 'a prevailing, dominant, or authentically contemporary view of the world by those artists who have most successfully intuited the quality of the human experience peculiar to their day and who are able to phrase this experience in a form deeply congenial to the thought, science, and technology which are part of that experience'.[10] The term 'Modernism' can hardly be taken in the former sense; for in any working definition of it we shall have to see in it a quality of abstraction and highly conscious artifice, taking us behind familiar reality, breaking away from familiar functions of language and conventions of form. It could be said that this is simply its initial shock, stage one of movement that leads us all into Modernism. And one can argue, to a point, that in graphics, architecture, design, and especially in the conventions of media like film and television, Modernism has become an invisibly communal style. Yet in some ways this is to defeat Modernism's presumptions; the shock, the violation of expected continuities, the element of de-creation and crisis, is a crucial element *of* the style. It has more commonly been urged that Modernism is our style in the second sense; these are the artistic forms consequent on modern thought, modern experience, and hence the Modernist writers and artists express the highest distillation of twentieth-century artistic potential. But many twentieth-century artists have rejected the label and the associated aesthetics, the modes of abstraction, discontinuity, and shock. And it can be well argued that the twentieth-century artistic tradition is made up, not of one essential strand, but of two – roughly antithetical, though meeting from time to time. This, for instance, is the view of Stephen Spender, who, in his book *The Struggle of the Modern*, sees two streams: the 'moderns' and the 'contemporaries'.[11]

The case for Modernism's total dominance has often been put and is easy to see. One of the word's associations is with the coming of a new era of high aesthetic self-consciousness and non-representationalism, in which art turns from realism and humanistic representation towards style, technique, and spatial form in pursuit of a deeper penetration of life. 'No artist tolerates reality,' Nietzsche tells us; the task of art is its own self-realization, outside and beyond established orders, in a world of abnormally drawn perspectives. 'What strikes me as beautiful, what I should like to do, is a book about nothing, a book without external attachments, which would hold itself together by itself through the internal force of its style' – this Flaubertian dream of an order in art independent of or else transcending the humanistic, the material, the *real*, has been crucially important to a whole segment of the modern arts. And what such artists have achieved can be considered – has been considered – the ultimate achievement of artistic possibility in the twentieth century, part of the progress and evolution of the arts towards sophistication and completion. The art that makes life, the drama of the artist's consciousness, the structure that lies beyond time, history, character or visible reality, the moral imperative of technique; are not these the basis of a great aesthetic revolution into literary possibilities greater than ever dreamt of? Hence Virginia Woolf, holding that the modern stylistic revolution came from the historical opportunity for change in human relationships and human character, and that modern art therefore had a social and epistemological *cause*, nonetheless believed in the aesthetic nature of the opportunity; it set the artist free to be more himself, let him move beyond the kingdom of necessity to the kingdom of light. Now human consciousness and especially *artistic* consciousness could become more intuitive, more poetic; art could now fulfil *itself*. It was free to catch at the manifold – the atoms as they fall – and create significant harmony not in the universe but within itself (like the painting which Lily Briscoe completes at the end of *To the Lighthouse*). The world, reality, is discontinuous till art comes along, which may be a modern crisis for the world; but within art all becomes vital, discontinuous, yes, but within an aesthetic system of positioning. Or, as Wallace Stevens puts it, the poet must be able to abstract reality 'which he does by placing it in his imagination', by giving it the substance or meaning of a fiction. There may be a poverty in the universe and a trauma in man, but the artist has the means to transcend both history and reality by the dispositions of his technique, creating Joyce's 'luminous silent stasis of aesthetic pleasure'.

The movement towards sophistication and mannerism, towards introversion, technical display, internal self-scepticism, has often been taken as a common base for a *definition* of Modernism. Certainly, a number of technical features do reappear from movement to movement, even when these are radically at odds in other ways: anti-representationalism in painting, atonalism in music, *vers libre* in poetry, stream-of-consciousness narrative in the novel. And certainly, as Ortega y Gasset has said, the aesthetic refinement involves a dehumanization of art, the 'progressive elimination of the human, all too human, elements predominant in romantic and naturalistic production'.[12] This has meant, though, not only radical remaking of form, but also, as Frank Kermode says, the tendency to bring it closer to chaos, so producing a sense of 'formal desperation'.[13] This, in turn, suggests that Modernism might mean not only a new mode or mannerism in the arts, but a certain magnificent disaster for them. In short, experimentalism does not simply suggest the presence of sophistication, difficulty and novelty in art; it also suggests bleakness, darkness, alienation, disintegration. Indeed Modernism would seem to be the point at which the idea of the radical and innovating arts, the experimental, technical, aesthetic ideal that had been growing forward from Romanticism, reaches formal crisis – in which myth, structure and organization in a traditional sense collapse, and not only for formal reasons. The crisis is a crisis of culture; it often involves an unhappy view of history – so that the Modernist writer is not simply the artist set free, but the artist under specific, apparently historical strain. If Modernism is the imaginative power in the chamber of consciousness that, as James puts it, 'converts the very pulses of the air into revelations', it is also often an awareness of contingency as a disaster in the world of time: Yeats's 'Things fall apart; the centre cannot hold.' If it is an art of metamorphosis, a Daedalus voyage into unknown arts,[14] it is also a sense of disorientation and nightmare, feeling the dangerous, deathly magic in the creative impulse explored by Thomas Mann. If it takes the modern as a release from old dependencies, it also sees the 'immense panorama of futility and anarchy' that Eliot saw in *Ulysses*.[15] And if an aesthetic devotion runs deep in it, it is capable of dispensing with that abruptly and outrageously, as in the auto-destructive dimension of Dada or Surrealism.

This leads us toward another kind of account as to why Modernism is our art; it is the one art that responds to the scenario of our chaos. It is the art consequent on Heisenberg's 'Uncertainty principle', of the destruction of civilization and reason in the First World War, of the world changed and reinterpreted by Marx, Freud and Darwin, of capitalism and constant industrial acceleration, of existential exposure to meaninglessness or absurdity. It is the literature of technology. It is the art consequent on the dis-establishing of communal reality and conventional notions of causality, on the destruction of traditional notions of the wholeness of individual character, on the linguistic chaos that ensues when public notions of language have been discredited and when all realities have become subjective fictions. Modernism is then the art of modernization – however stark the separation of the artist from society may have been, however oblique the artistic gesture he has made. Thus, to the Expressionist or the Surrealist for instance, it is the anti-art which decomposes old frames of reference and carries the anarchy of men's evolving desire, the expressive form of human evolution in energetic release. By this view, Modernism is not art's freedom, but art's necessity. The communal universe of reality and culture on which nineteenth-century art had depended was over; and the explosively lyrical, or else the ironic and fictive modes, modes which included large elements not only of creation but of de-creation, were inevitable. The assumption that the age demands a certain kind of art, and that Modernism is the art that it demands, has been fervently held by those who see in the modern human condition a crisis of reality, an apocalypse of cultural community. What, though, is clear is that not all artists have believed this to be so – that, indeed, ours has been a century not only of de-realization but of realism, not only of ironic but of expansive modes.

The paradox of Modernism lies in the relationship between these two very different explanations of and justifications for it; indeed one can distinguish, in the difference between (say) Symbolism and Surrealism, *two* Modernisms. On the one hand, modernism has been an arcane and a private art: as Ortega y Gasset says in *The Dehumanization of Art*, it tends to divide its audience aristocratically into two groups – those who understand it and those who do not, those trained in and acquiescent to its techniques and premises, and those who find it not only incomprehensible but hostile. Thus its main qualities – which Ortega sees as a view of art as 'play' or 'delightful fraud'; an aversion to the traditional; a tendency towards self-hate or irony; a self-diminishing quality, or belief that art has few consequences other than that of being itself – are not simply *avant-garde* but represent a privation and a hoarding of the artistic powers against the populace and the claims of time and history. On the other hand, specialism and experimentalism can be held to have great social meaning; the arts are *avant-garde* because they are revolutionary probes into future human consciousness. Then we could indeed say that the Modernist tendency is that which saw most deeply and truthfully into the situation of the arts and of man in our time, securing us a worthy art in an age which seemed not to grant us one; that most of our important writers have been of its tendency, and that its implications are inescapable for all other artists. By this view, Modernism, while not our total style, becomes the movement which has expressed our modern consciousness, created in its works the nature of modern experience at its fullest. It may not be the only stream, but it is the *main* stream. Like Romanticism, it originated with historical neatness about the beginning of a century, in a period of deep intellectual reappraisal and social and intellectual change, and has come increasingly to dominate the sensibility, aesthetics and mind of the hard core of our greatest writers, and to become the essential and appropriate vision to our most sensitive readers. Like Romanticism, it is a revolutionary movement, capitalizing on a vast intellectual readjustment and radical dissatisfaction with the artistic past – a movement that is international in character and marked by a flow of major ideas, forms and values that spread from country to country and developed into the main line of the western tradition.

Today it must surely seem to us that the truth lies somewhere between the view that Modernism is the supreme modern expression and the view that it is of marginal importance. Modernism is, clearly, more than an aesthetic event, and some of the conditions that lie behind it are discernible and clear. Yet it contains a highly aesthetic response, one which turns on the assumption that the registering of modern consciousness or experience was not a problem in representation but a profound cultural and aesthetic crux . . . a problem in the making of structures, the employment of language, the uniting of form, finally in the social meaning of the artist himself. The search for a style and a typology becomes a self-conscious element in the Modernist's literary production; he is perpetually engaged in a profound and ceaseless journey through the means and integrity of art. In this sense, Modernism is less a style than a search for a style in a highly individualistic sense; and indeed the style of one work is no guarantee for the next. This, perhaps, is what Irving Howe means when he remarks that 'modernism does not establish a prevalent style of its own; or if it does, it denies itself, thereby ceasing to be modern'.[16] The qualities which we associate with painters like Matisse, Picasso and Braque, with musicians like Stravinsky and Schoenberg, novelists like Henry James, Mann, Conrad, Proust, Svevo, Joyce, Gide, Kafka, Musil, Hesse and Faulkner, poets like Mallarmé, Valéry, Eliot, Pound, Rilke, Lorca, Apollinaire, Breton and Stevens, with dramatists like Strindberg, Pirandello and Wedekind, are indeed their remarkably high degree of self-signature, their quality of sustaining each work with a structure appropriate only to that work. The condition for the style of the work is a presumed absence of style for the age; and each work is a once-and-for-all creation, subsisting less for its referential than its autotelic constituents, the order and rhythm made for itself and submerged by itself. Modernism in this sense is indeed an international tendency, and we can predicate origins and causes for it and reflect on its significance. But it is hard to convert it into a universal style or tradition, despite the fact that its environment is not simply the work of individuals but of broader movements and tendencies. It is indeed a *part* of our modern art, not all of it. Yet there seems to be a discernible centre to it: a certain loose but distinguishable group of assumptions, founded on a broadly symbolist aesthetic, an *avant-garde* view of the artist, and a notion of a relationship of crisis between art and history. To this extent, one would also want to argue that there is an historical 'peak', where impulses from many varied sources begin to coalesce, and come through in a particular core of moments, out from which run many variant and diverse versions of the primary impulse.

3

Perhaps the oblique nature of Modernism explains why critics have found it so hard a movement to find a clear place or date for. For the potential of Modernism was long present in the development of literature; it is possible to discern its origins long before we see its fruition. If Modernism is movements, then movements had been coming in increasing waves right through the nineteenth century. If the movements have to be bohemian or *avant-garde*, then bohemia was active in Paris from the 1830s; and the theory of the artist as a futurist, an agent free and loose in the realm of dangerous knowledge, was active throughout romantic thought. If an explicit aesthetic of experimentalism is required, then Émile Zola published *Le Roman expérimental* in 1880 (though he used the word in a scientific or laboratory sense). The crucial idea of the modern as a special imperative and a special state of exposure exists in Nietzsche. If Modernism means the ruffling of the hard naturalistic surface by a state of multiplicity of consciousness, then Walter Pater in the 1870s in England and other thinkers in Europe were talking of 'quickened, multiplied consciousness'. If Modernism means a response of the imagination to an urbanized, *Gesellschaft* world, then Baudelaire spoke of the unreal city and the need for the imagination to produce 'the sensation of newness'. As for other aspects of Modernism – its use of anti-form or desecration of established conventions; its use of the hard, resonant and 'witty' image and its dependence on 'associated sensibility'; its sense of anguish and its dependence on what Lionel Trilling calls an 'adversary culture' – then we can trace these back through the western tradition, to Sterne, or Donne, or Villon. Modernism was indeed an international movement and a focus of many varied forces which reached their peak in various countries at various times. In some it seemed to stay for a long period; in others, to function as a temporary disturbance and then go away again. In some it seemed to do great violence to the received tradition – of Romanticism or Victorianism, Realism or Impressionism – and in others it seems a logical development of it. Indeed Modernism can look surprisingly different depending on where one finds the centre, in which capital (or province) one happens to stand. Just as 'modern' in the England of today can mean something very different from what it meant a century ago for Matthew Arnold, so it can also be observed varying significantly from country to country, from language to language. Because the essence of Modernism is its international character – one critic, indeed, has argued that 'Modernism, in short, is synonymous with internationalism'[17] – and because, lexically, the term 'modern' is itself internationally recognizable at sight and without translation, it is prudent to look briefly at these international connotations first.

Let us begin with one familiar version of the tendency. The title and sub-title of Cyril Connolly's 1965 book provide a usefully laconic definition: *The Modern Movement: One Hundred Key Books from England, France and America, 1880–1950.* Here, France is clearly identified as the source from which Anglo-American Modernism drew strength: 'The French fathered the Modern Movement, which slowly moved beyond the Channel and then across the Irish Sea until the Americans finally took it over, bringing to it their own demonic energy, extremism and taste for the colossal.'[18] Although, as Connolly is very ready to admit, it is impossible to fix on any one particular time as the start of the Modern movement, 1880 is taken as the point where the Enlightenment's 'critical intelligence' had combined with Romanticism's 'exploring sensibility' to stimulate the work of the first generation of truly modern writers, all owing something to Flaubert and Baudelaire – James, Mallarmé, Villiers de l'Isle-Adam, Huysmans, and 'the mysterious Lautréamont'. Thereafter followed wave after wave of writers, artists and musicians contributing to a very modern sensibility – Debussy, Yeats, Gide, Proust and Valéry; followed by Eliot, Pound, Lawrence and Joyce; Virginia Woolf, Edith Sitwell and Marianne Moore; Hemingway, Cummings, Faulkner, Malraux, Huxley and Graves; and thus to the present day. Within the outside limits of 1880 and 1950, it is clear that as Connolly sees it the high season was somewhere between 1910 and 1925. Somewhat similar views are to be found in Edmund Wilson's seminal book *Axel's Castle*, which relates the English and American modern movement to Symbolism, and in Maurice Bowra, who includes a great part of modern literature as a Symbolist heritage.[19] And though Graham Hough believes that English literature never really had a Symbolist movement proper, that what happened about the time of the First World War was at most 'symbolism without the magic', and that the nativist line predominated in England even if not in America, his basic interpretation of events is close to Connolly's.[20]

A more catholic Anglo-American view informed another book published in the same year as Connolly's: *The Modern Tradition*, the anthology of Modernist items edited by Richard Ellmann and Charles Feidelson. Not only do the editors acknowledge by their choice of items that there were key books in languages other than French and English, which Connolly, for stated (and honourable) reasons, does not; they extend their inquiry beyond the confines of literature as it is narrowly understood and into the wider realms of the imagination and the intellect; and they also embody in their book an awareness of 'a modern tradition that reaches well back into the romantic era and beyond'.[21] The outside limits, the envelope of their Modernism, assume a much more expansive shape; and their items range in kind and time, from Vico to Sartre, from Goethe and Wordsworth to Camus and Robbe-Grillet, from Blake to Picasso. Nevertheless, when they begin to focus upon the period of high intensity, they too give their closest attention to what is roughly the first quarter of the twentieth century, to Yeats and Joyce and Eliot and Lawrence and to their Continental coevals, Proust, Valéry and Gide, Mann, Rilke and Kafka. And if to other Anglo-American critics one turns with the two blunt interrogatives – who? and when? – to get a rough outline of their sense of Modernism, similar pictures emerge. Who is to be included in our identification parade of the Modernist spirit? Which are seen as the years of gathering force, of breakthrough, of concentrated change? A. Alvarez thinks that he who goes looking for Modernism must seek it in the first thirty years or so of this century, and that at the epicentre of the change will be found Pound and Eliot, Joyce and Kafka. For Frank Kermode the nineties are certainly forerunners of Modernism, but he claims that nevertheless 'anybody who thinks about what modernism now means will rightly look more closely at the period between 1907 and, say, 1925'. Neither Stephen Spender nor Graham Hough would seriously disagree with these chronological limits, though they further detect within them a period of enhanced intensity between about 1910 and the beginning of the First World War – years which, in Graham Hough's view, witnessed 'a revolution in the literature of the English language as momentous as the Romantic one'. As for personalities, because he recognizes that the Anglo-American developments were part of a larger European affair, he would set beside the names of Yeats, Joyce, Eliot and Pound also those of Gide, Valéry, and Thomas Mann, and perhaps also of Proust and Rilke.[22]

As the focus narrows and there is pressure to identify the really crucial event, the wholly significant work, the *annus mirabilis*, so the phrases grow in audacity. Tamping down an enormous cultural change into a brief moment in time, Virginia Woolf saw a quite explosive event: 'On or about December 1910 human nature changed ... All human relations shifted – those between masters and servants, husbands and wives, parents and children. And when human relations change there is at the same time a change in religion, conduct, politics, and literature.'[23] The year of the death of King Edward and the first Post-Impressionist Exhibition was doubtless crucial, though D. H. Lawrence used an equally apocalyptic assumption for a different year and with a different interpretation: 'It was in 1915 the old world ended,' he wrote in *Kangaroo*. Such comments confirm the contemporary sense of participating in a profound transition; and the Anglo-American focus on these years just before the war is utterly understandable, since – as later essays in this volume suggest – there is a sharpening of the claims of the new, manifest in literary texts and literary groupings, over this period. But there have been efforts to push things earlier; Richard Ellmann, for example, says that if a moment must be found for human character to have changed, 'I should suggest that 1900 is both more convenient and more accurate than Virginia Woolf's 1910', since the modernist theme sounds through the Edwardian period.[24] Other critics have transferred this point of intensity to the years after the First World War; Harry Levin, for instance, if pressed to identify *the* Modernist year, would rather want to point to the miraculous yield of 1922: the year of *Ulysses* and *The Waste Land*, of Rilke's *Duineser Elegien* (*Duino Elegies*) and *Die Sonette an Orpheus* (*Sonnets to Orpheus*), of Brecht's first play *Baal*, of Lawrence's *Aaron's Rod* and Virginia Woolf's *Jacob's Room*, of Proust's *Sodome et Gomorrhe* (*Sodom and Gomorrah*) and Eugene O'Neill's *Anna Christie*. Nor, he adds, would it be difficult to compile a list of comparable quality for the year 1924, and thus discover a peak of intensity in the early twenties[25] – a period which certain other critics would however regard as one in which the Modernist impulse was reaching a point of exhaustion. An even later emphasis may be found among those critics who would argue that Modernism, far from becoming exhausted, has continued as our essential art right to the present, and who see the entire inter-war period as the main phase of Modernist evolution – like Harold Rosenberg, who focuses particularly on the Paris of this period, 'the only spot where ... it was possible to shake up such "modern" doses as Viennese psychology, African sculpture, American detective stories, Russian music, neo-Catholicism, German technique, Italian desperation'.[26] The argument depends, in part, upon essential de-finitions about what characterizes Modernism, and also about whether the tendency has sustained itself, particularly via the surrealistic line, through into post-war art.

For if there is an argument about when Modernism began, and hence, implicitly, about what its causes and character are, then there is also one about whether it has yet ended. We have now amassed, on the basis of the art or anti-art of the post-war period – which at first appeared to be moving away from Modernism in the direction of realism and linearity – a new entity, called Post-Modernism. The term is acquiring high currency now to talk about a compound of that art of chance or minimalization, that 'literature of silence', in which, as in Beckett or Borges, the idea of absurd creation, random method, parody or self-exhausting fictionality is paramount; of the new *chosisme*, which expands to include not only the *nouveau roman* in France but the non-fiction novel in Germany and the States, where facts, objects or historical events are placed in the context of questioning narrative; of multi-media forms, like the happening or the street theatre; and of the anti-rationalistic anti-art of psychedelics, pornography, and revolutionary outrage.[27] Various aspects of this can be seen as continuous with the logic and the modes of Modernism – especially that part of it concerned with evolutionary psychic exploration, like Dada and Surrealism, or with romantic self-immersion, like Hermann Hesse, or with the revolution of the word, like Gertrude Stein or the later Joyce. The overall case for continuity has been forcibly put in the essay 'Modernisms' by Frank Kermode, which has appeared in several places, including the volume *Innova-tions*, where it is set against opposite views. Kermode holds that the contemporary art of the random – the squaring out of a piece of space or time, the specifying and signing of an environment, as in Cage or Burroughs – is blood-cousin to the earlier tendencies, though he draws a line across to distinguish early Modernism, which was much more formalist, or devoted to the paradoxes of form, from later or Neo-Modernism, which is anti-formalist, though compelled to use form to subvert it. The use of loose structure or aleatory art (i.e. art based on chance), as in Cage or Tinguely or the happening, or the art of conscious fictiveness, as in Nabokov, Borges, or Barthelme, is not outrightly at odds with its predecessors; it is a new disposition of old forces. Thus what Kermode calls Neo-Modernism and others have chosen to call Post-Modernism involves a change in what Harold Rosenberg calls the 'tradition of the new' – a change falling perhaps around Dada – but it is still that same tradition. But other critics in *Innovations* dissent; if there is now a new *avant-garde* and a new aesthetic or group of aesthetics – based, say, on Cage, Burroughs, Beckett and Borges, concrete poetry and the *nouveau roman*, but also on the happening, drugs, the counter-culture, and *négritude* – this is no longer simply a style; it is a form of post-cultural *action*, a politics.[28] The *avant-garde* has entered the streets, and become instinctive or radical behaviour; and we are in a new stylistic age, in which that enterprise of humanism and civilization Modernism attempted desperately to reinstate by its subversions of form is over. Anarchism and revolutionary subjectivism predominate; the uniqueness of the work vanishes; the cults of impersonality and pure form are done; art is either action, outrage, or play. In a spectacular essay called 'POSTmodernISM', Ihab Hassan has explored some of the continuities and the discontinuities, stressing that the new mood assumes a totally technological and dehumanized universe; and he argues that the newer developments must at least force us to reconsider Modernism and distinguish the obviously continuous elements in it.[29] Something of the same revisionism inhabits the new stress being put on the surrealistic wing of Modernism, and Modernism's affiliations with Romanticism. In short, the argument around Post-Modernism now adds to the abundance of versions of Modernism.

4

But what is clear is that there is in nearly all of these versions a sense of Modernism as an historical evolution coupled with a notion of crisis and a notion of a point of culmination. And, for most Anglo-American critics, that culmination falls in the first part of the twentieth century. Although the reports vary increasingly in their detail, as the lore begins to shift, they have in common an emphasis on the Anglo-American achievement following on from the innovations of French symbolism, behind which again stand two prime initiators, Flaubert and Baudelaire. The stress may then fall on the new classicism, or else on the continuation of Romanticism. But the period of highest intensity is seen by and large as the first quarter of the twentieth century, within which are two peaks: the years immediately preceding, and the years immediately following the First World War. Such is the concept of Modernism as it is commonly viewed from a New York–London–Paris axis. But what is not always adequately acknowledged is that Modernism or the Modern, when viewed, say, from Berlin, or Vienna, or Copenhagen, or Prague, or St Petersburg, is a thing with a quite different chronological profile, with a rather different set of representative figures and influential precursors, with a very different group of origins. Even if our task is less to make Modernism fit into line with contemporary experimentalism and radical attitudes than to straighten and clarify the record, which is the primary aim of this volume, this is something that deserves our best attention. This is not only because any account of Modernism that seeks to be genuinely synoptic and international must accommodate this sort of awareness, but also because these other manifestations of Modernism provide a broader, a thicker base for the generalizations to which all investigations like the present one are prone.

Let us try, then, to illuminate the conventional history of the tendency from the standpoint of Germanic Modernism. It would be convenient if Germanic Modernism could stand for the combined and conflated literature of Germany, Austria, and Scandinavia over these years; unfortunately, here too, such tidy simplifications will not quite fit. Berlin as it was in the nineties, especially the early nineties, may by its cultural and intellectual clamour draw attention to itself; but it would be a great mistake to allow Berlin to represent Germany in its totality at a time when Munich and Darmstadt and other provincial German cities were important and lively centres of literary activity. There is also the complex and ambiguous role of Vienna in these late-Hapsburg years, a multifarious role appropriate to a capital so influentially placed by history, geography and ethnic mix between north and south, east and west, past and present. In Vienna the modern ferment was strong; indeed, George Steiner tells us, 'from the eighteen-nineties until its enthusiastic swoon into Hitler's arms in 1938, Vienna was the foremost generator of our current sensibility'.[30] And there can be no doubt that the city of Karl Kraus, Freud, the Vienna Circle, Schoenberg and Wittgenstein was alive with Modernist perspectives. And then Scandinavia, with Ibsen, the age's most European figure of all, and Strindberg, whose influence was growing fast, made its own striking and peculiar contribution, had its own distinctive if Nietzschean passions of desperation and joy. Still, if from this complicated scene some identifiable range of phenomena that might approximately be designated as Germanic Modernism can be separated out, then the first and most striking thing is that it is – in its most significant manifestations – a good generation *earlier* than the Anglo-American Modernist upswing located by Connolly, Kermode and Hough. In Scandinavia, in Germany, and to a substantial extent in Austria, it was the eighties, nineties and early 1900s that witnessed a debate about the nature and name of Modernism of quite unparalleled passion and vehemence – years with, for the Germanic north, a much higher degree of self-consciousness, of articulateness, of documentation than perhaps any other part of Europe.

In trying to pin Modernism down – tentatively and crudely – in terms of men, books and years, attention is first drawn to Scandinavia: to the publication in 1883 of a series of critical essays by the Danish critic Georg Brandes with the significant title of *Men of the Modern Breakthrough* (*Det moderne Gjennembruds Mænd*). In no time at all – conceivably by virtue of the stature Brandes had achieved throughout the Germanic world – the epithet 'modern' became a rallying slogan of quite irresistible drawing power. One is, incidentally, struck by the contrast between this near-obsessive concern for the term 'modern' and the comparative disregard of it during these same years in

England, where between Meredith's *Modern Love* of 1862 and Michael Roberts's anthology *The Faber Book of Modern Verse* in 1936, the term is rarely used in any programmatic way. Though one might argue that its function, in English, is served by the word 'new': 'The range of the adjective [new] spread,' notes Holbrook Jackson, 'until it embraced the ideas of the whole period [the eighteen nineties], and we find innumerable references to the "New Spirit", the "New Humour", the "New Hedonism", the "New Drama", the "New Unionism", the "New Party", and the "New Woman".'[31]

In Germany, the anthology with which the new generation of iconoclastic poets announced their *credo* in 1885 was given the title *Moderne Dichtercharaktere (Modern Poet Characters)*.[32] The introductions to it, written by Conradi and Henckell, constituted a manifesto in which were defined the objectives for what was proudly called the 'modern' lyric – a manifesto, the programmatic urgency of which carried over into the poems themselves. Conspicuous is that poem by Arno Holz, one of the chief theorists of this Germanic age, which insisted:

> *'Modern sei der Poet,*
> *modern vom Scheitel bis zur Sohle.'**

From this moment on, and over the following decade, there were few writers in German who did not take some opportunity to discuss with rare vehemence the aims and ideals of so-called 'modern' literature. One of the most influential periodicals of the day, *Die Gesellschaft,* which began publication in 1885, was defined by its editor as *'ein Organ der modernen Bewegung in der Literatur'* ('an organ of the modern movement in literature'). In 1886 came the invention of that bewildering and disturbing term 'The Modern'; Eugen Wolff, in an address to the Berlin literary circle known as *Durch* ('Through') – in which there might well be an echo of Brandes's concept of 'The Modern Breakthrough' – invented and launched the term *'Die Moderne'*, 'the Modern', later elaborated and more widely disseminated in his article of 1888 entitled 'Die jüngste deutsche Literaturströmung und das Prinzip der Moderne' ('The most recent German literary currents and the principle of the Modern').[33] Articles with

---

*'Let the poet be modern,
Modern from head to toe.'

38

titles that announced their interest in 'Charles Darwin and the modern aesthetic', 'Truth in the modern novel', 'The significance of literature for the modern world', and so on, are conspicuous in these years.

The years 1890 and 1891 in Germany, as in Vienna, Oslo and to a lesser extent Zürich, witnessed a preoccupation with the concept of Modernism that approached the dimensions of a fever. There was a whole new range of 'modern' periodicals: *Freie Bühne für modernes Leben, Moderne Blätter* or even quite simply *Die Moderne*. Their pages were full of 'modern' contributions: 'Die Sozialdemokratie und die Moderne' ('Social democracy and the Modern') (1891); 'Moderne Wahrheitsdichtung' ('Modern poetry of truth') (1891); 'Moderne Bestrebungen' ('Modern aspirations') (1892); 'Der moderne Roman' ('The modern novel') or, more than once, 'Die Moderne'. Any bibliography of nineties literature in German would reveal an extraordinarily high concentration of titles making explicit reference to Modernism and the concept of the Modern, many of them crucial for an understanding of this decade: Hermann Bahr's *Zur Kritik der Moderne* (*On the Criticism of the Modern*) (Zürich 1890), Leo Berg's *Das sexuelle Problem in der modernen Literatur* (*The Sexual Problem in Modern Literature*) (Berlin 1891) and *Der Übermensch in der modernen Literatur* (*The Superman in Modern Literature*) (Leipzig 1897), and Eugen Dühring's *Die Grossen der modernen Literatur* (*The Great of Modern Literature*) (Leipzig 1893).

The flame of controversy burned bright, consuming a large part of the intellectual fuel of the writers and critics of these years. But it took its toll. By the time Samuel Lublinski drew up the pros and cons of these developments in his *Die Bilanz der Moderne* (*Balance Sheet of the Modern*) (Berlin 1904), the issue had become a spent force; having run its turbulent course for well over twenty years, it finally lost impetus. Five years later, its 'exit' was announced by the title of Lublinski's follow-up study, *Der Ausgang der Moderne* (*The Exit of the Modern*) (Dresden 1909); the literary world of Germany was surfeited and sickened by the term. 'The Modern', even the adjective 'modern', had become the sign of all that was old-fashioned and bourgeois, a term the connotations of which suggested nothing so much as exhaustion and decay. For the brave new generation of First World War writers in Germany, the term was something positively to be repudiated. The Expressionists went out of their way to declare how 'unmodern' they were – an irony surely not lost upon those whose view of Modernism is largely Anglo-French. The very moment of the Germanic repudiation of the Modern as a valid term marks the start of Anglo-American Modernism as it is currently understood; any comprehensive account of European Modernism must have as one of its major tasks the resolution of this discrepancy.

5

But it would not do to leave the impression that this Germanic 'Modern' was a simple, undifferentiated thing which grew predictably from its origins in the 1880s through to maturity and thence to inevitable decline in the early years of this century. For somewhere along the line of the semantic development of the term there was, not a break, not a rupture, not a reversal or revolution, but an abrupt change of direction, a realignment of thought. Something in its nature is not unlike the notion of the *Wendepunkt* (turning point), familiar to those acquainted with Tieck's theory of the *Novelle* – a point at which there is an unexpected yet in retrospect not unmotivated turn of events, a reorientation which one can see now is not only wholly consistent but logical and possibly even inevitable. It might be argued that it is precisely this same phenomenon, which, in the French–English–American line, constitutes that element of distinctiveness that the critics have sought for. But what is striking about this development in the Germanic Modern – and to place it somewhere about the year 1890 would not be far wrong – is that, because the moment was so unusually self-conscious and articulate, it is particularly well-documented and therefore accessible to investigation, like some dy by dx of a much larger configuration of change within which is contained the larger meaning of Modernism.

Some sense of the nature of this event is perhaps possible if we return to Lionel Trilling's comments on the modern. Trilling entitles his essay of 1961 'On the Modern Element in Modern Literature'; his title alludes to an event of over a century before – Matthew Arnold's lecture of 1857, called 'On the Modern Element in Literature'. Arnold was among those Victorians who had an active sense of modernity and change, and felt this generated new claims upon mind and art. The connotations of the term 'modern' were central to him; but they are connotations totally different from those of our day. They were substantially classical: the modern element was repose, confidence, tolerance, the free activity of the mind winning new ideas in conditions of material well-being; it involved the willingness to judge by reason and search for the laws of things. If Arnold felt, as we know he did, the power of unreason, chaos, deep personal depression, a strong sense of social anarchy, he did not see these as the essential characteristics of the modern element. Yet, as Trilling says, the modern element to our mind is almost the opposite of what Arnold sees – it is nihilism, a 'bitter line of hostility to civilization', a 'disenchantment with culture itself'.[34] Somewhere in the sequence – Trilling notes the importance here of Nietzsche, Freud, Conrad, and Sir James Frazer's anthropology – a radical alteration takes place to give us the intellectual conventions of Plight, Alienation, and Nihilism; the idea of the modern is bound up with consciousness of disorder, despair, and anarchy. So words like 'modern' can alter suddenly in content; a body of sensibility can recede and another grow without the terms changing. Imagine then such a cycle of development focused and concentrated into a brief span of time – a few months, at most a year or two – and one begins to sense the nature of our *Wendepunkt*.

Suffusing the entire 1880s sense of the modern was a confident faith in social advance, a readiness to believe that to expose abuses was to invite their annihilation, that to repudiate the conventional past was to clear the way for a healthy moral growth, for welcome ideals. Hard work, clear vision, courage, purposefulness – these were the keys to the future, to the evolution of new types of men, of society, of art. In Eugen Wolff's article of 1888 in which he first enunciated and defined the concept of the modern – a concept the detail of which one can find expressed in the Anglo-American line, too – he invents a spokesman who explains how that concept might be expressed in plastic, sculptural terms:

As a woman, a *modern* woman, filled with the modern spirit, and at the same time a typical figure, a *working* woman, who is nevertheless saturated with beauty, and full of ideals, returning from her material work to the service of goodness and nobility, as though returning home to her beloved child – for she is no young virgin, silly and ignorant of her destiny; she is an experienced but pure woman, in rapid movement like the spirit of the age, with fluttering garments and streaming hair, striding forward . . . That is our new divine image: the Modern.[35]

But this salutary ikon was not to remain such for long. A few brief years, and the modern was associated with a very different set of images. An earlier ally of Wolff's, M. G. Conrad, writing in 1892, could not repress the scorn and bitterness he felt for the spirit of transformation that was coming over the Modern and its representatives; and in a welter of mixed metaphors he abused the new literary leaders:

> The only true poetry now is the virtuoso art of the nerves, that which feeds us with the most outrageous sensations, which titillates us with techniques gathered from literary clinics all over the world, all tested for refinement; and it is with these that we are to march at the head of the cultural movement in Europe, we immoralists by the grace of Nietzsche, we magicians of the hypererotic sporting world, we mystics of the international passing show, we raging Rolands blessed by impotence and foolishness . . . For the healthy-minded man of today it is a matter of complete indifference what alien cuckoo's eggs the more extreme specialists of the Modern hatch out in their little *fin-de-siècle* chapels and brothels, wagging their little 'isms' like tails behind them: symbolism, satanism, neo-idealism, hallucinism . . . Give things a few years, and no cocks will crow for any of this ultra-modern charlatanism practised by these comic turns of literature and art.[36]

Conrad's statement, despite its own comic aspects, thus confronts a spectacle that was to complicate the revolt of the 1890s and is much more familiar to us in the observations of Max Nordau: the crossing of the 'modern' spirit with the spirit of Decadence and Aestheticism.

To get at the quality of this change, it is useful once again to take a roll-call. When, in the early 1880s, Georg Brandes wrote of the 'modern minds', as he called them, of the men of the Modern Breakthrough, of whom did he speak? Of Ibsen and Bjørnson, of Jacobsen and Drachman, of Flaubert, Renan, John Stuart Mill. But particularly of Ibsen. When the German writers of the late 1880s thought of 'modern' literature, of whom did *they* think? Of Ibsen, of Zola and Tolstoy, Daudet, Bret Harte, and Whitman. But particularly, again, of Ibsen. When, however, the 1890s generation of critics – often the same men as before – looked for specifically 'modern' qualities, to whom did *they* turn? To Strindberg and Nietzsche, Büchner and

Kierkegaard, Bourget and Hamsun and Maeterlinck. But especially to Strindberg. This is a sharp change, and nowhere is it more dramatically revealed than in two successive articles by the Viennese critic, Hermann Bahr – one of 1890, in the first of his series of studies called *Zur Kritik der Moderne* (*In Criticism of the Modern*), and the other of 1891, in the second series.[37] In the former he defined the task of 'modern' literature as that of achieving a synthesis of naturalism and romanticism, and urged the example of Ibsen as the supreme exponent. Within a year he speaks of 'the wild frenzy of the galloping development' that had so exceeded expectation that things half-anticipated for the end of the century had arrived after no more than six months; he points to Strindberg and the group of Scandinavians gathered about him – Ola Hansson and Arne Garborg, for example – as the most modernistic literature of the day. And here, in this brief time-span, one gets a sense both of the displacement and of the nonetheless essential *continuity* of events. The Ibsen vogue and the Strindberg vogue in Germany – and indeed throughout Europe – might be traced to one chief source, Georg Brandes: the Ibsen vogue to Brandes' elaboration of the concept of the Modern Breakthrough, and the Strindberg vogue to the seminal lectures given by Brandes in Copenhagen in 1888, which stimulated not only Strindberg but the whole German nation (which had hitherto virtually ignored him) to discovery of Nietzsche, and spread his importance right through Europe and into England and the United States.

This same crossover point, which (in crude terms) comes when something happens to the fortunes of realism and naturalism, themselves modern but not quite Modernist movements, can be seen elsewhere. In 1891, when the Parisian journalist Jules Huret enlisted from Paul Alexis, the novelist and Zola-disciple, what must be the classic literary telegram – 'Naturalism not dead,' it said, 'letter follows' – he stirred the hornets' nest; out of its buzz Modernism derives. Alexis, in the letter that did indeed follow, defended the claims of the naturalists to be *the* movement of the modern: it was not a school but a mode of knowledge, and its scientizing, rationalizing, democratizing tendency would bring into the domain of literature for the twentieth century 'the broad general current which carries our age toward more science, more truth, and no doubt more happiness'. As for the tendencies toward symbolism, decadence and psychology in art, he found these out of date and 'merely comical'. Yet it is precisely in the breaking up of the naturalistic surface and its spirit of positivism that one senses the growth of Modernism; as H. Stuart Hughes points out, 'nearly all students of the last years of the nineteenth century have sensed in some form or another a profound psychological change'[38] – a reaction against positivism, toward a fascination with irrational or unconscious forces. But, looking at the two Germanic Modernisms, early (before 1890) and late (after 1890), one can see clearly in this context – something that the more confused events elsewhere perhaps disguise – the one *growing out* of the other. That one might then, with some expectation of reward, polarize Modernism along an Ibsen–Strindberg axis is a natural consequence; especially since during the years about 1890 Scandinavian leadership in European drama coincided so provocatively with such ferment in German cultural life, and reached elsewhere as well – to, for instance, those very different modern talents Shaw and Joyce. It is almost symbolic that scarcely had Ibsen left Germany in 1891, after long years of residence there, to return to his native Norway than Strindberg himself arrived at Berlin to shock and provoke its cultural world with his and his associates' goings-on at the Black Boar tavern. It is equally appropriate that in the closing years of a century which had been gradually accumulating a body of apocalyptic, historicist, Nietzschean and indeed Dionysian aesthetic theories and presumptions, increasing in proportion as the modern age was seen as historically novel and distinct, one should sense, right across the European countries, not simply an extension but a *bifurcation* of the impulse to be modern.

6

The reader who has followed our exercise in Modernist revisionism thus far is now likely to ask the obvious question: what follows from such recognitions? Perhaps what follows first is that the suspicion, already strong, of current nomenclature as a guide to events is further reinforced. It is clear that many of the standard labels – Naturalism, Impressionism, Symbolism, Imagism, Futurism, Expressionism, to go no further – were forbiddingly intertwined and overlapped, producing a doubtful synthesis of many movements radically different in kind and degree. What is clear is that Modernism, whether used as a term within the sequence or a term to describe the sequence, is no exception, and is subject to extreme semantic confusion. But what is equally clear is that the terminological confusion should not be used as an excuse to disguise some of our difficulties. It is tempting to suppose that Anglo-American Modernism and the Germanic Modernisms were two quite different things, happening at different times, which just happened to acquire cognate labels. And so, if we are looking for significant similarities, we might cast our eyes across and try to equate Anglo-American Modernism of the early twentieth century with the contemporary movement in the German tradition, which would be Expressionism. In fact the notion that the common factor among Modernisms is, precisely, Expressionism has been advanced by R. P. Blackmur.[39] However, Graham Hough has pointed up some of the dangers of this generalization and comparison:

Mr Blackmur has referred to the whole European movement, with which the English one belongs, as Expressionism. I should not be very happy with this as far as our domestic affair is concerned. Expressionism in art has Germanic connotations, and the literature we are considering is Anglo-American profoundly influenced by France. And Expressionism is a name for a kind of critical doctrine, a doctrine of personality and self-expression, that is precisely the one *not* held by our twentieth-century school.[40]

Hough, therefore, is talking about one obvious bifurcation within Modernism, and he is referring, of course, to the doctrines of impersonality and classicism that mark much Anglo-American Modernist thought, and especially that vein in it that concentrates into Imagism, which becomes in every sense the hard core of the Anglo-American tendency.

What this shows us is that there are severe difficulties within any standard chronology of events (which sees the same things as happening at the same time in different countries), and that many of the basic ideas and motifs of Modernism were distilled over an extended time-span in a variety of different circumstances. But there is a further complication: divergence between Expressionism and Imagism is not the whole story either. Briefly looking at it from the Anglo-American end for a moment, we can now see that there are links between various Germanic developments and various phases of Anglo-American experiment. The impact of Ibsen and Nietzsche has long been known in both England and America. But there is also growing evidence of links between D. H. Lawrence and the early phases of Expressionism, through his wife Frieda; of strong Expressionist elements in John Dos Passos and Eugene O'Neill; and so on. Similarly Futurist developments, which tended to share with Expressionism a buoyant *acceptance* of the modern city, the modern machine, the sense of contingency, clearly pass on into English-language experimentalism. The Anglo-American line is not single, as becomes clear when we look at the differences between a Lawrence poem and a Pound poem in an Imagist anthology, or note the way in which poets like William Carlos Williams and Hart Crane could, while respecting *The Waste Land*, believe that it had, by virtue of its nihilism and despair, set poetry *back* twenty years.[41] In short, Modernism was in most countries an extraordinary compound of the futuristic and the nihilistic, the revolutionary and the conservative, the naturalistic and the symbolistic, the romantic and the classical. It was a celebration of a technological age and a condemnation of it; an excited acceptance of the belief that the old régimes of culture were over, and a deep despairing in the face of that fear; a mixture of convictions that the new forms were escapes from historicism and the pressures of the time with convictions that they were precisely the living expressions of these things. And in most of these countries the fermenting decade was the eighteen nineties.

Modernism does have, then, its distinct phases and its distinct lines and traditions, but there is great profit in trying to relate and reconcile them. And, of the many reassessments and realignments that this salutary exercise brings in its train, we might note one of especially large order. For the earlier and the wider we push in our attempts to get at the roots of Modernism, the more we are likely to ask questions about the relationship between Modernism and two of the essential mental and artistic movements of the nineteenth century: Romanticism, and positivistic Naturalism. A number of critics have been tempted to see Modernism as a resurgence of Romanticism, though conceivably in a more extreme and strained form of pure irrationalism. Thus Frank Kermode and A. Alvarez, while taking the tendency as a whole, and recognizing the 'classical' elements within it, both suggest that the intense subjectivity of the Romantic spirit remains central to the modern arts.[42] And an even more elaborate case has been put by recent scholars of Romanticism like Geoffrey Hartman, Harold Bloom, Robert Langbaum, Morse Peckham and, with more qualifications, Hillis Miller, who in various ways propose a continuity into Modernism of the primary Romantic concerns with consciousness, with self–object relationships, and with intensified experience.[43] But most of these arguments do have to recognize an element of discontinuity hidden somewhere in the sequence; as Hillis Miller puts it, 'a new kind of poetry has appeared in our day, a poetry which grows out of romanticism, but goes beyond it'.[44] And an examination of the period between 1880 and the turn of the century, both in the Germanic and the Anglo–American line, should bring home the fact that we are concerned with more than a swing back to the spirit of Romanticism. For if anything distinguishes these decades and gives them their intellectual and historical character it is a fascination with evolving consciousness: consciousness aesthetic, psychological, and historical. And the preoccupation arises under the pressure of history, the push of modern times, that carry with them new evolutionary hopes and desires, and new underlying forces, psychic and social. The new registers of consciousness alter our sense of history, and our sense of the stability of consciousness itself, taking us into new concepts of mental and emotional association. 'Since they are modern characters,' says Strindberg of his people in *Miss Julie* (1888), 'living in an age of transition more urgently hysterical at any rate than the age that preceded it, I have drawn them as split and vacillating . . . conglomerations of past and present . . . scraps from books and newspapers . . .'[45] This is much the sort of comment that might have been made by any Modernist writer between the 1880s and the 1930s; and, in its consonance between fragmentation, discontinuity, and the modern age of transition, it is itself modern.

It is one of the larger commonplaces of cultural history that we can distinguish a kind of oscillation in style over periods of time, an ebb and flow between a predominantly rational world-view (Neo-Classicism, Enlightenment, Realism) and alternate spasms of irrational or subjective endeavour (Baroque, *Sturm und Drang*, Romanticism). The resultant temptation is to regard ages as being identifiably one or the other: head or heart is in command, reason or emotion dominates, the cultural pattern is *'naïv'* or *'sentimentalisch'*, Apollo or Dionysus claims allegiance. It may help us to understand Modernism if we recognize that these spirits can cross and interfuse. They are, arguably, not fixed poles between which the spirit oscillates, but are subject to the dynamism of change, moving on convergent paths. Suppose, then, that the period we are calling the Modern shows us not the mere rehabilitation of the irrational after a period of ordered Realism, or for that matter the reverse, a period of Classicism after a phase of Romanticism, but rather a compounding of all these potentials: the interpenetration, the reconciliation, the coalescence, the fusion – perhaps an appallingly explosive fusion – of reason and unreason, intellect and emotion, subjective and objective. Let us recall one of the central tenets of the Anglo-American Modern, the Imagist definition of Image, in the words of Ezra Pound: 'An image is that which presents an intellectual and emotional complex in an instant of time.'[46] Pound is here talking about the juxtaposing of contradictions for resolution, and we may extend that notion of fusion into other areas of experience. Or consider Paul Klee, speaking of painting: 'Formerly we used to represent things visible on earth, things we either liked to look at or would have liked to see. Today ... things appear to assume a broader and more diversified meaning, often seemingly contradicting the rational experience of yesterday. There is a striving to emphasize the essential character of the accidental.' Immediately, again, we recognize the quality common to many of the most characteristic events, discoveries and products of this modern age: in the concern to objectify the subjective, to make audible or perceptible the mind's inaudible conversations, to halt the flow, to irrationalize the rational, to defamiliarize and dehumanize the expected, to conventionalize the extraordinary and the eccentric, to define the psychopathology of *everyday* life, to intellectualize the emotional, to secularize the spiritual, to see space as a function of time, mass as a form of energy, and uncertainty as the only certain thing.

An explosive fusion, one might suppose, that destroyed the tidy categories of thought, that toppled linguistic systems, that disrupted formal grammar and the traditional links between words and words, words and things, inaugurating the power of ellipsis and parataxis and bringing in its train the task – to use Eliot's phrase – of making new juxtapositions, new wholes; or, in Hofmannsthal's words, of creating 'from man and beast and dream and thing' an infinity of new relationships. And if, finally, one were to seek the precisely defining event, the supremely symbolical point, one would surely turn back to the nineties; and to, for instance, Strindberg's complete, desperate and protracted attention to alchemy, that unique fusion of reason and unreason, science and magic; or to Yeats's evolutionary cosmology, with its search for unity between time and the timeless, the dancer and the dance. One would turn to the intensifying discovery that the thrust of modern consciousness raised issues that were more than representational, were crucially aesthetic, problems in the making of structures and the employment of language and the social role of the artist himself. One would need to contemplate the uneasy awareness that the spirit of naturalism, with its implied optimistic scientific temper, its sense of political emancipation, must find some way of comprehending the strange pressures of unconscious forces and answer to those luminous, unpositivistic metamorphoses that art uniquely could produce. The great works of Modernism live amidst the tools of modern relativism, scepticism, and hope for secular change; but they balance on the sensibility of transition, often holding in suspension the forces that persist from the past and those that grow from the novel present. They turn on ambiguous images: the city as a new possibility and an unreal fragmentation; the machine, a novel vortex of energy, and a destructive implement; the apocalyptic moment itself, the blast or explosion which purges and destroys – images, like Forster's Marabar Caves, which are potentially a synthesis of all possible experience, globally conceived, or of the empty multiplicity and anarchy of the world. It is the image of art holding transition and chaos, creation and de-creation, in suspension which gives the peculiar concentration and sensibility of Modernist art – gives it what one of the contributors in this volume calls its 'Janus-faced' quality.

It is perhaps, then, characteristic that Modernist writers tend to suppress certain features of modern sensibility – some of its optimism in history, science, evolution and progressive reason – while choosing to release others. The sequence of Modernism, we have said, is a very various sequence running through different subversions of the realist impulse: Impressionism, Post-Impressionism, Cubism, Vorticism,

Futurism, Expressionism, Dada and Surrealism. They are not all movements of the same kind and some are little more than coterie names; and writers tended to move in and out of them. But one feature that links the movements at the centre of sensibility we are discerning is that they tend to see history or human life not as a sequence, or history not as an evolving logic; art and the urgent now strike obliquely across. Modernist works frequently tend to be ordered, then, not on the sequence of historical time or the evolving sequence of character, from history or story, as in realism and naturalism; they tend to work spatially or through layers of consciousness, working towards a logic of metaphor or form. The symbol or image itself, whether romantic or classic, whether it be the translucent symbol with its epiphany beyond the veil, or the hard objective centre of energy, which is distilled from multiplicity, and impersonally and linguistically integrates it – helps to impose that synchronicity which is one of the staples of Modernist style. By such means can occur that compacting, that sense of generative distillation which can – to borrow Eliot's phrase about compacting contemporaneity and antiquity in *Ulysses* – 'make the modern world possible for art'. Hence there is a preservative element in Modernism, and a sense of primary epistemological difficulty; the task of art is to redeem, essentially or existentially, the formless universe of contingency. Reality is not a material given, and nor is it a positivistic historical sequence. The act of fictionality thus becomes the crucial act of imagining; and Modernism thus tends to have to do with the intersection of an apocalyptic and modern time, and a timeless and transcendent symbol or a node of pure linguistic energy.

Now if these propositions about the complexity and nature of Modernism do have any validity, we can find nearly all the significant manifestations at dates much earlier than those points in the 1920s which some of our critics have seen as the heyday of it all. The significance of de-creating the given surface of reality; intersecting historical time with time according with the movement and rhythm of the subjective mind; the pursuit of the luminous image, or else of fictional order sustained against consecutive story; the belief in perception as plural, life as multiple, reality as insubstantial; these crucial notions form into a creative compound long before the First World War and are there in the last century, as symbolism and naturalism cross and interfuse. One reason why the post-war period has seemed so crucial is that the war itself can be recognized as the apocalyptic moment of transition into the new. But in this matter we might better look at the significance of the turn of the century itself, a topic on which Frank Kermode writes brilliantly in *The Sense of an Ending*, a book which does much to distil the character of modern theories of fictionality and also the apocalyptic and historiographic features of Modernist sensibility.[47] Kermode suggests that the turning of a century has a strongly chiliastic effect; it helps distil men's millenarian disposition to think about crisis, to reflect on history as revolution or cycle, to consider, as so many *fin-de-siècle* and *aube-de-siècle* minds did consider, the question of endings and beginnings, the going and coming of the world. The sensibility itself has, of course, an extended history, going deep into the Judaic tradition and the kind of importance we attach to secular time. What Modernism does is to raise in ferment the notion not only of form but also of significant time, and this is one reason why audacious attempts to discern a moment of transition (Henry Adams's 1900; Virginia Woolf's 1910; D. H. Lawrence's 1915) are themselves a feature of Modernist sensibility. The consequences of this apocalyptic ferment of order help explain much of Modernism. It illuminates the symbolist effort to transcend historical sequence by intersecting with it the timelessness of artistic revelation: the artist, like Scott Fitzgerald's Gatsby, tips back the clock on the mantelpiece and sees beauty, form, dream. It illuminates the desire to reappraise the structure and operation of mind: 'To appreciate the pagan manner of thought,' D. H. Lawrence tells us, 'we have to drop our own manner of on-and-on-and-on, from a start to a finish, and allow the mind to move in cycles, or to flit here and there over a cluster of images. Our idea of time as a continuity in an eternal, straight line has crippled our consciousness cruelly.'[48] It illuminates, too, that passion in Modernism to see the universe as contingent, poverty-stricken, denuded until it has been reimagined, its local virilities apprehended through the planes and conjunctions available to the fictionalizing mind.

This crucial compound persists until after the war, and certainly up to 1930. After that it seems that certain elements of Modernism seem to be reallocated, as history increasingly came back in for intellectuals, as, with the loss of purpose and social cohesion, and the accelerating pace of technological change, modernity was a visible scene open to simple report, and as the world depression tends increasingly to bring back political and economic determinism into the intellectual ideologies. Our own concentration in this book is therefore on the period before 1930, even though the lines of demarcation here cannot be clear, for the broader view of Modernism we have offered must suggest an extraordinary range of continuities through into present art. There is a further reason for this concentration; for perhaps one of the most remarkable features of this period between 1890 and 1930 is the extraordinary galaxy of talent that we find there. Few historical phases contain such an extraordinary wealth of major writers – European, English, American – whose complexity of aesthetic inquiry, whose generative sense of style, whose sustaining and self-risking intelligence offers so much work worthy of detailed consideration. Modernism may be a stylistic abstraction, one exceptionally difficult to formulate. But it does catch under its loose but invigorating label a large number of writers who manifest art for us in a major way. It does not, as we have said, catch *all* the important writers of the twentieth century. But enough to make a volume devoted to Modernist experimentalism an exploration of some of the most interesting and essential literary creation to be found in our difficult century.

Notes

1 Herbert Read, *Art Now* (London, 1933; revised edition 1960).
2 C. S. Lewis, *De Descriptione Temporum: An Inaugural Lecture* (Cambridge 1955). The lecture is reprinted in his *They Asked for a Paper* (London 1962), pp. 9–25.
3 Roland Barthes, *Writing Degree Zero* (*Le Degré zero de l'écriture*), translated by Annette Lavers and Colin Smith (London 1967), p. 9.
4 G. S. Fraser, *The Modern Writer and His World* (London 1953); Richard Ellmann and Charles Feidelson (eds.), *The Modern Tradition: Backgrounds of Modern Literature* (New York and London 1965).
5 Lionel Trilling, 'On the Modern Element in Modern Literature', in *Beyond Culture: Essays in Literature and Learning* (London 1966).
6 Northrop Frye, *The Modern Century* (New York and London 1967), p. 23.

7 A. O. Lovejoy, 'On the Discrimination of Romanticisms' (1924), reprinted in M. H. Abrams (ed.), *English Romantic Poets: Modern Essays in Criticism* (New York 1960).

8 See especially Georg Lukács, *The Meaning of Contemporary Realism*, translated by John and Necke Mander (London 1962).

9 Alfred North Whitehead, *Science and the Modern World* (London 1927); quoted in Wylie Sypher, *From Rococo to Cubism in Art and Literature* (New York 1960).

10 Wylie Sypher, *From Rococo to Cubism in Art and Literature* (New York 1960), p. xix.

11 Stephen Spender, *The Struggle of the Modern* (London 1963).

12 Jose Ortega Y Gasset, 'The Dehumanization of Art', in *The Dehumanization of Art, and Other Writings on Art and Culture* (Garden City, N.Y. 1956).

13 Frank Kermode, 'Modernisms', in *Modern Essays* (London 1971).

14 This is Harry Levin's interpretation of a primary characteristic of modernism in 'What Was Modernism?', in *Refractions: Essays in Comparative Literature* (New York and London 1966).

15 T. S. Eliot, '*Ulysses*, Order, and Myth', *Dial*, no. 75 (New York 1923), pp. 480–83, reprinted in Richard Ellmann and Charles Feidelson (eds.), *The Modern Tradition: Backgrounds of Modern Literature* (New York and London 1965).

16 Irving Howe, 'Introduction to the Idea of the Modern', in Irving Howe (ed.), *Literary Modernism* (Greenwich, Conn. 1967), p. 13.

17 A. Alvarez, *Beyond All This Fiddle: Essays, 1955–1967* (London 1968).

18 Cyril Connolly, *The Modern Movement: One Hundred Key Books from England, France, and America, 1880–1950* (London 1965), p. 4.

19 Edmund Wilson, *Axel's Castle: A Study in the Imaginative Literature of 1870–1930* (New York 1931); C. M. Bowra, *Heritage of Symbolism* (London 1943).

20 Graham Hough, *Image and Experience: Studies in a Literary Revolution* (London 1960).

21 Richard Ellmann and Charles Feidelson (eds.), *The Modern Tradition: Backgrounds of Modern Literature* (New York and London 1965), p. vi.

22 A. Alvarez, *Beyond All This Fiddle: Essays, 1955–1967* (London 1968); Frank Kermode, 'Modernisms', in *Modern Essays* (London 1971); Stephen Spender, *The Struggle of the Modern* (London 1963); Graham Hough, *Image and Experience: Studies in a Literary Revolution* (London 1960).

23 Virginia Woolf, 'Mr Bennett and Mrs Brown' (1924), reprinted in *Collected Essays, volume 1* (London 1966), p. 321.

24 Richard Ellmann, 'The Two Faces of Edward', in R. Ellmann

(introd.), *Edwardians and Late Victorians* (New York 1960); reprinted in his *Golden Codgers: Biographical Speculations* (New York and London 1973).

25 Harry Levin, 'What Was Modernism?', in *Refractions: Essays in Comparative Literature* (New York and London 1966).

26 Harold Rosenberg, *The Tradition of the New* (New York 1959, London 1962).

27 For useful comments on Post-Modernism, see Ihab Hassan, *The Literature of Silence: Henry Miller and Samuel Beckett* (New York 1967), and his *The Dismemberment of Orpheus: Toward a Postmodern Literature* (New York 1971). Also see George Steiner, *Language and Silence: Essays 1958–1966* (London 1967), and Susan Sontag, *Against Interpretation and other Essays* (New York 1966).

28 Bernard Bergonzi (ed.), *Innovations: Essays on Art and Ideas* (London 1968). In addition to Kermode's essay, see that by Leslie Fiedler on 'The New Mutants' and that by Leonard B. Mayer on 'The End of the Renaissance?'.

29 Ihab Hassan, 'POSTmodernISM', *New Literary History*, vol. III, no. 1 (Autumn 1971), pp. 5–30; reprinted in I. Hassan, *Paracriticisms: Seven Speculations of the Times* (Urbana and London 1975). Other essays on the same topic are to be found in this issue. For a more critical view, see Gerald Graff, 'The Myth of the Postmodernist Breakthrough', *Tri-Quarterly*, no. 26 (Winter 1973), pp. 383–417. Other essays in this same special issue – especially that by Philip Stevick – are relevant.

30 George Steiner, 'From the Vienna Woods', *New Yorker* (23 July 1973), pp. 73–7.

31 Holbrook Jackson, *The Eighteen-Nineties* (London 1913; reprinted in Pelican Books, 1939). The quotation comes from p. 19 in the Pelican edition.

32 Wilhelm Arendt (ed.), *Moderne Dichtercharaktere* (Leipzig 1885).

33 In *Literarische Volkshefte*, vol. III (1888).

34 Lionel Trilling, 'On the Modern Element in Modern Literature', in *Beyond Culture: Essays in Literature and Learning* (London 1966).

35 Eugen Wolff, 'Die Moderne', reprinted in Erich Ruprecht (ed.), *Literarische Manifeste des Naturalismus, 1880–1892* (Stuttgart 1962), pp. 138–41.

36 M. G. Conrad, 'Moderne Bestrebungen', reprinted in Erich Ruprecht (ed.), *Literarische Manifeste des Naturalismus, 1880–1892* (Stuttgart 1962), pp. 254–6.

37 Hermann Bahr, *Zur Kritik der Moderne* (Zürich 1890); second series (Dresden 1891).

38 H. Stuart Hughes, *Consciousness and Society: The Reorientation of European Social Thought, 1890–1930* (London 1959), p. 34.

39 R. P. Blackmur, *Anni Mirabiles, 1921–1925: Reason in the Madness of Letters* (Washington D.C. 1956).

40 Graham Hough, *Image and Experience: Studies in a Literary Revolution* (London 1960), p. 8.

41 Thus William Carlos Williams comments: 'I'd felt at once that it [*The Waste Land*] had set me back twenty years, and I'm sure it did. Critically Eliot returned us to the classroom just at the moment when I felt that we were on the point of an escape much closer to the essence of a new art form itself – rooted in the locality which should give it fruit . . . ' (William Carlos Williams, *Autobiography* (London 1968), p. 174).

42 Frank Kermode, *Romantic Image* (London 1957) and A. Alvarez, *Beyond All This Fiddle: Essays, 1955–1967* (London 1968).

43 Geoffrey Hartman, *Beyond Formalism: Literary Essays, 1958–1970* (New Haven 1970); Harold Bloom, *Yeats* (New York 1970); Harold Bloom (ed.), *Romanticism and Consciousness: Essays in Criticism* (New York 1970); Robert Langbaum, *The Poetry of Experience* (New York 1963); and Morse Peckham, *Beyond the Tragic Vision: The Quest for Identity in the Nineteenth Century* (New York 1962). Also see the essays in David Thorburn and Geoffrey Hartman (eds.), *Romanticism: Vistas, Instances, Continuities* (Ithaca and London 1973).

44 J. Hillis Miller, *Poets of Reality* (Cambridge, Mass. 1965).

45 August Strindberg, 'Preface' to *Lady Julie* (1888).

46 Ezra Pound, 'A Retrospect' (1918), reprinted in T. S. Eliot (ed.), *Literary Essays of Ezra Pound* (London 1954), p. 4.

47 Frank Kermode, *The Sense of an Ending* (London and New York 1966).

48 D. H. Lawrence, *Apocalypse* (London 1832), pp. 97–8.

TWO

The Cultural and Intellectual Climate of Modernism

THE problem of Modernism's social, cultural and intellectual origins
has generated a considerable amount of discussion, in part because
Modernism, as a highly complex aesthetic tendency, has not been
much given to a direct, realistic expression of the social and intellectual forces and conditions underlying it. Clearly it is an art of a
rapidly modernizing world, a world of rapid industrial development,
advanced technology, urbanization, secularization and mass forms of
social life. Clearly, too, it is the art of a world from which many
traditional certainties had departed, and a certain sort of Victorian
confidence not only in the onward progress of mankind but in the
very solidity and visibility of reality itself has evaporated. It contains
within itself that tendency, so apparent at the end of the nineteenth
century, for knowledge to become both pluralistic and ambiguous,
for surface certainties no longer to be taken on trust, for experience
to outrun, as it seemed to many to be outrunning, the orderly control
of the mind. In the two following essays, Alan Bullock examines the
seeming contradiction between the apparent cultural and commercial security of the turn-of-the-century period and the simultaneous ferments in thought and art; and James McFarlane examines
some of the changes in the mode of thought that underlie the tense
encyclopedia of Modernist writing.

THE DOUBLE IMAGE

ALAN BULLOCK

I

THE Great War which tore Europe apart between 1914 and 1918 was so shattering in its impact, so far-reaching in its consequences, that it is profoundly difficult to recapture what preceded it – difficult to avoid exaggerating the sense of conflict in the pre-war years, difficult not to see them building up into a general crisis of European society in which a crash, a resolution by force, was inevitable and felt to be inevitable. Yet, whatever the intimations, whatever the elements of disturbance and the feelings of change, the elements of stability and tranquillity are quite as apparent as the elements of schism. Trying to look back, then, at the years as they appeared to the people of the time, I find myself turning to two contrasting pictures. One is a photograph of a London street-scene taken in the summer of 1904; it shows the busy crossing in front of the Royal Exchange. Along the pavements under the gaslamps, businessmen in top hats and frock coats rub shoulders with clerks in bowler hats, a ragged newspaper boy with his placards, and one or two women with long skirts and large hats, carrying parasols; the roadway is crowded with hansom-cabs, brewers' drays, waggons and horse-drawn buses – the animated everyday scene on any day of the week in the largest and wealthiest city in the world, caught suddenly and pinned down in black and white. The second is a picture, *Les Demoiselles d'Avignon*, painted by Picasso in 1907, a painting fertilized by Spanish and African influence which has been called the first truly twentieth-century painting: five naked women painted in a series of geometrical lozenges and triangles, with total disregard of anatomy and perspective, a famous point of distillation in Cubism. To translate into words the meaning and associations instantaneously conveyed by this double image is to convey something of the span of experience represented by the period between the turn of the century and 1914.

2

The London street-scene is a kind of visual shorthand of the bourgeois civilization which reached its apogee at the beginning of the twentieth century. In the 1900s the European capitals, London, Paris, Berlin, were at the centre of a network of industrial, commercial and financial communications which is perhaps the nearest we have ever come to a world-wide economic system, based on the capitalist premiss of free enterprise and private profit. The half-century before the First World War was the most remarkable period of economic growth in history, not excluding our own time. In the years 1870–1913 the expansion of the international economy, measured by increase in industrial output per head, was more rapid than ever before or since. Britain, Germany and France between them commanded 60 per cent of the world market for manufactured goods and between 1900 and 1910 Germany virtually doubled her steel, iron and coal producing capacity. Overlapping with this great industrial expansion was a technological revolution which, in the 1890s and 1900s, produced a series of key developments that remain the foundation of the technology of the twentieth – as distinct from that of the nineteenth – century.

These were:

the internal combustion engine, the diesel engine and the steam turbine;

electricity, oil and petroleum as the new sources of power;

the automobile, the motor bus – the first London motor buses appeared in 1905 – the tractor and the aeroplane;

the telephone, the typewriter and the tape machine, the foundation of modern office organization;

the production by the chemical industry of synthetic materials – dyes, man-made fibres and plastics.

Industrialization had been accompanied by a great increase in urban populations. By 1900 there were already eleven metropolises in the world with populations of over a million. By 1910 Greater London and New York had populations of over five million, Paris of nearly three, Berlin of more than two.

This was the shape of twentieth-century European and American society: urbanized, industrialized, mechanized, its life shaped to the routine of factory or office. Ford in the U.S.A. and William Lever in Britain were only two of the businessmen who, well before 1914, had grasped the secret of successful business in such a society: mass production for a mass market. The advertising business had already been born in response to the same opportunities, and with it the mass entertainment industry, the history of which has still to be written. In 1896 Alfred Harmsworth began publishing the *Daily Mail*, a landmark in the history of popular journalism. The year before the Lumière brothers had invented the cinematograph, and Marconi wireless telegraphy; the first motion picture theatre in the world, the Nickelodeon, opened in Pittsburgh in 1905. The media had been created.

Europe dominated the world politically as well as economically. Only two nations outside Europe enjoyed real independence – America and Japan. The rest of the world was either parcelled out between the rival European empires or under the rule of states – China, Persia, the Ottoman Empire, the South American states – too feeble, corrupt, or both, to withstand economic penetration or political pressure. This was the great age of imperialism, based not only on the material superiority but, as the great majority believed without a shadow of doubt, on the cultural and racial superiority of the white races of European stock. The British Empire in 1900 covered one quarter of the land surface of the globe and numbered 400 million people. London was the imperial capital *par excellence*. Nor was imperialism simply a system of power politics and economic exploitation; it was also an ideology, a faith, fascinating intellectuals and writers, business men, soldiers, missionaries and politicians alike.

The transformation of Europe by industry and empire during the latter part of the nineteenth century produced far-reaching social and political changes. At the top, the traditional European élites, based on birth and the ownership of land, survived by accommodating themselves to the upward thrust of new groups drawn from industry, banking and the professions. The great estates of the European aristocracy, all the way from Scotland to Hungary, from Spain to Russia, were still intact. But ancient families kept strange company now, a hybrid society with wealth as its single common denominator, arrogant and ostentatious in the vulgarity of its taste, the world of the Ritz, Monte Carlo, Deauville and Biarritz, with Queen Victoria's son, Edward VII, as its royal patron. Below the top, Europe remained a society governed by class distinction, with undisguised inequality between rich and poor. The difference between the leisured and the working classes found expression not simply in their clothes, their food, their housing and their education, but in their physical appearance and mentality. The poor who thronged the overcrowded slums of the big cities were a lower order of humanity, and treated as such, valued only as the vast pool of surplus labour on which the social as well as the economic system depended. By 1900 the workers had learnt to organize and to protest; there were frequent strikes in the next fourteen years, and socialist parties steadily collected more members and more voters. Social questions began to figure more and more prominently on the agenda of politics. Yet we must beware of letting our knowledge of what was to come colour the picture too highly: up to 1914 there was no serious revolt against the existing order, except in Russia, where the loss of the Russo–Japanese war was followed by the confused outbreak of 1905. Even Russia, the most vulnerable régime in Europe, once it recovered nerve, was also well on the way to recovering its power by 1914. Indeed, it is arguable that, but for the War, there would have been no violent revolution in twentieth-century Europe; Lenin would have remained in obscure and vituperative exile in Switzerland. Certainly no European government hesitated to go to war in 1914 for fear that its subjects would refuse the call to arms or use their weapons against their own rulers; and they were right.

Well before 1914, Europe was divided into two hostile camps, France and Russia on the one hand, the Central Powers on the other, each arming against the other, with the British pursuing their own naval arms race with the Germans. Sooner or later this threatened war, a prospect which, however, evoked little of the widespread horror it did in the 1930s – partly because both the threat and the use of force were accepted parts of the power politics which all states practised, most of all because few even among the soldiers had any idea of what modern technological war would mean, not only for individuals but whole societies. Few believed the War would last beyond Christmas; none supposed that, when it was finally over, the Europe of 1914 would be gone for ever. The crowds who cheered the declaration of war in every European capital did so not out of some collective death urge, but out of ignorance.

If this picture of Europe before 1914 appears unattractive, it is because, in concentrating the main features into a few paragraphs, one distorts the cultural texture. Much has been written nostalgically about *la belle époque* and the Edwardian peace, much of it exaggerated in reminiscence. But there is a truth in this, especially if one was born into the right class. Despite periodic threats of war, strikes, suffragettes, fears of social conflict, the middle and upper classes of England and of Western Europe enjoyed a freedom and a security almost impossible to recapture today. And the benefits of this state of affairs, if very unfairly distributed by modern notions of social equality, were enjoyed by many more people than they had ever been before. With light taxation, no inflation, cheap food, cheap labour, a plentiful supply of domestic servants, many ordinary middle class families with modest incomes lived full and comfortable lives. No wonder that so many who came from such families and survived the War, looking back, felt that there was a grace, an ease, a security in living then which has since been lost for ever. And, curiously, this is not the antithesis of the other factors: open, uninhibited acceptance of inequality, power and wealth, class and racial superiority. Indeed one of the strongest impressions left on the external observer examining this world of the 1900s is of an age remarkably unselfconscious, self-confident, far less troubled by the anxieties, fears and fantasies, the self-consciousness and guilt which may tremble underneath a few of its writings but which have found such vivid expression and subscription in Europe since then. Perhaps it is precisely this that makes that world seem remote to us today.

3

But against this must be set that second image – Picasso's *Les Demoiselles d'Avignon*, and the entire break it stands for: a move away from the tradition in the representation of the human form, a profound cultural shock, one that had, however, been assimilated, become a new tradition, by 1914. For the 1900s were a period of the most extraordinary originality and vitality in the history of art. This was particularly true in Paris. Among those working there at this time – besides Cézanne, who did not die until 1906 – were Matisse, Marquet, Rouault, Utrillo, Derain, Vlaminck, Braque, Léger, Arp, Picasso, and Duchamp. If we add the names of those who visited Paris during these years, we draw in Nolde, Franz Marc, Brancusi, Archipenko, Marc Chagall, Paul Klee, Juan Gris, Modigliani, Soutine, Piet Mondrian, and Chirico, giving us a total list which starkly suggests the flowering of genius and modes these years saw. But Paris was not the only centre. In Dresden, between 1905 and 1913, German artists of the same generation of the 1880s, the generation to which Picasso and Braque belonged, formed *Die Brücke* group, one of the sources of Expressionism. More important still was the *Blaue Reiter* group formed in Munich in 1911, numbering among its members Paul Klee and the Russians Kandinsky, Jawlensky, and Naum Gabo. Klee – whose catalogue of work dates from February 1911 – and Kandinsky were both later to become members of the famous post-war Bauhaus in Dessau. Kandinsky was one of the founders of Abstract Art, and his book *Concerning the Spiritual in Art* was published in Munich by the same firm – R. Piper and Co. Verlag – that published two other key documents in the history of modern art: Wilhelm Worringer's *Abstraction and Empathy* (1908) and his *Form in Gothic* (1912). The Russians in Munich provided a link with another group in pre-war Moscow, including Kasimir Malevich, the founder of Suprematism, and the Constructivists, Rodchenko, Tatlin and the brothers Antoine Pevsner and Naum Gabo. Nor does this nearly complete the list of the major modern artists active before 1914: one must add James Ensor, the Belgian predecessor of the Surrealists; Oskar Kokoschka, whose first one-man show was held in Berlin in 1910; Edvard Munch, the Norwegian expressionist, and the Italian Futurists, whose manifestos and exhibitions between 1909 and 1914 drew into art the forms and forces of the world of the machine and technology.

This world particularly affected the architects and designers. In neither field was the pre-war period so rich in achievement as painting, but there is no doubt that the foundations of the Modern Movement in both architecture and design were laid before 1914. To select some names – in France, Perret and Tony Garnier with his designs dated 1901–4 for a linear industrial city; Robert Maillart, the Swiss engineer who opened up the possibilities of reinforced concrete in his Tavanasa Bridge of 1905; the Austrian Adolf Loos, who denounced ornament as a crime, and some of whose buildings, like the Steiner House of 1910 in Vienna, might well be dated in the 1930s; Peter Behrens, the German architect who became adviser to the German General Electrical Company in 1907, and his more famous pupils Walter Gropius, born in 1883, and Mies van der Rohe, born in 1886. (Notice again the generation of the 1880s.) The Bauhaus, which made Gropius famous, was founded in the 1920s; but the foundations for its work were laid before the war by the Deutscher Werkbund (1907) and Herrmann Muthesius, Superintendent of the Prussian Schools of Arts and Crafts, who broke through the barriers between the artist and industry in order to establish the possibility of good design for the machine-made, mass-produced product.

Once one begins to think in such terms, to examine painting or the new movement in architecture and design, the 1900s no longer seem remote, as they do when one examines their politics, their economics, their mundane everyday life: an age which can seem more difficult to understand than the mid Victorian age suddenly comes close, becomes an essential part of our century, the Great War no longer appearing as the great dividing line between the nineteenth century and contemporary history but rather as an event within our own history. But is this true only of the visual arts? What of music? In one of his conversations with Robert Craft, Stravinsky remarked that the richest musical years in this century were those immediately before the 1914 war, years of radical exploration which were to decline into a period of formalism in the late 1920s and 1930s. His own career supports this: the dates of three of his best known works are *The Fire Bird* – 1910; *Petroushka* – 1912; *Rite of Spring* – 1913. One may question Stravinsky's opinion, but there is no doubt that the language of twentieth-century music was created in these years – by Stravinsky himself, Debussy and Ravel in Paris; by Schoenberg and his two pupils Webern and Alban Berg in Vienna; by Bela Bartok, who was appointed professor at the Budapest Conservatoire in 1907.

In literature the matter is complex and extensively discussed in this book. But I suggest that the modern movement in literature begins rather earlier and that there are two age groups to notice. The first is a number of writers who, although, like Cézanne, clearly nineteenth-century by their date of birth, produced in the late 1890s and the

1900s work which belongs very much to modern literature; central here are Strindberg and Chekhov. Strindberg died in 1912, and some of the greatest of his plays – *To Damascus, There are Crimes and Crimes, Easter, The Dance of Death* and *The Ghost Sonata* – belong to the years between 1899 and 1907. Chekhov died in 1904, but his plays were all written in the last eight years of his life: *The Seagull* (1896); *Uncle Vanya* (1897); *Three Sisters* (1901) and *The Cherry Orchard* (1904). Henry James, in his later period, which began with *The Spoils of Poynton* and *What Maisie Knew* in 1897 and ran on to *The Golden Bowl* in 1904, should also be included in this group; and Conrad, whose *Under Western Eyes* (1911) is a startling preview of twentieth-century revolutionary politics. The second group is a younger generation, who were to become major literary figures in the 1920s, but who were all at work before the War. In France this included Gide and Proust – a first draft of the whole of Proust's great work was written between 1905 and 1911, and the first part, *Du côté de chez Swann* (*Swann's Way*) published in 1913; Alain-Fournier, whose short novel *Le Grand Meaulnes* (*The Lost Domain*) was also published in 1913; the poets Paul Claudel, Paul Valéry and Guillaume Apollinaire. In Germany it included Thomas Mann – *Buddenbrooks* was published in 1900, *Tonio Kröger* in 1903, and *Der Tod in Venedig* (*Death in Venice*) in 1913 – Kafka and Hermann Hesse, Stefan George and Rilke. In English and American literature there were Yeats (*Responsibilities* – 1914); D. H. Lawrence (*Sons and Lovers* – 1913, *The Rainbow* – 1915); Ezra Pound; James Joyce – *Dubliners* was published in 1914, *The Portrait of an Artist as a Young Man* serialized and the seven years' work on *Ulysses* begun in the same year – and those two middle men between the worlds of art and literature: Wyndham Lewis, who was editing *Blast* in 1914, and Gertrude Stein, who settled in Paris in 1903. These names are enough to establish that, in literature as in art and architecture, the modern movements of the twentieth century were born not after but before 1914. The same can be said of the modern theatre – Komisarjevsky, Stanislavsky in the Moscow Art Theatre, Max Reinhardt in Berlin, Gordon Craig and Appia in Western Europe – and of the modern ballet created before the war by Isadora Duncan, Fokine, Pavlova, Nijinsky and Diaghilev.

Thus, then, the arts; but let us now ask whether what was happening in science before 1914 in any way resembles that activity. Leaving aside biology and the establishment of genetics in the 1900s, the most striking case is physics. The revolution in physics is one of the greatest intellectual achievements of this century, and it is largely the working out of discoveries made and hypotheses formulated before the War. If there is a year from which to date the beginning of this revolution it should perhaps be 1895, the year of Röntgen's discovery of X-rays, which was followed by Becquerel's discovery of the radioactive properties of uranium and the Curies' of radium. In 1897–9, J. J. Thomson, working at the Cavendish in Cambridge, detected the existence of separate components, which he called electrons, in the structure of what had hitherto been regarded as the indivisible atom. In 1902 appeared Rutherford and Soddy's historic paper on the cause and nature of radioactivity; Soddy went on to discover (and name) isotopes in 1912, Rutherford in 1911 to introduce what Eddington called 'the greatest change in our idea of matter since Democritus', his revolutionary model of the atom as a small, positively-charged nucleus containing most of the mass of the atom, around which the electrons moved in orbit like the planets round the sun. These discoveries threw the classical theory of physics into confusion; the first step in re-formulation was Max Planck's quantum theory of energy, presented in a paper to the German Physical Society in Christmas week 1900, and revised by Niels Bohr working with Rutherford in 1913. Between these two versions of the quantum theory, Einstein published his *Special Theory of Relativity* in 1905, while he was still an examiner of patents in the Berne Patents Office, and started on the ten years' work which in 1915 produced his *General Principles of Relativity* with its model of a non-Euclidean four-dimensional space–time continuum. Thus, in the twenty years between 1895 and 1915 the whole picture of the physical universe, which had appeared not only the most impressive but also the most secure achievement of scientific thought, was brought in question and the first bold attempts made to replace it by a new model.

Finally we might note that the same radical exploring attitude found among the painters and the physicists of the 1900s was also being applied to the study of man and of society. The most famous name here of course is that of Freud. Born in 1856, he began as a neurologist and only became interested in psychology in the 1890s. (1895 is the date of the joint volume by Freud and Breuer, *Studies on*

Hysteria, usually taken as marking the beginning of psycho-analysis.) In 1898 he published his first paper on infantile sexuality; in 1899 (dated 1900) his *magnum opus*, *The Interpretation of Dreams*. There followed in 1904, *The Psychopathology of Everyday Life*; in 1905, *Three Essays on the Theory of Sexuality*; and in 1913, *Totem and Taboo*. No single man, probably, has exercised a greater influence on the ideas, literature and art of the twentieth century than Freud: not only was his most original work done before 1914, but the controversy to which his views gave rise was already in full swing. The first psycho-analytical congress was held in 1908; three years later came the breach with Adler and in 1913 the much more serious breach with Jung.

At the same time that Freud was challenging accepted views of psychology, Max Weber and Emile Durkheim were laying the foundations of modern sociology. Durkheim was born in 1858 and died in 1917; the dates of his three most important books are 1895, 1897 and 1912. Max Weber, born in 1864, died in 1920 and did the bulk of his work, much of it left unfinished, between 1903 and 1914. Although not comparable in intellectual stature with Weber and Durkheim, one can add at the same time other contemporary founders of the social sciences: in the U.S.A., Thorstein Veblen (1857–1919) who wrote the *Theory of the Leisure Class* (1899) and invented the phrase 'conspicuous consumption'; in London, J. A. Hobson, from whose *Imperialism* (1902) Lenin borrowed much of his own theory of finance-imperialism, and Graham Wallas, who published *Human Nature in Politics* in 1908; in Italy, Pareto and Mosca, the creators of the theory of the élite; in France, Gustav le Bon, whose *Psychology of Crowds* was published in 1895, and Sorel, whose famous *Reflections on Violence*, with its brilliant conception of the function of the myth in modern society, appeared in 1908.

In making this catalogue of names and dates, I am well aware that I have ignored the demarcation lines between different disciplines, and risked over-simplification, even inaccuracy. The risk is surely worth running, because while every specialist is aware of what was done before 1914 in his own field, he is not always aware of the importance of what was happening over the rest of the range of intellectual and cultural activity.

4

What does this catalogue of names and dates add up to? Let me first make clear some of the things I am *not* saying. First, the activities of the men and women I have mentioned represented only a minority, even within that minority which is ever interested in the arts and ideas. The dominant literary, musical and artistic taste, not to speak of the scientific outlook, of the 1900s was founded upon nineteenth-century, not twentieth-century, models, a cultural time-lag which is characteristic of every age of innovation. Second, most of them had precursors. The date 1900 is obviously an artificial boundary line. If one wanted to do full justice to this theme, it would be necessary to go back to the 1880s. (Roger Shattuck, for instance, whose book *The Banquet Years* is a study of the *avant-garde* in France, takes the dates 1885–1918.) In literature this is particularly true, where the modern movement has roots in Baudelaire, Flaubert and Dostoyevsky, as indeed in Nietzsche, Ibsen and the twentieth century's own discovery, Kierkegaard, who died in 1855. Nor, thirdly, do I wish to suggest that innovation came to an *end* with the War. Many of the names I have cited went on to produce their finest work in the 1920s and 1930s and the impulse released in the period before the First World War was still at work up to the Second.

None the less, when all this is said, it is surely true that the work of the individuals and groups I have considered not only makes this pre-war period one of extraordinary creativity and originality but marks a change in sensibility and a change in consciousness comparable with the impact of the Romantic movement, the scientific revolution of the seventeenth century, or the Renaissance. Many of those involved in these movements were certainly convinced that they were living at the beginning of a new age. They believed, rightly, that they were developing new ways of looking at the physical universe, both artistically and scientifically, new ways of understanding man and society, new forms of expression for what they saw and felt, which were different from any that had gone before. Nor, looking back from the last half of the century, does it appear that they were wrong. Time tests innovation harshly; how many of the 'new waves' of the past hundred, hundred and fifty, years are remembered today? But the period of the 1900s stands the test well; its works retain something of that original power to shock, surprise and excite. Anyone who wants to understand the origins of twentieth-century art or thought or science in any of the fields mentioned here must still go back to these years. And the origins are represented, in many cases, not by a modest inching forward, but by a bold leap – the originality of which is not diminished when later generations take up and develop the possibilities further.

Any attempt to put that change of consciousness and feeling into a single form of words seems to me inadequate. It is as full of cross-currents, shifting moods and contradictions as any of the other great cultural shifts, those complex movements which for convenience's sake we label the Renaissance, the Enlightenment or the Romantic movement. Particularly so in this case, for it is easy to see a parallel between, say, the scientists breaking up the accepted view of the physical universe and the painters breaking up the accepted view of art as representational of an external world; in neither case has the work of demolition been followed by the creation of an accepted alternative. Certainly it is possible to see a common temperament at work, radical, innovatory, experimental – but continuing so, not settling down with any new grand certainties or remaining content with the achievement of one set of new forms or a common language of expression. The old patterns have been broken up: this time they were not replaced.

Yet, surely, the break-up of the old patterns in so many different spheres at roughly the same point of time cannot have been accidental; it has common causes. Let me go back to the double image with which I began. The first was a picture of the society of the 1900s, a society rapidly changing under the impact of technological invention, economic growth and political tension. The second was an example of an artist's imagination at work in creating a revolutionary new form of expression. But the artist's, the writer's, or thinker's imagination, if it is to prove fruitful, does not work in an arbitrary fashion, creating in a vacuum. It is more likely that the artists, the writers and the thinkers of the 1900s with their more highly developed sensitivity were responsive to trends and conflicts – social, moral, intellectual, spiritual – already beginning to appear over the horizon, and sought for new forms, new languages, in which to project these in advance of their time. Vladimir Tatlin put it perfectly when he saw the ideas and art of the Constructivists taken up with enthusiasm in revolutionary Russia: 'We created the art before we had the society.' One clear example of this is the interest of architects and designers in the possibilities of machine production and their attempt to create an architecture and design for the technological age which was being born. Another, working the other way, is the violent reaction of many of the Expressionist painters to the dehumanizing pressures – the insecurity and loneliness – which they felt were being created by increasing urbanization. These were two opposite reactions to the same trend towards a much more highly urbanized, technological society which was rapidly developing behind the façade of what we might call Baedeker's Europe, reactions commonly shaped and caused.

What these radical new developments – in art, thought, literature, science – have in common is their awareness of the future. What they had to say was listened to and understood by only a minority at the time; only later, when the War had swept away the old order of European society and finally destroyed its values in a way which everyone could see, was it recognized that the imagination of the painters and poets, the scientists and the thinkers of the 1900s had reached out to see in advance the world (which they were helping to create), that improbable, disturbing, fragmented world in which we still live.

THE MIND OF MODERNISM

JAMES MCFARLANE

I

WHEN, in 1893, Hugo von Hofmannsthal remarked that to be 'modern' meant at that time two separate and distinct things, his lack of evident bewilderment was something which in itself struck a prophetically 'modern' note. 'Modern', he explained, could mean analysis, reflection, a mirrored image; or it could mean escape, fantasy, a dream image:[1]

> *Heute scheinen zwei Dinge modern zu sein: die Analyse des Lebens und die Flucht aus dem Leben . . . Man treibt Anatomie des eigenen Seelenlebens, oder man träumt. Reflexion oder Phantasie, Spiegelbild oder Traumbild. Modern sind alte Möbel und junge Nervositäten . . . Modern ist Paul Bourget und Buddha; das Zerschneiden von Atomen und das Ballspielen mit dem All; modern ist die Zergliederung einer Laune, eines Seufzers, eines Skrupels; und modern ist die instinktmässige, fast somnambule Hingabe an jede Offenbarung des Schönen, an einen Farbenakkord, eine funkelnde Metapher, eine wundervolle Allegorie.**

What these phrases acknowledge is the subsumption, within a single, newly emerging and as yet semantically unstable concept of the 'modern', of two distinct *Weltanschauungen* – the mechanistic and the intuitive[2] – which the earlier nineteenth century had so productively kept separate. The century's intellectual achievement had largely derived from the creative rivalry between these two anti-

---

*'Today, two things seem to be modern: the analysis of life and the flight from life . . . One practises anatomy on the inner life of one's mind, or one dreams. Reflection or fantasy, mirror image or dream image. Old furniture is modern, and so are recent neuroses . . . Paul Bourget is modern, and Buddha; splitting atoms and playing ball games with the cosmos. Modern is the dissection of a mood, a sigh, a scruple; and modern is the instinctive, almost somnambulistic surrender to every revelation of beauty, to a harmony of colours, to a glittering metaphor, to a wondrous allegory.'

thetical modes of intellectual inquiry; now the new concept brought them into a relationship of novel and unexpected intimacy.

Nearly forty years later, with the high peaks of European Modernism already past, Virginia Woolf's *The Waves* (1931) remarked the peculiar way in which the news of Percival's death saddened for Bernard the day on which his own son was born. Specifically, it was no simple invasion of joy by grief: 'Such is the incomprehensible combination, such is the complexity of things,' Bernard reflects, 'that as I descend the staircase I do not know which is sorrow, which joy.' The coalescence, the fusion to the point of indistinguishability of two concepts which the structure of everyday language was designed to keep separate and distinct, echoed Hofmannsthal's concern of the eighteen nineties.

Bernard's bewilderment, his finding the combination 'incomprehensible', was an acknowledgement that understanding does not come easily. Practice, said Rilke sternly, was essential; the intellect required exercise to equip it to meet the strain of comprehension: '*Deine ausgeübten Kräfte spanne bis sie reichen zwischen zwein Widersprüchen*'[3] ('Stretch your practised powers till they reach between two contradictions'). The defining characteristic of Modernism was its insistence that the mind be subjected to this wholly new kind of stress. Poetry became an 'intolerable wrestle with words and meanings', a hauling and straining, a racking of the mind's powers of comprehension. Older and more traditional definitions of poetry – the spontaneous overflow of powerful feeling, the best words in the best order – were impatiently dismissed. Obsessive attempts to say 'the unsayable' made extreme demands on the mind's elasticity. Not only literature but all art of the period seemed to be intent on stretching the mind beyond the very limits of human understanding.

2

The two modes of thought identified in 1893 by Hofmannsthal as the chief 'modern' preoccupations were far from enjoying comparable status; not until the turn of the century itself was it that their standing relative to each other underwent any radical revaluation. Although many of the individual philosophical systems and named doctrines which the nineteenth century had thrown up were now being subjected to sceptical and even hostile scrutiny, the prestige of natural science and of scientific method in general still stood high in these years. Positivism and utilitarianism in the field of social philosophy, naturalism in the field of literature, might be considered by those abreast of affairs to have had their day, but the intellectual assumptions, the modes of thought which had served as foundation for that kind of philosophical system-building, still retained in the minds of many an unquestioned validity. It only required a catalogue of the achievements of nineteenth-century science, not merely those which had afforded startlingly new insights into the nature of the physical universe but also those which had made impressive contributions to the material well-being of the individual and of society, to assure for the orthodoxies of scientific method a continuing respect: in the work of Charles Lyell in geology; Bunsen and Kirchoff in spectroscopy and cosmology; Mendel in genetics; Joule, Lord Kelvin and Helmholtz in thermo-dynamics; Örsted, Faraday, Clerk Maxwell and Hertz in electro-magnetism. A special and outstandingly influential role, within this general advance of scientific inquiry, attached in the nineties to the work and ideas of Darwin. By offering a new, exhaustively documented and entirely plausible pattern of cause and effect, based on the slow processes of sexual and natural selection and the reductive effects of environmental factors, Darwin stimulated a search in a great many other areas of intellectual endeavour for similarly long-term and slow-acting causal chains in the explanation of natural and social phenomena. The theory of evolution, as it had been outlined in *On the Origin of Species by Means of Natural Selection* and *The Descent of Man*, took its place alongside the earlier Newtonian theory of gravity and the 'uniformitarian' theory of geology as one of the seminal ideas in the history of thought.

The continuing success of a method of inquiry that placed its faith firmly in precise and detailed observation, in the painstaking collection and collation of data, in the rational basis of causality, and in the reduction of the particular and the various to some form of comprehensive generality also had an irresistible appeal for those enquiring into the nature of social and individual behaviour and into the ontology of art, culture and civilization. The conviction that behavioural phenomena were reducible to the same kind of general laws as were seen to apply in the physical world, using similar methods of observation and verification, became deeply rooted in nineteenth-century social thought. In, for example, Comte's exclusive concern with the immediate data of experience, and in his repudiation of anything metaphysical, mystical or supernatural, there is an argument for the existence of a 'positivist' universe, that is, a whole which is not an accumulation of self-willed individuals but an ordered organism, ruled by general and definable laws and within which the chief and indisputable agency was reason. For Comte and for those who took their cue from him, the study of society took on the characteristics of a science.

The same dedication to the abstract, the general, the classified also marked the thought of Taine. A declared anti-romantic, he repudiated what he considered to be Romanticism's mere pose and pretence, deploring its lack of high seriousness. For him, literature could never be a social factor, never an active force in the shaping of man's destiny, but only a social product that had little to do with individual talent or even individual volition: a great writer could only be an end-product of a multiplicity of impersonal factors – the determinants of race, environment and time. For him, real elegance and beauty could only manifest themselves where economy and reason were supreme. *'C'est beau comme un syllogisme'* ('It's beautiful like a syllogism') was a habitual remark of his which betrayed the true cast of his mind.

Deep distrust of any form of introspective study of the individual mind as a reliable source of truth was something that Buckle shared with Taine. For him – and in this he was characteristic of much nineteenth-century thought – the impact of the individual on human progress was as naught compared with the great momentum of social and community action. In his eagerness to establish what would virtually have been a science of history, he was moved to place great reliance on statistical 'proof', and on the concept of the average: here, he felt, was the surest way of establishing those general laws which he was convinced governed the course of human progress as rigorously as the laws of science held control over the physical universe.

The possibility of some ultimate and overriding synthesis of all empiric knowledge was something that underlay the endeavours of many of the system builders of these decades; and nowhere more persistently than in the thought of Herbert Spencer. Following his *Social Statics* of 1850 and his *Principles of Psychology* of 1855, he dedicated the ten volumes of his *Synthetic Philosophy* (finally completed in 1896) to great sweeping formulations of his faith in rational progress and in the efficacy of scientific method. Though accused of lacking real scholarly rigour, this work proved to be an eloquent and influential statement of the basic tenets of 'scientific' inquiry, and in particular prepared the way for an extended application of the assumptions of biological evolutionary theory to other aspects of life. A belief that totality of detail must inevitably betray something of the essential nature of existence, that an object asserts its own importance, is self-insistent, that it must ever be part of the author's intent to invest it with significance, sustained many forms of cultural and intellectual endeavour.

The tradition of thought represented by this – positivist, analytical, objective, generalized, logical, absolutist, impersonal, determinist, intellectual, mechanistic – also in large measure fed the aspirations of literary naturalism, which by 1893 was reputedly (or disputedly) already dead. The attitude of mind and the patterns of thought from which it drew its strength nevertheless continued to survive, sustained in large measure by the immense reserves of accumulated prestige, and creating in these years a situation of some cultural complexity.

Despite the manifest and impressive achievements of science, interest in what the Society for Psychical Research (founded 1882) primly called 'debatable phenomena' grew rapidly during the last quarter of the century. With the creation of the Theosophical Society in America in 1875, the beginnings of a switch of emphasis from social to individual preoccupations received an early measure of formal recognition. Not only did the newly formed society institutionalize the growing interest in the nature and development of the individual personality or ego; it also stimulated the serious and systematic investigation of 'occultism' – all those mystic, anti-positivist and irrational potencies of life and matter which now, progressively as the century moved towards its turn, occupied the attention of thinkers and writers. Deriving many of its articles of faith from Oriental sources, especially Vedic and Buddhist, but also from Greek and Cabbalistic ideas, theosophy was concerned to effect *individual* rather than social change as the key to human advancement, to achieve a radical revision of the aims and motives of the person, to transform not merely the everyday conduct of the common man but also his very thought and speech habits. In flat contradiction to the statistical abstractions of the positivist view of things, it believed ardently in the existence of an ego-entity, the nature of which could not only be changed by spiritual exercise but which could thus contribute effectively to the fuller development of mankind.

Powerful reinforcement of this trend towards 'individualization' came with the great revival of interest in the course of the nineties in Max Stirner's *Der Einzige und sein Eigentum* (*The Individual and His Property*), first published as early as 1845 but now given new currency by the expository zeal of John Henry Mackay. The doctrine of anarchism it advanced gave explicit emphasis to the importance of individual liberty in place of social constraint, to the free exercise of man's inherent powers guided only by his own personal understanding, to the rehabilitation of the individual and to the declared supremacy of subjective thinking. Hand in hand with this went a vastly increased attention to the whole range of problems connected with the nature of the unconscious or subconscious or subliminal self, and especially with the nature and the extent of the influence which one mind might succeed in exerting over another. Chief among the 'debatable phenomena' of the Society for Psychical Research was hypnotism – a term which around mid-century had come to displace the earlier 'mesmerism' or 'animal magnetism'. But the list was soon extended to include also such phenomena as somnambulism, animism, automatism, telepathy and hallucinatory experience.

It was nevertheless a characteristic of this spate of new inquiry that, whilst asserting the validity of a whole range of 'non-scientific', 'non-positivist', irrational and even mystic phenomena, it turned to the traditional 'scientific method' for the conduct of its investigations. Eduard von Hartmann, whose *Die Philosophie des Unbewussten* (*Philosophy of the Unconscious*) had by 1890 passed through no fewer than ten editions in twenty-one years, made much of his claim to have used the methods of inductive science in arriving at conclusions which we today recognize as essentially speculative. Most of the influential inquiries of the eighties and early nineties into clinical or morbid psychology – Charcot's examination of hysteria and hypnotic states; Liébeault's *Étude sur le zoo-magnétisme* (1883); Bernheim's *De la Suggestion* (1884), which insisted on a psychological rather than a physiological explanation of hypnosis, together with his *Hypnotisme, suggestion, psycho-thérapie* (1891); and Lombroso's studies of criminal states of mind, of mental and nervous anomalies – adopted as the basis of their approach what was clearly an orthodox 'scientific method'. The rational still held unquestioned dominion over the irrational; the full force of 'unscientific method', the invasion of the rational strongholds of thought by the concepts of irrationality, had still to be experienced.

As the European mind began to face the challenge of the nineties, the supremacy of scientific method was nevertheless progressively brought into question. Brunetière's is probably the most representative voice. From an initial faith that evolutionary principles must surely apply just as clearly in literature as in biological science, he swung over to a very real hostility towards scientific criteria. The slogan of 'the bankruptcy of science' – an idea which had already been given some currency by Paul Bourget – was stridently taken up by Brunetière, who argued for the replacement of 'purely positivistic demonstration' by 'purely visionary intuition'.

3

As though in mimetic enactment of its own dualistic processes, the decade of the nineties responded to two powerful though fundamentally different agencies of change: one positivist, and the other – in the peculiar sense of those days – 'debatable'. On the one hand, and in the tradition of Taine, one can point to the shaping force of the 'milieu' and the 'moment', to the very marked rise in intensity, over a wide range, of social and cultural pressures. On the other hand there occurred the largely contingent, devastatingly explosive impact of Nietzsche.

Appreciably, the dimensions of time and space had begun to alter. As communications improved, distances shrank. As the more hectic rhythms of urban living imposed themselves over wider areas of society, so events moved faster and the whole tempo of life quickened.

The chance of casual international encounter (like colliding atoms in conditions of rising temperature) was greatly increased, and with it the rapidity with which ideas and opinions were exchanged across national frontiers. A chart of the movements of artists, writers and thinkers in time and space during these years would doubtless reveal an astonishing incidence of random encounter – above all in Paris, Berlin and London – to create that spread of internationalism which (it has been suggested) is the main merit and sign of Modernism. Translations proliferated, and this was accompanied by a marked improvement in their general quality, and a quickening of the speed with which they tended to follow the original publication. The whole Goethean concept of *Weltliteratur* began to reassert its appeal. There was a palpable increase in intellectual traffic of all kinds, in ideological trade, in cultural exchange.

It also seemed as though, under the general press of events, the oscillations of the spirit became more rapid, and a new shrillness of tone began to manifest itself. Conspicuous in the early nineties is a growing sense of impatience; frustration becomes one of the more usual motivating forces; anti-movements reveal themselves often as those with the greatest driving force, and the desire to remove, to supplant, to replace becomes the overriding consideration. The cultural situation, most markedly perhaps in Germany, was revolutionary. The assault on the old guard in literature – and the new became the old with a speed which to some was astounding – was no mere stylistic swing but a vociferous demand for fundamental change: new attitudes, new areas of exploration, new values. Irreverence became a cult; ruthlessness was admired. Unexpectedly – as Samuel Lublinski commented in his *Die Bilanz der Moderne* (*The Balance Sheet of the Modern*) – it was the artists and intellectuals who provided the greatest revolutionary passion, the real sense of *Ekstase*; the more committedly political activists, sustained by their Marxist faith in the historical inevitability of change, often seemed content to work for limited or partial and sometimes rather prosaic objectives: prohibition or vegetarianism or theosophy. Not infrequently, writers became infected by a kind of political self-consciousness that led them to organize themselves on the analogy of political parties. They formed groups and alignments; they issued declarations and manifestos. The virtues of solidarity found new recognition; denunciation of some recognizable 'other side' was much practised. Relevance to the modern situation was demanded: to city life, to industrial problems, to political change. Re-adjustment, re-alignment, revaluation – change in infinite variety – lay at the basis of expectation.

It was a situation deeply vulnerable to the new ideas of Nietzsche, the date of whose impact can be placed with considerable precision, and the subsequent spread monitored with more than usual accuracy. Despite his prolific authorship of the seventies and eighties, Nietzsche was almost unknown before May 1888, when he was made the subject of a series of lectures in Copenhagen by the Danish critic Georg Brandes. From Brandes (who read the Germans a stern lesson on their neglect of this thinker in their midst) the word spread via the Scandinavian colony of writers and critics in Berlin and through the excited advocacy of Strindberg first to Germany's *avant-garde* and then to Europe at large. Nietzsche's letters to Brandes and Strindberg in the autumn of 1888, despite the clearly megalomaniac tone, have a strangely prophetic quality. Announcing in the November the impending promulgation of his 'revaluation of all values', he declared: 'I swear that in two years time the whole world will be in convulsions. I am sheer destiny.' The following month he wrote to Strindberg that he now felt possessed of the strength 'to cleave the history of mankind in two'.

His apocalyptic vision, his profound conviction that the history of man had arrived at a point of destiny, at the terminus of a long era of civilization, and that all human values must be subjected to total revision found a reverberent echo in the aspirations of western man in these years. By his violent assault on the tenets of Christianity, his advocacy of what Brandes (to Nietzsche's own declared pleasure) defined as his 'aristocratic radicalism', his ruthless questioning of the nineteenth century's *idées reçus*, his total repudiation of traditional morality, he won a response from the generations of the *fin-de-siècle* and the First World War which gave him a uniquely influential role in the Modernist period.

4

An early voice raised in repudiation of two of the most cherished beliefs of the nineteenth-century liberal mind – that society at large and not the individual was the real custodian of human values, and that 'truth' once established was absolute – had been that of Ibsen's 'enemy of the people' in 1882. 'The majority is never right,' announced the excited Dr Stockmann. '*I* am right – I and one or two other individuals like me.' And he went on to declare the essentially impermanent nature of truth: 'The life of a normally constituted truth is generally about seventeen or eighteen years, at most twenty. Rarely longer.' (Looking back from the twentieth century on the changes which these words heralded, the philosopher George Santayana took very much the same line: Science, he said, which had in his early years seemed like a family of absolute monarchs – sovereign axioms, immutable laws – was very shortly transformed into 'a democracy of theories elected for a short term of office'.) Individualistic, relativistic, Stockmann's outburst marked the start of a complex and protracted change in the European mind, in which a growing instability was to be its most conspicuous feature.

Initially, the emphasis is on fragmentation, on the breaking up and the progressive disintegration of those meticulously constructed 'systems' and 'types' and 'absolutes' that lived on from the earlier years of the century, on the destruction of the belief in large general laws to which all life and conduct could be claimed to be subject. As a second stage – though, as in the case of all these changes, never in obedience to any tidy or consistent chronological pattern – there came a re-structuring of parts, a re-relating of the fragmented concepts, a re-ordering of linguistic entities to match what was felt to be the new order of reality. Naturalism, which – as Philip Rahv has suggested[4] – exhausted itself in taking an inventory of the world while it was still relatively stable, could not possibly do justice to the phenomena of its disruption. Finally, in its ultimate stages, thought seemed to undergo something analogous to a change of state: a dissolving, a blending, a merging of things previously held to be forever mutually exclusive. A sense of flux, the notion of continuum, the running together of things in ways often contrary to the dictates of simple common sense (though familiar enough in dream) alone seemed able to help in the understanding of certain bewildering and otherwise inexplicable phenomena of contemporary life.

'Fragmentation' is the declared basis of Strindberg's dramatic strategy of 1888. His Preface to *Miss Julie* impatiently rejected nine-teenth-century notions of 'fixed' dramatic characters deriving identity from some abstracted notion of villainy, say, or jealousy or miser-liness, whose actions were explicable by some simple one-to-one relationship of cause and effect, who were definable, predictable, typed. Because – as he said of his own created figures – 'they are modern characters, living in a period of transition more feverishly hysterical than its predecessor', he had deliberately made them 'un-certain, disintegrated':

> My characters are conglomerations of past and present stages of civilization, bits from books and newspapers, scraps of humanity, rags and tatters of fine clothing, patched together as is the human soul.

It is the classic declaration in these early years of Modernism that human nature is not to be contained by vast and exhaustive inven-tories of naturalistic detail arranged and sorted under prescriptive heads but instead is elusive, indeterminate, multiple, often implausible, infinitely various and essentially irreducible.

This urge to fragmentation, of which Strindberg is here the early spokesman of an entire generation, was to override all merely stylistic distinctions of these years. It is present both in the naturalistic *Sekundenstil* – an attempt to break down into successive fragmentary moments of time even the most commonplace events of life (like the path of a falling leaf) in order that a 'realer' level of reality might be recorded – and also in those more impressionistic attempts to catch something of the moment-to-moment workings of the mind, such as Knut Hamsun wrote of in 1890:[5]

> They last a second, a minute, they come and go like a moving wink-ing light; but they have impressed their mark, deposited some kind of sensation before they vanished . . . Secret stirrings that go unnoticed in the remote parts of the mind, the incalculable chaos of impressions, the delicate life of the imagination seen under the magnifying glass; the random progress of these thoughts and feelings; untrodden, trackless journeyings by brain and heart, strange workings of the nerves, the

whisper of the blood, the entreaty of the bone, all the unconscious life of the mind.

Both strategies represented forms of stylistic microscopy that sought to penetrate below the surface of massed detail to some deeper level of literary cognition, to a veracity that no longer depended on accretion and painstaking enumeration but on the significantly random. And both relate to Bergson's *Essai sur les données immédiates de la conscience* (*Time and Free Will*) (1889), which argued for the recognition of a special kind of subjective logic, found at the deeper levels of the mind, and differing in essence from the conventional logic of the common-sense world of naturalistic time and space.

Yet it is revealing that, in much of this, the practices of science and of scientific method were still deeply respected: careful observation, precise recording and close attention to detail. An unspoken loyalty to traditional notions of causality, even determinism, still persisted, though the mechanics of it were no longer narrowly positivistic. Real hostility was reserved for abstraction and generality. The distinctiveness of select phenomena, the unique essence of individual personality, and the changing relationship between the individual and 'the whole' (however variously that might be conceived) constituted the new concern. The wanderer, the loner, the exile, the restless and rootless and homeless individual were no longer the rejects of a self-confident society but rather those who, because they stood outside, were uniquely placed in an age when subjectivity was truth to speak with vision and authority. Perceptibly in the nineties and even more markedly in the early years of the new century, the custody of life's integrities began to pass from society to the individual – to an individual who necessarily commanded some unique perception of the things of life, who embodied some secret essence which alone gave the world its legitimization.

Within this situation of growing fluidity, 'myth' (as Sorel was soon to argue) commended itself as a highly effective device for imposing order of a symbolic, even poetic, kind on the chaos of quotidian event, and offering the opportunity – to use a phrase of Frank Kermode's – to 'short circuit the intellect and liberate the imagination which the scientism of the modern world suppresses'.[6] Born of the irrational, and obeying a logic much closer to the subjective and associative promptings of the unconscious mind than to the formal progression of scientific inquiry, myth offered a new kind of insight into the wayward realities of social phenomena, gave – as Eliot was to say of Joyce's myth – 'a way of controlling, of ordering, of giving a shape and a significance to the immense paradox of futility and anarchy which is contemporary history'.[7] The result was, in Stuart Hughes's phrase, 'a kind of sociological mysticism'.[8]

A sense of the total relatedness of things, altogether different from those tightly drawn causal links by which the positivist world had held together, stimulated a search for that mystic 'world of relationships' – Hofmannsthal's *Welt der Bezüge* – in which the role of the poet was that of 'silent brother of all things', who saw the world not as an accumulation of categories, abstract concepts and general laws but as an infinitely complex lattice of relationships, personal to him, of which his mind was the centre and coordinator. In this he was helped by having as his main instrument the metaphor, that which (as Shelley had remarked before) 'marks the before unapprehended relations of things and perpetuates their apprehension'; in consequence the poet was able to coordinate, in patterns appropriate to the new thinking, those disparate elements which, following the fragmentation of the positivistic world, would otherwise have remained merely chaotic and unrelated. Hofmannsthal's call to the poet to create 'from past and present, from beast and man and dream and thing ... the world of relationships'[9] defined for the modern age the role of the poet in terms that astonishingly anticipated Eliot's now classic formulation a quarter of a century and more later: 'A poet's mind ... is constantly amalgamating disparate experience; the ordinary man's experience is chaotic, irregular, fragmentary. The latter falls in love, or reads Spinoza, and these two experiences have nothing to do with each other, or with the noise of the typewriter or the smell of cooking; in the mind of the poet these experiences are always forming new wholes.'[10]

Signs of change in collective sensibility are – as Ortega y Gasset has said[11] – likely to show first in art and in pure science, precisely because they are the freest activities, the least dependent on social conditions. From the bridgehead that had been won in poetry, this sense of an inter-relatedness of things greater than traditional concepts and linguistic categories seemed prepared to acknowledge soon began to invade science and philosophy. Barriers between subject and object, between the Cartesian *res cogitans* and *res extensa*, between man the observer and nature the observed were progressively demolished. Science admitted that to persist in rigid differentiation between objects in time and space and the mind in which they were reflected was no longer helpful in clarifying the nature of modern reality. For the philosopher Ernst Mach, there was an intimate interpenetration between things inner and things outer: 'There is no gulf between the psychical and the physical, no "within" and "without" ... There are only elements of one kind which according to the moment of their observation are "within" or "without".' Heisenberg allowed into the *Naturbild* of modern physics the recognition that 'science no longer stands in front of nature as an observer but acknowledges itself as part of the interplay between man and nature'.

New concepts in science more and more took on the nature of poetic conceits; the crucial advances in science (not merely in the relatively new field of psychology but also in the more traditional physical sciences) followed the exploitation of the same kind of imaginative, intuitive insight that went towards the making of a poem. The physicist found himself having to acknowledge the existence of new and disturbingly different laws, in which conventional logic and common sense played a greatly diminished role. Below the microscopic and above the telescopic thresholds of human vision – like Hofmannsthal's poet 'splitting atoms and playing ball games with the cosmos' – imaginative and even fantastic speculation invaded scientific thought on a scale as never before. The sculptural models of the micro-biologist, the mathematical models of the theoretical physicist shared something of the nature of the novelist's fictive world. New 'unscientific' concepts like a-logicality and a-causality demanded formal recognition, even experimental verification; the uncertainties of probability usurped the sovereignty of precise knowledge, of confident predictability. In some instances there was a shared distinctiveness. The Freudian concept of 'ambivalence' fused into a single entity the totally contrary ideas of love and hate. Jungian psychology was driven to operate with the concept of enantiodromia, 'the turning of each thing into its opposite'. The quantum physicist, faced with the problem of defining the nature of the so-called 'elementary particles', abandoned the classic common-sense distinction between mass and energy and accepted the existence of a wholly 'ambivalent' entity which was *both* wave *and* particle, and yet in a strict sense neither. The Special Theory of Relativity argued that space and time, instead of being the discrete and distinct dimensions they had always been taken to be, were in crucial and extreme circumstances actually functions of each other. In Minkowski's four-dimensional geometry, a single line represented the whole history of a body through the space–time continuum. And the very shape of the world was altered by this new knowledge.

Within this pervasive shift in the modern *Weltbild*, the dream came to enjoy a novel and special status. At the very turn of the century, with the publication of *Die Traumdeutung* (*The Interpretation of Dreams*) in 1899, Freud's theories gave the respectability of clinical proof to much that the popular mind had long known about the symbolic content of dreams. It was 'proved' that the action of the dreaming mind in collecting and ordering the heterogeneous and disconnected elements peculiar to it achieved a special kind of coherence, a new 'logic'. Although our recollection of dreams could only be uncertain and fragmentary, the eloquence of even such imperfect testimony was seen as a mode of communication of an entirely different order. The apparent incongruence and incoherence of the dream was nevertheless recognized as the mind's way of communicating the most complex and subtle things, often with a most admirable economy and elegance – things which the mind had perhaps never consciously or supraliminally perceived.

Bracketing in time Freud's clinical exploration of the nature of dream were those dramatic experiments of Strindberg that deliberately set out to exploit a dream logic: *To Damascus I* and *II* of 1898, *A Dream Play* of 1902, and the third part of *To Damascus*, much of it written in 1900 but the whole not published until 1904. In his preface to *A Dream Play*, Strindberg clearly set out his dramatic intentions:

In this dream play, as in his previous dream play *To Damascus*, the author has tried to reproduce the disconnected but apparently logical form of a dream. Anything may happen; all things are possible and probable. Time and space do not exist: against an unimportant background of reality, the imagination spins and weaves new patterns; a blend of memories, experiences, free ideas, absurdities, improvisations.

The characters split, double, multiply; they evaporate, crystallize, scatter and converge. But a single consciousness holds dominion over them all: that of the dreamer.

For a great many of the artists and writers of the first two decades of the twentieth century, the dream became – as Arnold Hauser has stressed – the paradigm of the whole *Weltbild* in which reality and unreality, logic and fantasy, the banal and the sublime form an indissoluble and inexplicable unity. The peak was reached in Surrealism:

The meticulous naturalism of the details and the arbitrary combination of their relationships which surrealism copies from the dream not only express the feeling that we live on two different levels, in two different spheres, but also that these regions of being penetrate one another so thoroughly that the one can neither be subordinated to nor set against the other as its antithesis. The dualism of being is certainly no new conception, and the idea of the *coincidentia oppositorum* is quite familiar to us . . . but the double meaning and the duplicity of existence, the snare and the seduction for the human understanding which lie hidden in every single phenomenon of reality, had never been experienced so intensively as now.[12]

5

The same point was made with greater, more epigrammatic, economy by Gottfried Benn:[13]

Der Phänotyp des 12. und 13. Jahrhunderts zelebrierte die Minne, der des 17. vergeistigte den Prunk, der des 18. säkularisierte die Erkenntnis, der heutige integriert die Ambivalenz, die Verschmelzung eines Jeglichen mit den Gegenbegriffen. *

The cross-references are endless. To Hesse's novel of 1919, *Demian*, in which the presiding deity, Abraxas, is both man and woman, god and devil, whose embrace is both an act of worship and a crime, and whose presence evokes both terror and bliss. To the moment in Joyce's

*The phenotype of the twelfth and thirteenth centuries celebrated courtly love; that of the seventeenth spiritualized ostentatious splendour; that of the eighteenth secularized knowledge; and that of today achieves an integrated ambivalence, the merging of each thing with its opposite.

Ulysses when Bella Cohen in the brothel turns her deeply carboned eyes on Bloom and asks in the language of the fan whether he remembers her and he replies 'Nes. Yo.'; and how, subsequently, this same Bella, the mannish woman with the sprouting moustache, undergoes transformation into Bello Cohen, a womanish man with bobbed hair. To Rilke's own explanation of the meaning of the *Duino Elegies* and the *Sonnets to Orpheus* as expressing 'the identity of terror and bliss' and 'the oneness of life and death'.[14]

Were this all that is characteristic of Modernism – a viper's tangle in which yes and no, life and death, man and woman, terror and bliss, crime and worship, god and devil lose their separate identity and merge – there would be little real novelty. The notion of the reconciliation of opposites is in itself at least as old as Heraclitus. As Hauser has pointed out, the idea of the *coincidentia oppositorum* is familiar to us from the philosophy of Nicholas of Cusa and Giordano Bruno. The nineteenth century itself produced many variants on the idea: Schelling went exploring a territory beyond human individuality, a womb of darkness where all distinctions, especially those of subjectivity and objectivity, disappear; Goethe detected in Nature a vast incomprehensible force, the 'Daemonic', which was compounded of contradictions and which in itself was both arbitrary and necessary; Hegel attended to the Absolute, in which were resolved things not merely contrary but contradictory; and Kierkegaard called on Man to leap in faith across the abyss of paradox.

To call the Modernist manifestation of this 'ambivalence', as Benn has done, is less than satisfactory. Strictly, our dictionaries lack the word which would embrace all the diverse ways of interconnecting opposites and contraries and contradictions, which would gather within one semantic category such notions as polarity and dualism and dialectic and schizophrenia and synthesis and ambivalence, which would admit the simple oxymoron as well as the Aristotelian idea that 'the highest harmony springs from opposites', and which would run right through to the sophistications of Freudian and Jungian psychology.

What is distinctive – and difficult – about the Modernist mode is that it seems to demand the reconciliation of two distinct ways of reconciling contradictions, ways which in themselves are also contrary. On the one hand, it recognizes the validity of a largely rational, mechanistic, Hegelian synthesis, a higher unity which preserves the essence of the two conflicting elements whilst at the same time destroying them as separate entities. As in the case of the character in Strindberg's *To Damascus*, for whom a Hegelian synthesis of 'yes' and 'no' was the way to ultimate understanding:[15]

Thesis: affirmation. Antithesis: negation. Synthesis: comprehension! ... You begin life by accepting all things. Then you proceed on principle to deny all things. Now finish your life by comprehending all things. Be one-sided no more. Do not say 'either ... or', but instead 'both ... and'!

But at the same time, the Modernist mind also seems to want to acknowledge Kierkegaard's 'intuitive' repudiation of this as merely shrouding everything in a great fog in which it is impossible to recognize anything, and to approve instead his concept of 'either/or' in place of the Hegelian 'both/and'. 'Either/or', Kierkegaard claimed, should not be considered as disjunctive conjunctions; rather, they belong so inseparably together that they ought really to be written as one word. Their unique function is to bring life's contraries into the most intimate relationship with each other, whilst at the same time preserving the validity of the contradiction between them. It is then as though the Modernist purpose ought to be defined as the resolution of Hegel with Kierkegaard; committing oneself neither wholly to the notion of 'both/and', nor wholly to the notion of 'either/or', but (as it were) to both – and to neither. Dauntingly, then, the Modernist formula becomes 'both/and and/or either/or'.

It comes as no great surprise that, although this highly ambiguous stance is one that might be detected at the heart of a number of more expressly Modernist works of literature, there has been a natural reluctance on the part of writers to try to say 'in simple words' what it was they were at. The very notion itself is elusive enough to be best served by the subtle complexities of poetic or symbolic language, or by the resources of fictional or dramatic communication. One of the very few to make the attempt was Hermann Hesse, who tried in an essay to define in straightforward terms what exactly he wished to try to do with words. If he were a musician, he wrote, he could without difficulty write a two-part melody in which the two lines of notes and sounds would complement, combat, determine and correspond to each other, which would at every point be mutually and reciprocally related in the most vital and intimate way: and yet anyone able to read music would always be able to see and hear each separate note along with its contrary and complementary note, its brother, its enemy, its antipode. It was precisely this two-part melody, this antithetical progression, this double line which he wanted to express in words:[16]

Beständig möchte ich mit Entzücken auf die selige Buntheit der Welt hinweisen und ebenso beständig daran erinnern, dass dieser Buntheit eine Einheit zugrunde liegt; beständig möchte ich zeigen, dass Schön und Hässlich, Hell und Dunkel, Sünde und Heiligkeit immer nur für einen Moment Gegensätze sind, dass sie immerzu ineinander übergehen. Für mich sind die höchsten Worte der Menschheit jene paar, in denen diese Doppelheit in magischen Zeichen ausgesprochen ward, jene wenigen geheimnisvollen Sprüche und Gleichnisse, in welchen die grossen Weltgegensätze zugleich als Notwendigkeit und als Illusion erkannt werden. *

These 'magic symbols' of Hesse's thus form a kind of meta-language in which things kept apart by conventional language are brought together within a new universe of discourse which allows workaday contraries to have at one and the same time a separate and a shared identity, to be indifferently both 'same' and 'different'. There is, in this, massive support for the view of Roland Barthes that the chief concern of modern literature – in his estimate since as far back as Flaubert – has been with the problematics of language.[17]

6

The testimony of *The Waste Land* (1922) suggests that this peculiarly Modernist kind of vision might appropriately be termed 'Tiresian'. The central importance to the poem of the lines

*Constantly I desire to point with delight to the blessed motley of this world, but equally constantly to bring to mind the fact that at the basis of this motley there lies a unity; constantly I desire to show that beautiful and ugly, light and dark, sin and sanctity are opposites only momentarily, and that they continually pass over into each other. For me, the highest words of humankind are those few mysterious phrases and images in which the great opposites of the world are seen to be both necessary and illusory at one and the same time.

> I Tiresias, though blind, throbbing between two lives,
> Old man with wrinkled female breasts, can see
> At the violet hour . . .

is something that Eliot himself has emphasized. His comments, in the 'Notes to the Waste Land', have been often quoted:

> Tiresias, although a mere spectator and not indeed a 'character', is yet the most important personage in the poem, uniting all the rest. Just as the one-eyed merchant, seller of currants, melts into the Phoenician Sailor, and the latter is not wholly distinct from Ferdinand Prince of Naples, so all the women are one woman, and the two sexes meet in Tiresias. What Tiresias *sees*, in fact, is the substance of the poem.

Thus, all the men, though individually identified, are one man; all the women one woman; and man and woman meet in Tiresias, the blind seer, who is both a mere spectator and 'the most important personage', is at the same time pivotal and peripheral.

Though blind, Tiresias can nevertheless see at the violet hour – at that precise moment when day and night lose their separate identity and merge into one another. Clear sight, it is suggested, is incompatible with real vision; to focus sharply on the separate phenomena of life is to reduce them to a succession of isolated, unrelated things, is merely to say 'Here is . . . and here is . . . and here is . . .,' as does Madame Sosostris, the famous clairvoyante, with her wicked pack of cards; she has won a (spurious) reputation as 'the wisest woman in Europe' as a result of directing her clear-sightedness, her clairvoyance, with such exclusive concentration on the objects within her range of vision that she cuts them off from any wider context that might give them fuller meaning or significance. To 'fix' the eyes is to give the whole attention to each thing separately and to neglect what lies about it; it is to apprehend the world as an aggregate of unrelated things, is to differentiate too strictly – a common frailty (according to Rilke) in all men: '*Aber Lebendige machen alle den Fehler, dass sie zu stark unterscheiden*' ('But all the living make the mistake of distinguishing too strictly').[18] The vision of Tiresias is otherwise. Watching at the violet hour, he shows no concern for this power of discrimination that ordinary men hold in such high esteem. To him, squalor and grandeur are indistinguishable, all beds are one bed, and all love-making the same undifferentiated enactment; he is indifferent to common-sense distinctions between life and death, seeing the shuffling crowd on London Bridge as a procession of dead men; he recognizes no difference between past and present, and greets one of the present-day generation as one who had been with him in the ships at Mylae; and unlike Madame Sosostris, who clearly sees as distinct individuals the Phoenician Sailor, the one-eyed Merchant and the rest, he sees all men as one man, all women as one woman, and resolves within his own androgynous person even this last distinction of male and female.

That the blindness of Tiresias is not to be interpreted in merely negative terms – as though he were simply bereft of the positive faculty we call good eyesight – is something that *The Waste Land* is very concerned to say. His seeing blindness derives from a very Modernist logic, a logic which is then embodied in the structure of the poem as a whole. An unexpected commentary to this point came a few years later with Elias Canetti's novel of 1935, *Die Blendung* – the German title of which, translatable variously as *The Blinding, The Dazzling* or even *The Delusion*, relates to the matter in hand more surely than that of the published English translation, *Auto-da-Fé*. The hero of this novel, a professor of Oriental studies, also discovers for himself by chance the full visionary power of blindness (or at least of controlled 'defective' vision) as a cosmic principle. Finding his attention distracted from his books and his research by the sight of the tawdry bedroom furniture his wife has placed in his library, he teaches himself to find his way among his shelves with his eyes shut, to select his books 'blind'. Although inevitably he makes what the logic of normal sight would regard as errors, the result nevertheless astonishes and delights and impresses him. There is recognition of the value of contingency, of chance juxtaposition, of luck that again recalls Barthes' notion that 'thought' is prepared by the contingency of words, and that 'this verbal luck . . . brings down the ripe fruit of meaning . . .'

Not that the intention is to evoke a picture – attractive though that might be – of Eliot padding blindly round his shelves, feeling for his Shakespeare, his Milton or his Dante and laying hands instead on Chapman's *Handbook of Birds of Eastern North America* or *The Proposed Demolition of Nineteen City Churches* or any of the other books that make their unexpected contribution to *The Waste Land*. Rather, it is that Canetti's hero recognizes in his adventurous raids into the library an active principle at work: in his kind of seeing-blindness he discovers a way of relating or linking things that would otherwise seem not in the least to relate to each other. Blindness becomes the means wherewith to come to terms with life, permitting a wholly new philosophy of contingency. Canetti's hero decides that 'blindness is a weapon against time and space, and our existence a unique monstrous blindness. It makes possible the placing together of things which would be impossible if they were to see each other.' His visionary blindness, like the blindness of eyes filled with tears or pain, or of those who close their eyes that they might dream or love or die, or the blindness that comes with much seeing, with 'looking into the heart of light' – such blindness, it is claimed, yields much more reliable testimony about the real meaning of life than does the report of witnesses enjoying conventional good sight.

To many minds this could only represent chaos – chaotic accounts of a twentieth-century situation which was in itself chaotic, a threat to the rules by which our existence had been traditionally ordered. 'Order' tends to commend itself as something in the nature of a planetary system, an arrangement of things 'held together' by cohesive force, the failure of which results in simple disintegration:

> Things fall apart; the centre cannot hold,
> Mere anarchy is loosed upon the world ...

The very vocabulary of chaos – distintegration, fragmentation, dislocation – implies a breaking away or a breaking apart. But the defining thing in the Modernist mode is not so much that things fall *apart* but that they fall *together* (recalling appropriately the derivation of 'symbol' from *symballein*, to throw together). In Modernism, the centre is seen exerting not a centrifugal but a centripetal force; and the consequence is not disintegration but (as it were) superintegration. The threat to (conventional) order comes not from the break-down of a planetary system but from the repudiation of a filing system, where order derives as much from keeping separate as from holding together, with dockets and folders and pigeon-holes to distinguish and hold things apart – rather as language itself sorts and separates those things it was at one time felt needed distinguishing. But in a situation where conceptual categories change at a pace different from linguistic ones, the tensions are immediate. When the pattern which thought necessarily imposes on experience demands fundamental revision, and when the linguistic system which is required to verbalize the new situation has a formidable built-in inertia to overcome, a crisis of culture and with it the inauguration of a wholly new 'civilizational phase'[19] is inevitable.

Notes

1 Hugo von Hofmannsthal, 'Gabriele D'Annunzio', in *Gesammelte Werke* (Stockholm 1946ff.), Prosa vol. I (1956), p. 149.

2 To adapt A. N. Whitehead's terminology: 'The literature of the nineteenth century . . . is a witness to the discord between the aesthetic intuitions of mankind and the mechanism of science.' (*Science and the Modern World*, Cambridge 1927, p. 108.)

3 R. M. Rilke, *Ausgewählte Werke* (Leipzig 1938), vol. I, p. 364.

4 Philip Rahv, *Literature and the Sixth Sense* (London 1970), p. 86.

5 Knut Hamsun, 'From the unconscious life of the mind' ('*Fra det ubevidste Sjæleliv*'), in *Samtiden* (1890), pp. 325ff.

6 Frank Kermode, *Puzzles and Epiphanies* (London 1962), p. 37.

7 T. S. Eliot, '*Ulysses*, Order and Myth', *Dial*, No. 75 (New York 1923), pp. 480–83.

8 Stuart Hughes, *Consciousness and Society* (London 1959), p. 176.

9 Hugo von Hofmannsthal, 'Der Dichter und diese Zeit' (1907), in *Gesammelte Werke*, Prosa vol. II (Frankfurt am Main 1951), p. 283.

10 T. S. Eliot, 'The Metaphysical Poets', in *Selected Essays* (London 1932), p. 287.

11 J. Ortega y Gasset, *The Modern Theme* (London 1931), p. 26.

12 A. Hauser, *Social History of Art* (London 1951), vol. IV, p. 224.

13 Gottfried Benn, *Gesammelte Werke* (Wiesbaden 1959), vol. 2, p. 156.

14 R. M. Rilke, *Briefe* (Wiesbaden 1950), vol. II, p. 382.

15 Father Melcher, in *To Damascus III*, Act IV, ii.

16 In Hesse's analysis of his own *Kurgast*, quoted in Richard B. Matzig, *Hermann Hesse* (Stuttgart 1947) pp. 13ff.

17 Roland Barthes, *Writing Degree Zero* (London 1967) p. 9.

18 R. M. Rilke, in the first of the *Duino Elegies*.

19 The term is David Jones's: see his *Epoch and Artist* (London 1959), p. 139.

THREE

A Geography of Modernism

ONE of the more striking features of Modernism is its wide geographical spread, its multiple nationality. Scanning the pattern of its development in east and west, from Russia to the United States, one notes the emergence of artistic phenomena, explosions of consciousness, generational conflicts which – even if not always contemporaneous – show remarkable similarity. Yet each of the contributing countries has its own cultural inheritance, its own social and political tensions, which impose distinctively national emphases upon Modernism and leave any account which relies on a single national perspective misleadingly partial. One reason for this, as Malcolm Bradbury suggests in the first essay here, is that Modernism found its natural habitat in cities – cities which themselves in turn became cosmopolitan centres. The essays which follow look selectively at some of Modernism's more important urban foci at periods of high cultural intensity: at Berlin, Vienna and Prague, essentially centres of Germanic Modernism, in the earlier part of the period; at Moscow and St Petersburg in the Symbolist phase before the Revolution; at Paris at the height of the battles fought for Modernism; at London, New York and Chicago. Inevitably there are gaps – the Scandinavian *Bohème*, the turbulence of Italian Futurism, the Berlin of the Expressionist decade, the Paris post-war scene – some of which are however caught up elsewhere in the volume. This section cannot aim to be comprehensive; instead it attempts to show something of the variety of ferment of Modernism in a number of its cultural settings.

THE CITIES OF MODERNISM

MALCOLM BRADBURY

In many respects the literature of experimental Modernism which emerged in the last years of the nineteenth century and developed into the present one was an art of cities, especially of the polyglot cities, the cities which, for various historical reasons, had acquired high activity and great reputation as centres of intellectual and cultural exchange. In these culture-capitals, sometimes, but not always, the national political capitals, right across Europe, a fervent atmosphere of new thought and new arts developed, drawing in not only young native writers and would-be writers, but artists, literary voyagers, and exiles from other countries as well. In these cities, with their cafés and cabarets, magazines, publishers, and galleries, the new aesthetics were distilled; generations argued, and movements contested; the new causes and forms became matters of struggle and campaign. When we think of Modernism, we cannot avoid thinking of these urban climates, and the ideas and campaigns, the new philosophies and politics, that ran through them: through Berlin, Vienna, Moscow and St Petersburg around the turn of the century and into the early years of the war; through London in the years immediately before the war; through Zürich, New York and Chicago during it; and through Paris at all times.

Of course such cities were more than accidental meeting places and crossing points. They were generative environments of the new arts, focal points of intellectual community, indeed of intellectual conflict and tension. They were mostly cities with a well-established humanistic role, traditional cultural and artistic centres, places of art, learning and ideas. But they were also often novel environments, carrying within themselves the complexity and tension of modern metropolitan life, which so deeply underlies modern consciousness and modern writing. There has always been a close association between literature and cities. Here are the essential literary institutions: publishers, patrons, libraries, museums, bookshops, theatres, magazines.

Here, too, are the intensities of cultural friction, and the frontiers of experience: the pressures, the novelties, the debates, the leisure, the money, the rapid change of personnel, the influx of visitors, the noise of many languages, the vivid trade in ideas and styles, the chance for artistic specialization. Writers and intellectuals have long abhorred the city: the dream of escape from its vice, its immediacy, its sprawl, its pace, its very model of man has been the basis of a profound cultural dissent, evident in that most enduring of literary modes, pastoral, which can be a critique of the city or a simple transcendence of it. And the forms and stabilities of culture itself have often seemed to belong, finally, outside the urban order.[1] Yet writers and intellectuals have, after all, constantly gone there, as on some essential quest into art, experience, modern history, and the fullest realization of their artistic potential. The pull and push of the city, its attraction and repulsion, have provided themes and attitudes that run deep in literature, where the city has become metaphor rather than place. Indeed, for many writers the city has come to seem the very analogue of form – for Pope and Johnson, Baudelaire and Dostoyevsky, Dickens and Joyce, Eliot and Pound. But as the breadth of this list suggests, the city has not remained one thing; and the forms have not either. And if Modernism is a particularly urban art, that is partly because the modern artist, like his fellow-men, has been caught up in the spirit of the modern city, which is itself the spirit of a modern technological society. The modern city has appropriated most of the functions and communications of society, most of its population, and the furthest extremities of its technological, commercial, industrial and intellectual experience. The city has become culture, or perhaps the chaos that succeeds it. Itself modernity as social action, it is both the centre of the prevalent social order and the generative frontier of its growth and change.

Thus it is that Modernist art has had special relations with the modern city, and in its role both as cultural museum and novel environment. The Modernist tendency has its roots deep in the culture-capitals of Europe: culture-capitals being, the sociologists tell us, those cities which appropriate certain functions to themselves and become centres of cultural exchange, places where the tradition in a given field is preserved, where the significant news gathers, the specialists are thickest, and innovation is most likely. But most of these culture-capitals were indeed typical modern cities, generating change as much as continuity. They were foci of intellectual activity at a time when the intelligentsia was expanding, acquiring greater self-consciousness as a caste, feeling increasing separation from dominant social orders, and increasingly orientating itself toward the future and belief in change. They were foci of migration from the countryside, places of population growth, new psychic stresses, new technologies and styles, climates both of emancipation and exposure, in societies growing more democratic and mass under the solvency of the second-stage industrial revolution. They were centres of new political actions and groupings. It was becoming clear to many at the end of the nineteenth century that the city was part of a total process of dissolution of old feudal and class relationships and obligations. This process in turn affected the status and self-image of artists and encouraged them to seek aesthetic distillation from the same context of heterodoxy and fluidity with which we associate the modern city – the *Gesellschaft* of Ferdinand Tonnies's famous definition.[2] It was no accident that the nineteenth century is both the great century of western urbanization and the century in which writers and artists, freed from dependence on patrons and particular cultural strata in the total audience, found themselves in that paradoxical position of independence and social indeterminacy that we often today call alienation. Nor is it any accident that the growth of cities as vast agglomerations of people in widely contrasted roles and situations, and hence as places of friction, change and new consciousness, coincides with a desire for extreme cultural novelty and with a feeling of crisis in value and expression which particularly touched the arts. In the United States, where the phenomenon of rapid urbanization could be seen in its most extreme forms, Josiah Strong called the modern cities – with their proliferating social problems, their melting-pot of classes and races cheek-by-jowl, their social contrasts, their inbuilt mixture of expectation and disillusion, and their tentacular and mysterious growth – the 'storm-centres of civilization'. So they were: civilization, as culture, was what they both created and destroyed. Formal echoes of that process are clear in the shape and shapelessness, making and unmaking, of Modernist art. The cultural chaos bred by the populous, ever-growing city, a contingent and polyglot Tower of Babel, is enacted in similar chaos, contingency and plurality in the texts of modern writing, the design and form of Modernist painting.

The art of Modernism was not the first art to reach this. These awarenesses are in realism and naturalism; one might argue that the unutterable contingency of the modern city has much to do with the rise of that most realistic, loose and pragmatic of literary forms, the novel. Certainly many of its themes – from the realistic stress on the dominance of the new fact to the naturalistic stress on the power of the external environment, the movement of masses, the exposure to forces – are responsive to the idea of the great city of modern life. In, for example, Stendhal, Balzac, Dickens, Zola, Dostoyevsky and Stephen Crane, we can see the novel-form expanding the urban metaphor or pursuing the urban experience, and taking up those postures – those of the journalist, the social scientist, the visionary or surrealistic prophet, the underground man – which can best probe the contingency, multifariousness, and principles of conflict and growth in urban life. 'I am bound to be in London,' wrote George Gissing, 'because I must work hard at gathering some new material'; the city was, in every sense of the term, *material*, its specificity yielding up an artistic shape. ('A symmetry is established,' wrote Zola, 'the story composes itself out of all the collected observations, all the notes, one leading to another by the very enchainment of the characters, and the conclusion is nothing more than a natural and inevitable consequence.') Modernism, however, seems to subtract that 'natural and inevitable consequence', to substitute for the 'real' city – that materially dominant environment of sweat-shops and hotels, shop-windows and expectation, that Zola or Dreiser, for example, convey so well as the total field of action for human will and desire – the 'unreal' city, the theatre of licence and fantasy, strange selfhoods in strange juxtapositions that Dostoyevsky and Baudelaire, Conrad and Eliot, Biely and Dos Passos convey as an unresolved and plural impression. The modern urban novel, Raymond Williams tells us, reveals an awareness 'intense and fragmentary, subjective only, yet in the very form of its subjectivity including others, who are now with the buildings, the noises, the sights and smells of the city parts of this single and racing consciousness'.[3] Realism humanizes, naturalism scientizes, but Modernism pluralizes, and surrealizes. Where in much realist art the city is the emancipating frontier, the point of transition into hopeful possibilities, and where in much naturalism it is a vast system both throbbing with and passing beyond human will, a jungle, abyss or war, in much Modernism it is the environment of personal consciousness, flickering impressions, Baudelaire's city of crowds, Dostoyevsky's encounters from the underground, Corbière's (and Eliot's) *mélange adultere du tout* (adulterous mixture of everything).[4]

Modernist writing has a strong tendency to encapsulate experience within the city, and to make the city-novel or the city-poem one of its main forms.[5] Hence Dostoyevsky's *Notes from Underground*, Hamsun's *Hunger*, James's *The Princess Casamassima*, Stephen Crane's *Maggie*, Döblin's *Berlin Alexanderplatz*, Biely's *St Petersburg*, Conrad's *The Secret Agent*, Pound's *Hugh Selwyn Mauberley*, Hesse's *Steppenwolf*, Mayakovsky's poems, Svevo's Trieste novels, Eliot's *The Waste Land*, Hart Crane's *The Bridge*, John Dos Passos's *Manhattan Transfer*, Virginia Woolf's *Mrs Dalloway*, Canetti's *Die Blendung* (Auto da Fé), William Carlos Williams' *Paterson*, and Sartre's *Nausea* belong to a consistent Modernist species. What is particularly important is that their pervasive assumption about the compellingly urban nature of the landscape in which we live, in which the city is, as has often been urged on us, 'a system of life constructed on a wholly new principle', tends to localize the modern artist in the city, not because it is his modern material, but his modern point of view. Much Modernist art has taken its stance from, gained its perspectives out of, a certain kind of distance, an exiled posture – a distance from local origins, class allegiances, the specific obligations and duties of those with an assigned role in a cohesive culture. In his increasing immersion in the city the artist has come to approximate to the condition of the intellectual. And, just as the modern intelligentsia has become something like a classless grouping, disposed to novelty, attempting to advance consciousness, seeking to provide an independent and futuristic over-view, so likewise with Modernist artists – who have so often cut themselves off, like Stephen Dedalus, from family, race and religion to forge the uncreated conscience of their race. This has encouraged much of that specialized aesthetic questioning, that obsessive concern with craft and form, that distinguishes one part of Modernism. But equally it has encouraged the exploration of the social environment out of which cultural novelty was transmuted. If one theme of Modernist literature is disconnection and loss, then another is that of artistic emancipation – so that not only Dedalus in *A Portrait of the Artist as a Young Man* but Paul Morel in *Sons and Lovers*, George Willard in *Winesburg, Ohio*, and many another literary hero all stand at the end of their novels on the edge of some urban redefinition of themselves – as if the quest for self and art alike can only be carried out in the glare and existential exposure of the city, where, as Julius Hart puts it in a compelling phrase in his poem *Journey to Berlin*, one is 'born violently into the wild life'.[6]

It is this plot that restores art to the cities, and the cities to art. For Modernism is a metropolitan art, which is to say it is a group art, a specialist art, an intellectual art, an art for one's aesthetic peers; it recalls, with whatever ironies and paradoxes, the imperium of civilization. Not simply metropolitan, indeed, but cosmopolitan: one city leads to another in the distinctive aesthetic voyage into the metamorphosis of form. The writer may hold on to locality, as Joyce did on to Dublin, Hemingway the Michigan woods; but he perceives from the distance of an expatriate perspective of aesthetic internationalism. More, he may become the kind of modernist writer whom George Steiner has seen as distinctive to our age in his book *Extraterritorial* (1972): the 'unhoused' writer, the writer who conceives language itself as polyglot – as Wilde did when he wrote *Salomé* in French, as Pound did in his multilingualism, as Beckett and Nabokov, who have written in more than one language and used the fact to reflect on the nature of language, do today.[7] Thus frequently it is emigration or exile that makes for membership of the modern country of the arts, which has been heavily travelled by many great writers – Joyce, Lawrence, Mann, Brecht, Auden, Nabokov. It is a country that has come to acquire its own landscape, geography, focal communities, places of exile – Zürich during the First World War, New York during the Second. The writer himself becomes a member of a wandering, culturally inquisitive group – by enforced exile (like Nabokov's after the Russian Revolution) or by design and desire. The place of art's very making can become an ideal distant city, where the creator counts, or the chaos is fruitful, the *Weltgeist* flows. So George Moore expresses a spirit that pressed many of his English contemporaries in the late nineteenth century:[8]

France! The word rang in my ears and gleamed in my eyes. France! All my senses sprang from sleep like a crew when the man on the look-out cries, 'Land ahead!' Instantly I knew that I should, that I must, go to France, that I would live there, that I would become a Frenchman. I knew not when or how, but I knew I should go to France . . .

Gertrude Stein distilled the appropriate phrase – 'writers have to have two countries, the one where they belong and the one in which they live really' – and added a word on her own allegiances: 'America is my country and Paris is my home town.'9 The other country healed the patent materialism of the first, gave form to matter; the cultural capital was the academy that sustained the modern artist's ability to function. In some cases it was the national capital, pulling writers in from the national hinterland. In others it was somewhere else again: Berlin and Paris for Scandinavian and Russian writers, Paris, again, for American writers in the 1920s. One can draw maps showing artistic centres and provinces, the international balance of cultural power – never quite the same as, though doubtless intricately related to, the balance of political and economic power. The maps change as the aesthetics change: Paris is surely, for Modernism, the outright dominant centre, as the fount of bohemia, tolerance and the émigré life-style, but we can sense the decline of Rome and Florence, the rise and then the fall of London, the phase of dominance for Berlin and Munich, the energetic burst from Norway and Finland, the radiation out of Vienna, as being essential stages in the shifting geography of Modernism, charted by the movement of writers and artists, the flow of thought-waves, the explosions of significant artistic production.

Within the great cities lay cosmopolitan villages of the arts, the bohemias and neighbourhoods where the aesthetic function was pursued: Montparnasse, Soho, Greenwich Village. Roger Shattuck's neat definition of the climate in his study of the French *avant garde*, *The Banquet Years*, is appropriate: he speaks of the 'cosmopolitan provincialism' of these communities.10 But they were cosmopolitan because they radiated influence and maintained contact, and it is largely because of this effectiveness of communication and contact that Modernism is an international movement. It depended considerably not only on the action in particular cities but on the readiness of writers to continue the journey to the city they had begun through many cities. So Gertrude Stein, moving from the U.S.A. to Paris in 1903, and then twenty years later becoming the great point of influence for a succeeding generation, linked the American novel and Cubism. Likewise, Strindberg, moving south, linked Scandinavian drama to mid-European Expressionism. Imagism was largely a derivative of expatriate Americans in London immediately before the war, as Dada was largely a derivative of expatriates from Germany and elsewhere in Zürich during it. In the 1920s Paris tended to become the supra-city of Modernism, drawing in Russian émigrés, Dadaists from Zürich, and a whole generation of young American writers of experimental disposition. In a state of economic and moral collapse following the war, it maintained the climate, the appropriately fluid but semi-permanent cultural institutions, which young writers needed. In fact it became, both in its chaos and its continuity, the ideal cosmopolitan city, cultured, tolerant, feverish and active, radical but contained. To some extent, with the Second World War, it was New York City that would inherit. But Modernism was more than any one city; it was, as later essays will show, the distillation of many capitals and nations, and many different intellectual and aesthetic endeavours and moods.

Notes

1 This topic is discussed in Morton and Lucia White, *The Intellectual Versus the City* (Cambridge, Mass., 1962).

2 Ferdinand Tonnies, *Gemeinschaft und Gesellschaft* (Leipzig 1887), translated by Charles P. Loomis as *Community and Association* (London 1955).

3 Raymond Williams, *The English Novel from Dickens to Lawrence* (London 1970). Williams very valuably extends his discussion of the topic in his *The Country and the City* (London 1973).

4 On the urban theme and the urban poem, see particularly Monroe K. Spears, *Dionysus and the City: Modernism in Twentieth Century Poetry* (New York and London 1970). Also see Frank Kermode's discussion of *The Waste Land* as a poem contrasting two cities – the *urbs aeterna* and the Babylon of Apocalypse – in his essay 'T. S. Eliot', in *Modern Essays* (London 1971).

5 For further comments see the essays in this volume by George Hyde ('The Poetry of the City') and Donald Fanger ('The City of Russian Modernistic Fiction').

6 The context of this is discussed in Richard Sheppard's essay 'German Expressionist Poetry' in this volume.

7 George Steiner, *Extraterritorial: Papers on Literature and the Language Revolution* (London 1972).

8 George Moore, *Confessions of a Young Man* (London 1888).

9 Gertrude Stein, *Paris France* (New York and London 1940); and Gertrude Stein, *The Autobiography of Alice B. Toklas* (London 1933).

10 Roger Shattuck, *The Banquet Years: The Arts in France, 1885–1918* (London 1959).

BERLIN AND THE RISE OF MODERNISM
1886–96

JAMES MCFARLANE

I

IN the summer of 1893, Arno Holz confided to his colleague Paul
Ernst his plans for writing a great cycle of plays under the general title
of *Berlin in Dramen* (*Berlin in Dramas*). This was intended to do for
Berlin what Zola's *Les Rougon-Macquart* had done for French society
under the Second Empire. Some reports spoke of ten dramas, others
of as many as twenty-five; but by the time the first and only drama of
the cycle, *Die Sozialaristokraten* (*The Social Aristocrats*) (1896) appeared three years later, the series title and indeed the whole scheme
had undergone a significant change. It now read: *Berlin: das Ende einer
Zeit in Dramen* (*Berlin: The End of an Age in Dramas*). It provides an
index of how, in the Berlin of 1896, the sense of an ending was
strong. For an entire decade, since the establishment in 1886 of the
literary society 'Durch', the city had known a tumult of literary activity. With writers endlessly issuing manifestos, founding movements,
forming coteries, establishing theatre groups, publishing periodicals,
pronouncing, protesting, declaring, associating and dissociating and
again reassociating, politicking, polemicizing, manoeuvring, enthus-
ing and abusing, the city had generated an intense cultural excitement.
Now it seemed finally to have spent itself. Stridency had yielded to a
strange, unaccustomed silence. A contemporary observer, Franz
Servaes, noted sadly in 1896 that no longer was it obligatory on a
young writer to come to Berlin if he wanted the authentic literary
experience. It seemed that the first phase of Berlin Modernism was
over – though, with another decade gone by, the vehemence of
Expressionism was soon to restore excitement.

But in 1896, to those who had earlier known Berlin in all its gregar-
iousness and intense sociability, the city now seemed virtually empty.
Gerhart Hauptmann might occasionally be seen; and indeed, when

in February an outraged bourgeois audience hissed his new drama *Florian Geyer* off the stage, it seemed for a brief moment as though the old embers might be blown into flame again. Arno Holz was sometimes seen around, but was never very much in evidence; Richard Dehmel, now living a comparatively withdrawn life out at Pankow, was threatening to move still further out of town; Stanislaw Przybyszewski, the Polish *Wunderkind* of Berlin in the early 1890s, found his magic failing; the Swede Ola Hansson and his wife 'Laura Marholm', whose ideas had earlier stimulated many new and exciting departures, had some time ago moved away to Bavaria; Max Halbe and Ernst von Wolzogen had gone off to Munich, Otto Julius Bierbaum to the Tirol, Julius Meier-Graefe to Paris, Max Dauthendey to parts unknown. Furthermore, a number of promising enterprises had seemingly failed to live up to expectations, to the dismay of those who looked for a resurgence of Berlin's cultural drive. The re-vamping of the periodical *Freie Bühne* in 1894 under the new title of *Neue deutsche Rundschau* had signally failed to rally the younger writers of the day; *Pan*, instead of the vigorous pioneering journal that had been hoped for at its launching in 1895, seemed to many to have become disappointingly tame, calculating, passive. In Servaes's view, all this contributed to break the spirit of *die Jüngeren*: 'Solidarity quickly disappeared; the forces distintegrated, latent antagonisms broke out, and one felt greatly sobered. Things crumbled on all sides; and, palpably, the capital city lost its prestige.'[1]

2

This seeming emptiness about the city in 1896 was qualitative not quantitative. In physical and demographic terms, Berlin was still expanding at an alarming pace. Following the unification of Germany and the adoption of Berlin as its capital, the city had grown rapidly. From 826,000 in 1871, its population increased to 1,100,000 in 1880, to nearly 1,600,000 in 1890, and was to rise to over two million by 1905. In sheer size it was third only to London and Paris. It was the seat both of the Imperial Parliament and of the Prussian Diet, and it held the principal residence of the German Emperor. The inflow of new residents was overwhelming; rents rose out of all proportion; both the military and the forces of officialdom expanded as never before; there was a thrusting determination to rival Paris both in material well-being and in the arts of peace. New and far-reaching measures were taken in sanitation and in public health; housing was rapidly improved, though the boom conditions brought endless opportunities for economic exploitation. Moreover, alongside the sheer growth in numbers, there came a spread of industrialization without parallel in any other German town of the age. Munich, for a brief period in the eighties Berlin's rival for the cultural leadership of Germany, was small by comparison: less than a quarter of a million inhabitants, of whom only a very small proportion were working-class. One in seventy of its inhabitants, it was excitedly claimed, was either a poet, a painter, a sculptor or a musician. As for the other smaller provincial towns of Germany, they offered little excitement or stimulus to the artist or intellectual. Even as late as 1891, Max Dauthendey discovered to his chagrin that nobody in the Würzburg university bookshop had so much as heard the name of Nietzsche, let alone thought it worthwhile to stock any of his works. Dauthendey later commented ruefully:[2]

The provincial towns of Germany, even those which were university towns, lived at that time by the classic authors, and their knowledge of modern literature stopped short at Paul Heyse . . . There were no literary societies in academic circles. Consequently young artists had to congregate in the larger cities of Paris, Munich and Berlin in order to hold together in the new spirit against bourgeois prejudice.

As Berlin slowly began to shake itself free from the cultural sterility of the Seventies, the city exerted with each passing year a growing attraction, and drew businessmen and industrialists, professional men and workers, writers and artists like a magnet. Many of those who later contributed to the literary ferment came in the first instance as university students; but when, like Heinrich Hart, they discovered that the city, not the university, was the great educative force, they stayed to make their lives there: 'A time of study such as we have never known opened up for us. But it was not in the auditoria of the *alma mater* that we gratified our urge to study – for there we were rare visitors. Our auditoria were streets, drinking places, coffee houses, occasionally also the Reichstag.'[3] Heinrich Hart and his brother Julius

– who together, as early as 1878 in their *Deutsche Monatsblätter*, had drawn attention to the innovatory significance of Ibsen, Bjørnson and Turgenev, and who by their editorship of the *Kritische Waffengänge* (1882–4) and the *Berliner Monatshefte für Literatur, Kritik und Theater* (1885) exercised an important formative influence on the early development of Berlin Naturalism – were among the first to respond to the pull of the city, moving there from Münster at the start of the eighties. Their example was soon followed by many who later played a significant part in the literary revolution: Arno Holz from Rastenburg, Johannes Schlaf from Querfurt, Bruno Wille from Magdeburg, Wilhelm Bölsche from Cologne, Paul Ernst from the Harz, Gerhart Hauptmann from Salzbrunn, Max Halbe from Danzig, Max Dauthendey from Würzburg, and many others. The city, especially after 1890, also drew in many from across Germany's national frontiers, particularly from Scandinavia and from Poland.

Clearly these were exhilarating years for a young ambitious writer to live through, one consequence of which was an unusually heavy crop of volumes of reminiscence in later life: Hauptmann's *Das Abenteuer meiner Jugend* (*The Adventure of My Youth*); Heinrich Hart's *Literarische Erinnerungen* (*Literary Memories*); Halbe's *Scholle und Schicksal* (*Glebe and Destiny*); Ernst's *Jünglingsjahre* (*Years of Youth*); Dauthendey's *Gedankengut aus meinen Wanderjahren* (*Thoughts from My Wanderings*); Przybyszewski's *Erinnerungen an das literarische Berlin* (*Memories of Literary Berlin*). In sum, they bear witness to an overwhelming sense of *shared* experience, of belonging, of participating, of being swept along in a powerful stream of events – political, ideological, literary – and of serving as part of some great and mystic *corpus* that had developed a will and a purpose all its own. Hauptmann, who later wrote of observing the city from 'a frog's eye view', remembered the surging crowds of humanity round the Rosenthaler Tor, and how one's very individuality seemed to be consumed: 'How often, at night by the light of the gas lamps, did I not allow myself to be pushed and jostled backwards and forwards, fascinated by the infinite variety of human kind. One scarcely felt an individual any longer; one was drawn into the body of the *Volk*, into the soul of the *Volk*.'[4] And permeating all was the intense political consciousness of the age, the thrill of giving one's allegiance to the proscribed social-democratic movement, and the passionate belief in its future promise.

Those who gave their loyalty to it, wrote Heinrich Hart, thought of it as some great brotherhood; and they waited as in a kind of ecstasy for the coming revolution.[5]

Not unnaturally within a social and intellectual climate of this kind, literature was marked by a sense of urgency and impatience and violence, by an eagerness to assault the old strongholds wherever they could be identified. The notion of literature as fire-power was obsessive: did not the Harts (to take one example) give the title *Kritische Waffengänge (Critical Armed Conflicts)* to their new journal in 1882? The printed word became a weapon in the service of social and political advancement. The prime target was public apathy: 'Away with public indifference, and away with all other forms of rubble and lumber. Let us release the young spirits from the spell that binds them; let us give them air and courage.' The literary old guard – Heyse, Geibel, Spielhagen, Lindau, Freytag – came under attack; alliances were formed, in spirit at least, with writers in distant parts of Europe, with Zola, Ibsen and Bjørnson, with Tolstoy, Dostoyevsky and Turgenev.

The pursuit of literature became increasingly collective. Hence in 1886 Konrad Küster, Leo Berg and Eugen Wolff – a physician, a writer, and a literary historian respectively – formed the society known as 'Durch'. This was intended to provide a meeting place primarily for 'the young and most modern poets and authors'. Shortly its members included not only the most active young writers resident in Berlin – Hauptmann, Holz, Schlaf, the Hart brothers, Bruno Wille, Wilhelm Bölsche, John Henry Mackay, Karl Henckell, Hermann Conradi and Paul Ernst – but also scholars, actors and others of like mind. The members were much concerned with the basic assumptions of their art, with debating the relationship between literature and science, with clarifying and defining concepts like idealism, realism and naturalism. Its members drafted 'articles of faith', 'theses', 'declarations'. It took itself seriously, and kept minutes of its meetings. Literature was for them pre-eminently a thing of ends and means – social ends and scientific means. They conceived of their works as 'imaginative experiments'; intellectual honesty became the supreme virtue; their determination to speak the undistorted, unbiased, unadorned truth was paramount. They put candour before subtlety, courage before sensitivity, precision before insight, authenticity before inventiveness. The fifth of *Ten Theses* drawn up for the Society in

1887 by Eugen Wolff – a document which for the first time established the term *die Moderne* – declared: 'Modern literature should, with merciless truth, show people with flesh and blood and passions, yet without thereby transgressing the limits set by the work of art itself, but rather indeed enhancing the aesthetic effect by the sheer extent of the truth to nature.'[6]

3

The rivalry between Berlin and Munich for cultural leadership continued throughout the rest of the eighties, and even some way into the nineties. In *Die Gesellschaft*, begun in 1885 and edited by M. G. Conrad, Munich continued to have what was probably the most influential periodical of these years; it found space in its pages not only for South German authors but also for many of the Berlin circle. Nevertheless, as the *Schwerpunkt* of literary endeavour shifted with the years from the novel to the drama, and Zola was progressively supplanted by Ibsen as the real giant of the age, so did Berlin, with its wealth of theatrical life, begin firmly to assume leadership. It was from the Berlin epicentre that the shock tremors of Ibsenism began to spread out through Europe. Ibsen's was not a new name in Berlin. Both Otto Brahm – in 1889 to become the first director of the new Freie Bühne – and Paul Schlenther – later to become the director of the Vienna Burgtheater – could recall the miraculous moment in February 1878 when *Pillars of Society* had taken Berlin's theatrical world by storm. Brahm claimed that even at that early date they had recognized the profound significance of the occasion:[7]

Then it happened one day that we [Schlenther and Brahm] found ourselves in the tiny Stadttheater in the Lindenstrasse, at *Pillars of Society*. And we immediately felt the first presentiments of a new poetic world; we felt ourselves encountering people of our own day in whom we could believe; and from an all-embracing social criticism of the present day we saw the triumphant emergence of the ideals of freedom and truth as the pillars of society. From that moment on we belonged to this new realistic art, and our aesthetic life was filled with meaning.

But the real shock came a decade later, with *Ghosts*. In 1887 the Berlin Residenz-Theater planned a production which, despite intervention from Brahm, Schlenther and others, was banned from public performance by the police. A closed performance was given on 9 June 1887, and twenty times over-subscribed. Controversy was immediate and passionate, and was given widest coverage by the daily and periodical press; copies of the German translation sold in large numbers. An Ibsen banquet two days later, attended by the author, brought speeches declaring the dawn of a new age. A rush of Ibsen plays followed in Berlin: in March the Ostend-Theater gave *An Enemy of the People*; in April the Residenz-Theater produced *Rosmersholm*; in March 1888 it put on *The Wild Duck*. On 20 March 1888, Ibsen's sixtieth birthday, there were countless tributes from the press of Berlin and of Germany at large. March 1889 saw an *Ibsen-Woche* with three separate productions: *The Lady from the Sea* at the Royal Theatre; *The Wild Duck* at the Residenz-Theater; and *A Doll's House* at the Lessing-Theater. On 29 September 1889 came the ultimate sensation, when the newly established Freie Bühne selected *Ghosts* for its opening production. The effect, as Franz Servaes reported, was terrific:[8]

Some people, as though inwardly shattered, did not regain their calm for days. They rushed about the city, about the Tiergarten. Destiny itself had revealed itself to them ... Such ineluctability, such inevitability of tragic fate! Wrapping itself round us like a snake, holding us in a captive embrace, round our limbs, round our breast. Then closing upon our throat. No wonder the public cried out in fear and in indignation.

When, three weeks later, the Freie Bühne followed with a production of Hauptmann's *Vor Sonnenaufgang* (*Before Sunrise*), all Berlin believed that here at last was the native Shakespeare to Ibsen's Marlowe.

The Ibsen fever raged for another two years before showing signs of abating. In May 1891, according to Ibsen's biographer Halvdan Koht,[9] a long five-stanza poem appeared in Berlin's *Der Zeitgeist* (*The Spirit of the Age*) to testify to the impact of the Scandinavian dramatist on the life of the city, part of which ran:

> *Ibsen, Ibsen überall!*
> *Da geht nichts mehr drüber!*
> *Auf dem ganzen Erdenball*
> *Herrscht das Ibsen-Fieber!*
> *Alle Welt wird Ibsen-toll,*

Wenn auch wider Willen,
Denn die ganze Luft ist voll
Ibsen-Ruhm-Bacillen!
Keine Rettung! Überall
Kunden Ibsens Namen,
Preisend mit Posaunenschall,
Moden und Reklamen.
Auf Cigaren, Damenschmuck,
Torten, Miedern, Schlipsen,
Prangt das Wort in gold'nem Druck:
Ibsen! A la Ibsen!*

The fortunes of the Freie Bühne itself – a 'theatre group' possessing neither theatre nor company of its own, and instead mounting closed performances for its members in existing theatres – are characteristic of the fragmentation that assailed the Berlin 'Moderns' after 1890. Its first director, Otto Brahm, provoked the hostility of a number of the founding members; consequently, a rival theatre group – the Freie Volksbühne – was formed with Bruno Wille as its first director, and intended for a working-class membership. Yet within two years a new dispute arose about where the real power ought to lie in the group: with the independently minded intellectuals or with the committed political activists. This conflict produced yet another splinter group in 1893: the Neue Freie Volksbühne.

The instability in evidence here – and comparable switches and changes marked also their magazines and periodicals – was the outward symptom of a growing malaise; behind the confident and clamorous declarations of these years were signs of a profound spiritual conflict. Two different and separate pairs of incompatibles left the Moderns uncertain about their own aims and purposes. On the one hand there was that uneasy alliance between the emergent chauvinism of the new Reich and the eager cosmopolitanism of a culture which for too long had remained inbred and in-turned. A great upsurge of national pride, most strongly marked in Berlin as the

*Ibsen, Ibsen, everywhere! There's nothing like it! Over the whole globe Ibsen fever rages. The whole world is Ibsen-mad, even though unwillingly, for the entire air is full of Ibsen-germs! No salvation! Fashions and advertisements everywhere proclaim Ibsen's name, trumpet his praise. On cigars, ladies' trinkets, pastries, bodices, ties is flaunted the word in letters of gold: Ibsen! A la Ibsen!

capital city, had followed the victories of the Franco–Prussian War and the unification of Germany; and for many it was clearly a matter for regret that this military and political triumph was without its cultural counterpart. Yet alongside this narrowly focused nationalism went an internationalism, at least in matters literary, the like of which Germany had not known for generations. Close and admiring attention was given to writers from many other parts of Europe and the world, in particular from Russia, France, Scandinavia, England and America. A deep desire to be culturally independent and self-sufficient thus came into conflict with an ardent cosmopolitanism. Elaborately racialist proposals for resolving this conflict, particularly in respect of Scandinavia and the Low Countries, sought acceptance: like Leo Berg's attempt to annex Ibsen for 'Germanic tradition' in his essay of 1887 'Henrik Ibsen und das Germanenthum in der modernen Literatur' ('Henrik Ibsen and German-ness in modern literature'); or Julius Langbehn's astonishing best-seller *Rembrandt als Erzieher* (*Rembrandt as Educator*) (over 100,000 copies sold within a few brief months of its publication in 1890), which sought to confine within a single ethnographic category artists and writers from a wide area of Northern Europe.

One other contradication remained which its Modernist practitioners were unable to resolve: that between the passionate and the dispassionate in their art. Here, on the one hand, was a deeply-felt sense of social outrage, a vehement repudiation of the *ancien régime*, an impatient rejection of prevailing bourgeois standards and values, coupled with an at times quite savage hostility towards the older generation of writers. In the manner of Julius Hart, one set one's face against 'the brilliant salons and the perfumed boudoirs . . . the dancing, laughing dinner-table world of the *ancien régime*, to enter instead the cottages of the poor and the oppressed'.[10] There, on the other hand, and not easily reconcilable with this highly-charged social motivation, was the desire to achieve for literature a scientific detachment (and thereby to win for it something of the current prestige attaching to science), to allocate to the writer the task of documenting life and of substantiating – by the special kind of evidence which literature was able to adduce – those laws which were held to control and determine human existence. Because Man was viewed primarily as a constituent part of the natural world, of Nature, and therefore subject to the same kind of laws and susceptible to the same sort of investigation as any other part of that natural world, it was believed that minute observation and scrupulous objective recording would (on the analogy of science) inevitably reveal the existence and the nature of those causal laws. When stripped of its surface sophistication, a great deal of the Modernist polemic of these days then reduced to a discussion how most properly to resolve the two elements: the 'slice of life' and the author's 'temperament'. By the time Arno Holz had fully formulated his theory of 'consistent Naturalism', in *Die Kunst: Ihr Wesen und ihre Gesetze (Art: Its Nature and Its Laws)* (1891), by which 'temperament' is largely discounted as a formative influence in literature, the entire naturalist movement had entered upon its decline. It was becoming increasingly apparent that such initial unity as the early Modernists had enjoyed was largely negative in origin, derived from shared hostilities, from common political and literary hatreds, from collective frustration. The literary 'enemy', the older generation of writers, had shown little capacity for fight; and when the conditions of political repression changed materially with the repeal of the Socialist Law in 1890, the encouragement given to internal dissension among the Moderns was immediate.

4

The first clear shift of enthusiasm to reveal itself was in their attitude to big city life, to the thrill of the crowd. Living within the city, they discovered, made group identity difficult to sustain; they felt the need of some refuge, of a measure of detachment, of solitude and quietude to allow them to think their ideas through. Nevertheless, it was important that the urban tumult should still be accessible, for to abandon the city completely would be a betrayal of earlier loyalties. Friedrichshagen am Müggelsee, conveniently situated near the newly extended municipal transport system but – with its lakes and hills and pine forests – peaceful and rural seemed to offer a solution. The first to move out, in 1888, were Bruno Wille and Wilhelm Bölsche. They were joined not long afterwards by the Hart brothers. Soon the whole centre of gravity of literary Berlin had shifted to this largely rural spot, where Berlin itself was still at hand and indeed continued as a presence, though only as a glow in the evening sky. Not that life in its economic aspects was any great idyll, however; the poverty of the group was proverbial and their material standard of living often barely above subsistence level. Moreover, there were other grounds for feeling dispirited: in particular, the hopes they had cherished as progressively-minded writers of forming an alliance with the working-class movement had been grievously disappointed. They were made to feel rejected, even harried. 'Neither the state, nor the nation, nor even the people in the old sense of the word concerned themselves with literature – only the *police*' was the way one writer put it in these years.

Some took up permanent residence in Friedrichshagen; some others – among whom were Holz, Schlaf, Henkell, Conradi and Mackay – were regular visitors; others again might be found there from time to time, like Wedekind, Paul Ernst, Dehmel, and Halbe, along with other painters, actors, and musicians. And also – often fatefully – foreigners, particularly Scandinavians. It was not simply that the group was greatly and generously receptive, both to new people and to new ideas. Scandinavia enjoyed a particularly high esteem, partly because Ibsen (and, to a lesser extent, Bjørnson) had already left a deep impression on German and European theatre but also because, within the climate of opinion that had made a book like *Rembrandt als Erzieher* into a best-seller, the appeal of Scandinavia on emotively ethnic grounds was considerable. (When the – on first publication, anonymous – 'Rembrandt author' wrote to thank a Scandinavian critic for a particularly fulsome review, he advanced the notion that, on the analogy of Nietzsche's *Übermensch*, he might perhaps refer to the Scandinavians as *die Überdeutschen*.) Young Scandinavian authors and artists seeking wider horizons found themselves turning naturally to Berlin in these years. Ola Hansson, a Swedish critic, was among the first to set up house in Friedrichshagen; and his influence on the domestic literary scene was profound. Other Scandinavians resident for shorter or longer periods in Berlin in the early nineties included also the Norwegian novelist Arne Garborg and his wife, the (by now quite senior) Danish poet Holger Drachmann, the painter Edvard Munch, the dramatist Gunnar Heiberg, the poet Sigbjørn Obstfelder (often claimed as the model for Rilke's Malte Laurids Brigge), the sculptor Gustav Vigeland; the young Finland movement was represented by Axel Gallén and Jean Sibelius. And, briefly but over-whelmingly, there was August Strindberg.

Chronologically, Hansson was the first to infect the group with radically new ideas. His essays, some of which were published in the *Freie Bühne*, came precisely at a time when the Friedrichshagen Modernists were most receptive to new ideas, especially now that a fair measure of scepticism about Holz's extreme or 'consistent' naturalism was being canvassed. Taking his cue from Georg Brandes's seminal lectures in Copenhagen in 1888 on Nietzsche (which virtually 'discovered' Nietzsche for Europe), he expressed wonderment that Germany should so have addressed itself to Zola, Ibsen and Tolstoy, when it had Nietzsche's important and stimulating ideas so immediately to hand. He had already begun to direct German attention to a new range of foreign authors and artists – among them Huysmans, Richepin and Bourget – whom he considered much more rewarding and exciting than the (by now) aging old-guard of European naturalism; and went on to commend Barbey d'Aurevilly, Stirner, Böcklin and Edgar Allan Poe. He published in German a number of critical studies of contemporary Scandinavian writers, including Strindberg, Hamsun, Garborg and Jacobsen, which gave a very different view of current writing from that represented by Ibsen and Bjørnson of the eighties.

The new names in themselves plot a very distinct swing away from the earlier social preoccupations and towards the psychological. 'Honesty' was still required of the writer, but now it betokened a readiness to acknowledge and record not the lower depths of society but the deeper sub-strata of the mind. Man, who in the pages of the naturalists lived by bread and work, now lived on his nerves. The fascination of the writer is less for crowded streets than for teeming brains; social organization suddenly matters less than mental patterns. The new catchword is *Nervenkunst*.

Largely as a result of Hansson's initiative, another new and foreign visitor joined the Friedrichshagen circle: Stanislaw Przybyszewski, an emigré Pole, whose arresting ideas and even more startling personality made him a central and influential and in time notorious figure of literary Berlin. His two critical studies – one on 'Chopin und Nietzsche' and the other on 'Ola Hansson' – were published together in 1892 under the title of *Zur Psychologie des Individuums* (*On the*

Psychology of the Individual), a book in which he set out his views on the essential relationship between 'individuality' and 'personality', and between the 'soul' and the 'brain', and which emphasized the dominant role of sex as a force in human behaviour. In the music of Chopin he claimed to find the tonal correlative of Nietzsche's philosophy. His own rendering of Chopin on the piano, wild, impassioned, abandoned, became legendary. People who had heard Przybyszewski play Chopin (wrote Julius Bab in later years) counted it as one of the most powerful artistic experiences of their lives. It seemed to symbolize the chaotic spirit of the new European *Bohème*: 'The . . . piano became a Hell which he opened with wild groping hands,' wrote Max Dauthendey. 'The sounds blindly swallowed up all thought, all law and order from within the minds of his listeners, and sounds and men and times turned to chaos. Life no longer retained form or sense.'[11] The term *Chopinisieren* was coined to describe the nature of this peculiar form of assault on life and art. It was a call for literature to concern itself with *die nackte Seele* ('the naked soul'), the inner and especially the sexual workings of the mind, using where necessary the *techniques* of scrupulous and detailed recording commended by the orthodox naturalists and their *Sekundenstil*, but rejecting absolutely their purely materialistic preoccupations.

It was however Strindberg who for a few brief months in the Autumn and Winter of 1892–3 became the indisputable focus of attention in literary Berlin. For some weeks he lived in Friedrichshagen, in the house of the Hanssons, during which time he astonished his friends and acquaintances by busying himself more with chemistry, photography and painting than he did with writing. In this he was aided and abetted by Przybyszewski, who had started his career as a medical student and was familiar with many of the fashionable scientific theories; together they would sit far into the night discussing biology, chemistry, alchemy and magic. Predictably, Strindberg lost patience with the Hanssons after a few weeks. He moved back into metropolitan Berlin, and gave his patronage to a small restaurant, the name of which he successfully urged the proprietor to change from *Das Kloster* ('The Cloister') to *Zum schwarzen Ferkel* ('The Black Boar'). Quickly the word went round Berlin that this was the new centre of literary affairs. As one of the *habitués* put it, this tavern then became 'within a short time the most famous or rather the most infamous drinking house of the *Bohème*'. They excitedly discussed the new *Nervenkunst* (art of the nerves), urged *psychischer Naturalismus* (psychic naturalism) in place of *konsequenter Naturalismus* (consistent naturalism), vehemently argued the place of sex in life and literature, demanded utter honesty in the examination of one's motives, and tirelessly explored links between poetry and painting and music. Still strong, however, was their sense of being social outcasts. Defiantly they demonstrated their contempt for bourgeois society by calculatedly scandalous behaviour. Selectively, they gave themselves to Satanism, to anarchism – and to alcohol. The group – which apart from Strindberg and Przybyszewski included the Germans Dehmel and Scheerbart and the Scandinavians Drachmann, Krogh, Munch and Lidforss – led a brief but intense existence; but with Strindberg's departure in the spring of 1893, and despite Przybyszewski's efforts to hold it together, the group broke up.

Its disintegration together with the collapse of any kind of residual collective naturalistic movement was clearly what Holz responded to when he amended the title of his drama cycle to *Berlin: das Ende einer Zeit in Dramen (Berlin: The End of an Age in Dramas)*. The one completed work of the cycle, *Die Sozialaristokraten (The Social Aristocrats)*, made savage fun of the communal endeavours of the early nineties. The play centres round the founding of a new political magazine. Gehrke, transparently modelled on Bruno Wille, is depicted as abandoning both 'evolution and revolution' and embracing in their place a new anti-Semite nationalism in order to further his own personal ambitions. He is set in the context of similarly identifiable figures: Stycinski standing for Przybyszewski, Bellermann for John Henry Mackay, and Herr Hahn for Holz himself. The play ends on a note of bitter hilarity with the establishment of the new periodical to a chorus of *Deutschland, Deutschland über alles* (Germany, Germany above all). Neither the one-time 'consistent naturalists' nor the Bohemians of the *Schwarze Ferkel* could have conceived an end of greater finality than that.

Notes

1 Franz Servaes, 'Jung Berlin I, II, III', in *Die Zeit* (Vienna), 21 and 28 Nov., 5 Dec. 1896.

2 Max Dauthendey, *Gedankengut aus meinen Wanderjahren, Gesammelte Werke* (Munich 1925), vol. I, p. 696.

3 Heinrich Hart, 'Literarische Erinnerungen 1880–1905', in *Gesammelte Werke* (Berlin 1907), vol. III, pp. 27ff.

4 Gerhart Hauptmann, 'Das Abenteuer meiner Jugend', in *Gesammelte Werke* (Berlin 1942), vol. 14, p. 726.

5 Heinrich Hart, 'Literarische Erinnerungen 1880–1905', in *Gesammelte Werke* (Berlin 1942), vol. 14, p. 726.

6 Reprinted in Erich Ruprecht (ed.), *Literarische Manifeste des Naturalismus 1880–1892* (Stuttgart 1962), p. 142.

7 Otto Brahm, *Kritische Schriften* (Berlin 1913–15), vol. I, p. 447.

8 Franz Servaes, 'Jung Berlin I, II, III', in *Die Zeit* (Vienna), 21 and 28 Nov., 5 Dec. 1896.

9 Halvdan Koht, *The Life of Ibsen* (London 1931), vol. II, p. 279.

10 Julius Hart, in *Freie Bühne für modernes Leben*, no. iv (Berlin 1893), p. 593.

11 Max Dauthendey, *Gedankengut aus meinen Wanderjahren, Gesammelte Werke* (Munich 1925), vol. I, p. 646.

VIENNA AND PRAGUE 1890–1928

FRANZ KUNA

I

LYING on the eastern fringe of the map of European Modernism, Vienna and Prague have a certain provinciality of appearance. They were both polyglot cities, and both intellectual centres stirring with very varied ideas; but they were also in many other respects incorrigibly traditional or conservative, and they irritated some of their livelier citizens by their inescapable smugness and provincialism. Between them, they produced some of the most central works, and stimulated some of the most fecund ideas we associate with Modernism; they spawned some of the major writers of the age (Hofmannsthal, Schnitzler, Rilke, Kafka, Musil); to one of these cities we owe the Vienna School of composers, the Vienna Secession in the arts; and in new science a figure without whom much Modernist thought is inconceivable, Sigmund Freud.

Yet several of these despaired of their environment, and some even went into exile. When applied to these cities, therefore, the term 'modern' is dubious. The fight for modernity was no real war, not that kind of *lustige Krieg, von London bis München, von Paris bis Petersburg* (merry war from London to Munich, from Paris to St Petersburg) of which *Ver Sacrum*,[1] the journal of the Secessionist painters and artists, spoke. The word 'Modernism' passed into general vocabulary around 1890, was a key-word about 1900, and by 1910 had given way to other '-isms' deriving from the creative ferment of the new century. But those who claimed modernity were many, and often of varied temperament: those who felt 'different', or 'sensitive', or 'nervous', or at odds with their age. Thus Theodor Billroth, the greatest surgeon in Vienna, a member of the conservative intellectual and social elite, writing in 1893 to Brahms, claimed his modernity in the following terms:[2]

After all, you admit yourself that pieces in a minor key are more easily absorbed by us, *the moderns*. I suppose this can be considered a parallel to the fact that we find muted, gentler colours on the whole more agreeable in our immediate surroundings than more dazzling ones . . . Modern people do not like dazzling light in their rooms either. The modern predilection for painted windows!

There was however conflict between the 'moderns' and the 'conservatives' (*die Konservativen*), a conflict which was usually good-natured, but at times became bitter and violent, and ran through the churches, medicine, the law, the arts. Men like Ludwig Wahrmund, professor of church law at Innsbruck, sacked for his pamphlet on *The Catholic Attitude and Free Learning*, lost their posts for being 'Modernists'; and when students rallied to Wahrmund's defence, the mayor of the city called the University a 'hotbed of subversive ideas, revolution, godlessness, and anti-patriotism'.[3] The older generation categorized the younger as 'decadent', 'mad', 'pathological'. Only rarely did the young hit back (as did Karl Kraus) in similar language; rather they took the hint and proceeded in their fiction, in their plays, and elsewhere to present the decadent, the mad, and the pathological as the new heroes of the age. When Kakfa's father called his son *'ein Ungeziefer'* ('an insect'), Kafka did not return the rhetoric but instead turned to the portrayal of a hero, Gregor Samsa, whose life became the problem of coming to terms with this very transformation into an insect. The feeling of not quite fitting into the age, of being strangely out of tune, was a matter of considerable moral and psychological concern to the 'moderns'; and they contrasted the solid bourgeois spirits who seemed to sit so harmoniously in the world with their own situation: passive, nervous, decadent, ugly, men without qualities. Thomas Mann often points to this essential contrast, as in the terms he uses of the 'young gentleman' in his story *Der Bajazzo* (*The Dilettante*) (1903):[4]

It was plain that he had made his way – not necessarily by pushing – and was on the straight road to a plain and profitable goal. He dwelt in the shade of good understanding with all the world and in the sunshine of general approbation.

Similarly, in his novel *Der Mann ohne Eigenschaften* (*The Man without Qualities*), Musil portrays the same personality type, more clinically and with more obvious satiric intent, in his portrait of Ulrich's father, the man *with* qualities:[5]

As with many men who have achieved something of note, these feelings, far from being selfish, sprang from a deep love of what might be called the generally and suprapersonally useful; in other words, from a sincere veneration for what advances one's own interests – and this not for the sake of advancing them, but in harmony with that advancement and simultaneously with it, and also on general grounds.

There were the moderns of new thought and of new forms; there were the pathologically modern; and there were the moderns who adjusted to the new as to fashion. But the term did acquire certain more precise associations among the younger generation of artists and writers. In his *Studien zur Kritik der Moderne* (*Critical Studies of the Modern*) (1894) Hermann Bahr, the Viennese critic and writer, lists four possible meanings all fairly close to the 'decadent' mood of the decade; to be 'modern' meant to practise *Nervenkunst* (the art of the nerves); or to pursue the urbane and artificial (from which nature is banned); or to yearn feverishly for the mysterious, the mystical; or, in Wagnerian fashion, to run to unbounded emotion. Following Ernst Mach, who postulated the fictive, arbitrary, accidental nature of the Self, who defined it in virtually untarnishable terms as an '*ideelle denkökonomische, keine reelle Einheit*' ('imaginary, hypothetical unity rather than an actual unity'),[6] Bahr also stressed the need for modern man to search not simply for subjective truth, but specifically for the truth of sensations: 'the sensations alone are truth . . . the Ego is but construction'. Hofmannsthal went further, linking Mach with Schopenhauer and Nietzsche. He defined the 'modern' as the desire to escape individual will and become one with the 'rhythm of the universe'. The periodical *Ver Sacrum* declared war on *dem thatenlosen Schlendrian, dem starren Byzantinismus und allem Ungeschmack* ('the idle slovenliness, the crass byzantinism and every act of tastelessness'), and stressed the *hohe Kulturmission* ('noble cultural mission') of all art. Architects like Otto Wagner, the author of *Moderne Architektur* (1895), and later Adolf Loos, together with the craftsmen of the Vienna *Werkstätte* justified the 'new art' by its ability to give expression to new ideals of man and society. Out of such a climate came the special achievement, as well as the special failures, of Central European Modernism.

2

Fin-de-siècle Vienna was a city of many faces. Politically it contained a motley collection of creeds and movements: 'A shapeless medley of ideologies and programmes ranging from anti-capitalist municipal planning to rabid anti-socialism in the name of the old order, from political catholicism to virulent antisemitism; . . . a cult of Viennese insularity and a publicity image of Old Vienna.'[7] Socially it offered an even more colourful array of classes and races, from the newly militant workers in Ottakring, the notorious sixteenth district, to the withdrawn aristocracy of the 'Inner City'; from the strong colony of Czech immigrants in the Landstrasse district to the steady trickle of East European Jews who, to the embarrassment of established Jewry, sought 'a new life' in Vienna. Culturally it ranged from the mass of traditional artists and craftsmen serving the New Bourgeoisie to the first wave of the Viennese Modernist movement – the writers of *das junge Wien* (Young Vienna), and the artists who called themselves 'Secessionists'. To the outside world, the social and intellectual life of the city presented an impression of unity, an amalgam of collective fictions about what it was to be typically Viennese. Behind this façade were wide differences. The Viennese have a great capacity for enjoying, in Kant's phrase, the 'manifold of existence' as long as the familiar background, the *gemütlich*, is undisturbed. When, on 1 May 1890, the city saw its first Socialist procession along the Prater – in the event one of the most peaceful and disciplined First of May demonstrations – a panic set in. The entire police force was posted in the Prater, the military held in reserve, and the terrified liberal middle classes hid in their large houses or spent the day in the country. 'The merchants let down the iron shutters in front of their shops,' wrote Stefan Zweig, 'and I can remember that our parents strictly forbade us children to go out in the streets on this day of terror which might see Vienna in flames.'[8] And a like distrust prevailed then, and still prevails, in the spheres of art, culture, and social intercourse.

Today it is tempting to speak of the 'flowering of the arts', and especially of modern music, in *fin-de-siècle* Vienna. The metaphor is inaccurate: it supposes a favourable soil and a good climate. But this is hardly true of the *avant-garde* activities of Schoenberg, or his pupils

Anton Webern and Alban Berg. Their first public concerts caused a scandal – not the explosive outrage set off by the performance of Stravinsky's *Sacre du Printemps* (*Rite of Spring*) in Paris, but a more lasting, nagging, demoralizing and damaging hostility. In the arts Gustav Klimt, who presided for eight years over the 'Secession', Egon Schiele and Oskar Kokoschka were regarded as *enfants terribles*. Viennese Modernist literature – which despite its modern content remained strangely traditional in form and style and little touched by the new naturalism elsewhere – gave less provocation, though Arthur Schnitzler did lose his rank as officer in the Reserve for exposing the emptiness of the military code of honour in *Leutnant Gustl* (1901) and provoked a major scandal by his analysis of the boredom of sexual routine in his ten-dialogue *Reigen* (*The Round Dance*) (1900), better-known in the popularized film version *La Ronde*.

Wholly characteristic of the age was the almost farcical history of misunderstanding between Gustav Mahler and the Vienna Philharmonica, whose conservatism and set habits in their rendering of the classics Mahler vainly attempted to break. Eventually he resigned, and the orchestra returned to its familiar routines, completely ignoring the new and exciting Viennese School of composers. If 'nothing could damage the golden tone of the strings of the Philharmonic',[9] then nothing – not even the new and urgent spirit abroad – could really undermine the habits, tastes, convictions and illusions of traditional Vienna.

Rooted in this kind of reactionary progressivism is the central paradox of the Vienna of these years: that whilst the city produced one of the most lively and important movements in modern art, music, and literature, it did not come up with a single major work of art. Works like *Ulysses*, *The Magic Mountain* and *The Waste Land* were not written there. The major, and truly modern, writers of the old Austria came from the less metropolitan city of Prague, which made far less noise about 'Modernism' than did Vienna. Vienna's traditionalism – self-conscious, clever, political, 'a gay apocalypse' in Hermann Broch's phrase – exerted a powerful pull on the modern movement; indeed it drew it steadily toward the alluring slogans of the old ideologies, encouraging the association between 'modern' sensibility and a feeling for the past. Hence it encouraged a peculiar love–hate relationship in Austrian writers for their capital city, drawing some in, pushing others into exile. Freud, Rilke and Kafka came to hate Vienna unambiguously for being what it could not help being: Viennese.

Yet the centres of Modernism existed. One such was the Café Griensteidl, where from about 1890 to 1897, a group of young writers and bohemians met (they later moved on to the Café Central and Café Herrenhof) and became known as 'Jung Wien' ('Young Vienna'). The best-known members were Hermann Bahr, founder and for many years spiritual leader; Hugo von Hofmannsthal; his friend Leopold von Andrian-Werburg, author of intimate impressionistic prose; the *doctor poeta* Arthur Schnitzler; the writers and journalists Stefan Zweig, Richard Beer-Hofmann, Theodor Herzl, Roaul Auernheimer, Peter Altenberg, and Siegfried Trebitsch, the translator of Shaw. Bahr (1863–1934) was the epitome of an important turn-of-the-century type: the brilliant reporter and restless analyst of a changing age. His plays and novels are strangely traditional accounts of the over-abundant energy and the vague creativity of otherwise conservative souls; his essays, inspired by a belief in the genius of the age and by the desire to assist the 'spirit of the times' to fulfil itself, are nevertheless still very much worth reading. Bahr was less an original talent than a great discoverer of the validity and modernity of others: he 'discovered' Hofmannsthal, and was one of the first to explain to his contemporaries the significance of Nietzsche, Mach, Freud and of Naturalism, Impressionism and Expressionism. Though the description 'Jupiter in Lederhosen' ('Jupiter in leather shorts') is not wholly unmerited, he was the essential focus for the many scattered talents and ideas circulating in the city, bringing them together round a single table, or displaying them in his liberal weekly *Die Zeit*. The journalistic tradition thus established was brilliantly sustained by Karl Kraus's *Die Fackel* (*The Torch*), a periodical which from its launching in Vienna in 1899 conducted a sustained, irreverent, and sardonically witty campaign against what its editor (who also very soon became virtually its sole contributor) had identified as the besetting social and cultural abuses in the Austrian life of the day: the hypocrisy of public morality (especially the blinkered attitudes to sexual problems), the mindless conventionality and conformity in matters of declared standards of conduct, and any manifestation of portentous or stupid or culpably insensitive use of language, especially by the proliferating officialdom.

One of his protégés was Arthur Schnitzler (1862–1931), who – with the obvious exception of Hofmannsthal – was the only writer of the period to achieve lasting importance. A doctor and neurologist, he conveyed in depth the society and the neurasthenia of the Vienna of Freud; his subjects were nearly always local, but the subtlety of portrayal and analysis were remarkable: 'He is the chronicler of all the moods and intrigues, the social events, the affairs and betrayals of the middle- and upper-class strata of Viennese society in the first decades of this century,' says J. P. Stern.[10] His literary fame dates from the publication of *Anatol* (1893), a series of dramatized episodes showing the love-affairs of a young man about town, and wittily analysing his 'sexual neurasthenia'. *Liebelei* (*Playing with Love*) (1895) explores the inner emptiness of a young officer play-acting with charm, and the tragedy arising from the integrity of his innocent party, 'the sweet girl' from the suburbs. *Leutnant Gustl* (1901) leads Schnitzler into complex technique; it is the first and the only sustained interior monologue of any quality in German literature – the fictional record of a young lieutenant's confused 'stream-of-consciousness' stirred when a vulgar civilian lays hands on the lieutenant's sword in the crowded cloak-room of the opera. The story's importance lies not so much in its outspoken social criticism, exploring as it does the clichés and sickness of a conventional mind, as in its adaptation of psycho-analytical methods – as Freud had outlined in *Studies in Hysteria* (1895) and *The Interpretation of Dreams* (1899) – for literary purposes. To quote Stern again: 'The literary correlative of the psychoanalytical method is the *monologue intérieur*, of which *Leutnant Gustl* is the most powerful and most consistent example in German literature.' Few such developments came out of German and Austrian literature; only the works of Kafka, Musil and Broch invite comparison. Schnitzler's own work does not attain such experimental modes again, but his powers as a social and moral critic – particularly obvious in his novel *Der Weg ins Freie* (*The Road into the Open*) (1908) and his comedy *Professor Bernhardi* (1912), about the conflict of old guard and new in the medical profession – and his sympathy for human weakness never left him. Until his death he remained the supremely representative Viennese writer, deftly manipulating the masks and fictions of life – Viennese especially.

The dominating figure of this period was however his friend Hugo von Hofmannsthal (1874–1928). 'Early ripe and sad and tender,' as he said in a famous line of his verse-prologue to Schnitzler's *Anatol*, Hofmannsthal published his first poem at sixteen, attended the Café Griensteidl in his father's company, quickly emerged as the major writer, critic, and man of letters of the 1890s, and produced most of the poetry he felt he wanted to write by the age of twenty-six. His essays between 1891 and 1900 are the pure distillation of contemporary sensibility; they embrace the spectrum of 'modern' heroes from Ruskin to Ibsen; they mirror every feeling and impulse the *fin de siècle* experienced, or thought it experienced; they portray the agonized conflict between moral passion and social consciousness on the one hand and the cult of the aesthetic on the other. This conflict is the predominant theme of his 'lyrical plays', like *Der Tor und der Tod* (*The Fool and Death*) (1893), *Das Bergwerk zu Falun* (*The Mine at Falun*) (1899), *Der Kaiser und die Hexe* (*The Emperor and the Witch*) (1900), and is also, in more pointed and particularized form, present in stories like *Das Märchen der 672. Nacht* (*The Tale of the 672nd Night*) (1895), and the dramatic *Reitergeschichte* (*Stories of Horse*) (1899). Hofmannsthal's poetry, the most 'polished' achievement in the history of German poetry, establish that 'three are one: a man, a thing, a dream' and that 'my part is greater than this slender / Life's ascending flame or narrow lyre'.[11] In those of his works written after 1900 – opera libretti (for Richard Strauss), allegorical morality plays, the comic *Der Schwierige* (*The Difficult One*) (1921), and a less successful 'political' play, *Der Turm* (*The Tower*) (1925-7) – Hofmannsthal betrayed a growing compulsion to preserve what he considered to be absolute European values of a religious, cultural, and aesthetic kind from the threat of destructive forces all around him. He initiated (very largely) the Salzburger Festspiele, for which his morality *Jedermann* (*Everyman*) (1912) was the first big production. The main impulse behind the project was an attempt not so much to rejuvenate drama but to assert spiritual values.

In 1927 Hofmannsthal crowned his politico-cultural ambitions by delivering a speech at the University of Munich on the theme of 'Das Schrifttum als geistiger Raum der Nation' ('Writing as the spiritual space of the nation'), a kind of Romantic manifesto of an overheated, twentieth-century brand of conservatism. Following Dostoyevsky and Moeller van den Bruck in their more apocalyptic moods, Hofmannsthal enthusiastically painted the picture of a moral leader emerging out of the debris of nineteenth-century liberalism, a 'genius . . . marked with the stigma of the usurper', 'a true German and absolute man', a 'prophet', 'poet', 'teacher', 'seducer', and 'erotic dreamer'. The spiritual passion of this leader will be such that it will transform his own ego, and with it the whole world, melting all fragmentary manifestations into unity and changing all matter into 'form, a new German reality'. What Frank Kermode says about Yeats is true also of Hofmannsthal, as it is also of many other European 'Modernists': that there is a correlation between early Modernist literature and authoritarian politics.[12] As H. Stuart Hughes has pointed out: the peculiar pathos of the period 1890–1930 rests 'in its combination of intellectual creativity with a conviction of what Germans call *Epigonentum*: the very individuals whose work established the guiding patterns of thought for the next fifty years were haunted by a sense of living in an age of merely derivative philosophy and scholarship'.[13]

It would nevertheless be misleading to end an assessment of Viennese Modernism on a negative note; for its main achievements were such that it is difficult to find parallels anywhere else. Modernism, wherever it occurred, generated a healthy mistrust of the impersonal and abstract in philosophy; it fostered a creative perspectivism and 'open systems' in the sciences; and it encouraged the dismantling of any rigid lines of demarcation between literature, philosophy, and the sciences. *The Interpretation of Dreams*, Freud's major work, still reflects this variety and open-endedness of approach and of subject matter; it is still read with equal interest and benefit by scientists, philosophers, lettrists, and laymen alike. Freud was one of the first to recognize this degree of interpenetration; writing to Schnitzler on 8 June 1906, he acknowledged that he had long been aware of the 'far-reaching coincidence' between their respective psychological interpretations, but that he had only recently dared to admit the fact that he had a 'double':[14]

I have often asked myself, wonderingly, whence you were able to draw that secret knowledge which I have had to acquire through laborious research into the subject; and in the end I have come to envy the poet whom earlier I had merely admired.

Modernism proved to be a pervasive force, and its influence is traceable at many levels. What is true of Freud is also true of many of his contemporaries. Ernst Mach (1838–1916), an eminent physicist who was also an important psychologist, nevertheless devoted himself in his later Vienna period almost exclusively to philosophy and ethics; moreover, his 'scientific' *Beiträge zur Analyse der Empfindungen* (*Analysis of Sensations*) (1866) greatly influenced creative writers. Musil, who wrote his Ph.D. thesis on Mach, began as a student of technology and later switched to philosophy before becoming the novelist we know; Hermann Broch (1886–1951) had an even more varied career as engineer, manager, mathematician, philosopher and author. But in arriving at these writers, one has moved from an earlier to a later and distinct stage of Viennese Modernism, to that second generation of Viennese Schools – of economists, composers, philosophers and writers who were born and brought up in Vienna but who, for complex reasons, found themselves developing and flourishing elsewhere; a secondary explosion the fragments of which were later found lodged in Berlin, Paris, London, Harvard, Princeton, and Cambridge.

3

The German literature of Prague never had an early wave of Modernism of any significance. In the 'city of the golden spires' the nineties were on the whole an uneventful affair, at least intellectually; writers like Hugo Salus (1866–1929), Friedrich Adler (1857–1938), Camill Hoffmann (1878–1944), and even Paul Leppin (1878–1945) were either thoroughly traditional or else only mildly infected by the Modernist spirit, Europeanly understood. When the first 'modern' writers began to make their voices heard, from about 1906 onwards, they were virtually doomed to be derivative.

The social background of the city provided little encouragement for the budding writer, particularly if he happened to be German, or Jewish, or both – as is the case with many of the writers who invite attention. Johannes Urzidil, himself an early emigrant from the 'Dublin of the East', has attempted an objective account of the social situation in Prague:[15]

The German-speaking poets and authors of Prague had simultaneous access to at least four ethnic sources: the Germanic tradition to which they belonged culturally and linguistically; the Czech tradition, which everywhere surrounded them as an element of life; the Jewish tradition, even when they were themselves not Jewish, since it formed one of the main historical and ubiquitously evident factors in the city; and the Austrian tradition, into which they were all born and within which they all grew up . . .

Even this account disregards the frictions, the almost unbearable fragmentation of all creative and intellectual efforts in this relatively small city. The statistical distribution of the various groups is also eloquent: in 1900 Prague had a population of 414,899 (92·3 per cent) Czechs, plus some 10,000 non-Jewish Germans and some 25,000 Jews, 14,000 of whom spoke Czech and 11,000 German. The minority groups had scarcely anything in common; nor, in their turn, did they have much in common with the dynamic and nationalist ambitions of the vast majority of Czechs. Despite a number of idealistic attempts at collaboration in intellectual circles, the situation in Prague remained one of fragmentation – a peculiar hothouse atmosphere in which all kinds of creeds, such as Socialism, Zionism, German nationalism, bohemianism, humanism, and an artificial type of cosmopolitanism clashed vehemently. Whatever apologists like Max Brod have said fifty years after the event, Prague in the early decades of this century provided a classic environment in which intellectuals were free to develop mass hysteria and claustrophobia. At least three major waves of emigré writers left Prague for no other reason than the drab atomization of life in their city. Rilke left as early as 1896; by 1906, Victor Hadwiger, Gustav Meyrink, Camill Hoffmann, and Leo Heller had also gone; Franz Werfel left in 1912, to be followed within the next eight years by Egon Erwin Kisch, the 'roaming reporter', by Willy Haas, one of the editors of the *Herder-Blätter*, by Paul Kornfeld and several others. In 1915 Kafka commented in his diary: 'Always this one principal anguish: What if I had gone away in 1912, in full possession of all my forces, with a clear head, not eaten by the strain of keeping down living forces?'[16] By about 1912, Modernism in Prague had ceased to exist as a significant force. There was left, on the one hand, a small group of writers of widely different outlook, of whom Max Brod was to some extent the leading spirit, dedicated to the propagation of a vague liberal humanism (for which Herder came to be adopted as the defining symbol) but productive only of a flat and unsophisticated *Epigonentum*; and, on the other hand, the man destined to become one of the greatest writers ever to use German as his medium: Franz Kafka.

Franz Kafka (1883–1924), whose main works did not reach the public until after his death, thoroughly mistrusted the noisy political activities of his contemporaries, and on a more general level, felt threatened by the typical manifestations of Central European politics and Hapsburg myth-making. Living largely in what he defined (in 1922) as that 'borderland between loneliness and fellowship', Kafka was uniquely qualified for the kind of literature which broke away decisively from literary traditions and conventions, and which developed original patterns of its own. Kafka's mistrust of literature as an institution was complete. His idea of paradise was a place where there were no books. But he had a compulsive interest in fictional works of a strongly autobiographical kind (Goethe, Dostoyevsky, Strindberg, Grillparzer, Kleist, Kierkegaard) and in works which use language analytically (biblical exegesis and works of a scientific, psychological or philosophical nature). The idea of language as pure exorcism fascinated him. There is a sense in which Austrian literature right down to Peter Handke can very largely be seen as a rhetorical ritual of exorcism. In the works of Schnitzler, Musil, Broch, and most contemporary Viennese writers, the spiritual muddledom and what is frequently referred to as 'the sickness of the Austrian mind' (in the widest sense of the phrase's geographical and teleological meaning) has been consistently on trial – a trial which normally ends with the hero condemned to silence. Kafka is the climax of this tradition. But where others might highlight a collective malaise, Kafka focuses on a single individual, as he does most rigorously in his novel *The Trial* (1914, 1925). His plans for collecting his three early stories *The Judgment* (1912, 1916), *Metamorphosis* (1912, 1916), and *In the Penal Settlement* (1914, 1919) into one volume under the title *Punishments* was never realized; but it clearly reveals his intention of relating his own personal perspectives to society (and society's relation to the past) as a whole.

Kafka is perhaps the most significant of 'post-Nietzschean' writers. Musil and others 'discussed' Nietzsche or 'adapted' certain Nietszchean habits of thoughts for their own purposes; but Kafka's very art is grounded on the one hand in the kind of nineteenth-century radical pessimism which we know from Schopenhauer, and on the other in Nietzsche's vision of life and art which resulted from a commitment to this pessimism.

Alongside the nightmare aspects of Kafka's work there is much that is comic and ironic. When he switches to the horrors of existence it is not to 'prove' the tragedy of it all but to create a desire and curiosity for existence redeemed. His works – particularly the novels *America* (1912f., 1927), the 'brightest' of Kafka's works, and *The Castle* (1922, 1926), his most ambitious attempt to explore man's existential dilemma, and the short stories like *Metamorphosis* and the *Hunger-artist* (1924) – offer a unique celebration of life. Long after Kafka's death, and well beyond the confines of Prague, a body of literature sprang up which is frequently referred to as the 'Kafka tradition'. But the 'tradition' is easily distinguished from its radical initiator. The difference between, say, Camus and Kafka appears to lie in the fact that Camus allows his characters to rediscover solace in an (admittedly absurd) spiritual position, whilst Kafka questions the validity of the human urge to embark on a spiritual quest as such. The religious hero, with his temptation to impose an alien order on reality, and the artist, with his temptation to assert the timelessness and impersonality of his art, are the first ones to be sent up for trial.

Notes

1. 1. Jahrgang, Heft 1 (1898).
2. Quoted from Ilsa Barea, *Vienna: Legend and Reality* (London 1966), p. 286.
3. Quoted from Arthur J. May, *Vienna in the Age of Franz Josef* (Norman, Oklahoma 1966), p. 136.
4. Thomas Mann, 'The Dilettante', in *Stories of a Lifetime*, vol. I (London 1961), p. 54.

5 Robert Musil, *The Man Without Qualities*, vol. I, translated by Eithne Wilkins and Ernst Kaiser (London 1953), p. 11.

6 Ernst Mach, *Beiträge zur Analyse der Empfindungen* (Jena, 1886), p. 18.

7 Ilsa Barea, *Vienna: Legend and Reality* (London 1966), p. 317.

8 Stefan Zweig, *The World of Yesterday* (London 1943), p. 56.

9 Ilsa Barea, *Vienna: Legend and Reality* (London 1966), p. 362.

10 J. P. Stern, Introduction to his edition of Arthur Schnitzler, *Liebelei. Leutnant Gustl. Die letzten Masken* (Cambridge 1966).

11 Hugo von Hofmannsthal, *Poems and Verse Plays. Bilingual Edition*, edited by Michael Hamburger, with a preface by T. S. Eliot (London 1961), pp. 31, 35.

12 Frank Kermode, *The Sense of an Ending: Studies in the Theory of Fiction* (London 1966), p. 108. This book contains one of the most intelligent analyses of a difficult theme: the general critical failure in early Modernism.

13 H. Stuart Hughes, *Consciousness and Society: The Reorientation of European Social Thought 1890–1930* (London 1959), p. 14.

14 Sigmund Freud, quoted in Ilsa Barea, *Vienna: Legend and Reality* (London 1966), p. 326.

15 Johannes Urzidil, *Da geht Kafka* (Zürich and Stuttgart, 1965), p. 6.

16 Franz Kafka, *The Diaries of Franz Kafka 1914–1924*, edited by Max Brod, translated by Martin Greenberg (New York 1949), p. 145.

MODERNISM IN RUSSIA 1893 – 1917

EUGENE LAMPERT

I

A N allusive historical reminiscence in Boris Pasternak's *Doctor Zhivago* provides an illuminating comment on Modernism in Russia:[1]

The time contained the foretaste of new things. In it were those portents and promises which before the war had appeared in Russian thought, art and life, in the destiny of Russia as a whole and in his own, Zhivago's.

Zhivago, we learn, longs to go back 'to that climate, once the war is over, to see its renewal and continuation, just as it was good to be going home'. From the context, and from indications earlier in the novel, it emerges that the time which evokes Zhivago's nostalgia is the period shortly before and after the revolution of 1905. It may be a sign of Zhivago's tragically confused mind that he should remember this of all times on the very eve of the October Revolution. But it is more or less exactly the period, 'with its portents and promises in Russian thought, art and life', to which the spirit of Russian Modernism most attaches.

It cannot be said with certainty when this period began – in 1893, or in 1900, or, still later, in 1905. But we know for certain that it ended in 1917. In the climate of this period we can find many of the features of artistic change that dominated the contemporary European scene as a whole. Measured in economic and political terms, it was a time marked by the advent to prominence of industrial society in Russia, by attempts to modernize the political structure, or at least to remove some of the crutches of the régime on which it had grown accustomed to limp, and by an accelerated growth of the middle class – which, after 1905, restrained its own disaffection and sought political salvation in a liberalized tsardom. The process was partly frustrated by the heavy residue of feudalism, by the peculiar position of the

Russian bourgeoisie which, compared with its western counterpart, was particularly closely geared to the needs of the state, by the rigidity of the autocracy, and by Russia's economic dependence on the West. But the feudalization of the bourgeoisie went hand in hand with an *embourgeoisement* of feudalism. Even the huge rural population was affected by the process – not the poor peasants, of course, but the propertied ones, the beneficiaries of Stolypin's agrarian reforms which brought wealth to the wealthy. Economic expansion and political differentiation were plainly at work, although at the back there was a deeply-felt fear that change would mean collapse, and although the forces impelling the process were so constricted within the old order that they had to burst it.

There was a corresponding change of pace and temper, a differentiation and variegation, in the cultural and artistic sphere. The change owed something to the remarkable reserves of cash and leisure among the middle classes, to the fact that for the first time in Russia art, in all its forms, really began to pay and the artist and writer became producers of commodities to be bought and sold on the open market. Even the erstwhile *kulaks*, the ex-serf peasant merchants, the primitive capital accumulators who used to inhabit a grim world of rapaciousness and piety pickled in dill-water and suffocated by eiderdowns, became culture-conscious: the Muscovite Medicis turned Maecenases, producing such remarkable patrons of the art as Tretiakov, Mamontov, Morozov, Riabushinskii, and others. Unlike their early western European counterparts they seldom tended to sober calculation and the puritanical slide-rule, and they quickly discovered art as an investment, an embellishment of private life, even a real aesthetic need. Artistic activity itself became an occupation part-romantic, part-commercial, part-escapist, part-subservient to a conglomerate of nameless consumers.

The cultural consumer – a creature that appeared in the West some fifty years earlier, after 1848 – was a new phenomenon in the cities of Russia, although faint symptoms can be detected as early as the eighteen sixties. It has scarcely been studied. It was a kind of gutter-intelligentsia (*bul'varnaia intelligentsia*), ranging from the relatively up-holstered variety, which flourished especially among the merchants and their scions, to the Chekhovian genteel hairdressers, telegraphists and bank employees who shared (with the bugs) the tenements of both the capitals, Moscow and St Petersburg, and the larger provincial towns. They showed a rising demand for sub-culture products and pulp fiction (in the manner of Kamenskii, Verbitskaia, Nagrodskaia, or the more sophisticated *boulevardier* novelist Artsybashev). They were supplied with a mass-produced periodical literature (such as *Vestnik znaniia* and *Damskii zhurnal*). The better-off had their *vie de bohème*, as often grimy as gaudy. They not only caroused with the gipsies (*u Yara*), but sat in artistic night clubs, drinking treacly champagne with the juice of modernist verse in the company of aesthetes and prematurely seedy sixth-formers who fed on Artsybashev. They joined in the widespread love of shocking the bourgeois: it was a luxury, a slap in the face to obtain and to give pleasure but render any further steps unnecessary, to get into the swing and leave everything intact. Often they were confused, disorientated and vulgar; but these attributes were not confined to this milieu alone. They were also present among those artists who withdrew from such coteries and made sensibility supreme, a sensibility which, when pushed beyond its relevance, became equally false.

These writers and their constituencies represent no uniform movement; rather an intellectual, moral and imaginative experience which comprises many conflicting elements, but which has, none the less, acquired a distinct period quality. There was, on the one hand, an extraordinary display of artistic, literary and intellectual talent, lively and eloquent; a fresh cosmopolitanism, an intense concern for aesthetic and spiritual values. On the other hand, much of this crystallized into fastidious prejudice and evasion, into a whimsical and uncompassionate view of the human situation, a readiness to sacrifice truth to aesthetic satisfaction or metaphysical comforts, a Jamesian 'sickness of one's own exquisite taste'. Who influenced the trend? Virtually everybody: the Greeks, the Italians, German Idealist philosophy, Baudelaire, Verlaine, Nietzsche, Dostoyevsky, Ibsen, to mention only a few. There was, in addition, the dominant international style of *art nouveau* and the whole end-of-century cultural climate which characterized European cosmopolitan arcadia and, outside Russia, survived the First World War. But the hunt for influences, however attractive, would be unhelpful. There are, in any case, no external influences, except where internal conditions are ready for it. One can borrow everything. The Russians were eager to borrow from a variety of sources, but they could not borrow the history and the imagination which impelled them to do so: and this is the crux of the matter.

2

I mentioned 1893 as one of the possible dates for the beginning of the period: it is the publication date of a book somewhat cumbersomely entitled *On the Origins of the Decline of Russian Literature and on New Currents in It* (*O prichinakh upadka i o novykh techeniiakh sovremennoi russkoi literatury*), which served as a manifesto for the new trend, and is held to have pioneered Russian Symbolism. Its author was the novelist and poet Dimitri Merezhkovskii. Together with his wife, Zinaida Gippius, and the neo-Nietzschean writer Minskii he signalled a protest against the politically committed radical intelligentsia, which largely dominated the literary stage in Russia for almost half a century, against its brash assertions and reasoned assessments of tangible issues, and its search to engage in art and literature the force of politics and society. Strictly speaking, Merezhkovskii did not oppose ideology in art or in politics (with which he also concerned himself). Very few Russian writers above a certain level of mediocrity ever did, perhaps (a very smug 'perhaps') because social injustices were more obvious in Russia than in the West. Merezhkovskii merely sought to replace articulate opinion by myth and mystery – which however he immediately proceeded to rationalize. He was endowed with astounding mytho-poetic or myth-hunting gifts – dark, apocalyptic and humourless – combined with a maniacal discursiveness and a simple lack of proportion. Together with many of his contemporary fellow writers, he fitted more or less exactly Stendhal's definition of a decadent person: *'quelqu'un qui se sacrifie à ses passions, mais à des passions qu'il n'a pas'* ('Somebody who sacrifices himself to his passions, but to passions which he does not have'). He was full of cerebral ecstasies of the flesh and equally cerebral invocations of the spirit, reading significance into trivia, insisting on some buried treasure of meaning, some abysmal, terrifying profundity, and touting mysteries like some saleable real estate. In his imaginative work, especially in his novels (many of which exist in English translation), he devoted himself to the creation of stylized, roaring metaphysical worlds, of a kind of occult intellectual comedy or tragi-comedy. Merezhkovskii's message met with immediate response. It suggested that a whole new shimmering universe of discourse was being opened up. It electrified the pioneers of what appeared to be a Russian cultural renascence, induced a sense of escape from the surrounding flatness and from the imperative issues of the day. It is not by chance that the heyday of Merezhkovskii and his group was also the heyday of mediums in Russia, of apparitions, of clairvoyants, of extra-sensory phenomena and creepy-crawlies, chiming with the orgy of mystery-mongering at the Rasputinizing Imperial court and the widespread readiness to mythologize uncomfortable facts into conspiracies and scapegoat-hunting.

Merezhkovskii's wife, Zinaida Gippius, also a novelist and a poetess, was a less influential but more talented figure. A Russian Messalina who tended to arouse desires which she never committed herself to gratifying, a metaphysical flirt intent on tempting the devil, she was formidable, immensely clever, and sharp-tongued. Unlike her dwarfish, somewhat marionettish husband, she was flamboyant and regal, appearing in green salamander-skin robes, with a cross dangling over her abdomen and fingers playing with beads. She tried to be a *Kulturträgerin* and was a literary tiger-lily. Her prose work whips characters into intensity and, like her husband's, turns people into states, genders and depersonalized ideas in a kind of would-be Dostoyevskian frenzy (the novels *The Devil's Doll* and *Roman Tsarevich* are cases in point). Her poetry, though, is superior to her husband's, less formless, more controlled and discriminating. Yet it generates an atmosphere of constriction. It creates a world tucked away in a private corridor, of interior life as narcissistic magic and sticky hot-house eroticism, paradoxically combined with a spinsterish distaste for other bodies.[2]

The Merezhkovskiis – in their capacity of trend-setters, literary practitioners and cultural impresarios – had a number of more or less gifted, more or less important protégés: poets, critics, novelists, religious thinkers and mystical dervishes. One was the writer Vasilii Rozanov – a figure as typical of the period as he was outstanding, although he himself, from a deep instinct for and enjoyment of fickleness, periodically betrayed or cracked down on its representatives. As a writer Rozanov is unclassifiable: his most striking and startling utterances are contained in footnotes to private letters to himself, which he published without the permission of their senders. He uses an extraordinarily resourceful and idiosyncratic style full of whimsical typographical devises – parentheses, brackets, inverted commas, question marks. His language breaks up the conventional pattern of discourse and turns into a kind of disjointed, insidious whisper. He is the nearest to a Russian D. H. Lawrence – plus a sense of play, but minus the social passion. He longed for the human race to surrender to the intestinal flow, beyond good and evil. What gave him fulfilment was slopping around in the amniotic fluid. He believed in salvation through sexual intercourse and dreamed of the *paradisus voluptatis* of Genesis and an association between the brothel and the church. He was not a pornographer: he had no desire to excite and titillate, nor did he have the pornographer's coldness. He sought protection in a merging of identities. His mood was one of passivity, tenderness and warmth, with a distinctly effeminate complexion, hospitable, ever clamorous for petting and with nothing to hide.

Indeed, the feminine trait is characteristic of a great deal in this cultural milieu – a monosexual milieu which seemed to claim for man the same alluring vanities which traditionally belonged to woman. It was a reaction from the austerity of the radical intelligentsia, from the heightened masculinity of social and revolutionary struggle, and a direct or indirect result of disablement in the face of the facts of real life. The effect was inevitably blurred, androgynous, self-admiring.

The same trait can be detected even in some of the prevailing religious and metaphysical ideas. The whole complex of religious symbolism in the thought of Soloviev, Florensky, Bulgakov, and similar burning amateurs of philosophy is a case in point. Longing for the myth from which a desacralized world had dissociated itself, they too were torn by the irrational and incoherent and searched for a single, comprehensive metaphor, for the ultimate equation of reality, the Holy Grail, in the feminine image of Saint Sophia, Holy Wisdom (which also provided a source of inspiration for some of the Symbolist poetry of the time). These 'sophiologists' were far from Rozanov's apotheosis of primitive urges and from cultivated decadence, but the association of the erotic with the metaphysical is unmistakable. Conscious of the divisive forces in the world, they believed that the mystical Lady, Saint Sophia, had bridged the gulfs by transcending and embracing them. They felt at one with her and with the world, endorsing it and the whole wretched empirical reality as part of the preternatural order. Hence the theocratic schemes of Soloviev, of his disciple Sergei Trubetskoi, of Bulgakov. Hence the tendency to confer divine, eschatological status on national and social phenomena, which gave the illusion of redeeming them and which, in Bulgakov's case, resulted in a vision of the reign of the last Romanov as white sophianic tsardom shrouded in mystery.

It must be said that, while feeling a growing pull towards the Orthodox Church, the Russian religious thinkers had grave doubts about the ecclesiastical establishment. They believed its vocabulary to have lost Christian substance. They hesitated to accept its preaching of the doctrine of the transvaluation of lost or unowned goods into the securities of an imperishable order. They hankered after a deity that would fill the explanatory gaps, and they were convinced that the survival of society and civilization was the reward for return to divine allegiance. They quoted Dostoyevsky but forgot that God was Dostoyevsky's misadventure, and that he did not get anything out of his faith except a deepened sense of conflict. They were metaphysical totalitarians, claiming the licence of prophets but involved, almost against their will, in legitimizing everything by explaining everything.

Such positions were not shared by all. Berdyaev, who for a time became identified with Merezhkovskii's literary circle, was different. He was the noble *homme fatal* among the religious thinkers – outrageous, proud of his non-conformity, jerky in the manner of his writing no less than in the paradoxes of his thought, having so many ideas that he was exhausted by the time he got down to them. Reason for him was, and should be, the slave of the passions. The notion of comprehensive intellectual structures, of metaphysical master-keys (which, in Soloviev's and Bulgakov's view, was what philosophy and religion meant) was anathema to him. But the cragginess of his philosophical matter and manner conceals a number of dominant themes, of which the idea of *creativity* is the most important. He advocated creation with no 'objective correlative' (in T. S. Eliot's phrase) – the creative impulse with no embodiment, for embodiment was 'objectification', a running down, an exhaustion of the impulse, a congealment. This was the romantic dream which outruns reality. Yet by rights Berdyaev's own books ought to have remained unwritten. As it is he could be said to have fostered the illusion that the creative process had found its resting place. He ought to have pressed forward towards silence. He did not. He wrote thirty-five books and 135 articles. In the last analysis, they can be reduced to the proposition that life is like a Sisyphian stone, falling repeatedly from the edge into crushing failure, that man's limitless urge to create issues is powerlessness, and that every achievement is a servitude. The position came to this: on the one hand, the corrupt objective world in which nothing really significant can or must happen, on the other, man with his untarnished creative subjectivity and a sense of life conducted in the innocence of private values.

Berdyaev was a contributor, together with six others, to a symposium entitled *Landmarks* (*Vekhi*) – the most celebrated and best-selling moral tract in late pre-revolutionary Russia. Although nothing, except perhaps political speeches, dates so much as a moralizing sermon, *Landmarks* encompasses a very important slice of Russian intellectual history and constitutes an important element in the Russian Modernist trend. It is in many ways a remarkable document, written by some of the most gifted and clever members of the intelligentsia. It is basically a case of 'treason of the clerisy'. From every possible angle the *Landmarks* men (*vekhovtsy*, as they are now referred to) called in question the assumptions and implications, the views and habits of mind of the Russian intelligentsia which, throughout most of the nineteenth century, stormed the established order and smashed their heads against its walls, preparing the way for those who came after them. The *vekhovtsy* were beset by a sense of guilt of the kind to which the Russian intelligentsia was prone for generations, but now in an opposite direction. Ashamed of the intelligentsia's part in the abortive revolution of 1905 and in the struggle that led up to it, they sought to efface their guilt and repent of what they considered their own and their predecessors' youthful follies.

Ideologically they were concerned to indict the belief that man can control and transform his environment, the belief which offers radical solutions to intractable problems and defies or oversteps the limits of caution, the belief whose audacity had blinded people to human irrationality and appealed to the future instead of the past or the world above, the belief which, in the words of Bulgakov, another contributor to the symposium, substituted *geroizm* for *podvig*: that is, the heroic deed, the decisive action for the deep, slow, patient, interminable endeavour. To make heroes of the saboteurs of history was to sentimentalize them. The task was to shrivel their reputations, to show that their shrill, implacable proposals concealed a mere desire to impose their unaccommodating juvenile ideas on a world from which they were deeply alienated, an inability to understand that their precipitate behaviour merely served to provoke the authorities into repressive measures, thus causing a chain-reaction of unrest.

There is hardly a single important argument in the whole body of meliorative, liberal European thought since Tocqueville which has not been skilfully seized upon and indeed anticipated with remarkable foresight by these writers. Some of them were ex-Marxists and they were the first to engage in what has since become the favourite academic indoor sport of burying Marx. Overshadowed as they all were by the traumatic experience of the 1905 revolution, the *vekhovtsy* lamented that people should think of circumstances, instead of realizing that it was all a matter of a change of heart (and head). They appealed to their readers to jettison the great utopia of the radical intelligentsia, the starry-eyed unsound posture, the revolutionary dream, as if Russia could have been cured of revolution any more than of the proletariat and the ninety million peasants. But the proletariat and the peasants hardly figure in the *vekhovtsy*'s appeal to spiritual regeneration, except as an ominous and terrifying threat. One of the contributors to the symposium writes:[3]

In our condition we should not only stop dreaming of solidarity with the people: we should be much more afraid of them than of all the executionary works of the powers that be, whose bayonets and prisons protect us from the people's wrath.

A historian is not concerned to fight past battles, let alone to fight them differently. His duty is to explain. It is not impossible to explain why the *vekhovtsy* were frightened. Ironically, by the time they had issued their challenge the revolutionary forces were no longer represented by the intelligentsia, except for the as yet relatively small Bolshevik section of it, but by 'the people', by the proletariat and the landless or land-hungry peasants. This was the threat which in the cir-

cumstances imposed a choice between following the Bolsheviks and
conniving in the existing order, thus pre-empting the works of the
executioner. The *vekhovtsy* were by no means opposed to change.
They were aware that the order was tottering, or at least visibly and
awfully deteriorating. They recoiled fastidiously from the torpid
reality of their surroundings. But they were pursued by the perennial
dilemma of the Russian liberals of all shades and persuasions, who
could not expect real change so long as they accepted the régime, but
could not effectively attack the régime without ceasing to be liberals
and becoming revolutionaries. In a way, it was a situation that reminds one of Flaubert, who declared himself ready to go and '*baiser le
derrière de Louis Philippe*' ('kiss the backside of Louis Philippe') were
it not that so many others were queuing up to do the same.

As it happened, most of the *vekhovtsy*, or those who were not
openly playing the political game, believed they had found a way out
of the dilemma in aristocratic idealism which gave a feeling of being
beyond the social predicament, of having attained salvation for the
gifted and isolated few. Berdyaev, whose view of the *Vekhi* venture,
and indeed of the whole climate of opinion around it, became much
more critical in exile after the Revolution, wrote this in his autobiography:[4]

Our misfortune lay in [our] isolation . . . from the wider social
movement of the time – a fact which proved fatal in the light of the
subsequent development during the Revolution . . . We lived in a different age, estranged from the historical struggle . . . It was not the Word
that had become flesh here but, on the contrary, the flesh became word,
and facile constructions were taken for the real things . . . I cannot help
realizing now that we were living in an ivory tower where mystical
discourse was pursued, while below the tragic destiny of Russia took its
course.

3

The essential role however – both in the preparation and in the subsequent development of the cultural trend – belonged not so much to
philosophical or metaphysical debate as to art and literature, particularly to poetry and, still more particularly, to Symbolist poetry. It

must be given its due for an enormous extension and deepening of the imagination and sensibility, although it led – above all in the person of Alexander Blok – to a revaluation of the whole trend.

Symbolism in this connection implied not only the technical procedure in poetry of substituting images for direct description or statements about facts and feelings, but a *Weltanschauung*, a longing for life to be transfigured. It embodied a mixture of boldness and fear in which a desire to find life more than it is is combined with an impotence in the face of what it is. Soloviev – a Symbolist poet as well as a philosopher, whose oracular reporting of visions heralded, in the manner of Descartes' and Rousseau's dreams, his philosophical vocation – was the first to turn for relief to the distant in time and space and induced in his poetry the sense of an eerie twilight. Over his shadow-land there gleamed the sophianic inscription: 'Lighten our darkness, O Beautiful Lady!'

In a sense, Symbolism is a refinement and concentration of the romantic experience, whose premise is a consciousness of the isolated self, and of a world unrelated and possibly hostile. Yet neither Byron's, nor Heine's nor Lermontov's poetry suffers from oppressive, paralysing self-consciousness, for they sought to reach out from their solitude, to assimilate the visible world and render it back charged with meaning. And this is true, if not of Soloviev, of Alexander Blok – the towering figure among the Russian Symbolists. His most impressive work belongs to the immediate pre-revolutionary and post-revolutionary period, when he exchanged the current high-pitched language of myth and symbol for the language of simplicity. He captivates because like Pushkin (and no other comparison would do him justice) he could make poetry out of everything. What puts him in a special sense beyond Symbolism is an extraordinary conjunction of the visionary and the sense of concrete situation. He was haunted by the *sound* of events, objects, thoughts, his own inarticulate thoughts, and the faintest signs which showed where the sickness of the old world lay and the drama of the new one was enacted. His last and most important poem was *The Twelve* – as it were, the apocryphal Gospel of the Twelve (twelve Red Army Guards), marching like a haughty host, driven by blizzards and shambling through the snowy streets, between the bleak houses of hungry Petersburg in the first winter of Bolshevik Russia. Their procession was to him mankind processing through the twentieth century.[5]

Most of the other Russian Symbolists, on the contrary – to say nothing of those post-Symbolist poets whose declared aim was 'not to offend the imagination by anything concrete' (Kruchenykh) – gave voice to the great retreat of the Russian imagination, to its self-deliverance from life and history, whether through art, or mumbo-jumbo or intoxicating spasm or whoop. They announced that artists were men seeking to be above all inhuman. Their romanticism was a tired, trapped and impotent posture, despite the occasional Nietzschean drawing-room purring about 'living dangerously'. There was a link between this and the hermetic elaboration of private images, the secret cellars and shut doors, the standardized pessimism, the phrase-making and mechanized eroticism of their verse.[6] In the end, they will be remembered not for what they said in their poetry, or even how they said it, but for exemplifying a human condition and a time whose meaning exceeded their understanding.

The other cultural sphere where an incompatibility declared itself between sensibility and evasion, between art and limited sympathies, was that of painting and art criticism. Cubism, Cubo-Futurism, Constructivism, pure abstraction in painting, indeed almost every artistic movement reverberated and, in some cases, originated in Russia during the period in question. Some painters representative of these trends – Tatlin, Malevich, Lissitskii – were imbued with a tremendous revolutionary energy, which impelled them to assume an almost impossibly daring social responsibility, bending art towards extreme practical application, sweeping aside all barriers between art and life and mingling all areas of art activity. They produced the visual equivalents of the dynamite of Mayakovskii's revolutionary poetry. But this happened with the first years after 1917, when artists were free to fling their pots of paint at or with the public. Before the break with the pre-revolutionary bourgeois forms occurred, the artistic climate carried all the symptoms of imaginative dissociation. The dominant responsibility for fostering this climate belonged to the art critics. Their role, and the financial support of the wealthy merchant patrons (the *kupecheskie millionshchiki*), were in fact decisive not only in the development of modern Russian art but also in the re-discovery of old Russian art, and in the propagation of a wider knowledge of western art. The journals *World of Art* (*Mir iskusstva*) and *Golden Fleece* (*Zolotoe runo*) were leading channels for this activity, with Benois, Diaghilev, Grabar' and Muratov as its distinguished promoters. They were extremely cultivated men, at home in the art world of Renaissance Florence and Venice as much as in that of pre-Muscovite Russia. They eagerly discovered, carefully nurtured and lovingly developed talent wherever they found it.

There is a diary by Alexander Benois (published in English a few years ago) which conveys the atmosphere that prevailed in these circles. Benois was a painter in his own right as well as a writer on art – a décor painter, who designed for Diaghilev's ballet. With the dissolution of the old order, others (Larionov, Goncharova, Dobuzhinskii) also decided for the glamorous dream with Diaghilev, while Kandinskii opted for the Bauhaus, and Chagall, Pevsner and Gabo for Paris, where art seemed to be still for art's sake. The diary depicts a charmed life in highly civilized surroundings, in the upper social regions of the author's beloved Northern Palmira, with himself as an amiable, perceptive connoisseur, successful enough to be patronized by the Emperor, enjoying the not inconsiderable fruits of that patronage and bathing in an environment where personality found room to expand in mildly eccentric shapes. No shadow of Russia's predicament ever disturbed the tenor of this life. An artistic erudite of unflawed urbanity and taste, Benois loved Sèvres china, Fabergé gilded lilies and gem-encrusted Easter eggs, and delighted in toys. Making acquaintances was his passion. He leaves the impression of patent leather shoes in the heart of the country, of a sort of genuine phoneyness. But it was typical of those exclusive enclaves of Petersburg society where the artistic climate was generated, although the performance of the few really gifted artists themselves cannot, of course, be reduced to this.

Now it is in these circles that the idea was mooted that Russian Modernism represented a cultural Renaissance analogous to the Italian one. The analogy was eagerly taken up and extended beyond the sphere of artistic activity by Berdyaev, Viacheslav Ivanov and others, and it has become axiomatic in post-revolutionary émigré circles. It is not easy to pursue the analogy because, if for no other reason, historically and culturally the concept of the Renaissance is notoriously vague. If the European Renaissance means a 'renewal' of classical culture, then the Russian renewers must have been involved in a vicarious experience not of its elements of luminous humanism but of its dark and most decadent side, its *terror antiquus*. They were at the mercy of Dionysiac powers, lured by the prospect of dissolution in a cosmic vortex. This accounts for the incontinent, incoherent, overloaded style of so much in the period, for the general obscurity which took over and which was due not so much to depth as to a polarity between a bewildering and chaotic outer world and the inner private one that failed to connect. This style cannot, strictly, be attributed to the Benois circle. While celebrating with the rest the infinitude of the private man, they preferred the quietly 'minor' to the vehemently 'major', the decorative to the cavernous. But they offer an additional avenue for pursuing the Renaissance analogy to which the spokesmen of the new trend in Russia laid claim.

It could be said that a resemblance exists between certain aspects of this Russian cultural scene and a period in the Italian Renaissance between Dante and Michelangelo, during the *Quattrocento*, when the epigonian elaboration of Gothic symbolism began to give way to the pressure of the Baroque *Sturm und Drang*: a time known for its exquisite surfaces, for costume and gesture, for façades and courtyards, for ornament and embellishment. These were the Renaissance *bizzareries*. They were matters predominantly of social privilege and prestige for those Venetians, Siennese, Florentines whose economics and theology had finally made them see life as a *Magnificat* in reverse, with the mighty secure in their seats and the humble and poor sent empty away; matters which never touched the people even in Florence. The man for whom 'the people' had ears was Savonarola, the subverter of the Medicis – a character of quite another spiritual and social order.

4

Who, then, one might ask, was the Russian Savonarola? The role fell to Lenin, the relentless, ungraceful revolutionary and most fascinating political genius of the twentieth century, whose shadow grows longer as his successors seem to grow shorter.

Genius is a way out that one invents. Lenin's way out was not and could not be a gentleman's agreement out of John Locke. It meant not a modification in the rules of the game, but a change of the game itself. In undermining the foundations of the edifice, however, he did so with an inevitability which high-lighted its inexorable disintegration. Genius is also a gathering into one's own life and work the central experience of one's time. Lenin embodied the century-long search by the much-spurned radical intelligentsia – sometimes a pathetic and hopeless, sometimes a hopeful and certain search – for 'the people' and for the force that would re-fashion human life. And he gave – at least to those who had nothing to lose but their chains – a shock of recognition similar to the Florentine rabble's reception of Savonarola, or to the *sans-culottes'* reception of Rousseau, or to the British artisan's reception of Paine, but in a situation that stirred conflicts far more decisive and unleashed forces far larger than those involved in the greatest upheavals of the past.

To allow myself a final incongruity, who, one might ask, was the Russian literary Savonarola? Surely not Chekhov, however deep and, in a way, classical his view was of the experience of a sinking civilization or, at any rate, of a class and cultural milieu whose complexities (or the little he saw of them before he died) were to him not signs of richness but of confusion and obfuscation, or which evoked merely his gentle irony. Perhaps Tolstoy? He had nothing but contempt for the cultural élite and all it stood for. But this was no more than a minor item in the huge subversive sacrifice he made, or *tried* to make, of all human truths and falsehoods, and in the end, of his own life and work. The man to whom the role of literary Savonarola belonged during the period in question was Maxim Gorky – the 'stormy petrel' from the lower depths, who sent shivers down the spines of the cultural élite and whom they dubbed 'the Great Cad' (*Velikii kham*). He was no longer able to believe in the possibility of even ideal escapes from real situations. Striding across all barriers and curiously belying his pen-name – the Bitter – he created an image of man with all the marks of the soiled underground from which he came, but also of all the features of the future of which he dreamt. The question of what man *is* really meant, for Gorky, what man can become.

Much insight is needed to distinguish between the death-throes of the old world and the birth-pangs of the new. Gorky, just as the infinitely more vulnerable Alexander Blok, seemed to possess this insight to a high degree, and it made him look at the Modernist trends in pre-revolutionary twentieth-century Russia as a decline, not a renewal. On the whole, and for the reasons I have tried to put forward, the conclusion seems irresistible. Admiration for a marvellous window-box display is bound to be diminished, although it was not diminished for Yuri Zhivago, if the building incorporating it happens to be rotten to the core and/or if it is on fire.

Notes

1 *Doctor Zhivago*, English translation (London 1958).
2 For an example of Gippius at her best, see 'Ona' (She), in *The Penguin Book of Russian Verse* (Harmondsworth 1956).
3 M. O. Gershenzon, in N. A. Berdyaev, S. N. Bulgakov, M. O. Gershenzon, A. S. Izgoev, B. A. Kistiakovskii, P. B. Struve, S. L. Frank, *Vekhi, Sbornik statei o russkoi intelligentsii (Landmarks, Collection of Articles on the Russian Intelligentsia)*, 2nd edition (Moscow 1909).
4 N. A. Berdyaev, *Dream and Reality* (Engl. transl.) (London 1950).
5 To illustrate the ironic fusion of, and sometimes the alternation between, the romantic, the visionary, the semi-somnabulistic and the acute sense of the world's real presence in Blok see his well-known poem, *The Stranger*, in the excellent translation by Frances Cornford, and the translation of *The Twelve* in Maurice Bowra's edition.
6 A few quotations from Symbolist verse will convey the mood and the intonation:

Мне мило отвлеченное:
Им жизнь я создаю ...
Я все уединенное,
Неявное люблю.
Я – раб моих
   таинственных,
Необычайных снов ...
Но для речей
   единственных
Не знаю здешних
   слов ...

'I rejoice in the abstract: I make my life from it ... I like all that is secluded and recondite./I am a victim of my mysterious, uncommon dreams ... But I have no earthly words to express the unrepeatable.' – *Gippius*

Я ненавижу
  человечество,
Я от него бегу, спеша.
Мое единое отечество –
Моя пустынная душа.

'I hate mankind, I flee from it in haste. My one home is my deserted soul.' – *Balmont*

Я не знаю других
  обязательств
Кроме девственной веры
  в себя.

'I know of no other commitments/save a virginal faith in myself.' – *Briusov*

For an account of the more vacuous, not to say blank, post-Symbolist poetry in which poets such as Burliuk or Kruchenykh were avowedly exercising themselves in abracadabra, see Kruchenykh's own *Declaration of Transrational Language* (*Zaumnyi iazyk*), an English translation of which will be found in V. Markov, *Russian Futurism* (London 1968), pp. 345f.

CHICAGO AND NEW YORK:
TWO VERSIONS OF AMERICAN MODERNISM

ERIC HOMBERGER

I

IN 1888 the novelist William Dean Howells, then fifty-one and at the height of his creative powers, moved from Boston to New York. 'But at the bottom of our hearts,' Howells wrote to Henry James, 'we all like New York, and I hope to use some of its vast, gay, shapeless life in my fiction.' Howells's move is a portent of a significant shift in American cultural life. The decline of Boston, and the rise of the great commercial centres of New York and Chicago, mark the beginning of 'modern' American culture. Fastidious young men from Harvard, such as Wallace Stevens, who found New York 'fascinating but horribly unreal', were ambivalently absorbed by the spectacle of disorder and energy on such a profuse scale. In June 1919 the poet Hart Crane explained to a correspondent that 'New York is a series of exposures intense and rather savage which never would be quite as available in Cleveland, etc. New York handles one roughly but presents also more remedial recess – more entrancing vistas than any other American location I know of.' Whether in the great height of the skyscrapers (a new word in the 1880s), the size and variousness of the population, the misery of the poor, the bitterness of the battle between labour and capital, the extravagance of the rich, the venality and crusading courage of the press, the ruthlessness of the cartels and trusts, and the shattering indifference of urban society towards the individual (' "We're not exactly in need of anybody", he went on vaguely, looking her over as one would a package,' is how Dreiser expressed it in *Sister Carrie* in 1900), New York and Chicago stood for everything *new* in American society.

New York was a magnet, attracting the peasant from Sicily and the Ukraine as well as the worldly, sophisticated graduates of Yale and Harvard. The small-town boy from Iowa or from the villages of

Indiana and Ohio, where a new writing had been growing, turned as if by instinct to Chicago. The contingent differences between New York and Chicago, historical and geographical, suggest an important difference in the culture of the two cities. While both embody the *laissez-faire* ethos of the Gilded Age, and shared a healthy indifference to the idea of 'culture' which was at the same time appallingly obsequious (the motto of the Chicago Columbian Exposition in 1893 was 'Make Culture Hum!')[1], New York and Chicago stood for different kinds of 'newness'; and that difference is seen in the literary milieu of each city, and in the major literature which is most closely associated with that milieu.

What mattered in Chicago could always be measured, counted or weighed, whether in the thousands of bushels of grain shipped east, the millions of head of beef brought by train to the Union Stockyards for the meat-packing industry, or by the tons of steel produced by the mills in Gary. Carl Sandburg wrote in 1919:

You might say at first shot that this is a hell of a place for a poet but the truth is it is a good place for a poet to get his head knocked when he needs it. In fact, it is so good a place for a healthy man who wants to watch the biggest, most intense, brutal and complicated game in the world – the economics and waste – so good a place is it from this view-point that I think you will like it.

The economy of the city was dominated by a small number of giant industries whose oligarchs were Chicago's leading citizens, and whose names (McCormick, Armour, Marshall Field, Sears Roebuck, Montgomery Ward) still matter in America. Chicago prided itself on the giant scale of its achievements, from the cheque for $2,600,000 given by John D. Rockefeller to found the University of Chicago in 1893, to the riot in Haymarket Square in 1888 and the bitter Pullman strike in 1894. Travellers from Europe might be repelled by the roughness of Chicago, and by its corrupt and insatiable materialism ('Having seen it,' Kipling wrote of Chicago, 'I urgently desire never to see it again. It is inhabited by savages'); but to the tens of thousands of young Carrie Meebers, and to those who read of her ambiguous rise to 'success' in *Sister Carrie*, Chicago was the pinnacle of sophistication and luxury. Wallace Stevens noted in his journal on 1 August 1899 that 'modernity is so Chicagoan, so plain, so unmeditative'.

The small literary community of the nineties with its clubs, polite manners, and Anglophile aestheticism (*The Chap-Book*, published in Chicago in 1894, and Thomas Mosher's *Bibelot*, brought the *Yellow Book* writers to a small reading public of cognoscenti in America) was submerged in the growth of a semi-bohemian literary society drawn to the South Side by the availability of cheap housing thrown up for the Columbian Exposition. In Old Town, and in the South Side near the University, the young novelists just escaped from the village, the populist bards and the sensitive souls trapped in an unfriendly environment, found a congenial, undemanding, milieu. It was a small world, socially uniform, with a few periodicals to encourage their efforts. The 'Renaissance' *circa* 1912 has in retrospect seemed an incomplete gesture rather than an accomplished fact; the writers were not asking enough of themselves. Many turned to writing from other careers: Dreiser and Sandburg were originally journalists, Sherwood Anderson was a businessman, Edgar Lee Masters was a lawyer. The contrast with Edwin Arlington Robinson, precariously supporting himself by the patronage of a few friends in New York, is illuminating. Robinson did not turn to poetry – he was simply a poet, and would not make the slightest concession to become anything more than that. The modern movement in Chicago stood for a new liberation, in manners and morals as well as in thought, as Sherwood Anderson wrote in his memoirs:

Then the week ends at some little town on the lake shore six or eight of us men and women sleeping perhaps, or at least trying to sleep, under a blanket by a bonfire built on the shore of the lake, even perhaps going off in the darkness to a secluded spot to bathe, all of us in the nude, it all quite innocent enough but such a wonderful feeling in us leading a new free bold life, defying what seemed to us the terrible stodgy life out of which we had all come.

But the revolt against the gentility of the established quarterlies and reviews soon subsided into a new kind of modern gentility. The best little magazines (the *Dial* and Margaret Anderson's *Little Review*), and some of the writers too, moved to New York. What remained was the most famous of the Chicago magazines, Harriet Monroe's *Poetry*. Financially supported by a small but influential group of cultured Chicago bourgeoisie, for a brief period *Poetry* was at the forefront of the Modernist movement in America. It was due less to the efforts of Miss Monroe, however, than to the labour and good taste of her foreign editor, Ezra Pound. Pound, who had studied Romance languages and literature at Hamilton College, and then at the University of Pennsylvania, settled in London in 1908. By 1912 he was brilliantly established as perhaps the most important of the younger poets. He was the conduit through which the work of Yeats, Tagore and Ford Madox Ford reached Chicago, and it was Pound who in 1915 insisted that Miss Monroe print T. S. Eliot's 'Prufrock'. Pound's relationship with *Poetry* is in effect the story of his struggle against the taste of the genteel tradition; every sign of hesitancy from Harriet Monroe, every puzzled reaction, drove him further towards the direction of the most extreme developments of art and literature on the continent. By 1916 their uneasy relationship was at an end. Pound sent his best work elsewhere (*Poetry* printed the 'Homage to Sextus Propertius' in an emasculated, incomplete text), and *Poetry* survived for many years upon the reflected glow of the brief period when it was genuinely open to the work of the most advanced poets. *Poetry* is a measure of the limitations of the Chicago 'Renaissance' as well as its most enduring monument.

The novelists and poets of Chicago cared ultimately for matter over manner. The fiction of Sherwood Anderson and Sinclair Lewis introduces significant new areas of experience into the literary culture (as do the novels about Chicago in this period, Frank Norris's *The Pit* [1903], and Upton Sinclair's *The Jungle* [1906]), but make little or no advance beyond the canons of realism. Their work stands more for a vivid regional phenomenon, but one which remains outside the achievement of a distinctively modern literature. Anderson partly assimilated Gertrude Stein and Freud. But generally it was too modest, in the worst sense. In the verse of Sandburg, Masters and Lindsay there is a genuine, naïve disrespect for 'tradition'. They wanted a literature open to new freedoms and new experiences, and the old and established modes of mediating this experience were dismissed. Their work sustained no more than a primitive historical sense, and one cannot find in the Chicago milieu anything like the programmes, manifestos and obsessive concern for technique which existed in New York and the cosmopolitan centres of Europe. There was something brash and exciting in Vachel Lindsay's *Rhymes to be*

Traded for Bread (1912), and in the 'higher vaudeville' of his later poetry. But by the standards of Wallace Stevens and William Carlos Williams in New York, of Pound and Eliot in London, Lindsay was not a *serious* artist when he explained that he wrote his poetry 'not by listening to the inner voice and following the gleam – but by pounding the table with a ruler and looking out at the electric sign'.

2

The great size of Chicago meant that land was relatively cheap. Where Chicago encouraged large-scale capital intensive industry, New York, and particularly Manhattan, was severely limited. The population was rapidly expanding, land values were high, and the industries in which New York was preeminent (clothing and printing) characteristically were carried out on a small scale. Most of the small firms and workshops were family businesses; most required a skilled and reasonably well-paid workforce. The nature of the economy left great scope for a particular kind of individualism which was enhanced by the staggering rush of immigrants who passed through Castle Garden. Between 1890 and 1919 some thirteen million arrived, primarily from East Europe and Southern Italy. What the immigrants brought with them, from the Mafia to the Yiddish Theatre, deeply altered the culture of New York. The immigrants felt the pressure to assimilate, to become 'real' Americans, with particular immediacy. But some of them, a small number, of first- and second-generation immigrants were able to act as cultural mediators between Europe and America, and provide a cosmopolitan base for the new developments that were to give American artistic experimentalism an international as well as a nativist spirit.

The experimental spirit was particularly visible in Greenwich Village, an irregular hatchment of streets south of West Fourteenth Street which had been the country estate of an English governor in the eighteenth century. By the 1840s it was being deserted by the wealthy – the process was later described by Henry James in *Washington Square* (1881) – and began to acquire a shifting bohemian and immigrant population, in the European style, based in stables and studios. 'Early in the twentieth century,' notes the recorder of American bohemia, Albert Parry, 'the stage was set for America to have a huge and definite Montmartre of her own,'[2] and he notes that between 1910 and 1917, after the appearance of the magazine the *Masses*, the spirit became very novel, radical, political; its open, various milieu took in a vastly expanded new constituency of those devoted to experimentalism in politics, morals and the arts. The *salon* of Mabel Dodge provided, for a brief period before 1914, a place where radical politics, via John Reed and Big Bill Haywood, the I.W.W. leader, progressive cultural attitudes, and figures like Max Eastman could intermingle. As Hart Crane wrote back to Ohio, New York – especially the Village – was a uniquely auspicious place for a young writer; he was one of many who moved there to write for or edit the vast number of new little and *Tendenz* magazines that the Village spawned: the *Liberator*, *Smart Set*, *Others*, *Glebe*, *Seven Arts*, *New Republic*, the *Freeman*, *Nation*, *Masses* which, with the *Little Review* and *The Dial* as émigrés from Chicago, were the base for the literary *risorgimento* of the 1910s and 1920s.[3] So too were theatre groups like the Provincetown (later the Greenwich Village) Players, producing O'Neill, Floyd Dell, Dreiser and Edna St Vincent Millay, which from 1916 did a winter season in the Village, and the Washington Square Players, involving Robert Edmond Jones, Philip Moeller and others, much influenced by German developments in theatre. The rampant individualism of Village life was an apparent alternative, in life-style and philosophy, to an acquisitive, increasingly regimented economic order. When the veterans returned in 1919 the old gay life of the Village, with its costume balls, saloons, and bohemian camaraderie, seemed inexcusably frivolous. The Left was crushed by the Palmer raids and deportations; the *avant-garde*, despairing of America, discovered the meaning of expatriation.

Yet before that there were others, immigrants to America, expatriates from it, who were aware of the artistic needs of an America on the verge of an international role; these were to contribute to the development of an *American* Modernist tradition. Among these were Pound in London, Stein in Paris, and in New York City Alfred Stieglitz (1864–1946), the Berlin-educated son of German-Jewish parents, whose Little Gallery of the Photo-Secession, founded back in 1905, sustained links with the German and Austrian Secession groups. He staged the first American exhibitions of Matisse, Toulouse Lautrec,

Rousseau, Picasso, Picabia, Brancusi and Severini, and is one of a number of indications that an American Modernism was well-established long before the famous 'coming-of-age' of 1912–13. It might be noted that the Armory Show of 1913, that great point of transition, so immensely successful in publicising the new painting and sculpture, was, as the work of a *bien-pensant* committee, lacking in Stieglitz's discrimination; there were three works by Braque, eight by Picasso, but forty-one by Redon. Before this Stieglitz's friend Marsden Hartley established contact with Kandinsky and the *Blaue Reiter* group in 1912. Stieglitz's *salon* attracted the most brilliant young critics in New York (Van Wyck Brooks, Waldo Frank, Randolph Bourne and Lewis Mumford).[4] What they found in Stieglitz was a nearly mystical evocation of America (he explained his efforts as an artist as 'trying to establish for myself an America in which I could breathe as a free man'), and a searching re-examination of what it meant to be an American artist. Stieglitz's brilliant series of photographs of New York (arguably the most wholly satisfying artistic response to urban life in America) suggested the possibility of an elite, international *avant-garde* art held in a fructifying relationship with a strongly-felt sense of place. The subsequent history of Modernism in America is the story of the disintegration of what in Stieglitz's work was a dialectical relationship between the two.

3

Van Wyck Brooks (1886–1963) in his early work was at the cutting edge of the new mood in American letters. A more serious figure than H. L. Mencken, whose iconoclasm tempted him to play the buffoon too often, Brooks's *The Wine of the Puritans* (1909) and *America's Coming of Age* (1915) were important contributions towards a new cultural analysis of America. His argument was that the materialism of the society, and its idealistic transcendental philosophy, emerged from the decline of Puritanism, and had lead to a split, an impasse, to a 'genteel' tradition (that 'slightly becalmed' state which affected the American mind, as George Santayana put it in his famous lecture at Berkeley in 1911 'The Genteel Tradition in American Philosophy'). Brooks provided the tools for a diagnosis in depth of the American writers who had been damaged by a split in their culture, and the result was *The Ordeal of Mark Twain* (1920), a book which is of greater interest for its extension of Brooks's argument than for the specific and tendentious application to Twain. Brooks argued that writers in America needed a critical sense of their inheritance, a 'usable past' in other words. The literary and cultural nationalists were at heart contemptuous of the European tradition, and optimistic in their interpretation of America. They were uninterested in experimental literature, and by the mid-twenties were regarded as conservative influences by the younger generation of writers.

The opposition between the literary nationalists and the *avant-garde* Modernists was latent in the early years: their enemy, the genteel, gave them a shared but insecurely based sense of cohesion. But when Pound, in his introduction to *The Spirit of Romance* (1910), declared that the 'tradition' was nothing less than the whole of European literature, and when Eliot (who had remained in London after 1914) said similar things in 'Tradition and the Individual Talent' (1919), it was clear that the immediately local, and even national, traditions from which Brooks defined a 'usable past' had been rejected. The criticism of Pound and Eliot, which was strikingly congruent in the period before *The Waste Land,* argued in effect that the really serious artist must be as international, polylingual and professional as a scientist. The only thing which could be allowed to 'flow' from him was discipline in his craft. The modernist poets in New York – Wallace Stevens, E. E. Cummings, Hart Crane and Marianne Moore – were committed to an idea of poetry which was astringent, uncompromising and difficult. By refusing to be 'poetical' in the old sense the Modernist poets chose to exclude most of the things that older readers understood by poetry itself. They wrote for a new audience of fellow artists and those sympathetic to the new experimentalism. W. C. Williams's description of Marianne Moore's use of language suggests the difference: 'With Miss Moore a word is a word most when it is separated out by science, treated with acid to remove the smudges, washed, dried and placed right side up on a clean surface.'[5] To praise a poem as 'a triumph of explicit ambiguity' (Marianne Moore on Stevens) was the purest praise a Modernist poet could bestow. The obvious, the sentimental, the lyrical (the 'ordinary universe', as Denis Donoghue suggests)[6] were suspect, and a new vocabulary (irony, complexity, tension, structure, ambiguity, toughness) enters the lexicon of modern critics. Pound's 'Homage to Sextus Propertius' (1917), and *Hugh Selwyn Mauberley* (1920), Crane's *The Bridge* (1930), Stevens's 'The Comedian as the Letter C' and 'Sunday Morning' in *Harmonium* (1923) and Eliot's culminating triumph in *The Waste Land* (1922) form the essential canon of the heroic era of Modernism in American literature. Only Crane's poem has an American subject or locale. The novel was a more congenial genre for a specifically American art. The nature of American society as seen in Sherwood Anderson's *Winesburg, Ohio* (1919), Sinclair Lewis's *Main Street* (1920), and Fitzgerald's *The Great Gatsby* (1925) suggested that something had gone desperately wrong. The social concern of Anderson, Lewis and Fitzgerald did not, however, require the wholesale importation of European experimental techniques. John Dos Passos (*U.S.A.*, 1930–36) and E. E. Cummings (*The Enormous Room*, 1922) went further into Cubism and Expressionism, but perhaps only the intense regionalism of William Faulkner's *The Sound and the Fury* (1929) can be offered as an art fully contemporary with that of Proust, Joyce or Lawrence; ironically, the writer closest to the Europeans in spirit, Hemingway, was never their equal in talent.

The sheer excellence of the Modernist writers, and the intensely doctrinal nature of their view of art, could not but establish a tradition of its own. In Harold Rosenberg's fine phrase, this was a 'tradition of the new'; it has been compelling in American writing. But it was not the self-conscious heirs (such as Archibald MacLeish) who have meaningfully extended the achievement of the Modernists. The dialectic between the local, immediate pressures on a writer, and the imperatives of technique, produced in William Carlos Williams one writer capable of using this creative tension. His *In the American Grain* (1925) attempted, through a collage of the lives and prose styles of representative Americans, to define such a tradition, and from his impetus there have emerged several long poems which mix geography and history in pursuit of a sound basis for cultural localism. In the late poem *Paterson* (1946–58), Williams drew strength from the dialectic of place and Modernist poetic technique. The poem is uneven, and in parts scarcely readable, but its ambitiousness contrasts with the polished facility which the students of Stevens and Yeats were affecting in the post-war period. Williams' principal heir in contemporary American poetry was Charles Olson, whose *Maximus Poems* (1953–68; a third book appeared in 1975) attempts a synthesis of traditions in the manner of Williams. Olson is no less a moralist than Williams (he condemns 'perjorocracy' with the patrician fervour of a Henry Adams), but his elitism was arrogantly uncompromising. Both *Paterson* and *Maximus Poems* exhibit a highly self-conscious historical sense, which presupposes that the culture of the present can be nourished on the past. The greatest uncertainty of the Modernist legacy is here: how can any historical sense remain relevant to a culture that has no respect for its own past? The physical restlessness of Chicago and New York, and the disappearance of so much that would be preserved in England, is a metaphor in some sense for the destruction of a whole series of past cultures. Modernism remains a radical movement because it urges what, in terms of American society, is little less than utopian.

Notes

1 The Laureate of the Exposition was Harriet Monroe, who subsequently founded *Poetry*. She describes the composition of her 'Columbian Ode' in *Chosen Poems* (New York 1935): 'The Columbian Ode was written at the request of the Joint Committee on Ceremonies of the World's Columbian Exposition, accepted by that honorable body, and delivered on the four-hundredth anniversary of the Discovery of America, October 21st, 1892, before an audience of over one hundred thousand persons . . . By authority of the Committee, Mr Theodore Thomas, Director of Music, requested Professor George W. Chadwick, of Boston, to set to music the lyric passages. Professor Chadwick admirably fulfilled the obligation. The song beginning, 'Over the wide unknown', and the passage of eight lines beginning 'Lo, clan on clan, The embattled nations gather to be one', were given by a chorus of five thousand voices, to the accompaniment of a great orchestra and military bands.'

2 Albert Parry, *Garrets and Pretenders: A History of Bohemianism in America* (1933; revised edition, New York 1960). Also see Caroline Ware, *Greenwich Village, 1920–1930: A Comment on American Civilization in the Postwar Years* (New York 1935).

3 For full details of these see Frederick Hoffmann, Charles Allen and Carolyn Ulrich, *The Little Magazine: A History and a Bibliography* (Princeton 1947).

4 Their tribute in *America and Alfred Stieglitz: A Collective Portrait*, edited by Waldo Frank, Lewis Mumford, Dorothy Newman, Paul Rosenfeld and Harold Rugg (New York 1934) is an important affirmation of Stieglitz's role.

5 W. C. Williams, review of Moore's *Observations*, *The Dial*, May 1925.

6 Denis Donoghue, *The Ordinary Universe: Soundings in Modern Literature* (London 1968). The essay on Williams is of particular interest.

REVOLT, CONSERVATISM
AND REACTION IN PARIS
1905–25

ERIC CAHM

I

ON 29 May 1913, Diaghilev sprang on the fashionable and tradition-
ally-minded audiences which he had created in Paris for the *ballets
russes* the most revolutionary music they had yet heard: it was Igor
Stravinsky's *Rite of Spring*. The music, marked by apparent caco-
phonies and insistent primeval rhythms, caused a riot among the
first-nighters. Fighting broke out, and the hubbub practically drowned
the music; the refined innovations of Debussy were one thing, but
these primitive rites of Russian tribalism another. 'Wherever were
these ruffians brought up?' demanded the following day's newspapers. Diaghilev called the scandal *le moment de la musique moderne*, a
turning point in musical history – for, whatever the first-night
hubbub, within a few days the *Rite of Spring* won acceptance and
acclaim. A decisive battle in the Modernist campaign in music had
been fought and won in Paris, and the ripples were to spread far
abroad.

This was, though, only the most dramatic and celebrated of the
clashes between Modernist rebels and the cultural and sociopolitical
establishment in Paris in the early years of the century. For, in the
first decade of the century, Paris was at the centre of many of the most
significant Modernist developments. Its long-standing reputation as a
focus for European culture, and the earlier movements and bohemian
tendencies it had sheltered, may have attracted the innovators like
Diaghilev, Stravinsky, the Cubist painters, Apollinaire, Gertrude
Stein who now gathered there. Whatever the reason, the variety,
importance and concentration of these Modernist developments,
particularly between about 1905 and 1914, is striking.

It was in pre-war Paris that Cubism had matured rapidly into an internationally recognized movement, in the few short years since Picasso painted *Les Demoiselles d'Avignon* in 1906–7, a painting of outright challenge to the laws of composition and perspective of the past. It was in the French capital, too, that Guillaume Apollinaire had begun writing poetry, which, advancing beyond the Symbolist tradition, was equally explicit in its dismissal of the past; he rejected punctuation, regular typography, recognizable verse-form, and introduced into poems like *Zone* (1913) subject-matter like townscapes, aviators, shorthand-typists and other gimmickry of the modern world. Within four years of the *Rite of Spring* he was to be hailed by the review *Nord-Sud* as the leader of the Modernist movement in poetry. Likewise, in the novel and politics, there were still other trends involving the rejection of past values which became widespread around this time. André Gide's *Les Caves du Vatican* (The Vatican Cellars) (1914), in which Lafcadio commits an 'unmotivated crime', came to be regarded as the inspiration of a whole post-war generation of young writers dedicated to the apologia of Lafcadio's gratuitous personal affirmation. Anarchist militants became prominent in the trade union movement, urging the workers towards revolution through the general strike, while an anti-patriotic trend appeared in the socialist movement itself after 1905, when Hervé launched his campaign for a general strike of reservists in case France declared war. Capitalism and state power, especially in its ultimate form, military force, were now openly rejected by a number of the workers, who saw themselves as alienated from the state, and indeed the whole French nation and its past, and owing no loyalty except to their class. Strike action intensified. In political affairs as in cultural ones, pre-war Paris was the storm-centre of revolt against all that France and Europe had once stood for. The First World War then brought home to everyone the precariousness of civilization in a France already shaken to the roots by the Modernists and anti-patriots: as Paul Valéry remarked in 1919: 'We civilizations now know we are mortal.'

It was the destructiveness of the war itself, both physical and moral, which finally undermined the fabric of the national past, and led the way into the total cultural nihilism of the Dadaists and the total political and social transformation envisaged by the 1917 Russian Revolution. Before the war Paris had been one of the centres of revolt; during the hostilities, it became a focus of bellicose conformity, and the centre shifted. Switzerland became the rebel refuge; from here Romain Rolland led his humanitarian, internationalist resistance to the war; here Lenin worked out his anti-war policy and his exploitation of the wartime situation to pave the way for revolution; here, finally, in Zürich, Dadaism was born in 1916. The message of revolution and Dadaism did not reach Paris until 1920. It was then that Cachin and Frossard, the Socialist Party's emissaries to Moscow, returned to address enthusiastic meetings on the new Russia, after which the majority at the historic Socialist Tours Congress voted to adhere to the Moscow-based Communist International and to set up the French Communist party. At about the same time Tristan Tzara, the Dadaist, burst on the Parisian literary scene, preaching artistic and social anarchy. He began nihilistic poetry readings, presenting, as a poem, a newspaper article read to the sound of bells and rattles. Traditional French civilization, already shaken by the violence and destructiveness of the war itself, found itself challenged again by doctrines even more extreme than those it had known before 1914: Communism and Dadaism, the latter coming to a head in the *Manifeste Surréaliste* of 1924.

2

However, the Paris of revolt and experiment was not the only Paris of the years between 1900 and 1925. From the beginning, Modernist trends met vigorous opposition from the defenders of tradition. There appears to have been a pattern of Modernist revolt and traditional response in early twentieth-century Paris which offers some clues toward an understanding of the cultural and social dynamics of early twentieth-century Europe. Modernism, cultural and social experimentation, sparked off in every case both moderate conservative protest and extremist reactionary backlash. The conflict in France between the rebels, on the one hand, and the conservatives and reactionaries on the other, was concentrated in Paris by a number of factors. Paris had always largely dominated France's cultural and social life, and most of the significant developments took place there; it had, too, a central position as a European focus for the artistic and musical *avant-garde*; at the same time, official taste in the city, and even the taste of the Parisian public in general, was dominated by the canons of the past. In music, Debussy had hardly shaken the hold of Wagnerism; in painting and poetry, Impressionism and Symbolism remained dominant; in prose, Anatole France and Maurice Barrès remained the arbiters of taste. In politics and society, Radical Republicanism and parliamentary Socialism had now become practically a part of the Establishment. It was because of this climate that Stravinsky ran up, not only against Debussy, who blocked his ears at the first night of the *Rite of Spring*, but against the still solid ranks of the Wagnerites; the Cubists found the state galleries of Paris harder to conquer than those of other capitals (as Apollinaire noted in 1913, they could not get a foothold in the major Paris galleries at a time when in Amsterdam Picassos were already hanging side by side with Rembrandts); while Gide, Apollinaire and of course Marcel Proust remained marginal, and almost unknown, figures to Parisians in the period before 1914. Finally, the political and social rebels were opposed politically, not only by the Republican political leadership, but by a rising tide of right-wing nationalism and xenophobia – which was much more prevalent in Paris, indeed, and in the Parisian press, than it was in the country at large, as was evidenced by the left-wing victory in the 1914 elections.

What were the basic factors underlying the conflict between the rebels and the establishment and reactionaries? What set off the atmosphere of cultural scandal and social conflict, of which the first night of the *Rite of Spring* and the strikes of 1906 and 1909 were only the most notable examples? The fact was that the older cultural and social norms, while they maintained their domination among the Parisians at large, had exhausted their creative impetus: a mood of uncertainty had set in among artists, poets, writers and political thinkers, as nineteenth-century standards began to lose their meaning. The old norms had hardened into accepted formulae and dogmas; as Péguy put it, the *mystiques* had given way to *politiques* – freedom and creativity had been replaced by authority and the mechanical application of outmoded schemas. Freedom from the authority of the past was therefore the rebels' central demand: Stravinsky sought freedom from the tyranny of accepted patterns of harmony in music, the Cubists wanted to shake off the stranglehold of perspective and chiaroscuro in art, Apollinaire rebelled against the tyranny of punctuation and regular typography in poetry. It was this essentially anti-authoritarian temper of all the pre-1914 Paris rebels that brought down on their heads the wrath of conservatives and establishment figures: and the dominant mood of cultural and politico-social uncertainty, combined with revolutionary experimentation, whipped up, too, an unprecedented backlash against them among the devotees of reaction, who went scurrying back to the lumber-room of the *ancien régime* in search of the long-dead values of Classicism and monarchy, while at the same time tarring all innovations with the brush of anarchy.

The movement of cultural reaction had been sparked off by an article Barrès wrote in *Le Figaro* in 1892 bemoaning the domination of French literature by Romanticism, a barbarous foreign import, identified with Ibsen, Tolstoy and Maeterlinck. French literature must return to classical and national values, he affirmed. Charles Maurras was soon singing the praises of the 'classicism' of the poet Moréas, the incarnation of traditional Classical France, who had re-introduced the Alexandrine. Rapidly, reaction spread to politics, with the birth of a new virulent nationalism of the extreme right, sparked off by the passions of the Dreyfus Affair. What began in 1898 as a wave of xenophobia and anti-semitic street rioting was to grow into a new, authoritarian, anti-semitic and reactionary form of nationalism, which Maurras soon influenced towards royalism. The new France, the nationalists hoped, would have done with Jewish traitors and their champions, and restore France's military defences. Those defences had been undermined by a Republican régime which, according to Maurras, was as putty in the hands of Imperial Germany: it ought to be swept away, together with its supporters – anti-French Dreyfusards, Republicans who were simply anarchists in disguise, and Socialists like Jaurès and Hervé who were no more than agents of the German Emperor.

In the xenophobic atmosphere whipped up in Paris by Maurras's *Action Française* after the Agadir crisis in 1911, when war began to seem a virtual certainty to many Frenchmen, it is easy to see how hostile the Parisian environment was to the experimentation of the *avant-garde*, how all demands for freedom were dubbed 'anarchic'. The cosmopolitan character of the movement did not help. Experimentation of all kinds was readily identified by the reactionaries and their fashionable followers with foreign 'barbarism', as in the case of the *Rite of Spring*. Xenophobia in Paris led to attacks on the Cubists as *métèques*, 'damn foreigners', based on the fact that Picasso, for example, was a Spaniard. Louis Vauxcelles, the art critic, wrote in 1912:

Foreigners are very much to blame. The *Salon d'Automne* and the *Indépendants* are full of Moldo-Walachians, Munichers, Slavs and Guatemalans. These *métèques*, as Binet-Valmer calls them, are settling in Montrouge and Vaugirard. Sickened by the café-scene at home, they have landed here in hordes, crowding in at Matisse's studio, and with neither culture, talent nor integrity, have got up the new recipes in four months, and are practising them in even more extreme forms. What anarchy and excess! . . .

We have put up with the barbary of cubism and the chaos of epileptic futurism. They have no idea what the aims of art are . . . Picasso, who had some talent a decade ago, is now the leader of the cubists, like Father Ubu-Kub.

These attacks on the Cubists, in 1912, were followed by questions in Parliament on their 'anti-artistic' and 'anti-French' activities. Apollinaire, whose own origins were not French, suffered in the same way: he was in 1911, quite without evidence, jailed on suspicion that he had been responsible for the theft of the Mona Lisa!

The fusion, in Maurras, after the Dreyfus affair, of cultural and political nationalism, and his insistence on classical values, were, it should be noted, no more than a reassertion of the traditions of the seventeenth century. The concept of Universal Man central to seventeenth-century French classicism had led Frenchmen to confuse their own civilization with civilization as a whole: they tended to see the French language, French values and French concerns, as those of all civilized men. And this tendency was reinforced by two centuries of French military, diplomatic and cultural dominance in Europe. Frenchmen had for long been quite unable to distinguish between an attack on 'civilization' – identified with French classicism – and an attack on France herself. 'Barbarism' had always been at the gates, waiting to destroy France, and with France civilization itself. So that Maurras found fertile ground for his association of classicism with French nationalism.

His xenophobic prejudices were shared, to a considerable extent, by the Parisian public, of whom Apollinaire remarked 'People here are too suspicious of foreign taste'. Small wonder that Ernst Robert Curtius could write in his *Civilisation of France* that they were particularly reserved 'when foreign countries are lavish in their praise'. The protectors of French tradition, Curtius observed,

usually arise and stigmatize the new tendency in art as 'un-French'! This means that aesthetic controversy is carried into the political arena. Because artistic taste in France is regarded as a national possession, it must be preserved from becoming falsified or foreign in its form. When the national tradition is based upon the standard of the Classical School, naturally everything which is non-Classical is an alien importation, poisonous and harmful.

3

In the light of this picture of revolt, conservatism and reaction, a fascinating question arises concerning the pre-1914 Parisian rebels. They faced denunciation from the backwoodsmen of the right as cultural and political anarchists, but just how revolutionary were they?

In order to answer this question, it is necessary to consider briefly what the fundamental values of classical French civilization were. Only then will it be clear whether the pre-1914 rebels rejected that civilization completely. Three basic strands can perhaps be isolated in the value system of French classicism. The first of these is the concept of a harmonious order in cultural and political affairs, an order which can be achieved by the voluntary, or enforced, adherence of the individual to norms laid down from above, let us say by the Académie Française and the monarchy: any assertion of individuality is here seen as anarchic and harmful. The concept of a harmonious order persisted into the Romantic and liberal-democratic age, for, until the coming of revolutionary socialism and anarchism, the liberal conception of the non-violent resolution of conflicts within a generally accepted state structure was not decisively challenged by any alternative based on violence and hostility to the state. Romanticism, too, whatever its individualistic atmosphere, and its links with 1848, never lent itself to any fundamentally anarchic cultural forms. The second strand in the classical tradition is the unshakeable adherence to reason and logic as the supreme guides to understanding the workings of the universe and the springs of human action. Once again the spread of the scientific attitude from England to France in the eighteenth century did nothing to dethrone reason: if for Descartes reason came from God, for the Enlightenment it came from man: the sanction was now simply human rather than divine. The third strand in the classical tradition is the vision, already referred to, of man in universal rather than individual terms, or in terms of a specific time or place. This universal vision is seen as compatible with a feeling for France because of the confusion between Universal Man and the Frenchman. This led the French to see their classical tradition as a peculiar national possession, and to an association between classical universalism and nationalism which persisted right down to the emergence of the Socialist left and beyond: as late as 1941 Léon Blum was still prepared to claim, in *A l'Échelle Humaine (Human Proportion)*, that French socialists – like all good Frenchmen – could reconcile 'patriotism' (i.e. nationalism) with an internationalism stemming from the Universalism of the French eighteenth century – which itself echoed the Universalism of the seventeenth century.

It is in the light of these three criteria that we can see just how far the pre-1924 Modernists of Paris remained rooted in the traditions of the past. The pre-1914 *avant-garde* of Paris was not fully revolutionary in the way Dadaism and Surrealism were to be revolutionary, in the years after the war. It was a culture of transition. Stravinsky was right, I believe, to reject for himself the revolutionary label. And likewise the aesthetic experiments of the Cubists did not imply a total departure from order and reason. They looked towards a freeing of painting from the laws of perspective, certainly; but they pursued their aims via a re-ordering of the elements of our visual experience at another level, via the creation of a new order. The different planes of an object might be reassembled in a painting in a dislocated pattern, so that they could all be perceived simultaneously, a feat that was impossible if the object were painted according to the old rules, as if seen from a single viewpoint. The new order was thus not to be dictated by the pseudo-scientific logic of perspective, but by a personal and poetic logic, springing from the vision of the individual artist, and worked out in artistic terms. Much the same sort of analysis might be applied to Stravinsky and Apollinaire. Maurice Bowra has pointed out, for example, that a typographically eccentric poem of Apollinaire such as *Le Jet d'Eau* (*The Fountain*) can be punctuated and arranged in regular lines; typographical fantasy is here a disguise for the classical Alexandrine. All this is a far cry from cultural anarchy.

It is possible, too, to point to the semi-classical viewpoint of a pre-1914 political leader as far left as Jaurès, whose acceptance of order and state authority, whose fanatical attachment to reason, and whose ardent patriotism were only challenged on the anarcho-syndicalist extreme-left, where Sorel and Hervé preached precisely the rejection of order, harmony, the state and patriotism, and explicitly preached the revolutionary general strike to replace capitalism and the state by a social order based on independent workers' organizations. The transitional situation of the cultural *avant-garde* in pre-1914 Paris can be seen expressed discursively in unmistakable terms in Apollinaire's lecture of 1918 on the 'New spirit and poets'. For all his talk of freedom in poetry in both presentation and subject-matter, he declared:

The new spirit stands above all for *order and duty* which are the great qualities displayed by the French mind in its highest form . . . You will not find in this country any of those 'liberated words' which are simply the excesses of the new spirit.

The homage to tradition, and the rejection of the Futurist and for that matter Dadaist anarchy that were so soon to hit Paris are clear here. 'France detests disorder' he went on, and he concluded:

I don't believe society will ever reach a point where we can no longer speak of national literature. Similarly the new spirit, which seeks to reflect the universal mind, and has no intention of confining its activities to any particular sphere, is at the same time – and means to adhere to this – a particular lyrical expression of the French nation, a sublime expression of the French nation.

The accumulation here by Apollinaire of the traditional themes of French classicism: order, reason and the reconciliation between Universalism and patriotism, should remove all doubt about the transitional cultural situation of the *avant-garde* up to 1920.

The pre-war *avant-garde* in Paris was still attempting, in 1918, to create a new culture out of the ruins of the old, at a time when the fully revolutionary doctrines of the post-war world were so soon to burst on Paris. It was now indeed becoming part of the establishment:

Proust, Gide and Valéry, the Cubists and Apollinaire were now seen as the leading figures we know them as today. In Dadaism and later in Surrealism, however, as well as in the first flush of the Russian Revolution and French Communism – before the reversion to authoritarianism set in in Moscow, and was imposed on the infant French party – Paris was at last to come face to face with a culture totally alien to classicism and the whole of the French national past. The revolutionary mood already seen in pre-war anarcho-syndicalism emerged clearly in Dadaism and Communism. Order, authority and harmony gave way to their opposites: anarchy, total conflict and violence, a violence which, for Lenin, was the essential handmaiden to revolution. Reason was replaced by the total irrationalism which led to the verbal extravagances of Dadaist poetry and the automatic writing of the Surrealists. Patriotism was rejected in favour of a noisy anti-patriotism, handed on to the Surrealists: their 1924 banquet to Saint-Pol Roux ended in a riot with cries of 'down with France'. The parallel with Lenin's anti-patriotic 'revolutionary defeatism' is evident. So that the pre-1914 revolt of the Paris Modernists – Stravinsky, the Cubists and Apollinaire and Gide – has to be seen as not totally revolutionary, when placed in the context of the total revolution of Dadaists, Surrealists and early Communists. It was only after 1920 that Paris witnessed the emergence of cultural and social values representing a complete break with the past: these values were, however, elaborated elsewhere, so that Paris cannot be seen, in the last analysis, as the real birthplace of the new revolutionary culture of the early twentieth century.

LONDON 1890–1920

MALCOLM BRADBURY

'The richest town in the world, the biggest port, the greatest manufacturing town, the Imperial city – the centre of civilization, the heart of the world! ... it's a wonderful place.'

H. G. Wells, *Tono-Bungay* (1909)

'Beside this thoroughfare
The sale of half-hose has
Long since superseded the cultivation
Of Pierian roses.'

Ezra Pound, *Hugh Selwyn Mauberley* (1919–20)

I

IN the history of Modernism, London has always had a somewhat ambiguous reputation. It is the obvious centre of English-language Modernist activity, and between 1890 and 1920 it sustained and generated a vital sequence of experimental movements and phases. Yet it is also in the record as one of the dullest and most deadening of capital cities, one with no real artistic community, no true centres, no coteries, no cafés, a metropolis given to commerce and an insular middle-class life-style either indifferent or implacably hostile to the new arts. Its image lives in Modernist writing itself. Its fascination and its repulsion, its status as the centre of vivid multiple impressions and as the city of dreadful night, have entered deeply into poetry and fiction, where a cluster of unforgettable associations surrounds it; it is the city of 'horrible numerosity' in James's *The Princess Casamassima*, the focus of a mass of vivid nocturnes and 'impressions' for the urban poets of the Decadence, the place of a 'darkness enough to bury five millions of lives' in Conrad's *The Secret Agent*, of 'hidden but magnificent meanings' in Wells's *Tono-Bungay*, of civilization thrust out by commerce in Pound's *Hugh Selwyn Mauberley*, and it becomes the city of modern cities, the Unreal City, in Eliot's *The Waste Land*. Its imperial role, as a magnet of the nations, has seemed to some to be paralleled by its cultural role, which made it a great capital of the cosmopolitan arts; yet by other hands its characteristic culture has been reported as traditionalist, parochial, anti-cosmopolitan. There can be no doubt, in fact, of its high achievement in the arts over these years, but this too is strangely reported. It has been judged on the one hand as a distillation of the English tradition, a disturbance, yes, but also the realization of the sequence. On the other hand, it has been seen as largely a cultural accident, one of line with what went before or came after – a chance importation of foreigners, these often temporary expatriates, from Ireland or America, who went elsewhere for their greatest work, and whose real contribution was not to the English tradition, which never fully assimilated Modernism at all, but to an international movement whose English-language realization is most apparent in the United States.[1]

The mixed judgements exist in part because many of the Modernist writers who settled in London themselves reported in contradictions. So, for example, Henry James, who chose London over Paris – his choices of residence had always symbolic overtones – for its settled density, its energy and mass of life, yet who in his later years became increasingly uneasy with London itself, and found the English cultural scene of which it was the centre increasingly stifling, provincial, and above all uncritical. And Joseph Conrad, who became a British citizen, and was also drawn by the civilization and stability of English life, was always aware of the darkness underlying its imperial and urban light, as *Heart of Darkness* makes quite clear. Ezra Pound, who had so much to do with London Modernism, arrived via Venice from the United States in 1908, mainly to see W. B. Yeats. He settled, married, and was later to persuade T. S. Eliot, a refugee from Marburg in 1914, to follow the same course; yet shortly thereafter he was condemning London for its artistic desolation, and roundly declaring that the significant developments in English verse after 1910 were not a native achievement at all, but the work of Americans. Arnold Bennett, with one eye on the comparable situation in France, regarded the British middle-class audience with a characteristic mixture of outright suspicion and good business sense ('Only sheer ennui,' he wrote, 'sometimes drives [the middle class] to seek distraction in the artist's work'), and constantly stressed the regressive effect of the culture on ambitious writing.[2] If England had the reputation for being hospitable to writers, it had also the reputation of disregarding or rejecting their work, especially if it were experimental. The Vitezelly trial, which had put the works of Zola in the dock, the Wilde–Queensberry trial of 1895, and the significant refusal of Thomas Hardy to write further novels after *Jude the Obscure*, all pointed to the notion that the English audience was inherently philistine and Victorian, that in England art was not taken seriously, that, as Ford Madox Hueffer put it, the 'critical attitude' simply did not have a place.[3] Hueffer saw a change in the atmosphere after 1910, as many observers did; the 'serious artist', in the fashionable phrase, seemed to prevail. But, like Pound and Lawrence, he was to despair again and, the War over, he went off to find craft and perfection in Paris, another of the English Modernist expatriates.

The belief that Paris was the true capital of the Modernist arts, and London an anti-capital, was familiar enough from the 1880s onward. In some ways the Paris in question was a fantasy city; and at times it seemed that literary London was populated by natural Parisians who could not quite summon up the cross-channel fare. In fact there had grown up, from the 1880s, an obvious dialectical relationship between the two capitals. One reason for this was the gradual disintegration of the mainstream Victorian literary culture, with its social centrality and its sense of progress and positivism, a disintegration which left the artist isolated either in the precisions and the revelations of his own artistry and his commitment to formal revelation, or else in a new and stressful view of his own relationship to society and social subject-matter. Developments in the European arts now began to acquire a fresh importance, and Scandinavia, Germany and Russia were all to press new influences into English culture. So did the Japanese craze that came after Whistler. But, as writers tended to move toward the alternative claims of naturalism and aestheticism, and as they tended to lose confidence in their power or willingness to act at the centre of English cultural life, the transactions between London and Paris especially multiplied.[4] It became commonplace for English writers and painters to spend an apprentice phase in Paris, the Paris of George

Moore's *Confessions of a Young Man*, George du Maurier's *Trilby*, Wyndham Lewis's *Tarr*, Somerset Maugham's *Of Human Bondage*, of bohemianism, *art nouveau* and Symbolism, of schools, garrets and movements. There was in Paris a standing British atelier population, mostly consisting of painters, who became points of contact and transmission; and in consequence most of the new tendencies of Paris in painting and writing – Naturalism, Symbolism, Decadence, Aestheticism, Impressionism, Post-Impressionism, Fauvism, Cubism – acquired English adherents and were quickly assimilated though sometimes they underwent strange mutations on the cross-channel ferry. What in fact tended to happen was not a direct imitation, but a complex grafting of European tendencies onto the English tradition. We can trace the naturalism of George Moore to French origins, just as we can find in such origins many of the principles and some of the spirit of James's or even Arnold Bennett's realism. We can similarly see the importance of the Ibsenite vogue that swept Europe in the 1880s and 1890s for the work of Shaw, Galsworthy and Joyce. The 1890s are a high point of this kind of assimilation; cross-channel contact was particularly close, and the decade that begins with George Moore's *Impressions and Opinions* and Wilde's *The Picture of Dorian Gray* and ends with Arthur Symons's book *The Symbolist Movement in Literature*, the decade in which a wealth of Parisian lore about Aestheticism and Decadence, Impressionism and Symbolism is taken even into the realms of dress, decoration and music-hall, is unmistakably cosmopolitan.[5] Yet we can also trace an internal or native history for these developments, and equally unmistakable is the modifying process by which these importations were grafted onto an ongoing native tradition, according to a distinctive rhythm and evolutionary structure crucial to English-language writing.

In fact the idea of a fruitful symbiosis of the cosmopolitan and the nativist becomes a profoundly important aspect of the aesthetics of the entire period from the 1880s through to the First World War; it takes on especially complex forms in the work of Henry James in the novel, and Yeats and Eliot in poetry. The 1890s climate of *Yellow Book* aesthetic depravity, of the veil trembling on the brink of revelation, of superfine consciousness active before the impression, is incomprehensible without reference to Huysmans, Mallarmé, and Valéry – but is equally incomprehensible without reference to Pater, Blake, and the

Irish folk-tradition. In various blends, a like mixture of cosmopolitanism and provincialism persists through the subsequent run of movements and tendencies. T. E. Hulme, for example, so important to the early Imagist climate, looked to French and German sources (especially Worringer) but also reasserted an English tradition of 'classicism'.[6] D. H. Lawrence, as we are increasingly coming to see, was both a rooted native intelligence and an eclectic cosmopolitan, with slightly unusual sources; through Frieda Lawrence, he was very much in touch with the early stages of German Expressionism in Munich in the pre-war period when he was looking for an anti-nihilistic, post-Nietzschean synthesis. Bloomsbury was famously Francophile; it was the source of the crucial Post-Impressionist exhibition of 1910 organized by Roger Fry, and also of what was so clearly needed, an aesthetics of modern form – for which it went to Gallic and Germanic sources, but also to Ruskin, Pater, and, for its broader aesthetic attitude, the spirit of Cambridge philosophers like G. E. Moore.[7] As for the later stages of Imagism, between 1912 and 1915, these had a considerable American contingent in them (Pound, Eliot, H. D., John Gould Fletcher) and a deep debt to French sources. It was in part F. S. Flint's magazine reports on the contemporary French movements that produced the notion of having a movement at all, while that movement was itself a synthesis of various Symbolist inheritances from the Anglo-French literary concords of the 1890s, with new novelties: Symons, Laforgue, Corbière, Mallarmé, Valéry, but also Bergson, Remy de Gourmont, *Action Française* and Apollinaire. Yet despite the eclectic cosmopolitan tradition that Pound, that early product of comparative literature studies, amassed behind it, we well know that the indebtedness back to Donne and the Metaphysicals, and the dramatic monologue of Browning, is quite as central.[8] Likewise with Vorticism: Wyndham Lewis had been resident in Paris, and his tendency was a curious cross between French Cubism, Italian Futurism – which Marinetti actively promoted in London – and a strong vein of Anglo-Saxon celebration.[9] The ferments of the period from 1890 to 1920 were a complex mixture of ongoing native preoccupations and a hospitable assimilation of foreign tendencies, to a degree unusual in the history of English writing and thought. This means that English-language Modernism had its own distinctive preoccupations and character, and that its tendencies and movements were not exact analogues of those elsewhere. It also means that London in this period was alive with the same essential mixture – of ideas and forms both internationally and locally derived – which made the characteristic spirit of Modernism.

As with the movements, so with the personnel; the period was one of a remarkable infusion of writers from elsewhere who, for short or long periods, settled in London. 'For one who takes it as I take it,' wrote Henry James, who made his home in the city in December 1876, 'London is on the whole the most possible form of life. I take it as an artist and a bachelor; as one who has the passion of observation and whose business is the study of human life. It is the biggest aggregation of human life – the most complete compendium of the world.'[10] What fascinated James was London's bustle and density, and its depth of custom and manners; you might say he chose the London of the aesthetic realist. His choice was to be followed, over the next forty years, by many other writers from the United States, the Commonwealth, and Ireland, all of whom found London a cultural magnet, though for a mixture of reasons. By the 1890s Joseph Conrad, Henry Harland, and Stephen Crane, as well as Moore, Wilde, Yeats and Shaw, had settled there, in the London of Impressionism, Naturalism, and Symbolism. In the years shortly before the War came another generation that included Ezra Pound, Hilda Doolittle, Robert Frost, T. S. Eliot, Katherine Mansfield and Wyndham Lewis, looking for the new arts of twentieth-century *risorgimento*. There are important differences among these generations; James, for example, was concerned with the inherited cultural density of English society, while Pound, though devoted to the question of cultural polity, was in search of new forms and a multiplicity of assimilable traditions.[11] By 1920 much of the attraction of London for such people had gone, and Paris was the primary centre of attraction, above all for the new generation of American expatriates. Pound, complaining 'now . . . there is no longer any intellectual *life* in England save what centres in this eight by ten pentagonal room [his own]: now Remy [de Gourmont] and Henry [James] are gone and Yeats faded, and NO literary publication whatever in London . . .', made his angry farewell in *Hugh Selwyn Mauberley* and moved on to Paris, as did Ford Madox Hueffer, now Ford.[12] 'For the post-war years up till 1924 or 1925 the activity of both America and England was perhaps more apparent in

Paris than anywhere else,' Pound tells us.[13] Joyce and Lawrence were also expatriates by now, and the axis of English-language Modernism was clearly changing. But English-language traditions – British, Irish, and American – cross and interfuse in London.

One thing is clear; it will hardly do to take this as simply a chance infusion from outside There is the question of the state of the English tradition itself. From the 1870s onward the vigorous, central phase of Victorian literary achievement was weakening. Dickens had died in 1870, seven years after Thackeray; George Eliot died in 1880, the 1880s saw the death of Arnold and Browning. The sense of positivistic, liberal hope, which, however qualified by underlying notes of despair, ran through Victorian literary achievement began to weaken, and so did the belief in the centrality of the literary imagination. *The Origin of Species*, published in 1859, spread an entirely new intellectual ferment through the late Victorian age. But quite as much importance was the growth of a new mass audience which sociologically altered the bases of artistic production. It was now, with the vast commercial expansion of literature and literacy, that the cult of the serious artist grew, and the search for purified language and form intensified. Over successive decades the entire motion of English literary culture began to be redirected.[14] The hospitality of English writers to foreign tendencies is partly the consequence of this directional change, part of a larger breakdown of inherited beliefs and aesthetic and moral conventions. While writers who came in from elsewhere had an important catalytic effect, their presence coincided with the emergence of two, perhaps three, of the most remarkable English literary generations to emerge since the Romantics and early Victorian periods, stirred into mental ferment by the need for a great revaluation, Thomas Hardy, Samuel Butler, George Gissing, Ernest Dowson, Arthur Symons, D. H. Lawrence, E. M. Forster, Ford Madox Hueffer, Arnold Bennett, H. G. Wells, T. E. Hulme, Lytton Strachey, Virginia Woolf, Dorothy Richardson – the names are an exceptional roster by any standards. And what, despite their extraordinary differences of temper and intention, unites them is a prevailing sense of dislocation from the past, and a commitment to the active remaking of art. The truth of the matter is that there is a distinguishable English brand of Modernism, founded in the sense of transformation, often of liberation, affecting those who believed the era of Victorianism was ending, a new phase in society, art and thought beginning. As a result of such convictions, London saw extraordinary artistic turbulence over the crucial years of 1880 to 1920. That turbulence did not come alone from those who would have accepted the label of 'Modernist', running through the developments of the period is a line much less apocalyptic, more empirical, meliorative and liberal than that term suggests. The fact remains that there was a great reshaping of experience and form in the turn-of-the-century period in England, a mood of experiment of which what we conventionally label Modernism was an essential seam.

2

Were there any special reasons for London's drawing power over this period – a drawing power that attracted not only expatriate writers from elsewhere but pulled English writers into urban groups and coteries? As James said, the London of this time was a complete compendium, and it had generated a folklore. It was – this was part of its essential attraction – the world's biggest city, still expanding with extraordinary rapidity, generating a remarkable cityscape and a fascinating technology. Between the 1860s and the century's turn, the population of its conurbation had grown from three and a half to some six and a half million, a development which continued and concentrated a process of urbanization which had been happening throughout the century, part of the English industrial and commercial revolution. The visible fruits of that revolution filled the streets, so that the technological face of the city made for a sense of excitement and stimulus. London had now become the outright point of concentration for English national culture, overtaking and preempting the role of the provincial large cities. It had acquired utter dominance in communications, commerce, banking and, of course, most forms of cultural activity; through it and from it came the newspapers, the books, and the ideas of the country at large. It was a great burgher city, and is conventionally portrayed as a solid, even a stolid, middle-class entity, marked by imperial confidence, expanding trade, and social stability – a stability greatly in excess of that felt in most of the other European capitals. Certainly it had not experienced to the same degree the kinds of social and political disturbance that had provoked new accountings elsewhere. Yet the times were generally recognized as times of great social and intellectual restructuring; as Rupert Brooke said, at the end of the Edwardian period in 1910, 'The whole machinery of life, and the minds of every class and kind of men, change beyond recognition every generation. I don't know that "Progress" is certain. All I know is that change is.' Both the confidence and the sense of change were stimulated by the fact that London was not simply a national capital, but a cosmopolitan city. It was the capital of an Empire and the centre of world trade: and, as Baedeker noted, it contained more Scotsmen than Aberdeen, more Irishmen than Dublin, more Jews than Palestine, more Roman Catholics than Rome. In Asa Briggs's phrase, it was a 'world city' with a world hinterland, an entrepôt for culture, publishing, finance and shipping, a magnet both for internal migration, from other parts of England, and for external migration from the rest of the world.[15]

It was thus a city of radical contrasts and complex mixtures of peoples, contrasts visual, social, and ideological: 'the whole illimitable place,' says H. G. Wells in *Tono-Bungay* (1909), a novel which dwells on the city's most remarkable characteristic, its extraordinary cell-like growth and proliferation, 'teemed with suggestions of indefinite and sometimes outrageous possibility, of hidden but magnificent meanings'. Beneath stability was fluidity, strangeness. If its middle-class life-style was the object of international envy (Herbert Hoover reported it as, up to 1914, the pleasantest place in the world to live) and it was associated with the density of an achieved culture, it was also famous for its fantastic sprawl and mass. It confronted social thinkers and writers too with the problem of agglomeration and scale, the strangeness of what Gissing called its 'nether world'. It was a jungle and abyss as well as a civilization, as General William Booth of the Salvation Army stressed when he entitled his book on the East End, in imitation of the explorer Stanley, *In Darkest London and the Way Out* (1890). By the end of the century, as the problem of mass and the masses came to seem crucial for writers, and as the cause of social reform spread, the stark contrasts within the culture were becoming famous. Sociologists reported on unexplored areas of poverty, and the West End was set against the East End, poor and polyglot and anarchic – the world another American visitor with a different eye from James's, Jack London, stalked through in disguise to report on in his documentary *The People of the Abyss* (1903), or which Shaw examined in his early *Plays Unpleasant* (1898). Images of anarchic proliferation and growth underlie the culture at this time; they help explain the sense of intellectual ferment; and they certainly generate much of the structure and content of contemporary writing.

So the London cityscape, as a scene and a set of social contrasts, becomes important literary subject-matter and the source of new forms. One reason for this was that, like many of their fellow men, writers were being urbanized, following the tide of metropolitan migration, feeling those emotions of isolation and separation, despair and hope that characterize city life. The aesthete is the dandy, and the dandy is an essentially urban figure, a style-maker standing out in the general display. The naturalist, too, is the solemn explorer of the conflicts of urban life. And thus Naturalism, Impressionism, and the Symbolist novel designed round motif or moving consciousness rather than stabilized character are all, in part, responses to the agglomerated city experience. James, in his Preface to *The Princess Casamassima* (1886), speaks of the book as one derived from the 'great grey Babylon' of London: 'the attentive exploration of London, the assault directly made by the great city on an imagination quick to react, fully explains a large part of it'. In the same year another imagination quick to react, but working from a different social location and another perspective on life, George Gissing, produced *Demos*; this was one of a number of Naturalist novels based on London much as Zola had based novels on Paris and urban France. The London of strange, unreal contrasts and encounters had been in fiction since Dickens; it certainly has much to do with those strange exchanges between Naturalism and Impressionism, Realism and Surrealism, Determinism and Aestheticism, that make up the turn-of-century mood. Thus the Naturalist's London – of Gissing, Arthur Morrison (*Tales of Mean Streets*, 1895), Somerset Maugham (*Liza of Lambeth*, 1897) and others – shades into the aesthete's London: the poem written by analogy to the Whistler urban nocturne becomes a characteristic form of the 1890s. Richard Le Gallienne's 'London, London, our delight,/Great flower that opens but at night...' is a fair example; it appears to pastoralize the urban scene, while doing the reverse, and celebrating the *art nouveau* of the city. Naturalism and aestheticism cross in William Morris's Utopian novel *News from Nowhere* (1891), where the disorderly metropolis, reformed, becomes charged with medievalism. As Holbrook Jackson says, many writers of the 1890s reasserted 'the romance of London as an incident in their new-found love of the artificial'.[16] The urban artist, unmistakably encapsulated in the city, here to stay, attempts by his techniques less to humanize or limit the city than catch at its mixture of onerous reality and strange unreality, its unexpected forms and masses, its odd disjunctions, fleeting exchanges, inviting corruptions.

In this metropolitanizing process, London increasingly comes to typify the great city of modernity, rather as New York City has since done; an abrasive, dionysian milieu, it sets process against art and growth against containment.[17] These things become part of the matter of those later Modernist works which use the city to take a modern culture-reading, to compare the historical civilization of the past with the seamless, disorganized impressions of the present. One distinctive feature of London-based Modernism, as compared with its New York or indeed Berlin equivalent, is that it tends toward cultural despair in the face of the contrast. Conrad gives it with high irony in two of his works: *Heart of Darkness* (1902), which threads out from the imperial city to the dark places of the earth, and ambiguously links the two; and *The Secret Agent* (1907), which starts from a vision of London in all its inordinate mass – 'a monstrous town more populous than some continents, . . . a cruel devourer of the world's light . . .' – and juxtaposes, in what will become recognizably Modernist fashion, the city of light and of darkness, the façades of order in the harsh sunlight set against underlying anarchy and exposure in the dark shadows of the East End. Visions like this get yet bleaker after the War: Pound's attempt to 'bottle London' in *Hugh Selwyn Mauberley* (1919–20) depends on superpositioned images of art and commerce, aesthetic potential and cultural waste. And T. S. Eliot's *The Waste Land* (1922) extends the metaphoric process by making London the figure for all the great imperial cities of commerce and politics, in their Byzantine dignity, and also for the undercutting obverse, the broken apocalyptic cities of ruin and falling tower, overwhelmed by the invading hordes.[18] The sense of cultural stress and strain is of course also an explanation of the need for a new art, an art of fragments and images, an art of language retrieved from chaos and misuse, an art which encounters the modern city but also arises from out of it in a new translucent form.

3

There can indeed be no doubt that, as Holbrook Jackson suggests, the obsession with the city and the obsession with new forms and styles were closely related. For Modernism was of course very much an urban phenomenon – as Jackson puts it, 'a product not of England but of cosmopolitan London' – and it depended on the activity of those various urban artistic groupings which filled the cultural scene over our period. In the period before the First World War, there are two phases when such groups are mostly visible: the 1890s when the movement towards Impressionism, Decadence and Symbolism distilled itself, and the years between 1908 and 1914, when Imagism, Post-Impressionism, Fauvism, Futurism and Vorticism surfaced. In both these phases groups clustered and contested; formal debates became great issues; new magazines and new presses grew up to express new opinions in new formats; and the displays of shock and outrage that tend to go with *avant-garde* activity became regular features of the London scene. Both of these two phases have left behind them a considerable folklore and a body of records of the prevailing excitement. Holbrook Jackson tells us of the eighteen-nineties:[19]

The experimental life went on in a swirl of song and dialectics. Ideas were in the air. Things were not what they seemed, and there were visions about. The Eighteen Nineties were the decade of a thousand 'movements'. People said it was a 'period of transition', and they were convinced that they were passing not only from one social system to another, but from one morality to another, one culture to another . . .

A similar folklore of excitement and innovation has attached itself to the immediately pre-war years, as Ford Madox Hueffer tells us:[20]

It was – truly – like an opening world . . . For if you have worried your poor dear brain for at least a quarter of a century over the hopelessness of finding, in Anglo-Saxondom, any traces of the operation of conscious art – it was amazing to find these young creatures not only evolving theories of writing and the plastic arts, but receiving in addition an immense amount of what is called 'public support'.

A further significant period occurs in the 1920s, when the original contacts of the pre-war phase had dissolved, and many writers had now left London, but when some of the greatest classics of English-language Modernism, including *The Waste Land* and *Ulysses*, appeared. What has more recently become apparent is that many elements of continuity connect these periods of high activity – even though overall they do amount to a large transition away from the late Romantic spirit of the 1880's, through the classical revival of 1912–14, to the ironic nihilism that prevailed in many quarters after the War.

There are various useful sources for testing the vitality of such periods – memoirs are sometimes not a good guide – and one of them, for the purposes of a brief sketch like the present one, is to examine the general presence of coteries, tendencies and the magazines and presses which transmit and support them. The 1890s is visibly a period given to new groupings, new magazines, new publishing houses, new forms of relationship between writer and public. Among the groups which tended to centre on cafés or pubs, probably the best-remembered, though mostly for exotic reasons, is the Rhymers' Club, founded by Yeats and Ernest Rhys, and including Lionel Johnson, Ernest Dowson, John Davidson, Richard Le Gallienne, Selwyn Image, and Arthur Symons, who distilled the transaction from Decadence to Symbolism in his book *The Symbolist Movement in Literature* (1899), dedicated to Yeats, which was to reacquire new importance later, when it led T. S. Eliot to Laforgue, Rimbaud, Verlaine.[21] Pound also invokes this group in *Mauberley* and suggests its relation to later events, noting in a paradoxical passage, the presence of 'Image impartially imbued / With raptures for Bacchus, Terpsichore, and the Church' (the Image in question is presumably Selywn, but Pound must have liked the ambiguity). But Yeats, who reports the group in his memoir *The Trembling of the Veil* (1922), recalling it meeting each night 'in an upper room with a sanded floor in an ancient eating-house in the Strand called the Cheshire Cheese', was moving across a London of other groups, of mystics and mediums, Celtic groups and the Socialist League; and this range is typical of the period. A more complete portrait comes if we look to the work of the new presses like the Bodley Head, which was initially run by John Lane and Elkin Mathews before they split to become the two most important publishers of newness in the decade. From the joint source came the *Yellow Book*, which ran from 1894 to 1897 under the flamboyant editorship of Henry Harland, an expatriate American with eyes turned to Paris, and, for a while, Beardsley as art editor, and which printed across the range from Henry James to Max Beerbohm.[22] Beardsley transferred to the rival venture, the *Savoy*, promoted by another central publisher, Leonard Smithers, which mixed Verlaine and Beardsley with Shaw, Conrad, and Havelock Ellis. Here and in other ventures like the *Dome* there was more than decadence; and journals like the *New Age* and the *New Review* suggested that dawns as well as dusks were on the way. The 1890s interfused Symbolism and Naturalism, aestheticism and social conscience, decadent despair and glimpses of Nietzschean or Ibsenist hope. And, if certain of the figures fled, or died, or descended, as Yeats said, from their barstools, around the turn of the century, some of the most significant careers in Modernism are those of writers who, like James, or Yeats, or Conrad, were deep in the spirit of Symbolism or Impressionism in the 1890s and went forward to meet early twentieth-century history and experience. And indeed that evolution is apparent in many of the writers who were to be involved in Hueffer's 'opening world' of 1908–14.

The 1900s certainly turned the mood, and began on a more modest note, though, as Richard Ellmann says, the degree of recession has been much overstated.[23] The century started with great ferment in the world of philosophy, ideas, and political thought, and many novel artistic energies – especially *in* the novel, for between 1900 and 1905 came, for example, Henry James's most Modernist works, *The Wings of the Dove, The Ambassadors* and *The Golden Bowl*, Conrad's *Lord Jim* and *Nostromo*, and E. M. Forster's *Where Angels Fear to Tread*. But by 1908–9 there was a marked resurgence of *avant-garde* activity as such, a fresh move against realism, and a new phase in which the novelties of several arts – literature, music, painting – in several nations compounded into an eclectic modern fusion. 1908, the year Matisse named Cubism, saw early poems by T. E. Hulme and Pound, and the start of Ford Madox Hueffer's *English Review*, intended as an '*aube-de-siècle Yellow Book*', which mixed older talents like Hardy's with the work of discoveries like D. H. Lawrence, Wyndham Lewis, and Pound, just come to London. This was the first of a large new wave of modern-centred magazines which were soon to emerge; Hueffer's 'opening world' was opening. 1909 saw T. E. Hulme's 'school' at the Eiffel Tower Restaurant, which began discussing the image and classicism, the 'forgotten school' which led to later developments. And now the mood was shifting into a tone of intellectual innovation, high experiment, artistic display, aesthetic carnival: 'It was a sort of *mi-carême* festival of big drums and little tin whistles and fancy dress. A new show of Post-Impressionist pictures had much the same character and purpose as the marches of flustered suffragettes on Whitehall,' reports one participant, R. A. Scott-James.[24] The new show of Post-Impressionist pictures was in 1910 – the year in which King Edward died, drawing from the *New Age*, the 1890s review now reconstituted under A. R. Orage, the judgement that the Victorian Age was at last over, and a startling new epoch on hand.[25] The feeling was widespread. These were now the years of what Robert Ross calls 'the Georgian revolt',[26] including not only the new Georgian poetry, promoted in anthologies by Edward Marsh, but the growth of many other movements and campaigns – including, of course, Imagism, which now looks historically the most significant, but was one of many of its type.

The atmosphere of accelerating and novel activity is widely reported. Ford Madox Hueffer had sought to link the Old Lions – James, Hardy, Shaw – with the new writers who were coming to notice, *'Les Jeunes'*, in an entire new post-representational campaign:[27]

Les Jeunes, as they chronologically presented themselves to us, were Mr Pound, Mr D. H. Lawrence, Mr Norman Douglas, Mr Flint, 'H.D.', Mr Richard Aldington, Mr T. S. Eliot . . . [In] our editorial salons they found chaises longues and sofas on which to stretch themselves while they discussed the fate of an already fermenting Europe. So, for three or four years, culminating in the London season of 1914, they made a great deal of noise in a city that was preparing to reverberate with echoes of blasts still greater . . . They stood for the Non-Representational in the Arts; for *Vers Libre*; for symbols in Prose, tapage in Life, and Death to impressionism . . .

Hueffer's editorial salons were, however, to be only one corner of the total little magazine activity. In 1911 John Middleton Murry and Michael Sadleir set up *Rhythm*, later to be the *Blue Review*, on a London–Paris, literature–art axis. Murry had taken up Hulme's interest in Bergson, while Sadleir stressed Fauvism as the new movement of energetic, non-mechanical art, a mode for remedying 'the formlessness of Impressionism' while keeping its brilliance. Into this climate came, eventually, both Katherine Mansfield and D. H. Lawrence, who welcomed in the *Review* Marsh's *Georgian Poetry: 1911–1912* as the new, dawning mood of the times, a breakthrough from nihilism: 'The nihilists, the intellectual, hopeless people – Ibsen, Flaubert, Hardy – represent the dream we are waking from.'[28] In 1912 Harold Monro, whose Poetry Bookshop was a key coterie centre, began the *Poetry Review*, a year later shifting to a new quarterly called *Poetry and Drama*, which eclectically amassed material from Imagism, Futurism, Impressionism, etc. 1913 saw Pound's takeover of the literary pages of the feminist *New Freewoman*, quickly to be renamed the *Egoist*, where Imagism flourished, along with Eliot, Joyce, and a massive new American constituency, including William Carlos Williams. In 1914 came the two issues of Wyndham Lewis's *Blast*, 'a review of the Great English Vortex', promoted from the Rebel Art Centre in Great Ormond Street, a movement made up of Lewis, Pound, Gaudier-Brzeska and others, devoted to transforming art, literature, music, architecture and house-furnishings. According to Lewis, the fundamental demand Vorticism made was for an art of invention: 'there must be no echo of a former age, or of a former manner'. The result of all this activity was a conscious belief that the arts were now in the hands of an *avant garde* who, having cast off the past, were remaking art for the present and the future. Aesthetic debate proliferated in the face of the claims of the urgent now; and in this climate many of the ideas and major works of Pound, Eliot, Joyce, Lawrence, and Lewis were forged. The mood intensified further until in the two years before the War the excitement among what Wyndham Lewis called 'the Men of 1914' was profound. 'If we had no Offenbach to set everyone whirling frantically to tunes in which mad gaiety blended with the tom-toms of a dance of death,' said Douglas Goldring, 'there was nevertheless a close resemblance between the Paris of the last days of the Third Empire and the London which woke with a hangover to face the deluge of blood in 1914.'[29]

Goldring was not alone in sensing that the entire mood was related to and conditioned by forces that would threaten, amend, perhaps destroy it; the forces gathering towards war. Lawrence's moment of dawning was to be brief; soon he was to see not a dawn but a dusk, an old world ending rather than a new one starting. Perhaps the best judge of the turn brought by the War, which brought modernity rather than Modernism into most subsequent English art, is Wyndham Lewis, who noted that the entire episode represented a new spirit. In 1914, he said, 'a ferment of the artistic intelligence occurred in the west of Europe', which was 'full of titanic stirrings and snortings'; it appeared a great new historic school was in process of formation. Everywhere 'the structural and philosophical rudiments of life were sought out'; everywhere 'a return to first principles was witnessed'. The school would have been, says Lewis, more significant, more mature, technically better than anything in nineteenth-century romanticism:

These arts were not entirely misnamed 'new' arts. They were arts especially intended to be the delights of this particular world. Indeed they were the heralds of great social changes. Then down came the lid – the day was lost, for art, at Sarajevo.

And how does it appear in retrospect? Lewis, writing in 1937, goes on to suggest the subsequent view. The phase will come to seem, he proposes, the key period of modern *avant-garde* activity, the great era of collective advance: it will 'appear an island of incomparable bliss, dwelt by strange shapes labelled "Pound", "Joyce", "Weaver", "Hulme"':[30]

As people look back at them, out of a very humdrum, cautious, disillusioned society . . . the critics of that future day will rub their eyes. They will look, to them, so hopelessly *avant garde!* so almost madly up-and-coming! What energy! – what impossibly spartan standards, men will exclaim! . . . *We are the first men of a Future that has not materialized!*

Examining the records, it is hard to say that England did not have its new arts; in the long term Lewis's judgement has its real truth.

Notes

1 For the more negative view, see especially Graham Hough, *Image and Experience* (London 1960) and A. Alvarez, *The Shaping Spirit* (London 1958), which notes: 'The experimental trappings of modern-

ism are a minor issue in English verse. It is largely an American importation and an American need.' Neither critic denies, though, that English literature underwent 'modernization'. Pound's later statements about London, however, grow increasingly hostile: English literary culture refused the modern and was hence dead and exhausted (see *The Letters of Ezra Pound, 1907–1941*, edited by D. D. Paige (London 1951)).

2 Arnold Bennett, 'Middle-Class', in *Books and Persons: 1908–1911* (London 1917). For comments on what became a widespread attack on the British audience, see C. K. Stead, *The New Poetic: Yeats to Eliot* (London 1964), chapter 2.

3 Ford Madox Hueffer, *The Critical Attitude* (London 1911), *passim*.

4 For studies of this contact see Enid Starkie, *From Gautier to Eliot: The Influence of France on English Literature, 1851–1939* (London 1960).

5 On these contacts see especially Frank Kermode, 'Poet and Dancer before Diaghilev', in *Modern Essays* (London 1971), and Richard Ellmann, 'Discovering Symbolism', in *Golden Codgers* (London and New York 1973).

6 A. R. Jones, *The Life and Opinions of T. E. Hulme* (London 1960).

7 See on this J. K. Johnstone, *The Bloomsbury Group* (London 1954).

8 On this see Natan Zach's essay 'Imagism and Vorticism' in this volume.

9 There is a good report on this overall climate in Robert H. Ross, *The Georgian Revolt: The Rise and Fall of a Poetic Ideal, 1910–22* (London 1965).

10 Henry James, *The Notebooks of Henry James*, edited by F. O. Matthiessen and K. B. Murdock (New York 1947), p. 28.

11 Alan Holder explores this contrast in detail in his *Three Voyagers in Search of Europe: A Study of Henry James, Ezra Pound, and T. S. Eliot* (Philadelphia and London 1966).

12 Ezra Pound, letter to William Carlos Williams, 1920; quoted in Charles Norman, *Ezra Pound: A Biography* (London 1969), p. 227.

13 Ezra Pound, 'Date-Line' (1934), reprinted in *The Literary Essays of Ezra Pound*, edited by T. S. Eliot (London 1960), p. 82.

14 I have explored this evolution in English literary culture, and its implications for the growth both of modernization in society and Modernism in literature, in my book *The Social Context of Modern English Literature* (Oxford 1971), where many matters discussed here are considered further.

15 Asa Briggs, *Victorian Cities* (London 1964). I have drawn on this fascinating book for several points here.

16 Holbrook Jackson, *The Eighteen-Nineties* (London 1913). Quotation from p. 105 of the Penguin reprint.

17 This topic is extensively discussed in Monroe K. Spears, *Dionysus and the City: Modernism in Twentieth-Century Poetry* (New York and London 1970), which also has many suggestive comments on the evolution of Modernism in London.

18 This double image is admirably explored in Frank Kermode, 'T. S. Eliot', in *Modern Essays* (London 1971).

19 Holbrook Jackson, *The Eighteen-Nineties*, Penguin reprint, p. 29.

20 Ford Madox Hueffer, *Thus to Revisit* (London 1921), pp. 136–7.

21 See Richard Ellmann, 'Discovering Symbolism', in *Golden Codgers* (London and New York 1973).

22 A useful book on this phase is Kathleen Lyon Mix, *Study in Yellow: The Yellow Book and Its Contributors* (London 1960).

23 Richard Ellmann, 'Two Faces of Edward', in *Golden Codgers* (London and New York 1973).

24 R. A. Scott-James, 'Modern Accents in English Literature', *Bookman*, vol. LXXIV (New York September 1931).

25 On the importance of this journal in the London scene see Wallace Martin, *The New Age Under Orage: Chapters in English Cultural History* (Manchester and New York 1967).

26 Robert H. Ross, *The Georgian Revolt* (London 1965).

27 Ford Madox Hueffer, *Thus to Revisit* (London 1921), pp. 59–64.

28 D. H. Lawrence, 'Georgian Poetry', *Rhythm*, vol. II, no. 7 (March 1913); reprinted in D. H. Lawrence, *Phoenix* (London 1936).

29 Douglas Goldring, *South Lodge* (London 1943). Goldring was Hueffer's assistant editor on the *English Review*.

30 Wyndham Lewis, *Blasting and Bombardiering* (London 1937), pp. 254–62.

FOUR

Literary Movements

AT the centre of any account of Modernism must be the great names and great works; but beyond the individuals there were the movements. It has been generally recognized that Modernism was very much a movement *of* movements; the broad tendency divides into a sequence of phases, theories, social groupings, occurring in different places at different times, yet having sufficient in common to make up a controlling set of aesthetics and tempers. Some of the movements were social groups; others were broad intellectual and aesthetic theories that passed from country to country; yet others were small groups of activists. The movements were often the behavioural dimension of Modernist writing; they helped sustain its image as a neo-political force, a true *avant-garde*. The other essays in the following section are largely documentary, concerned with the larger, more theoretically significant, more productive movements, and with the where, when and what of them. The list ranges from the broadest of international tendencies, like Symbolism, to more local, once for all, yet crucially important movements, like Vorticism. But what should be kept in mind is that many of the major writers of Modernism did not specifically align themselves with these movements; they worked in their ambience, and picked up their ideas, while the movements themselves were very often the main work of more minor figures, whose achievement was, in the end, the movements, the manifestos, the displays that they created.

MOVEMENTS, MAGAZINES AND MANIFESTOS: THE SUCCESSION FROM NATURALISM

MALCOLM BRADBURY AND JAMES MCFARLANE

'A Movement in the Arts – *any* Movement – leavens a whole Nation with astonishing rapidity; its ideas pour through the daily, the weekly and the monthly press with the rapidity of water pouring through interstices, until at last they reach the Quarterlies and disturb even the Academicians asleep over their paper baskets...'

Ford Madox Ford, *Return to Yesterday* (1923).

I

'I REALLY don't care any more than you do about the word "Naturalism",' Émile Zola told Flaubert, who had objected to his use of this programmatic term. 'However, I repeat it over and over again because things need to be baptized, so that the public will regard them as new.' There is a dispute – one which we shall go on to consider – about whether what came to be baptized Naturalism is, strictly speaking, one of the truly Modernist movements; but there can be little doubt that, in expressing his conviction of the need to name and advertise his tendency, to give it a programme and a manifesto, Zola was acting very much in the Modernist spirit. For the movement principle was an essential constituent of Modernism, a basic part of its cohesion and its evolution. When Pound, that master-tactician in literary politics, surveyed the scene in London in 1912, he decided that what was needed was a movement. He organized one, with some friends in a Kensington teashop, calling it *Imagisme*; he had one of these friends, Hilda Doolittle, sign her poems 'H. D., Imagiste'; he produced manifestos and took over parts of magazines for movement promotion. He drew in other writers, most of them only hazily familiar with the Imagist precepts, into volumes with programmatic titles; and in general, as Wyndham Lewis was to remark, he behaved like a Baden-Powell getting everyone under canvas. The result was a sharp concentration of the experimental mood, with long-extended consequences; like Zola (or, later, Tzara and Breton) Pound recognized that the *avant-garde* functioned best, made its mark, when it performed as a campaign, or when its writers operated as a cadre.

In his suggestive book *The Theory of the Avant Garde* (1968), Renato Poggioli has some very useful comments on the social and the political role of movements, which were quite as important as their aesthetic role. One of the distinguishing features of the modern arts, he suggests, is to be found in the milieu and life-style from which they are generated – the *avant-garde* life-style in which the artist functions as a kind of aesthetic guerrilla (sometimes as a frankly political one as well), given to distinctive mannerisms, outrageous social display, withdrawal from bourgeois norms, and manifestations of group cohesion and solidarity.[1] Of course many Modernist writers, often the most important, did not allow themselves to be drawn into such *avant-garde* action, such group performance – though they often abstractified as a principle something that for others served primarily as a basis for group solidarity, a party cause. Still, they draw upon, even if they were not drawn into, the ferment of movement activity. At the other end of the spectrum, there were, of course, many movement performers who did not allow themselves to be drawn into the distraction of writing, or into dangerous individualism; part of the significance of a Tzara, a Marinetti, a Breton is that he is less a writer than an event, indistinguishable from the movement enterprise he created. The implication indeed was that the new arts were not created but performed, enacted, demonstrated, thrown into the public eye, or the public face. This was always one dimension of the movement impulse, which of itself long pre-dated Modernism. But the notion of radical performance itself becomes in some modern aesthetics a theory of anti-art, an act of negation denying the formal significance of perpetuated, monumentalized expression; and this notion reaches its high point in Futurism, Dadaism, and Surrealism, continuing into much current theory about the movement as theatre. Thus, gatherings of coteries were replaced by happenings; the behaviour of the participants was itself what Marinetti called 'art as aggressive action'; the traditional genres were transformed into multi-media events, operating as immediate cultural newspapers, acts of consciousness-raising, or unsigned communal performances. Manifestos, cabarets, happenings, displays could thus become the new environments that modern art required, and acts of attack on the old conventions – one common feature of movement activity being its dissent from all or most extant propositions or presumptions about the aesthetic and social character of art and the artist.

But of course there were many types of movement, from general stylistic 'isms' to local coteries; and the movement dimension is itself not peculiar to Modernism. In the sense of schools or aesthetic theory-clusters, movements had long been significant in art, and especially in the visual arts. In the sense of *avant-garde* groupings of the futuristically inclined, movements certainly go back to Romantic-ism; and there is a clear statement of the *avant-garde* spirit in Shelley's *Defence of Poetry* (1821, published 1840), where poets are 'the hiero-phants of an unapprehended inspiration; the mirrors of the gigantic shadows which futurity casts upon the present'. In the sense of flam-boyant, aggressive, socially dislocated coteries of artistic specialists, gatherings of the lumpenproletariat of the creative world, they certainly reach back to the early days of the Bohemian tradition. Bohemia emerged in the Paris of the 1830s, a buoyant and impover-ished milieu, which Henri Murger records for us; here the traditional Grub Street crisis – an overplus of active creators coupled with a shortage of monied patrons – became transformed into a gay seed-bed of the unacceptable arts, the art of the *refusés*, virtuous because of the very neglect it suffered. Bohemia provides an exemplary sociology for much of the movement impulse, as Cesar Graña shows in his book *Bohemian Versus Bourgeois* (1964), the very title of which sums up part of the social division underlying the display, the moral unconventionality, the dirt, the poverty.[2] And, in justifying both his flamboyant poverty and his flamboyant yet neglected genius, the Bohemian gave the essential *avant-garde* explanation: his work was adjusted not to the present but to the future, not to contemporary consciousness but to consciousness that must learn to come, and his task was the discovery of a new language of forms which must be learned before understanding could occur. In consequence Bohemia got most of its own support from within itself; it was self-policing, self-judging, making its own reputations for later approval, creating its own institutions outside the orthodox culture. And much of this would pass on to Modernism.

But when, therefore, does this desire of the movements to *be* modern become Modernism? We have already seen how difficult that date is to fix, and of course it was contentious among the movements themselves. Part of the answer, though, does lie in the very momentum *of* those movements themselves; it lies in the acceleration of the sequence, the growing pace of stylistic generation, the intensification of lore that occurs when various forms of stylization turn into a style, which is, as Wylie Sypher puts it, 'based on the techniques it transcends'.[3] And it also lies in the multiplication of many *types* of movement, so that tendencies substantially philosophical in emphasis cross with others predominantly aesthetic in emphasis and with yet others predominantly behavioural in emphasis (such a compound exists in the relationships between Naturalism, Symbolism, and Decadence). It lies further in the intrusion of certain new theories of consciousness, of inwardness, of technical complexity, of abstraction and of hard form into the equation. But the cultural analyst, surveying the nineteenth century and seeking a place among the tendencies to start from, is well advised to contemplate Naturalism and the evolution out and beyond from it – that *Überwindung des Naturalismus* (conquest of naturalism) which was so frequently and eagerly announced as the 1880s yielded to the 1890s, and out of which a whole body of new programmes begins to develop.

2

The dissolution of Naturalism is perhaps best caught in an image. In the lamplight of Maeterlinck's *L'Intérieur* (1894), an old man broods sadly on a girl's suicide by drowning. 'Why?' he wonders. 'Nobody knows. What can anybody know? . . . You can't look into the soul as you can into a room.' Here, with that phrase, is both the nature of the new challenge and the defining limitations that the writers who sought to press beyond Naturalism into Impressionism, or Symbolism, or Psychologism must have felt: here is the continuity and the rupture. Interiors had always fascinated the Naturalists. By 'removing the fourth wall' (to use the standard idiom of their practice) they had opened up a range of domestic interiors, arenas of social and familial tension within which had been played out those terrible conflicts that so preoccupied the late nineteenth century: the conflict of individual aspiration and social obligation, the pull of personal inclination against the duties of kinship, the clash of tradition and self-fulfilment. Within these domestic interiors, the positivist, determinist and environmental proclivities of many late nineteenth-century writers found an appropriate setting. Here were distilled those extra-personal forces that pressed on the late nineteenth-century individual: heredity, environment, strict moral imperatives, the coercions of politics, press, religion. But the new preoccupations, of which Maeterlinck is the witness, are with a different kind of interior: with the inner life, the soul, *l'âme, die Seele, sjælen*. Paul Bourget – whose *Essais de psychologie contemporaine (Essays on Contemporary Psychology)* (1883–5) stimulated so many of the new ideas, much as did William James's in the English-speaking countries – urged that *'notre âme est le palais des légendes'* ('our soul is the palace of legends'). Already in the eighties Strindberg became obsessed with the phenomenon of 'soul murder' or 'psychic murder', from which he was led on to an exploration of what he called 'the soul's irradiation and dilatability'. Przybyszewski, so eloquent a spokesman of the Post-Naturalist group in Berlin, saw the poet's task as exposing *'die nackte Seele'* ('the naked soul'). As early as 1890, Knut Hamsun urged his contemporaries to attend to those 'fractional feelings' that characterize 'the unconscious and even today almost wholly uninterpreted life of the soul'.

The English 'soul' disturbingly disguises the range of reference of *l'âme* and *die Seele*. The latter reach into the life of the mind, the heart, even the nerves. It was a point not lost upon Henry James when, in 1892, he characterized *Hedda Gabler*: 'It is essentially that supposedly undramatic thing, the picture not of an action but of a condition. It is the portrait of a nature, the story of what Paul Bourget would call an *état d'âme*, and of a state of nerves as well as of soul, a state of temper, of health, of chagrin, of despair.'[4] But to this soul – mind, spirit, nerves, psyche, consciousness – there is no fourth wall to be opened to permit direct observation: nothing immediately audible, visible, accessible to the five standard senses. And on the other side, there was much that was beyond the reach of reason. There *were* signs that betrayed to the sensitive, intuitive witness those secret shifts of the endless flux and infinite change of the inner life, that reality which was not objectively given but was something subjectively perceived through consciousness, an active motion of mind that William James in his *Principles of Psychology* (1890) caught in a famous analogy: 'A "river" or a "stream" are the metaphors by which it is most naturally described. In talking of it hereafter, let us call it the stream of thought, of consciousness, or of subjective life.'[5] It was a reality caught only in some flow of consciousness, a character's, the artist's, a reality like the inside of a hot-house, as in Maeterlinck's *Serres Chaudes* (*Hot-houses*), sealed, steamy, hidden behind bottle-green panes of glass; or like the hidden depths supporting Rodenbach's water-lily, so innocently riding the surface of the water. To Hofmannsthal, writing in 1893, two things were overwhelmingly modern: on the one hand, psychic self-dissection; and, on the other, escape.

It is central to the spirit of the eighteen-nineties that such new intuitions were asserting themselves, and in the arts. The problem was often how to define and name them. Some felt that this made of Naturalism a spent force, a mechanical and basically unimaginative mode in the arts, dependent upon careful imitation rather than imaginative grasp, and stemming from a limited and mechanistic *Weltanschauung* rather than intuitive understanding. The natural consequence was then to declare an allegiance to Symbolism or Impressionism or Neo-Romanticism or Decadence. Others, by contrast, generously recognized the very real *technical* debt which the new style owed the old, and honoured the courage and honesty with which the Naturalists had exposed that which timidity had previously concealed, suppressed or ignored. 'Naturalism' was too honourable a designation to be lightly cast aside; what was new was, in their eyes, a mutation of Naturalism not a repudiation of it. 'Psychic Naturalism' was a term that found much favour. In a number of instances, the new was simply a matter for annexation – as when Friedrich Michael Fels, at the opening of the Viennese Freie Bühne, declared that 'Naturalism' was so comprehensive and admirable a term, nobody need hesitate to adopt it:[6]

Ultimately, everybody is a Naturalist. The man who tries with the most painstaking care to imitate the external world in all its details, strictly preserving all the disorder of coincidental or insignificant or inconsequential things, is a Naturalist. The man who immerses himself in the inner world and traces with anxious care every little nuance of the life of his soul is a Naturalist. Finally, every Romantic is a Naturalist ... Every good poet is a Naturalist, no matter what idealistic, romantic or symbolic gestures he may make.

3

But, if here we find the footings of Modernism, we might add that Fels's semantic eclecticism was very typical of the course of the Modernist developments that take place from the decline of Naturalism in Europe to the rise of Expressionism. Within this period – as in many another – innovation sometimes develops out of what has gone before; equally it sometimes repudiates it. There are unmotivated leaps, unforeseen mutations; even the laws of change sometimes appear to change. Terminology varies with the locality: what Berlin charts as Neo-Romanticism, Vienna calls Impressionism. In some circles Symbolism, Neo-Romanticism, Impressionism and Decadence pass for the same thing; in others, where the distinctions are perhaps finer, the notion that Symbolism achieves a compounding of subject and object, whereas Neo-Romanticism does not, makes for further sub-divisions. In some company, Decadence was obviously a term of opprobrium; in others a proud defiant banner. Here, the Symbolist movement is related to an Aesthetic movement; there, the latter enjoys no recognition. Names, in short, are not final guides to styles.

Essential to an understanding of Modernism's movements (and those movements consequent upon Naturalism which the following section goes on to consider in detail) is a recognition that they vary greatly in type and reach over a long range of historical experience. Some (like Decadence) are distillations of broad generational moods; others (like Imagism) relate to precise aesthetic programmes or theories. Some are belated names for already extant activities (as with German Expressionism); others find the name first and the programme afterwards. Some enjoy a general kinship, flourish in a variety of places and pass from nation to nation (like Symbolism), sometimes with the same name, sometimes different; others (like Vorticism) were once and for all small groups. In some instances, the single movement defines the work of a particular generation or country (like Russian Futurism or German Expressionism), whilst in others it manifests itself as a small constituent of a vastly larger creative enterprise. To look across them all, from movement to movement, from country to country, is to see not one interlocking system but a frenzy of forms and artistic energies variously expressed and variously justified, to see strange channels of influence and shifts of meaning, to recognize different conventions and symbols, as on maps drawn to different projections and scales.

However, some attempt to order and distinguish the different levels of magnitude could be helpful. First, then, come those terms which, in their order of magnitude and their scale of abstraction, claim affinity with earlier and larger historical shifts of sensibility. In the enduring record, the distinction between Romanticism and Classicism shows the greatest persistence. On this level the Neo-Romanticism of the nineties was (by a kind of inverted historicism) succeeded by the Neo-Classicism of the early years of the new century. Neo-Idealism was a term favoured by some of those conscious of the philosophical content of their authorship; Neo-Naturalism as a term had an enduring appeal for, among others, Strindberg; and Neo-Rococo had a brief vogue as an alternative to *Bohême*. But the contemporary efforts are often imprecise, and they shift from phase to phase within Modernism. Looking back on it all, other terms have been preferred. Classicism has had some persistence. But Wylie Sypher, for cogent reasons, has (we have seen) urged the claim of Cubism as the best word in this large-scale class. And this is the level at which the term Modernism itself most commonly does service. However, after these large historico-stylistic terms, there come next, on a reducing scale, those concepts that derived in the first instance from stylistic developments in painting and the visual arts, and normally have a precise technical association: most conspicuously Impressionism, Expressionism, and (in time) Surrealism, as well as Fauvism, Futurism, and – in its usual usage – Cubism. Art Deco, Art Nouveau, and Post-Impressionism are useful blanket terms.

Then, as one moves down the scale from styles and movements to policies and attitudes and thence to 'schools' and groups, the classifications grow both narrower and ever more particularized. *Jugendstil* (which is frequently if not wholly accurately taken as the German equivalent of Art Nouveau) occasionally serves as the above type of blanket term covering an entire phase of art and literature. But despite the similarity of names, 'Junges Österreich', 'Jüngstdeutschland', 'La Jeune Belgique' and 'Unga Sverige' are of a different order and had little in common amongst themselves save youth, zeal and indignation. (A half-hearted attempt by a member of the last group to establish a 'Young France' failed rather sadly, presumably because there were already so many.) As for the implications of *fin de siècle* and *die Jahrhundertwende*, they were incomparably further apart than the simple difference in chronology they seem to denote; similarly the links between the English writing of the nineties – with its greenery-yallery connotations – and the Swedish *nittiotalet* are tenuous. Apparently analogous names do not link up; they hide distinct and particular climates. It is when one reaches the level of what are self-evidently national categories and distinctly local units that one is on safer ground – *la belle époque, die Gründerzeit*, the Celtic Twilight, and The Georgians are fairly clearly located. And when we move to the level of the Rhymers' Club, the Cafe Griensteidl or Zum schwarzen Ferkel we know where we are: among distinctive coteries of people with a common debate or a cause to make. Yet of course the entire spectrum comes under the movement heading, from the largest of technical styles to the smallest of personal coteries.

This is why it is useful and necessary to try to consolidate all these phases and groupings and labels and actions into some comprehensive European design, but also why great caution is necessary. Conspicuous in the age of Modernism is an unprecedented acceleration in the intellectual traffic between nations, but sometimes terms themselves crossed boundaries faster than the actual philosophies or techniques they implied. One clear example of this is to be found in our starting point, with the 'decline of Naturalism' itself. For, even in those countries where Naturalism had become a dominant mode and therefore something provoking change or reaction, the change did not take place uniformly. Indeed, even *within* one country, or one linguistic community, one can see that it differently affected the different genres of novel, drama and lyric poetry. Germany showed a significant time lag compared with France, Scandinavia or (less obviously) Russia; America showed a greater time lag still. 'It is strange for me as an outside observer,' wrote the Danish critic Georg Brandes to two leaders of German Naturalism (Arno Holz and Johannes Schlaf) in 1890, 'to note that strict Naturalism is only now making its presence powerfully felt in Germany, just at the very moment when in France and Scandinavia it is on the point of being pushed out by new developments.' What is so striking is that the turbulence engendered by this uneasy and in some ways paradoxical transition was of international magnitude – and perhaps even of far greater impact than the dominance of Naturalism itself. For other forces were simultaneously dissolving: forms of Romanticism, forms of realism, forms of positivism, forms of culture. There was an avid search for the new arts, a great sense of the transition of forms. In this climate, international exchanges and unacknowledged borrowings flourished. Translations increased, startlingly in number and gratifyingly in quality. The simultaneous publication or performance in a number of different languages of an author's work – Ibsen, in the nineties, was the supreme example – showed an extraordinary upswing. In a wide range of European cultural capitals, the theatres made audiences familar with the latest dramatic authors. Publishers extended their foreign lists. Distinctly *European* reputations proliferated. 'Cultural emigration' began to exert a growing attraction for creative minds: periods of residence abroad, if not outright expatriation, became – as has already been noted – commonplace for writers and artists, with Paris as a notable magnet. All this had clear formal consequences. Cross-fertilization of ideas, not only among the separate nations of Europe (and America) but also among the various arts of literature, music, painting and sculpture, was on a scale as never before.

In sequence and in sum, the different movements build up into a shift away from the romantic nuances of Symbolism towards a harder, mechanized, more impersonal or classical form of the image; from an assertive aestheticism towards a more crisis-ridden view of the modern artistic situation; from an ambition of artistic wholeness to a fascination with decreation. Most offer similar forms of self-justification: a loss of faith in objective reality and in the 'word', established language; a fascination with the unconscious; a concern with the pressures of industrial environment and accelerating change; a desire to discover significant artistic structure in increasing chaos. The variations could nevertheless be radical and significant; often they led to wholly different politics (as, for instance, with Surrealism and Futurism), to different artistic procedures and to differing views of the importance of art and its possibilities of survival. Yet the similarities remain striking, expecially if one looks not to the justifications offered but to the art itself: to its growing interest in abstraction and perspectivism, in the break-up of traditional generic frames and realistic forms, in the personalization of language, in various neo-symbolistic or imagistic forms, and in its attention to certain distilling objects, like the machine or the modern city. Here it is that one senses something like a common artistic style. At the same time, to recognize the widely differing uses to which, say, spatial form, the doctrine of impersonality, the stream of consciousness mode of narration, *vers libre* or collage were put brings a warning that radically different issues could underlie very like-seeming modes. The movements are not a dialectical growth leading to one true synthesis, even though significant lines can be run through them to trace a path from, say, Expressionism to Dadaism and Surrealism. There is no one common understanding, and the moments of optimum creation come at random points in the sequence.

4

As is a tendency of 'isms', Modernism was an intensifying atmosphere of aesthetic, cultural and political differentiations with a certain common psychology, sociology and formalism. As in all sects, religious or political – and it was on such analogues that the movements formed and acted – 'ism' tended toward schism, denominationalism. So they appropriately rallied followers, mounted displays, enacted themselves in public. Hence of considerable importance to their history are the manifestos they presented and the magazines they promoted or published. A great many of the movements did in fact assert themselves through documents of this kind: fusions of form and content. The manifestos of Marinetti are, for example, superbly fascinating documents in themselves. In similar fashion, Wyndham Lewis made *Blast*, the magazine of Vorticism, with its puce cover, largely a manifesto itself. And for Tzara, Breton and others, with causes to announce like the Revolution of the Word, or the Surrealist Revolution, the manifesto *was* the art form. As for the little magazine, this was often an analogue or extension of the manifesto formula. Virtually a new phenomenon, it frequently represented a privatization of the publishing process, functioning as the logical obverse to the solemn, serious, debating Great Review. It was largely through such magazines that the evolving works of Modernism achieved their transmission, sought out their audiences, as *Ulysses* did through the American *Little Review*. And, gradually, it was the self-consciously small paper, in an era of large publishing ventures, that began to take over not only the localized work of particular movements but the larger tasks of cultural transmission. Such papers, with a limited but distinctive readership, specialized and usually advanced in taste, disposed (often) to bring the various arts together, became the primary expressions of new talent. By the end of the nineteenth century such journals were a crucial part of the literary scene; and, as we have seen in earlier essays, they are a very useful index of the general level and range of experimental activity in the particular national cultures.

And as the movements can be roughly arranged into types, so can the magazines. Some are especially notable for creating a comprehensive aesthetic environment in which new developments in writing and the visual arts compound to distil an attitude, a distinctive graphic and typographic complex: so, in Holland, *Van nu en straks* (1892); in England the *Yellow Book* (1894); in Germany *Pan* (1895); in Austria *Ver Sacrum* (1898) carried out this important stylistic function. Others were specifically *Tendenz* or movement magazines, like Tzara's *Dada* or Louis Aragon, Philippe Soupault and André Breton's *Littérature* (founded in 1919) which in turn sponsored the *Premier Vendredi de Littérature (First Friday of Literature)*, a manifesto-reading event at the Palais des Fêtes in Paris, and similar large extensions beyond the printed page. There were many such journals in all the Western countries, with particularly large numbers in France and the United States, pushed into being by the widespread activity in experimental writing. Often they were given to generating an air of outrage by any means from a small-type title (*transatlantic review*) to a violent title-word or phrase (*Die Aktion, Der Sturm, Secession, Broom*). Not all the magazines, however, were closely attached to one single movement; some were hosts to several, or were simply committed generally to experimental literature. Both the *Egoist* in London and *Poetry* in Chicago carried Imagism, largely because Pound infiltrated both, but they also carried a wide range of Modernist modes; so did many of the expatriate magazines – like *Secession* and *Broom* – in Paris in the 1920s. With greater or lesser degrees of commitment, they functioned as centres of aesthetic debate and as clearing houses of ideas. Indeed as the little magazines became the primary centres for establishing new taste, they also found a role in establishing new writers. In fact, as Frederick Hoffman, Charles Allen and Carolyn Ulrich note in their survey of English and American small-press ventures, *The Little Magazine* (1947), these journals first published some 80 per cent 'of our most important post-1912 critics, novelists, poets, and storytellers'.[7] And, increasingly as time went by, there came a more solemn form of Modernist publishing: the Modernist review, like the *Criterion*, the *Dial, Die Neue Rundschau* or *La Nouvelle Revue Française*, where, with various degrees of hospitality, the movements and experiments acquired a format of respectability and inevitably stimulated fresh counter-assertion from a newer wave of experimenters. It is important to note that this development is more than a symptom of human compromise: it is an important indicator of the way in which the sensibility of Modernism acquired more than coterie or shock acceptance, acquired critical and commercial recognition and therefore more extended stylistic resonance.

Here, perhaps, is an index of the success of the movements – and also of their failure. For it was characteristic that what they made drew on novelties elsewhere, and equally that what they helped to create passed beyond them, into more general hands. Experimentalism generally began, it may be said, in a climate of apparent neglect; and made its way by spectacle, establishing its practices and its norms, asserting its distinctive significance for the times. By the twenties many of the battles for acceptance were won; apart from Surrealism, a good deal of the original movement excitement had passed, though many new coteries were appearing. Now the great, achieved works of the entire endeavour began to stand out in their significance; and newer ones began to appear, their creation made possible by the already large stockpile of *avant-garde* debate and achievement. Here you could see the Modernist impulse transcending, often, the tendencies which had pushed and forced forward new modes, new presumptions. And works like *Ulysses, The Waste Land* or the *Duino Elegies* are acts of modernized imagination for which no movement explanation can ever properly fit. We need to look at the clashes and fusions of the many movements to help understand how such works came into being, while recognizing, in the end, that Modernism was more than its movements, magazines, and manifestos, and close to being, finally, a comprehensive modern style.

Notes

1 Renato Poggioli, *The Theory of the Avant Garde*, translated by Gerald Fitzgerald (Cambridge, Mass. 1968).

2 Cesar Graña, *Bohemian Versus Bourgeois: French Society and the French Man of Letters in the Nineteenth Century* (New York and London 1964). See also Helmut Kreuzer, *Die Boheme* (Stuttgart 1968).

3 Wylie Sypher, *Rococo to Cubism in Art and Literature* (New York 1960). Sypher's proposition in this book is that a period's style comes to maturity as a consequence of the accumulation of techniques which fuse into a coherent or compatible method of representation 'deeply in harmony with the thought and science of that age'. He hence distinguishes between 'style' and 'stylization': 'To distinguish: a technique does not become a style until it can be used to represent adequately a contemporary view of the world, and like the areas of the early renaissance, the nineteenth-century arts are an area of competing techniques of representation. It is only in cubism – a style summarizing and conciliating the many techniques devised by impressionism, post-impressionism, and Art Nouveau – that an authentically modern style is achieved' (p. xxii).

4 Henry James, 'On the Occasion of *Hedda Gabler*', *New Review*, June 1891.

5 William James, *Principles of Psychology* (New York 1890), vol. I, p. 239.

6 Friedrich Michael Fels, 'Die Moderne', *Moderne Rundschau*, no. iv, 1891, pp. 79ff.

7 F. J. Hoffman, C. Allen and C. F. Ulrich, *The Little Magazine: A History and a Bibliography* (Princeton 1947), p. 1.

SYMBOLISM, DECADENCE AND IMPRESSIONISM

CLIVE SCOTT

I

THE end of the nineteenth century was prolific in awarding names to its literary movements, thus lending disproportionate emphasis to the differences among them. Today one sees more clearly the manifold affinities, and takes the differences as mainly those of emphasis. At the same time, the tendency to overlap, to trespass from one art to another, to allow the senses to usurp each others' functions was accompanied by an attempt on the part of the arts to develop their own peculiar and distinctive assets. For some, poetry was becoming purer; painting was approaching two-dimensional composition of line and colour. Among the names, three stand out: Symbolism, Impressionism and Decadence. Their overall importance for our century is unquestioned; what they do leave is a continuing controversy about priorities. Those who value in Modernism its pursuit of raw experience, its primitivism even, and who see Impressionism as the common denominator of the movements current round the turn of the century, may side with Hauser who, in *The Social History of Art*, calls Impressionism the 'last universally valid "European" style'. Those others who esteem Modernist literature as a liberation of the text, of the word, will probably point to Symbolism as the source of the self-subsistent work that lives among the multiple privacies of its language, and side rather with Edmund Wilson who in *Axel's Castle* saw the foundations of modern literature in 'the development of Symbolism and its fusion or conflict with Naturalism'.

2

Symbolism contains within itself a shift from a romantic to a modernly ironic aesthetic. The task of understanding it is primarily

that of understanding Stéphane Mallarmé (1842–98). But it is Paul
Valéry (1871–1945), Mallarmé's 'direct' successor, who indicates
most explicitly the shift in reading habit that Symbolism presupposes
and on which much of its aesthetic is built:[1]

> *Longtemps, longtemps,* la voix humaine *fut base et condition de la* lit-
> térature . . .
> *Un jour vint où l'on sut lire des yeux sans épeler, sans entendre, et la lit-
> térature en fut tout altérée.*
> *Évolution de l'articulé à l'effleuré, – du rythmé et enchaîné à l'instantané, – de
> ce que supporte et exige un auditoire à ce que supporte et emporte un œil
> rapide, avide, libre sur une page.**

The Symbolist poem is the poem animated, not so much by the voice
breathing life into it, as by the mobile eye wandering restlessly
forward and back over the page, ensnared in an ever-recurrent and
variously momentous instant. The absence of what Mallarmé, in
Crise de vers (1886–92–96), calls *la direction personnelle enthousiaste de la
phrase* (the enthusiastic personal direction of the phrase), permits an
art that owes more to forms than to the poet. Form multiplies meanings even as it articulates them; the poem becomes a multitude of
unified, total utterances. Mallarmé's eccentric but fastidious syntax
decentralizes the sentence, challenging rather than anticipating a
resolution. And often, this most scrupulous *grimoire* is momentarily
exploded by sudden parenthetic collections of nouns, grammatically
unconstrained, impatient, wonderfully erratic:[2]

> *Tison de gloire, sang par écume, or, tempête!*
>
> *Nuit, désespoir et pierrerie*†

Jean Moréas, in his 'Manifeste du symbolisme', enumerates some of the stylistic devices peculiar to the synthetic language of Symbolism:[3]

. . . d'impollués vocables, la période qui s'arcboute alternant avec la période aux défaillances ondulées, les pléonasmes significatifs, les mystérieuses ellipses, l'anacoluthe en suspens, tout trop hardi et multiforme; . . . ★

What we usually call lyric poetry is necessarily elliptical, since much of its business is to trace emotional and intellectual short-circuits. The lyric line can never properly contain itself; it is ever reaching out for that which it is too impatient to express, which makes the pause at the line's end crucial to its self-fulfilment. Pauses in Romantic poetry are by and large filled with the implications of the voice; here the rhetorical punctuation of the line is translated into sounded silence, the reverberations of exclamation, the expiration of despair, the baffled silence of question. The pauses – more accurately, the spaces – at the end of Mallarméan lines are filled with mental exercise; here the meanings with which the line is pregnant collect, collide, coalesce. When Mallarmé uses traditional rhetorical punctuation, he largely empties it of its rhetorical force. Exclamation marks, for example, are sometimes a way of casting an aura about a word (*Anastase!*, *Lys!*), sometimes the visual sign of a word's meaning (*Hyperbole!*, *Vertige!*), sometimes a notification to the eye of the criticalness of an idea (*Naïf baiser des plus funèbres!* (Naïve and most dismal kiss!)).

Mallarmé was never afraid of overestimating the amount of poetic responsibility that can be borne by blank space:[4]

L'armature intellectuelle du poème se dissimule et tient – a lieu – dans l'espace qui isole les strophes et parmi le blanc du papier: significatif silence qu'il n'est pas moins beau de composer que les vers.†

The blank space has the utter virtuality of thought: '*Penser étant écrire sans accessoires, ni chuchotement mais tacite encore l'immortelle parole*' ('To

---

★. . . unpolluted words, the period which creates a single supporting arch alternating with the period of undulant cadences, significant pleonasms, mysterious ellipses, suspended anacoluthon, a pervasive sense of extreme audacity and multiformity; . . .

†The intellectual substructure of the poem conceals itself, is present – is active – in the blank space which separates the stanzas and in the white of the paper: a pregnant silence, no less wonderful to compose than the lines themselves.

think being to write without accessories or whispering, but with the immortal word still implicit') he notes in *Crise de vers*. But the 'supreme' language which the Symbolists so avidly sought, and which might convey such thought, keeping intact the word's tacitness, is lacking. Mallarmé's task therefore is to use an imperfect language in such a way as to *communicate* the blank space upon which language has trespassed. Hence an aesthetic of suggestion. Because blank space is a condition of its existence, poetry most nearly approaches the 'supreme' language. For all his respect for the individual word, Mallarmé's basic working-unit is the line, because its prosodic integrity is endorsed by the white paper that envelops it and serves as its conceptual counterpart. The line '*rémunère le défaut des langues*' (compensates for the shortcomings of language) (*Crise de vers*). Writing is for Mallarmé a limiting process which form manages to outwit; language itself seeks to define and analyse, whilst form and the space it begets liquefy and reintegrate. Writing poetry becomes a means of activating what is missing.

The poem is compounded of word and erasure; the symbol is compounded of object and idea, presence and absence. Mallarmé's poems are negating processes, in which what is affirmed is promptly denied and made semantically evanescent. From all denials is derived the absence that is undeniable, the symbol, which cannot be superseded and which *is ' l'objet tu'* :[5]

Évoquer, dans une ombre exprès, l'objet tu, par des mots allusifs, jamais directs, se réduisant à du silence égal, comporte tentative proche de créer . . . *

So the '*rose dans les ténèbres*' (rose in the shadows) can only emerge magnificently at the end of 'Surgi de la croupe et du bond' ('Risen from the crupper and leap'), because the vase is empty; conversely, the poet can only *evoke* the amazon's absent breast by *invoking* his mistress's(?) present breast in 'Mes bouquins refermés' ('My books closed'). What then differentiates symbol from metaphor is that while metaphor has only a local existence within the poem, the symbol informs the whole poem and can subsume it, rather as a title does.

---

*To conjure up, in a specially created penumbra, the negated object, with the help of allusive and always indirect words, which constantly efface themselves in a complementary silence, involves an undertaking which comes close to the act of creation . . .

Indeed, the emergence of the symbol usually coincides with the poem's discovery of its subject. Thus, in poems like 'Tout Orgueil fume-t-il du soir' ('Does every evening's pride smoke'), 'Surgi de la croupe et du bond', 'Le vierge, le vivace et le bel aujourd'hui' ('The virginal, living and beautiful day'), 'Au seul souci de voyager' ('To the sole concern of journeying'), the symbol – object or person – is both the tacit occasion of the poem, an ordinary reality, and the goal and culmination of the poem, a symbol, with dimensions enough to repossess all the ideas which, as the occasion of the poem, it engendered. The symbol is the precipitate of all the '*tiers aspects*' ('third aspects')[6] that have grown out of the metaphors of the poem.

The transformation of the simple object into the symbolic object often manifests itself as the transformation of a common noun into a proper noun, as we see in Mallarmé's 'Toast funèbre' to Gautier:

> *Le Maître, par un œil profond, a, sur ses pas,*
> *Apaisé de l'éden l'inquiète merveille*
> *Dont le frisson final, dans sa voix seule, éveille*
> *Pour la Rose et le Lys le mystère d'un nom.* *

In 'Le vierge, le vivace et le bel aujourd'hui', *un cygne* indeed becomes *le Cygne*, the indication being, not that the swan has become a personification of the poet but that a particular swan has somehow become its own paradigm. *Cygne* joins a higher order of words whose references lie not outside and accessible to everyone, but within, in the world to which they as words are the only key. In the same way, the 'supernatural' quality of the line of verse is due in large measure to the *pieuse majuscule* (pious capital letter) (*La Musique et les lettres*) with which it is endowed and whereby it is shown to transcend the commonness of the words that constitute it.

Some of the sources of this aesthetic may lie in Baudelaire's *surnaturalisme*, a state of perception which intensifies the existence of things, makes them *hyperbolically* themselves. This state is accompanied by an expansion of time and space which allows things to break their bounds, to become vibrant, resonant, and enlarges the poet's ability to spiritually encompass the world; and connected with this is the total

---

*The master, by means of his profound eye, has quieted the restless wonder of Eden about his steps, whose final shudder in his voice alone awakens the mystery of a name for the Rose and the Lily.

sentience made possible by *correspondances*. It is in this state that the poet has a direct sense of the depth of life:[7]

> *Dans certains états de l'âme presque surnaturels, la profondeur de la vie se révèle toute entière dans le spectacle, si ordinaire qu'il soit, qu'on a sous les yeux. Il en devient le symbole.**

Preciosity, that over-meticulous inventiveness, was an inevitable concomitant of Symbolism. But in its hands, it was no idle intellectual caprice. Valéry is in no doubt about its value – indeed its centrality – in the Symbolist aesthetic: '*Vous nous dites* précieux*? Mais le contraire du précieux, c'est le vil!*' ('You charge us with *preciosity*? But the opposite of the precious is the vile') (*Existence du symbolisme*). Preciosity might well be called verbal dandyism, if dandyism is '*avant tout le besoin ardent de se faire une originalité, contenue dans les limites extérieures des convenances*' ('above all the burning need to create an originality for oneself, but kept within the external limits of social propriety') (Baudelaire, 'Le Dandy'). The precious image is one that is both outrageous and tactful, that shows that the imagination flies highest not when it liberates itself from convention but when it discovers that convention is liberating. Rare rhyme, of which the Symbolists were very fond, is perhaps the most convincing demonstration of this truth, for in rare rhyme, convention condones a combination of words that flaunts conventionality. The rhyme that most tortures meaning, the rarest, can also be the most perfect of rhymes, the richest. Poetry-making approaches Pound's notion of 'Logopoeia', 'the dance of the intellect among words' (*How to Read*); and the poem becomes a transformation of the arbitrary into the necessary, something highly prized by Valéry.

Pound applies the term 'Logopoeia' to the work of Jules Laforgue (1860–87). It is precisely when it appears in structures – like Laforgue's free verse – which expressly avoid the gravity that regular forms inevitably confer on matter, that preciosity recovers some of its capriciousness. But in these reaches of Symbolism, the functions of the precious image and rare rhyme are markedly different from those just discussed. If we are to believe Duhamel and Vildrac (*Notes sur la*

---

*In certain, almost supernatural, spiritual states, the profundity of life is revealed in all its fullness in the thing, however banal, which one is looking at. It becomes the symbol of that profundity.

technique poétique, 1910) to whom Pound refers us, the function of rhyme in free verse is to '*fignoler des pastiches*' ('give a real finish to pastiches') and '*faire d'amusantes petites blagues*' ('crack amusing little jokes'). Poets like Laforgue (and, later, Eliot) stress the gratuitousness of rare rhyme without covering it, as do Mallarmé and Valéry, with the mask of poetic inevitability. This they are able to do by exploiting the fragmentariness and discontinuity of free verse. Thus the a-logicality of their rare rhymes moves not towards mental sophistication but towards what those other storehouses of rare rhyme, the limerick and nursery rhyme, capitalize upon: rationality without reason, need without motive.

What then did the Symbolist revolution achieve? Most fundamentally, it awakened an acute consciousness of language. Language was no longer treated as a natural outcrop of the person but as a material with its own laws and its own peculiar forms of life. The plausibility of old-guard Symbolist[8] poetry owes much to our awareness that the reflective gap between poet and language is filled with scruple. It is different when the climate changes and the gap is filled with ironical consciousness, which is tempted to make a cliché of a diction and turn the high-sounding into the brassy. The ironist's consciousness of language is an invitation not to renew our faith in language but to distrust it, to admit that language may be all surface, all verbalism. In the hands of the ironist, language easily becomes something hollowed out, to wrap round a mask or a persona or a pretence. Laforgue, perhaps the first of the 'Modernist' poets and a seminal influence on Eliot, uses generously polysyllabic adverbs and adjectives with the same relish as Mallarmé:[9]

> *Les Jeunes Filles inviolables et frêles*
> *Descendent vers la petite chapelle*
> *Dont les chimériques cloches*
> *Du joli, joli dimanche*
> *Hygiéniquement et élégamment les appellent.**

But in doing so, he underlines the disproportion between their weight and the flippant intention behind them, thus effectively transforming

---

*The inviolable and delicate Young Girls go down towards the small chapel whose unreal bells, the bells of prim, prim Sunday, summon them hygienically and elegantly.

pomp into pomposity. The words '*Hygiéniquement*' and '*élégamment*' are full of significance only because they are full of themselves; the empty ritual of language apes the empty ritual of Sunday. The polysyllabic word, by the play of its modulating vowels, can suggest several meanings at once. For Mallarmé, this is the source of its richness; for Laforgue, it is a sign of its duplicity and guile. It has too much to say to be able to tell the truth.

3

The origins of Laforgue's ironic adverb are perhaps to be found in the Verlaine (1844–96) of *Fêtes galantes* (*Amatory Entertainments*) (1869), in lines like:[10]

> *Et les amants lutinent les amantes,*
>
> *De qui la main imperceptible sait*
> *Parfois donner un soufflet, qu'on échange*
> *Contre un baiser sur l'extrême phalange*
> *Du petit doigt ; et comme la chose est*
>
> *Immensément excessive et farouche,*
> *On est puni par un regard très sec,**
> *. . .*

where the adverb points up the discrepancy between the restraint and sophistication of the action and the extravagance of the reaction, introduced by the careless banality '*et comme la chose est*'; the adverb acts as a brake while indignation is inflated. With its sphinx-likeness, its mixture of grace and impudence, that Barbey d'Aurevilly finds characteristic of dandyism, the passage displays that 'over-subtilizing refinement upon refinement' which Arthur Symons (1865–1945) picks out as one of the marks of Decadence. It depicts the peculiarly modern brand of love that Proust finds in Watteau, in which conversation, *gourmandise*, the melancholy of disguise and the walk play a

---

*And the lovers tease their ladies with little intimacies which the ladies occasionally repay with a slap, imperceptibly administered. And in their turn, the lovers repay the slap with a kiss on the smallest knuckle of the smallest finger. And as the whole thing is unspeakably excessive and done with a shy sullenness, they are punished with a very sharp look.

greater part than pleasure itself, *une sorte d'impuissance ornée* (a sort of ornate impotence).

For the English poets in whose eyes Mallarmé had overreached himself, Verlaine was the French master, but particularly the pallid, more poignant, less piquant Verlaine. George Moore spoke for many when he declared: 'Hence all pallidities of thought and desire were eagerly welcomed: Verlaine became my poet.'[11] Symons, too, frequently tries his hand at the suggestive adverb:[12]

> And now the stealthy dancer comes
> Undulantly with cat-like steps that cling;
> ...

In an effort to capture the pleasurable insidiousness and hypnotic effect of the dancer – a prime decadent effect – the long word lovingly traces her every movement. But, as so often in Symons's work, the verbal inaccuracy obtrudes ('cat-like steps that cling'). Indeed the attempts of English decadents to subtilize sensitivity are frequently marred by Swinburnian ponderousness. We find polysyllabic non-entities in the work of Ernest Dowson (1867–1900), like 'oblivious lands', 'ulterior land', 'ultimate night', which do little more than give phonetic weight and stateliness to shame-faced nouns. We find too, in Symons, accumulations of adjectives – 'Dear soft white little morbid hands' ('Hands') – which suck the sense almost to skin and bone. And in place of the conscious imbalance that sets the nerves on edge, creates verbal collisions and rhythmic disorientation, we often find the mindless, soporific equilibrium of Swinburnian oscillation:[13]

> Beyond the need of weeping
> Beyond the reach of hands

> Some rich as sin and some as virtue pale

Baudelaire is perhaps the first to portray the modern and decadent artist as someone with an overdeveloped nervous system; but for him the nerves are motors of creative energy, of gigantism, stridency, multiplication, as well as hyper-sensitive registers of sensation. For him, dandyism is not so much eye-catching arrogance as a necessary ethic of control and exercise of the will – and not just the will to surprise but the will to do a day's work – and Satanism is not so much perversity as an exultant assertion of personal irreducibility. And if Baudelaire undergoes his share of remorse, it is a remorse that can regenerate itself in its aesthetic equivalent, nostalgia. There is plenty of play between Baudelaire's moral propensities as a man and his moral needs as an artist.

But Verlaine and his English contemporaries adopt an essentially passive stance in which nervous awareness is heightened by physiological atrophy; vicarious experience, via memory, disguise, desire, becomes the only attractive form of experience, and all actual experience has the habit of seeming vicarious. It is this that accounts in Verlaine for the spiritual crisis that lies behind so many of his poems as he attempts to relate sensation to a sentient identity.

The curious anguish which results from the decadent's frenetic pursuit of experience relates, in English poetry, less to the whole being than to the merely moral being:[14]

> When I kissed her for your sake
> My lips were sobbing your name

'For your sake', 'for her sake' are phrases that recur in the poetry of Dowson and Symons. There is an obsession with considerateness and with being understood (e.g. Symons: 'I take her hands into my hands/ Silently, and she understands'; Dowson: 'Ah, she who understands'). The concern for responsibility and consent permits an indulgence in forbidden pleasure without loss of honour. In Symons' 'Stella Maris' we find an incongruous combination like 'frank delight'; the delight of the thorough-going decadent has no need to apologize for itself with a word so rich in self-righteousness. Even Dowson's insistence on silence, communication by sensory signals, is explicable not in terms of the bodyless music of passion, but by a fear of double-dealing. If no promises are made, none can be broken:[15]

> Silence were fitter:
> Lest we should still be wishing things unsaid. ('You would have understood us had you waited.')

Ultimately the nineties poet is rather more concerned with the fruit of experience than with what Pater argued for: the experience itself. Hence, even the more overtly erotic poems are tendentious. Symons's 'Bianca' cycle (*London Nights*, 1895) can be usefully compared in this respect with Verlaine's 'Filles' cycle (*Parallèlement*, 1889). Symons has

not the verbal control to deal with physical contact unembarrassingly;
his sublime moments involve contortion and over-intensity:

> And on my lips your lips now pressed
> Cling moist and close; your lips begin
> Devouringly to gather in
> Your kisses that my lips possessed.

All pleads in the end for the essential amorality of pleasure. This is
sensual wallowing beyond the glancing, flirtatious contact of the
Verlainian decadent, where even in his most erotic enterprises is
interposed between the poet and the girl a fine literary foam. Verlaine
is a master of ceremonies, delighted with his own sensuality, but demonstrating that sexual pleasure has some difficulty in holding its own
against literary pleasure.

One of the poets most representative of the Decadence is perhaps
Albert Samain, in whose collection *Au Jardin de l'Infante* (*In the
Garden of the Infanta*) (1893) are developed those paradoxes and
ambiguities so typical of the trend. Here is to be found that conjunction of feverishness and fadingness, that uncertainty whether sensory
perceptions are thresholds or vestiges of experience, those conflicting
elements of Baudelairian dandyism, the pride and the apathy of
excess:[16]

> *Des soirs trop lourds de pourpre où sa* fierté soupire.*

The pressures of ornate sensuality and the balm of cool effacing
nostalgia are pointed up in clusters of imagery – on the one hand,
night, perfume, warmth, rich colours and materials, and on the other,
evening, water, flowers, music, light colours. Frequently these inter-
fere with each other in complex relationships (e.g. '*ô Nuit volup-
tueuse et pâle*'; '*Les fleurs dorment dans le velours*' ('O pale and voluptuous
night'; 'The flowers sleep in velvet'). Like Dowson, but without an
eye to broken vows, Samain finds essential communication in '*des
frôlis d'âme*' ('glancing contact of souls'), in the intimacy of silence
('*Je ne dis rien, et tu m'écoutes*') ('I say no words and you listen to me').
Like Dowson, Samain focuses amorous energy in the lips, the point
where souls are imbibed and exhaled:[17]

*Evenings too heavy with purple when her pride sighs.

> *L'Amour sanctifié . . .*
> *Buvait à l'urne exquise et profonde des lèvres . . .* *

This wishful attribution of a third dimension to the exquisite-superficial highlights a problem which all decadents must face: how to charge an epidermic experience with profundity. There is no reason to doubt its profundity, as Valéry points out:[18]

> *Je tiens qu'il existe une sorte de mystique des sensations, c'est-à-dire une 'Vie Extérieure' d'intensité et de profondeur au moins égales à celles que nous prêtons aux ténèbres intimes et aux secrètes illuminations des ascètes . . .* †

But how is the depth to be expressed? Of course literary techniques are at hand. Perhaps the most common is repetition, whereby a word, a sensation, becomes an incantation, investing itself and its context with an uncanny abstractedness. Varying its grammatical character and its position in the line underlines its inescapable versatility. So the sensation, initially random, becomes compelling: Symons's Renée is

> Ever desiring, ever desired in vain.
> Mother of vain desire.

But a more fundamental solution is the transference of substance to the accidents of life. Make-up, costumes and the like still perform their illusionist task, acting as decoys for the sentimentally vulnerable Pierrots, plastering over a premature spiritual maturity to put character in accord with age, as in Verlaine's 'Nevermore' ('*Allons, mon pauvre coeur . . .*') ('Come, my poor heart . . .)'. But even here the gap between appearance and reality is deceptive. For Baudelaire, fashion is not a mask concealing triviality but a symptom of the '*goût de l'idéal*' ('aspiration to the ideal'), and the red and black of make-up represent '*une vie surnaturelle et excessive*' ('a supernatural and hyperbolic existence').[19] Man's nature is to be found not only in his shortcomings, but also in those aspirations which are embodied in the image of himself he strives to project. Man strives always to be more than natural; thus his nobility is in proportion to the artificialities

---

*Hallowed Love . . . drank at the deep and exquisite urn of lips.
 † I maintain that there exists a kind of mysticism of sensations, that is to say an 'External Life' of an intensity and depth at least equal to those we ascribe to the intimate shadows and secret revelations of the ascetics.

with which he surrounds himself. Make-up, the music-hall milieu with its garish lights, costumes, and other forms of ostentation are at once the *art* of being oneself and the way that, for others, knowledge of a self becomes a series of sensory delights. In this essentially baroque world of fluid roles, identity depends on the particular sensory stimulus one transmits at a given time: a Proustian experience, so that one's potential for growth and diversification is unlimited. One lives in one's mirror and the eyes of others. And looking forward, we find in Impressionism an art in which appearance *is* vision, revelation.

It is hardly surprising then that the city-experience initiated by Baudelaire – in which the city does not dehumanize but rather searches out in man the lowest common denominators of his humanity – should have been replaced, for the decadents, by a city that was all spectacle, a city of patterns of gaslight (e.g. Lord Alfred Douglas, 'Impression de Nuit'), a land of sexual promise, where light and night achieve magic transformations. Richard Le Gallienne, decadent despite himself, put it:[20]

> Within the town the streets grow strange and haunted,
> And, dark against the western lakes of green
> The buildings change to temples . . .

It was from non-decadent nineties poets like Henley and Davidson that the city-poetry of the following generation got its impetus.

4

The vision of the Symbolist and the Decadent has accustomed us to the sensorily acute begetting the semantically or modally indefinite. It is typical of Verlaine, for instance, to *apprehend* things sharply but to *see* them only just, to catch distinct voices and cries which coalesce in the monotony of lament and under the sedation of memory. This must suggest a comparison with Impressionism, with a way of building up a unified impression of light (or meaning or mood) by first breaking the subject down into specific energy-filled fragments. What drew Monet to the river at Argenteuil and the sea at Antibes was the fact that water acted as a prism and broke light up into its primary colours. The brush-stroke when seen from close-up looks bright and unambiguous, but from a distance and in the overall picture, it is nothing more than a half-tint.

Verlaine's characteristic perspective on sensation is a withdrawing one; sensory perception abstracts itself in feeling, interrogation, translates itself into the lives of others. Ultimately his sense of fleetingness increases; he tries to hold on by turning inwards or turning away. But in Rilke's 'Das Karussell' ('The Merry-go-round') (*Neue Gedichte (New Poems)* 1907–8), on the other hand, a contrary movement is evident; the circular movement does not threaten dispersal as much as achieve precipitation:

> *Ein Rot, ein Grün, ein Grau vorbeigesendet,*
> *ein kleines kaum begonnenes Profil – .* *

Fleetingness approached is shown to comprise a collection of momentary stillnesses, just as in Degas' work, Verhaeren finds those split-second poses and gestures which are the choreography of transience:

> *Poses qui durent un instant, gestes ébauchés ou à faux, . . . désarticulations savantes, équilibres instables, allures étranges, voilà ce qu'il poursuit et traduit.*†

Like the Symbolist meaning, the Impressionist subject is often situated somewhere in between, in the unsung and often ungainly transition between states of confident repose.

Impressionism, like Symbolism, disengages quality from object; in literature this often leads to the substantivalization of verbs and adjectives, while in painting colour tends to exceed the object; the object becomes a function or temporary rationalization of its colour. In extreme cases, we find ourselves half-way along the road to abstract art: Symons says of Monticelli, for instance: 'He tries to purify vision to the point of getting disembodied colours.' Both in literature and painting, we find things not so much identifying themselves, as expressing themselves, by their colours; and this coincides with a turn towards those contemporary subjects which are pretexts for fashionable display like tennis-parties, horse-racing, seaside resorts, picnics.

---

* A red, a green, a grey sent flashing by, a slight, half-sketched profile.

† Poses which last only a moment, incipient or ungainly gestures, . . . subtle disarticulations, unstable equilibria, unfamiliar attitudes, that's what he is looking for and rendering.

One thinks of such scenes in Naturalistic novels like Zola's *Nana* (1880) or George Moore's *A Modern Lover* (1883) or of Mallarmé's journalistic enterprise *La Dernière Mode* (*The Latest Fashion*) (1874). The red of a dress is contingent, no necessary concomitant; its arbitrariness gives it glamour, it becomes a tone in a temperament. The dress is a machine for colour, liberating fantasy and allowing the wearer to leap the barriers of class and condition. Colour in this unstable state lends itself to all areas of experience, erotic, moral, aesthetic. The green of a leaf, on the other hand, is an integral part of an inescapable chemistry, an ingredient, which, with others, *adds up* to spring. Green foliage is a decor of reassurance, a pledge of preordainedness, against which we may view chance with impunity. But the Impressionists sought to give these 'natural' colours the same volatility, the same nonchalant exuberance, as the artificial ones: flowers vie with dresses, networks of metaphorical correspondence are established by colour between, say, a flag, a flower, a glove, a glint in the water. And similar processes are to be found in literature; in Rilke's 'Blaue Hortensie' ('Blue Hydrangea') (*Neue Gedichte*), the ups-and-downs of the hydrangea's secret life disclose themselves in the range of its unpredictable blues; the uncertain *'ein Blau'* ('a blue') after a temporary dilution and dissolution into yellow, violet and grey, becomes the source-colour, the unmistakable, *'das Blau'* ('the blue'); the green (foliage) *behind* the many blues (of the umbels) becomes, triumphantly, the single blue *in front of* a generalized green background. It is otherwise in poems like Wilde's 'Symphony in Yellow', where colour is not used to register an object's internal energy nor graded to dramatize those intimate tensions within a colour which that colour alone can reconcile – what Proust calls *'l'unité multicolore de la couleur'* ('the multi-coloured unity of colour'). Instead, yellow is merely a structuring *leitmotiv* to hang bric-à-brac on and is given point by a closing modulation into crystalline green (jade). Wilde's impressionist poems are altogether too homogeneous, iambic tetrameter quatrains, rhyming abba, where images are juxtaposed in pairs of lines and given bare momentum by a verb at the beginning of the second line, introducing the timely rhythmic variation of an inverted first foot:[21]

> An omnibus across the bridge
> Crawls like a yellow butterfly

But Wilde himself seems to have no illusions about the purely *decorative* function of such poems (see his 'Fantaisies décoratives'). A German poet close to Wilde's kind of Impressionism is Max Dauthendey (1867–1918) (see particularly his collection *Ultra Violett*, 1893); but Dauthendey, like Van Gogh in painting, already shows how inevitably a part of Impressionism Expressionism is; Dauthendey half projects a consciousness into the environment, making phenomena into the images and instruments of that consciousness, rather than arranging incoming data.

But all such parallels between colour-use in painting and in poetry must be qualified by an awareness of certain linguistic factors which make direct transpositions from the visual impossible. Most obviously, there is acoustic interference; in Symons's line[22]

> The pink and black of silk and lace

the hard abruptness of the short vowels and 'k's' in 'pink', 'black', and 'silk' convey the bright but brittle surface, the kaleidoscopic speed of the changing perception, while 'lace', to which 'black' seems to belong, conveys something quite different, with its long vowel, soft lateral consonant and fading final sibilant – a gentleness, a vulnerability which in fact becomes the poem's concern. There is some transition between these two areas of association in the common 'l', but a fundamental difference is manifest between a material and its colour. We need to take into account also the way that the position of a colour-adjective affects its force; in the phrase 'scarlet satin slippers', it may be felt that 'scarlet' is the quality, 'satin slippers' the commodity, while in 'waving black hair', the 'wavingness' is the significant fact while the 'blackness' is merely a generical attribute It might equally be argued, however, that as one moves through adjectives towards the noun, one moves towards more essential, more indispensable qualities. Similar problems occur in other languages, complicated in French by the pre- or post-positioning of adjectives, in German by compounds. And we must recognize too that the literary Impressionist who is anxious to restore a primordial power to colour must combat both the fact that literature has accustomed us to accept colours as the culmination of a great deal of cultural experience and therefore as elementary symbolic signs – 'blood-red', 'black as pitch', 'lily-white' – and also the view that colour can only function as colour in literature if it is hyperbolized, given help from other areas – 'emerald', 'ruby-red', 'raven-haired'.

Literary Impressionism is, not surprisingly, a matter of linguistic techniques, the attempt to make language the act of perception rather than analysis of the act, to make language experiential activity rather than a description of activity. There are several solutions, the commonest being to weed out particles, conjunctions and so on, the syntactic tools of location and hierarchization. The Impressionists wish us to look at reality without prejudice, though this impulse may be jeopardized, among the painters, by deeply ingrained ways of making pictures, like the portrait (Renoir) or the genre-painting (Morisot, Degas) and the natural visual privileges of certain colours, red in particular. Exercises like Monet's Rouen Cathedral series (1892–4) may be necessary attempts to paint pictures despite the subject, to let relativity make a nonsense of great names. Another method of making language as dynamic as perception is the punctuational solution of Dujardin's novel *Les Lauriers sont coupés* (*We'll to the Woods No More*) (1887), where semi-colons are a *passe-partout* punctuation, isolating phenomena while not hindering the flow of the consciousness on which they register. 'Stream of consciousness' technique is as much a result of Impressionism as of advances in psychology.

Any view that has relativity at its centre must propound an ethic and an aesthetic of the moment. This is not the narrational 'moment of Truth', which is the culmination of a continuity; it is not the moment of dramatic convenience, in which can be concentrated the momentous decisions of a lifetime. It is, rather, the moment of coincidence, of confluence, in fact any moment where the relationship between experience and time-sequence is haphazard; it is the moment of discontinuous flux, of mere and therefore pure existence; as memory destroys the present (unless it replaces it entirely), so meaning destroys sensation and the sense of an object's function destroys its reality. All coincidence reveals the profound *concertedness* of life.

Thus despite their high degree of composedness, Impressionist pictures are thoroughly on the brink of *a* – rather than *the* – next moment (do not all Impressionist paintings imply that they are one of a series?), thoroughly contiguous to an adjacent space (so the 'cut off' figures of a Degas). Thus the art-form is doubly absolute because doubly arbitrary. The 'significance' of, say, Pissarro's 'The Church of

Saint Jacques at Dieppe. Morning, rainy day' (1901) lies in the fact that no ulterior motive, no concern of human vanity interferes in its collusion with the art-form that represents it; the absolutely occasional becomes absolutely self-justifying by virtue of paint alone.

But our sense of the instability or the randomness of the subject is necessary to our sense that the world is our continuous experience of it, that the made is the being made and unmade, and that the painter has not painted the merely paintable (the picturesque), the already existent picture, but has had a picture disclosed to him in the rawest of materials. In the animation of the picture surface is one of the sources of a belief in the essential optimism of a Monet, a Renoir, a Sisley. Light and shade are no longer cordoned off for separate inspection; light no longer falls in uncomplicated highlights, is no longer endowed with a preternatural artistic tastefulness. Light scintillates across the scene without bias, clings to any obstacle; all things are equal in the light that embellishes them. Rilke calls Impressionism the 'pantheism of light' ('Impressionisten', 1898).

Mallarmé often uses the image of the play of light to convey the kind of verbal activity he is trying to create in his poems:[23]

> [*Les mots*] *s'allument de reflets réciproques comme une virtuelle traînée de eux sur des pierreries**

He 'mobilizes' his words by '*le heurt de leur inégalité*' ('the shock of their inequality'), quantitative, semantic, acoustic, grammatical etc. Verlaine achieves this by the disequilibrium of the imparisyllabic and the volatility of his caesuras and *coupes*. Rimbaud uses the pluralization of nouns, so that while the preponderance of nouns gives his world a solidity, a simple 'thereness', the pluralizing process makes these nouns multiform, makes them animate in a teeming way, like the teeming Impressionist atmosphere, makes them susceptible to metamorphosis, uncontrollable.

But the painter is not subject to paint – though he may be subject to its limitations – in the way that the poet is subject to words; language can never be fully subdued. The present tense, or the implied present of a predominantly substantival, notational prose, the tense of Impressionism, of unrehearsed contact with an environ-

---

*[Words] light one another up with mutual reflections like a virtual trail of fire upon precious stones.

ment, carries within it inescapable risks; with the present it is not always easy to distinguish between description and action, the continuous and the momentary; the poet forgoes the sedateness of the past tense[24] where all has fallen into place and where the desire to *re*count is a tacit guarantee of significance, and instead surrenders himself to a tense that guarantees nothing, neither a direction, a meaning nor indeed an ending. At the best of times the reader may find it difficult to decide whether phenomena are *décor* or subject:[25]

> *Die*
> *Luft so weich;*
> *die*
> *hohen, grauen,*
> *hässlichst balkoniüberklatschten Häuser*
> *ringsum*
> *fast*
> *schimmernd,*
> *schleierdünstig, silberschillerig;*★

For Rimbaud, the present tense is a safeguard of his creative autonomy, is part of the leap into the exhilaration, and the linear and architectural world, of Futurism. For others, it is part of an anguish, of a feeling of being assaulted by the world; reality is no longer encompassed, but collided with in an interminable series of encounters. Only those like Mallarmé, Rilke or Proust, who use a resilient periodic syntax, can approach the apparent equanimity of a Monet, a Renoir; for others, a contemplative participation *in* the world grows, by degrees, into a paralysing oppression *by* the world. Perhaps some distinction should be made between the Impressionism of, say, a Monet or a Rilke, and a sensation-Impressionism like Holz's. The former is already a step away from the raw sensory shock of sensation, is either a single sensation generalized or a group or series of sensations reconciled and appeased by a synthesizing structure; the latter is a group or series of sensations untranscended, intractable, erratic, and hostile. Inevitably, therefore, literary Impressionism not only runs parallel with Naturalism, not only opens up into Expressionism and Futurism, but also may be regarded as the early manifestation of the peculiarly

---

★The air so mild; the high, grey, most loathsomely balcony-plastered houses round about almost shimmering, veil-of-misty, silver-twinkling;

modern plight of an exploded consciousness caught in a fragmented universe.

Literary Impressionism, and sensation-gathering, must always fight a running battle against their own gratuitousness. It is no good breaking a scene down if it only adds up to itself again. Literary transcription alone cannot make the thing seen the thing said, and, vice versa, we are too used to meaning to have to picture it. Whether visual images, unaided, lead to reflection or not is a matter of chance. Verlaine's solution is often precisely to ask what it does all mean. Symons frequently transforms foreground into background: sense-data become album-reminders of amorous and other encounters. For Wilde the answer is simile, near-metamorphosis, impression within impression; simile provides the guarantee of its own literariness, has the useful appearance of a significant poetic act. The Imagists in their turn fall back on this device, despite Pound's hopeful claim that 'the natural object is the adequate symbol'; and we should not forget just how much Pound and others owed to nineties sensationalism, a debt that Pound himself acknowledges in an article on Symons:[26]

And with all our past ten years' talk of direct treatment and hard phrasing I do not know that the 'next generation' has gone much further toward the desirable plainness of Villon than had Symons.

For Symbolists like Mallarmé and the Rilke of *Neue Gedichte*, Impressionism was a means rather than an end, a means of expressing the process of exploration as a process, a means of groping among phenomena for the revealing detail or combination that would call forth the absent subject, a means of seducing essence from circumstance.

'Atomization of the world of the mind and of matter, relativism and subjectivism characterize the impressionist synthetic vision of the world' (Kronegger).[27] To escape the unregenerate partiality of the single view, views are multiplied, and in their multiplication lie the twin dangers of randomness and anonymity. Many of the poets here treated perceived the change, took part in it, and yet either avoided or postponed any cataclysmic showdown. This they did by compelling environment to remain *décor* for subjects for the subjective treatment of which there were time-honoured sanctions, by creating new absolutes, symbols, whose area of compass is the totality of the perceptions contained in the work, by demonstrating the continuing validity of old absolutes, form and conventions. They also initiated a more lasting and by now characteristic solution, irony; not that aggressive irony that seeks to cut dead wood from a tradition, but the irony that is the only way to maintain the relativistic view without a compromise, in good faith, namely, the countering of the variable transmissions from the world with one's own variability.

Notes

1 Valéry, 'Littérature', *Tel quel*.
2 Mallarmé, 'Victorieusement fui . . .'; 'Au seul souci de voyager'.
3 Moréas, 'Manifeste du symbolisme', *Le Figaro littéraire*, 18 September 1886.
4 Mallarmé, 'Sur Poe'.
5 Mallarmé, 'Magie'.
6 Mallarmé describes the art of metaphor-making when he writes in *Crise de vers* (*Crisis in verse*): '*Instituer une relation entre les images exacte, et que s'en détache un tiers aspect fusible et clair présenté à la divination*' ('To institute an exact relationship between the images, and let there stand out from it a third aspect, bright and easily absorbed, offered to divination').
7 Baudelaire, *Fusées*, XI.
8 To the Symbolist poets who gravitated around Mallarmé, poets like Georges Rodenbach (1855–98), Stuart Merrill (1863–1915), Adolphe Retté (1863–1930), Henri de Régnier (1864–1936), Francis Vielé-Griffin (1864–1937), there is no room to do justice. Their strengths have yet to be properly represented and acknowledged. Their weaknesses lie chiefly in the ways they made Symbolism easy. They tended to prefer an allegorical mode, where objects merely represent abstractions for narrative purposes, to a symbolic one, where abstractions are contained by an object; they consolidated a diction with a prefabricated suggestiveness and by failing to stiffen it with real intellectual motive, they let their work become a collection of seasonal mood-poems, bland and wistful.
9 Laforgue, 'Dimanches'.
10 Verlaine, 'A la promenade'.
11 George Moore, *Confessions of a Young Man* (London 1888).
12 Symons, 'Javanese Dancers'. (For a convenient collection containing a number of the poems cited, see R. K. R. Thornton (ed.), *Poetry of the 'Nineties* (Harmondsworth 1970).)

13 Dowson, 'Vanitas'; Wratislaw, 'Hothouse Flowers'.

14 Symons, 'To One in Alienation'.

15 Verlaine's lovers belong to an entirely different breed:

' *Trompeurs exquis et coquettes charmantes,*
  Coeurs tendres, mais affranchis du serment,
     . . .'

(Exquisite deceivers and charming coquettes,
tender hearts, but set free from vows)
('A la promenade'; my emphasis).

16 Samain, Liminary poem; my emphasis.

17 Samain, 'Visions III'.

18 Valéry, 'Autour de Corot'.

19 Baudelaire, 'Eloge du Maquillage', in *Le Peintre de la vie moderne* (1863).

20 Le Gallienne, 'Sunset in the City'.

21 Wilde, 'Symphony in Yellow'.

22 Symons, 'Impression'.

23 Mallarmé, *Crise de vers.*

24 It is, of course, possible to create present-tense effects with the past tense, to seem to re-establish an immediate contact with the data of the past, by imitating the patterns of perception and reaction contemporary with those data. Thus *A la recherche du temps perdu* (Remembrance of Things Past) is not a novel about memories, but is made of remembering; and thus, too, we find fully Impressionist passages in Zola, e.g. '*C'étaient des signes d'appel, des froissements d'étoffe, un défilé de jupes et de coiffures, coupées par le noir d'un habit ou d'une redingote . . .*' (There was much attention-catching, rustling of material, a procession of skirts and hairdos, intermittently interrupted by the black of a dress-suit or frock coat) (*Nana*).

25 Arno Holz, *Phantasus* (1898–1929).

26 Pound, in the *Athenaeum*, 21 May 1920.

27 Kronegger, 'Impressionist tendencies in lyrical prose: 19th and 20th centuries', *Revue de littérature comparée*, vol. 43, 1969, p. 529.

IMAGISM AND VORTICISM

NATAN ZACH

I

OVER half-a-century after Hulme's, Pound's and Amy Lowell's various groupings have ceased to exist, Imagism is still the subject of scholarly disagreements and partisan squabbles. The movement has been variously described as the centre of a 'revolution in the literature of the English language as momentous as the Romantic one' (Graham Hough) and as 'little more than a recognition that something was wrong with poetry' (F. R. Leavis). T. S. Eliot, close to Pound's school in his early London years, considered its accomplishment in verse 'critical rather than creative', whereas Herbert Read, himself the author of Imagist verse, felt that T. E. Hulme, F. S. Flint and H. D. (the American Hilda Doolittle) had written some of 'the only certainly perdurable poems in our century'. Hugh Kenner, whose *The Poetry of Ezra Pound* (1951) has probably done more than any post-war book to reactivate Imagist ideas, concedes no Imagist besides Pound and dismisses the movement's history as 'a red herring'. The doctrine of the Image has in turn been interpreted as a 'modernized, but essentially traditional, aesthetic of Symbolism' (Frank Kermode) and a hesitantly realist reaction against Symbolist aesthetics (Donald Davie).[1] While some critics insist on a basic difference between T. E. Hulme's and Pound's theories, others see Pound as little more than impresario to Hulme's speculations. Hulme himself has been variously labelled the philosopher of the 1914 *avant-garde*, a Ruskin *manqué* whose career as art critic and aesthetician was cut short by his death in the war, and – less flatteringly – as an able propagandist for other people's ideas (Bergson, Georges Sorel, Pierre Lasserre and Wilhelm Worringer were some of his main inspirations).

Even contributors to Imagist anthologies cannot agree on the nature and significance of the movement they took part in. Thus,

Richard Aldington – with H. D. the earliest convert to Pound's new ideas – considers in retrospect that he and his colleagues did 'some useful pioneering work', made free verse popular in England and tried to attain 'an exacting if narrow standard of style'. Frank Stewart Flint, a member of both Hulme's earlier and Pound's later cenacles, considers Imagism 'a general movement, a product and impulse of the time', but doubts whether Pound himself was Imagist in the 'hard strict sense of the word'. Pound for his part describes Flint and D. H. Lawrence, another contributor to Imagist anthologies, as Impressionists, later dissociating himself from the entire school and accusing it of 'diluting' his ideas. William Carlos Williams, who accepted the basic Imagist principle about the need to move away from 'the word as symbol towards the world as reality', nonetheless arraigns the 'flat Hellenic perfection' of much Imagist verse, its neglect of structure, and the eclecticism of Pound's 'literary cuisine'.[2] Finally, Lawrence, who never conceded theoretical allegiance and wrought his own brand of Whitmanesque Imagism, saw what Ford Madox Ford describes as 'the only well-organized movement in English poetry since the days of the pre-Raphaelite Brotherhood' as no more than one of Pound's 'illusions', dismissing most of its work with the exception of H. D.'s.

Contradictions, real or apparent, and differences are rooted in the very nature of Imagism. As a movement, it contained three distinct phases: (1) Hulme's 1909 group of obscure, non-combative poets who for a year or so discussed a new 'dry and hard' poetic in their weekly meetings in a Soho restaurant, the Eiffel Tower;[3] (2) Pound's much more ambitious and belligerent 'school of 1912'; and (3) the post-Poundian Imagists whom a disillusioned Pound dubbed 'Amygists', after Amy Lowell's takeover. Yeats, Eliot, Lawrence, Williams, Wallace Stevens, Robert Frost, Marianne Moore, Carl Sandburg, Hart Crane and some of the other prominent names in twentieth-century Anglo-American Modernism all come within the Imagist field of radiation, which, however, may mean no more than exposure at some stage to Pound's indoctrination or familiarity with his experiments.[4] With Vorticism, its successor in the fine arts, Imagism belongs to what is now often called 'classical Modernism'. It thus occupies in English-language literature the position held by such Continental – and roughly contemporaneous – movements as

Futurism, Unanimism and Expressionism. But for a movement with such claims, its immediate impact, particularly in England, was negligible: 'It has no vogue in England,' Flint stated in a 1915 letter. Lastly, while some of Pound's (by no means voluminous) strictly Imagist work is generally ranked among his best, that of most of his colleagues is far from exciting, and, were it not for the doctrine with which it is associated, would probably attract little critical attention today.

2

Called by their initially French name, *Les Imagistes* are first publicly mentioned in Pound's October 1912 *Ripostes*, where they are said to be the descendants of Hulme's 'forgotten school' of 1909. Included in Pound's volume was a reprint of five of Hulme's poems ('The Complete Poetical Works of T. E. Hulme'), reproduced, Pound wrote, 'for good fellowship', but also because 'they recall certain evenings and meetings' with Hulme and others of his so-called 'School of Images'. 'As for the future', Pound promised mystifyingly, '*Les Imagistes* . . . have that in their keeping.' A month earlier he responded to Harriet Monroe's invitation by sending her poems described as Imagist for her *Poetry* magazine, about to make its first appearance: first his own 'Middle-Aged', followed by three poems by Richard Aldington and three by H. D., whom he made sign 'Imagiste' (probably in emulation of Jules Romains, who at that time similarly added 'Unanimiste' to his name).

In the January issue containing H. D.'s first published poems, Pound indicated the existence of a programme urging precision. *Poetry* for March 1913 saw publication of the first Imagist manifesto, presented as an interview with Pound by Flint, but mainly written by Pound himself. It was accompanied by the now famous 'A Few Don'ts by an Imagiste'. Flint's note contained the three tenets, agreement on which constituted the first act of the new school:

1. Direct treatment of the 'thing', whether subjective or objective.
2. To use absolutely no word that does not contribute to the presentation.
3. As regarding rhythm: to compose in the sequence of the musical phrase, not in sequence of a metronome.

The 'Don'ts' were intended as a little manual for the 'candidate' wishing to write the kind of 'harder and saner' poetry which, Pound was predicting, would be written 'during the next decade or so'. Pound decreed:

Use no superfluous word, no adjective which does not reveal something.

Don't use such an expression as 'dim lands of *peace*'. It dulls the image. It mixes an abstraction with the concrete. It comes from the writer's not realizing that the natural object is always the *adequate* symbol.

Go in fear of abstractions. Do not retell in mediocre verse what has already been done in good prose. Don't think any intelligent person is going to be deceived when you try to shirk all the difficulties of the unspeakably difficult art of good prose by chopping your composition into line lengths . . .

Don't imagine that the art of poetry is any simpler than the art of music, or that you can please the expert before you have spent at least as much effort on the art of verse as the average piano teacher spends on the art of music . . .

In 1912 – the year in which Pound's little group made its first appearance – a culturally provincial London experienced some of the agitation accompanying the advent of the Modernist movement on the Continent and across the Atlantic. In January, Harold Monro's *Poetry Review* had opened with a call for a re-definition of the function of poetry and a shaking off of the 'fetters of stereotyped poetic language'. The *Georgian Poetry* anthologies, edited by Edward Marsh, made their first appearance and proclaimed a new 'Georgian period' which 'may rank in due time with the several great poetic ages of the past'. Following the great publicity success of Roger Fry's 1910 Post-Impressionist exhibition, the first Futurist display in London opened on 1 March at the Sackville Gallery, its book-long catalogue heralding a new epoch in painting. Marinetti, supported by the painters Balla, Boccioni, Carra and Russolo, visited London to lecture on Futurist ambitions and provoked the predictable scandal. Another visitor was the Unanimist Charles Vildrac, whose lectures on modern French poetry were attended by Flint and possibly by Pound. Wyndham Lewis exhibited his large *Kermesse*, the first canvas by an English artist to indicate awareness of recent Cubist developments in Paris. Diaghilev's Ballets Russes repeated their Continental triumphs:

T. E. Hulme was one of many to be captivated by their endeavour to bring the ballet into line with the non-humanistic ideas that inspired Egyptian, archaic Greek and Polynesian art.[5] In a special issue of the *Poetry Review*, Flint introduced no less than eight Neo-Symbolist and Post-Symbolist schools. Schools and coteries were very much in the air. Attracted to the Modernist's Mecca, Pound, H. D. and Aldington spent most of May in Paris, getting their first glimpse of what was generally described as a Reawakening. Pound's 'Effects of Music upon a Company of People' – an early testimony to the impact of this French encounter – set out to evoke imagistically the collective emotion of a concert audience, in the manner of Romains in his *La Vie Unanime* (*Unanimous Life*) and *Un Être en marche* (*A Being on the move*). Pound was later to describe the whole period as '*temps des unanimistes*'. Back in London, the three young poets decided, in a Kensington teashop, that they had 'as much right to a group name . . . as a number of French "schools"'.

As a result of Pound's proselytizing, the triple alliance soon expanded and was looking for suitable platforms. Harriet Monroe's *Poetry* was the first, American outlet. In the latter half of 1913 Pound persuaded Harriet Shaw Weaver to turn over the literary pages of her somewhat nondescript feminist paper, the *New Freewoman*, to Imagist hands. Renamed the *Egoist*, it became the school's British stronghold, with Aldington as assistant editor, a post he held until 1917, when he was succeeded by H. D. and later by T. S. Eliot. Equally significant was the appearance in 1914, in both England and the U.S.A., of the first Imagist anthology, *Des Imagistes*, edited by Pound. Of the eleven contributors, however, one – James Joyce, at that time still in Trieste – knew virtually nothing of Imagist principles. Another – Ford Madox Hueffer (later Ford) – cannot be considered a true Imagist, though his Impressionist ideas greatly influenced Pound. The rest, besides the original three, were Flint, Skipwith Cannell, Allen Upward, John Cournos, William Carlos Williams and Amy Lowell, whose contributions now seem exceedingly tame and unadventurous by any Modernist standard. Shortly after the appearance of the anthology, internal disagreement, especially with Amy Lowell, caused Pound to sever his ties with the school. All his strictures of it postdate the break. But he continued to promote his Imagist creed under the banner of Vorticism – Wyndham Lewis's art movement which Pound helped organize and to which he had given its name. Leadership of the Imagist school passed to Amy Lowell who shifted its centre to the U.S.A. Under her shrewd and less provocative sponsorship, three more anthologies, entitled *Some Imagist Poets*, appeared in Boston in 1915, 1916 and 1917, for which the six contributors (Aldington, H. D., Flint, Amy Lowell, John Gould Fletcher and D. H. Lawrence) chose their own work. With these, containing further statements of Imagist doctrine, on the whole faithful to Pound's tenets,[6] the name of the school was achieving some currency. In 1917 Amy Lowell announced that 'the collection had done its work'. By that time a broader Modernist movement, by no means synonymous with Imagism, was already breaking new ground in the English-writing world. One more Imagist Anthology – a product of nostalgia rather than a new venture – appeared under that title in 1930. Introduced by Ford Madox Ford and Glenn Hughes, it contained, Aldington wrote in his autobiography, 'poems by everyone who had contributed (including James Joyce and Carlos Williams) except poor Amy who was dead, Skipwith Cannell whom we couldn't trace, and Ezra who was sulky'.[7]

3

Despite some arguments to the contrary, the continuity of Imagist work from Hulme's circle to Pound's school can be readily traced. Joseph Campbell's 'The Dawn Whiteness' illustrates the kind of Imagist poem coming from the former:

> The dawn whiteness.
> A bank of slate-grey cloud lying heavily over it.
> The moon, like a hunted thing, dropping into the cloud.

Slight without being trivial, the poem's concentration on the image echoes the Symbolist stress on essential form to the exclusion of all allegedly extra-poetic matter. Though mildly suggestive of mood or state of mind, it minimizes the poet's personal involvement, and is not manifestly symbolic in the sense of standing in for anything distinct from its own delimited surface meaning. The poem strives for verbal economy, its lightness of touch recalling the Japanese *Haiku*.

Hulme's 'Above the Dock' throws further light on such characteristically Impressionist,[8] but uncommonly condensed, 'nuclear' poems:

> Above the quiet dock in midnight,
> Tangled in the tall mast's corded height,
> Hangs the moon. What seemed so far away
> Is but a child's balloon, forgotten after play.

The great poems of ancient times, Hulme argued, resembled pyramids; the old poetry 'dealt essentially with big things', its authors contaminated with the 'disease, the passion, for immortality'; in Romanticism the pyramidic urge became the craving for a boundless, impertinent, anarchic infinitude. By contrast, the new poem, corresponding to a new or revived metaphysical attitude, which regards man as 'an extraordinarily fixed and limited animal', would be that of small, dry things and 'street emotions'. Like Barrès – a major inspiration to the *Action française* he admired – Hulme saw the shift from absolute to relative as the mark of modern art. To the Symbolists he conceded the significance of metaphor, which alone can represent with any accuracy 'an object or an idea in the mind', without having recourse to language's ever-ready stock of abstract counters and threadbare clichés. Nature, he wrote, 'presses in on the poet to be used as metaphor'. Since the old, symmetrical verse-forms, in which stanzas were 'shaped and polished like gems', had reached inevitable exhaustion, and no efflorescence of verse was possible without a new technique, Hulme went on to advocate an irregular versification, close to but not identical with the specifically French *vers libre*, as the new instrument appropriate to the new sensibility.

On many such points Pound's doctrine remains markedly close to Hulme; though the poetry written by the two men to exemplify that doctrine differs greatly. For Pound, Imagism is that 'sort of poetry where painting or sculpture seems as if it were "just coming over into speech"'. The *Image* – 'that which presents an intellectual and emotional complex in an instant of time' – thus envisages a fusion of spontaneity, intensity and critical discipline. It is also – and here Pound submits an idea which has been credited with fathering Eliot's

Objective Correlative – an 'equation' for an emotion. The image-equation inheres in a relation between things, and is not the verbal snapshot of A thing. Pound may have read Mallarmé, in the original or in Arthur Symons's quotation: '*Instituer une relation entre les images exacte, et que s'en détache un tiers aspect fusible et clair . . .*' ('To establish a precise relationship between images to that a third aspect emerges there from which is integrated and clear'). He may also have come across Bergson's notion that 'no image can replace the intuition of duration, but many diverse images, borrowed from very different orders of things, may, be the convergence of their action, direct consciousness to the precise point where there is a certain intuition to be seized'. But he must surely have been familiar with Hulme's Bergson-inspired ideas:

> Say the poet is moved by a certain landscape, he selects from that certain images which, put into juxtaposition in separate lines, serve to suggest and to evoke the state he feels . . . Two visual images form what one may call a visual chord. They unite to suggest an image which is different to both.

Pound's most notable contribution has to do with the fact that such Imagist ideas, on many points heavily indebted to Symbolist-Impressionist thinking, gradually developed into an anti-Symbolist, anti-Impressionist platform. He put forward his own not quite accurate notion of the Symbolist method:[9]

> The symbolists dealt in 'association', that is, in a sort of allusion, almost of allegory. They degraded the symbol to the status of a word. They made it a form of metonymy [Pound writes metonomy]. One can be grossly 'symbolic', for example, by using the term 'cross' to mean 'trial'. The symbolist's *symbols* have a fixed value . . .

As part of an all-out campaign against nineteenth-century aesthetics, he arraigned Symbolism for its 'softness' and arbitrariness, its ultimate renunciation of the '*de facto* world' and aspiration after infinitude, its experiments in synaesthesia, and the Satanic posturings associated with Symbolists and Decadents. Since Imagism aimed at genuine and 'permanent' relationships, it was also set off, in theory if not always in practice, from the Impressionists' fleeting, fanciful word-pictures. Hulme had similarly condemned Yeats's attempts to 'ennoble his craft by strenuously believing in a supernatural world, race-memory, magic, and saying that symbols can recall these where prose couldn't,' all of which he regarded as 'an attempt to bring in an infinity again'. But his devotion to Bergson and his regard for the initially Symbolist *vers libre* made him stop short of branding the whole movement as yet another incarnation of 'blurry' Romanticism.

Thus, though his roots be in Hulme, Pound takes Imagist theory a considerable step forward, his own work underlining the progress. As the doctrine develops it accommodates not only metaphoric or suppository complexes, but any kind of utterance that is direct, un-embellished and economical. Originally focused on brief 'points of maximum energy', it is in time extended or converted to allow for larger and more ambitious work. Since logical development is ruled out, and traditional narrative composition discarded, an architectonic of concatenation, sometimes described as *collage*, is rationalized, and the 'logic of the imagination' upheld against the 'logic of concepts'. 'The reader,' Eliot instructs the uninitiated in his introduction to St-John Perse's *Anabase*, 'has to allow the images to fall into his memory successively without questioning the reasonableness of each at the moment; so that, at the end, a total effect is produced. Such selection of a sequence of images and ideas has nothing chaotic about it.' Beyond this, ideas of the total or governing image were gaining hold. Dante's *Paradiso*, Pound wrote, 'is the most wonderful *image*'; and a whole *Noh* play 'may consist of one image'.

Pound's collaboration with the Vorticists brought more modifications as well as some apparent retractions. The Vorticist insistence on movement, energy and intensity, a universal trait of pre-war (Bergson-inspired) art, strengthened Pound's conviction that the 'permanent' or 'absolute' image-complex-juxtaposition must be active rather than static and fixed – as Gautier's, H.D.'s and Aldington's word-sculpture had often tended to be. His later, influential ideas of 'active patterns' have their origin in this phase of his development. His own Vorticist images swirl, whirl, flutter, strike, fall, move, clash and leap, with a new emphasis on conflict and distortion. Impressed by Vorticist (geometrical-abstract) art, Pound produced *The Game of Chess* in which chess-board, figures and game are made to move and clash in an angular, 'intensive' manner. From Cubist Paris, Wyndham Lewis had imported the Douanier Rousseau cult; and Pound obliged with a surrealistic piece, *Heather*, which (he wrote) was impersonal and fell in with the new pictures and the new sculpture. Such experiments, however, were not pursued. As so often, having scored his technical or doctrinal point, Pound lost interest and turned elsewhere. But the new 'sense of [artistic] form' gained in the process was to have a lasting effect on his work. He now re-defined the image as Vortex:

> The image is not an idea. It is a radiant node or cluster; it is what I can, and must perforce, call a VORTEX, from which, and through which, and into which ideas are constantly rushing.

Less essentially perhaps, the Vorticist anti-representational bias ('We want to leave Nature and Men alone') was imparting to his thinking an abstract, 'musical' colouring. Constantly on the look-out for allies, contemporaneous or otherwise, Pound read and quoted Kandinsky's *Über das Geistige in der Kunst* (*On the Spiritual in Art*), excerpts from which were reproduced in Lewis's publication *Blast*, Apollinaire's pioneering *The Cubist Painters* (*Blast* itself was partly modelled on the latter's *L'Anti-tradition futuriste* (*The futurist anti-tradition*)) and Whistler's 'Ten o'Clock' lecture. Putting forward his Vorticist ideas of a 'musical conception of form', paraphrasing Pater's 'All art constantly aspires toward the condition of music', Pound may not have fully realized that he was thereby realigning himself, in at least this respect, with the mainstream of Romanticism and Symbolism.

The *image* projected by Pound's mature, but never satisfactorily resolved, doctrine can be described as content conceived of as form. It provides a medium for exploration, rather than a territory to be explored. It is, in Pound's words, a 'new focus'. The combination of such a new focus with some of the old *materia poetica* is responsible for a good deal of the striking new–old physiognomy of early Imagist verse.

Hulme's thought was similarly developing, though his interests had by then almost entirely shifted to the fine arts. Inspired by his reading of Worringer, Hulme credited modern geometrical art with the overthrow of the vital and humanistic tradition reigning since the Renaissance, which he associated with ego-centred Romanticism. Chiefly attracted by prospects of 'dehumanization' – in his *Blast* manifesto, the French sculptor Gaudier-Brzeska had made human self-adoration the harbinger of artistic decay – Hulme laid the foundations for a theoretical edifice that attempted to account for the work of

Picasso, Epstein, Gaudier, Lewis, Nevinson, Bomberg and Wadsworth. Forms follow needs, he maintained, and modern Western man may use 'formulae' derived from archaic civilizations to express his changed sensibility and needs. Hulme's January 1914 *Modern Art* lecture is as important a landmark in the history of English modernism in the fine arts as his *Romanticism and Classicism* is in that of poetry. At the time he was killed, in September 1917, he was busy writing a book on his friend Epstein. His other friend, Gaudier, to whom Pound devoted a book in 1916, was killed in action in early June 1915.

4

Imagism is perhaps best viewed as a doctrine of *hardness*, the commonest, widest-ranging concept in the movement's vocabulary. On a naïve level, the Imagist's 'hardness' may simply express his preferences in the selection of materials – thus, hard stone or hard bones as against mellow notes of music, soft hues, soft perfumes or the softness of silk, all of which had enthralled the alternately melancholy and hedonistic spirit of the Nineties. More radically, it applies to style, rhythm and emotion. Judging by Imagist pronouncements, verse becomes hard (1) through being concise and paring away all ornamental frills; (2) when, in remaining close to everyday speech, it conveys some of the harshness of quotidian reality; (3) when it tends towards concrete objectivity, thus avoiding sentimental effusions; (4) because, in rendering what purports to be an accurate account of its subject, it approximates the scientist's 'hard' methods, his hard observation of detailed fact; (5) when it 'dares to go to the dust-bin for its subjects' (Pound's praise for Fletcher's work); (6) when it avoids symmetrical, isochronic metres, which are branded soft, monotonous and soporific, and instead traces in its rhythms the 'rough' (i.e. irregular) contours of 'things'. Even the concentration on the image may be interpreted in terms of the desire for a resistant hardness, the image being one of the least 'convertible' elements of poetry.

In its preoccupation with hardness, Imagism constitutes a truly twentieth-century movement. In this it is as close to Futurism, with which it shares some basic tenets, as to Expressionism, from which it differs in many crucial respects. When it aspires to the condition of sculpture rather than to that of music, Imagist work manifests an affinity with the German *Dinggedicht* (the object-poem) and Rilke's Rodin-inspired work. Williams's red wheelbarrow glazed with rain-water – nothing more nor less than just that – is Imagism at its most objective. Pound's *Make it New* ideology bears comparison with what Brecht, the Surrealists and the Italian and Russian Futurists understood by the same slogan. Finally, in Russian Imaginism, sensitive to Futurist 'errors' but equally condemnatory of Symbolism and Decadence, Imagism finds a curious counterpart whose existence it ignored.[10] Viewed in this Continental perspective, it becomes clear that Imagism was 'a general movement, a product and impulse of the time' in a much wider sense than Flint perhaps suspected. Indeed, broadly speaking, one may distinguish two conflicting impulses at work in much of early twentieth-century poetry: the purist aesthetic of the image, with its aversion to rhetoric and non-artistic concerns and its elitist disposition, and a democratic creed of expression and representation, with its emphasis on the human condition, on art as involvement, and its mystically heightened sense of communion.

As well as bringing these two closer together, indeed synthesizing them in many cases, the outbreak of the First World War seemed to vindicate Imagism as a philosophy of style. The hardness which the movement required for its modern medium suddenly became the common experience of a generation on both sides of the trenches. The 'softness' of late nineteenth-century Aestheticism, itself a re-action from a hardened world, was now being superseded by a state of mind in tune with an even harsher reality. But its 'Religion of Beauty' ancestry will always provide characteristic Imagist work with that uneasy 'soft' streak which no desired or affected hardness ever manages to eliminate entirely.

5

An assessment of Imagism depends to a large extent on one's view of its boundaries. If one considers the whole of Pound's later work Imagist, or if one goes even further and takes Eliot, the later Yeats, Wallace Stevens and Dylan Thomas for Imagists, as some critics have done, then the little 'Eiffel Tower' gatherings and the 1912–17 groupings assume a momentous significance. In Pound's case, however, a distinction between Imagist and non-Imagist work seems warranted. In turn, Wallace Stevens's adage about the poet being the 'priest of the invisible' is at odds with the very fundamentals of Pound's creed, as is his belief that 'reality is a vacuum' to be filled by words. Neither should Eliot's undoubted sympathies be mistaken for conformity. Though his famous Objective Correlative bears a formal resemblance to Pound's 'equation', his theory (as Donald Davie justly argues) in fact runs the other way from Pound's. Such affinity as exists in this and other instances may be safely attributed to a common Symbolist heritage and a common *Zeitgeist* (the Futurists, too, were claiming that '*nous créons ainsi en quelque sorte une ambiance émotive en cherchant à coups d'intuition les sympathies et les attachements qui existent entre la scène extérieure (concrète) et l'émotion intérieure (abstraite)*') ('In this way we create some kind of emotive mood by searching out through flashes of intuition the sympathies and attachments which exist between the external (concrete) picture and the internal (abstract) emotion').[11] Eliot's insistence on depersonalization and 'art emotions', Williams's 'low-life' attentions, Marianne Moore's irregular rhythms and prosaicisms can all be linked up one way or another with Imagist tenets. But a French-European tradition running from Flaubert, Rimbaud and the Parnassians down to the self-styled *Action française* 'classicists' affords a sounder background and perspective.

It is all too easy to make too many or too few claims for Imagism. The 1909–17 succession of groups anticipates a turning-point in English and American poetry, and to a limited extent embodies it. More specifically, it seems justified to say with Stephen Spender that the movement 'isolated the basic unit of the modern [English] poem', besides campaigning to redress Romantic excesses (though arguably itself a Romantic phenomenon, as Babbitt indeed branded it). Along with many other contemporaneous schools and individuals, it upheld the craft of poetry, preached the experimental approach to art,[12] and reaffirmed the importance of living speech to a living poetry. It introduced irregular rhythms on a massive scale and emphasized that poetry cannot for long afford to lag behind prose if it does not wish to become irrelevant to a new, hardened sensibility. In common with other modern schools which had renounced the Beyond, it argued persuasively that poetry should not distance itself from the world of things if it does not wish to end up with 'pure' music and sheer mood. It had earnestly endeavoured to chart its own tradition but ended by substituting a cosmopolitan provincialism for a national one (here both credit and discredit go equally to Pound). Adjusting itself to an intellectual climate that placed its emphasis on action, it blundered seriously by diagnosing the image – the most flow-resisting element of poetry – as its most 'moving' and dynamic. Equating abstraction with empty rhetoric (thus undermining its own intellectual ambitions), banning descriptiveness and ornament, neglecting syntax, structure, development, subordination and – on a different level – the exploration of psychic processes, and often incurring a certain frigidity and triviality of the emotions, it proceeded to reconstruct the modern poem from what it rightly or wrongly considered as its smallest, most organic and most reliable cell. Ideas similar to its own reverberate through Williams's and Zukofsky's Objectivism of the early thirties, Charles Olson's 'Projective' poetics of the fifties and the Minimalism of the sixties well into the present day.

Notes

1 Graham Hough, *Image and Experience* (London 1960): F. R. Leavis, *New Bearings in English Poetry* (London 1932); T. S. Eliot, in the *Criterion*, July 1937; Herbert Read, 'What is a Poem?', in his *Collected Poems* (London 1966), and *The Contrary Experience* (London 1963); Frank Kermode, *Romantic Image* (London 1957); Donald Davie, *Ezra Pound: Poet as Sculptor* (London 1965).

2 See *Selected Essays of William Carlos Williams* (1954), pp. 10, 11, 23–4.

3 Flint lists as members, besides Hulme and himself, Edward Storer, F. W. Tancred, Joseph Campbell and Florence Farr. Pound also attended but at this stage apparently did little more than 'attempt to illustrate (or refute) our theories occasionally' with the help of quotations from the troubadours (F. S. Flint, 'The History of Imagism', *Egoist*, 1 May 1915). For further data, see Peter Jones (ed.), *Imagist Poetry* (Harmondsworth 1972).

4 A major source of Imagist ideas, Hulme exerted much of his influence through Pound, his key essays appearing only posthumously, in *Speculations* (1924). Edward Storer, prominent in the Eiffel Tower discussions, gave the main points of Hulme's teachings

in an essay contained in his 1909 *The Mirrors of Illusion* and in his introduction to a William Cowper selection (1912), the first written form of ideas which would wait twelve more years before being printed under their proper author's name.

5 A. R. Jones, *The Life and Opinions of Thomas Ernest Hulme* (London 1960), pp. 92–3.

6 See in particular the introduction to the 1915 anthology – written by Aldington with some alterations by Amy Lowell. Herbert Read considers this the *locus classicus* for Imagist doctrine, and quotes its six principles in *The Contrary Experience* (London 1963).

7 Richard Aldington, *Life for Life's Sake* (London 1968), pp. 130–31. But Aldington forgot Allen Upward, another early contributor, by that time also dead, who was equally unrepresented in the 1930 anthology.

8 See in this context Stephen Ullmann's *Style in the French Novel* (Oxford 1964), pp. 121–6.

9 Ezra Pound, *Gaudier-Brzeska* (Hessle 1960), p. 84.

10 The Imaginists were however made aware of the London group's efforts through a long article 'Angliiskie Futuristi' (Strelets 1915) by Zinaida Vengerova, who had had a personal interview with Pound.

11 See Introduction to the Futurist Bernheim-Jeune and Sackville Gallery exhibition (1912) in *Archivi del Futurismo* (Rome, undated), vol. I, p. 108.

12 Stanley K. Coffman, *Imagism* (Norman, Okla., 1951), p. 225.

ITALIAN FUTURISM

JUDY RAWSON

I

THE *Futurist Manifesto* first appeared in *Le Figaro* for 20 February 1909. Its author was an Italian, Filippo Tommaso Marinetti, who, though making his mark first of all in Paris, had also been active in Milan since 1905 as editor of *Poesia*, one of the aims of which was the publicizing of the works of the French Symbolists in Italy. (Later, Marinetti was also to claim[1] Zola, Whitman, George Kahn and Verhaeren among his predecessors – in an article characteristically entitled 'We deny our Symbolist Masters, the last Moon-Lovers'.) In this, the first of his many Manifestos, Marinetti declared: 'It is from Italy that we broadcast this manifesto of ours to the whole world . . . because we want to free this country from the stinking gangrene of its professors, archaeologists, tourist guides and antique dealers.' Italy had been a junk shop for too long, he insisted; now it was time to burn her libraries, flood her museums and galleries, and tear down her sacred cities.[2]

Compared with the French, the Italian literary scene was unexciting. D'Annunzio was now the chief literary figure of the day; Carducci, whose 'strength' appealed to Marinetti more than did the 'femininity' and delicacy of D'Annunzio, had been dead for two years. Other writers like Pascoli, Fogazzaro and even Verga were by international standards rather low-keyed. The *Manifesto* was however not addressed solely to Italy, but from Italy to the world; and the challenge was taken up outside Italy in a number of bitter disputes: with the Cubists, for instance, with Apollinaire's Orphists, and with Wyndham Lewis's Vorticists. These disputes quickly acquired a nationalistic flavour, particularly during the early years of the First World War. It was this nationalistic element in Futurism which made its confusion with Fascism so easy.

The preamble to the eleven points of the *Manifesto* describes how it was written by Marinetti with his friends (seemingly Buzzi and Cavacchioli) one night in his flat in Milan. They were aggressively proud of sharing the night hours with the ships' stokers, the railway firemen, the drunks, the trams and the 'hungry motor cars'. The cars are spoken of as wild beasts – *'fauves'* in the French version. (The Salon exhibitions of the Fauves were held in 1905–6.) There follows the description of a journey they make in their three cars, a flight from reason into the Unknown which will itself devour them; the outing ends when Marinetti's own car, swerving to avoid two teetering cyclists, overturns in a ditch. Unexpectedly, however, this is a moment of rebirth; for when the car is fished out of the rich maternal factory mud, it is still functioning but has lost its 'coachwork of common sense' and its 'soft upholstery of convenience'.

Already in a poem of 1905, 'A l'Automobile de Course', Marinetti had declared an admiration for the machine which amounted almost to a romantic love and death relationship; and with it an exaltation of speed as a new beauty (point 4 of the *Manifesto*):

> *Hourrah! Plus de contact avec la terre immonde! ...*
> *Enfin, je me détache et je vole en souplesse*
> *sur la grisante plénitude*
> *des Astres ruisselant dans le grand lit du ciel.* *

Soon this was to develop into still greater excitement over the possibility of flight, which took on an almost mystical significance for Marinetti. In the preamble to the first *Manifesto*, he claimed that 'soon we will see the first angels fly'. In his novel *Mafarka le Futuriste*, contemporary with the first *Manifesto*, the climax comes when Mafarka, the African king, dies in the act of creating his own son Gazurmah, an Icarus Superman figure, who successfully defies the sun and makes 'total music' with his wings as he flies off into the heavens at the end of the novel. Beneath Gazurmah the mountains topple, towns are ruined and the sea is cloven into an abyss with the facility of a scene from Walt Disney's *Fantasia*, while he bandies erotic nothings with the breezes and shouts defiance at the sea and the sun. So far as any

---

*Hurrah! No more contact with the filthy earth!
At last I take off and, supple, fly
Over the intoxicating fullness
Of the stars, streaming in the great bed of Heaven.

metaphysics is implied it is an amoral exaltation of action for its own sake – as prescribed in the first three points of the *Manifesto*. 'Dynamism' was in fact a name that was contemplated for the movement during these early days. Again one can see how this easily-communicated ideal foreshadowed Fascism's cult of action and drive. In *The Technical Manifesto of Literature* (1912) the motor car is replaced by the aeroplane flying two hundred metres above Milan.

The first *Futurist Manifesto* speaks always of poetry, of 'singing'; yet the visual nature of its prescriptions is very obvious. Point 11 illustrates how closely Futurism was bound to be involved with the visual arts, and indeed with the cinema:

We will sing of great crowds engaged in work, pleasure, or revolt: we will sing the many-coloured, polyphonic tides of revolution in modern capital cities: we will sing of the clangor and the heat of nights in the shipyards and docks blazing with violent electric moons; of gluttonous railway stations devouring smoking snakes; of factories hanging from the clouds by the twisted threads of their smoke-trails . . .

Marinetti was himself an artist; more than that, and even more importantly for Futurism, he was a great patron and organizer of artists, with a flair for advertising and a propensity for long-distance travel which did more than anything else to publicize the movement. Today Futurism is largely remembered as an artistic movement and not a literary one. Paintings such as Russolo's *Sleeping City* (1909–10) and *The Revolt* (1911) and Boccioni's *Fight in the Galleria* (1910) are obviously inspired by Marinetti's ideas. Dynamism and simultaneity – key Futurist terms to express the beauty of speed – came in painting to mean those strange studies of movement suggested by current experiments with film, as in Balla's *Girl Running on a Balcony* with its eight split-second views of the running girl, or his *Lead in Motion* with its many-legged, many-tailed dachshund walking out on his four leads. A visual element is also an essential component of the literature of the movement, not only in kinetic and technicolour descriptions such as the flight of Gazurmah in *Mafarka le Futuriste* but also in the typographical revolution which the Futurists provoked. Marinetti's Free Word broadsheet *Mountains+Valleys+Roads×Joffre* (1915) is so close to the *Papier collé* creation of Carrà, *Patriotic Festa* (1914), and to Severini's *Serpentine Dance* (1914) that the difference is negligible.

That all three works are concerned with the swift communication of propaganda – in this case, propaganda for Italy's entry into the First World War – does not go unnoticed.

'The new beauty, the beauty of speed', the fourth point of the first *Manifesto*, was given renewed emphasis in the *Technical Manifesto of Literature* of 11 May 1912; but now the aeroplane has taken over from the motor car as the dynamic muse. The new eleven points are dictated by its propeller:

> In an aeroplane, sitting on the petrol tank with my stomach warmed by the pilot's head, I realized the ridiculous stupidity of the old grammar inherited from Homer. A furious need to set words free, to drag them from the prison of the Latin sentence. Like any idiot this naturally has a shrewd head, a stomach, two legs and two flat feet, but it will never have two wings. Hardly enough to walk, to run a moment and stop almost straight away, out of breath.
>
> This is what the whirling propeller said to me as I flew at two hundred metres above the powerful smoke stacks of Milan.

The call is for a new poetry of intuition: to hate libraries and museums, to repudiate reason, to reassert that divine intuition which is the gift of the Latin races. Their poetry is to depend on analogy instead of logic; the old Latin grammar is to go, and nouns are to be placed as they come; verbs are to be used only in the infinitive; adjectives, adverbs and punctuation to be abolished (though mathematical and musical signs are allowed); and human psychology is to be replaced by a lyrical obsession with matter. He writes of an intuitive psychology or 'physicology' of matter. They will invent Wireless Imagination; they will give only the second terms of analogies, unintelligible though this may sometimes be. The result will be an 'analogical synthesis of the world embraced at one glance and expressed in essential words'. These are the '*Parole in libertà*', or '*Parolibere*': 'After Free Verse' – the invention of Gustave Kahn whom Marinetti much admired – 'we have at last Free Words.' In his *Replies to the Objections* to this *Manifesto* (11 August 1912), Marinetti describes the intuitive act of creation almost as if it were automatic writing: 'The hand that writes seems to detach itself from the body and reaches out independently far away from the brain . . .' It reads like some early foreshadowing of Breton's 'magic Surrealist art'.

Marinetti's *Zang Tumb Tumb* (dated Adrianople, October 1912) is in

Free Words. Published in 1914, prefaced by a further Manifesto written the year before, and entitled *Destruction of Grammar – Wireless Imagination – Free Words*, it decrees that the new style is only to be used for the lyric, and not for philosophy, the sciences, politics, journalism or business, or indeed for Marinetti's own *Manifestos*. The basis of the new Futurist art forms – pictorial dynamism, noise-music, Free Words – lies in the new sensibility which has been conditioned by the new speed in communications. He held, as he put it, that a great daily paper is the synthesis of one whole day in the world. Each individual has multiple and simultaneous consciousnesses. He needs to see everything at a glance, to have everything explained in a couple of words. A war correspondent (before the age of television, which would presumably have delighted Marinetti) will need to explode the mechanism of Latin grammar in order to communicate in essential words his impressions – which will be largely sense impressions – and the 'vibrations of his *ego*'. Like wireless, he will link distant things through his poetry. Typographic revolution will help to express different ideas simultaneously. Twenty different types and three or four different colours can be used on one page if need be, to express ideas of differing importance and the impressions of the different senses. Molecular life, for instance, will always be expressed in italics.

This is the style of *Zang Tumb Tumb*. The impact of the new typography is immediate, particularly when contrasted with what Marinetti called the 'mythological greengroceries' of the *art nouveau* decorative style he was replacing. Words in a variety of types are splayed out over the pages, interspersed with mathematical signs, and sometimes arranged in graphic designs as in the very explicit 'hanging'. The spelling too bears witness to the liberation advocated in the opening Manifesto and to some extent achieves the marriage with onomatopoeia that Marinetti was hoping for. The 'sssssssiii ssiissii ssiissssssiiii' of the first page, describing a train journey to Sicily while correcting the proofs of the book, expresses both the positive hopes he has for Futurism and the whistling of the train. The 'chapters' of the book are impressionistic vignettes with titles such as 'Mobilization', 'Raid', 'A Train full of Sick Soldiers'. This last is a very graphic and telegraphic account of the smells and sounds, the hopes, dreams and anguish, and the medical conditions of 1500 soldiers being taken in a locked train, under fire, from Karagatch to Istanbul. It is remarkably successful if one can break through the intelligibility barrier. In the last words of *The Destruction of Grammar* Marinetti gives a clue as to how this might be done when he speaks of the need for special 'declaimers' for his poetry. Different parts of *Zang Tumb Tumb* were declaimed by him in a number of European cities during 1913 and 1914, including London from 16 to 20 November 1913, and again at the Doré Gallery on 28 April 1914. Wyndham Lewis gives a description of one of these occasions at which he was present:

> The founder of Fascism [sic] had been at Adrianople, when there was a siege. He wanted to imitate the noise of bombardment. It was a poetic declamation, which must be packed to the muzzle with what he called '*la rage balkanique*'. So Mr Nevinson[3] concealed himself somewhere in the hall, and at a signal from Marinetti belaboured a gigantic drum.
> But it was a matter for astonishment what Marinetti could do with his unaided voice. He certainly made an extraordinary amount of noise. A day of attack upon the Western Front, with all the 'heavies' hammering together right back to the horizon, was nothing to it.[4]

Seemingly, there are no recordings of any of these performances; but certainly the Marinettian method of declamation and his own personality must have been of vital importance. This in turn shows how very close he was to the theatre – particularly Variety Theatre – which he very much admired.[5]

The last technical literary *Manifesto* of the pioneering days was contemporary with the publication of *Zang Tumb Tumb*; it uses passages from this book as examples. (Later literary *Manifestos* such as the introduction to the anthology of *New Futurist Poets* [Rome 1925] and the 1937 article on *The Technique of the New Poetry* do little more than summarize the history of the movement and reiterate the definitions of Free Words.) With the baffling title *Geometric and Mechanical Splendour and Numerical Sensitivity*, it first appeared in *Lacerba* in March and April 1914. Here the technique of Free Words is brought even closer to the aesthetics of the machine; first it is likened to the controlling of a Dreadnought at war, and then to the control panels of a hydro-electric station with the sparkling perfection of their precise machinery representing the synthesis of a whole range of mountains. The depreciation of human psychology which had been noticeable in the *Technical Manifesto* of 1912 ('The warmth of a piece of iron or wood is now more exciting to us than the smiles or tears of a woman') and which Lawrence had pointed out in a letter to Garnett, not without some qualified sympathy, has become much more pronounced. At the front in 1911 Marinetti had noticed 'how the shining aggressive muzzle of a gun, scorched by the sun and by rapid firing, makes the sight of tortured and dying human flesh almost negligible'. In this way 'the poetry of the human is to be supplanted by the poetry of cosmic forces. The old romantic, sentimental and Christian proportions of the story are abolished.'

Another theme taken up from the earlier *Manifestos* was the use of the verb in the infinitive, instead of in the forms related to persons or tenses. This gave 'action' to the new lyric, using the verb like the wheel of a train or the propeller of an aeroplane, and reduced human representation. As with a number of his linguistic suggestions, one is conscious that the language Marinetti is dealing with does not lend itself to this kind of experiment. English or American might have proved a much more malleable instrument for his purposes than Italian. The new 'numerical sensitivity' derives from a love of precision which prefers to describe the sound of a bell in terms of the distance over which it is audible – 'bell stroke distance 20 sq. km.' – rather than by 'imprecise and ineffectual' adjectives. Similarly, the formula $+ -+ -+ +\times$ describes a car changing speed and accelerating.

2

It is natural to concentrate on *Manifestos*, partly because they give the essence of the Futurist movement as its founder saw it, but also because they were the movement's literary form *par excellence*. Marinetti possessed the flair for setting out his ideas attractively and aggressively in this form. Apollinaire followed suit with his *Futurist Anti-tradition* of 22 June 1913, as did Wyndham Lewis in his two Vorticist manifestos in the first number of *Blast*.[6] One notable difference between the two is that Marinetti comes first on Apollinaire's list for 'Roses', whereas he draws harsh words from Lewis, although not actually on the list for 'blasting'.

In the early history of the movement, Marinetti's greatest political triumph was probably his conversion to Futurism of that flourishing school of Florentine writers who were connected with the periodical *Lacerba*. Perhaps the most interesting of these figures was Papini, whose vicious criticism in the form of '*Stroncature*' reflects the aggressiveness of the movement. He wrote a number of essays on Futurism in 1913, and spoke in its favour during its heroic years; later he grew away from it. Palazzeschi was strongly defended as a Futurist by Marinetti in 1913, because he threw 'intellectual bombs' at the Romantics, at the love and death mystique, and at the cult of women. Marinetti particularly praised Palazzeschi's poem 'The Sick Fountain' with its onomatopoeia ('*Clof, clop, cloch*') which was 'spitting on the Altar of Art'. Ardengo Soffici was the third member of this group and the only one who made a name as a painter as well as a writer. He also wrote a *Futurist Aesthetics* between 1914 and 1917. His main contribution to the literary side of the movement, beside his *Futurist Aesthetics*, was his *Bïf§zf+18. Simultaneità. Chimismi Lirici* (1915), which attempts the Free Word style. These three Florentines brought prestige to the movement. But the uneasy marriage between Florence and Milan did not last, and by 1915 the Florentines were claiming that they were the true Futurists – the others were Marinettists. To our eyes they seem less experimental, particularly in the prose writings and novels by which they are more usually remembered; while Marinetti's name remains linked with Futurism and the pioneering days of the movement which he never really outgrew.

After the break with the *Lacerba* writers the Futurist cause was not, however, lost in Florence. It was taken up by another group of writers including Carli, Settimelli, Corra, and Ginna. These last three had a particular interest in theatre and cinema, and it is noticeable that from 1915 onwards the new Futurist pronouncements have to do mainly with this new area. In 1915 Marinetti, Corra and Settimelli brought out a collection of thirty-six 'theatrical syntheses' under the title *Futurist Synthetic Theatre*. In the *Manifesto* of the same name they explained how they were now looking to the theatre rather than to the printed word in order to reach the general public. They asked for a theatre that would be 'synthetic', unlike the 'Pastist' theatre which left the audience 'like a group of idlers sipping their anguish and pity and watching the slow death of a horse that has fallen on the cobbles'. Simultaneity would mean that several actions could take place at once; nothing need be reported as having taken place off-stage; old techniques, such as the climax coming in the fifth act, would go; so would logical arguments explaining cause and effect, since they are never fully present in real life. Action would overflow from the stage into the auditorium, and eventually a new, more theatrically conscious audience would grow up used to this continuous contact with the Futurists and having absorbed their 'dynamic vivacity'.

Early in 1916 Settimelli and Corra founded the review *L'Italia Futurista* – the mouthpiece of the so-called Second Florentine Futurism. Here Marinetti published his *Manifesto* on *The New Religion of Speed* (places particularly sacred to the cult being, among others, restaurant cars and the Strand); here, later in 1916, the Futurist experiments with the cinema were announced. Corra and Ginna were brothers (their real name was Ginanni-Corradini, but Balla had persuaded them to take different and more Futurist names)[7] who had already experimented with short films between 1910 and 1912. Marinetti proposed a Futurist film, and together the group made *Futurist Life* in the summer of 1916 in Florence. Balla, Settimelli, Corra, Marinetti and others all took part; Ginna was responsible for production and camera work. The film was a series of sequences, some of them dealing with Futurist social and psychological problems. The first showed some dynamic young Futurists led by Marinetti attacking an old man at a restaurant in Piazzale Michelangelo because he was drinking his soup in an old-fashioned way. There was also – recalling the title of Marinetti's manifesto – the 'Dance of Geometric Splendour', with strong beams of light projected on to girls dressed only in tin foil, so that 'the flashes of light criss-crossed and destroyed the weight of their bodies'. The film ended with an inquiry into 'Why Franz Joseph did not die', which the censors cut. As it was, the film aroused a great deal of emotion, and objects were hurled at the screen at every showing. Of the few copies made, all are now lost.

Out of this experience the *Manifesto of Futurist Cinema* was written and signed by Marinetti, Corra, Settimelli, Ginna, Balla, and Chiti. The cinema was seen as the new art form which was to fulfil the need for poly-expressivity. Marinetti contributed the idea that 'the universe will be our vocabulary', which echoes his views on analogy. Balla introduced simultaneity with the trick of showing shots of different places and times at once. Ginna and Corra's views on 'chromatic music', 'symphonies of gestures, actions, colours, lines', are also there, foreshadowing what was to be realized in Walt Disney's *Fantasia*. It is a less coherent manifesto, perhaps because so many people contributed, perhaps because Marinetti's flair was lacking (he must have spent some time at the front that year) or because he was more interested in theatre than cinema. Certainly it was to dance and to theatre that he returned in later pieces – though these, like his later literary *Manifestos*, add little new. Indeed, by the outbreak of war, the first impulses of the heroic days of Futurism were spent. By the end of it, the second Florentine Futurism had also worn itself out, and after it Marinetti did little more than anthologize and justify himself. The last expressions of Futurism took on political form; they must have reflected the feelings with which not only many Futurists but many Italians returned from the front; and the movement's social place changed.

3

Futurism had always had a political side. As early as 1909 a short political *Manifesto* with an anti-clerical message had been published for the elections. In 1911 a second *Manifesto* appeared in favour of the Libyan war. For the elections of 1913, a more evolved *Futurist Political Programme* was brought out, its first phrase reiterating, from the 1911 *Manifesto*: 'The word Italy must dominate the word Liberty.' The ideological basis was anti-clerical and anti-socialist, and what constructive proposals there were supported modernization in industry and agriculture, Irredentism, and an aggressive foreign policy. These three *Manifestos*, with other politically aggressive writings, were published together in *War the only Cure for the World* in 1915 – the year of Italy's entry into the First World War.

Marinetti published his *Manifesto of the Futurist Political Party* in *L'Italia Futurista* in February 1918, and again in September that year in *Roma Futurista* – a new magazine recently founded in Rome by Carli and Settimelli as the 'Journal of the Futurist Political Party'. Anti-clericalism, still one of the chief points, was reflected in the programme for State education and for easy divorce. Parliamentary changes would mean a younger Chamber of Deputies and the abolition of the Senate in favour of a government of twenty technical experts elected by universal suffrage. Other items were the introduction of proportional representation, nationalization of land, waterways and mines, modernization in industry, the eight-hour day, equal pay, national assistance and pensions, legal aid, provisions for ex-combatants and the abolition of bureaucracy. One of Marinetti's main concerns both here and in his *Futurist Democracy – Political Dynamism* of 1919 was to differentiate between the *avant-garde* artistic movement and the new political party. He went to great lengths to point out the difference between artistic Futurism, which had aroused so much antagonism among ordinary people, and the Futurist party to which anyone might belong who wanted progress and loved Italy. At this time the Futurists formed links with the Association of the Arditi (ex-combatants). Carli was the founder of the Rome group, while the Milanese group founded by Vecchi met at Marinetti's house. In March, 1919, Marinetti, Vecchi and other Futurists took part in the foundation of the Fasci di Combattimento, the fighting squads who were to constitute the original Fascist party; and in April Futurists and Arditi made up the Fascist forces that attacked the offices of the Socialist paper *Avanti* in Milan. After losing to the Socialists in the elections, Marinetti spent twenty-one days in prison in December with Mussolini, Vecchi and other Arditi, charged with endangering the security of the State and organizing armed bands. During that time he wrote *Beyond Communism* which was the Futurist condemnation of Communism as bureaucratic, pedantic and Pastist. He looked beyond Communism to a future when the new education would produce a race of heroes and geniuses in Italy. Art would be the means and the end in this process; and finally 'we will not have an earthly paradise, but economic hell will be brightened and comforted by countless festivals of art'. One can see here how it could be that the Futurists were not always taken seriously as politicians.

It was because of practical politics and the necessity to compromise over the issues of the Monarchy and the Church that Marinetti and Carli left the Fasci di Combattimento in May 1920. However, by the time Marinetti came to anthologize the speeches and accounts of these times in *Futurism and Fascism* in 1924, the differences were patched up and he was concerned to present Futurism as a forerunner and partner of Fascism. The last piece is a *Manifesto* on *The*

Italian Empire signed by Marinetti, Carli and Settimelli in 1923, and addressed to 'Mussolini, leader of the New Italy'. It stresses Futurist aggression and patriotism, although it still persists in seeing the new Empire as anti-clerical. But the preceding piece on *The Rights of Artists Proposed by the Italian Futurists* showed quite clearly that Futurism had ceased to be a political movement. It was now reverting to the area of the arts, leaving the government of the country in the capable hands of 'a President of the Council with a marvellous Futurist temperament'.

This alliance with Fascism has ever since been the greatest stumbling block to an appreciation of Futurism. Futurism certainly contributed to the aggressive rhetoric of Fascism that allowed Mussolini to speak with pride of 'punching the stomach of the Italian *bourgeoisie*',[8] as also to the Fascist programme of toughening up the Italians. The 'Fascist Saturday' was to be given over to gymnastics and physical training, and Mussolini wanted the Appennines reforested to 'make Italy colder and snowier'.[9] Other ideas actually detrimental to the national cause are traceable to Futurist sources. For instance: 'Italy did not have aircraft carriers since Mussolini had proudly announced that Italy herself was a huge aircraft carrier extending into the Mediterranean.'[10] As early as 1911 Marinetti had said in his *Second Political Manifesto*: 'Today Italy has for us the shape and the power of a Dreadnought battleship with its squadron of torpedo-boat islands.' Again during the war, when economic collapse was imminent, Mussolini apparently thought he would avoid trouble by selling off Italian art treasures – a proposal in line with the early Futurist dream of destroying museums and art galleries, as well as a later idea of capitalizing on works of art.

Futurism of course sought antagonism from its audiences. At a Futurist happening an enlivened audience was all part of the show. Marinetti was called 'the caffeine of Europe' because of his ability to annoy and disturb. He antagonized Pound, who said in a letter to Joyce on 6 September 1915 that Futurism was 'spliced cinematography in paintings and diarrhoea in writing'[11] – though later an Italian critic quotes him as having said 'the movement which I began with Joyce, Eliot and others in London would not have existed without Futurism'.[12]

Critics have pointed out that many of the ideas of Futurism were in the air during the early years of the century, and Pavolini writing in 1924 could say that there would have been some kind of Futurism without Marinetti. But the synthesizing and aggressive publicizing of these ideas in the Futurist style was important. Many of them were taken up and fought over by other movements, particularly the Dadaists.[13] It has also been suggested, with reference to Dos Passos, that 'perhaps the most important discovery of the Futurists was the realization that fragmentation, contrast, and the interplay of apparently discordant materials constituted a direct expression of the speed and diversity of modern life'.[14] Certainly the technique of the newspaper headlines and the 'Camera Eye' in Dos Passos's *U.S.A.* recalls Marinetti's remarks about the daily paper being the synthesis of a day in the life of the world. It is perhaps time that the literary and theatrical experiments of Futurism were revalued and not allowed to be entirely overshadowed by the work of the painters and sculptors[15].

A chronological list of the principal Manifestos *of the Futurist Movement.* For a fuller list see C. Baumgarth, *Geschichte des Futurismus* (Reinbek bei Hamburg 1966), pp. 299 f. For further documentation see *Archivi del Futurismo*, edited by M. D. Gambillo and T. Fiori, 2 vols. (Rome 1958).

1909 *The Futurist Manifesto*, Marinetti.
      Let's Kill the Moonlight, Marinetti.
      First Political Manifesto, Marinetti.

1910 *Manifesto of the Futurist Painters*, Boccioni, Carrà, Russolo, Balla
      and Severini.
      Technical Manifesto of Futurist Painters, Boccioni, Carrà, Russolo,
      Balla and Severini.
      Against Pastist Venice, Marinetti, Boccioni, Carrà and Russolo.

1911 *Second Political Manifesto*, Marinetti.

1912 *Technical Manifesto of Futurist Literature*, Marinetti.
      *Preface to Catalogue of Exhibitions at Paris, London, Berlin, Brussels,
      Munich, Hamburg, Vienna, etc.*, signed by Boccioni, Carrà,
      Russolo, Balla and Severini.

1913 *Destruction of Grammar – Wireless Imagination and Free Words*,
      Marinetti.

Futurist Manifesto against Montmartre, Mac Delmarle and Marinetti.

The Variety Theatre, Marinetti.

The Futurist Political Programme, Marinetti, Boccioni, Carrà, Russolo.

Futurist Anti-Tradition, Apollinaire.

The Painting of Sounds, Noises and Smells, Carrà.

First appearance of *Lacerba*, edited by Papini and Soffici.

1914 *Geometric and Mechanical Splendour and Numerical Sensitivity*, Marinetti.

Weights, Measures and Prices of Artistic Genius, Corradini and Settimelli.

Futurist Architecture, Sant'Elia.

My Futurism, Papini.

Futurist Painting and Sculpture, Boccioni.

Cubism and Futurism, Soffici.

Vital English Art, Marinetti and Nevinson.

1915 *War the Only Cure for the World*, Marinetti.

Futurist Synthetic Theatre, Marinetti, Settimelli, Corra.

Warpainting, Carrà.

Italian Pride, Marinetti, Boccioni, Russolo, Sant'Elia, Sironi, Piatti.

1916 *Futurist Cinema*, Marinetti, Corra, Settimelli, Ginna, Balla, Chiti.

The New Religion of Speed, Marinetti.

First appearance of *L'Italia Futurista*, edited by Corra and Settimelli.

1917 *Manifesto of Futurist Dance*, Marinetti.

1918 *Manifesto of the Italian Futurist Party*, Marinetti.

First appearance of *Roma Futurista*, edited by Marinetti, Settimelli and Carli.

1919 *Futurist Democracy*, Marinetti.

1920 *Beyond Communism*, Marinetti.

1921 *Tactilism*, Marinetti.

The Theatre of Surprise, Marinetti.

1924 *Futurism and Fascism*, Marinetti.

After Synthetic Theatre and the Theatre of Surprise we invent Anti-

psychological Abstract Theatre of Pure Elements and the Tactile Theatre, Marinetti.

Notes

1 *Opere di F. T. Marinetti*, edited by L. De Maria (Verona 1968), vol. II, p. 261.

2 'Manifesto del Futurismo', *Opere di F. T. Marinetti*, edited by L. De Maria (Verona 1968), vol. II, p. 11.

3 C. R. W. Nevinson and Marinetti signed the Futurist Manifesto *Vital English Art* which Marinetti read at the Doré Gallery and Cambridge and published in June 1914. Like *Blast* it echoes the *Against and For* approach of Apollinaire's *Futurist Anti-Tradition*, cf. *Opere di F. T. Marinetti*, edited by L. De Maria (Verona 1968), vol. II, p. 95. Nevinson was a Vorticist at this time, but was dropped by Wyndham Lewis because he was too Futurist, cf. M. W. Martin, *Futurist Art and Theory* (Oxford 1968), p. 182.

4 Wyndham Lewis, *Blasting and Bombardiering* (London 1967), p. 33.

5 The *Manifesto on The Variety Theatre* was first published in the *Daily Mail* on 21 November 1913, cf. *Opere di F. T. Marinetti*, edited by L. De Maria (Verona 1968), vol. II, p. 70. This is the first Manifesto which is directly concerned with the theatre. The *Manifesto on Dynamic and Synoptic Declamation* of 11 March 1916 describes his technique with its dehumanized voice and geometric and mechanical gestures which must have commended itself to Mussolini. It also describes the Doré Gallery declamation referred to above. *Opere*, p. 104.

6 *Blast*, no. I, 20 June 1914.

7 This was a frequent practice among Futurists. Corra means 'run', and Ginna has a suggestion of gymnastics. Balla means 'he dances'.

8 *Italia nuova, pagine di trent'anni di storia contemporanea 1918–1948*, edited by F. Cecchini and G. Gabelli (Rocca San Casciano 1962), p. 101.

9 C. Hibbert, *Benito Mussolini* (Harmondsworth 1965), p. 156.

10 L. Fermi, *Mussolini* (Chicago 1961), p. 410.

11 *The Letters of Ezra Pound to James Joyce, with Pound's Essays on Joyce*, edited by F. Read (London 1968), p. 43.

12 A. Frattini, *Da Tommaseo a Ungaretti* (Rocca San Casciano 1959), p. 102. In the manifesto *The Synthetic Novel* of 1939 Marinetti accused Proust and Joyce of 'corrupting our synthetic, dynamic,

simultaneous Free Words into a diarrhoea of words'. *Opere di F. T. Marinetti*, edited by L. De Maria (Verona 1968), vol. II, p. 193.

13 H. Richter, *Dada* (London 1965), p. 217.

14 E. D. Lowry, 'The Lively Art of *Manhattan Transfer*', *Publications of the Modern Language Association*, vol. 84, no. 6, Oct. 1969, p. 1628.

15 This article was written before the Exhibition of Italian Futurism organized in November 1972 by the Northern Arts and Scottish Arts Council which went some way towards redressing the balance.

RUSSIAN FUTURISM

G. M. HYDE

I

IN his major poem of 1915 'The Cloud in Trousers', Vladimir Mayakovsky – the largest if not the most innovatory talent of the Futurist movement in Russian literature – designated himself 'the loudmouthed Zarathustra of our day'. It was not the only grandiose title he gave himself (he also saw himself as the Christ of *Revelations*) but it was the aptest: the prophetic stance of the schismatic seer formally inaugurating – indeed, inventing – the new era and speaking the funeral dirge of the old world and the old self suited him best. And Mayakovsky shared with Nietzsche a stridency and a desire to lay all waste in the cause of renewal, together with a neurotic urge to subdue and dominate, at great cost, the passive, intuitive side of his personality. Mayakovsky's special contempt was reserved for the immediately preceding Symbolist generation, and their literature of nuance and allusion, self-consciously located in a late phase of civilization of which it was the decadent flower. Indeed Futurism's general debt to Nietzsche was substantial; of the movements devoted to the Nietzschean passion for shaking off a decadent past and asserting the human will against determinism and habit, it was probably the most extreme and violent.

It is not surprising that many contemporary critics saw no more in the doings of Mayakovsky and his friends than gross extravagance and self-advertisement. They did not seek to please: the notorious manifesto concocted by Mayakovsky with the help of Khlebnikov, Kruchonykh, and David Burlyuk in 1912, appropriately called *A Slap in the Face of Public Taste*, seemed simply the written expression of the noisy hooliganism typical of the public appearances of the group almost up to the Revolution in 1917. Khlebnikov advertised himself stridently as 'President of the World'; Larionov and Goncharova, two of the most talented Futurist painters, paraded the streets in grotesque costumes and masks; 'happenings' were staged in cafés and restaurants, resembling Dada's feasts of misrule. Mayakovsky himself mounted aggressively ill-mannered performances – declaiming verses, shouting obscenities – at public functions, such as his notorious appearance at the opening of the Petrograd exhibition of Finnish paintings in 1917. Yet Boris Pasternak, whose different poetic make-up makes it hard to accuse him of *parti-pris*, describes his first meeting with Mayakovsky in 1914 in terms which evoke a personality of enormous creative power, a power extending beyond eccentric shock-tactics, in a manner extraordinarily sensitive and evidently just:[1]

He sat on a chair as on the saddle of a motor-cycle, leant forward, sliced and rapidly swallowed a *Wiener Schnitzel*, played cards, shifted his eyes without turning his head, strolled solemnly along the Kuznetsky, hummed sonorously and nasally, as though they were fragments of liturgy, some very deep-pondered scraps of his own and other people's work, frowned, grew, drove about and read in public; and, in the background of all this, as though in the wake of some skater dashing straight forward, there always loomed some particular day of his own, which had preceded all the days gone by – the day on which he had made his astonishing flying start that gave him the look of being so hugely unbent and unconstrained. His way of carrying himself suggested something like a decision when it has been executed and its consequences are irrevocable. This decision was his very genius; his encounter with it had so astonished him at some time that it had since become his prescribed theme for all time, and he had devoted his whole being to incarnate it without any pity or reserve.

The motor-cycle image is apposite, invoking as it does the Futurist love of rapid movement, the rush into the distance that parallels spatially their rush into the future, as in Marinetti's '*Automobile ivre d'espace*' of his early poem 'A mon Pegasse' ('A L'Automobile de Course'), 1905. And Mayakovsky's rapid, ungainly movements enact the nervous rhythms of urban life and the multiplicity of simultaneous but unrelated stimuli which the Russian Futurists, like their Italian predecessors, incorporated into their aesthetic theories, on the principle that their art must be as discontinuous as modern life, must liberate the energies, analogous to those of the machine and the city, which will thrust man forward in his conquest of time and space. As Mayakovsky wrote in his *How are verses made?* (1926):[2]

In order to write about the tenderness of love, take bus no. 7 from Lubyansky Square to Nogin Square. The appalling jolting will serve to throw into relief for you, better than anything else, the charm of a life transformed.

The great human emotions are dramatized in relation to the dynamics of the city, set free from what Mayakovsky called the 'trembles and palpitations' of Decadent and Symbolist verse. The technique resembles that of a Futurist painting like Umberto Boccioni's *The Noise of the Street Penetrates the House* (1911) or Carlo Carrà's *Jolts of a Cab* (1911), where violent discontinuities assault and distort the sensibility: if there is no exact equivalent in Russian painting, Natalia Goncharova's *The Cyclist* (1913) or Malevich's *The Knife-Grinder* (1912) are analogous. This passage from Mayakovsky also reveals that eccentric kind of materialism that led him to submit to the Bolshevik leaders that he was committed as they were to revolutionizing consciousness. Mechanization shapes not only perception (as for the Impressionists) but consciousness; though Russian Futurism, in contradistinction to Italian, seeks not so much to mechanize man as to celebrate man as victor over nature. To the Russian mind at this time, machines, primitive as they were compared with those in the West, had a revolutionary role in society, a role reflected in art; this distinguishes them from the streamlined racing-cars Marinetti eulogized, as it also distinguishes politically Russian from Italian Futurism.

Bolshevism, as Futurists pointed out with more or less enthusiasm, was like their own movement an endeavour to seize hold of the future and tie it by the tail to the lumbering ox-cart of the present. Pasternak's striking image of a skater evokes a man who has overtaken himself in his impatience with the backwardness of Russia and the stupefying irrelevancies of an exhausted literary tradition: it also suggests a certain precariousness. Leon Trotsky, in his *Literature and Revolution* (1924), was unequivocal about the fact that 'a Bohemian nihilism exists in the exaggerated Futurist rejection of the past, but not a proletarian revolutionism'. Undeniably, though, the work of the Futurists was shaped by the Revolution; indeed (through propaganda art of diverse kinds and often of high artistic merit) played a part in shaping the Revolution. Mayakovsky had been involved in revolutionary agitation long before 1917, even when he was still a schoolboy. His sometimes naïve *Schwärmerei* for power stations (he designates himself in *A Cloud in Trousers* a 'praiser of the machine and England') fed his revolutionary urge to wipe out the economic backwardness that resulted from, and upheld, Russia's autocratic régime. In the witty autobiography he sketched in 1928, *I Myself*, he reports that the boyhood sight of Prince Nakashidze's Rivet Works lit up by night persuaded him to reject nature in favour of electricity: nature was 'not up-to-date enough'. His early techniques of self-advertisement, developed in the halcyon days of the early Futurist happenings, gave way to a platform manner carefully contrived to communicate to a mass audience the truths of Socialism and of poetry without vulgar simplifications; his success here is remarkable, given the problems this synthesis presents. The style and diction of his verse draw inventively on popular (particularly urban) speech and ballad-forms in a heroic attempt to reverse Mallarmé's celebrated dictum by galvanizing the dialect of the man of letters rather than purifying the dialect of the tribe. *How are verses made?* defines the problem thus:[3]

The Revolution . . . has thrown up on to the streets the unpolished speech of the masses, the slang of the suburbs has flowed along the downtown boulevards; the enfeebled sub-languages of the intelligentsia, with its emasculated words 'ideal', 'principles of justice', 'the transcendental visage of Christ and Antichrist' – all these expressions, pronounced in little whispers in restaurants, have been trampled underfoot. There is a new linguistic element. How can one make it poetic? . . . How can we reduce the spoken language into poetry, and extract poetry from the spoken language?

But by now Mayakovsky had come far from the early days of Futurism; and these comments show a degree of commitment to the socialist state that other Futurists were incapable of. His work spans Futurism from its origins to its development into a more rationalistic, abstract Constructivism, with its remarkable projects in architecture and theatrical design. But many of the other adherents of so-called Cubo-Futurism[4] were too anarchic to adapt their art to the drawing-boards of Socialism. As Trotsky rightly said, Futurism was substantially pre-revolutionary, and Mayakovsky's deliberate tough committedness was far from being dominant in the movement. Its total break with tradition left many political possibilities open: indeed Italian Futurism gravitated toward Fascism.

2

Central to the Futurist aesthetic is the effort to liberate the word itself from the overlays of literary tradition. One way of doing this was that urged in the previous passage from Mayakovsky; another was the insistence on the autonomy of the Word and the autonomy of the literary text. If the first of these propositions runs counter to Symbolist exploration of the allusive and associative power of language, the second clearly has links with Mallarmé's famous comment to Degas: 'Poems, my dear Degas, are made not with ideas but with words.' Words are set free from the constrictions of everyday discourse in being named by the poet, chosen to enter the liberated structure of his text; but where the Symbolists devoted their art to the redemption of a fallen world, the Futurists saw the world, and the language that adheres to it, as not fallen but petrified. The Futurist poem is functional – is the drill that splits rock to disclose the precious metal. Marinetti had recommended that poets use only the infinitive of the verb, 'so that the action should not be limited to a single agent: we are more aware of actions than of actors'. He thus confirmed what Ortega y Gasset calls 'the dehumanization of art' in our time – mass man is a series of functions. The conception of human personality has changed, as D. H. Lawrence's well-known letter to Edward Garnett of June 1914, which expresses interest in Marinetti's physiology of matter, argues. Many of Marinetti's works are shaped on the page not by humanized syntax but by certain typographical devices, forming an original visual whole; likewise many of Mayakovsky's poems appeared in volumes given inventive typography and layout, either by Mayakovsky himself (who was a considerable graphic artist) or by one of his colleagues. So, as with Marinetti, words acquire new functions as they disport themselves up and down the page, growing larger and dwindling away to nothing, or forming shapes and patterns that may endorse or alternatively violate their semantic content. Futurist art is in many ways an irreverent reworking of the Wagnerian dream of the *Gesamtkunstwerk*. The attack on grammar and syntax, the emphasis on sonic and pictorial qualities of words, attacked the book as such, those rows of words trooping dutifully across the page which had become the dominant mode of communication in European society. The Futurist theatre in Russia as in Italy – and Futurism was all theatre, one way and another – demanded the total participation of the audience in a spectacle by no means tied to a text; similarly their poetry demanded the active collaboration of the reader in *making* the text (though less freedom, perhaps, than in the work of the Dadaists, whom the Futurists partly anticipated). The Ferroconcrete poetry of Vassily Kamensky (1864–1961) was as much of a random construct as the newest concrete poem or cut-up; and, like them, can be read or 'performed' in different ways, revealing each time a different significance. Velemir Khlebnikov's poem 'Exorcism by laughter' ('Zaklyatiye smekhom') (1910), which takes the Russian word for laughter (*smekh*) and makes it perform extraordinary acrobatics as different inflexions and endings build up words (mostly 'non-existent') from this root, is a way of liberating the word and thus the reader. It is an experiment in morphology rather than semantics, exploiting processes of word-formation characteristic of the Russian language; its incantatory pattern enacts the liberating effect of laughter by means of the sympathetic magic of the shaman – the witch-doctor who curiously becomes a favourite analogue for the poet in Russian Futurism, part of the strange primitivistic element so important in the movement. Of course this poem is also a stunt, like flying an aeroplane under Tower Bridge – the sort of exploit the Futurists loved, absurdly daring and exhibitionistically up-to-the-minute. Khlebnikov had been one of the signatories of the important *Slap in the Face of Public Taste* manifesto: this group of Cubo-Futurists shared common aims, though it is likely that the assault on language in this document is the work of Khlebnikov and Kruchonykh, the assault on tradition that of Mayakovsky and Burlyuk. The manifesto demands that poets be given the right to

enlarge the vocabulary of the people with factitious and fabricated words. The word is making new ... Declare boundless loathing for the language handed down to us.

Khlebnikov and Kruchonykh also produced the manifesto *The Word As Such* (*Slovo kak takovoye*) (1913), which Kruchonykh followed up with his *Declaration of the Word as Such* (*Deklaratsiya slova kak takovovo*) (1913) – a bibliographical inelegance produced by the Futurists' scorn for permanence. The first of them parallels Marinetti's title *Parole in libertà* and has comparable intentions. The Italians have a more evolved plastic sense, their Futurist movement quarrelling with Italy's museum-culture. The Russians emphasize oral and auditory effects; they draw on folk poetry and on the Scythian myth – a complex phenomenon which for present purposes may be defined as an extreme and mystical nationalism invoking the imminent triumph of primitivistic irrationalism, symbolized by the Scythians, over European rationalism and materialism – hence the shamanism already referred to, which readers unfamiliar with the phenomenon may recognize in Stravinsky's *The Rite of Spring* (1913). The earlier of these two manifestos begins with examples of expressive sound in poetry, the most abstract of which is Kruchonykh's notorious[5]

> dyr bul shchyl
> ubeshchur
> skum
> vy so bu
> r l ez

This is the complete text, as meaningless in English (or rather transliterated, as here) as in Russian, although in Russian the sounds do suggest a number of possible words or morphemes that might be made out of them. The author claimed them as extraordinarily Russian sounds (some have no real equivalent outside the Slav languages); and, under the 'Scythian' impulse to reject European influences, Khlebnikov and Kruchonykh asserted that this poem was more Russian than the whole of Pushkin. The international Pushkin, the greatest Russian poet, had been named in the *Slap in the Face* as one of the first writers to be 'thrown overboard from the steamer of modernity', a remark analogous to Pound's assertion that you needn't read Shakespeare, you could find out all you needed to know about him from 'boring circumjacent conversation'. The language of poetry should be 'transrational' (*zaumniy yazyk*), freed from the rigid forms of logic which had been attributed at least since the time of Dostoyevsky to Western thought: its expressive sonic powers should make their impact without an intermediate conceptualizing process, which dissipates energy. The effect is comparable to the 'physical transcendentalism' that Boccioni called for, and may owe something to Marinetti's *Parole in Libertà* declaration of 1912 that the liberation of the word from traditional constraints of meaning would facilitate direct communication of one 'wireless' imagination with another. The sounds created tend to be dissonant: partly in order to startle the reader into attention, but more, as Kruchonykh says, because the dissonances in our soul will know how to resolve them. There is no harmony other than the equivalence of two dissonances at an energized point: a dynamism to be found again in Imagist and Vorticist theory. Everywhere in the manifesto, and other such manifestos, is a stress on enactment and an enactment of stress. In 1913 two enactments (or plays, for want of a better word) were presented in St Petersburg which exhibited the combined talents of the group: Mayakovsky's *Vladimir Mayakovsky: A Tragedy* and Kruchonykh's extraordinary opera, for which Khlebnikov wrote a preface and Malevich designed the sets, *Victory over the Sun*.

The theme of the opera is echoed in a later poem by Mayakovsky, 'An Extraordinary Adventure which befell Vladimir Mayakovsky in a Summer Cottage' (1920). It is central to Futurism in all its manifestations: the triumph over time, conceived not as a movement into the past, as for Proust and Eliot, but as a leap into the future. In Mayakovsky's poem the poet invites the sun to tea in order to interrupt its eternal rising and setting, with which he has grown bored; by a nice conceit, the sun acknowledges that Mayakovsky, slaving over his propaganda posters all night, is manufacturing light and warmth to be disseminated like the heat of the sun, a process which demonstrates the power of the human will over nature. In Kruchonykh's opera (1913), for which Malevich executed what he said were his first Suprematist (geometrically abstract) designs, the so-called Strong Men from the Future Land, together with a team of sportsmen and a heroic aviator, overcome a Quarrelsome Man and an Ill-Intentioned Man and sundry historical personages, and celebrate a Futurist world liberated from time. Put in these terms, it sounds like a heady mixture of Expressionism and Stalinism; in fact, since the whole thing is written in *zaum*, in which grunts and whistles of the 'dyr bul shchyl' kind predominate, and the action is so chaotic that it is almost impossible to follow, it is more comic than fearful. Boris Tomashevsky, in his reminiscences of the first night (*Teatr* no. 4,

1938), makes it clear that, like the Cocteau–Picasso–Satie *Parade* of 1917, the whole venture could be enjoyed as a kind of circus entertainment, an event in which the boundaries between high art and vaudeville were trampled under-foot in the enthusiastic *mêlée*. The audience were, it seems, caught up in the affair and very good-humoured, except when direct insults were aimed at them at one point, where they became restive. *Victory over the Sun* was the most elaborate of the Futurists' advertisements for themselves.

3

After the Revolution, the Futurists dominated Soviet cultural life for a brief period. This was not because there were no other *avant-garde* movements to challenge their supremacy: the twenties were, in Russia as elsewhere, an extraordinarily rich period of artistic experiment. Their dominance was really attributable to the efforts of the talented and politically committed Mayakovsky, who put his indefatigable energies (and a sophisticated dialectical aesthetic comparable to Brecht's) at the disposal of the Bolsheviks, in his capacity as poet and propagandist of the new régime. The short-lived journal *Iskusstvo Kommuny* (*The Art of the Commune*) – produced under the taxing conditions of war communism – in which Mayakovsky and the brilliant but doctrinaire Osip Brik played a major part, printed in its first number in 1918 Mayakovsky's poem 'Directive to the Army of Art', where he called upon the Futurists to join with the Bolsheviks in a combined political and aesthetic thrust to defeat the forces of the past. It was a summons which those Futurists who were closer in spirit to the Symbolist generation, like Shershenevich (Marinetti's Russian translator) and Igor-Severyanin (founder of so-called Ego-Futurism, distinct from Mayakovsky's Cubo-Futurism) could rally to. Brik's demand for a concrete, anti-idealist art, in which artistic creation was classified as an aspect of productive process (as in Mayakovsky's *How are Verses Made?*), and the artist was seen as a worker rather than as a hero (as the Romantics and Symbolists had seen him), set the tone for a pseudo-materialist theory of the *avant garde* which persisted throughout the twenties – holding on to the designation 'Futurist' even after the term had become politically suspect, simply because only under this revolutionary banner could a coherent materialist apologia for abstraction be formulated. Meanwhile an important 'functionalist' school of criticism and theory (today known under the blanket name of Formalism) had come into being, inspired by the new linguistics of Saussure, and taking the verbal experimentation of the Futurists (with whom it was closely allied) as the necessary challenge to outworn methods of literary scholarship and as the grounds of a new critical method and total theory of literature.[6] The most remarkable essay in this context is without doubt Roman Jakobson's *The Newest Russian Poetry* (1919; revised 1921),[7] written while he was still a member of the Moscow Linguistic Circle (he subsequently emigrated to Prague, where the second edition was published, then to America); it is worth brief attention to show the link between Futurist poetry and Formalist criticism.

Jakobson does not doubt that the 'newest' Russian poetry is that of the so-called Futurists, though he declines to give any typological definition of what the movement stands for as a whole. He quotes with approval Khlebnikov's remark that 'the homeland of art is the future', and he uses this as a jumping-off point for an analysis firstly of the process by which innovation (like that of Pushkin, whom he quotes frequently and provocatively) is turned by time and platitudinous convention into orthodoxy, then of the contrary process by which poetry both of the present (taking Khlebnikov, whose work he analyses in great detail, as representative) and of the past is made new. Poetry, he maintains, is renewed from within, by specifically linguistic means; he treats poetic language throughout his essay as a kind of metalanguage. New subject matter of 'content' (to which, like I. A. Richards, he denies a distinct existence) can do no more than provide what he calls the 'motivation' for new linguistic forms – sonic, syntactic, rhythmic, etc. Analyses of innovation based upon external or social causation are therefore erroneous. Jakobson thus contrasts Marinetti's false, impressionistic, 'reportage' theory (Jakobson's own term) of the renewal of literary forms under the pressure of new forms of experience, whether inner or outer, with Kruchonikh's claim that a new form, arising from within poetic language, generates a new content – and ultimately a new world. On the basis of this comparison, Jakobson distinguishes between what he calls a poetic linguistic system (that of the Russians, and Khlebnikov in particular) and an emotional or affective linguistic system, that of Marinetti: thus poetry is characterized as obeying immanent laws, and its communicative function reduced to a minimum. Just as all the other arts consist in the shaping of self-validating 'material', so too does poetry: its 'material' is words. Consequently the study of literature is properly defined as the study of literariness ('*literaturnost*'). Biography, psychology, politics, etc., are relegated by this theory to an insignificant role; and indeed at this early date Formalist theory was content for polemical purposes to ignore extra-literary material, only later (in a work like Voloshinov's *Marxism and the Philosophy of Language*)[8] drawing it into a more elaborate scheme of sign systems. What Jakobson designates 'the world of emotion and spiritual experience' (i.e. the traditional stuff of poetry) is accounted for in his theory as a 'justification' ('*opravdanie*') of literary language: he demonstrates that even the Romantics, when their work first appeared, were received as innovators in form rather than in experiential content, the latter being understood as no more than the 'justification' of the former (Jakobson quotes from contemporary reviews to prove this). The most significant fact about the work of Khlebnikov in this context is that it moves away from a justification in the earlier work of 'irrational' poetic devices by means of an appeal to plot-structure, and toward a characteristic 'laying bare' ('*obnazhenie*') of the device without justification, as in folk narrative and ballads. The sound (or some other linguistic element) controls the sense and generates ambiguities, parallelisms, and (a favourite device of Khlebnikov's) what Jakobson calls 'metamorphoses' (various in nature but basically reversed or negative metaphors which, to employ Shklovsky's key term, 'defamiliarize' the referent).[9] The interest in folk material, in the structure of anecdotes and jokes, and in wit in all its manifestations, and the provocative exploitation of this 'low' material in a scholarly context, is characteristic of much of the literary *avant garde* of the period (Dada, Joyce, and of course Freud may be cited as analogous).

Jakobson notes that the difficulty and feeling of strangeness in Futurist texts obliges the reader to participate in the process of their realization (*realizatsia*). This formula, and the concept of 'complication' or 'making difficult' ('*zatrudnenie*') which underpins it (again the key texts are by Shklovsky), anticipates Roland Barthes' ideological distinction between the *lisible* and the *scriptible*: a formulation which certainly adds nothing significant to the discoveries of the Formalists. It is clear enough that the alliance between Futurism and the Bolsheviks belongs in this area of *realizatsia* (later to be more austerely defined in the aesthetics of Constructivism); but Jakobson does not touch on this and a full investigation of it would be extremely complex. On the purely stylistic level, it is a feature of Khlebnikov's texts that their components are related to one another by juxtaposition, or simultaneously, rather than sequentially, and this device in combination with the typical Futurist practice of realizing concretely familiar literary tropes (oxymoron, hyperbole, enallage) creates an autonomous system of relationships. There is therefore a poetic 'space' (*'prostranstvo'*), analogous to pictorial space, wherein language is multi-dimensional rather than purely sequential (as it strives to be in rational, non-poetic, discourse) and literature emulates the temporal complexity of the cinema. Among the syntactic devices employed by modern poets, and especially the Futurists, one of the most effective in the matter of creating a non-linear time continuum is 'verblessness' (*'bezglagolnost'*), and Jakobson cites instances of it from both Futurist and other poets (e.g. Marienhof). The implication of 'verblessness' is that the whole poem becomes a kind of verb. Khlebnikov himself distinguished between the words with which you can see ('Word-eyes') and those with which you can act ('Word-hands'): the antithesis may not be very sophisticated, but one can at least grasp the crucial distinction here between Symbolist semanticism and Futurist functionalism. From this it follows that Khlebnikov's poetry (and by extension that of the Futurists generally, since all who mattered learnt from Khlebnikov) is a poetry of dissociation rather than of association. This typically tendentious formulation (it appears in Jakobson almost in these exact terms, as in in the work of other Formalist critics) is of course diametrically opposed to T. S. Eliot's doctrine of re-association as he formulates it in his influential discussion of the Metaphysical poets – an essay which, however distinguished, is clearly traditionalist in intent and symbolist in practice. Jakobson enjoys himself collecting examples of dissociation and defamiliarization in children's songs, folk incantations and ceremonials, urban ballads (the *chastushki* which Mayakovsky appropriated and imitated), relating them tellingly to Khlebnikov's plays on words, puns, etc., which he classifies under the heading of 'poetic etymology' (defining this as a special category of etymology related to other kinds of etymology but in this *form* peculiar to poetry). Phonetic and semantic deformation and new meanings generated by them are an inextricable part of poetic etymology, and contribute to what Jakobson describes as the 'significant potential' of neologism: that is, its potential for abstraction (which is Jakobson's way of bringing his essay back to its initial objections against Marinetti's 'impressionism': in point of fact the Russian word *bespredmetniy* might perhaps be better rendered 'non-objective' than 'abstract'). Thus his conclusion is that, if rhyme had in its earliest historical manifestations been semantically motivated, in Khlebnikov's rhymes (and by implication in Mayakovsky's) we are made aware of what Jakobson happily describes as 'words in search of a meaning'.[10] The inventiveness and tricky exactitude of Jakobson's essay – it is itself a remarkable piece of creative writing – may stand as representative of Formalist criticism at its most iconoclastic and provocative.

The history of this critical movement has of course been fully documented and it need hardly be said that the work of Jakobson and his colleagues, whether they remained in Russia or not, progressed far beyond the context of Russian Futurism: the best work of the *Opojaz* and Moscow Linguistic Circle in the twenties and thirties is by no means confined to their studies of the *avant garde*. They effected a revolution in criticism and a radical revaluation of earlier Russian and foreign literature very like the achievement of the New Critics of England and America who, despite their greater conservatism, emerged in a similar fashion from the context of Modernism. The influence of the Russians has, however, extended further, and in more directions, than has that of the New Critics. Apart from Jakobson's own major contribution to linguistics, it is the Russian Formalists who have contributed most to modern semiotic theory, and Tsvetan Todorov's collection of French translations of Formalist essays, *Théorie de la Littérature* (1965), has been enormously influential. It is interesting to note that the crucial rapprochement between linguistics and other branches of semiotics, inaugurated by Lévi-Strauss's *Structural Anthropology*, has led to a major revival of structural poetics in the U.S.S.R.[11]

Velemir Khlebnikov, the main subject of Jakobson's essay, died in 1922. If not unambiguously the founder of Futurism in Russia, he was at all events a great innovator whose work became a bottomless mine of experiment from which other poets, including the great Mayakovsky, drew much rich ore. His output was large and is only now being assigned its proper place in Russian literary history. Very little is translated, at least into English. When he died, the anarchic experimentalism of the pre-revolutionary period died with him. Mayakovsky's journal *LEF* (an abbreviation signifying Left Front of Art), founded in 1923, forcefully upheld Futurism and non-objective (or at least non-representational) art. It terminated in 1925, and its replacement *Novyi Lef* (*New LEF*), founded in 1927, struck a curiously uncertain note in which Mayakovsky's strenuous radicalism (he was happy to see the end of the compromise New Economic Policy) was tempered by assurances, in an ever more conservative political climate, that Futurism did not reject the past as such, but only the attempt to validate outmoded styles in the present. Mayakovsky continued to produce important work up to his suicide in 1930, but the creative rapture of Russian Modernism was gone. By the time Kruchonykh published his *Fifteen Years of Russian Futurism* (1928) the movement was at an end, although Kruchonykh himself a comparatively minor talent, continued publishing until 1934, finding himself thereafter, like Pound's M. Verog,

> Detached from his contemporaries
> Neglected by the young
> Because of these reveries

– though he escaped the brutal fate of so many of the writers of his generation. So passed the most iconoclastic movement in Russian Modernism, leaving behind it the by now institutionalized figure of Mayakovsky, one of the most quoted and least understood writers in the world. It also left behind an ambivalent functionalism which, in the form of Constructivism, survived into the thirties, to leaven the dough of Socialist Realism and to inspire artists outside the U.S.S.R. Its proper place in the rich Soviet Modernist movement – and indeed the significance of that movement as a whole – is only now becoming understood.

Notes

1 Boris Pasternak, *Safe Conduct* (1931), translated by George Reavey.
2 Vladimir Mayakovsky, *How are Verses Made?*, translated by G. M. Hyde (London 1970).
3 Ibid.
4 The various (and often mutually contradictory) strands of Futurism are thoroughly documented by Vladimir Markov in his standard work *Russian Futurism* (London 1969).
5 Printed in transliteration by Vladimir Markov, *Russian Futurism*, (London 1969).
6 The best general survey remains Victor Erlich, *Russian Formalism: History, Doctrine* (The Hague 1969).
7 The Russian text and a German facing translation are included in *Texte der Russischen Formalisten Band 2*, edited by Wolf-Dieter Stempel (Munich 1972).
8 V. N. Voloshinov, *Marxism and the Philosophy of Language*, translated by L. Matejka and I. R. Titunik (London and New York 1973). First published in Leningrad in 1930.
9 Two important essays by Victor Shklovsky, *Art as Technique* and *Sterne's Tristam Shandy: Stylistic Commentary*, are included in *Russian Formalist Criticism: Four Essays*, edited and translated by L. T. Lemon and M. J. Reis (Lincoln, Neb. 1965).
10 For more on the implications for the general study of Modernism in these theories, see David Lodge, 'The Language of Modernist Fiction – Metaphor and Metonymy', pp. 481–96 below.
11 Dmitri Segal's study, *Aspects of Structuralism in Soviet Philology*, to be published in T. A. Sebeok's forthcoming volume *Structuralism Around the World*, provides impressive evidence of this.

GERMAN EXPRESSIONISM

RICHARD SHEPPARD

I

AT the time of its inception, the term Expressionism had no literary connotations. Originally used in French in 1901 as a label for eight paintings exhibited by the dilettante painter Julien Auguste Hervé in the Salon des Indépendants in Paris, it seems to have first appeared in German in April 1911 in the Foreword to the catalogue of the twenty-second exhibition of the Berliner Sezession to characterize a group of young French painters who included Picasso, Braque and Dufy. By the middle of 1911, according to the critic Karl Scheffler, it was being 'gossiped around by those who are mesmerized by words'; though, before the year was out, the authority of the art historian Wilhelm Worringer had helped to legitimize it by his reference to 'the young Parisian Synthetists and Expressionists' among whom he included Cézanne and Van Gogh. By the end of 1911, the term was being applied to any painter who was in reaction against Impressionism. The first to apply the term to German *literature* was apparently Kurt Hiller in the July 1911 supplement to the *Heidelberger Zeitung*: '. . . At least, those aesthetes who know only how to react, who are nothing more than wax-tablets for impressions, or delicately exact recording machines really do seem to us to be inferior beings. We are Expressionists.' Nevertheless the term was slow to win acceptance within literary criticism; not until the second half of 1913 did it begin to establish itself. No writer of any real standing seemed anxious to apply it to his own practice before late 1914 or early 1915. Kasimir Edschmid claimed to be completely unaware of the term until critics applied it to his stories *Die sechs Mündungen* (*The Six Outlets*) as late as 1915.

There is thus no sanction for assuming the existence of any tightly knit group conscious of themselves from the outset as Expressionists, consistently pursuing a clearly defined and commonly accepted set of objectives. Kurt Hiller, a central figure of early Expressionism, acknowledged that he did not represent any coherent movement when, in the Foreword to the first Expressionist anthology *Der Kondor (The Condor)* (1912), he wrote: 'A direction? *Der Kondor* intends to follow no particular direction.' Looking back to the early days, Expressionists often stress that early Expressionism was not a collectively held ideology, but simply the interaction of independently creative individuals. Franz Jung wrote of the group that formed round the periodical *Die Aktion* that it 'did not seem to have any particular common bond'. Jacob Picard confessed that 'one heard only vague talk about it being a total movement: it still didn't have a proper name'. And Kurt Wolff has even cast doubt on the validity of the term itself: 'People are still (and even more than ever nowadays) trying, through the concept "Expressionism", to give a group of writers who were getting into print between 1910 and 1925 the stamp of a collectivity which they never possessed.'[1] In sum, one does better to think of Expressionism as a series of explosions rather than a programmatic movement. As Paul Fechter puts it: 'The very absence of a clear, conscious formulation of tasks and ends, the confusion in the utterances about the meaning of the new art, testified to its inner necessity.'[2]

2

In the light of this, and despite the many 'definitive' theoretical pronouncements made during the years of ferment, 1910–19, the complex phenomenon called Expressionism is best looked at with caution. The term covers a multitude of people working in a variety of fields – poetry, drama, painting, cinema, architecture – and is not amenable to simple definition. Furthermore, with certain conspicuous exceptions like Kurt Pinthus's 'Zur jüngsten Dichtung' ('On the latest poetry') (1915) or Otto Flake's 'Von der jüngsten Literatur' ('On the latest literature') (1915),[3] early theoretical writings about the phenomenon tended to be either wildly ecstatic or exaggeratedly partial; and it was only when the initial explosive enthusiasm had diminished that more balanced, analytical accounts began to emerge. One thinks above all of Kasimir Edschmid's two famous lectures

'Über den dichterischen Expressionismus' ('On Literary Expressionism') (1917) and 'Über die dichterische deutsche Jugend' ('On the young generation of German writers') (1918), of his article of 1919 entitled 'Die Situation der deutschen Dichtung' ('The situation of German poetic writing')[4] and of his address with which he opened the first Expressionist exhibition in Darmstadt on 10 June 1920.[5]

Uncertain though they may have been about the positive significance of their new art, the early Expressionists were in no doubt about its destructive intent. In the Foreword to the first number of the periodical *Der Sturm* (*The Storm*) (March 1910), Rudolf Kurtz flatly declared that the journal was setting out to undermine existing society: 'We want insidiously to demolish their comfortable serious-sublime image of the world. For we consider their seriousness to be an existential inertia, the stupor of backwoodsmen ...' This violent hatred of bourgeois society common to all the Expressionists derived from their conviction that the institutions of industrial capitalism were maiming and distorting human nature by developing the intellect and the will in the service of material production and neglecting the spirit, feelings and imagination. The apparent purposefulness and technological order of contemporary society concealed, they claimed, an increasing psychic disorder. Thus, Paul Fechter:[6]

The Spirit [*Geist*] which at the beginning of the Nineteenth Century stood at the zenith of its freedom becomes, as time goes on, forced into the service of a function; is no longer an end in itself, but has meaning only insofar as it can be applied to practical life, to scientific technological matters and to the organization of the bourgeois state. The shift of emphasis from inner to outer matters is victorious all along the line. Looked at in this light, the war is the consequence, consummation and reversal of this tendency: the applied Spirit, dragged away and bound to material and technological affairs, rigidifies in the organizations of an idea long since dead (that of the state), breaks loose from its bonds in order to attain its freedom in a gigantic catastrophe of self-destruction, and as it does so, smashes the technological order through martial tools of destruction and the organizations of the state through its second phase – revolution.

Somehow or other, increased ability to manipulate the external world had been acquired at the expense of the inner life. So the price of the prevailing social order was held to be the 'mechanization of the Spirit'[7] and the transformation of human beings into de-substantiated 'relations and functions'.[8] An essential dimension (*Geist*) common to both the interior and the external worlds seemed to have been forcibly thrust out of sight, the essential unity of these two worlds destroyed: 'Gradually, of course, the ability to use our Spirit (*Geist*) disappeared. Language still provided adequate concepts for dealing with economic phenomena alone, and when that stage had been reached, it was only in economic affairs that any vitality could still be found in Germany.'[9] The human *Geist*, claimed Kurt Hiller, was increasingly unable to express itself in the affairs of everyday life and confined within a realm of inwardness, the dimensions of which were continually shrinking as the institutions of materialism and utilitarianism tightened their hold on men's personalities. These convictions were directly related to the father–son conflict in Expressionist dramas: the father symbolized all the forces of repressive and insensitive authority which had to be smashed if the son were to realize himself. In a diary entry of 3 November 1911, George Heym summed up this sentiment when he wrote: 'I would have been one of the greatest poets, if only I hadn't had such a swine of a father.'

If the Expressionists rejected the banal world of industrial society on the grounds that its artefacts were skeletal and synthetic, they also rejected Impressionist art and literature because they provided a beautiful outer 'surface' without inner substance, and disguised the perniciousness of the society from which they arose. By contrast the Expressionist artist inclined to see himself as a prophetic visionary who was called to explode conventional reality, to break through the crust that had formed around men's psyches in order to give uninhibited *expression* to the energies there imprisoned. Unable to represent, describe or imitate the 'fallen' conventional world, the visionary artist of Expressionism aimed to abstract the objects of the everyday world from their normal context, and recombine them into radiant beacons of lost inner *Geist*. As with the Vorticists, the Expressionist's respect was 'not for the subject-matter, but for the creative power of the artist; for that which he is capable of adding to the subject from himself'. Hence the appeal of the '*Ich*-Drama': a play is built around one central figure (the Son, the Beggar, the Young Man) who is seeking total self-expression and release from an oppressive environment, and to whom all other characters and events are subservient. And hence the belief in 'Revolution as an act of the spirit', in Lothar Schreyer's phrase. The artist was returning to art's essentials, he said, 'to the "inner resonance", as Kandinsky calls it, to the break-out of the creative power in man . . .'[10]

Analogously, everyday language, desiccated by functionalism, was said to have become inadequate in itself for the 'expressive' task. Words in current usage had ceased to be signs of the creative *Geist*, had lost their resonance and been reduced to one-dimensional counters. Where the late Romantic poets had tried to conserve traditional linguistic hierarchies based on the noun and to re-present the world as it had impressed itself on them, the Expressionists sought to rid themselves of the notion that words were known quantities which intellect could synthesize into an elegant, mimetic surface, and to see them as charged reservoirs of energy awaiting release by the visionary writer. Hence they were concerned with conventional syntactical relationships only insofar as these could be recharged with psychic energy. Otherwise hierarchies of language were repudiated, parts of speech held to possess equal status, interchange of conventional linguistic functions encouraged to release the inner potencies of language. The adjective, the principle agent of description, was to change function: instead of describing the impression made by the external world, it was to bring forth the hidden metaphorical dimension of the poet's subjective vision. Nouns were to be used not for referential qualities but for the expressive charges latent in them. Clearly, Expressionist writing always risked degeneration into mere rhetoric; but where that was avoided, the result was poetry and drama of startling novelty and vitality. Edschmid, in characteristically epigrammatic manner, tried to define the essence of this newness:[11]

Thus, the whole space becomes a vision for the Expressionist artist. He doesn't see, he envisions. He doesn't depict, he experiences. He doesn't reproduce, he fashions. He doesn't take, he searches. Now the chain of facts exists no more: factories, houses, disease, whores, tumult and hunger. Now there is only the vision of these.

However, the Expressionist concepts of liberation and re-spiritualized art are not as straightforward as they may appear. What exactly was meant by the authentic Self, the *Geist* which was to be re-discovered and released? Was it Spirit or Energy, the transrational or the irrational? This ambiguity was nothing new: nor was it peculiar to the Expressionists. Nietzsche, one of the principal fore-bears of Expressionism, had talked of Dionysus both as amoral, anarchic energy and as self-regulating energy. Similarly, and more recently, Herbert Marcuse has defined Eros as that which 'knows no value, no good and evil, no morality', yet goes on to suggest that there is a 'natural self-restraint' in Eros.[12] Erwin Loewenson, one of the founders of Der Neue Club, regarded self-fulfilment as 'heightening of vital intensity', whereas Kurt Hiller, his co-founder, described the power of regeneration as 'idea-alistic', a concept which implies some sort of immanent order and restraint rather than formless ecstatic intensity. Though this ambiguity was never resolved, it is clearly crucial. Taken to one extreme, it can lead to various forms of political or religious commitment. Taken to its other, it can lead to nihilism and self-annihilation.

The notion of art as expressive vision was, as Herwarth Walden realized at the time, not new. The unique defining feature in Expres-sionism was, rather, the nature of the symbols employed to give this vision form. Although it had a neo-Romantic side – as in Else Lasker-Schüler's fragile, fairy-tale world – the real innovators among the Expressionists were men like Stadler, Kaiser and the Bauhaus archi-tects who chose to refashion the tough, sinewy language, rhythms and materials of contemporary industrial civilization, to see 'humanity in the whores and the divine in the factories'.[13] This it is, then, that provides the final term for a tentative definition of Expressionism: the attempt to create a visionary world, liberated from the language and values and patterns of bourgeois society, expressive of the deepest levels of the personality (*Geist*, variously understood), and utilizing symbols derived from the modern industrial world. As Kurt Pinthus put it:[14]

To free reality from the confines in which it appears, to free ourselves from reality, to transcend it not with its own means or by running away from it but, by grasping it all the more passionately, to defeat it and dominate it through the penetration, flexibility and desire for lucidity of the mind and the intense, explosive power of feeling . . . That is the common will behind present-day poetic literature.

3

The question of the relationship of revolutionary art to social revolution adds a further complexity to the problem of defining Expressionism. Although most Expressionists felt this problem was crucial, few agreed about the answer. Nevertheless, three conceptions of the relationship of art to politics seem distinguishable in the period up to the end of the First World War. First, there was the meliorist view, subscribed to by the anarcho-humanist Franz Pfemfert and, from about 1914, by the Activists around Kurt Hiller. For these, art related to politics through its social content and humane idealism, contributing to the 'redemption of the world' and assisting in 'the building up of the Kingdom of God'. Not surprisingly, they frequently lapsed into fantastic utopianism and too easily assumed that the significance of a work of art resided in its conscious message. Second, there was that 'ecstatic destructivism' typified by Ludwig Rubiner's influential essay 'Der Dichter greift in die Politik' ('The poet takes a hand in politics'),[15] where he held that the poet must create the 'Will to Catastrophe' and shatter conventional institutions and illusions by creating images which released intense psychic energies into the everyday world. This was an approach whose limitations became only too apparent with the outbreak of war, when the problem became how to turn expressive energy from destruction to creation. Third, there was the view – developed, for example, by Herwarth Walden from about 1914 – which succeeded in finding a positive role for art within the state while avoiding both the *naïveté* of the reformists and the daemonism of the ecstatics. Although Walden is usually thought of as the a-political Expressionist *par excellence*, his a-politicism derived from the assumption that art was about the organization of energies and not the propagation of ideas. Denying that it was the business of art to have an overtly political *content*, he nevertheless accepted that art could have far-reaching political *effects*; and his essay 'Das Verstehen der Kunst' ('The Understanding of Art') asserted that the effect of all visionary art was to break down the walls which men have constructed around themselves and to evoke in them the 'senses and impulses' in which the 'generally human' consisted. Art was thus to effect a psychic revolution in the individual, not to project ideal revolutionary possibilities into some unknown future.

The social upheavals in Germany of 1918 and 1919 put these theories to the test; and, without exception, all were found to be unsatisfactory when measured against the realities of social and political change. Consequently, after about 1919, many Expressionists, feeling either the impotence of their moderate theories, or disillusion with the middle-class Socialism of the Weimar Republic, moved over to the doctrinaire left. Others lapsed into vapid political intellectualism; others still moved from a rejection of industrial capitalism to an obscurantist rejection of all science, technology and industry in the name of pre-industrial organizations – became, in other words, proto-Nazis.

Such wide disagreements on fundamentals meant that the Expressionist scene was one of highly fluid relationships and intensely personal hostilities. Friedrich Schulze-Maizier says of Der Neue Club:[16]

The latent malice of intellectuals rarely affected me so intimately as it did in the midst of this certainly highly-gifted Berlin circle. Now and then it felt as if one had landed in a tribe of headhunters.

Alfred Richard Meyer described the acrimony of Expressionist Berlin even more graphically:[17]

With the best will in the world, you simply cannot imagine today the excitement with which we sat of an evening in the Café des Westens or on the street by Gerold's by the Gedächtniskirche, quietly sipping our drinks and waiting for the appearance of the *Sturm* or *Aktion*. We weren't thinking so much about the intoxicating feeling of getting into print as keeping a watchful eye open for the possibility of being attacked in words which could bite like quick-lime or sulphuric acid. Incredible animosity which we had to counter was all around us in the air . . . Had new fronts developed? Was another turncoat due to be exposed? What camp threatened to split? Were ominous creakings to be heard in the timbers of a friendship? Who was winning? Who was falling?

There were many who found this hyper-sensitivity and neurotic intellectualism remarkably stimulating. When, for example, Heym joined Der Neue Club in Spring 1910, his poetic style matured strikingly. Acrimonious the atmosphere may have been; but this acrimony was the product of the interaction of highly creative individuals who were experiencing, with Georg Trakl, the 'nameless disaster' of the collapse of their worlds, and so felt compelled to discover a new identity. Unfortunately the seriousness underlying this intent frequently degenerated into a self-dramatizing egomania, unrelieved by self-irony. Faced with a world drained of meaning, many Expressionists attempted to flood the vacuum with their own egos; when this attempt failed, or the world recoiled, they often succumbed to madness or annihilating despair, or sold out to a totalitarian system.

4

Throughout the entire Expressionist decade, the principal centre was Berlin, whither aspiring writers most naturally gravitated and whence provincial Expressionism took much of its tone. Within the complexity of the Berlin scene itself, two major focus-points are discernible: the journals *Die Aktion* and *Der Sturm*. Consideration of these and their associated institutions gives a useful impression of the character of the movement.

In the spring of 1909, a group of students at the University of Berlin left the student *Verband* known as the Freie Wissenschaftliche Vereinigung (Free Academic Association) and, under the 'eternal presidency' of Kurt Hiller, founded Der Neue Club. Other prominent members included Erwin Loewenson, Erich Unger, Simon Ghuttmann, David Baumgardt, Armin Wassermann, Fritz Koffka, Ernst Blass, Jakob van Hoddis, Robert Jentzsch, and, from about March 1910, Georg Heym. At the first public session, held before an audience of several hundred students on 8 November 1909 in Neumanns Festsälen, Loewenson and Hiller attacked the decadence and apathy of the age, and invited men of like mind to join with them in trying to discover new modes of feeling and new directions in art. From then on, the Club met every Wednesday evening in an upper room of the Nollendorf-Kasino to discuss literary subjects. From an initial Wildean aestheticism, the Club turned to problems of personal regeneration and social reconstruction. Accordingly, between 1 June 1910 and 3 April 1912, it staged eight public sessions, the so-called

Neopathetische Cabarets, in such semi-formal venues as the Neue Sezession on the Ku-damm or the back room of the old Café Austria on the Potsdamerstrasse. (The term *Neopathos*, coined by Loewenson, was defined by him as 'the will to a new, revolutionary vitalism'.) Cabaret, they insisted, was not 'dirty songs sung to a piano' but serious readings of prose and verse, mainly concerning the growing emptiness of city life and the approaching threat of disaster. A quarrel between van Hoddis and Hiller – they differed, it seems, about the meaning of *Geist* – took Hiller and some others away from the Club in February 1911 to found their own literary cabaret called Das Gnu, and, by mid-1912, the disintegration of the group was complete. But it was out of the intellectual and aesthetic mood stimulated by the Club together with the left-wing humanist politics of the journal *Der Demokrat* (*The Democrat*) that *Die Aktion* (*Action*), perhaps the main Expressionist periodical, came into being on 20 February 1911. Here was a journal whose novel combination of literary (and later graphic) art with various forms of non-aligned political radicalism exactly corresponded to the needs of the growing number of young writers.

At first, *Die Aktion* confined its external activities to sponsoring reading evenings and lecture evenings, and associating itself with informal literary cabarets. But in time its activities began to diversify. Taking his cue from other Expressionist publishing houses such as the Alfred Richard Meyer Verlag, with its series of *Lyrische Flugblätter* (*Lyric Fly-sheets*) (1907–23), Pfemfert began to issue, in October 1916, the first numbers of the four series of *Aktion* books. These were: *Aktionsbücher der Aeternisten* (*The Action Aeternist Series*), works which in Pfemfert's view were of imperishable worth; the *Aktions-Bücher*, the best-known of which was the anthology of war poetry entitled *1914–1916*; the *Politische Aktions-Bibliothek* (*The Action Political Library*); and, from 1917, the series of pamphlets called *Der rote Hahn* (*The Red Cock*) which, after the 1918 Revolution, concerned itself almost exclusively with left-wing politics. On 1 November 1917, Pfemfert opened a bookshop in the Kaiserallee 222 where, after the fashion of *Der Sturm*, exhibitions of graphic art were held and the *Aktion* books were sold. The shop closed down in October 1918. In 1915 *Die Aktion* had even founded its own miniscule political party – Pfemfert's Anti-Nationale Sozialisten-Partei – which, although an underground group during the war, published a political manifesto in *Die Aktion* in November 1918, the signatories to which included Albert Ehrenstein, Karl Otten and Carl Zuckmayer. Nothing is heard of this party after the uprisings of 1919, and it probably died a natural death in the general disillusionment of the left which followed upon the murders of Karl Liebknecht and Rosa Luxemburg in January 1919 and the suppression of the Spartakists in March of the same year.

The editor of *Der Sturm*, Herwarth Walden, was, in contrast to Pfemfert, a highly sophisticated and cultured man; an aesthete who was equally at home in the worlds of music, literature and the visual arts. During the first years of its life, however, *Der Sturm* (which had first appeared on 3 March 1910) concerned itself primarily with the graphic arts. Only later, with Walden's discovery of the poetry of August Stramm, did literature and literary theory assume a central place in its pages. Consequently, whereas the *Neopathetiker* and *Aktivisten* tended to associate themselves with *Die Aktion*, the *Kubisten*, the *Futuristen*, the neo-Romantics, the politically indifferent and all those concerned more with formal theories than with 'content' found *Der Sturm* and its institutions more congenial. At the beginning of 1912 *Der Sturm* moved from Berlin-Halensee to the Potsdamerstrasse 18; and later that year, Walden rented a house which was about to be pulled down, the Tiergartenstrasse 34a, to stage the first of the two *Sturm* exhibitions of graphic art in March and April 1912. The first of these presented, *inter alia*, 'Der blaue Reiter' ('The Blue Rider') and a selection of paintings by Oskar Kokoschka; the second had paintings by the Italian Futurists. Both exhibitions were very successful: the Futurist exhibition – the opening day of which ended in a brawl between the invited audience and the foreign guests of honour which had to be broken up by the police – sometimes attracted a thousand visitors a day. The bourgeois press were outraged by the new art; *avant-garde* painters were delighted that here at last was a man who was prepared to exhibit and even partly finance their work. 'Sturm-Ausstellungen' ('Storm Exhibitions') were held regularly thereafter for more than a decade, exhibiting work by many of the significant modern painters at a time when they were unknown. In June 1913 Walden moved the entire enterprise – periodical, publishing firm, exhibition rooms, private dwelling and the 'Sturm-Kunstschule' ('Storm Art School') – to their permanent site at Potsdamer-strasse 134a. Here, starting on 1 September 1916, the famous and occasionally tempestuous Sturm-Abende were held every Wednesday evening, largely in order to promote the poetry of August Stramm and his epigones. In 1917 a *Sturm* art bookshop section was added; in 1918 two experimental theatres were founded under the direction of Lothar Schreyer in Berlin and Hamburg. Not only was *Der Sturm* a more comprehensive organization than *Die Aktion*; it was also a more missionary one. During the pre-war and post-war years, travelling exhibitions were staged throughout the world – in March 1914 alone, twelve exhibitions were open in various cities. Even during the war years, *Sturm* exhibitions were mounted throughout Germany and in neutral countries like Sweden. In 1914, a subsidiary office was established in Paris. During the winter months of 1916–17, public Sturm-Abende were held in Dresden, Frankfurt, Jena, Hamburg, Hannover and Leipzig. The break-up of this organization – which for all its size and ambitiousness was not run commercially, and partially financed from the part-time earnings of Walden's wife – followed Walden's growing disillusionment with those of his collaborators who he felt had betrayed him and the ideals of *Der Sturm*, and his growing commitment to Communism. This allegiance caused him finally to emigrate in 1932 to Russia, where he disappeared without trace in the great purges.

In the provinces, the Expressionist institutions – the café, the periodical, the back-room press, the reading evening, the little book – were with local variations not unlike those of Berlin. Nevertheless, each city managed to develop its own distinctive Expressionist character. Munich, for instance, was more of a cosmopolitan centre than Berlin; and with its tradition of artistic bohemianism attracted graphic artists from Scandinavian and Slav countries. In Leipzig the central figure of a highly enterprising group was the publisher Ernst Rowohlt, who had founded his press in a single room in 1908 and held court daily at the Mittagstisch in the back room of Wilhelms Weinstuben. Kurt Pinthus was his principal reader; from late October 1912, Franz Werfel was one of his sub-readers. Associated with this group were Kurt Wolff (who had financed Rowohlt and who in February 1913 took single control of the Rowohlt Verlag, changing its name to the Kurt Wolff Verlag) and the dramatist

Walter Hasenclever. Between them, this group brought off several publishing coups: Georg Heym's first volume of poems *Der ewige Tag* (*The Everlasting Day*) in April 1911; Franz Werfel's first volume of poems *Der Weltfreund* (*The Friend of All Men*) in December 1912; Georg Trakl's first volume of poems in May 1913. The Leipzig group was also responsible for the periodical *Die Weissen Blätter* (*The White Leaves*) which, produced in Switzerland between 1916 and 1918, provided German writers with one of their few war-time platforms for the expression of radical and pacifist political views. The Prague Expressionists, who formed a German-speaking enclave within a Slav culture and included such men as Max Brod, Franz Kafka and Paul Kornfeld, were rather more introverted than their German contemporaries, and maintained a certain distance between themselves and the rest of the movement.

5

Unexpectedly, the most interesting provincial centre of the Expressionist decade proved to be Zürich, where many Expressionists sought refuge from censorship, conscription and scarcity, and where Dadaism originated. Although several of the Zürich Dadaists – foremost among whom were Hugo Ball, Richard Huelsenbeck, Hans Arp, Emmy Hennings and the Rumanians Marcel Janco and Tristan Tzara – had previously worked on Expressionist journals in Germany, the German Dadaist movement attained self-consciousness partly in reaction against the politically utopian, activist Expressionism encountered in Zürich (represented chiefly by Albert Ehrenstein, Leonhard Frank, Ludwig Rubiner, René Schickele and Franz Werfel). Whilst Expressionists and Dadaists united in rejecting the civilization which had 'produced the flame-thrower and the machine-gun', the Dadaists gradually became convinced that something vital was missing from midwar literary Expressionism. Somehow the aesthetic politics, utopian dreams and abstract intellectualism which characterized the literary side of the movement by 1916 were felt to be an inadequate and even conservative response to the realities of the twentieth century. Consequently, from within Dada, one finds the emergence of a radical critique of Expressionism as it stood half-way through the war. Where the Expressionists had tried to evolve a new 'expressive' language and attempted to make reality conform to that language, the Dadaists, through their totally a-syntactical and non-referential language, declared the inability of human institutions to capture a protean reality. Where the Expressionists frequently stood poised above the twentieth century, unsure of their commitment to it, simultaneously looking back to an ideal past and forward to a utopian future, the Dadaists, though their commitment was always ironic, refused to abandon their involvement with the banalities of the twentieth century. Where the Expressionists were frequently afflicted by a messianic consciousness which showed itself politically in their desire to be leaders of 'redeemed communities', aesthetically in their desire to assert the subjective *Ich* as the centre of the universe, the Dadaists were always conscious of the relativity of their own egos within the flux of becoming. Where Expressionist despair was frequently that of men who find their image of a concentric universe overwhelmed by a vision of a universe in flux, the Dadaists committed themselves joyfully to this universe in flux and created 'disposable' works of art to celebrate it. Where the Expressionists sought to fill the vacuum which was opening up before them with their subjective expressive energies, the Dadaists attempted to concretize the fluctuating energies which were already at work in the vacuum, declared that these 'concretions' were in themselves images of an interior world and claimed that what to the unattuned eye looks like nothingness was in reality plenitude. Where Expressionism was frequently the declaration that an end had been reached and that hope lay in the ecstatic and possibly destructive release of pent-up energies, Dada was the affirmation that a new beginning had taken place, that creative life went on in new ways, and that the oppressive father-figure of the Expressionists could become the harmless 'Daddy' if the life-force were trusted.

It took a long time for German Dada to develop its full critique of Expressionism. Zürich Dada went part-way, but after Richard Huelsenbeck's return to Berlin in January 1917, the Swiss group became conservative and aesthetic to such an extent that Huelsenbeck called it a 'manicure-salon of the fine arts'. That this remark was not entirely unjustified can be seen from the following extract from their *Manifesto of Radical Artists* which was published on 4 May 1919:[18]

... We artists want to exist within the state, within its very life and take a share in all its responsibilities. We affirm that the laws of art of our age have already been formulated by and large ... We oppose lack of system ...

Berlin Dada began with the foundation of the Club Dada in February 1918; and here the critique of Expressionism reached its zenith. In the turmoil of Berlin where hunger and death were obtrusive realities, Dada became concerned with aggressively anti-establishment politics, and the Dadaists there gradually came to see that, contrary to appearances, the utopianism and revolutionary rhetoric of much latter-day literary Expressionism concealed a deep-seated will to conform. Hence, Huelsenbeck attacked Expressionism on the grounds that it was providing an official literature for the emergent bourgeois Socialist parties and that it offered an escape from the horrors of the trenches and the realities of radical social reconstruction:[19]

In Germany, the Expressionist movement had developed with the most transparent consistency into the established style of art. Its tendency to inwardness, its hankering after the mysticism of Gothic cathedrals, its proclamation of humanity were therefore construed as a beneficial reaction to the ghastly slaughter of the trenches. People saved themselves through an art which promised its proselytes intense pleasure through that abstraction and turning-away from things which was mentioned above. The Dadaist saw in Expressionism a withdrawal, a flight from the hard angularity of things.

The accuracy of this analysis can perhaps be gauged from the fact that shortly after Noske's troops had bloodily put down the Spartakist risings and murdered Karl Liebknecht and Rosa Luxemburg, an officially sponsored evening was held in the Berlin Blüthnersaal at which 'revolutionary' Expressionist poems by Paul Zech, Johannes Becher, Walter Hasenclever and Franz Werfel were read. At this gathering, Kurt Erich Meurer is reported to have said: 'May the state look upon the artist, who is called to raise the level of thought and feeling of the people, as an official of humanity, and may it reward him as such.'[20] Hence, the Berlin Dadaists developed a radically left-wing stance, a non-ideological *Gefühlskommunismus*. But the left-wing stance of the Dadaists differed from the left-wing stance of the Expressionists of the later war years because the Dadaist call for revolution went hand in hand with a disbelief in the power of social revolution to alter things in any final way. Where the Expressionists appeared to desire the once-and-for-all revolution, the Dadaists were committed to permanent revolution – to the process of running in order to stay on the same spot.

If Berlin Dada is the ironic acknowledgement of the need for and the impossibility of revolution, then the history of the final years of literary Expressionism is the record of the disillusion of men who had hoped for everything and found themselves unable to live with the ambiguities of a situation far short of their utopian hopes. In 1917, Expressionist drama (after four lean years) came again to life, proclaiming the hope of the new humanity and the redeemed revolutionary community in plays such as Fritz von Unruh's *Jüngster Sohn* (*Youngest Son*), Ernst Toller's *Die Wandlung* (*The Transformation*) and Ludwig Rubiner's *Die Gewaltlosen* (*The Non-violent Ones*). By 1920, however, Toller's *Masse Mensch* (*Mass Man*), Fritz von Unruh's *Platz* (*Square*) and Georg Kaiser's *Gas I* and *II* registered the shattering of these utopian dreams. These men, like most of the other Expressionists who survived the war, had hoped that a new order would arise, phoenix-like, from the holocaust and grant legitimate release for their expressive energies. When, however, they discovered that the German Revolution was not the Parousia which, by their own rhetoric, they had persuaded themselves would succeed Armageddon, disillusionment was boundless. Some wandered into exile, others committed suicide, not a few died early deaths. Others turned to mysticism, became Roman Catholics, or allied themselves with totalitarian political parties. In contrast, the German Dadaists, who had never deluded themselves with their own prophetic rhetoric, did not generally undergo such a profound experience of disillusionment. Realizing all along that the distorted structures which the pre-1914 Expressionists had so fiercely attacked still prevailed, even though their semi-feudal surface had been stripped away by the war, they were prepared for a long and probably hopeless struggle against a de-personalized civilization. Thus, whereas German Dada ended as the sardonic, self-ironizing commitment against an established and continuing state of affairs, Expressionism finished as a cry of incredulous and disorientated despair that their situation had not been revolutionized once and for all. If the post-war Expressionists were so confused that they were unable to decide whether Dr Caligari was a megalomaniac dictator or a compassionate therapist, and whether they themselves were his zombies, his victims, or simply patients who were to be healed back into conformity by his benevolence, the German Dadaists at least knew that they were the inmates of Caligari's asylum, and saw that the original Expressionist dream, the overthrow of a repressive order, was only realizable by a change of vision rather than a revolutionary act. Expressionism seems now to have foundered on the mistaken belief that it is possible to change the world by forcing it to conform to a set of pre-existent ideals. Dada, in contrast, seems to declare that the first step towards change consists in the acceptance of things as they are, in their absurdity; that the second step consists in persuading a situation to change under the impetus of its own inherent dynamic; and that the third step consists in laughter at the realization that in reality nothing has changed at all.

Notes

1 See Paul Raabe and Karl Ludwig Schneider (eds.), *Expressionismus: Aufzeichnungen und Erinnerungen der Zeitgenossen* (Freiburg 1965), pp. 125, 141, 292.

2 Paul Fechter, *Der Expressionismus* (Munich 1920), p. 17.

3 Both are reprinted in Paul Raabe (ed.), *Expressionismus: Der Kampf um eine literarische Bewegung* (Munich 1965), pp. 68–79 and 53–65.

4 All three items are reprinted in Kasimir Edschmid, *Frühe Manifeste* (Darmstadt 1960), pp. 13–43 and 85–90.

5 In Paul Raabe (ed.), *Expressionismus: Der Kampf um eine literarische Bewegung* (Munich 1965), pp. 173–6.

6 Paul Fechter, *Der Expressionismus* (Munich 1920), p. 3.

7 See Kurt Hiller, *Gustav Wyneken's Erziehungslehre und der Aktivismus* (Hanover 1919), p. 9.

8 See Gottfried Benn, 'Bekenntnis zum Expressionismus' (1933), in Paul Raabe (ed.), *Expressionismus: Der Kampf um eine literarische Bewegung* (Munich 1965), pp. 235–46.

9 Carl Sternheim, *Die deutsche Revolution* (Berlin 1919), p. 11.

10 Lothar Schreyer, 'Herwarth Waldens Werk', in *Der Sturm: Ein Erinnerungsbuch* (Baden-Baden 1954), p. 114.

11 Kasimir Edschmid, 'Über den dichterischen Expressionismus', in *Frühe Manifeste* (Darmstadt 1960), p. 32.

12 Herbert Marcuse, *Eros and Civilization* (London 1969), pp. 41, 181.

13 Edschmid, 'Über den dichterischen Expressionismus', in *Frühe Manifeste* (Darmstadt 1960), p. 33.

14 Kurt Pinthus, 'Zur jüngsten Dichtung', in Paul Raabe (ed.), *Expressionismus: Der Kampf um eine literarische Bewegung* (Munich 1965), p. 70.

15 *Die Aktion*, 22 May and 5 June 1912.

16 Georg Heym, *Dichtungen und Schriften*, edited by K. L. Schneider, vol. 6, p. 24.

17 Alfred Richard Meyer, *Das Maer von der Musa Expressionistica* (Düsseldorf 1948), pp. 12, 13.

18 Quoted in full in José Pierre, *Le Futurisme et le Dadaisme* (Paris 1967), p. 120.

19 Quoted in Paul Raabe and Karl Ludwig Schneider (eds.), *Expressionismus: Aufzeichnungen und Erinnerungen der Zeitgenossen* (Freiburg 1965), p. 354.

20 Quoted by J. C. Middleton, 'Dada versus Expressionism or The Red King's Dream', in *German Life and Letters*, vol. 15, 1961–2, p. 45.

DADA AND SURREALISM

ROBERT SHORT

I

THE pre-war Modernist movements had attempted to recreate the syntax of art to accommodate modern experience, and had increasingly proposed that notions of a fixed and immutable reality and of wholly self-conscious and rational man were discredited. Dada and Surrealism went further; they suggested that the transformation was so great as to question the meaning and purpose of art itself, and rejected the idea that the creative licence this new awareness held out should merely take the form of a proliferation of aesthetic '-isms', each characterized by nothing more radical than certain innovations in the language of form. As beneficiaries of the inventiveness of the previous generations, Dadaists and Surrealists freely exploited the stylistic breakthroughs that had been made. What they disputed was whether, in the light of new knowledge about man's psychology and the nature of the universe which was his environment, the production of works of art or literature was any longer feasible, morally justifiable or socially worthwhile. The Dadaists suggested that reality was too elusive and incoherent to be formally represented. Our senses fed us misleading information; the lucid concepts of classical rationalism could not grasp its protean nature; words – by definition instruments of public communication, continuity and order – deformed and betrayed life's authentic character as a discontinuous sequence of immediate experiences. Hence, Dadaists and Surrealists claimed that there was no longer any point in writing *about* experience: the act of the poet or artist should be to put his whole sensitivity in direct contact with the universe in a stance of cosmic passivity. In place of the maker of forms, Surrealism posited a new image of the artist as someone who was characterized by his availability to chance, to the promptings of the unconscious and internal impulses, who welcomed everything that occurred spontaneously. The poet was a spiritual adventurer or explorer: productivity was of only secondary importance, art as commonly understood a restriction. Poetic significance was attributed to a certain style of life and to the ability to give free rein to desire; a moral exigency was given priority over an aesthetic one. Thus the urge to perfect authenticity which Dada and Surrealism carried to its ultimate threatened to end up as complete abdication: poet and artist were being invited, not to art, but to silence or action.

Although cultural factors might by themselves have eventually produced a movement of such radical doubt, it was the impact of the First World War which persuaded poets of the younger generation that western culture was mortal and had been touched in its foundations, that the victor countries had suffered a débâcle in ideas and ethics as dramatic as that of the régimes, aristocracies and frontiers among the defeated. The war confirmed a growing conviction – hardly there in the pre-war Cubists and Futurists – that the West's obsession with technological advance and the over-estimation of reason at the expense of feeling led straight to destructive megalomania. The exploding of the myth of progress encouraged the Dadaists' tendency to identify life with the instantaneous and the ephemeral: the ambition to make durable, classic works for posterity died. But the Dadaists and Surrealists also despised the contemporary public that patronized the arts: thus the anguished self-interrogation, 'Why do you write?', thrown down as an open challenge in the Pre-Surrealist Parisian review, *Littérature*, in 1919, was supplemented by the equally disturbing question, 'For whom do you write?' A civilization that had condoned such inhumanities did not deserve the satisfactions of art. Language had been debased by its use in propaganda to the point where the disparity between word and truth rendered it worthless. More, the war revealed the fraudulence of bourgeois pretensions to separate cultural issues from economic and social ones; erstwhile champions of a spiritual life 'above the struggle' had set new records for war-mongering chauvinism. The Dadaists and Surrealists welcomed the demolition of the ivory towers. The highly volatile post-war situation, the success of the Bolshevik Revolution, itself an achievement largely of intellectuals, gave an appearance of viability, albeit short-lived and illusory, to the most utopian visions of a younger generation of rebels. Simultaneously artistic, linguistic, moral and social, the pressures on the imagination to issue out of the laboratories of the experimental artist and to take the offensive in the world at large were irresistible. It is these circumstances that explain why Dadaism and Surrealism, both in process of formation between 1915 and 1920, were not so much new schools of poetry and art as movements of the spirit involving definite moral, philosophical, and, in the case of Surrealism, political commitments.

2

Who invented Dada? Where and when did it begin? New York, Barcelona, Zürich, Berlin, Hannover, Cologne and Paris, were all centres of Dadaist activity at one time or another between 1915 and 1923. The former Dadaists themselves, as if still pursuing their campaign against history, have done their best to confuse the traces of its origins. Claims for priority have been made on behalf of the activities of Marcel Duchamp and Francis Picabia in New York in 1915. Their mutual taste for destructive paradoxes and blasphemies against all manner of received ideas, the irony behind Duchamp's 'Readymades' and Picabia's representations of men and women as functionless machines, the frigid humour with which they emptied life of its spiritual content: all these were later recognized as Dadaist in spirit. But it was in Zürich, another neutral city offering a haven to a disparate band of refugees from the military conflict, that occurred that essential 'magic fusion of ideas and personalities' (Richter) that launched the movement. Although the accounts of the participants themselves are so conflicting that no one will ever know which among Tristan Tzara, Hugo Ball or Richard Huelsenbeck discovered the seminal word, Dada, its first appearance in print was in Hugo Ball's introduction to the unique number of his review, the *Cabaret Voltaire*, which came out in June 1916. With its multiple meanings in a variety of languages – an enthusiastic affirmation in Slav, an obsessional preoccupation in French, a hobby-horse in baby-talk – Dada was ideally apt for infuriating the *bourgeoisie*. It was almost a manifesto in itself.

Dada was not identifiable with any one personality, viewpoint or style, nor did it ever acquire a single coherent programme. The focus of emphasis within the movement was continually shifting, never more so than during the war years in Switzerland. The heterogeneity that characterized the Zürich community of expatriates, pacifists, deserters and revolutionaries (Lenin, Romain Rolland, Wedekind, and James Joyce among them) extended to the group that staged entertainments at the ironically named Cabaret Voltaire and mounted exhibitions at the Galerie Dada in the Bahnhofstrasse. The only native Swiss among the original Dadaists was Sophie Taeuber, who married the Alsatian painter and poet, Hans Arp. Tristan Tzara and Marcel Janco were Romanians, Walter Serner was from Austria, Marcel Slodki from the Ukraine; the other central figures, Hugo Ball, his wife Emmy Hennings, Richard Huelsenbeck and Hans Richter were Germans. Though all shared a common hatred of the war being fought beyond the frontier, the exacerbated individualism, universal doubt and aggressive iconoclasm that now appears as Dada's hallmark did not prevail without a struggle over other conceptions of what Dada might be. For the first two years it was the mystical, naïve and constructive-minded Hugo Ball who set the tone rather than the mercurial and increasingly nihilistic Tristan Tzara. A contradictory personality himself, Ball was at once a fervent Catholic and a Bakuninist Anarchist, mystic and entrepreneur, idealist and sceptic. His journal, *Die Flucht aus der Zeit* (*Flight out of Time*) (1927) reveals the earnest intent behind the rowdy provocations, primitivist dance, cacophony and Cubist theatricals that went on at the Dadaist soirées. Image-smashing was only a preliminary act of mental hygiene after which the real task of rehabilitating art as a 'meaningful instrument of life' could begin. As Hans Arp put it: 'We were seeking an art based on fundamentals to cure the madness of the age and a new order of things that would restore the balance between heaven and hell.' The scandal and subversion were only the obverse side of a deep moral concern to regain a lost purity: Dada was to restore the mind to health and not just measure the ravages of the disease.

This view of Dadaism was especially prevalent among the painters – among them Richter, Janco, Baumann, Arp and Alberto Giacometti – for whom the unlimited freedom to experiment offered by Dada was a main attraction. For all that Dadaism might be a 'state of mind' shared by all, the writers could much more easily express absolute negation by means of verbal protest than could the painters deny constructive form by plastic means. From the summer of 1918, by which time Hugo Ball had left Zürich for the Ticino, and Tzara, in alliance with the recently arrived Francis Picabia, had become the impresario of Dada, the artists and writers found themselves moving in opposite directions. While the latter progressed towards nothingness with ever gayer blasphemies and ever more playful scepticism, the artists were seeking to become once again 'a positive force in life'. In April 1919, after forming the Association of Revolutionary Artists, they published a manifesto the terms of which were closer in their cloudy idealism and vacuous demagoguery to the spirit of the tamed activist wing of Expressionism, now turned social-democrat, than to anarchistic Dada. 'The spirit of abstract art,' they said, 'represents an enormous widening of man's sense of liberty. We believe in a brotherly art: this is art's new mission in society. Art demands clarity, it must serve towards the formation of a new man.' With the appearance of this text and the return of the exiles to their native lands when peace was signed, Zürich Dada came to an end.

The Dada virus was carried to Berlin by Richard Huelsenbeck, the phonetic poet who had employed savage negro rhythms 'to drum literature into the ground'. The German capital, its resistance sapped by defeat and civil war, was quickly infected after Huelsenbeck published his Dadaist manifesto in April 1918. A formidable Dada Club was established to which rallied, among others, Raoul Hausmann, Georges Grosz and John Heartfield, who together developed the technique of photomontage into a powerful instrument of subversion, Wieland Herzfelde, the left-wing publisher, and Johannes Baader, self-styled 'Super-Dada' founder of Christ Co. Ltd, whose manic genius for arousing scandal led him to invade the Weimar *Diet* and hurl down armfuls of leaflets declaring himself President of the State. Berlin Dada waged a running battle with the Expressionists whom it denounced for becoming middle class like the Republic and for their typically Germanic proclivity for Romantic soul-searching and inwardness. Action, increasingly violent and political, was what counted for the Berlin Dadaists. They campaigned in turn with the Spartakists and the Communists, promoting a whole series of little reviews with titles like *Jedermann sein eigener fussball* (*Everyman his own Football*), *Der Blutige Ernst* (*In Bloody Earnest*) and *Die Pleite* (*Bankruptcy*), often no sooner distributed than banned by the authorities on the grounds of anti-militarism or obscenity. Communism satisfied their instincts for aggression but only Herzfelde went so far as to join the Party. The rest set too much value on their freedom, dwelt more on the absurdity of the present than on future reform and were generally sceptical about schemes for the betterment of man. After a triumphant series of 'lectures' in the provinces and in Czechoslovakia followed by a climactic International Dada Fair in the capital in June 1920, Berlin Dada went into decline; by 1922, thanks to bitter rivalries, the rout of the revolution and a series of decisions by individuals to devote themselves exclusively to either art or politics, it was no more.

Dada had also petered out by this time in Cologne where in 1919 and 1920, animated by Max Ernst, Johannes Baargeld and Hans Arp, a highly distinctive offshoot had enjoyed a brief but brilliant existence. The Cologne Dadaists refused to sacrifice poetic revelation to the demands of propaganda but insisted, as the Surrealists were to do later on, that a combination of external action and internal freedom was indispensable to the revolutionary movement. Their most original contributions to Dadaist expression were the so-called Fatagagas: disquieting collages manufactured collectively and anonymously by the Cologne triumvirate. German Dada showed the greatest capacity for survival in Hannover largely because here it was the operation of one man, the painter-poet Kurt Schwitters, who was an artist through and through and had no truck with politics. Schwitters stood on the individualist, fantastic wing of Dadaism. He made an ironically sentimental *Merz-poem*, *Anna Blume* (1919) out of a patchwork of newspaper cuttings, publicity jingles, phrases from pop-songs and homely sayings, and an endless series of *Merzbilder* or collages assembled from lovingly collected litter off the streets.

Although it would be misleading to judge the importance of Dadaism solely by reference to its artistic achievements, it is nevertheless paradoxically true that in both the German-speaking countries and in Paris, where the Dada episode will be considered separately, the repudiation of art proved to be a stimulus to art. But it is not easy to identify Dada's originality through its products, since the movement's main contribution was to posit a new conception of the artist rather than a new style. The Dadaists were unabashed about borrowing from a whole variety of pioneers: collage from Cubism, typographical acrobatics and 'bruitism' from Futurism, unconstrained use of colour from Expressionism, spontaneous techniques from Kandinsky and poetic inventions of Apollinaire and Max Jacob. The 'phonetic poetry' that was universally popular among the German Dadaists and also exploited by Tzara derived largely from Marinetti's theories of 'words at liberty' and from the Expressionist Auguste Stramm. Typical of this genre were Richard Huelsenbeck's *Phantastische Gebete* (*Fantastic Prayers*) (1916). The aims behind these 'sound poems' varied: Hugo Ball seems to have sought a pure language free from the contamination of meaning; Schwitters, in his *Ursonate* (*Primal Sonata*) (1932), was most interested in the non-figurative plastic effects to be achieved by disposing words about a page. With 'Simultanéist' poems, the intention was to create 'an illusion of many things happening at once': they were the spontaneous creation of a group and everything depended on performance. According to Arp, 'the poet crows, curses, sighs, stutters, yodels as he pleases'. These poetic acts represented the dissolution of the psyche and perhaps of the world at large by forces outside man's control, by chance and by the unconscious.

It was only appropriate that a movement born in the same year as the Congress of Kienthal and which faded away in 1922 as hopes died for the international revolution should have made the manifesto its very own genre. All the Dadaists, apart from the very few who were exclusively painters, wrote manifestos, but Tristan Tzara was undisputed master in the field. Tzara had left behind in Romania the Post-Symbolist preciosity of his early poems and had developed an incoherent, savage language which set aside logic and syntax, exemplified in *La Deuxième aventure céleste de M. Antipyrine* (*The Second Celestial Adventure of Mr Fire-extinguisher*) (1917) and *Cinéma calandrier du coeur abstrait* (*Cinema Calendar of the Abstract Heart*) (1918). While owing a good deal to the aggressive, raucous, tub-thumping manifestos of the Futurists who had employed the medium to publicize what they imagined to be the style of art to come, Tzara's manifestos were intended to desacralize all art. Contradiction was the very lifeblood of Tzara's method; it is his surefootedness on the brink of chaos that make texts such as his *Manifeste Dada 1918* and *Dada Manifeste sur l'amour faible et l'amour amer* (*Dada Manifesto on Lukewarm and Unrequited Love*) (1921) the classic expressions of Dada sensibility.

As if he were fulfilling some wager, Tzara successfully employed the didactic manifesto form as a vehicle for his irrational *credo*, while at the same time refusing to falsify the latter by giving it a rational formulation. Metalanguage about the writing of manifestos and poetic language repeatedly sabotaged the 'message'; continual ruptures occurred between comprehensible if outrageous declarations of principle and passages of verbal delirium. Tzara's manifestos were extended statements to the effect that there was nothing to state. Their very redundancy was their message, their *raison d'être*. Tzara was more keenly aware than any of his comrades, except Picabia and Duchamp, that Dada had to remain fugitive and imponderable, that it would die the moment it began to take itself seriously or become fixed in any stance. For six years this indefatigable juggler kept his quoits spinning in the air until even he ran out of energy and found his capacity to invent new tricks exhausted.

Tzara's belated arrival in Paris in January 1920, bearing the spirit of Dada like the arc of the covenant, opened Dadaism's final and most spectacular phase, which was also the most fraught with misunderstandings. A sympathetic reception had been prepared for Dada among the first of its Paris adherents, André Breton, Louis Aragon and Philippe Soupault, who together edited the Modernist review *Littérature*, by the personal example and remarkable wartime letters of Breton's friend, Jacques Vaché (*Lettres de guerre*, 1919). Intuitively developing Alfred Jarry's highly idiosyncratic brand of Symbolism, Vaché had carried humour to the point of demolishing conviction that anything in life, including the early literary efforts of Breton and his comrades, could be worthwhile. Refusing to grant any reality to the war, Vaché had 'deserted' into himself in much the same way as several of the German Dadaists deserted to Zürich. He died in mysterious circumstances in 1919. The *Littérature* group, the nucleus of the movement which in 1924 was to be christened Surrealism, evidently understood Dada to be an enterprise that would force the public at large to undergo the moral shock-treatment of Vaché's *umour*: a sharp and salutary cauterizing operation on corrupted forms after which a fresh start could be made. With the enthusiasm of evangelical crusaders, the Dadaists employed every cultural megaphone that Paris could provide to proclaim the dominion of nonsense. A plethora of reviews appeared. Apart from *Littérature*, which gave itself over to Dada in May 1920, there were Paris numbers of Picabia's *391* and of Tzara's *Dada*; there was Paul Eluard's *Proverbe* and Picabia's new *Cannibale*, the latter being a vain attempt to bring some order to the anarchic Paris Dada scene, and a host of still more ephemeral plaquettes like Céline Arnauld's *Projecteur*, Paul Dermée's *Z* and Tzara's *Le Coeur à Barbe* (*The Bearded Heart*). Among the books appearing under the Dada label were Picabia's *Pensées sans langage* (*Thoughts without Language*) (1919), Eluard's *Les nécessités de la vie et les conséquences des rêves* (The *Necessities of Life and the Consequences of Dreams*) (1921), Aragon's *Anicet* (1921) and Benjamin Péret's *Le passager du Transatlantique* (*The Transatlantic Passenger*) (1921). Dada's season of *soirées*, lectures and *salons* between January and May 1920 brought public indignation to a crescendo. On these occasions, everything was calculated in advance. Experiment and improvisation which had been integral to Zürich entertainments was sacrificed to a single end: assault on the public. The technique was to arouse expectations with tantalizing publicity and then to so disappoint these hopes that the audience would be forced on the rebound to realize the futility of its motives, to look over into an abyss of nothingness.

Paris Dada might have repeated these cultural guerrilla exercises for many years if Tzara, Picabia and Georges Ribemont-Dessaignes had had their way. That it did not was partly because the Dadaists soon began to turn their derision on each other and, more important, because the *Littérature* group had quickly found reason to revise Vaché's judgement about the 'theatrical and joyless uselessness of everything'. In the spring of 1919, months before Dada came to Paris, Breton and Soupault had conducted a series of experiments using the psychoanalytic technique of automatic writing. They discovered that by turning themselves into 'recording machines' of the unconscious murmur, they could release a language that was by no means absurd or arbitrary but which glittered with an unlikely display of brilliant poetic images. Little by little, during the period in which they had ostensibly rallied to Dadaism, Breton and Soupault began to draw lessons from these texts (published in 1920 as *Les Champs Magnétiques*) (*Magnetic Fields*), lessons which had never occurred to the haphazard practitioners of automatism in Zürich such as Ball, Huelsenbeck and Arp. First of all they recognized the similarity between their automatic imagery and that of Rimbaud's *Illuminations* and parts of Lautréamont's *Les Chants de Maldoror*. Admiration for these two poets had been the original bond between Breton, Soupault and Aragon; it was to remain one for all Surrealists in the future. Secondly, they recognized that in the speech of the unconscious, words 'lost their wrinkles', ceased to play the part of intellectual policemen and gave voice to new and active thoughts. This meant that unlimited credit could now be extended to language; a new reason for writing had been found, however little the results might have in common with what was generally accepted as art. Automatism revealed that the flux of the inner mind was linguistic in character. If, at one level, language was an alien social institution as corrupt as society itself, at a deeper level it was a natural phenomenon expressive of the entire being. The images thus bodied forth were not artificial but part of reality itself, of 'natural history' as René Crevel was later to say. Holding the keys to the real motivations of our conscious thoughts, poetry, as it was eventually defined by André Breton in the first *Manifeste due surréalisme* in 1924, rejoined the sciences as a route towards the understanding of man. It became once more what Rimbaud had intended it to be: an adventure after knowledge. At the same time, Lautréamont's demand that poetry be a communal affair rather than an individual one might be satisfied since the evidence of automatism suggested that 'inspiration' would grant its favours to all men once they had broken the shackles of habit, and a constricted notion of reason.

3

Surrealism was not 'the French wing of Dada', nor was it simply Dada 'changing its name and adding to its goals' – as the historians Michel Sanouillet and Herbert S. Gershman respectively have claimed. Nor was it Dadaism that had turned constructive – the evolution of the Zürich painters described earlier shows what 'positive' Dada became. Surrealism was heir to an indigenous tradition with its roots in Romanticism. Paris Dada was an unsuccessful graft onto what was already a healthy native growth. It undoubtedly helped the nascent Surrealists to cut free of their remaining inhibitions and it was a useful apprenticeship in the art of scandal but beyond this the Surrealist state of mind (and it has been shown states of mind and not techniques or styles are the real issues at stake) diverges sharply from Dada. The two movements drew different lessons from a similar experience. Tzara's Dada stopped short at parody and mockery; the Surrealists attend to the privileged moments of existence. Dada was scatological; Surrealism lyrically exalts love and eroticism. After automatic writing, the *Littérature* group, soon joined by René Crevel, Robert Desnos and Paul Eluard, developed a whole arsenal of methods for soliciting revelation and plumbing the obscure regions of the mind; but the hypnotic sleeps and dream analysis had to be carried on outside and against the Dada of Picabia and Tzara. Freudianism, which for Breton held out the prospect of revolutionary self-awareness, was dismissed by Tzara as 'a dangerous illness'. Although Breton and Tzara were equally convinced of *le peu de réalité* (the dearth of reality), of the meaninglessness of the world as it was, the Surrealists laid new stress on the responsibility of man for the meaning that was accorded to things – any derogation of matter implied a correspondingly higher valuation of the imagination. Thus while rejecting, as vehemently as the Dadaists, all fixed categories, dogma (including revolutionary dogma), and rationalizations that threatened to impoverish man and diminish the options open to him, the Surrealist is confident in the capacity of the mind to sustain itself in the midst of chaos, to swim in the waters of discontinuity like some *poisson soluble* (soluble fish) as if they were its natural element. The Surrealist believes that the greater the virtualities of metamorphosis, the greater is the likelihood that desire will have its way.

The Surrealist contention is that the world would cease to be a conglomeration of unrelated fragments in which man feels himself to be alien and lost if the associative faculty of the mind could be re-stimulated and developed. This means regaining the use of powers we once possessed before they were emasculated by a materialistic civilization; powers which children, primitive peoples and the insane seem to be the last among us to retain. In place of, or at any rate supplementary to, logical analysis that has been proven inadequate, the Surrealists propose analogical thinking which can permit the reclassification of experience in an emotional and intuitive way. They claim that the poetic analogy has the power to reveal the principle of identity between the human mind and the exterior universe and hence to change man's idea of his place in the world. The poetic or plastic image, especially when it brings together a pair of elements which reason would regard as having nothing in common, often generates a mysterious luminosity and appears to be inexplicably appropriate, even inevitable. As André Breton put it in *Les Vases Communicants* (*Communicating Vessels*) (1932):

The spirit is marvellously prompt to seize the faintest rapport that exists between two objects selected by chance and the poets know that they can always, without fear of deceit, say that the one is like the other: the only hierarchy that may be established among poets can rest solely upon the greater or lesser liberty which they demonstrate in this respect.

This attitude is clearly shared by Surrealist painters like Magritte, Dali, Max Ernst and Hans Bellmer; it also accounts for the proliferation in Surrealist poetry of images such as 'my flaming plane castle soaked in Rhenish wine' (Péret), 'the rainlands revealed by pearls' (Breton) and 'the Earth blue as an orange' (Eluard). In the Dadaist poetry of Tzara, one senses that the nascent images have been repeatedly aborted and lyricism cold-heartedly denied. Much Dada poetry does no more than faithfully reflect chaos; the Surrealist image by contrast, 'leads somewhere'. It is itself, as Julien Gracq has noted, an invitation to poetry. Although gratuitous in origin, it is experienced as an approach towards knowledge that has hitherto been veiled.

The Surrealists are well aware that to propose a new language is to propose a changed life for men and an alternative and revolutionized society. Their art is not diversion, but a challenge to the *status quo*. The Mexican Surrealist poet, Octavio Paz, has written: 'Surrealism proposes not so much the making of poems as the transformation of men into living poems.' The criterion that the Surrealists apply to a work of art is its susceptibility to provoke a real change in those who encounter it, to call forth an affective response similar in quality to that evoked by the sight of the woman one loves. Their art is sometimes obscure because they refuse to sacrifice truth to the inner vision, or 'interior model' as Breton called it in *Le surréalisme et la peinture* (*Surrealism and Painting*) (1928), for the sake of immediate communicability. The latter is a traffic in false currency because it is tied up with a purely contingent, external and unacceptable reality. The Surrealists believe that 'matter follows information', that words when

stripped of deforming accretions have a power to act on the world
and that like magic spells they are a means of realizing desire. Hence
eventually the poet's words and the artist's new signs will be read and
understood. The intimate relationship which the Surrealists posit
between language patterns and social values, between our powers of
enunciation and the mediocrity of the universe, means that the artist
has to assume a heavy burden of moral and even political responsibility.
Surrealism seems serious and even at times desperate to the point of
suicide and insanity in contrast to the playful nonchalance of Dada,
because the Surrealists have never been complacent in the face of life's
absurdity or injustice. It was a moral issue that occasioned the first
public split between Tzara's Dadaists and Breton's Proto-Surrealists:
in May 1921 the latter staged a mock trial of the nationalist writer,
Maurice Barrès, at which they indicted him with 'crimes against
the security of the mind'; Tzara and Picabia tried to turn it into a
farce. Ever since then, which means up to the events of May 1968 and
beyond, Surrealism has stood for revolt against everything that
mutilates man's inner life, or stifles his imagination for the sake of
'peace and quiet', law and order and the smooth running of the social
machine. Crediting humanity, once liberated, with immense potential,
the Surrealists have battled against all forces which encourage renunciation – against religion with its craven doctrine of original sin,
against the institution of the family in which love is crucified, against
work and the eight-hour day, the paradigm of regimented dehumanized existence. It is not for nothing that the movement's
reviews have had titles like *La Révolution surréaliste* (1924–9), *Le
surréalisme au service de la révolution* (1930–33), and *La Brêche* (*The
Breach*) (1961–5). Among the works of individual Surrealists are
some of the most intransigent expressions of rebellion ever made:
Breton's 'Confession dédaigneuse' ('Disdainful confession') (1923),
Aragon's *Traité du style* (*Treatise on Style*) (1928), Eluard's brutally
stark 'Critique de la poésie' (1931), René Crevel's *Les Pieds dans
le plat* (*Putting One's Foot in It*) (1933), Péret's *Je ne mange pas de ce
pain-là I* (*I Won't Stomach that*) (1936) or Bunuel's film *L'Age d'Or
The Golden Age*) (1930) to pick just a handful at random.

From the moment in 1924 when Breton and his friends fought off
rivals to win exclusive right to Apollinaire's term *surréaliste* and applied
it to the whole gamut of activities that they had been pursuing under

cover of Dada since 1919, it was clear that Surrealism required of its participants a total commitment. It is a corporate experience which amounts to a complete way of life: attendance at daily meetings, drawing up collective tracts, demonstrating at reactionary theatre productions, playing all manner of games that stimulate the imagination, sharing the mysteries of the capital. The Surrealist group has assumed a wide variety of guises. It has resembled in turn a magicians' coven, a bandit gang, a sect of heretics or a revolutionary cell. It is both an underground movement subverting the *status quo* and a retreat within the confines of which life can be regulated according to desire. Curiously, despite all vicissitudes, a balance has been roughly kept between admissions and expulsions, so that the number of active participants in the group at any one time has been such they can gather without too much discomfort in a café. Allowing for a good deal of overlap, one can distinguish separate generations of Surrealists: the initiators were quickly joined by Antonin Artaud, André Masson, Joan Miro, Yves Tanguy, Raymond Queneau, Pierre Naville, Jacques Baron, Roger Vitrac, Michel Leiris, Jöe Bousquet, Georges Limbour and René Crevel. The departure by 1929 of Desnos, Soupault, Artaud, Vitrac, Prévert and Naville was compensated for by the arrival of René Char, Tristan Tzara, Salvador Dali, Alberto Giacometti, and Luis Bunuel. This rhythm has been maintained ever since.

Although the Surrealist adventure has always been open to all and not just to writers and artists, its essentially libertarian character has been qualified by the knowledge that Surrealism makes its own special demands; a high degree of self-discipline is required to maintain oneself in a condition of total availability to the solicitations of the marvellous. Like the early alchemists, the Surrealists believe that the *magnum opus* can only be successful if its practitioners preserve a personal *asepsie* or purity. Between the wars the prevailing sense of commitment was strengthened by the politicization of the Surrealist programme for converting the imaginary into the real and by their stubborn but unreciprocated courtship of the French Communist Party. They made heroic efforts to extend the field of application of the Marxian dialectic beyond surplus value and the labour process to the antimonies of subjective existence such as dream and conscious life, the pleasure principle and the reality principle.

They refused to be blackmailed when the Communists ordered them to make a definitive choice between poetry and politics. They have always insisted that there is no 'hierarchy in evil' and that any action designed to transform man's social condition must be accompanied by the interpretation and reform of his internal condition. Unlike Dada where every Dadaist was a president, Surrealism has been dominated by the unique moral and intellectual authority of André Breton who until his death in 1966 played the roles alternately of arbiter, theoretician, venerable father, conscience, prophet, exemplar and when occasion required, lord of misrule. All these factors help to account for the remarkable coherence that the Surrealist movement presents despite the countervailing irrationalism of its premises. They also help to explain how Surrealism could become worldwide, with successful transplantation first to Belgium in the twenties and then, in the following decade, to Czechoslovakia, Yugoslavia, Holland, Scandinavia, Britain, Japan, the Canaries and virtually the whole continent of South America.

If commitment and a highly idiosyncratic kind of self-discipline assured Surrealism such a long and stormy history, they did not on that account condemn the movement to uniformity and rapid ossification. The immense variety of works produced by Surrealism and the continuous development of its original theses are proof of a great capacity for self-renewal. The Surrealists have resorted to art because, 'lamentable expedient' though it is, it remains the best way of recording the inner life, or endowing subjective imaginings with the forms of reality and of projecting desire. But the work of art is still a means for Surrealists rather than the end of their activity. Thus it is a waste of time to look for a unifying style or technique behind all the works that the Surrealists claim as their own. That which makes a painting Surrealist, as Max Ernst has suggested, is something which is itself 'beyond painting': the artist's drive for spiritual emancipation. E. L. T. Mesens, the Belgian poet and collage-maker, recommends that Surrealist works be read as so many marks on the rim of a compass indicating different roads for the Surrealist quest. Since the image is not exclusive to any one medium, the Surrealist sensibility has found expression in all the arts except perhaps music and ballet. It has shown even less respect than Dada for the autonomy of the individual arts; most of the painters and sculptors have written, and the poets, even if they have not taken up the brush, have made collages or poem-objects. Not only have they pioneered hybrid forms like the happening and the *objet à fonctionnement symbolique* (object with a symbolic function), they have invented a repertoire of techniques for provoking inspiration such as Ernst's *frottage* (rubbing), Paalen's *fumage* (smoke picture), Dominguez' *decalcomania* and the collectively executed *cadavre exquis* (exquisite corpse). Moving on from their original researches into automatism and dreams, the Surrealists have reached out into areas where imagination would seem to have as much to contribute as the sciences: sexuality (the subject of a long series of inquiries in Surrealist reviews from 1928 onwards), clairvoyance (Breton, 'Lettre aux voyantes' ('Letter to the Clairvoyants') (1929)), the language of mental illness (Breton and Eluard, *L'Immaculée conception* (1930)), magic (Breton and Gérard Legrand, *L'Art Magique* (1957)).

The consistent aim of Surrealist art has been to show the degree to which the world is porous to the imagination. Poets and painters alike seek to demonstrate that the fantastic belies its fantasy by being obstinately real. Individual Surrealists have chosen to cultivate their own particular sectors in the boundless domains of the marvellous. Among the painters, Dali, Tanguy, Ernst and Bellmer for example, photograph the landscape of the oneiric world with such hallucinatory conviction that we are compelled to accept their images as tangible components of reality. Others, like Masson or Miro, elicit the inner flux in the act of painting and thus trace out a seismographic record of the mind's most profound vibrations. Among the writers, Robert Desnos, the oracle of the *époque des sommeils* (period of trances), was master of the dreamworld where he quarried the elaborate punning sentences credited to Rrose Sélavy (*Eros c'est la vie*). Aragon prospected for the marvellous in contemporary Paris, unearthing mysterious beauty just beneath the commonplace surface of things. In *Le Paysan de Paris (Paris Peasant)* (1926), he reveals how encounters in the street evoke the same thrill as poetic images. Breton in *Nadja* (1928) and *L'Amour Fou (Mad Love)* (1937) deduced from personal experience that all manner of subtle exchanges occurred between exterior determinisms or chance and the inner workings of the mind. Unlike the Dadaists who deliberately drew attention to the vulnerability of the psyche to invasion by chaos, Breton argued that it was external circumstances that often responded to the unspoken demands and desires of the human psyche. From the notion of '*le hasard*', Breton thus moved on to that of '*le hasard objectif*' (objective chance). All Surrealists exalt love as the archetypal Surrealist act because it brings about the seemingly impossible fusion of the 'self' with the 'other', because it is a perpetual challenge to the life-denying equation of the useful with the good and because it is the supreme manifestation of the pleasure principle. The poet of love *par excellence* was Paul Eluard. In poem after poem in *L'Amour la poésie (Love: Poetry)* (1929), *La Rose publique (Public Rose)* (1934), *Les Yeux fertiles (Fertile Eyes)* (1936), for example, Paul Eluard celebrated love with a simple purity that conferred sacredness on profane sensuality.

Despite the often shocking and anarchic appearance of their work, the Surrealists are making a plea for greater control by man over his destiny and are searching behind the disorder of experience for a higher principle of order. They are not content merely to keep faith with chaos but expect a richer and more open rationalism to emerge from reason's confrontation with its opposite. They are not mystics or transcendentalists: they situate the absolute squarely in man himself and conceive of the Surreal as a strictly 'immanent beyond'. They recognize that it is as urgent to remedy man's material as it is his spiritual deprivation. Their vision is not naïvely anthropomorphic; rather they look forward to a day when it will be possible, as Michel Beaujour has put it, for 'a humanized nature and a naturalized man to converse together free from hindrance in exalting clarity'. Of course, theirs is a utopian doctrine. Of course, the victory of the Surreal is still as distant as the kingdom of the saints. But the Surrealistic life remains as an example and the Surrealist works as witness to a stirring and, for all its affinities with the past, an essentially modern aspiration. The Surrealist sensibility is of the here and now. And the Surrealists at least have not begged the questions that they themselves were among the first to raise about the viability of art in the present. On the contrary, they have sponsored the revolutionary idea of the artist as everyman and of every man as potentially and as of right *un homme complet*. The question then remains – to quote a caption in Max Ernst's book *La Femme 100 Têtes* (1929) – whether, in the eyes of the society in which we live, the 'compleat man' is a 'crime or a miracle'.

PART TWO

PART TWO

FIVE

The Lyric Poetry of Modernism

WE generally understand that the crisis of Modernism was felt particularly sharply in poetry, because poetry, above all the genres, tends to experience changes of relationship and belief in a culture at the direct levels of subject-and-object relationship, and at the very base of form and language. Yet in some ways there is, in poetry, more than elsewhere, a peculiar continuity between Romantic and Modern writing, in part because the changes of consciousness brought about throughout the nineteenth century had been so sensitively monitored and responded to by earlier poets. The new economy of the Modernist poet is perhaps most visible in the use of new metrics and modes like *vers libre*, the look of the poem on the page, as Clive Scott puts it in one of the following essays. But it was based too on a fresh concept of the symbol and the image, which tend in Modernist poetry no longer to involve an easy metaphoricization but an arduous process of fiction-making, as Ellman Crasnow shows. The following essays are designed to come at the problems of Modernist poetry from several angles – through its new lyric economy and its tendency to withdraw from narrative forms (Graham Hough); through its sense of linguistic crisis (Richard Sheppard); through the changing social milieu to which it had to relate (G.M. Hyde). We have also sought in these essays to add to and vary emphases already discussed in the book – to set, for example, against the Imagist or objectivist tradition considered earlier by Natan Zach the Expressionist tradition, important in German but not only in German verse; or to place against the classicist emphasis of Hulme and Eliot the romantic inheritance through Valéry, Rilke and Stevens.

THE MODERNIST LYRIC

GRAHAM HOUGH

I

WE may now be in a process of cultural change greater and more rapid that any that has been seen before – greater than the end of the ancient world or the close of the middle ages. A culture dominated by the word is turning into one dominated by number; and no one can foresee what place the arts of the word will occupy in the kind of society that is coming into being. Poetry has been a part of man's collective life from the earliest civilizations, but it has not always served the same function. It has been the vehicle of law and history, the repository of the folk memory, popular entertainment, the esoteric activity of a few. We must suppose that poetry will continue; but a change in its position has been discernible since the beginning of the modern world.

For Aristotle the supreme exemplars of poetry were tragedy and the epic; and during most of the span of Western civilization it is these major public forms, drama and heroic narrative, that typify verse. They change their shapes, develop innumerable extensions, colonies and minor flowerings; but men's thoughts about poetry, their organized consciousness of it, is dominantly of a shared public experience, the expression of a culture, a nation, or a ruling class. Romantic subjectivity did not fundamentally alter these expectations. It was Shelley who said that poets are the unacknowledged legislators of the world; however, it would not have been necessary to say this if it had been obviously true. Such exalted claims are likely to be made just when they are becoming difficult to sustain, and it is in the generation after the Romantics that the retreat of poetry from its public role first becomes evident. To consider the social aetiology of this change would be to write a large chapter of the history of modern culture; here we are concerned only with the symptoms as they appear in poetry itself. The principal ones are these; drama for the most part retires into the domain of prose; the epic function is taken over by the novel; and in consequence the archetype of poetry is no longer to be found in drama and heroic narrative, but in the lyric. Poetry finds its fullest expression, then, not in the grandiose, but in the exquisitely, restricted form; not in the public utterance but in the intimate communication; perhaps not in communication at all. Among many definitions of the lyric is a well-known one by T. S. Eliot; the lyric in the voice of the poet talking to himself, or to nobody. It is an interior meditation, or it is a voice out of the air, regardless of any possible speaker or hearer. For the last hundred years it has been this conception that is at the heart of our feeling about poetry.

2

Lyric poetry of the earlier European tradition had always of course had a private quality. We hear of Shakespeare's 'sugared sonnet among his private friends', and this way of speaking is typical. But the lyric had always attached itself to the public world in a number of recognized and established ways. The lyric poet traditionally claims one of a few recognized roles: the lover, the courtier, the patriot, the sage or the religious contemplative. But Baudelaire, the first of the moderns, cannot be assigned to any of these roles, and when he claims kinship with his readers (which he does by means of a calculated insult – '*Hypocrite lecteur, mon semblable, mon frère*' ('Hypocrite reader, my likeness, my brother') it is through the shadow side of their lives, '*la sottise, l'erreur, le péché, la lésine*', all that is unacknowledged or rejected by their social selves, that he professes to be at one with them. Folly, error, sin, meanness; he adds above all, ennui; and the almost hopeless aspiration towards an order that is for ever out of reach.

> *Là, tout n'est qu'ordre et beauté,*
> *Luxe, calme et volupté**

– but it is *there*, in the altogether elsewhere, not in the conceivably actual or the imaginably present.

Here we might introduce a distinction, originally made by Stephen

*There, all is but order and beauty, luxury, calm and delight.

Spender, between the modern and the Modernist. The modern, a matter of period and historical phase; the Modernist, a matter of art and technique, a peculiar twist of vision. Baudelaire is the first modern, the first to accept the de-classed, dis-established position of the poet who is no longer the celebrant of the culture to which he belongs, the first to accept the squalor and baseness of the modern urban scene; but he is not a Modernist. It is the peculiarity of his poetry to express a new alienation in the language of received tradition; the movement of his verse and even the diction can often remind us of Racine. For a new language and a new verse movement to match the changed status of the poet we have to wait for the next generation – for Rimbaud; and it is in the poems that Rimbaud wrote between 1870 and 1873 that the origins of the Modernist lyric are to be found. Their changed relation to established culture is not so much in their antinomianism – conspicuous though it is in Rimbaud's case – as in their unpredictable, occasional quality. It is the poetry of a wanderer, arising from none of the time-sanctioned provocations; a poetry of unorthodox celebrations and chance epiphanies. Ham sandwiches and beer undergo a transfiguration ('Au Cabaret vert') ('The Green Inn'); the peace that passeth all understanding is figured by two white sisters who gently crush the lice in the hair of a vermin-tormented child ('Les chercheurs de poux') ('The pickers of lice'); ridiculous customs-officers stand as the type of all the officious oppressiveness of social order ('Les douaniers') ('The customs-officers'). The language and imagery are not confined to the traditionally sanctioned sources, but can be in the same poem slangy, obscene, elaborately learned and conventionally poetic. The unique symbol of fulfilment is an innocence like that of childhood, which can be longed for hopelessly, or may suddenly reappear, momentary and unannounced, in the midst of sordid and alien circumstance. Above all, in prose-poems and ethereal song-like fragments, the firm outlines of pictorial presentation or narrative or logical sequence all disappear, and meaning arises uncertainly, through a film of unanalysable suggestion.

> *Elle est retrouvée.*
> *Quoi? – L'Éternité.*
> *C'est la mer allée*
> *Avec le soleil.*

Ame sentinelle,
Murmurons l'aveu
De la nuit si nulle
*Et du jour en feu.**

A remarkable visual presentation of this demonic divine child among the established functionaries of poetry is to be seen in Fantin-Latour's picture *Le Coin du Table* (*The Corner of the Table*). It portrays a group of contemporary French men of letters in studiously formal-informal attitudes; dark coats, bow ties, white linen, shirt-cuffs well in evidence (even Verlaine's); and in the middle of them Rimbaud, looking like a lost angel thirteen years old, bundled up in an old greatcoat five sizes too big for him, with an expression of remote unearthly beauty.

The description of Rimbaud's lyrics would serve equally well to characterize large areas of the Modernist lyric all over Europe, for the spirit of modern poetry soon became international, and for the most part took its inspiration from France. It would be deficient however in one particular. In its emphasis on the novel and the un-predictable it fails to notice the immense mass and weight of inherited culture – of belief, myth, legend and poetic habit. Newly invented codes are superimposed on the code of shared knowledge. Even Rimbaud's earliest works were the extremely accomplished Latin verses he wrote at school; and his earliest French poems were homages to Coppée and Banville, the established poets of his day. In other poets – in Yeats and Eliot, Mallarmé and Valéry, Rilke and George, Montale and Quasimodo, Machado and Lorca – the dialectic between tradition and innovation seems to be one of the mainsprings of their work. Even the Communists Brecht and Neruda, ideologically committed to the future, see it as rooted in history and the inescapable past. This acute consciousness of a tension between the modern sensibility and ancient ways of feeling is more marked in the poets of the last hundred years than in any previous phase of our culture. Indeed for modern poetry it is the general unignorable fact; the varied solutions imposed by differing social and political convictions become variations on this single theme. The solutions are certainly

* It is rediscovered. What? – Eternity. It is the sea mated with the sun.
  Sentinel soul, let us murmur the avowal of the night so empty and the day on fire.

various. There is the defiant assertion of antique modes of awareness, as in Yeats and George; there is the ironic juxtaposition of ancient grandeur and modern banality, as in Eliot. In Rilke all experience from the mythological to the trivial daily round is seen equally as material to be transformed by contemplation. And in Mallarmé the resolution is found only in the artistic process itself; the 'subject' of the poem becomes immaterial or non-existent, and the matter of the work is simply its own composition.

Hence the eclecticism of modern poetry. Poetry can no longer be derived, as that of most previous poetical schools had been, from a single cultural stream. Malraux has called attention to the profound change in the situation of the visual arts brought about by the existence of the 'Musée Imaginaire' ('Imaginary Museum'). With modern methods of reproduction the art of all civilizations, of all periods, is available to everyone, at the nearest public library. With some qualifications due to linguistic diversity, poetry finds itself in the same case. Classical culture has lost its unique authority; there is no ecumenical religion; the psychologists and anthropologists have revealed systems of symbolism anterior to the accepted cultural structures. The poet has all the myths of the world available to him; which also means that he has none – none that can impose itself as indubitably his own by simple right of inheritance. The one inevitable unifying intellectual force in the modern world is that of natural science; and since the poet is concerned with areas of experience that natural science does not touch, he is left to make his own myth, or to select one by an arbitrary existentialist choice, from the vast uncodified museum, the limitless junk-shop of the past.

From the standpoint of poetry the great mythological systems that are specifically of our own day – let us call them summarily the Freudian and the Marxian – are only myths like any others. Marxism gives to poetry no themes and no materials that it did not already possess; it offers only the possibility of organizing these materials into a scheme of social and political action – a possibility that poetry in general has been very little inclined to take up. The world in which modern poetry grew up was the world of high bourgeois culture, the heir of all the ages, and possessed of the technical resources to become fully aware of its inheritance. Yet even before 1914 the dominant attitude in poetry is the 'sense of an ending'. The notion of the *fin de siècle* has a more than chronological significance; and though it was linked with a self-conscious modernity, as far as poetry is concerned the awareness of what is passing is far more acute than the awareness of what is to come. This is apparent at a level below that of direct statement; the end of the day and the end of the year exercise a haunting fascination. In German poetry particularly – in Hofmannsthal, Rilke, Trakl and George – autumnal imagery seems almost obsessive, and extends itself easily from nature to culture. Rilke's poem 'Herbsttag' ('Autumn Day') closes with lines that make a shadowy parallel between the last over-ripe days of the harvest season and the end of a phase of human experience:

> *Wer jetzt kein Haus hat, baut sich keines mehr.*
> *Wer jetzt allein ist, wird es lange bleiben,*
> *wird wachen, lesen, lange Briefe schreiben*
> *und wird in den Alleen hin und her*
> *unruhig wandern, wenn die Blätter treiben.* *

And the Russian Revolution, even among those who hailed it as a hope or accepted it as a necessity, did little to turn the current of poetry in the other direction. In Russia Blok and later Pasternak are struggling rather to keep something alive through the turmoil than to bring something new into being. The English poets of the thirties are still emotionally held by the old world that they ostensibly want to abandon or change. Auden wrote a poem acclaiming 'new styles of architecture', but later dropped it from the canon on the ground that he really likes old styles best. The tide making for technical progress and the scientific organization of society flows on; but whatever our social and political desires we cannot plausibly pretend that poetry swims with it.

Depth psychology, on the contrary, is the leader of a journey into interior experience; but it was Freud himself who acknowledged that he was not the discoverer of the unconscious; the poets and artists had been there before him. Freud's great contribution to the natural history of the imagination is chapter 6 of *The Interpretation of Dreams*, and that has been powerful because it shows that the associa-

---

* Who now has no house will build no more. Who now is alone will long remain so; will wake, read, write long letters, and will walk restlessly up and down the alleys, in the driving leaves.

tive logic found in poetry is intrinsic to the human mind. His analysis of what is mainly clinical material has given a quasi-scientific status to the processes of the symbolic imagination – a partial re-establishment of poetry in the world from which it had withdrawn. But the poets have carefully guarded their own explorations, and have had little to do with psychoanalysis. Rilke refused to be analysed by Freud; Joyce refused to be analysed by Jung, and Lawrence thought he had refuted the whole psychoanalytic system.

For the most part then the poets have refused the great public mythologies of our time, and have evolved rival myths of their own, some grandiose and comprehensive, some esoteric and private, but none with any status in the world of organized scientific and historical knowledge by which the world conducts its business. (Homer to the Greeks was a guide to politics and generalship; we have only to mention this to see how far poetry has retreated from the world of action.) Yeats elaborated a large mythological system, which claims to include history, individual psychology and the fate of the soul after death. But he attributed it to the agency of disembodied spirits, communicating by trance and automatic writing, who announced the limits of their enterprise at the start by saying 'We come to give you metaphors for poetry.' At the other extreme, the extreme of particularity, Lorca makes a myth of his own province, Andalusia, in which the gipsies represent the forces of instinctual life and the *Guardias Civiles* the forces of repressive civilization. Rilke, perhaps the greatest myth-maker of all, used Christian symbolism, classical legend, pre-existent works of art, the bric-à-brac of many cultures and even of common daily life – to dissolve them all into a continued dream whose object was to transform the temporal and evanescent, to transcend mortality and absorb death into life.

Because all these endeavours stand aside from the pragmatic activity of their age they tend to move towards abandoned areas of knowledge, unrecognized sources of enlightenment – in short towards some sort of occultism. '*Weit. Wir wohnen dort draussen . . .*' ('A long way. We live out there . . .') say the guides of the soul. It is claimed that poetry gives access to forgotten wisdom or a secret doctrine. Sometimes this is seen as an actual system of archaic knowledge, the wisdom of the East or a long-deserted historical road. Sometimes it is reduced to a psychologism – the esoteric sources are and have always been in the interior life. The most powerful and persistent claim is that poetry itself is a kind of magic, the poet not only a seer but a magus, bringing into existence what he has seen in dreams. The fullest exposition of this claim, and its most decisive rejection, is to be found in the chapter of Rimbaud's *Saison en Enfer* (*Season in Hell*) called 'Alchime du Verbe' ('Alchemy of the Word'). With a less desperate commitment and more safely within the literary sphere Yeats says at one point 'Words alone are certain good,' and he hailed Blake as a prophet because 'he announced the religion of art, of which no man dreamed in the world he knew'. Mallarmé would reduce all other arts and all other activities to literature – '*Tout au monde existe pour aboutir à un livre*' ('Everything in the world exists to result in a book') – and for him all literature is poetry. So there arose a mysticism of poetry, openly announced and pursued by the systematic zealots, covertly underlying and supporting the work of many other poets less prone to theoretical absolutes. This faith becomes so pervasive that poets who owe allegiance to other orthodoxies have to take special pains to detach themselves from it. Claudel, by an improbable sleight of hand, turns Rimbaud into a Christian apologist; Eliot austerely remarks that the object of poetry is to amuse decent people; and Auden after his conversion, if that is what it was, continually re-emphasizes the Kierkegaardian primacy of the moral over the aesthetic.

But the world in which modern poetry grew up was neither Christian nor moral; and poetry in our age has felt little able to rely on any structure of belief outside itself.

3

A special quality has been given to this autonomous realm of poetry by the dominance of the lyric. The doctrine of Edgar Allan Poe that there is no such thing as a long poem was taken up by Baudelaire, and seems tacitly to have been taken up by his successors. In fact the long poem almost disappears: most of the large-scale poetical works of modern times are composed of sequences of short poems, like Rilke's *Duino Elegies* or Eliot's *Four Quartets*. Long narrative and philosophical poems do occasionally appear, but they seem antiquated contraptions, divorced from the spirit of the age. Sustained structures and fully worked-out conceptual schemes become superfluous to poetry. The epic poem expresses a settled ethical choice; the lyric can be the expression of a transitory mood or a momentary illumination. It is not demanded that it shall be consistent with any other lyric by the same poet. So poetry becomes habituated to startling changes of mood and style. Verlaine shifts from blackguardism to religiosity, Rilke from an almost coaxing familiarity to metaphysical abstraction, Gottfried Benn from the blatantly revolting to the alluringly exotic. Eliot's *Waste Land* is positively founded on this principle; it consists of a variety of lyric fragments, some of a nostalgic traditional kind, some Surrealist dream-songs, interspersed with passages of dramatic realism and satire. In poetry of this kind the larger unities are not visible on the surface or present in any readily analysable structure. They are given by a slow underground process of psychic development, often only discernible in retrospect. To write a series of lyrics is more like keeping a spiritual diary than anything. It has little resemblance to the organization of a large-scale literary work, with formal requirements outside the author's personal development. Much twentieth-century criticism has played down the biographical connection between the poet and his poems, and regards the work as an artefact, floating free from its creator. But this cannot disguise the fact that poetry which takes the lyric as its primary model will always tend to follow the contours of individual experience.

Modernist poetry has placed great weight on conscious craftsmanship. Baudelaire derived this emphasis from Poe and transmitted it to Mallarmé and Valéry. From France it found its way into the poetic thought of George in Germany, Pound and Eliot in England; and from these foci it has become widespread. Yet the deeper rhythms of poetry in our time seem to be conditioned in another way. The Surrealist protest has been powerful, with its reliance on unconscious organization; but there is no need to rely on the deceptive claims of automatic writing. We can look at the lyrical production of an individual poet not merely as the record of a psychic development, but as the actual means by which the psychic development has been realized. Psychic development has its own laws, and they are hard to generalize; at all events it is neither a willed activity of the ego nor a turning loose of the unconscious; it is an integration of the two. And it rarely proceeds in a straight unbroken line. It may do so for a time, but the mere specialization on a particular line leads in the end to a crisis, brought about by the need to integrate discarded and neglected material. Such crises are frequent in poetical life-stories of the last hundred years, and the sense of failure in dealing with them is also frequent. Yet without them the poetry itself would not exist.

> ... every attempt
> Is a wholly new start, and a different kind of failure
> Because one has only learnt to get the better of words
> For the thing one no longer has to say.

There are only three ways out of such psychic impasses: alienation in the clinical sense – breakdown or madness; reintegration on a lower level of insight and experience; and the successful individuation of disparate elements, leading to a more comprehensive experience on a higher level of insight. All three have occurred in modern literary history, and the number of truncated poetic careers show that the third is the least common. There are no Goethes in modern literature, and few poets whose lives show a long-sustained development, a perpetual re-creation of the self continued into late maturity or old age. Yeats is the outstanding exception. The slow organic evolution of his poetic life is in part the reward of his own energy and tenacity, and in part a gift of fortune – the fortune that cast his lot in with that of a small country, comprehensible by individual intelligence and will, rather than with the vast inhospitable movements of the wider world.

War, revolution and exile have broken many poetic careers, but even before they had begun to do their worst modern poetry was at odds with the world in which it grew up. Again and again we see the poets impelled to extraordinary journeys, unlikely from the start ever to reach their goal. The most startling example of a *voyage au bout de la nuit* (voyage to the end of night), dramatically broken off at its farthest point, is that of Rimbaud, who re-created French poetry before the age of twenty and for the rest of his life never thought of poetry again. His commitment to poetry was total, and when his expectations came to seem a vast delusion he made a complete rejection of the whole venture. He lived on for eighteen years, the fag-end of a life; but no more poetry. There are not many extremists of Rimbaud's calibre, though there are plenty of fakes, lacking the integrity and the genius. And outside these desolate regions, honourable and relative failures to integrate the poetic experience are many – almost inevitably in an age when the general culture offers no point of attachment and the poet is left alone with his own creative powers. So the poet who has ceased to be a poet becomes a critical impresario, or a teacher of 'creative writing' or a frequenter of cultural conferences. As Cyril Connolly has put it, the cow serves in the milk-bar.

C. G. Jung has advanced a theory of poetic creation – that the poetic faculty is an 'autonomous complex' within the psyche of the poet, split off from his total personality, his social and historical being. This is strikingly echoed in T. S. Eliot's image of the poet as a catalyst, in whose presence the poetry takes place, leaving his mind otherwise unaffected. As an account of poetry in general this seems grossly overstated, but we can see that the situation of the modern poet is singularly apt to provoke it. We are probably at the beginning of a period when the position of the arts in the total economy of our lives is likely to undergo a further rapid change. Such a period cannot be a happy one for the artist. When we consider the appalling history of Europe in the last sixty years to speak of a discomfort in the position of poetry seems trivial. And admitting that we live in a bad time, that none except the very old have ever known a good one, we must admit that the isolation of the poet is perhaps his only salvation. The fact that poetry is not of the slightest economic or political importance, that it has no attachment to any of the powers that control the modern world, may set it free to do the only thing that in this age it can do – to keep some neglected parts of the human experience alive until the weather changes; as in some unforeseeable way it may do.

THE CRISIS OF LANGUAGE

RICHARD SHEPPARD

I

THE notion of a crisis of language is not something entirely modern. Many poets have experienced, at one time or another, a sense of the inadequacy of established poetic idiom, and felt, for personal or broader cultural reasons, the urgent need to develop fresh means of harnessing the resources of language. So, for example, Holderlin's *Empedocles*, Hume's *Letter to a Physician*, Wordsworth's *The Prelude* all explore the poet's experience of spiritual death and rebirth, linguistic aridity and plenitude. Many writers undergo a period when it seems that an essential dimension, a vital energy, has gone from the forefront of consciousness; that the surface of language has ceased to be luminous and grown opaque. And with this experience we become more familiar as we approach the modern age. At first sight, the modern sense of literary language seems to contain, recurrently, this familiar dialectic of death, and of inevitable rebirth into new form. Eliot's essay on *The Metaphysical Poets* (1921) suggested that English poetry between the time of Donne and the present had undergone a progressive hardening and a cerebralization from which it had never recovered; this 'dissociation of sensibility' was crucial, but it was one that Eliot presumably hoped that his own harder, more ironic poetry might help remedy. Similarly, Pound's central cycle *Hugh Selwyn Mauberley* (1919–20) is both an analysis of the flat two-dimensionality of the poetry of Romanticism in decline and an investigation into the opportunities now available for restoring the missing third dimension to poetry. After completing the *New Poems* in 1908, Rilke produced no major poetry for more than a decade during which the First World War finally reduced to ruins the humanistic and aristocratic world from which the *New Poems* had taken their strength. Still, his cryptic letter to Witold Hulewicz of 13 November 1925 suggests that the *Duino Elegies* (1922) and the

Sonnets to Orpheus (1922) represent an attempt to discover what flowers might grow amid the ruins of language.

Nevertheless, a rapid comparison of pre-modern explorations of linguistic crisis with an archetypal modern statement, Hofmannsthal's Chandos Letter, reveals a crucial difference. The former represent a clearing away of lumber prior to a fresh burst of creativity; Chandos's letter suggests a real pessimism about the possibility of revivifying language, indicating both that the future lies with a language which is no language and that, until this language is found, the only possibility is silence. Chandos's pessimism can be seen in the list of objects which, in an imaginative desert, still ignite in him an occasional and momentary vision of eternity: a watering can, a deserted harrow in the fields, a dog in the sun, a wretched church-yard, a cripple, a peasant cottage. All of these ciphers suggest tired-ness, desertedness, decrepitude and pathos; all seem *residues* of a lost unity rather than pointers to a unity to come. A similar sense of pessimism about the possibility of revivifying language, a similar sense that all that remains are a few isolated and arbitrary symbols, runs through the writings of Eliot, Yeats and Rilke. Eliot ends *The Waste Land* by shoring a few arcane fragments of language against the ruin of the present. Rilke said to Hulewicz that his generation was 'perhaps the last' to have known the 'household gods', the 'laral objects' into which 'the hope and contemplation' of their fore-fathers had gone. Yeats confessed in *The Nineteenth Century and After*:

> Though the great song return no more
> There's been delight in what we have:
> The rattle of pebbles on the shore
> Under the receding wave.

Eliot, Yeats and Rilke seem, like Hofmannsthal, to be intent on pre-serving the sense of eternity which inhabits the few fragments left to them by the past, and without which, they suggest, all would be blackness, boredom and despair.

2

This overwhelming sense of the imminence of linguistic aridity and imaginative death is an aspect of a much wider socio-cultural problem: the supersession of an aristocratic, semi-feudal, humanistic and agrarian order by one middle-class, democratic, mechanistic and urban. Seen as retrogressive rather than neutral, the transition represented for these poets the abandonment of an order whose language was poetically amenable, whose structures were total and capacious, and whose forms were impressive in their apparent permanence and rootedness, for an order whose language was cerebralized, whose structures were partial and repressive, and whose forms were only superficially impressive. Hofmannsthal's Lord Chandos, like some of the Yeatsian aristocrats, partly analyses this problem. Previously he had felt himself to be part of a total, encompassing structure, the parts of which corresponded with and interpreted each other. Now, however, he feels that this edifice is disintegrating into even smaller fragments which no longer have any substantial unity. Formerly, social institutions had been vehicles through which the deepest corporeal and spiritual energies of the personality had been expressed and harnessed and all human and physical phenomena endowed with a transcendent aura. Now, however, the social edifice disintegrates; the unifying concepts of 'spirit' and 'soul' can no longer be uttered; the disappearance of its mysterious unifying centre has shut off entire areas of his personality and only rarely does he feel a 'flood of higher life' breaking through the crust surrounding him. Abstract concepts formerly real to him 'crumble in his mouth like mouldy fungi'; whole areas of social discourse become incredible. So Chandos can no longer feel that the historical work which he had planned is worth writing; nor can he use the classical myths as hieroglyphs which will interpret his civilization to itself. Because the social order has proved factitious, its wisdom not worth knowing, he can no longer bother to compile an *Apophthegmata*. The extent of his linguistic crisis Chandos sums up by saying that while once, 'beneath the stone arcades of the great square in Venice', he had found within himself 'that structure of Latin prose whose plan and order delighted him more than did the monuments of Palladio and Sansovino rising out of the sea', now such structures of prose appear impossible, because the man-centred social order they presuppose has become incredible.

This form of disturbance runs deep in modern poetry; and many modern poets have taken their sense of chaos and crisis into further reaches. Thus many Expressionists and Dadaists are ready to argue that the order which is replacing the artistocratic one ignores all the fluid parts of personality – the feelings, the spirit, the unconscious, the imagination – and that rationality, predictability, utilitarianism have torn the potentiating centre out of language. This conviction is crucial both to Yeats and Eliot, but also, for example, to Breton, no pessimist about the modern age:[1]

Experience . . . moves around in a cage from which it becomes more and more difficult to make it emerge. It too is sustained by immediate utility and guarded by commonsense. Under the garb of civilization, on the pretext of progress, we have managed to exclude from the mind everything which, rightly or wrongly, could be charged with being a superstition or a chimera, and to outlaw any means of seeking after truth which does not conform with established custom.

Carl Sternheim, the German Expressionist dramatist, similarly declared in 1919 that the economic values of efficiency and productivity had become so institutionalized in nineteenth-century Germany that 'language came to provide adequate concepts for economic phenomena alone' and that, hence, 'nothing was alive in Germany outside of the area of economics'.[2] This has been a recurrent suspicion of the modern mind; the belief that, variously, the industrial order, or mass democracy, or concepts of efficiency, have destroyed the still point within the spirit and that order has been sacrified to formless and entropic anarchy. Similarly, when the modern poet approaches the mass industrial city, the specific milieu of our century, that too is seen as a superficially tidy and rational complex, a surface hiding a forgotten substratum of history and civilization, or else of unorganized and festering psychic energy. In Baudelaire, the 'forest of symbols', the unity of correspondences, is superseded by the '*fourmillante cité*' ('swarming city'), the industrial waste land of spleen and boredom. The centre lost, Baudelaire turns to the voluptuous surfaces, trying to bury himself in them as if to reassure himself of their reality. However, sensuality takes on the quality of nightmare – the surfaces, no matter how seductive, prove without substance and threaten to throw him into the formless '*néant*' which he senses beneath. Eliot's *The Waste Land* associates this with failing language; while Gottfried Benn, Ivan Goll and Garcia Lorca all use the image of cancer to express the latent irrationality which erodes and breaks through the cracks of the apparently ordered surface of the 'petrified city'.

This is why the struggling pursuit of language culturally lost has been so crucial to modern poetry: to use Pound's metaphor, many modern poets have felt that the god is locked inside the stone. For the essential powers of language and the person, variously described as 'the Logos', 'the Word', the 'Self', 'Being itself', '*Anima Mundi*', 'the Unconscious', 'the older layers of the personality', are encrusted by the excessive cultivation of the will and the conscious powers of the mind which technological society requires. Cut off from the 'primal source', modern poetry is permeated by a sense of homelessness. To paraphrase a line from the *Duino Elegies*: many moderns feel that 'man is not very securely at home in the world which he interprets with his intellect'. Because a principle of unity is felt to have been lost, the present seems to lose its organic connection with the past and the future. Time becomes a series of fragmented instants, and a sense of continuity gives way to discontinuity.

Consequently, linear and progressive notions of history are rendered dubious. Institutions inherited from the past (including the institution of language) are felt to be magnificent but hollowed-out shells which give some semblance of continuity with the past but which in fact provide a beautiful surface for a repressive and pernicious reality. Writing from this sense, the Existentialist philosopher Martin Heidegger claimed that language had undergone 'a process of deformation and decay', and put forward a diagnosis of historical decline to which not a few modern writers could have given their assent:[3]

The spiritual decline of the earth is so far advanced that the nations are in danger of losing the last bit of spiritual energy that makes it possible to see the decline ... The darkening of the world, the flight of the gods, the destruction of the earth, the transformation of men into a mass, the hatred and suspicion of everything free and creative, have assumed such proportions throughout the earth that such childish categories as pessimism and optimism have long since become absurd.

Starting from similar statements about the 'de-potentiation' of language, Roland Barthes arrives at an even more extreme formulation: 'Writing therefore is a blind alley, and it is because society itself is a blind alley.'[4]

For the writer who feels that 'society is a blind alley', language ceases to exercise control over a fluid and elusive reality and comes to lie like a thick crust over his imagination; ceases to be a luminous vehicle for self-expression and turns into something like an oppressive super-ego; ceases to be a means of communication and becomes an opaque and impenetrable wall. Franz Kafka, whose imaginative world resembles the vision of an animal looking out from its burrow on to a world which in its flatness and greyness no longer belongs to him, voiced a similar despair: 'What I write is different from what I say, what I say is different from what I think, what I think is different from what I ought to think and so it goes on further into the deepest darkness.'[5] That which links thought with language, language with the external world, and man with man has disappeared. Like the mock tennis game at the end of Antonioni's *Blow-up*, all language games are felt to have become absurd because the ball, that which guarantees communication between subject and object, is lost.

Part and parcel of the modern crisis of language is the disjunction between social discourse and literary discourse. Where the 'surface' of classical writing takes strength from and corresponds with the authenticity of the social and linguistic structures which it presupposes and celebrates, the modern writer cannot assume this correspondence. He has to dismantle the structures of the conventional world and 'explode' language before he can create an adequate 'verbal ikon':[6]

'Poetic', in the days of classicism, never evokes any particular domain, any particular depth of feeling, any special coherence, or separate universe, but only an individual handling of a verbal technique, that of 'expressing oneself' according to rules more artistic, therefore more sociable, than those of conversation, in other terms, the technique of projecting out an inner thought, springing fully armed from the mind, a speech which is made more socially acceptable by virtue of the very conspicuousness of its conventions.

Rightly or wrongly, many modern writers feel that ordinary discourse is cripplingly deficient. Words get in the way of reality, to such an extent that language, 'the worst of conventions', has to be attacked if it is again to become a lens through which a lost *tiers aspect* may be revealed. From this comes the peculiarly modern notion of literary language as 'autotelic'. Because conventional language is held to be 'de-potentiated', 'de-substantiated', and hollowed-out, its syntax and vocabulary are rejected as unserviceable for poetry. Mallarmé liked the word '*ptyx*' precisely because it meant nothing and was therefore full of unrealized possibilities; Rilke at one point said that the word 'and' in a poem is entirely different from the same word in everyday speech. Furthermore, the Modernist poet rejects all notions of art as description or mimesis; because the 'real' world is felt to be 'fallen' to questionable ends, the task of art cannot be to reproduce this fallen world or manufacture a beautiful 'surface' for it with a language which is equally suspect. Thus the task of the modern poet becomes the creation of a redeemed, visionary world of language in which, as André Breton put it in *The Disdainful Confession* (1924), 'something fundamental' is given back to form and in which the lost dimension of language and the human psyche is rediscovered or preserved. He abstracts words from their conventionalized place in speech and recombines them in such a way that their forgotten secondary potential – connotative properties, rhythmic and aural possibilities, similarities with other words, forgotten meanings – becomes primary. The traditional role of the adjective becomes suspect; the modern poet becomes disposed to use it not so much to describe the surface 'look' or 'feel' of a noun as to bring out its latent metaphorical dimensions. In some modes of modern poetry, particularly in Dadaist a-syntactical and 'non-sense' poetry, the noun itself is suspected of being an oppressive dead-weight; ceases to be the fixed and governing centre of language, and becomes simply one among several component parts. The Modernist crisis of language is thus located not in the impotence of the creative individual or a literary style within a language which is assumed to be living and potentiated, but in the 'de-potentiation' of an entire language as such. Hence, the Modernist poet ceases to be the manipulator of fixed *quanta* and attempts to liberate the repressed expressive energies of language; ceases to be the celebrant of a human order and becomes the experimenter who searches for a barely possible 'redeemed and redeeming image' amid a protean universe in apparently chaotic process.

3

This raises the crucial problem: if there really is a polar opposition between the needs of the creative spirit and the values which have been institutionalized by mass industrial society, under what circumstances is it possible to break out of the prison and write poetry at all? How, in Yeats's words, can the arts overcome 'the slow dying of men's hearts that we call the progress of the world, and lay their hands upon men's heart-strings again, without becoming the garment of religion as in old time's?[7] Paradoxically, many of the major Modernist poets produced their poetry out of a marginal situation in which their sensibilities, nurtured on the still credible forms and symbols of a disappearing order, had come into headlong conflict with the antipathetic institutions of the rising industrial city. This conflict is seen in *The Waste Land*, where Eliot's New England sensibility expresses its alienation from the modern mass city, yet seeks to discover places there which, because they retain contact with the 'more authentic' institutions of the past, permit the encrustation of the city to be breached. It is seen in the city poetry of Baudelaire, where a Romantic temperament tries to construct refuges from the horrors of modern Paris; and seen also in Garcia Lorca's *The Poet in New York*, where Lorca, nurtured in rural Spain, seeks the salvation of the city in the pre-industrial primitivism of its black inhabitants. Thus, many Modernist poets become 'acrobats', 'tightrope walkers', 'dancers', required to maintain a precarious balance on the edge of a crumbling cliff.

Not surprisingly, the temptation is to turn one's back on the abyss, to refuse the threat of nothingness in order to return to the security of the milieu, the institutions, the mythology or the idiom of some pre-industrial order. Eliot is suspected in some quarters of having done just this, of having made his commitment to the past at the expense of the present. Pound clearly did draw back and, with what has been termed 'an Olympian apathein', returned in *Hugh Selwyn Mauberley* to seventeenth-century diction and conceptions to define the new direction post-Romantic poetry was to go. Hofmannsthal and Rimbaud faced the same situation of threat and resolved it by giving up writing poetry altogether. But, whereas Hofmannsthal identified himself with the magnificent but moribund public institutions of Catholic Austria, Rimbaud decided, with something approaching a diabolic cynicism, that the problems of poetry were either not worth solving or too difficult to solve, and became a gun-runner.

With Rilke and Yeats, the withdrawal from the abyss takes a different form. In their later years both men climbed, either metaphorically or literally, a winding stair which led to the topmost room of a lonely tower. After the collapse of the all-encompassing world of the *New Poems*, Rilke turned his back on the present and on the city and retired to a lonely manor house in an obscure Swiss valley, there to cultivate his inner world of residual images in the rarified air of the *Duino Elegies* and the *Sonnets to Orpheus*. After the disappearance of the faery world of his early poems and the shattering of his hopes for Ireland, Yeats turned away from the twentieth century to create the taut, complex world of his later poems, suspended in empty space through which sardonically reverberates the cry of Plato's ghost: 'What then?' Knowing that the past is slipping away from him, feeling the present intolerable, Yeats leaves those who come after him with the half-serious, half-mocking counsel to[8]

> Sing the peasantry, and then
> Hard-riding country gentlemen,
> The holiness of monks, and after
> Porter-drinkers' randy laughter;
> Sing the lords and ladies gay
> That were beaten into the clay
> Through seven heroic centuries;
> Cast your mind on other days
> That we in coming days may be
> Still the indomitable Irishry.

But in 'The Circus Animals' Desertion' he contemplates the bitter possibility that 'all the masterful images' which had grown 'in pure mind' may have been in some ways bogus for not having arisen from the 'foul rag-and-bone shop of the heart', the challenge of the urban waste land.

The world of the poets who come at the end of the Symbolist tradition is terrible and often inhuman. Finding the ground giving beneath their feet, they are plagued by the problem of responsibility and detachment. To whom does their poetry belong? By what right do they put pen to paper at all, seeing that they derive their authority from no one but themselves? Is their sense of being 'outside' simply an inability to adjust, or an extreme form of pride? Writing in a vacuum, do they do more than dramatize themselves and fill the void with their own egos? Can they be sure that their safeguarding irony is not cold detachment or indifferent *Schadenfreude*? Is their compassion merely sentimental condescension? Where the poet cannot root the lyric 'I' in a clear sense of literary tradition or social identity, he finds himself dancing an almost impossible dance amid terrible pitfalls. And if the essential achievement of the Dadaists was the discovery that this dance was a possibility, it is no small wonder that Hugo Ball, their founder and perhaps the most far-sighted of their number, decided that the cost for him was too great and fled out of time into the high mountains and the Roman Catholic Church.

In his fearsome world of isolation and solipsism, the Modernist poet seems to occupy a position like that of Kafka's Hunger Artist, who is as incapable of finding the right food outside society as within it. Or that of Thomas Mann's Adrian Leverkühn, beneath whose chilly intellectualism is the despair of saying anything at all. How then can the poet break out of this linguistic bankruptcy and deal with the experience of aridity and nothingness without self-compromise? How to achieve a breakthrough without falling deeper into solipsism? How to go forward without going back? Perhaps the people who first investigated and answered these problems to any extent were the Dadaists. They, by their linguistic experiments, first began to identify the assumptions on which the rear-guard action of Symbolism had been conducted; they it was who first ventured the daring conclusions that the experiences of nothingness and linguistic aridity can be dealt with not by retreat, resignation or withdrawal but by accepting them and that from this acceptance, new if transient patterns may be born. As Hans Arp said in his poem 'Geländer' ('Railings'), he who can bear the shock of being thrown into the abyss may grow wings and learn to fly. If the Dadaists begin to realize Chandos's desire for a new language which is no language, it is because they are prepared to accept the new situation of the modern age and do not label it hopeless *a priori*. If the great European

The Crisis of Language

Post-Symbolists felt themselves to stand at the end of a line, the Dadaists felt that the inescapability of their situation was forcing them to begin all over again. Together with the Surrealists in their quest for a new language which is no language, they invented the shock tactics by which the mind, conscious of its imprisonment, might in astonishment free itself. Multi-media, cacophony, abusiveness, dreams, children's games, drugs, psychedelia, automatic writing, nonsense and a-syntactical poetry, calligrams, violently incongruous images and surprise effects, all are declared legitimate in the attempt to break down conventionalized responses to words, to defeat the censorship which the surface areas of the personality, the conscious intellect and the will, had imposed upon the profounder levels of the psyche.

Essentially, both the Dadaists and the Surrealists were anti-art. With them, literature and poetry cease to be supreme and become instead only one psychedelic means among others. With them, poetry becomes 'disposable', created for no particular purpose, and useful in an undefinable way. With them, language is displaced from its pinnacle and reinstated simply as one means of communication among many. With them, language ceases to be *the* tool for asserting human lordship over the universe and becomes a natural force in its own right, which creates as it will and over which human beings have only limited control. With them, man becomes the servant of his language rather than its master. With them, poetry is removed from the hands of the élitist genius and becomes something which 'belongs' to the group. With them, the printed page yields to oral delivery. With them, the poet ceases to be the charismatic leader and celebrant of a human order and becomes a medium through whom earthy powers more freely flow. Both the Dadaists and, more systematically, the Surrealists say that the poet must leave his isolation, learn to accept 'le néant' ('nothingness') and put his talents at the disposal of a counter-cultural movement whose aims are social and existential and not purely aesthetic. Whereas many of the older Modernist poets predicated Armageddon on their own inability to adapt to a new situation, the Dadaists and the Surrealists, while not less aware of the modernist crisis of language, said that a way through this crisis existed, that the first step along this way was the acceptance of the new situation and that the second step was the evolution of a new understanding of language.

Paradoxically, both the Dadaists and the Surrealists seem to say that the way to overcome the industrial city is to accept it, learn to love it ironically, and to cultivate those forces at work there which are already eroding its established values from within. That a pre-industrial culture and its literature had reached a dead end should not beguile men into believing that all culture and life have come to a dead end, say the Dadaists and Surrealists. The revitalization of language, it is therefore concluded, must come from groups who have accepted the new situation and are trying to develop a 'counter-culture' from within it. Thus, Raoul Hausmann wrote in 1921 that 'the new language will only arise when the arbitrariness, chance and egoism of a limited individuality has been overcome by a consciousness of mutual obligation as the affair of a human community'.

Following ideas thrown out in part by the Dadaists and the Surrealists, the oral poetry of contemporary counter-culture, combined with other media (music, light and drugs), seems to aim at creating a transiently redeemed situation within the apparent nothingness on which so many of the older Modernist poets turned their backs. Born into the new situation, the members of the counter-culture seem to be trying to say things which were inconceivable for the older Modernist poets – namely, that *le néant* is empty only to eyes which do not know how to discern its hidden patterns, and that once *le néant* has been accepted, it is full of strange shapes and infinite possibilities as well as great dangers. The counter-culture seems to seek to overcome the crisis of language by redefining the status of language. It discards notions of language as a human bastion against chaos and nothingness and sees it as a force which, in conjunction with other media, shapes itself under its own impetus into constellations of meaning which are both as luminous and as transient as Chandos's vision of a water-beetle swimming in a forgotten watering-can beneath a dark tree. The counter-culture seems to be trying to say that the crisis of language can be overcome when man surrenders his claim to be lord of the universe who creates meaning by means of his language and consents to be a simple inhabitant of the universe to whom meaning is unpredictably given through various means, of which language is only one. Where older writers had unconsciously postulated a correspondence between the structures of human language and the structures of external reality, had assumed that their universe of discourse *was* the universe and were dismayed when they experienced the break-up of these fictions, the counter-culture, following the Dadaists and Surrealists, dispenses joyfully with these fictions, experiences their loss as liberation, and permits cosmic powers to do what they will with language if only this surrender leads to a way out of the impasse presented by technological civilization.

When poetry ceases to be a printed exercise in individual excellence and becomes a spoken sign of total sensory stimulation and corporate engagement, art (if that term is not anachronistic in this context) becomes revolutionary gesture. At this point, the 'discontinuous speech' of modern poetry becomes the symbol of the 'alternative way'; the poetic imagination open to linguistic experimentation turns into a political imagination susceptible to the idea of an industrial society based on a non-capitalist mythology; the group which responds as a unity to the language of concern becomes an image of a society based on co-operation not competition; the right of everyone to practise poetry as he wishes becomes the equivalent of the right of everyone to political self-determination; the lowering of the status of language implies the rejection of all forms of élitism. At the far end of modern poetry lies the conviction that if the Chandos experience is ever to be overcome completely, and the demythologized world of 'self-sufficient finitude' is ever to become a mythic landscape again, then the imaginative capacities of human nature must affirm themselves in what amounts to a social revolution. Whether this aspiration represents chaos rather than order, mob rule rather than democracy, destructive apathy rather than liberated purposiveness, or a crude anti-intellectualism rather than the assimilation of the intellect by the imagination remains indeterminate. Once all restraints have been removed, modern poetry and the utopian politicial aspirations which underpin it are as likely to be 'seduced by sea-girls' as they are to find the vision of the Chapel Perilous; are as likely to end in the demonic narcosis of the Third Duino Elegy as they are to end in the stasis and peace of the Fifth Duino Elegy – but perhaps that ambiguous possibility is the inescapable price of the acceptance of *le néant* and the open-ended desire to find transient meaning there.

The last word belongs to Mann's Adrian Leverkühn, an artist who knows the risks attendant on his marginal situation, and who is perpetually threatened by total imaginative bankrupcy. In one of those rare moments in Mann's novel when his voice is actually heard, he articulates the disillusions and the aspirations of a whole range of writers who have known a crisis of language:

> The whole temper of art, believe you me, is going to alter and become gay and more modest ... that's inevitable, and it's a good thing. A great deal of melancholy ambition will fall away from her and a new innocence, yes, an innocuousness even, will be her portion. The future will see in art, and art will see in herself the handmaid of a community which will encompass far more than 'cultivation' and won't possess 'culture' but which perhaps will be a culture. We can only envisage this with difficulty, and yet it will be so and it will be the natural thing: an art without suffering, spiritually healthy, unceremonious, not mournful and yet confidingly friendly, an art which exists on terms of the utmost familiarity with all mankind ...

Whether contemporary developments represent that 'art without suffering' remains to be seen.

Notes

1 André Breton, in *The First Surrealist Manifesto* (1924).
2 Carl Sternheim, *The German Revolution* (Berlin 1919), p. 11.
3 Martin Heidegger, *What is Metaphysics?*, edited by Ralph Mannheim (New York, 1961), pp. 11 and 33.
4 Roland Barthes, *Writing Degree Zero* (London, 1967), p. 63.
5 In a letter, July 1914.
6 Roland Barthes, *Writing Degree Zero* (London 1967), p. 48.
7 W. B. Yeats, 'The Symbolism of Poetry', in the *Dome*, April 1900, pp. 249–57.
8 W. B. Yeats, 'Under Ben Bulben'.

THE POETRY OF THE CITY

G.M. HYDE

I

IT could be argued that Modernist literature was born in the city and with Baudelaire – especially with his discovery that crowds mean loneliness and that the terms 'multitude' and 'solitude' are interchangeable for a poet with an active and fertile imagination:[1]

> *Multitude, solitude: termes égaux et convertibles pour le poète actif et fécond. Qui ne sait pas peupler sa solitude, ne sait pas non plus être seul dans une foule affairée.**

The closeness of these near-homophones (*multitude, solitude*) persuades us, through an arabesque of Baudelaire's active and fertile imagination, to see the masses as a generalized abstraction of the same order as the noun *solitude*: and Eliot's *Waste Land* is prefigured. Cities get less real as they get closer: or as one gets closer to them. This proposition defies the laws of perspective in a characteristically Modernist way:

> Jerusalem Athens Alexandria
> Vienna London
> Unreal.

Eliot, at that point in his poem, the nadir of the wheel of history, changes direction: his search for the point at which the time-bound and the timeless intersect takes on overtly the forms of Christian myth. The quest for the grail has more substance than the unredeemed urban multitudes, whom Eliot presses into service as specimens of degeneracy and sterility. Other major modernist poets (Crane, Mayakovsky) have explained the unreality of the unreal city as a failure of art rather than as a human failure: profoundly at odds with

---

*Multitude, solitude: equivalent and interchangeable terms to the shaping spirit of the poet. If you don't know how to people your solitude, you don't know either how to be alone in a busy crowd.

the anti-democratic attitudes of the Symbolist generation, Crane finds Helen of Troy in a streetcar, Mayakovsky contemplates with glee the urban proletariat as agents of the millennium, and in the work of both poets a renewal of cities goes along with a renewal of poetry, entailing an anti-Symbolist view of language as the property of the people, not of any purifying cultural élite. But Crane and Mayakovsky, the architects of the transfigured urban environment whose mythical worlds were too big for one man to sustain, also mark the demise of the Modernist city: Crane drowned himself in 1932, Mayakovsky shot himself in 1930. The work of both poets displays a confusion between the revolutionary power of poetry and the enacted apocalypse, the end of historical time. The dilemma is implicit in Baudelaire's work.

If multitude and solitude are equal and convertible terms, the city has no objective reality. In *Les Fenêtres*, Baudelaire enlarges on this proposition:[2]

> *Celui qui regard du dehors à travers une fenêtre ouverte, ne voit jamais autant de choses que celui qui regarde une fenêtre fermée. Il n'est pas d'objet plus profond, plus mystérieux, plus fécond, plus ténébreux, plus éblouissant qu'une fenêtre éclairée d'une chandelle.**

The word *fécond* recurs in a crucial position here: the city is inherently unpoetic (the basic Romantic attitude to the question; despite Wordsworth's Westminster Bridge sonnet, where the poet catches the city as it were off-guard, sleeping unawares in a remarkably natural posture); and yet the city is inherently the most poetic of all material. It depends how you look at it. The dominance of viewpoint over material is characteristically Modernist, and in Baudelaire's poetry point of view can be studied as it drags its scaly coils out of the Romantic cavern in which it was engendered. It naturally enough takes up residence in the pluralistic modern city. Baudelaire is uneasy about the status of his proposition, anticipating a sharp reply from the reader, and feels he has to defend his position. The stance (defensive yet arrogant) has become the classic pose of Modernist writers, the

---

*Looking through an open window from outside you never see as much as when you look at a shut window. Nothing exists more profound, more mysterious, more creative, more shadowy or more dazzling than a window lit up by a candle.

debate with an imagined, but for that reason only too real, interlocutor has become the very mode of existence of many Modernist works of art ('Let us go then, you and I'). Classically dialectic in Baudelaire, it becomes nervous and self-mocking in Laforgue, and reverberates plangently in *Prufrock* and *The Waste Land*. Often it is as much a dialogue with self as a dialogue with an other, and seems to relate to the characteristic disease of modern civilizations, schizophrenia. Even Baudelaire, of course, is in fact his own interlocutor:[3]

> *Peut-être me direz-vous: 'Es-tu sûr que cette légende soit la vraie?' Qu'importe ce que peut être la réalité placée hors de moi, si elle m'a aidé à vivre, à sentir que je suis et ce que je suis.*★

This solipsism finds a sad echo in Eliot's 'These fragments I have shored against my ruins': and it will serve as an introduction to another issue of Modernism that finds its fit metaphor in images of cities: the question of the individual talent's relation to the literary tradition, myself and my race, my race and its past.

2

The city Baudelaire wrote in was the expanding Paris of the Second Empire, Haussmann's splendid city, proliferating monumental neoclassical façades and served for the first time by roads that were planned (as opposed to being just the gaps between buildings), and sewers and water pipes quite separate and distinct from each other. It suggested a revival of the glories of ancient Rome (or was meant to); the primacy of roads embodied the dominant idea of communications integrating the whole. It offered to be a late flower of the Enlightenment: but like all such late flowers it took on the rigid forms of an *immortelle* rather than the living plasticity of a natural growth. The city and its life were dominated by the ideology of the *bourgeoisie*; it was inevitable that dissident elements would rise up within it and against it. The poet belonged literally and symbolically to the garrets and attics that lurked behind the huge façades: not dreaming, as yet, of a

★You will say to me, perhaps, 'Are you sure that your tale is a true one?' What do I care about the reality of the world around me, if only it helps me to live, to feel I exist and to know what I am.

transfigured city, a new order, but trying to explain to himself why he was necessarily damned in a society that was so sure of its salvation. The fate of Evgeny, in Pushkin's poem *The Bronze Horseman* (written in 1833, but first published posthumously in 1841), foreshadowed this condition as it foreshadowed indeed the great urban novels of Dostoyevsky. The little clerk, Evgeny, caught between the flood (Nature's revenge on man for his hubris in setting up his city in opposition to her will) and the rigid memorial of the enlightened despot who founded St Petersburg, goes mad. His room is let out to an impoverished poet, says Pushkin drily. Herein lies Pushkin's difference from Baudelaire and the reason why, despite his acknowledged place at the head of nineteenth-century Russian fiction, his sensibility does not strike us as modern. He saw the city of St Petersburg in Hegelian terms, as the embodiment of the idea of Freedom, and his premonitions of the tyranny emerging from the ruthless subjection of the natural (including man, for the rationalist Pushkin) to the dictates of the concrete embodiment of the Idea is refracted through an art that is at heart Apollonian, severe and graceful like the city itself. The contradictions inherent in the poem are radically different from the contradictions inherent in such a poem as Baudelaire's *Le Cygne* (*The Swan*), and they will all be acted out on the stage of history. St Petersburg, built in conscious imitation of Western cities like Amsterdam, growing in the course of the eighteenth century in a rational and harmonious wholeness, enacts in stone the disciplined urbanity of Pushkin's verse. For all the tragic contradictions embodied in the patterns of ironic parallels that constitute the structure of the poem, the early tribute to the city of light in whose white nights the poet can read and write without a lamp is a positive factor in the dialectic. Baudelaire's Paris presents by contrast only the travesty of classicism: its façades hide squalor (probably this was always so: only now, with the dissolution of social forms, the collapse of the natural hierarchies, it shows). The classical city which Auden described well in his essay *The Poet and the City*,[4] where institutions are a guarantee of freedom and public life expresses man's highest faculties, is parodied in the conspicuous consumption that shapes Haussmann's architecture. Uniformity of style and structure which once bore radiant witness to the fact that civilized men everywhere spoke the same language and could communicate with urbane ease now threatens to shut men in a hard carapace: the hypocrisies of the Second Empire. Spleen is above all a feeling of enclosure (the theme which dominates Blake's urban poetry: since historically enclosures populated cities), and freedom now is all inward. The language of poetry is a restrictive form: in France, Romanticism, despite Hugo's boast, had not dislocated the classical Alexandrine, or at least not dislodged it: the literary language is threatened by the clichés of dead forms of oratory (and the Romantics themselves were not blameless in this matter); the dialect of the tribe must be purified. Baudelaire's urban poetry is not marked by radical formal innovation (though sometimes, as in *Crépuscule du Soir* (*Evening Twilight*), he works on the Alexandrine from within, exploiting its formal balance as a vehicle for juxtapositions of lyrical and sordid material): but the problems that lead to modernist innovations in form are urgently expressed in his work. They arise from the problematic relationship of the poet to his audience, to his race, to his cultural inheritance, to his environment, to his reader. The problems are all, as I have said, essentially problems of relationship in a society which offers only a false and hypocritical account of how its parts inter-relate; the city is the metaphor, the only adequate metaphor, through which relational problems can be expressed. Exigencies of the market demand that the poet move to the city, like any artisan; and competitive pressures dictate that he shall precariously exist in a state of war with his society and all the other entertainers squabbling for the surplus cash of the rising *bourgeoisie* who alone guarantee the material basis of art: they are its consumers, and those who pay the piper want to call the tune. Isolated in this way, the poet turns inward with a desperate inwardness different from Romantic subjectivity, and puts together the cultural fragments that give him a private sense of belonging and a sense that an order exists, however personal. The poet then has his cultural context, even if he has to keep re-inventing it.

Baudelaire's poem *Le Cygne* focuses all these issues and anticipates the themes and methods of *The Waste Land*. Its opening invocation of a living classical tradition (transmitted through Racine) contrasts it, in an Eliotesque way, with a reduced present, and constitutes an early contribution to that inverted historicism that denies confident proclamations of progress and substitutes an assertion of regress: the myth of the Fall, the decline of the West. The river is eternal (cf. the

Neva in Pushkin's poem, the Thames in Eliot's) and waters give life (the favourite *fécond, fécondé*) as the river evokes other remembered and imagined rivers and the poet repossesses the fragments of a shattered cultural tradition, classical ironically juxtaposed with neo-classical, and is reassured by fragmentariness in the face of oppressive totalities which deny fertility:[5]

> *Le vieux Paris n'est plus (la forme d'une ville*
> *Change plus vite, hélas! que le coeur d'un mortel).*

The swan of the poem's title is one of Baudelaire's many urban outcasts, suffering firstly because it has escaped from its cage (a nice irony) and the pavement is hard, but more because it longs for the burst of thunder bringing rain, the epiphany that ends Eliot's *Waste Land*. The crucial stanza is placed vulnerably at the beginning of the second section of the poem:[6]

> *Paris change! mais rien dans ma mélancolie*
> *N'a bougé! palais neufs, échafaudages, blocs,*
> *Vieux faubourgs, tout pour moi devient allégorie,*
> *Et mes chers souvenirs sont plus lourds que des rocs.*†

Call it allegory, myth, symbol: the order to which the poet belongs can have only inner reality, when he is to this extent estranged from his society and intensely conscious of the fact that one cannot change essences by changing façades. This estrangement has nothing to do with Rousseau's complacent assertion that he may not be better than other men but at least he is different: Rousseau didn't doubt for a moment that he was better than other men. Baudelaire feels himself full of some painfully raw material which no forms can embody, yet which is the dearest thing he owns. It is the rock from which the blocks to build civilization are hewn; it is ages-old; it is his cultural inheritance, and ours; and it is a crippling burden to him. In such poems as *Le Cygne* and *Les Sept Vieillards* (*The Seven Old Men*), urban images, raised to what Eliot described with restraint as 'the first intensity', shape themselves into the allegory which begins to

---

*The old Paris no longer exists (the shape of a city changes more quickly, alas, than a mortal heart).

†Paris changes, but nothing has stirred in my gloom. New *palais*, scaffolding, blocks, old suburbs, everything turns into allegory for me, and my dearest memories weigh heavier than rocks.

express the tragic dividedness of the modern artist and, through him, of modern man.

3

Baudelaire's poetry has a moral stature that dwarfs the work of most of his followers and imitators. After him come many variations on the urban themes stated in his work. In England the greatest urban poetry is in prose, in the novels of Dickens: his follower and sensitive critic, George Gissing, though he lacked Dickens's profound originality and humanity, goes on to express in a way his master did not the rootlessness of the sensitive individual at the mercy of the commercial pressures of the metropolis. His very lack of creative richness adds to the pathos of his work by bringing home to the reader the defeating magnitude of the imaginative effort required to create one's own order from the void, as the modern artist must. The ghost of community haunts Gissing's world, in such a novel as *New Grub Street*, taking on mocking shapes of married happiness, secure family life, the fellowship of scholars: a longing for rest draws close to a longing for death. In the English poetry of the nineties there is a recognition of the truth of Clough's contention that the true province of the discrowned modern Apollo is the great metropolis;[7] but with the real life of English poetry flowing in quite other channels, it isn't surprising that for the most part the rhapsodies, voluntaries, theatrical décors and impressions of most of the city poetry of this period, bent on catching the fleeting movement and kaleidoscopic light of a changing environment, are parasitic upon French Symbolist verse and Impressionist painting, of which it reflects only the superficies. Two notable exceptions deserve mention: John Davidson, mainly for his extraordinary *Thirty Bob a Week*, and James Thomson, for the ramshackle masterpiece which must surely be the closest literary equivalent of mock-Gothic Victorian London, *The City of Dreadful Night*. Eliot, at all events, felt that both had contributed to the Modernist tradition a native English element that was not imitated from continental literature. Davidson's native Englishness is his strongest quality: the urban proletariat makes way for the British working man, diction and rhythms mime popular speech, and we are in the world of 'lonely men in shirtsleeves', the world Prufrock hurries through to reach the

deceptive drawing-rooms which welcome him mockingly with a
sham culture, the women who come and go and talk of Michelangelo.
Davidson's poem is a dialogue with the reader. In this it isn't original,
but its argumentative heckling tone, that of a dissenting voice at a
complacent public meeting – the way it makes the reader a member of
a complacent public meeting – is very disturbing; and its argot is used
to organize an intricate argument that by turns parodies high culture,
ironically dismisses the poetry of imperialism, and radically questions
the social Darwinism that directs Victorian society. It gives the impression of having been written under great emotional pressure: public
issues have forced their way back into verse, and refuse to be kept out;
the current language has insisted on making itself heard. For a moment,
the poet, spokesman of high culture, has joined forces with the victims
of anarchy: but whatever Eliot learned from Davidson about ways of
getting a living speech idiom into poetry, he learned nothing about
how to use the lyric for public discourse: he misleadingly praises
Baudelaire, we remember, for his deliberate eschewal of public issues
dear to the reforming nineteenth century.

James Thomson's *City of Dreadful Night* is rather a frighteningly
authentic document than an achieved literary work. Its large structure
is a deliberate Gothic ruin, its philosophy an odd perversion of Calvin-
ism. Thomson was a free-thinker: but the announcement that God is
dead, made to the hungry congregation of a huge cathedral, brings
no release from moral agony. Thomson was quite sure he was among
the damned, and no mere Darwinian theory about the origin of
species could shake his belief: this is his personal hell, a gigantic
reflector held up to Victorian doubts and scruples. But worse: if
God is dead, it means only that his purgatory is quite meaningless,
and there is no domain of timelessness to rescue man from his historical
trap, even by damning him. The eternal succession of the known is
the organizing principle of the universe as it is of time-bound Victorian urban life. Remove the hands from the clock, says one of the
ghostly interlocutors that loom in and out of the poem, in a very
modern image, and it still runs on:

> As whom his one intense thought overpowers
>   He answered coldly, Take a watch, erase
> The signs and figures of the circling hours,
>   Detach the hands, remove the dial-face;

> The works proceed until run down; although
> Bereft of purpose, void of use, still go.

The language of these wraiths, especially in the dialogues in which nothing is communicated, prefigures Eliot: here and in the poetry of Jules Laforgue he found the idiom of Prufrock, the language of a man handicapped by his sensitivity and frustrated in his attempts to throw a bridge across to the Other:[8]

> And you have after all come back; come back.
> I was about to follow on your track.
> And you have failed: our spark of hope is black.

> *Bref, j'allais me donner d'un 'Je vous aime'*
> *Quand je m'avisai non sans peine*
> *Que d'abord, je ne me possédais pas moi-même.*★

> . . . If one, settling a pillow by her head,
> Should say: 'That is not what I meant at all,
> That is not it, at all.'

These are all dialogues between lovers: attempts to escape the prison of self resultant upon the equivalence of solitude and multitude. If modern man is spiritually crippled, he bears still deeper wounds in his passional centres: one way or another, sterility is his lot. *The Waste Land* is about sterility: especially where it is about burning sexual desire, in the section founded on the Buddha's Fire Sermon. Crane's *The Bridge*, consequently, builds a bridge from modern man to Pocahontas, Indian princess, chaste, yet radiant with sexuality. His prothalamion, *For the Marriage of Faustus and Helen*, marries Spengler's time-bound Faustian man to his vision of eternal beauty, Helen. Both poems are inordinately conscious of Eliot: this is manifest in the deliberate polemic they conduct with the idiom and imagery of *The Waste Land*. Where Eliot's long historical perspective creates a powerful sense of the inescapable presence of the traditions embodied in the mind of Europe, against which the present is evaluated, Crane's wilful mythologizing presses what of the past can be made to work into the service of an eclectic imagination that celebrates the untrammelled future. The fine delight that fathers thought, the loss of

★In short, I was about to surrender myself, with an 'I love you', when, not without distress, I registered the fact that I wasn't really mine to give.

which Hopkins lamented in his sonnet, sustains Crane's art (or so he would have us believe: he is less than completely convincing); and his Dionysiac thrust finds expression in an eroticism quite alien to the world of *The Waste Land*, in which sexuality is presented only as sterile or sordid. The prostitute, stripper, and prim virgin of the *Three Songs* (Section Five of *The Bridge*) may all be 'wrong', but they are not wrong as Eliot's typist and young man carbuncular are wrong. Their unsatisfactoriness as images of sexuality lies in their one-dimensionality: they have been, in Crane's own phrase from *Faustus and Helen*, 'untwisted by the world dimensional', split off by the material world from the great totality to which all life aspires. Nevertheless, through them shines the form of Pocahontas (a mixture of Red Indian myth and Platonism, this), just as the girl in the street-car and the flapper in the night-club in *Faustus and Helen* are incarnations of Helen. One may imagine what Eliot made of Crane's pursuit of strange gods: the conceptual system of *The Waste Land*, however personal, rests upon an austere orthodoxy; an act of impurity has dried up the lifegiving water, and the land will not bloom again until it has been atoned. It is easy to see how *The Waste Land*, a poem sustained by a great culture, revaluing that culture from the stand-point of the present, and yet profoundly negative, should have challenged Crane to make good the optimism that had shaped America's history, and to do so in Eliot's own terms by making the metropolis central to his poem and using as his organizing symbol the artifice that rests on nothing, the suspension bridge. The sardonic mimicry of urban accents, in Eliot, gives way to what Crane himself described as 'an idiom for the proper transition of jazz into words'. Drawing on Whitman (and thus Emerson too) Crane raises an airy structure of unsupported metaphor in the shape of Brooklyn Bridge, Roebling's web of steel which enacts nature's subordination to man's heroic will.[9] The catenary curve of steel is stabilized by the weight of road-and-railway it bears: throwing a bridge across a river is an act symbolic of pioneering confidence and exploration, yet this bridge is thoroughly urban in its location and an advanced technical feat. It replaces the Brooklyn Ferry sung by Whitman and communicates not only with Manhattan Island but with the unknown body of America's future. Interestingly Eliot chose to print, in the *Criterion*, just one section of Crane's poem: the section devoted to the tunnel under the bridge, a descent into the underworld. The ideal engenders its dark antithesis: *The Tunnel* goes down as deep as Thomson or Eliot into the underworld of a bewildered and brutalized humanity, where the ghost of Poe lurks, the man who, as Crane says accusingly, 'denied the ticket'. But Crane's tunnel emerges reassuringly into the daylight: the subway train leads us through this urban hell almost unscathed, and without Prufrock's guilty sense of complicity; the city opens on to a river promising renewal (Crane working still with the symbols of *The Waste Land*) and imbued with a kind of manic innocence. If the dynamics of Crane's bridge are less accurately plotted than those of Roebling's, the power of the verse everywhere bears witness to the intensity of the need which engendered it.

Crane's poetry is in many ways paralleled by that of the Russian Futurist, Mayakovsky, who in his *A Cloud in Trousers* sings of a transfigured city in a public poetry which has as much of the tone of prophecy in it as Crane's, but a good deal more political oratory. As with the socialist Verhaeren, some of whose poems have a Maya-kovskyan millenarian ring, the city is for Mayakovsky not the jungle or desert of Thomson's imagery, but rather some monstrous creature, a *Ville Tentaculaire* (to borrow the title of one of Verhaeren's collections) endowed with the alienated life of the people whose blood it has fed on. Its institutions embody the distorted and exaggerated passions of its less-than-human inhabitants, turning back threateningly on its victims, negating human life and love – the poet presents himself both as prophet and sacrificial victim. Mayakovsky, who on the one hand realizes the dialectics of the city with a vividness that recalls Blake, on the other hand brings us close to the metropolis of German Expressionism, discussed in another essay in this collection. Nearly a century after Pushkin, Mayakovsky proffers a Marxist reformulation of enlightenment aspirations. The capitalist city must fall: its place will be taken by the Socialist community. No artist has yet built this city, though several have satirized (Zamyatin, in *We,* for example) the mathematics of its blueprint.

Notes

1 Baudelaire, *Le Spleen de Paris*, XII, *Les Foules*. Cf. Walter Benjamin, *Illuminations* (London 1970).
2 Baudelaire, ibid, XXXV.

3 Baudelaire, ibid.

4 W. H. Auden, *The Dyer's Hand* (London 1962).

5 Baudelaire, *Le Cygne*.

6 Baudelaire, *Le Cygne*.

7 A. H. Clough, 'Recent English Poetry: A Review', *North American Review*, vol. lxxvii, July 1853.

8 James Thomson, *The City of Dreadful Night*; Jules Laforgue, 'Dimanches'; T. S. Eliot, 'The Love Song of J. Alfred Prufrock'.

9 On this see Alan Trachtenberg, *Brooklyn Bridge* (New York and London 1965).

THE PROSE POEM AND FREE VERSE

CLIVE SCOTT

I

ONE of the principal concerns of emergent Modernism was the redemption from the aesthetic of the experiential and the existential. Ways were sought to make art not an imitation of reality nor an alternative reality but an intensification of reality. Regular verse seemed to many only to distract or to cushion; its formality meant that a lot of non-verbal matters were taken for granted or became achievement; words functioned primarily in relation to their position in a structure and what ultimately concerned the reader was what the poet *ended up* by saying. Many of the poets of the later nineteenth and early twentieth centuries wanted something which would allow them to say as they went along, they wanted meaning to reside in the process of experience. Hence the pressure towards *vers libre*, and the growing traffic between poetry and prose. Prose was looked to because it moves at a pace of its own making, has an option on itself at every step, is able to capitalize upon coincidence, creates its own impetus and is good at registering life's miscellaneousness. Why not a poetry of the odd thought that springs to mind and is as quickly forgotten? Prose is supremely impressionable and should be able to mould itself to the human condition at any particular historical moment; Brecht, for example, gives the following reasons for using free, prose rhythms in his verse drama *Leben Eduards des Zweiten von England* (*The life of Edward II of England*):

Ich bemühte mich um die Darstellung gewisser Interferenzen, ungleich-mässiger Entwicklungen menschlicher Schicksale, des Hin-und-her historischer Vorgänge, der 'Zufälligkeiten'. Die Sprache hatte dem zu entsprechen.*

*I concerned myself with the representation of certain interferences, of irregular developments in human destinies, of the erratic nature of historical events, of 'coincidences'. The language had to be appropriate to these needs.

349

Prose may have more difficulty in compressing meanings than verse, but it has the compensation of being able to compress many tones, by liberating or challenging the resourcefulness of the voice. The incursions of prose into poetry as a relevant and conventional form have been various and international – one might point to Wordsworth's *Lyrical Ballads*, to Tieck's *Reisegedichte eines Kranken* (*Travel poems of a sick man*), to the *alexandrin familier* of Sainte-Beuve and Maurice de Guérin, as one might point to a host of other examples. The incursions of poetry into prose are equally numerous. But nowhere perhaps is the attempt at reconciliation so thorough-going, nor so formally developed, as in the prose poem.

2

The prose poem is then part of a general movement toward a free verse. But it is a peculiarly French phenomenon, probably because the segregation of verse and prose practised in France was for so long so complete,[1] that the prose poem had an urgent liaisory function to fulfil. Its origins lay primarily and variously in poetic prose from Fénelon to Chateaubriand, biblical prose, and prose translations of foreign lyrics. The Romantics defended this generical hybrid, as they defended all hybrids, by calling the natural order to witness – Barbey d'Aurevilly's apology for the prose poem is reminiscent of Hugo's for the '*mélange des genres*' in his *Cromwell* preface:[2]

> *Dans l'ordre des créations de l'esprit comme dans les créations de la nature, il y a des créations intermédiaires entre les créations contrastantes. Le monde ne se rompt pas en* deux, *mais se relie toujours en* trois. *La Nature procède par nuances, l'esprit aussi.**

Indeed the history of the prose poem is the history of inquiry into the form and of avoidance of an answer. Each author tests the strengths and weaknesses of the short prose piece only to find that it has many of both and that he is moving further and further away from a formula. In fact, one of the fundamental qualities of the prose poem

*In the order of the mind's creations, just as in the order of nature's creations, there are intermediate creations between contrasting ones. The world is not divided into *two* but is always conjoined in *three*. Nature proceeds by gradation, as does the mind.

is its ability to retain its accidental nature, its *uncontrollable* novelty. And that discontinuous history makes it difficult to decide whether the prose poem has circumscribed itself sufficiently to make it generically distinct, whether it is a literary oddity used by odd poets, or whether it is best seen as something transitory and transitional, whose main value lies in its stimulation of new forms and of free verse in particular – which would seem to involve saying that all modern examples of the form, those of the Surrealists, for instance, are in some sense archaizing.

The prose poem is as often as not a gradual thwarting or suppression of narration or description. Most obviously perhaps, the writer produces a prose velocity that is either too fast for narrative, as with the notational prose of Laforgue's 'Grande complainte de la ville de Paris' ('Grand lament of the city of Paris'), or too slow – one of the ways that Lautréamont 'cretinizes' his readers is by taking all the time in the world to tell them that he is getting on with the story:[3]

(*Ce serait bien peu connaître sa profession d'écrivain à sensation, que de ne pas, au moins, mettre en avant les restrictives interrogations après lesquelles arrive immédiatement la phrase que je suis sur le point de terminer.*)*

Or alternatively, the writer translates the dynamic vigour of narration into the arresting vigour of image-making. Bertrand's poems in *Gaspard de la nuit* (*Gaspard of the Night*) (published posthumously in 1842) are often like heavily cut films, a selection of briefly held frames that threaten not to be sequential. The characters of 'L'Écolier de Leyde' ('The student of Leyden'), for example, are figures in a series of suggestive arrangements, and only become protagonists in an action when the absent footage is supplied or when the mind, disregarding the blank space between the frames, coerces them into continuity. In the work of the less worthy, this kind of immobilization too often takes the form of sheer 'adjectivalization', so that description becomes décor. The adjective that should show off and direct the noun ends by being the noun's reason for existing. Lautréamont double-crosses so-called 'artistic' prose by making the ascription of adjectives part of a tiresome routine:[4]

*(It would be a sure sign of one's ignorance of one's calling as a writer of sensational literature not at least to put forward these restrictive questions, which will be followed immediately by the sentence that I am about to bring to a close).

Les branches penchent sur lui leur élévation touffue, afin de le préserver de la rosée, et la brise, faisant résonner les cordes de sa harpe mélodieuse, envoie ses accords joyeux, à travers le silence universel, vers ses paupières baissées, qui croient assister, immobiles, au concert cadencé des mondes suspendus.★

Poetry can sustain a greater density of ornament simply because blank space lets air in. Prose can be alleviated only by its own 'prosyness', by lulls in meaning; ornamental prose either intercalates poetic space or congeals, as Lautréamont lets it.

Some prose poets also counter narrative by rhythmic means, by overlaying it with non-prosaic cadences. Reading an ordinary narrative, we accentuate its eventfulness by making our voice full of event, by variation of tone, pitch and speed. Prose cadences do not exist in themselves of course, they are merely the way any particular voice moulds itself to phrases and clauses of varying length and importance. Cadences become poetic when we find ourselves regularly returning to a particular one until we feel it controlling our reading; it assumes the proportions of an overseeing will, enveloping the narrative with an aura of absoluteness and depriving it of the capriciousness of a fiction. Maurice de Guérin's 'Le Centaure' ('The Centaur') (1840) and 'La Bacchante' (published posthumously in 1862) employ this technique. Biblical prose too has this poetic cadence: in Wilde's prose poems, we find ourselves *intoning* a narrative, we are aware of things happening but cannot prevent them happening ceremoniously; Hebraic history becomes divine law even in the reading.

All the techniques just discussed concern the medium only, prose; they tell us how prose becomes poetic, but not how it becomes poem. It would be idle to suggest any single source. Suffice it to say that the prose poem's poem-ness may lie in its brevity, inasmuch as some prose poems are prose versions of imagined verse originals; this brevity, as in the verse lyric, derives from the natural equation of emotion and ellipsis, depth and density, and the fulfilment of a form which is under too much sustained pressure to last long. But many prose poems create the sense of poem-ness by the way they end.

★The branches arch their tall foliage over him, to protect him from the dew, and the breeze, plucking at the strings of its tuneful harp, wafts light-hearted harmonies, through the universal silence, towards his lowered eyelids which have the illusion of participating, motionless, in the cadenced concert of suspended worlds.

Often in Bertrand as in Baudelaire, the poem is a field of vision, where people submit themselves to the poet's scrutiny before they reclaim their own peculiar privacies out of the picture. For Bertrand, this mode demonstrates that even chance cannot tolerate waste, that history is always in the making. Baudelaire's poems ('Les Vocations' ('Vocations'), 'La Belle Dorothée' ('The Beautiful Dorothy'), 'Les Veuves' ('Widows')) reach into that privacy, into an irreducible condition confidently typified; Baudelaire has compassion, but to some purpose. Other prose poems end, not with a clearing of the stage but with the recalcitrant persistence of the subject. This kind of poem ends in frustration, not consentingly, but because, quite suddenly, it is unable to go on.

Claudel's 'Jardins' ('Gardens') (*Connaissance de l'est* (*Knowledge of the East*)) (1900), for example, comes to a close as the poet's eye alights on a great rock, in which is concentrated the secret power of the whole view and the poet's sudden sense of alienation. The poem ends because prose can no longer cope, because it has not the resources to deal with dumbfoundedness. This sudden impotence of prose accompanies the refusal of the commonplace to remain docile, the realization that an object has designs on the individual's peace of mind. Again, in some of Baudelaire's depictions of Parisian characters in *Le Spleen de Paris*, the subject draws inexorably closer to the poet, until he alone is exclusively concerned, *'tout pour moi devient allégorie'* ('everything for me becomes symbolic'). Poems like 'Le Vieux Saltimbanque' ('The Old Acrobat') or 'Les Yeux des pauvres' ('The Eyes of the Poor') end with a failure of integration, a refusal to let involvement of the self become formal accomplishment, to let exclamation become apostrophe, a question become rhetorical. Rimbaud's *Les Illuminations* (written 1872–6), while providing examples of the paroxysmal ending when words fall short ('H', 'Being Beauteous'), also contains poems that end with negative forms of speechlessness, the speechlessness of lethargy, loss of interest, overwhelming dispiritedness ('Barbare' ('Barbarian'), 'Les Ponts' ('The Bridges'), 'Conte' ('Tale')). At the other end of the scale is the laconic ending, not the 'I can't say more' but the 'Need I say more'; Bertrand's 'Le Maçon' ('The Mason'), for instance, closes with the sight of a village set fire to by marauding soldiers, but it succeeds in being no more than a painterly image – *'une comète dans l'azur'* ('a comet in the sky') – and not the image of human brutality it should be; while the cathedral sleeps along with those who idly amuse themselves in its shadow, singular and sudden acts of god-lessness – there is a change of tense from present to past historic – take place.

3

Often the prose poem would seem to be a method of capturing the pre-poetic; the dynamism of Rimbaud's poems is owed largely to a coming to life, a taking or changing shape. Here the very fluidity of the genre derives from the fact that it aims at registering nothing more than the impulse to make poetry, the emergence of poetic raw material. It is gestation made visible, the often awkward attempt of something to be and to be uniquely. Rimbaldian prose poems are an exploration of many different kinds of formality, so that para-doxically we are left with the impression of a form's insufficiency or of the evasion of form; they offer a way of breaking out of the critical situation described, some years later by Hofmannsthal:[5]

> *Wir denken die bequemen Gedanken der anderen und fühlens nicht, dass unser bestes Selbst allmählich abstirbt. Wir leben ein totes Leben. Wir ersticken unser Ich.* *

The desire to replace a stylized lyric self with a self more intimate, more authentic, would appear to have been one of the reasons for adopting free verse – for Gustave Kahn, free verse provides the means *'d'écrire son rythme propre et individuel au lieu d'endosser un uniforme taillé d'avance'* ('to write one's own unique rhythm, rather than putting on an off-the-peg uniform') ('Préface sur le vers libre', 1897) – and for adopting a stanzaic form of free verse; any number of lines of any length can be combined in any number of *inimitable* ways. But no verse, however free, can avoid being an open invitation to read in terms of verse habit; no rhythm, no line can get far enough away from some conventional paradigm not at least to be an allusion to it and no freedom has any meaning unless we know what it is

---

* We think the reassuring thoughts of others and do not notice our most valuable self withering away. We live a death-in-life. We stifle our very self.

freedom from. Dujardin may claim *'Le vers libre ne modifie pas, il ignore le nombre des syllabes'* ('Free verse does not look to modify the number of syllables, it knows nothing of syllable-counting') (*Les Premiers Poètes du vers libre*, 1922), but this does not make them any less countable. In the cause of intimacy, the prose poem may fare better than free verse, but by the same token, it is likelier to have to regard its oddity as its supreme, if not sole, virtue.

When one cherishes the notion of being absolutely new and absolutely unrenewable, because one is always and never oneself from instant to instant, then one must work with devices that most nearly derive from nothing and beget nothing, one wilfully destroys literary continuity. But Rimbaud himself lost faith in his loss of faith. He is pathetically careful to supply an ancestry of *voyants*, and his confidence is always unstable, threatened by the possibility of regret. In many of the 'autobiographical' poems, in the past rather than the liberating present tense, the usual welter of undifferentiated phenomena, moored neither in time nor space, takes on the damning sequentialness, consequentialness, of anecdote. Ultimately Rimbaud is left not with a sense of achievement but with a sense of the ludicrous systematicness of his intentions. But he had left an example for that rhapsodic species of free verse which clings to the shaky idea that words are all communication and as it were simultaneous with the experiences they transmit, and not intervention, obstacle, and not capable of accidentally ageing the experience they transmit by several hundred years. Lawrence's 'Introduction' to his *New Poems* (1920) is an extreme declaration of Rimbaldian directions:

Give me the still, white seething, the incandescence and the coldness of the incarnate moment: the moment, the quick of all change and haste and opposition: the moment, the immediate present, the Now.

The notational prose which Rimbaud so often has recourse to, as do other prose poets, is an attempt to diminish that fictional, syntactical time between now (and) now, to make a prose that is recurrently instantaneous. Even his more extended sentences are not so much artificial prolongations of time in description as a continuous procession of coalescing images. Description itself dissipates the eruptive energy of the image and casts doubt on its self-sufficiency; in fact Rimbaud's 'Veillées I' would appear to be a demonstration of the ability of the image by itself to present 'an intellectual and emotional complex in an instant of time' (Pound, 'A Retrospect. A Few Don'ts'). Modernist, and in particular Imagist, literature gives us a whole aesthetic of speed and suddenness. Pound's enlargement on his definition of the image is well known, and T. E. Hulme asserts:[6]

Literature a method of sudden arrangement of commonplaces. *The suddenness* makes us forget the commonplace.

Literature is here approaching advertising techniques;[7] the conversion of the object into sensation, the equation of the rawness of that sensation with its significance, shock with persuasion. But if the abrupt presentation of the object liberates the object, the role of poetry differs from that of the poster in that it must be more than merely effective. The art of the Imagist poem is precisely to envelop the sudden and sensational with reflective quietness, to deliver the imaginatively loud *sotto voce*, in short, not to let it waste its meaning in its sheer unexpectedness.

Metaphor must be a central element in any aesthetic of speed, for metaphor is one perception overtaking another, a state of affairs that language is powerless to convey except by indirect means. Hofmannsthal makes much of metaphor's speed – he calls it an *'Erleuchtung, in der wir einen Augenblick lang den grossen Weltzusammenhang ahnen'* ('illumination in which, for no more than a moment, we have glimpses of the universal analogy') (*Philosophie des Metaphorischen*) (*Philosophy of the Metaphorical*) – as does Pound, quoting Aristotle in support ('A Serious Artist'). And it would not be too much to suggest that metaphor owed much of its new-found vigour to its use in prose or prosaic contexts. The matter-of-factness of tone might easily convince us that such metaphors are matters of fact. Anything out of context is more fully itself than in context; metaphor in prose is more nakedly and alarmingly metaphorical than in verse. It is no longer one of a particular form's habits of speech, part of the act, but a figure born out of a reality that has no knowledge of such figures. Its power is doubled by its borrowing the submissiveness of prose.

It might disturb to find Rimbaud treated as a precursor, however indirect, of two literary trends as far apart as 'Rhapsodism' and Imagism; that such a thing is possible derives from that fusion of first and third person perspectives which characterises the prose poem, and the

Rimbaldian one especially. For it is precisely this bizarre mingling of two perspectives that allows Rimbaud to discover the very world he is putting together; Rimbaud's poems involve both the lyric process of undergoing oneself and the more properly novelistic business of mapping out a behaviour.

4

But there is another kind of prose poem, the prose poem that has the look of the postpoetic. The presence of the translation in the ancestry of the prose poem should not be overlooked; indeed some prose poets have written their poems with the image of translation clearly in their minds. Barbey d'Aurevilly calls his 'Niobé' *'cette rêverie qu'on croirait traduite d'un poète anglais'* ('this reverie that one might believe to be a translation from an English poet') and explains elsewhere:[8]

> *Et de fait il y a dans le diable de* fouillis *qui est ma nature, . . . couché quelque part, un poète inconnu et c'est des oeuvres cachées de ce poète que ceci a été traduit dans la furie ou la Rêverie d'un moment.**

This may merely be a pretext for flaunting the para-poetry of the prose, but it does suggest too an attempt to rationalize the dual nature of the prose poem. The prose poem–translation is not resonant with its own significance so much as resonant with another poem, a verse original; and its peculiarly poetic flavour derives from its aspiration not to say more than it can, but to be more than it is. The prose poem–translation is at one and the same time investigation and interpretation of a lyric expression and an effort to regain that expression. Apostrophe and brevity are the only authentic relics of the original.

Baudelaire's prose companion pieces to verse poems in *Le Spleen de Paris* are equally translations of them, though the dating is obscure; in the prose 'L'Invitation au voyage' ('Invitation to travel'), he makes it wryly clear that he wishes us to use the prose poem as a springboard for the imaginative reconstruction of a verse original:

---

* And in fact there is, in this devilish muddle which is my nature, an unknown poet buried somewhere, and it is from the works of this poet that this piece has been translated in the poetic frenzy or abstractedness of a moment.

*. . . quel est celui qui composera l'*Invitation au voyage *qu'on puisse offrir à la femme aimée, à la soeur d'élection ?**

With the weakening of the sound ingredient of words in the shift from poetry to prose, words can no longer be their meanings; desire is no longer realized in the words that express it. Furthermore, deprived of the easy and continuous intercourse between the literal and the figurative that we find in poetry, words are reduced to a minimal meaning; the objective correlative becomes object again. Baudelaire's prose 'L'Invitation au voyage' can only manage the clichés of everyone's El Dorado in vulgar excess; the spiritual analogy is a desperate projection by the poet of himself into his image, which fails:

> *Vivrons-nous jamais, passerons-nous jamais dans ce tableau qu'a peint mon esprit, ce tableau qui te ressemble ?†*

But it is a nonsense to try and evaluate the prose against the verse; by translating the verse, Baudelaire does not wish to challenge it but to treat it as a document, to document himself. The verse poem is invulnerable to the prose, but the illusions that went into its making are not. Baudelaire retraces his verse poem back to his own weakness, his own ordinariness; if the prose poem does not manage to leap back into verse poem, it is because Baudelaire is more responsible for it, and insists on admitting responsibility.

Lautréamont also feels a compulsive need to embarrass himself with his own pretensions. As *Les Chants de Maldoror* (*The Cantos of Maldoror*) proceed, the eloquent period of the Romantic sinks imperceptibly into flat-footed over-insistence or the tiresome ramblings of a prematurely senile mind. And the precious periphrases and the inept but fulsome similes do not enhance fact which is already so startling or ugly as to be beyond enhancement, but are left to nurse their gratuitousness; Lautréamont teases poetry by inviting images and comparisons to fall prey to their own intricacy so that poetry-making becomes a form of incompetent casuistry. He mocks the poetry that nevertheless emasculates his prose. The epic dimension of Maldoror slips back again and again into paranoia.

Some of the most attractive effects in these two writers derive from

---

* Who is it who will compose the *Invitation au voyage* that can be offered as a tribute to the loved one, to the chosen sister?

† Will we ever live, will we ever pass into this picture which my imagination has conjured up and which so resembles you?

the poet's vying with his medium, he to establish the eloquent false-hood, and it to be superfluously truthful. Both prose and poetry are shown to be in some sense gratuitous, the former in its comprehensiveness, the latter in its embroidery; so that, precisely in betraying each other, they reveal the one quality that eloquence and veracity have in common. This is the point at which Mallarmé's word '*vespéral*' can meet Laforgue's phrase '*statistiques sanitaires*' :[9]

> *Le sobre et vespéral mystère hebdomadaire*
> *Des statistiques sanitaires*★

These lines demonstrate what much Modernist poetry demonstrates, that any scientific or technical term is poetically viable as long as it is thought of not in connection with a discipline but as a 'rare' combination of vowels and consonants with an exotic etymology, and that poetic diction is as much a technical jargon as any other.

5

Kahn acknowledges Baudelaire as a precursor of his free verse and prose in *Les Palais nomades* (*Nomadic Palaces*) ('Préface sur le vers libre'). If the prose poem was a peculiarly French form, free verse was at least a peculiarly French issue; and if it was treated as an issue in England and America, it was because the poetic upbringing of the new generation of poets – Pound, Eliot, etc. – had been based on French models. The Germans, with the longest and most celebrated tradition in free rhythms, stretching back to Klopstock, kept out of the turn of the century controversy by and large, and when they did come forward to dabble in poetic, it was to tell the rest of Europe that free verse was 'old hat', as Arno Holz did in his *Revolution der Lyrik* (*Revolution in the lyric*) (1899):

> *Die zeitgenössische französische vers-libre-Bewegung . . . scheint mir in Theorie und Praxis erst bis Goethe und Heine gelangt. Das heisst also, nur erst bis zu den sogenannten 'freien', noch nicht aber schon zu den natürlichen Rhythmen.†*

★The weekly sober, vesperal mystery of health statistics

† The contemporary French free-verse-movement . . . seems to me, both in theory and practice, to have got only as far as Goethe and Heine. That means then, only as far as the so-called 'free' rhythms, but still not yet as far as natural rhythms.

But why did the French make such a fuss about a form that had evolved so quietly in other countries? Certainly there is no shortage of sources: the prose poem as we have seen, *vers libéré,* and foreign example – Whitman's influence was probably considerable, and Mauclair argues for the centrality of Heine:[10]

> *Si Heine n'avait pas existé, Verlaine n'eût pas été ce qu'il fut. Il n'y aurait peut-être pas Laforgue, qui fut le premier à faire de vrais et beaux vers poly-morphes en langue française.**

But it should be realized that though the poetic masters of the time may have condoned free verse, they stubbornly refused to practise it; Mallarmé, before his 'Coup de dés' ('A Dice-throw') (1897), felt that poetry could continue to be public ceremonial only if it stayed within the conventions, and Verlaine, for all his own prosodic outrages, treats the *verslibristes* with some scorn in his *Épigrammes:*

> *Que l'ambition du Vers Libre hante*
> *De jeunes cerveaux épris de hasards!*
> *C'est l'ardeur d'une illusion touchante.*
> *On ne peut que sourire à leurs écarts.†*

Furthermore, *vers libre* seemed to involve the setting at nought of two elements that had been considered essential to French prosody, indeed its distinguishing characteristics: number and rhyme. It is number alone that defines the line and thus the line's rhythmic possibilities (i.e. the possible break-downs of the number) and it is rhyme that testifies to the integrity of the line and relates it to other lines. The French *verslibristes* could not really object that French rhythms were too regular because French prosody has always been by nature phrasal, that is to say moving hand in hand with normal syntax; within the limits of number, the line has enjoyed the maximum of suppleness.[11] Their quarrel was rather with the paucity of possible combinations of line-lengths and with the kind of rhyme that merely insisted on the consistency of those line-lengths and the regularity of their

---

*If Heine had not existed, Verlaine would not have been what he was. There would perhaps be no Laforgue, who was the first to write genuine and accomplished polymorph verse in the French language.

† How the ambition to write free verse obsesses young brains with a passion for risks! It has all the fervour of a touching illusion. One can only smile at their deviations.

patterning. Poets like Kahn set out to discredit the notion of the line as an autonomous rhythmic unit; for them, the line was to be the accidental product of the alignment of one or more '*fractions organiques*' (i.e. 'measures' in a traditional sense)[12] and would itself constitute a *fraction organique* of a stanza. The *fraction organique* is thus like a building brick which can interlock with any other brick of any other size as long as the overall structure (stanza) is stable. The quarrel of the English and German free verse poets, on the other hand, was neither with rhyme which had never been viewed as an essential ingredient of verse, nor indeed with the rigidity of line lengths – the iambic pentameter may be anything between eight and twelve syllables long. It was rather a quarrel with a particularly mechanical kind of metrical verse and more especially with a prosodic system in which habits of foot-scansion had begotten habits of foot-composition and a verse that could do little more than patter or lilt. Poets looked to the broader and more variable rhythms of prose to supply new prosodic resources.

What benefits then did free verse derive from using prose to make poems? There is after all a real sense in which much free verse is prose laid out in a special way, a making manifest of the poems lurking in every paragraph or sentence; in short, the unique art of the free verse poet, and not his underhand deceit, is the art of lay-out, is the art of making the most of those expressive potentialities of which the paragraph is sublimely unaware. By putting in relief, in lines of varying length, the constituents of the paragraph, the poet gets all he can from the variations in duration and cadence, makes them ends in themselves, makes them serve utterance rather than action. Even so of course the free verse poem is still only one interpretation of prose, still only one translation of it; here we have a process that is the reverse of the one mentioned in our treatment of the prose poem; it is now prose not poetry that is the pluri-significant and only partially translatable original. And within the paragraph, the grammatical units, phrases and clauses, which in regular verse had often been treated disrespectfully by rhythms and rhymes, as though grammar was the recalcitrant matter which poetry had to wrench about in order to liberate its secret meanings, now these became the very rhythmic foundation of the verse. And it was because poets took such care to safeguard the intactness of grammatical entities, that these outgrew the sentences in which they occurred; a phrase was no longer a phrase but a line of poetry, every part of the sentence had a right to grammatical absoluteness, that is to say, containing its own order, entering the sentence only on sufferance, self-determining. In the following stanza from Trakl's 'Elis' for example:

> *Ein sanftes Glockenspiel tönt in Elis' Brust*
> *Am Abend,*
> *Da sein Haupt ins schwarze Kissen sinkt.**

the adverbial phrase '*Am Abend*' is no longer a qualification of a particular verb, but a louring permanence with much more than a literal meaning, which actually *conditions* the verb. The prose sentence is thus shown to be full of entities all threatening not to fulfil their proper syntactical function, but to plane above it and infect it with a metaphysical eeriness. The properly subject '*Am Abend*' of an earlier line:

> *Am Abend zog der Fischer die schweren Netze ein.†*

has acquired a paralysing autonomy; syntax has failed to suppress or control the will to anarchy that every constituent nurses.

6

One of the misfortunes for the English analyst of the free verse that is prose-inspired is that his prosodic training has not provided him with the means of doing full justice to it; while phrase-outline or variation of pitch are at the base of French versification, in English these are factors that scansion takes little notice of; we have kidded ourselves for long enough that 'ebb and flow' or other metaphors of marine movement are as close as we shall get to describing cadence effects. And yet those English-speaking poets who envisaged an English poetry with a French kind of fluidity, have given us some warning that the traditional tools don't fit any more; Amy Lowell, for instance, calls the moderns[13]

> *A soft ringing of bells chimes in Elis's breast
> In the evening,
> When his head sinks down into the black pillow.
> † In the evening the fisherman hauled in his heavy nets.

perfectly conscious artists writing in a medium not less carefully ordered because it is based upon cadence and not upon metre.

By 'cadence', Lowell means not only a pattern of intonation but, like Kahn, a strophic rhythm retrospectively perceived, an overall balance rather than the balance continually disturbed and restored that we find in regular verse. Pound too values cadence most highly:[14]

Measure defines the quantity and equality of beats; Cadence is properly the spirit, the soul that must be added.

In this kind of free verse, the written poem is the indication to the voice of how it should group elements and of the degree of impulsiveness with which it should read them; the written poem reveals not a metric system but the organization of the poet-reciter's *chant profond*. Lowell insists, as does Kahn, that their brand of free verse should be read aloud:[15]

Where stanzas are printed in an even pattern of metrical lines, some sense of rhythm can be gained by the eye. When they are not, as in *vers libre*, the reading aloud becomes an absolute condition of comprehension.

Perhaps we can trace back to prose too that phlegmatic lyricism so common among modern *verslibristes*, though translations from Chinese and Japanese have also played a substantial part. The poem is not so much the expression of a lyrical state as evidence for such a state. The poet is out to avoid at all costs the poetry that is an 'asylum for [the] affections' (Pound, in a letter to Kate Buss, 9 March 1916) and instead is looking for the formulation that is no more than adequate. So the poem never quite surrenders its formal contingency and refines sensibility by discreetly disappointing it. There is not to be found here the understatement that is merely hyperbole turned upside down, but the understatement that is no figure of speech, the unassuming, innocent of its profundity:[16]

> I have eaten
> the plums
> that were in
> the icebox

and which
you were probably
saving
for breakfast

Forgive me
they were delicious
so sweet
and so cold

This poem of Williams's has the makings of regularity, with its occasional $\cup/\cup$ (note the parallelism '*for* breakfast/*For*give me'), the four-line stanza, the progression from I-focus, through you-focus, to they-focus, but still refuses to let us discover its real partialities. In this delicate resurrection of plums, we would perhaps like to stress the poignant vertebral 'were', but it dims and brightens with each reading. Should we make this a confession and stress hard the initial 'I' or a modest feast and stress only the 'eaten' or both equally and leave it doubtful? And so on. The voice has all the freedoms that prose usually allows it. The danger of such a lyricism is that our interest in it will remain a prose one, that the poem will represent to us an event without its context rather than an event become utterance, that it will have the tantalizing nature of news in brief, which fascinates by what it could be rather than by what it is.

Although all *verslibristes* may owe something to prose, particularly in the manipulation of tones, the source of some free verse – Laforgue, Verhaeren, Rilke, the early Eliot – lies evidently in verse, or *vers libéré*. And it is because English verse, and German for that matter, has always been *libéré*, inasmuch as syllables have been counted lazily, that Claudel could claim that blank verse is free verse,[17] and that Rilke's Eighth *Duino Elegy*, which is also in blank verse, does not seem out of place among the other more irregular elegies. These poets have more feeling for the line as a complete organism than for the line as a partial glimpse of a total poetic personality; this verse is written on the understanding that it will be scanned in the traditional way, because the line, as in regular verse, is a comment on an ideal abstract line. The French *verslibriste* has in this respect more to exploit, because in a versification in which one syllable is the difference between two entirely different rhythms, correctness is something more than academic fussiness. As has been seen, peculiar freedoms inhere in each type of

French line, and being correct is the only way of safeguarding those freedoms from promiscuity and consequent meaninglessness. In free verse the reader easily becomes the poet's plaything because his is the burden of defining the line; what could be more amusing and more damaging to prosody's good name than presenting a mongrel line and compelling the reader, if he would read it, to give it a pedigree? Surprisingly perhaps, lines can be far more doubtful in French, and more so when pronunciation habits are changing, simply because the line's identity depends on syllabic minutiae. In the opening lines of Laforgue's 'L'Hiver qui vient', for example:

> *Blocus sentimental! Messageries du Levant!* ... 2+4+3+3
> *Oh, tombée de la pluie! Oh, tombée de la nuit!*★ 3+3+3+3

we can only arrive at alexandrines as long as certain embarrassing mute e's are suppressed, the dignity of the alexandrine can only be maintained as long as we are prepared to countenance indignities like '*Messag'ri's*'. Can the reader derive much pleasure from reading when each line is a test of his poetic conscience, when each line, if it is to become a line, involves something more than reading, something more like connivance? In another, somewhat similar example, Eliot's[18]

> When lovely woman stoops to folly and
> Paces about her room again, alone

Goldsmith's iambic tetrameter, with an extra feminine syllable in odd lines, becomes pentameter. Here we find that equivocal mixture of respect and insolence that accompanies the inaccurate quotation. Eliot has in fact divided his lines in the 'wrong' place (Goldsmith has 'When lovely woman stoops to folly/And finds too late, etc.') and in so doing has provided enjambment and a rhyme of greater audacity and far greater vulgarity. The unnatural emphasis on the go-between 'and' endows Goldsmith's line with a brashness it could not have suspected itself capable of – the sense of folly is not real enough to produce pause, the pause of acknowledgement, and the improper haste of 'and (pause)' heralds no revelation but mindlessness reconquered. So the quotation is never more than inapposite, because

---

★Sentimental blockade! Levantine shipping companies! . . . Oh the falling of the rain! Oh the falling of the night!

'folly' is applied to a way of life in which the word, let alone the concept, is unenvisageable.

The sustained momentum and measuredness of regular verse created that unity of impression which was the poem's authority. In free verse however, which further localizes the already local effects of prose, such a unity is often out of the question. This has its advantages; there is nothing so resilient as a free verse poem, as Graves and Riding point out:[19]

The badge of the modernist poet might well be the one that the Stanley family gave to the Isle of Man – three legs conjoined at the middle and the motto 'Wherever you throw it, it will stand'.

But there are prosodic disadvantages; only by virtue of the regular recurrence of a regular pattern can simple variation become the much more meaningful 'variation on'. In regular verse variation is heard simultaneously with an abstract metrical constant, rhythm plays against metre; or in the case of French verse, rhythmic variation is heard both *against* an ideal pattern of measures and *within* a constant, the line or hemistich. Thus even the slightest variation is fraught with consequence; licences in regular verse can *afford* to be modest. The problem facing the free verse poet is how to create a variation beyond that variation which is the very principle of his verse, without falling into the strenuous and the ephemerally sensational. How is he to avoid a situation in which the various parts of his poem stand only in an aggressive relationship with one another? Until we can work ourselves into a position to imagine the difficulties of writing free verse, until we can assess something more than the poet's linguistic skills, we shall do free verse little justice. Pound and Eliot did not tire of telling us that writing prose is as demanding as writing verse, if not more so. Prose and all that it entails might well be a reasonable standard for judging poetry, if we understood it. But, even so, there may be dangerous Modernist prejudices and unverified assumptions lurking in one of the remarks with which Eliot prefaces his translation of Saint-John Perse's *Anabase*:

As a matter of fact, much bad prose is poetic prose; and only a very small part of bad verse is bad because it is prosaic.

Notes

1 See Maulnier, *Introduction à la poésie française* (Paris 1939), p. 35: '*La poésie française a, dans le langage français, son domaine propre, elle ne se mêle point à la prose, elle ne lui dispute pas ses thèmes, elle ne lui prête pas son secours dans les grandes occasions, elle ne donne aucune aide à la prose, et elle n'en attend rien.*' (French poetry has its own enclave in the French language, it does not mix with prose, it does not compete with prose for subjects, it does not lend prose its help on great occasions, in fact it gives prose no help at all and expects none in return.)

2 Barbey d'Aurevilly, letter to Trébutien, March 1852.

3 Lautréamont, *Les Chants de Maldoror* (1868–9), Chant sixième.

4 Lautréamont, *Les Chants de Maldoror*, Chant deuxième.

5 Hofmannsthal, 'Maurice Barrès' (1891).

6 T. E. Hulme, 'Notes on Language and Style', in the *Criterion*, vol. III (1925), p. 489.

7 Laforgue 'quotes' advertisement in his 'Grande complainte de la ville de Paris' and one might refer to the well-known lines of Apollinaire's 'Zone' (*Alcools*):
   Tu lis les prospectus les catalogues les affiches qui chantent tout haut
   Voici la poésie ce matin et pour la prose il y a les journaux.
(You read handbills catalogues posters singing aloud/That's what poetry is this morning and for prose there are the papers (Bernard, *Apollinaire: Selected Poems*, Harmondsworth 1965).)

8 Barbey d'Aurevilly, letter to Trébutien.

9 Laforgue, 'L'Hiver qui vient'.

10 Marinetti, *Enquête internationale sur le vers libre* (1909).

11 There are thirty-six possible combinations of measures in the alexandrine, for instance.

12 Kahn puts it thus: ' . . . *l'unité vraie n'est pas le* nombre *conventionnel du vers, mais un arrêt simultané du sens et du rythme sur toute fraction organique du vers et de la pensée.*' ('The true unit is not the conventional number of syllables in the line, but a simultaneous pause of sense and rhythm after every organic fraction of the line and of thought.') ('Préface sur le vers libre', *Premières Poemes* (Paris 1897), p. 26.)

13 Amy Lowell, 'Walt Whitman and the New Poetry', in *Poetry and Poets* (Boston 1930), p. 63.

14 Pound, 'Vers Libre and Arnold Dolmetsch', in T. S. Eliot (ed.), *Literary Essays of Ezra Pound* (London 1954).

15 Amy Lowell, 'Poetry as a Spoken Art', in *Poetry and Poets*, p. 23.

16 Williams, 'This is just to say'.

17 'Réflexions et propositions sur le vers français' (1928), *Réflexions sur la poésie* (Paris 1963), p. 13. Arthur Symons claims much the same: '*Dans un certain sens tous les vers anglais sont des vers libres. Du XII au XV siècle* [sic] *le vers anglais n'a jamais été obligé d'être syllabiquement exact*'. (In a certain sense, all the kinds of English verse are free verse. From the twelfth to the fifteenth centuries, English verse was never obliged to be syllabically exact.') (Marinetti, *Enquête internationale sur le vers libre* (Milan 1909), p. 75.)

18 Eliot, 'The Fire Sermon', *The Waste Land* (1922).

19 Graves and Riding, *A Survey of Modernist Poetry* (London, 1927), p. 251.

POEMS AND FICTIONS:
STEVENS, RILKE, VALÉRY

ELLMAN CRASNOW

I

A PREOCCUPATION with fictions has been one of the distinguishing marks of Modernist literature. The philosophers' interest in fictions goes back at least as far as David Hume, in the eighteenth century; but, in literary terms, they will here be considered in a perspective taken from Romanticism, from which Modernism was not so much a break as a complex continuity. Romantic thought gives a new status to sub-ectivity: in literature as elsewhere, the highest claims are made for creative imagination; the writer, particularly the poet, takes it upon himself to reveal truths and values to which his vision gives access. The hazards of subjectivity, the privacy and contingency of single vision, are countered by the Romantic interchange with a natural environment from which many of its pieties are drawn. Since the values are 'natural', only an unnatural corruption can prevent their endorsement; and since they are in some sense present in the environment, to elicit them is to participate, to belong to a potentially regenerative world in organic community, and thus to achieve salvation in a secular myth.

It is a noble myth, but fragile. Individual vision may falter or fail; communal acquiescence in natural value may prove utopian; the validating environment may be denied or destroyed. The risks are amply documented within Romanticism itself, and become still more evident later in the nineteenth century, as the writer's world seems increasingly alien: physically, socially, intellectually, it offers little continuity or consolation. An accelerated breakdown of traditional values seems to make Romantic creativity all the more necessary, but its exercise is baulked – on the one hand by estrangement from environment and community, on the other by doubt of the very idea of absolute value. Meaning, truth and the 'real' world are increasingly seen as merely human conventions, and hence contingent.

We can trace the shift in tone from Romantic assertion to Victorian nostalgia, to what Pater, looking back to Coleridge, diagnosed as 'that inexhaustible discontent, languor, and home-sickness, that endless regret, the chords of which ring all through our modern literature'.[1] This marks out a point of departure for one aspect of Modernism: a pessimistic world-view in which, amid worsening conditions, regret passes through despair into crisis and apocalypse. Here we are concerned with another, more constructive possibility. It arises, paradoxically, from that very sense of value as convention, as merely the work of man, which furthers pessimism and nihilism. But to this there is an alternative reaction, in which pessimism need not follow. Rather, the fact that value has a human origin can prompt celebration instead of apology: the capacity to add meaning, to construct reality, will then be acknowledged as an essential human resource. Such meanings are not given but made; they are fictions,[2] but fictions justified by their purpose – just as, in their restricted context, legal fictions are justified. Of course, the context of what we may call existential fictions is anything but restricted; indeed, it embraces the whole human universe, and profound arguments for its justification are accordingly involved.

This fictionalism acquires a new dimension when applied to literature. For the writer can play on the word 'fiction' as the thinker can not. As a writer, he produces literary fictions: these, classically, have been open to attack as 'untrue', or as inferior to 'reality'. But, from the standpoint of fictionalism, reality itself is seen as a personal and social construction. Its absolute value is thus denied; hence the attack on literary fictions fails. More: the artifice of constructing the literary world can be seen as analogous to, even as part of, the artifice of constructing the human world; both are fictional activities. And this convergence of literary and existential fictions is a key concept in modern poetics.

The acknowledgement of artifice is not confined to works of specially fictionalist orientation. It pervades Modernism, following the movement's radical concern to renew itself and its medium of expression. The Modernist work tends to be technically introverted, analytic, incorporating its own critique to the point at which this critique may form the true subject: the work is 'about' its own making, questioning its own practices and presuppositions. The contribution of fictionalism is to make this task more widely representative; to extend the critique, as we have seen, through the parallelism of literary and extra-literary artifice.

2

The analytic introversion of Modernism is not restricted to a single genre or mode; it is a marked feature of the novel and of drama. Poetry, however, building on prior traditions of lyrical meditation and reflection on the powers of language, is especially rich in examples. Nineteenth-century meditative verse persistently treated the Romantic and post-Romantic problems of experience that I have described above. The transition of this concern into the twentieth century is a key point in Modernist development, and I want to trace it through the work of three poets, Wallace Stevens (1879–1955), Rainer Maria Rilke (1875–1926) and Paul Valéry (1871–1945): an American, an Austrian and a Frenchman.

Modernism, while recognizably an international movement, was not homogenous. The personal and national identities of these three poets are quite distinct. Stevens's first publications formed part of the resurgence of American poetry in the second decade of the century; for a long time he was known primarily as an American stylist and dandy. And he does show the typical concern with local and national identity that preoccupies so many American writers; again, typically, he can temper his ironies with a broader native humour and allow just that fooling or *bêtise* that a Valéry would abhor. Valéry himself is firmly if not uncritically in the French rationalist tradition, and his elegant precision is the apotheosis of a national trait. As a friend and colleague of Mallarmé, he is the closest of the three to Symbolism, and his first verses, published in the 1890s, are exercises in the prevailing French modes. Another kind of influence shows in Rilke, who, like Stevens, was interested in modern art; the link is particularly strong for Rilke, through his association with Rodin. Rilke's roots in German culture show in an idealism and mysticism that separate him sharply from the other two. He can, for example, be curiously insistent on the demonic intensity of his inspiration – rather atavistically so, from a fictionalist point of view; but then, Stevens and Valéry are more explicit fictionalists than Rilke. On the other hand, Stevens and Rilke are similar in their avowed intent to cope with certain aspects of the human condition, while Valéry is reluctant to present his work as in any sense instrumental, preferring it to remain 'pure' – again, following a French tradition.[3]

All three, however, are distinctly part of the early Modernist generation (Proust, Hofmannsthal and Mann were also born in the 1870s) that is distinguished by its close contact with the nineteenth century, both chronologically and conceptually. Post-Romantic problems are still a live issue, demanding a new response. Stevens claims ('Of Modern Poetry') that he is writing

> The poem of the mind in the act of finding
> What will suffice. It has not always had
> To find: the scene was set; it repeated what
> Was in the script.
> > Then the theatre was changed
> To something else. Its past was a souvenir.

The established past of poetry is discounted as a 'souvenir'; the task of the modern poet will be to concern himself with the existential need of 'finding/What will suffice'. Since this cannot be done by prescription, the need will be met by fiction; hence the artifice, the 'act of finding', becomes itself the focus of interest. Nor is that interest merely conceptual; for the artifice also constitutes the literary object itself, 'The poem of the mind in the act of finding . . .'

It is not possible here to cover the poets' full range. Rather, I want to discuss the way they develop two essential themes to which I have already referred: first, questions of the self, its immediate experience of and relation to the world; and second, more general questions of meaning and value – in particular, the problem of transcendence. The two themes form extreme positions in the scale of human existence, and we can borrow terms from Rilke to mark their polarity – *das Nächste* and *das Namenlose*: literally, the nearest and the nameless, or the immediate and the ineffable. It is with *das Nächste*, the immediate, that we begin.

3

In their considerations of self and world, our poets find neither term sufficiently stable to allow for a final pronouncement on their relationship. As fictionalists, indeed, they must beware finality and authority, including their own. Accordingly, their work is not developmental or cumulative; it presents and analyses a discontinuous series of situational attitudes. The need for 'finding/What will suffice' underlies these explorations, but it may not and perhaps can not always be answered.

The most immediate datum of experience to be explored appears as an intransitive consciousness, unconcerned with outer objects except as counters in the game of positing the self. The attitude suggested by this mode of experience is one of subjective containment and withdrawal. Writing in a context in which aestheticism offered a recent example, the attitude is tempting. The poets' use of Narcissus figures shows their interest. Valéry, in particular, savours the purity of exclusion:[4]

> *J'appelle* Solitude *cette forme fermée où toutes choses sont vivantes. . . tout ce qui m'environne participe de ma présence. Le murs de ma chambre me semblent les parois d'une construction de ma volonté.* *

But even here, typically, Valéry is not so much enjoying the situation, as the aesthete might, but is watching himself create and sustain it. The emphasis is on artifice, which may indeed prove inadequate, as when Stevens shows the closed system under pressure from that which it excludes:[5]

> The scholar of one candle sees
> An Arctic effulgence flaring on the frame
> Of everything he is. And he feels afraid.

If we forsake the enclosure and move from the concerns of pure being to those of being-in-the-world, the question of an outward relationship arises. The task of fiction at this point is to present that

---

* *Solitude* I call this closed form where everything is alive . . . all that surrounds me shares in my presence. The walls of my room seem the shells of a structure of my will.

relationship in satisfactory terms. One possible aim is the revival of a Romantic interchange between self and world, 'the blissful liaison', as Stevens calls it. And Rilke uses the Romantic metaphor of organic process when he celebrates this interchange through the image of breathing, of participation in a yielding element:[6]

> *Atmen, du unsichtbares Gedicht!*
> *Immerfort um das eigne*
> *Sein rein ausgetauschter Weltraum. Gegengewicht,*
> *in dem ich mich rhythmisch ereigne.* ★

But this is an exceptional state of affairs. Scanning it as a sufficing fiction, we might say that it begs the question of a more resistant medium, or a more recalcitrant subject-matter; the poet's rhythms achieve cosmic status too easily. Now, many other poems do attempt to invoke a greater density: thus Stevens thickens the air with rain or crisps it with frost; Valéry's protagonist bends against the wind or plies his oars. But by attempting to do greater justice to the world's resistance, by making the environment more challenging, the blissful liaison is made progressively more difficult and finally impossible. The metaphoric concepts that invoke relationship – affiliation, reciprocity, centrality – give way to those that oppose it: alienation, confrontation, distance. It is this opposition, rather than an easy relationship, that is often seen as the norm:[7]

> *Dieses heisst Schicksal: gegenüber sein*
> *und nichts als das und immer gegenüber.* †

The drama of changing relations between self and world may, of course, be described in terms of personal relationship, allowing a current of personal feeling to colour the theme. Again, when this happens, individual emphases differ. Stevens's figures tend to be conceptual, personifications. Rilke's may be unapproachable, more than human. Valéry, by contrast, is sensual, even erotic, though very far from losing himself in sensuality:[8]

> *Ma nuit, le tour dormant de ton flanc pur amène*
> *Un tiède fragment d'épaule pleine, peu*

★ Breathing, you invisible poem! Pure world-space, constantly exchanged for this particular existence; counterbalance, in which I rhythmically happen.

† This is [our] fate: to be opposite and nothing else, and always opposite.

Sur ma bouche, et buvant cette vivante, dieu
Je me tais sur ma rive opposée à l'humaine. *

Physically, the observer is very close, almost touching; intellectually, he is separated by a topography of opposition that recalls *gegenüber sein*. The very physicality, as reproduced in the poem, suffers a sea-change from object to figment:

Tu respires l'enfant de ma seule chimère.†

– the last line is poised between pride for the achieved artifice and irony for its 'chimerical' status.[9]

Valéry is thus hinting that observation is not passive: the observer contributes to his experience which is in this sense never objective. This realization is a crux in modern thought, and it has repercussions far beyond literature. For the writer, however, it offers a kind of analogical justification for his fictions, the artifice of the eye serving as warrant for the artifice of the creative mind. Valéry's irony shows his awareness of the great flaw in this scheme: the risk is the loss of contact with an objective datum of experience, and this loss is one that all three poets must face. Valéry's reaction does not usually exceed irony; after all, even unsatisfactory experience is grist to his analytic mill. But for Rilke and Stevens, who press on past analysis towards meliorism, the loss of contact is more deeply felt. Hence their nostalgia for an unmodified datum, something 'which you can't spoil', as Rilke says. In Stevens there is a recurrent passion for[10]

> The poem of pure reality, untouched
> By trope or deviation, straight to the word,
> Straight to the transfixing object, to the object
>
> At the exactest point at which it is itself,
> Transfixed by being purely what it is.

Stevens is not only trying to retrieve the object; he thrusts 'straight to the word'. As before, we find an analogy between literary and existential situations: here, the renewal of perception prompts a renewal of diction. The special interests of fictionalists here link with a wider modern concern, the cleansing of language. We can also find parallels

---

* My night, the drowsy contour of your pure side leads to a warm fragment of ripe shoulder, scarcely touching my mouth; and drinking this live womanliness, a god, I am hushed upon my bank opposite the human being.

† You breathe, the offspring of my lonely fancy.

to their nostalgia for the 'pure' object; several *chosiste* movements in twentieth-century writing are rooted in just such a feeling. The naïve *chosiste*, however, presents an 'objective' description as if he thereby avoids all artifice. Fictionalists are more scrupulous.

Strictly speaking, this nostalgia for the self-sufficient object can never be satisfied. It is an emotional reaction to the rôle of an inevitably intrusive, metamorphic self. In their more confident moods, the fictionalists will claim that this self needs no apology. So we find Stevens abandoning the nostalgic, 'pure' reality of the previous quotation, and redefining the term as an inclusive, created, human universe:[11]

> What our eyes behold may well be the text of life but one's meditations on the text and the disclosures of these meditations are no less a part of the structure of reality.

One can see this as the neutral middle ground of fictionalism. But there is a more ambitious and extreme development, in which the hitherto apologetic self goes over to the offensive, as it were, and claims that the external world somehow depends on a human agent. Rilke develops this theme at two levels. He sometimes describes existence as dependent on a quasi-mystical *Raum* (space), a sort of lifeblood of being. This *Raum* may be gained or lost; when the self jealously hoards experience, it is leeching *Raum* from objects. But it can reverse the flow by opening itself to the objects, offering them its own inner *Raum* for their fuller being. It thus becomes the objects' host, instead of their uneasy guest. Rilke is really offering us another argument about the transmutation of objects, in terms of his own mythology. And he has an alternative version of this moralized, even loving relationship, expressed in more literary terms. Here, *saying* is the existential possibility that the self offers to objects:[12]

> *Sind wir vielleicht hier, um zu sagen: Haus,*
> *Brücke, Brunnen, Tor, Krug, Obstbaum, Fenster, –*
> *höchstens: Säule, Turm . . . aber zu sagen, verstehs,*
> *oh zu sagen so, wie selber die Dinge niemals*
> *innig meinten zu sein.**

*Are we possibly here to say: house, bridge, well, gate, jug, fruit tree, window, – at most: pillar, tower . . . but to say, you understand; oh, to say as even the objects never meant so profoundly to be.

Language itself, as embodied in saying and naming, becomes the carrier of being; a renunciatory gesture places it at the service of others, transforming what would otherwise be mere self-expression into what Susan Sontag aptly calls 'benign nominalism'.[13] When the poet speaks the object's name and articulates it through language he is not labelling but loving: offering it an added intensity of meaning that is only available through human intervention. That this addition aids the object-in-itself is, of course, a fiction; but a fiction whose exemplary gesture is relevant to the human world at large. This relevance is emphasised by a continuum of such acts in Rilke, including specifically interpersonal encounters in which a similarly moralized model of relationships is used.

4

In this final section I shall consider the fictionalist response to questions of value, and the effect on these of the concept of transcendence: whether of the transcendent subject, as in private mystical experience, or of the transcendent object, as in attitudes towards the divine. Both are attacked in nineteenth-century thought: by various forms of positivism, which are part of the background of fictionalism itself; and by the erosions of organized religion which culminate in Nietzsche's announcement that God is dead – a fictionalist statement in that it makes man both creator and destroyer. The transcendental, then, is a problematic category, as the anonymity of Rilke's *das Namenlose* implies. It has, of course, been problematic both before and since: God, like Charles II, is an unconscionable time-a-dying. But for these early Modernists his loss is felt with the force of an event, rather than merely noticed as a norm:[14]

To see the gods dispelled in mid-air and dissolve like clouds is one of the great human experiences.

Stevens is typical in registering both this experience, and the challenge he goes on to describe, 'to resolve life and the world in his own terms'.

Valéry's intense cultivation of his own resources is a case in point; a process chastely aloof from both private and public transcendence. At first sight, this may seem a largely negative reaction; it is hard to find an offer of new values in Valéry. And this is understandable in view of his horror of works that offer and recommend, that offend his ideal of a purity sustained by nothing more than the calm stringency of its self-analysis. In his determined detachment he almost goes so far as to announce the notion of ludic literature, writing as play. Almost, but not quite:[15]

> *Un poème doit être une fête de l'Intellect. Il ne peut être autre chose.*
>
> *Fête: c'est un jeu, mais solennel, mais réglé, mais significatif; image de ce qu'on n'est pas d'ordinaire, de l'état où les efforts sont rythmes, rachetés.**

'*Solennel*', '*significatif*', '*rachetés*'; Valéry's self-sufficiency is not neutral after all, but engaged in creating value (in true fictionalist fashion) through internally generated rules or sanctions. It is part of the 'game' to make these sanctions as strict as possible; hence Valéry's claims for craft and rigour, his pursuit of method, his recurrent scorn for mere writing. Despite its dispassionate air, this is a humanism. One might even trace its secular shrine, the Mediterranean shore whose *puissance salée* (salty power) marks an invigorative climax in 'Le Cimitière Marin' ('The Cemetery by the Sea') and 'La Jeune Parque' ('The Young Fate'), and whose resistance makes of Socrates[16]

> *un héros imaginaire, victorieux du vent, et riche de forces toujours renaissantes, toujours égales à la puissance de l'invisible adversaire ...*†

We have already met this concept of the world as resistance in section 3; and of course Valéry's picture of living as a continuous heroic exercise is simply the apotheosis of being-in-the-world: a secular apotheosis, emphatically in the world and not out of it. At this point his humanism joins that of Stevens and (with reservations) Rilke. Their anti-supernaturalism amounts to a polemic, recalling Nietzsche's injunction to be 'faithful to the earth'. 'Earth', indeed, becomes a charged, prestigious term in Stevens and Rilke; while its rival sphere is attacked by Stevens and Valéry through their scorn for supernatural iconography – what Stevens calls the 'flash drapery' of heaven.

Rilke, however, reminds us that Modernism is not an exclusively

---

*A poem must be a festival of the Intellect. It can be nothing else. Festival: it's a game, but solemn, ordered, significant; an image of what one usually is not, of a state in which efforts are rhymes, redeemed.

†an imaginary hero, triumphant over the blast, and rich in forces ever reborn, ever equal to the power of the invisible adversary ...

secular movement. Though the faith of his early devotional poems is later lost, the transcendent remains a live option for him: for all his faithfulness to the earth, he feels:[17]

> *dahinter aber ist das Namenlose*
> *uns eigentlich Gebilde und Gebiet.**

Yet he is also a brilliant diagnostician of beliefs as fictions. His model of exemplary perception, lending 'space' to objects, can extend to myth, as in his sonnet on the unicorn:[18]

> *Zwar war es nicht. Doch weil sie's liebten, ward*
> *ein reines Tier, Sie liessen immer Raum.*
> *. . . Sie nährten es mit keinem Korn,*
> *nur immer mit der Möglichkeit, es sei.†*

There are grounds for tension here between Rilke's transcendental leanings and his awareness of their possibly phenomenal origins. This tension emerges in his range of attitudes to a transcendent figure that has been widely used by modern writers: the angel.[19] For Rilke, it may be inaccessible, altogether superhuman, a daunting reminder of our finitude. Or, as intermediary between man and god, it may be a possible arbiter or sponsor of human achievement, and in this rôle it may be humbly sought or proudly rejected. Again, it may be a terminal fiction for the poet himself, an image of the imaginative process in full fruition. Obviously, no single value can be assigned to all these appearances. What has happened is not uncommon with theological terms in the modern period: they become free-floating metaphors which need not follow their original meaning, and may indeed deliberately invert that meaning as part of a humanist polemic. There is a fine example of this in Stevens's 'angel of reality', who proclaims:[20]

> I have neither ashen wing nor wear of ore
> And live without a tepid aureole,

and who turns men's eyes towards earth, not heaven, for their better seeing.

---

*behind, however, is the Nameless, our proper image and realm.

† Of course it didn't exist. Yet since it was loved, it came to be a pure beast. They always left space [for it] . . . They fed it with no corn, but always with the possibility of being.

We still have to account for the popularity of this figure. Why should the angel prove so perversely attractive? There is a clue in what the Catholic philosopher Jacques Maritain calls 'angelism': the sin of an attempted independence of the limits of human cognition, and a reaching after the modes of pure spirit.[21] Maritain finds this heretical pride endemic in modern thought, and traces it to Descartes; we need not share his Thomism to apply 'angelism' to the modern imagination, and in particular to the fictionalists. As their analyses dissolve the world into a network of artifice which then awaits re-ordering, there is an obvious temptation to see themselves as perfected intelligences with worlds at their disposal. One can see them struggle against it in their devotion to the earth, in their protestations of helplessness and humility. But all occasionally succumb to the arrogance of angelism, none more so than Valéry: he writes in his notebooks that Degas had called him an angel, and that Degas was more correct than he realized. It is fitting, therefore, to close with Valéry's prose poem on the angel, completed two months before his death, in which he triumphantly embodies and resists the temptation of pride. The angel, like Narcissus, is watching his reflection. Puzzled, he sees it weeping; his luminous intelligence performs miracles of precision (to which Valéry's prose is fully equal) but in vain: the grief belongs to another realm, the realm of the human, and thus he cannot grasp it. His incomprehension is both impressive and pathetic:[22]

'*Ô mon étonnement, . . . Tête charmante et triste, il y a donc autre chose que la lumière?*'*

Light is the angel's environment, the pure universe of a consciousness free from matter; yet it is at the same time a confining sphere, from which his diamond brilliance can never escape:

Et pendant une éternité, il ne cessa de connaître et de ne pas comprendre.†

This irony and paradox are like a touchstone of good faith for the fictionalist. It is his privilege and penalty to have to acknowledge both the power of mind, and its inherent limit.

---

*'O my amazement, . . . charming and sad Head, so there is something else besides light?'

† And through an eternity, he did not cease to know, and not to understand.

Editions

Wallace Stevens:
The Collected Poems of Wallace Stevens (London 1955).
Opus Posthumous, edited by Samuel French Morse (London, 1959).
The Necessary Angel: Essays on Reality and the Imagination (London 1960).
Rainer Maria Rilke:
Sämtliche Werke, edited by Ernst Zinn, 6 vols. (Wiesbaden and Frankfurt am Main, 1955–66).
Paul Valéry:
Oeuvres, edited by Jean Hytier, 2 vols. (Paris 1957, 1960).

Notes

1 W. Pater, *Appreciations; With an Essay on Style* (London 1889), pp. 105–106.

2 For a summing-up of nineteenth-century views of fiction, see Hans Vaihinger, *The Philosophy of 'As If': A System of the Theoretical, Practical and Religious Fictions of Mankind* (London 1924), especially part III.

3 See D. J. Mossop, *Pure Poetry: Studies in French Poetic Theory and Practice, 1746 to 1945* (Oxford 1971).

4 Valéry, 'Laure', *Nouvelle Revue Française*, vol. XXXVI, p. 8.

5 Stevens, 'The Auroras of Autumn', *Collected Poems*, p. 417.

6 Rilke, 'Sonette an Orpheus', II, i, *Werke*, vol. I, p. 751.

7 Rilke, 'Duineser Elegien', VIII, *Werke*, vol. I, p. 715.

8 Valéry, 'La Dormeuse II', *Oeuvres*, vol. I, p. 1663.

9 James Lawler has studied Valéry's image of the sleeping woman, including this poem, in 'Lucidité, phoenix de ce vertige . . .', *Modern Language Notes*, vol. 87, no. 4, May 1972, pp. 616–29; reprinted in *The Poet as Analyst: Essays on Paul Valéry* (Berkeley 1975), pp. 149–65.

10 Stevens, 'An Ordinary Evening in New Haven', *Collected Poems*, p. 471.

11 Stevens, 'Three Academic Pieces', *The Necessary Angel*, p. 76.

12 Rilke, 'Duineser Elegien', IX, *Werke*, vol. I, p. 718.

13 Susan Sontag, *Styles of Radical Will* (London 1969), p. 25.

14 Stevens, 'Two or Three Ideas', *Opus Posthumous*, p. 216.

15 Valéry, 'Littérature', *Oeuvres*, vol. II, p. 546.

16 Valéry, 'Eupalinos', *Oeuvres*, vol. II, p. 116.
17 Rilke, *Werke*, vol. II, p. 252.
18 Rilke, 'Sonette an Orpheus', II, iv, *Werke*, vol. I, p. 753.
19 See, for example, Michael Hamburger, *The Truth of Poetry: Tensions in Modern Poetry from Baudelaire to the 1960s* (London 1969), p. 28.
20 Stevens, 'Angel Surrounded by Paysans', *Collected Poems*, p. 496.
21 'Descartes, or The Incarnation of the Angel' in *Three Reformers: Luther, Descartes, Rousseau* (London 1928), pp. 53–89. Allen Tate has developed Maritain's argument in literary terms in his 1951 essay on Poe, 'The Angelic Imagination', reprinted in his *Essays of Four Decades* (London 1970), pp. 401–23.
22 Valéry, 'L'Ange', *Oeuvres*, vol. I, p. 206.

GERMAN EXPRESSIONIST POETRY

RICHARD SHEPPARD

I

THE originality of Expressionist poetry lies in the fact that it was the first German poetry to pass beyond the spirit of later Romanticism, the spirit of Rilke, George, and Hofmannsthal, seeking to encounter directly the phenomena and crisis of modern industrial capitalism, and searching for a new consciousness within this total setting. It was a poetry marked less by community of style than community of attitude – a modern poetry of urban life, of warfare, of visionary and radical politics, depicting, as Georg Trakl did in his *An die Verstummten* (*To the Silenced*) (1914) the city as a place of madness and disinheritance, but offering the promise that a new, suppressed energy might grow within it. It was also a poetry which encountered, described and interpreted the First World War, and the revolutionary movements and shocks which followed it. It was, in short, both for thematic and historical reasons a very contemporary poetry. Looking back now, it is possible to distinguish four phases of development.

The first and most spectacular phase of Expressionist poetry can be represented by four poets, Gottfried Benn, Georg Heym, Jakob van Hoddis and Alfred Lichtenstein.[1] They were poets of different tones and perspectives, but they united in a common vision – an essentially Expressionist vision of the repressed, demonic forces that were struggling to break through and destroy the apparently ordered surface of the industrial city. Their poetry is an apocalyptic verse, full of images of contrast and conflict: van Hoddis's *Weltende* (*End of the World*) contrasts the violent portents of disaster with the *bourgeoisie*'s apparent indifference; Heym's *Umbra Vitae* (*The Shadow of Life*) freezes the movements of chaos into a threatening, unnatural stillness which one knows will have to shatter; Lichtenstein's poems abound in bloated shapes about to dissolve into primal formlessness. In Gottfried

Benn's *Mann und Frau gehn durch die Krebs-Baracke* (*Man and Wife Walk Through the Cancer-Ward*), collected in his early volume *Morgue* (1912), the cancer patients, whom chthonic powers are seen to be reclaiming, are shown as victims of a society in dissolution. The motif of the city as a state of warfare runs through the verse. In Heym's poems, demons bring chaos to human affairs; in Lichtenstein's, people are perpetually tempted to surrender to irrational and destructive urges; in van Hoddis's a great storm seems always about to break. Heym, in *Der Krieg*, prefigures conflict, and in his diary for July 1910 noted: '. . . if only someone would start a war, it needn't be a just one. This peace is so stagnant, oily and greasy, like a patina on old furniture.'[2]

In general, the stance of the early Expressionist poets towards this situation is ambiguous: they stand not within the stricken city, but on its extreme edge, or some precarious vantage-point from which the panorama is valid both as an objective picture and as an image of their subjective condition. In this way they seem both involved in and detached from their vision, fascinated by and repelled by its horror, welcoming the irrational upsurge as a purgation, yet fearful of the devastation involved. The irony of Benn's collection *Morgue* is notably complex: his coldness conceals a compassion that fears to express itself lest it become part of the dissolution, and his detached observers in the cancer-ward seem to distance themselves to avoid their own inner cancer. Heym uses a strict verse-form, apparently to give an external, firm shape to a complex of energies that tends towards chaos; Lichtenstein and van Hoddis use a more off-hand, throw-away style to distance a vision that might engulf them. Generally, these poets seem to stand on an almost impossible point of intersection between a multitude of conflicting impulses: the poems are inherently unstable and derive little security from their relationship to the lyric '*Ich*'. They resemble unsecured scaffoldings within which an explosion seems about to occur. Not surprisingly, the second phase of Expressionist poetry deals with an eruption that was gradually to become the war itself.

Perhaps the two poets who best exemplify this development in Expressionism are Ernst Stadler and Ernst Wilhelm Lotz, from whose most striking poetry that sense of detached and precarious objectivity we have seen in Benn, Heym and the others has disappeared. The ice has given way, and the poet precipitated into the current beneath. Both Stadler and Lotz tap the frenzy always latent in the earlier Expressionist vision, allow it to flood the surface of their poetry, and then proclaim it ecstatically, as the means to reintegration and redemption. As Otto Flake puts it, '. . . they gradually penetrate deeper and deeper inwards from the surface and at last reach the centres, even if this way produces violent disturbances and even upheavals . . .'[3] Lotz, for example, in *Ich flamme das Gaslight an* (*I Light the Gas-lamp*) moves from the simple act of lighting a lamp into a raw, exultant vision of the dissolution of apparently stable forms of bourgeois life as irrational force floods in with the light. In Stadler's *Fahrt über die Kölner Rheinbrücke bei Nacht* (*Night Journey over the Rhine Bridge at Cologne*) – a poem that fascinatingly contrasts with Julius Hart's pre-Expressionist poem *Auf der Fahrt nach Berlin* (*On the Journey to Berlin*), a powerful piece which nonetheless finally celebrates the valuable wildness of the industrial city – a train-journey over the Rhine Bridge suddenly becomes a descent into the primeval oneness of the unconscious, and culminates in a frenzied acceptance of destruction. His poem *Leoncita* ends with the cry: 'In deine Welt!/Brich aus, Raubtier!/Brich aus!' ('Into thy world!/Break out, beast of prey!/Break out!'). And Lotz's poem *Aufbruch der Jugend* (*Revolt of Youth*) is a clear glorification of the coming war, very much in the spirit of Heym's diary-entry. Indeed, by 1913 and 1914 there was a clear sense among Expressionist poets that the institutions of society were such a travesty of human nature and energy that a violent shock from war or revolution was needed to smash and replace them. And if some of these poets saw war as a horror on the way to utopia, others rejoiced in it as an end in itself, with little heed for its human implications. Indeed when war came, it was, if for a brief while only, welcomed by certain Expressionist poets as the fulfilment of their earlier yearning. Something of this mood is to be found in Hans Leybold's *O Über allen Wolkenfahnen* (*O Above All the Banners of the Clouds*), written while the poet was dying of his wounds in September 1914. In this poem Leybold, in the manner of Stadler and Lotz, receives death gladly as the power which will unite him with the All:

Wir werden Äther, Luft und Wellen.
Oh, aus unsern Leibern strömen Quellen
spritzend in das ungewohnte Licht! Wir schenkten
uns dem All!★

2

The next important movement of Expressionist poetry comes when it is clear that reconstruction is not the inevitable consequence of destruction, and after about September 1914 the earlier mood fades. Once the war had begun to protract, the realization grew that those irrational powers in which the earlier poets had exulted were, when their true nature was revealed on the battlefield, totally destructive. The primal energies of ecstasy were seen to be those of death: they smashed, but did not reshape. Lotz, who had first greeted the war in a manner similar to Leybold, wrote home to his wife on 16 August, 1914:[4]

> I've had enough of all the martial sensations which could give pleasure to an inhuman boor. When I hear the word war I can see only what is unedifying: burst bellies, the whimpering wounded, the crying children of burning households and the brutal shell-bursts which rip whole columns to pieces.

As one commentator noted, Expressionism 'grows out of and is nourished by the growing chaos of human relationships; the immense dislocation, which the war produced even in the everyday minds of men, created all the organic prerequisites for the emergence of the new art'.[5] Nevertheless, the new art gradually turned against the war and refused to accept the ultimacy of the gods of destruction.

Having been exposed to and comprehended the nature of the forces of mechanized destruction, the third phase of Expressionist poetry consisted in an attempt to get beyond sheer irrationality to some transcendent sense of permanence and reconciliation. It is this spirit that produces the blank, shell-shocked refusal of Wilhelm

★'We become aether, air and waves.
O, from our bodies stream springs,
spurting into the unaccustomed light! We gave
ourselves to the All!'

Klemm's *Schlacht an der Marne* (*Battle of the Marne*); gives unity to the fragmented impressions and disordered terror of August Stramm's *Sturmangriff* (*Shock Attack*); creates the bitter irony and impotent anger of Albert Ehrenstein's *Der Kriegsgott* (*The God of War*), and issues in the fragile image of reconciliation of the silent sister in Georg Trakl's final poem *Grodek*. This latter poem is not simply the major Expressionist war poem, it is also, in a very real sense, the *non plus ultra* of all Expressionist poetry. If the first phase of Expressionist poetry was diagnostic in character, and the second phase ecstatic, then *Grodek* moves beyond both of these modes. It creates a silence out of cacophony and retrieves an enduring image from chaos, which somehow reconciles the polarities and cancels out the frenzy of the Expressionist poetry which had preceded it.

From October 1914 until the end of the War, the periodical *Die Aktion* alone published some hundreds of *Dichtungen* and *Verse vom Schlachtfelde* (*Poems* and *Verse from the Battlefield*). At first a powerful indictment and statement of belief, the war poetry of Expressionism tended with time to lose its measured lucidity and imaginative density and pass into its final phase – a phase of shapeless and facile denunciation, horrified rhetoric, melodramatic pathos and forced irony. (So Richard Fischer's *Den Schlachten Zu* (*To the Battles*) and Hugo Sonnenschein's *Ein Dichter stirbt im Kriege* (*A Poet dies in the War*), both published in *Die Aktion* of 9 February 1918.) Clearly, all war poetry is prone to such degeneration. War is so obviously terrible that it is difficult to say much new about it unless, like Trakl or Stramm, the poet is able to see through the carnage to something present in its midst which outlasts the chaos. Trakl died after *Grodek*, and, with few exceptions, the poetry of German Expressionism went into decline from then on. In contrast, Wilfred Owen's war poetry achieves what is needed: his initial sense of bitterness becomes an intense compassion, which enables him to bring into relief the pathos of the young soldiers on the battlefield and affirm that something essentially human can live on. Thus, whereas English war poetry began by being rhetorical (that is, providing a preconceived, two-dimensional gloss on a situation whose force remained beyond the poet's scope) and only with time became analytical and three-dimensional, the German poetry of the Great War followed the opposite evolution. The Georgian poets of pre-war England had known intimations of disease and disorder, and images of dark presentiment; they are clear in poems like Edward Thomas's *Tall Nettles*, W. H. Davies's *The Villain*, Thomas Hardy's *Channel Firing* and the uneasy jokiness of Rupert Brooke's nostalgic *Grantchester*. But because they had not poetically faced the consequences of their intimations, did not encounter them directly, the war came as something unexpected for them – as it did not for their German contemporaries, who had given themselves over to the disruptive powers they saw about them. Consequently the English poets took much longer to comprehend and assimilate the war; and it is probably not too much to say that whereas the major German war poetry had been written by the time of August Stramm's death in September 1915, the major English war poetry was only really beginning to get written from late 1916. Where the German Expressionists had grasped the Great War for what it was in the first months, the vision of many of the English poets was, until the slaughter on the Somme, obscured to greater or less extent by romantic rhetoric, notions of war as moral crusade, and nostalgic introversion.

Thus, where the English poets of the later war years learnt increasingly to handle the trench situation in terms and with a tone appropriate to that situation, the German poets of the later war years tended to turn away from war and social upheaval in order to provide an unreal humanitarian, utopian or apocalyptic gloss on those realities. Where Wilfred Owen and Isaac Rosenberg learned to *show* us, in recognizably human terms, the present pathos of the trenches, their German contemporaries increasingly left these realities in order to *tell* us abstractly about the future 'new man' and 'new society' they felt must emerge from the war. Erwin Piscator acidly characterized this poetry:[6]

Pfemfert's disciples can be divided up into: 'O Man!' dramatists and poets who pleaded with those brothers of theirs who were already threatening to smash in their heads with rifle butts again; Expressionists who made a style out of historical necessity; Dadaists who mocked art because they felt betrayed by it; right-wing, middle-of-the-road and left-wing Communists, who frequently, as Tucholsky put it, stood to the left of themselves; and the Resigned, who bowed to Necessity.

Hermann Lindeman's poem *Mensch (Man)*, published in *Die Aktion* of

9 March 1918, is a clear example of what Piscator means by the 'O Man' school:

> *Ich trage eine grosse Liebe*
> *Suche dich in allen Gassen,*
> *in Schmutzkaschemmen*
> *und glänzenden Terrassen:*
> *Dich Mensch! . . .* *

Other such rhetorically humanitarian poems were Franz Werfel's *Der Gute Mensch* (*The Good Man*), Yvan Goll's *Der Führer* (*The Leader*), and Karl Otten's *Wir Utopisten* (*We Utopians*). Karl Jakob Hirsch, looking back on the blithe utopian hopes for post-war Germany that were gaining currency in 1917 and 1918, admitted the failure of all such poetry when he wrote that: 'The sun of blissful humanitarianism stood high in our youthful heaven; we cared little for the reality in which much blood was flowing.'[7] Something similar might be said of the explicitly left-wing and revolutionary poems which appeared in print from mid-1918 and are characterized by the shrill revolutionary scream, the hectoring tone, and the predisposition toward abstractions. Of these, the best known are the Marxist poems, Rudolf Leonhard's *Prolog zu jeder kommenden Revolution* (*Prologue to any Future Revolution*), which rings the rhetorical changes on *Freiheit, Gleichheit,* and *Gerechtigkeit* (Liberty, Equality, Justice), and Johannes Becher's hysterical panegyric *Hymne auf Rosa Luxemburg* (*Hymn to Rosa Luxemburg*), which unequivocally describes the murdered revolutionary as a saint and finally as Christ.

By 1918 and 1919, in fact, the 'false image' of the world for which the Expressionists had attacked 'bourgeois' Impressionist poetry was replaced by an equally factitious Expressionist rhetoric of utopia and social revolution in which, as the Dadaists pointed out, the will to conform was evident. Thus, by the end of the war, the revolutionary impulse of the early Expressionists, which had been directed toward the destruction and eventual recreation of the city of industrial capitalism through the immanent power of Eros, had degenerated into a cerebralized attempt to superimpose an alien, idealized image on the

> *'I bear a great love,
>   Seek thee in every by-way,
>   in dirty dives
>   and gleaming terraces:
>   Thee O Man!'

realities of the world. The difference is clear if one compares Heym's *Umbra Vitae* and Becher's *Berlin*. Heym's gaze is fixed on the city in such a way that his language reproduces the horrors he actually sees there and within himself; Becher, who actually sees the city in conventional terms, gives that vision an Expressionist garb by using violent and dramatic epithets taken from sources extrinsic to the city. Heym translates a total vision, a *Gestalt*, into words; Becher merely concatenates preconceived ideas without having a total vision that could give them imaginative validity. Gottfried Benn suggested the great aim of Expressionism when he said that the movement travelled along an arduous inner path 'to those levels of the mind from which creation proceeds, to the archetypes, the myths, and wrestled compulsively, disciplinedly and in dead earnest amid this fearful chaos of disintegrating reality, in order to achieve a new image of man'.[8] Where Lorca and Eliot were able to penetrate through chaos to a new sense of meaning, the Expressionist poets never managed a comparable achievement. Franz Herwig, writing in 1916 after the best Expressionist poetry had in fact been produced, implied as much when he said he found it hard to believe that even one of these poets 'might grow essentially "into the ethical"'. He continued: 'What I sense in them is the impassioned cry for the ethical, the yearning for it which they themselves will never fulfil, but which some other human being will fulfil who matures far away from their group.'

There is an unmistakable sense in which the best Expressionists had known the ambiguity of their situation all along; had sensed that they were the last of a line fated to die of disillusion, and the first of a new generation questing amid chaos. This dual consciousness is essential to early Expressionism and it passed, after the deaths of Trakl and Stramm, to the Dadaists rather than the late Expressionists with their commitment to schematic and ready-made ideologies. Early Expressionism and Dada both knew the spirit of Trakl's *An die Verstummten* (1914), which saw in the mad, chaotic city the secret activity of a redemptive power:

> *Aber stille blutet in dunkler Höhle stummere Menschheit,*
> *Fügt aus harten Metallen das erlösende Haupt.**
>
> *But silent in dark caverns a stiller humanity bleeds,
>   Out of hard metals moulds the redeeming head.

And it was on this paradox that the best Expressionism turned. For where the preceding Impressionists had felt themselves the last guardians of a culture coming to an end, the Expressionists felt themselves on an intersection, at once looking backwards and forwards, mystical and revolutionary, desiring legitimate self-expression and falling prey to the daemonic will to power. Perhaps the word that best conveys their spirit is *Menschheitsdämmerung*, the title of the best-known anthology of Expressionist poetry, and a concept which can be rendered in English either as *Twilight of Humanity* or *Dawn of Humanity*. If Expressionist poetry was, all said and done, incapable of resolving the conflicts of twentieth-century existence, it was at least the first German poetry to take its strength from those conflicts, and explore the dangers and possibilities which engagement in them entailed.

Notes

1 Verse by most of the poets mentioned in this essay is to be found (with translations) in Michael Hamburger and Christopher Middleton (eds.), *Modern German Poetry 1910–1960* (London 1962). This volume also includes useful brief biographies of the poets.

2 Georg Heym, *Dichtungen und Schriften*, edited by Karl Ludwig Schneider (Hamburg 1960), vol. 3, p. 139.

3 Otto Flake, 'Von der jüngsten Literatur', *Die Neue Rundschau*, vol. XXVI, no. 2 (1915), pp. 1276–87. This essay is reprinted in Paul Raabe (ed.), *Expressionismus: Der Kampf un eine literarische Bewegung* (Munich 1965), pp. 68–79. Flake is comparing Expressionism with Impressionism, which has, he says, 'become a thing of the past' and which, though realistic, also helped to beautify bourgeois life.

4 A comparable response is to be found in Ludwig Meidner, the graphic artist, who looked back on the war which had killed his close friend Lotz in its first months, and indicated the later response of Expressionists when he wrote of the turmoil of Dresden turning to 'blasphemy and endless mockery,' and adds that 'in their madness [people] took the rod of chastisement for a feast of joy' (in Paul Raabe and Karl Ludwig Schneider (eds.), *Expressionismus* (Freiburg 1965), pp. 149–50).

5 Friedrich Marcus Hübner, 'Der Expressionismus in Deutschland', in *Preussische Jahrbücher* no. 173 (1920), pp. 176–88. Reprinted in

Paul Raabe (ed.), *Expressionismus: Der Kampf un eine literarische Bewegung* (Munich 1965), pp. 138–46.

6 Erwin Piscator, 'Die politische Bedeutung der *Aktion*', in Paul Raabe and Karl Ludwig Schneider, *Expressionismus* (Freiburg 1965), p. 195.

7 Karl Jakob Hirsch, 'Revolution in Berlin', in Paul Raabe and Karl Ludwig Schneider, *Expressionismus* (Freiburg 1965), p. 237.

8 Gottfried Benn, 'Expressionismus', in *Collected Works* (Wiesbaden 1959), vol. 1, pp. 240–56.

SIX

The Modernist Novel

IF modern poetry raises particularly sharply the question of the relationship between subject and object, poet and world, writer and language, then the novel, because of its prose character, especially raises problems in the representation of reality and logical sequential structure. The Modernist novel has shown, perhaps, four great preoccupations: with the complexities of its own form, with the representation of inward states of consciousness, with a sense of the nihilistic disorder behind the ordered surface of life and reality, and with the freeing of narrative art from the determination of an onerous plot. In all of these areas what is being questioned is linear narrative, logical and progressive order, the establishing of a stable surface of reality; and the following essays in different ways pursue this theme. John Fletcher and Malcolm Bradbury look at the concern of the Modernist novel with its own technicality and fictiveness; J. P. Stern examines the transition, in the work of Fontane and Mann, from the novel as burgher epic to the new concern with artistic consciousness; Michael Hollington looks at changing modes of spatial and temporal relation; Franz Kuna at the establishment of ironic and ambiguous modes of exploration; Melvin Friedman at the Symbolist techniques of modern novelists; Donald Fanger at the Surrealistic urbanism of Russian fiction. The final essay, by David Lodge, exactingly examines the changing use of language structure in modern fiction, showing by stylistic analysis how Modernist 'synaesthesia' is founded in the deep structure of Modernist prose.

393

THE INTROVERTED NOVEL

JOHN FLETCHER AND MALCOLM BRADBURY

I

IN the course of the nineteenth century, the novel established itself as a genre of unparalleled variety, range and depth. The Romantic, realist, and naturalist movements all deposited their alluvia on its shores, and left it with the familiar contours which we now take for granted. By the turn of the century, therefore, it seemed that this sophisticated medium had no more territory left to develop, for it turned in upon itself. Among some of its most important practitioners, the novel's degree of self-analytical presentation markedly increased; its obsessions with its own tactics of structure and design grew; it became markedly more 'poetic', in the sense that it became more concerned with precision of texture and form, more disturbed by the looseness of prose as popular written usage. The effect of all this was a radical revolution in technique and a vastly greater stress upon form; and the consequences of this are still very much with us, in two associated aspects. One is the obsession with formal matters, aesthetic wholeness, and the use of language and design, rather than contingency and imitation, to make novels; the other is the air not only of internal difficulty but of artistic crisis that was part of the same phenomenon, and has to do with the very problem – a problem both artistic and historical – of apprehending and making authoritative the traditional stuff of fiction, reality itself, in an effective order of words. These concerns are today present in the *nouveau roman*, the writings of Nabokov and John Barth, Muriel Spark and Iris Murdoch, Borges and Günter Grass; Nabokov, that great master of play in the space between formal order and orders taken from the world outside, that novelist of shades, mirrors, and reflections, appropriately says of a novel written by one of his own characters: '. . . the heroes of the book are what can be loosely called methods of composition . . .' We know many books like this now, books in which these 'heroes' occur, in a variety of dispositions, and showing both a sense of joy in the elegance of a fiction and a sense of crisis about the relations between a novel and God's fiction, the real universe. Contemporary variants proliferate; but this sense of the complexity and the paradox of a fiction clearly has its roots in the fictional structures, the aesthetic concerns of the early moderns.

The Modernist phenomenon of what might be called 'narrative introversion' needs to be carefully distinguished from something familiar in the entire history of fiction and somewhat analogous, the mode of self-conscious narration. The novel has always conducted complicated transactions between its propensity toward realism, empirical detailing, the illusion of facticity, and elements of form and making involved in the realistic illusion. Such self-awareness is familiar enough in the fiction of the seventeenth and eighteenth centuries,[1] and reached one kind of culmination in *Tristram Shandy*, a work which parodies most of the extant conventions of the already slightly less-than-novel novel, and exploits to the greatest lengths the narratorial convention. Though this species of writing greatly influenced the form and shape of fiction, its main effect was to draw attention to the narratorial role itself, to inculpate the reader with the narrative voice which claimed – and frequently exercised – ostentatious tyranny over that reader, anticipating and often cheating his expectations, frequently for comic effect. Modernist tactics contain this sort of authorial virtuosity, but they contain a good deal else. If the propensity toward drawing attention to the irredeemably fictional nature of fiction was already there in the form, and had been played with in the surrounding aesthetic debates, it had not reached that point of difficulty where, for instance, an entire writerly career might be founded on the evolution of adequate tactics for facing the problem, on an endless internal speculation about the nature of that art which, simultaneously, the artist is creating. It is in Modernism that one finds this happening, taking shape as an internal crisis of presentation, and resulting, among other things, in a penchant for forms which, by turning in upon themselves, show the process of the novel's making, and dramatize the means by which the narration is itself achieved. In other words, although there is a certain similarity of intention, most of the earlier devices served to draw attention to the autonomy of the narrator, while the later techniques drew attention to the autonomy of the fictive structure itself. And whereas the former versions of self-conscious narration functioned usually for humorous effect, the later ones were normally serious and 'literary' in a way that would have been incomprehensible a century or so previously. Putting the means and modes of art at the centre of the work, they demand the reader's involvement in its significant order; so they set limits upon the realistic level of the novel's operation, and require our comprehension of *this* particular order and structure as an articulated whole. One of the great themes of the Modernist novel has been, in fact, the theme of the art of the novel itself: a theme that, by forcing the reader to pass beyond the reported content of the novel, and enter into its form, has given Modernist fiction a dominantly Symbolist character. In a phrase of Ortega y Gasset's, it has made the novel today into an art of figures rather than an art of adventures – an art that does not *report* the world, but *creates* it.

2

These developments in the modern novel reach back certainly as far as Flaubert, but they belong particularly to that turn out of realism that comes toward the end of the last century: the most useful starting point is Henry James. James moved from an ironic complicity with his reader, in his earlier novels, to a deft connivance – in his later books – with his *characters*, a shift that strikingly gave him an intensified responsiveness to the possibilities of active form. So in *The Ambassadors* (1903), for example, we find that he lightly flits from one character to another in the dialogue, alternately illuminating the mystery which lies unspoken behind the spoken word:[2]

Strether could only listen and wonder and weigh his chance. 'And yet, affected as you are then to so many of your clients, you can scarcely be said to do it for love.' He waited a moment. 'How do we reward you?'

She had her own hesitation, but 'You don't!' she finally exclaimed, setting him again in motion. They went on, but in a few minutes, though while still thinking over what she had said, he once more took out his watch; but mechanically, unconsciously, and as if made nervous by the mere exhilaration of what struck him as her strange and cynical wit. He looked at the hour without seeing it, and then, on something again said by his companion, had another pause. 'You're really in terror of him.'

He smiled a smile that he almost felt to be sickly. 'Now you can see why I'm afraid of you.'

James, who calls himself Strether's 'chronicler', keeps in the background but not out of sight, supplying us with precious information while hinting tantalizingly at what he does not care to mention. The complicity is overt in a remark like this: 'it came over him that Miss Gostrey looked perhaps like Mary Stuart: Lambert Strether had a candour of fancy which could rest for an instant gratified in such an antithesis' – James, it's clear, is as gratified by the antithesis as Strether is. This is the novel aware of itself indeed; and an appropriate way of underlining it is the play on the forenames of Lewis Lambert Strether. 'It's the name of a novel of Balzac's!' exclaims Miss Gostrey delightedly, adding as a wry afterthought, 'but the novel's an awfully bad one.' These fictional characters are connoisseurs of fiction too. The complicity, the close relation that we sense between the author and his characters, extends through all the working of the action, to the point where it sometimes seems that the characters have read the novel in which they exist; certainly there is a sense in which we feel that, in the process of its making, they have amended it. In his preface to *The Awkward Age* (1899), James remarks: 'We are shut up wholly to cross-relations all within the action itself, no part of which is related to anything but some other part – save of course by the relation of the total to life.' The characters belong less to a world being imitated than to a process, and they seem to participate in the act of their own creation. They are part of the technical plot; and as in many modern novels they seem to assert against their author the right to greater freedom, to profounder psychological depth, or to life that reaches freely backward and forward in time (as, say, in some of Virginia Woolf's novels). In fact, though, the same techniques can be used to subordinate the characters to the design, to the pattern of the novel. Nonetheless, whether the result is freedom or irony,[3] one can recognize the appropriateness of Ortega y Gasset's suggestion that in this type of novel a certain sort of 'dehumanization of art' takes place.[4] The form is not simply an enabling means of handling the content, but in some sense it *is* the content; experience generates form but form generates experience, and it is in the delicate intersections between the claims of formal wholeness and human contingency that we find some of the central aesthetics and tactics of Modernist fiction.

In Joseph Conrad's novels, the same overt awareness of the complexity of fictional structure is taken further and moved in other directions. *Under Western Eyes* (1911), for example, has an extremely contorted narratorial procedure, itself embodying a kind of struggle with the material to be conveyed and constituting a distinctive logic. The book is narrated from two quite different points of view: that of an elderly British language-teacher, and that of a young Russian revolutionist, Razumov. The former introduces the story, but to supplement not only his obviously partial information but also his limited responses he has recourse to Razumov's confessional diary. The teacher remains the principal narrator: he not only uses the diary to supplement his account, but he edits it, building it in to his own narration, to the end of completing and diversifying it. All this is a good deal more than simply a convenient narrative device, as it might well have been in less sophisticated narrative structures of earlier date: it is in fact the very essence of the novel. For since *Under Western Eyes* is, as its title suggests, a study of pre-revolutionary Russian dilemmas seen by and for westerners, Conrad requires a narrator who will 'distance' the material and make it comprehensible to us; and the language-teacher effectively does this by acting as go-between. However, the diary itself, with all its immediacy, is present to render the complexity, irrationality and mystery of the problem. The mystery is partly cultural, a difference of values; but it is also the mystery of meaning that applies to all stories, for Conrad perpetually teases our desire to presume a simple significance. In *Under Western Eyes*, as in most of Conrad's novels, the narrative pattern therefore dramatizes the difficulty of establishing the material and ordering its significance, conveying its completeness; that becomes part of the story.

In his pursuit of his 'difficult' subject, then, Conrad deploys a considerable virtuosity of narration which draws our attention as readers. After a disingenuous disclaimer that the narrator is no artist and so must be content to tell the story naïvely and straight, the teacher's first part is based on Razumov's own account of how he betrayed the conspirator Haldin to the Tsarist police, and ends on a question: where will Razumov, thus compromised, take himself off to now? The second part abruptly brings the narrative back six months in time and moves in space, to the Russian expatriate colony in Geneva into which the language-teacher has his entrées; this part takes us up to the arrival of Razumov in the colony, where he is accepted as a fugitive from the Tsar. We have the answer to the question left at the end of the first part: he will infiltrate the Geneva colony as a police stooge. The narration can now revert to Razumov's viewpoint, and it does in the last parts, taking us forward now in time to the gruesome rough justice by which Razumov pays for his treachery. So the different viewpoints converge: the end is with the narrator, the language-teacher who has watched the whole tragi-comic episode unfold, not fully comprehending its import until Razumov's diary comes into his hands. Then only can he understand what happened, and take pen to paper and lay it before us, in all its Russian darkness and inscrutability. But, despite his denials, he *is* a competent story-teller – and he constructs fictions. He does not tell it straight, as a newspaper account might; nor does he take us through the stages he went through as the 'Razumov mystery' gradually sorted itself in his mind, as a sleuth might; he rather shapes the material into dramatic form, by immediately conjuring up Razumov in Petersburg on the basis of the diary, tactically the one available source of information on that experience. In other words, he undertakes, like any creator, an imaginative reconstruction, which in the terms of the story can be neither wholly true nor wholly false. He acts as a surrogate novelist, with Conrad as the real novelist behind him.

The novel, however, obscures this. It is coyly reluctant to be taken as a novel at all ('this is not a work of imagination' (Penguin edition, p. 90)): it is apparently unable to effect a smooth transition between, in space, St Petersburg and Geneva, and, in time, the shift from the execution of Haldin to a period six months earlier when Haldin is still alive and his mother and sister are living in the security of exile. But under the smokescreen of talk about not being able to effect a neat transition, the prose does just that. A similar tactic works in the following passage:

The diary of Mr Razumov testifies to some irritation on his part. I may remark here that the diary proper consisting of the more or less daily entries seems to have been begun on that very evening after Mr Razumov had returned home.

Mr Razumov, then was irritated. His strung-up individuality had gone to pieces within him very suddenly.

'I must be very prudent with him', he warned himself . . . (Penguin edition, p.78).

Here the language-teacher introduces an interpretation of Razumov's feelings which direct transcription of the diary could not give him; by sleight of hand he slips in the interpretation but as if it had emerged unassisted from his source-material. As he intends it should, the diary acts as a check on his own veracity, to carry conviction that the work is not a fiction, while enabling fictionalization to occur. In fact he functions as a skilled novelist, providing an object-lesson in how to handle a difficult theme, manage transistions, and exploit two different, though complementary, points of view.

Of course he is a surrogate: the novelist, the maker of it all, is Conrad. An eighteenth-century writer would have been happy enough to shield behind the alias and let the reader take the teacher as the author. But Conrad, in the modern way, takes the novel as an art-form; the tactics are overt. Thus he signs the novel in his own name, and later writes a preface for it; he recognizes that his readers will be sophisticated enough to take it for granted that the weaving of fictions is not a frivolous pursuit, but is the arduous labour of the artist; and that, therefore, he can create for their admiration a creator creating a fiction before their eyes, and all the while convince them of its basic verisimilitude. His aim is to make dense the feel of life, and the conditions of uncertainty and complexity under which it is lived. In this book, at least, the purpose is not to set us at a remote distance, though in a novel like *The Secret Agent* (1907) somewhat similar means do serve to provide a totally ironic artefact, a novel which diminishes all the human agents and the human civilization of which they claim to be a part. Nonetheless, his kind of narrator (or rather that complicated interaction between Conrad and his famous hierarchy of narratorial surrogates) has the effect not only of doing justice to the complexity of the 'material' and the density of experience, but also of putting that material into shape within the universe of forms by which it may be made. In a letter of 1923 Conrad spoke of his art as lying almost wholly in 'my unconventional grouping and perspective'; it is this that makes his writing 'fluid' and impressionistic, concerned with 'effects' rather than 'mere directness of narrative'. And it is clear that Conrad and James do introduce into fiction a new technical intensity, that theirs is an art of deliberated and articulated means. Mark Schorer has remarked that the virtue of the modern novelist, from James and Conrad on, is 'not only that he pays so much attention to his medium, but that, when he pays most, he discovers through it a new subject matter, and a greater one'.[5] The result is a writing of what he calls, in a compelling phrase, 'technique as discovery'– technique being 'any selection, structure, or distortion, and form or rhythm imposed upon the world of action', by means of which our apprehension of that world of action is enriched or renewed. Today we have learned to follow in such writing some hidden long logic, some figure in the carpet, and learned, too, a new critical discourse, a poetics of 'point-of-view', 'pattern', 'design', and 'symbol'. The process of making not only becomes part of the significant logic of the story: it can, indeed, *become* the story. As a result, novels come to seem more and more to approximate to their character as verbal constructs (though this, of course, *all* novels are), form being not simply an enabling means for handling the content, but in some essential sense *being* the content. At times, what we feel is that the techniques of introversion bring us closer to life; at others, we are more aware that they bring us closer to the art of the occasion, to the elegant consolations of their own being. The contemporary desire in poetry for a symbolist wholeness comes to preside in one whole strain of the modern novel as well; the world beyond the contingent detail and haphazard reality acquires that luminosity which, for instance, Virginia Woolf sought in fiction. One result is a progressive fading of that realism which has long been associated with the novel; language ceases to be what we see through, and becomes what we see. The novel hangs on the border between the mimetic and the autotelic species of literature, between an art made by imitating things outside itself, and an art that is an internally coherent making.

3

It is the possibility of such an art of fiction that constitutes the prime aesthetic subject-matter of Marcel Proust's multi-volume novel *À la recherche du temps perdu* (*Remembrance of Things Past*) (1913–27).

Proust wrote a few other things, but the novel was his essential life-work, a vastly ambitious enterprise, into which went the bulk of his own personal experience and the full depth of his aesthetic perceptions. The book is a voyage into the complexity of consciousness, instinctual and aesthetic, as well as a realistic document of a life and a society. In the last volume, both are on the wane: the narrator, Marcel, returns after many years' absence in sanatoria to the high Parisian circles of which he was once an assiduous member. Mingling with the guests at a large reception, he is astonished to see how old his friends appear; and it only gradually dawns on him that this is because he, too, has grown old. Many of those he once knew are dead; a few are dying, and so are not at the reception; the rest he brings once again all onto the same stage, and ends his chronicle with them all about him. But the novel extends far beyond its chronicle dimensions, and beyond the world of a social or historical time. It transcends such mere realism; it is in fact a poetic, indeed a Symbolist, quest for the lost reality of the past, and a search for the artistic means for its recreation. Man, says Proust, is a giant standing on the living stilts of his years; and it is possible, in rare and therefore joyous moments of illumination, to span the intervening decades and relive, in all its perfectly natural reality, a fragment of our past. For most of us the joy of such isolated instants is short-lived; but for the artist they have the resonance of symbols or revelations, since they carry the imperious command to preserve and hold the vision in words. Art is thus the central illumination; it alone can give pattern or form which in turn make significance out of what would otherwise be a contingent sequence. And *À la recherche du temps perdu* is therefore primarily the story of the birth of a literary vocation, of a sense of the relation between reality and art, and of the disciplined and sacramental power it can accrue, as well as a structure devoted to recapturing the past as a joy.

Marcel's confidence in literature as the remedy for the depradations of time is not, however, easily won. Early in the closing volume, the narrator describes how, before falling asleep one night, he dips into the Goncourts' journal. His reading depresses him: he is envious of the brothers' powers of observation, and yet he is simultaneously aware that their acute eye sees little that is worthwhile because, being realist, uncritical, it misses the essence. He is gloomy because the Goncourts at once convince him of his own lack of literary 'gifts', and strangely relieved because literature, which he had formerly esteemed so central, is apparently incapable of serving his ambition to resurrect the past. This is a crucial passage in the book, and two things about it are especially striking. In the first place, the eight pages he 'quotes' from the journal are not to be found there. Indulging in a favourite pastime, Proust is not excerpting but pasticching. The material he lends the brothers is not theirs at all, but his own, for he has them describe a dinner-party at the Verdurins', such as he himself described often enough, but in utterly different terms, in the early volumes of the novel. The result is, of course, an extreme of literary awareness: not only is Proust, like Joyce in *Ulysses*, describing a situation of his own imagining in the manner of another writer, but he is doing so in order that the narrator may seem to convince himself of his own inability to write. But secondly, the passage is only a preamble to the triumphant demonstration, a little later on, that the writer *can* find the incentive, the subject-matter, the means which will enable him to become a writer. After his mystical experience in the Guermantes library, he foresees the time when the literary work which, within the novel, he contemplates writing, will become that novel itself. And so the fictional wheel comes full circle – just as the two 'ways' of an earlier volume (Swann's Way and the Guermantes Way) are seen not to be irreconcilable, as the narrator in youth had believed; just as the George Sand novel *François le champi* (*François the Foundling*), which in the opening pages of the first volume painfully reminds him of his mother's capitulation to his neurasthenic lack of will, becomes the instrument of the literary self-discovery that will redeem that willessness when fondled in the Guermantes library. He sees that the 'essential book' he conceives there is the 'only genuine book', because it is the book which a writer does not have to invent but only to translate, for it exists potentially within him as within any of us: 'The duty and task of the writer are those of a translator', he concludes.

But he still insists that his book is not an autobiography but a fiction – which is to say art. Its construction will be elaborate, and he uses various metaphors, comparing it to a cathedral, or a gown: things which, in their different ways, are elaborate structures, themselves requiring duration, and patience, and the careful building of different materials into an overall scheme, the purpose of which only stands revealed when the whole is complete. Perhaps – like Musil's novel *Der Mann ohne Eigenschaften* (*The Man Without Qualities*) (1930–43) – it never can be complete, because incompleteness is, as in much modern fiction, its real form, just as some cathedrals, like the great chancel at Narbonne, stand unfinished 'as a consequence of the very scale of the architects' plan'. The novel on the grand scale may then draw on autobiographical material, because the writer may feel compelled to write of what he has known, felt, or experienced; but the work will transcend its locality. This is inevitable by virtue of the nature of readers, for 'every reader is, when he reads, reading only about himself'. But Proust's narrator, himself Marcel, has no regrets that his accounts of his love-affairs will commit infidelities toward the women he loved; 'this profanation of my memories by unknown readers' who apply their own situations to the novel 'was carried out myself beforehand' in the process of refracting them through the literary medium. In literary creation the individual experience is transformed into a 'spiritual equivalent'; in discovering ourselves, we uncover the world of art that lies within us. And because it is by art alone that we emerge from ourselves, a writer's style is not a matter of technique but a vision or a symbolist totality. So his novel discovers what it already is, as well as showing its own openness: thus it validates its slow accretive prose, its chains of complex association, its run of language and sensitive awareness, its self-engrossed quality. It acquires its own impersonality as it goes along, becoming a coherent symbol. But the becoming of the book is also the becoming of the writer, as it is with many Modernist novels, 'the true life, life at last discovered and illuminated, the only life really lived, is that of the writer', Proust observes.

À la recherche du temps perdu is both a portrait of the artist and a discovery of the aesthetic by which the portrait is painted; clearly, a Modernist aesthetic. The theme of the portrayed artist is a recurrent one in the Modernist novel, and one of the means by which the aesthetic self-consciousness of the species develops through the great classics of modernism. Proust's Marcel, Mann's Tonio Kröger, Joyce's Stephen Dedalus, Gide's Édouard are all 'portraits of the artist'; and nearly all are parts of plots that take us toward the centre of a symbolist possibility for art. The modern artist, often an exile, takes on shape as a spirit, a voyager into the unknown arts, and an embodiment of the difficulties in the form which surrounds him, taking his place in the complex perspectives of the writing itself. In this way, Joyce's entire *œuvre* composes a transaction much resembling that of Marcel in *À la recherche du temps perdu*. Each of Joyce's three major works – *A Portrait of the Artist as a Young Man* (1916), *Ulysses* (1922) and *Finnegans Wake* (1939) – is implicitly a redefinition of the work before it, and each constitutes part of a continuous aesthetic quest. There is unbroken thematic development, but the formal progression is discrete: the fictionalized confession of *A Portrait* and the jocose epic poem of the *Wake* have little, structurally speaking, in common, and yet they are part of a triptych of forms. *A Portrait* is a *bildungsroman* of the Symbolist-Modernist artist, Stephen Dedalus, which describes the pursuit of an artistic metamorphosis both as a sympathic autobiography and as a formally contained object set in several framing modes. Dedalus's containment within the world of forms continues into *Ulysses*, in which he takes a subordinate position, until he fades away into the impersonal, distanced world of *Finnegans Wake*, a world made and held together by its own language. In *A Portrait* Joyce prefigures this movement by setting up an aesthetic hierarchy; art moves from the lyric to the narrative to the dramatic, the last an art of authorial indifference, of the coherent and self-sustaining symbol. In the same process art loses specificity and becomes not only an intensified making but a myth. *Ulysses* seeks a form for such a myth, but a modern form, and the result is in fact the Modernist novel *par excellence*. The idea of reincarnating the wily Odysseus in a seedy advertisement canvasser, and of telescoping the hero's ten-year wanderings into the twenty hours of a Dublin summer day, is characteristic of the ironic literary self-consciousness of Modernism. The trivial and everyday are thereby mythologized, and the contemporary male attains to the stature of a legendary hero; by such means the novel transcends both the auto-biographical and the realist-naturalist documentation that goes into its making. Its art is located in the endless context of art; conversely, though, the ancient epic is reborn – like a Bach concerto transcribed by Schoenberg – into a new idiom. But that idiom is itself curiously compromised; the higher mode mocks the lower, and the book invokes, therefore, a world of lost or broken forms. Parody and pastiche, the use of plurality of language, demonstrate the lack of plot and discourse in the contemporary world. The novel contains the degenerate history which the symbol must transcend; the compulsion towards technique becomes a feature of a world in which there is no coherence to give outside the coherence of art. *Ulysses* turns, in fact, on the element of destruction of art as well as of creation of it that lies in Modernist introversion; and the aspiration toward the unknown arts and the new forms embodied in Stephen Dedalus's priestly and sacramental vocation is given a dimension of scepticism, which questions not only the Dedalus figure but indeed the total environment in which modern art is made.

In a curious way, therefore, the portrait of the Modernist artist exists in Joyce's work to compromise him as well as to validate him. And this is true in the work of Thomas Mann as well. Like Joyce's, Mann's work becomes increasingly Symbolist. This aspiration toward the redemptive symbol emerges slowly into sight from within the structure of his first novel, *Buddenbrooks* (1901), a long family chronicle, apparently in the naturalistic mode, about the decline of a Lübeck bourgeois family. But the novel is a complex metaphor for the way art is born out of a dying culture; the important figure here is the delicate and in a sense deathly Hanno, an obvious surrogate for the author (the first of many – Tonio Kröger, Gustav von Aschenbach, Felix Krull – in Mann's work). But just as Hanno emerges from the dense, naturalistic web of *Buddenbrooks*, and so belongs within, as well as transcending, the historical conditions that have made him, so likewise does Mann's own aesthetic predicament. When *Buddenbrooks* was read as a naturalistic novel, and the writer was accused of plagiarizing from life, Mann gave the classic Symbolist defence: 'When I have made a sentence out of something, what has that something to do with the sentence?' It is not the 'subject' but the making which is the object of contemplation. This is central to Modernism; it sets form over life, pattern and myth over the contingencies of history; the power of the fictive presides. And yet that artistic absoluteness ('I should like to think of art as an absolute', he commented) is persistently compromised in Mann's work. Symbolist purity is always part of the quest; the novels and stories tend increasingly toward the symbolist, the mythological, the timeless in *Der Zauberberg* (*The Magic Mountain*), *Doktor Faustus*, *Joseph und seine Brüder* (*Joseph and His Brethren*), and yet they insistently assert, often within the symbolist form, that which stands against the symbol: contingency, reality, history. In Proust and Joyce and Mann we can see, as one of the results of Modernist introversion, the desire for pure form – for what E. M. Forster calls in *Aspects of the Novel*, and in all respect, 'faking': that making of pattern and wholeness which makes art into an order standing outside and beyond the human muddle, a transcendent object, a luminous whole. All three writers embody the desire; all three struggle with it; and the result is a profound element of irony presiding in the spirit of Modernism. Mann's irony is however the most complete, and because the claims of history, of naturalism, of the present, are intensely real to him. His heroes are usually given in their historical location, part of the complex struggle of aestheticism in the late bourgeois culture. In *Der Tod in Venedig (Death in Venice)* Aschenbach is killed by his own symbol, a tainted object of contemplation in part made by the intensification of his own creativity beyond its controllable limits. In *Der Zauberberg* symbolist stasis struggles with intellectual dialectic and the more onerous dialectic of history; once again art emerges as a deathly magic. Mann always compromises the metamorphosis that his own art creates; that is the basis of his famous irony. But the irony is recurrent in Modernism – an irony that recognizes the chaos and the abyss that underlie and condition artistic perfection. The world of art becomes a strangely dangerous world, a world of perceptions and illusions generated by powers themselves capable of coming under suspicion. And similarly the completeness and coherence of the work of art can be paradoxically no more than an elegant fiction. This Mann saw, and for the artist who makes such a world Mann created a highly appropriate metaphor about which he wrote twice, at the beginning and the end of his career. The figure he gives us is Felix Krull, the artist as confidence-trickster, a man whose self-conscious gift for creation is in the end a gift for deception. And against Joyce's famous portrait of the artist, the elegant artificer, the secular priest, we need, if we are to catch the total spectrum of Modernist self-questioning, to set Krull and his wry implication about the status of art and the meaning of it.

4

As we consider the new introversion that came into the novel in the later years of the nineteenth century, and effected a radical change in the form, we might therefore see in that development two somewhat contrary impulses. One is the desire to free the novel from its earlier limitations – its flat, external realism, its dependence on the material world and the loose contingencies of prose – and to probe more freely and intensely the fact of life and the orders of modern consciousness. This is the desire that Virginia Woolf expressed in a famous essay:[6]

If a writer were a free man and not a slave, if he could write what he chose, not what he must, if he could base his work upon his own feeling and not upon convention, there would be no plot, no comedy, no tragedy, no love interest or catastrophe in the accepted style, and perhaps not a single button sewn on as the Bond Street tailors would have it. Life is not a series of gig lamps symmetrically arranged; but a luminous halo, a semi-transparent envelope surrounding us from the beginning of consciousness to the end. Is it not the task of the novelist to convey this varying, this unknown and uncircumscribed spirit, whatever aberration or complexity it may display, with as little mixture of the alien and external as possible?

This is of course a plea to situate fiction within the flow of human consciousness, and Virginia Woolf is Paterian enough to believe that consciousness is itself aesthetic; it is a kind of poeticized, subjective vision in which we all (though especially women) live, an unconditioned state of high reverie and awareness analogous to the condition of the artist. The modern novel thus becomes the novel of fine consciousness; it escapes the conventions of fact-giving and story-telling; it desubstantiates the material world and puts it in its just place; it transcends the vulgar limitations and simplicities of realism, so as to serve a higher realism. The modern novel is the freer novel, and its freedom is the freedom not only to be more poetic, but also truer to the feel of life. Her great novels of the twenties and early thirties, therefore, and especially *Mrs Dalloway* (1925), *To the Lighthouse* (1927) and *The Waves* (1931), are novels of pattern rather than plot, novels in which the high sensibilities of the central characters consort and co-operate with the consciousness of the author to produce form. 'I insubstantise, wilfully to some extent, distrusting reality – its cheapness,' she noted; but the result is not simply formal purism but the representation of the flow of a sensitive human mind – and so a fiction which redisposes the assumed relationship between authors and characters, characters and time, the mind and time, and redefines all the significant elements – story, plot, catastrophe – of the novel species. We experience an exploration both of the aesthetics of consciousness and the aesthetics of art, pursued simultaneously and without any real sense of artistic crisis – rather with a kind of joyous artistic freedom. Her works are thus, like Joyce's *Ulysses*, self-manifesting; they constitute a total universe and sustain themselves within the completeness of their own vision.

This is one vein in the Modernist novel, but beside it we can see the evolution of another: the novel fleeing from material realism not in order to convey consciousness or the feel of life more intensely, but in order to explore the poverty of reality and the powers of art, of perspective and form which lie in the spaces between the data and the creative object. This is the desire that André Gide expressed in *Les Faux-monnayeurs* (*The Coiners*, sometimes translated as *The Counterfeiters*) (1926) through his surrogate Édouard – who complains, as Virginia Woolf does, that the novel has 'always clung to reality with such timidity', but proposes an alternative aim: a novel about the relations of reality and form, a novel of free inclusiveness, a novel which pluralizes techniques, cuts all ways at once, a novel about everything. Gide proposed to call this book his only novel; his other works of fiction were, he considered, partial, and he called them 'tales' or 'farces' instead. But *Les Faux-monnayeurs* is his distillation of the novel-form; it contains a novelist named Édouard who is writing a novel also called *Les Faux-monnayeurs*; he concurrently keeps a diary from which quotations are liberally taken by Gide, who during the writing of the book also kept a journal which he considered publishing in it and which he did indeed publish soon after. The result is, undoubtedly, a novel which is an artificial game with Chinese boxes, a highly pleasurable game; but Gide is a serious and sincere mind, and the book is a sophisticated reflection on the nature of a fiction. It is constructed in a complex but in fact an exceedingly neat and tidy fashion; the life it reflects, the reality it encapsulates, is, in conscious contrast, muddled and cruel – a life of murder, suicide, loveless defloration and adultery by proxy, though also of consummated (but homosexual) passion and paternal devotion. It contains a story represented as true, but it is a desperate reality, and the fact that in the end the unhappiness, after some bloodletting, is resolved and a precarious order restored is itself an ironical comment: literature is a tidying up after life's chaotic bungling. And Édouard is himself something of an imperfect novelist, so that there is a further dimension of ironic distance – not only between Édouard and the fiction he tries to make, but between Gide and Édouard. The baroque technicalities make it significant that Édouard cites as his aesthetic ideal Bach's *Art of Fugue*, though another character dismisses this as an abstract and boring monument. Gide's recognition of the writer's cardinal problem – the fact that fiction is the artist's ever-renewed and ever-inadequate means of embracing the shifting and lively forms of reality – turns him therefore not only to the history of the book's making, but to a questioning of it. One character remarks that good novels are written more naïvely than this; and the title raises the question of the total falsity of all fictions, which are counterfeit coin. This central paradox is not, though, a sterile one; Gide means it to disturb complacency about both fiction and reality, and he succeeds. The result is something close to the Flaubertian ideal of a 'novel without a subject', to the extent that the book seems to eliminate from itself all elements which do not belong specifically to it, the simple stuff of exterior life, the data from life that the reader can himself supply. The description that Musil applied to *Der Mann ohne Eigenschaften* – 'what the story that makes up this novel amounts to is that the story that was supposed to be told in it is not told' – fits *Les Faux-monnayeurs* very accurately, and not only because Édouard's novel is never finished and therefore not imparted to us. Gide portrays the autonomy of the fictional material, which gets out of hand and commits violence before being brought to heel and restrained to some semblance of order; the implication is that if life were not sanguinary disorder the story that is not told could always *be* told. Yet the story half-told enables another telling – that of the creation not of the world but of the word, of those perspectives and those difficulties beyond the stuff of reality where the artist makes, shapes, imposes, in elegant forgery.

5

In *The Dehumanization of Art*, Ortega y Gasset remarks that one consequence of the modern novel's shift away from realism and humanized representation is that art tends to become a game or a delightful fraud. And indeed it is the case that the grand thrust of the modern novel towards its fulfilment as art – its stress on the power of form and technique, on the drama of the artist's consciousness, on the musicalities of composition, on the disposition of thematic and spatial aesthetic blocks, which stitch a novel together from inside, and appeal not to the reader's sense of history but his sense of aesthetic harmony – has also been part of an intense questioning of art, and a sense of the existence of a difficult divergence between art and reality. Awareness of the ephemerality and discontinuity of modern reality, of the evanescence of character, the disorderly sequence of time, invades the Modernist novel. And indeed once the artist has succeeded in making his reader, in Max Ernst's phrase, 'a spectator at the birth of his work', as so many modern novelists have, then what the reader comes to share is a knowledge not only of the power and the potential transcendence of the creative energy, but also of its paradoxical unreality. The novel becomes for the reader a creation, 'something aesthetically compact', as Forster puts it; but the creation is itself a fiction, a pattern or grid placed over reality, a God-like intervention. It is a forging, but also a faking; it partakes of orders discerned in reality, but discovers its own orders which are the orders of art. Latterly Iris Murdoch has warned us of the dangerous 'consolations of form', and has spoken of the need for the novel to be open to an unutterable contingency, and to the opacity and complexity of persons.[7] Behind that urging lies the most powerful debate of the modern novel – the debate between the art that makes life, and the art that would assert it *is* life; between the art that makes its appeal to its own internal universe, and the art that makes it to the reality and texture of the material world and the social order and our familiar concepts of 'person' and 'time'; between the art of long or complex perspectives and the literature of 'that middle distance which places individual people in one working perspective'[8] – and the debate is still with us. But it would not do to forget that the dialogue exists not only between the modernist novelist and his antithesis (as between James and Wells, for instance[9]) but also *within* the Modernist novel; it is indeed a part of the introversion which we have explored. For, time and time again, the Modernist novel has explored the space between the 'something aesthetically compact' and the muddle of human life, between Poetry and History, between the metamorphic symbol and the place it takes in disorderly time; it has hung curiously poised between the energetic powers of aesthetic making and the countervailing claims of history or contingency, between the artifice of eternity and the conviction that this artifice is no more than a consoling fiction. The modern novel has gone on playing with these paradoxes since, and we might add that it is an intensely serious game, for the nature of fictions implicates us all.

Today the relationship between the fictive and the real remains an active matter of debate around fiction; and, too, within it. The dilemma of which Iris Murdoch speaks she also embodies, in her own writing, though in softer forms than the great Modernists did; so too do Muriel Spark (says Caroline, the heroine of *The Comforters*: 'I intend to stand aside and see if the novel has any real form apart from this artificial plot. I happen to be a Christian') and John Fowles, notably in *The Magus*. In France, Samuel Beckett has achieved the feat of composing novels which disintegrate into silence as they unfold, crucified on the paradox that 'you must either lie or hold your peace', a convention common to all fiction but explored with particularly obsessive logic by Beckett; and the end of Claude Simon's recent novel *La Bataille de Pharsale* (*The Battle of Pharsalus*), the 'observer observed' technique of which is clearly Modernist, rejoins its beginning, as in the Viconian *Finnegans Wake* and Beckett's *Molloy*. In Argentina Jorge Luis Borges has published his *Ficciones* (*Fictions*), which turn the short-story form back upon itself, and involve a universe of fictional imaginings which speculate not only on the claims of the real world to inhere reality but on the superior power of orders derived from the resources of language structures themselves. In the United States, that elegant cosmopolitan Vladimir Nabokov has chased the butterflies of fleeting reality with nets of words themselves aspiring to the condition of ordered game; similarly John Barth, reacting against a too literal universe ('reality,' he says, 'is a nice place to visit but you wouldn't want to live there'), has produced a literature in which the formal properties of fiction turn into their own fiction, mirroring the fact that all human order is an imposition on the absurdity of experience; and the mode, so recurrent as nowadays to be a prevailing convention, has popular expression in the science-fiction of Kurt Vonnegut, in which the escape from the space–time continuum and from the familiar exigences of plot and sequence are analogous acts. Today, indeed, it has become almost a matter of prevailing convention to suppose that the realistic novel is dead; that fiction is yet another plot imposed on that world of many fictions we call reality and history; that there is no commonly apprehendable experience out there that we all share in common and all value in common. Hence the novel is implicitly design and design only, a form of art and joy, a world pleasured by its own making. Reality itself being offensively literal or hideously surreal, the novel has thus tended to become, for a substantial and international group of writers, a particular occasion of order – or disorder – to set against all other orders, or disorders.

Most of this reaches back to the spirit of the paleo-moderns, though there are some significant differences. Indeed the whole question of whether the tradition of introversion and experiment has been continuous, or whether it has been severely interrupted, is a difficult one. It is often held that in the 1930s the novel reverted to social realism and politics, and equally it has been argued that, in England at least, the post-war years saw a reaction against Modernist experimentalism. Yet in England, the United States, and France there are figures of continuity: Faulkner, Beckett, Malcolm Lowry, Hemingway, Sartre. The vexed question is perhaps best considered in the light of what happened in France over the rage for commitment of the thirties, and the existentialist heart-searching of the 1940s. The fact is that the genuinely durable novels of this period – Malraux's *La Condition humaine* (*Man's Estate*) (1933), Sartre's *La Nausée* (*Nausea*) (1938), Camus's *L'Étranger* (*The Outsider*) (1942) – are considerable formal achievements, the nature of which, now the dust has settled a little, should not be obscured by their obvious referential and realistic bias, their concern to use prose, as Sartre urged it must be used in 'Qu'est-ce que la littérature?' (*What Is Literature?*) (1947), as a medium of communication, of action, of history. Despite these obvious attributes, we cannot fail to be struck by the formal intricacy of these novels. Malraux's is constructed like a tragic drama in five acts, framed by a prologue and an epilogue, and, as a later article here argues,[10] shows many symbolist features; *La Nausée* self-consciously harks back to the 'diary-discovered-among-the-papers-of' mode of much eighteenth-century fiction; *L'Étranger* is an elaborate exercise in rhetoric conducted by a self-conscious narrator of whose fundamental innocence Camus is concerned to persuade us. It was these writers, quite as much as the so-called *nouveaux romanciers*, who developed what John Sturrock sees as the distinguishing feature of the works of Robbe-Grillet and Claude Simon, namely narration by a 'problematic first person [whose] narration is his own objectification of himself', and the abandonment of traditional forms of preterite narration in favour of the present tense.[11] The formal curiosity of the Modernists, in fact, has been alive in many post-modern writers who have been concerned with realism and history, from Sartre to Angus Wilson to Norman Mailer. To some extent, they have amended the debate; and craft has yielded to history. Hence it is still in the classic moderns that we can see the full force of what the novel of aesthetic introversion might be and do: and here we can perceive the intensity of strain and pressure under which it was created, as well as the symbolist luminosity to which it might aspire. An art-form so preoccupied with its own aesthetics is, of course, the kind of rare flower that only a fully mature plant can produce. There is an obvious danger of decadence from inbreeding, as there is a danger of avoiding the force and pressure of history. But in these writers we have looked at structural introversion is more than the narcissistic contemplation of art. The consolations of form, when they are won, are hard-won, and out of constant and often exposed and unresolved struggle. As a result, these works at their greatest attain to the lucidly critical self-awareness of art of a uniquely fertile and original kind.

Notes

1 Wayne Booth valuably discusses this in *The Rhetoric of Fiction* (Chicago 1961).

2 Henry James, *The Ambassadors*, Part First, Chapter 1.

3 On the 'freer' form of the modern novel, the 'flux of consciousness' finishing in 'the experience of incompletion', see Alan Friedman, *The Turn of the Novel* (New York and London 1966).

4 Ortega y Gasset, *The Dehumanization of Art and Other Writings* (New York 1956).

5 Mark Schorer, 'Technique as Discovery', in William Van O'Connor (ed.), *Forms of Modern Fiction* (Minneapolis 1948) and in Mark Schorer, *The World We Imagine* (London 1969).

6 Virginia Woolf, 'Modern Fiction' in volume 2 of *Collected Essays* (p. 106) (London 1966). Originally published in *The Common Reader* (first series).

7 Iris Murdoch, 'Against Dryness', *Encounter* (January 1961), pp. 16–20.

8 J. P. Stern, 'Reflections on Realism', *Journal of European Studies* (March 1971), pp. 1–31.

9 For the famous literary quarrel between these two, see Leon Edel and Gordon Ray (eds.), *Henry James and H. G. Wells: A Record of Their Friendship* (London 1958).

10 See Melvin J. Friedman, 'The Symbolist Novel: Huysmans to Malraux,' pp. 453–66 below.

11 John Sturrock, *The French New Novel* (London 1969), p. 33.

THE THEME OF CONSCIOUSNESS:
THOMAS MANN

J. P. STERN

I

OUR point of departure is the conservative wing of German fiction around the turn of the century. Theodor Fontane's last novel, *Der Stechlin*, was published in 1899, a year after its author's death at the age of 79; Thomas Mann's *Buddenbrooks: the Decline of a Family*, the masterpiece of a young man of 26, appeared two years later, in October 1901. Both are leisurely novels of good society, affectionate tributes to a style of life whose decline they describe; both are cast in a form regarded as outmoded by the literary vanguard of the day.

Fontane's Stechlins are *Krautjunker*, Prussian landed gentry short of cash, with a ramshackle castle on a lake and in a village whose name they bear, with connections among the military and in the upper civil service. At the centre of Fontane's tableau is old Major Dubslav von Stechlin; round him are grouped his servants and family, including his son and heir, Woldemar, and his sister, Domina Adelheid, deaconess of a Lutheran conventicle, besides a conservative village schoolmaster and a sceptically progressive young parson; while the rich and cosmopolitan Barbys with their elegant Berlin residence form a counterpoint to the mildly eccentric 'originals' of provincial Stechlin. The plot, such as it is, involves the defeat of the paternalistic politics of Old Prussia by a social-democratic candidate 'with principles', and the marriage of Woldemar to the less exacting of the two charming Barby sisters. Throughout most of his career as a novelist Fontane had conformed to the formal precepts of European realism by placing action, plot and characterization at the centre of his novels and stories; allowing mood and atmosphere to emerge from the action; and displaying no interest in ideas except as means of character depiction. His last work too displays those high skills of the conversational and socially accommodated novel – the worldly novel – of which he is the first serious practitioner in German literature. Yet the plot of *Der*

Stechlin is something of an excuse. The novel's dominant aspect is its mood, old Dubslav Stechlin's gentle decline towards death. Though there are a few intimations that this decline is part of a wider historical picture, they amount to hardly more than casual hints, musings that remain unexplored. The old century is drawing to a close, but the realistic novelist is too deeply interested in the present and its roots in the past to be much of a prophet of the dark things to come.

The young Thomas Mann's scope is a good deal broader and more ambitious, and his narrative means are a good deal more sophisticated. The Buddenbrooks are North German (Lübeck) merchants and corn shippers, fully involved in the public life of their city as senators and honorary consuls. The socio-historical dimension of the plot that covers the years 1835 to 1877 is rather more explicit than in Fontane. The decline in the fortunes of the family firm is traced out over three-and-a-half generations, and is given its partial and proximate cause in the Buddenbrooks's inability to adjust to the changes from mercantilism to financial capitalism which are taking place around them. Hand in hand with their economic decline goes a gradual loss of physical stamina and moral fibre, ending with the death of the family firm's last head, Thomas Buddenbrook, in the prime of his life, and the subsequent liquidation of the firm; the decline is completed in the precocious and sad little life of Thomas's son Hanno, who dies of a typhoid infection, aged fifteen. The richness and complexity of the social and psychological substance from which the two-volume work is built, the assurance with which the various threads of the narrative are handled, the dovetailing contrasts of mood, and the interplay of action and ideas – all these have never been surpassed in German fiction; and when, more than forty years later, Franz Werfel on his deathbed said to Thomas Mann that he had just re-read *Buddenbrooks* and still regarded it as his one 'immortal masterpiece', Mann himself noted his bemused agreement and added: 'It may well be a case like that of *Der Freischütz*, which [Weber] followed up with all sorts of music, some of it even better and finer – and yet, it alone has survived among the people.'

Among the people? The remark, in Thomas Mann's Californian diary of January 1944, recalls the enormous popularity his first work achieved, and which no later book of his ever equalled. But it is also an echo of all those early polemics – some barbed with political intent –

in which he defended his work against charges of 'modernist decadence' and pessimism. He never ceases to identify himself with the ethos of the Hanseatic patrician *Bürgertum*, but his traditionalism, somewhat like T. S. Eliot's, is part of his literary strategy. In the very act of paying homage to the past he voices his own nostalgic awareness of the distance that separates him from its values and beliefs, its decencies and taboos. The past is available to him not in its continuity into the present, not as a living tradition, but as the reconstructed object of his detached and ironical art.

If there are any *esprits forts* among the writers of the early twentieth century, Thomas Mann is not one of them. Throughout his long life he feels a paramount need for reassurance, a need to shore up his complex literary undertaking by pointing to its – and indeed his own – roots in the nineteenth century. In several essays he has paid generous tribute to Fontane, and on many occasions he has stressed his indebtedness to Flaubert and Zola, Paul Bourget, Tolstoy and Goethe. He regards the 'epic monumentality' and 'immense creative patience' of *War and Peace* as a shining example 'which it is my dream somehow to imitate'; and he traces back his own use of the *leitmotif* technique, in *Buddenbrooks* and throughout his later work, to Tolstoy's 'literal and significant retracing of narrative relations'. The very size of Tolstoy's achievement gives him, a young man with no more than a few stories and literary articles to his credit, the freedom and courage he needs for his own enterprise: which is epic in size though emphatically not in manner. For whereas the Tolstoyan epic manner rests on the creative trust that a narrative of people and their actions unaided by ironic indirection and stylistic self-consciousness will tell its own significant tale, sustained confidence of this 'naïve' kind is not to be found in Mann's most characteristic work. His relationship to the homelier Fontane is somewhat similar; and again the Schillerian distinction between the (relatively) 'naïve' and the 'sentimental' (= reflectively self-conscious) poet suggests the significant difference. The gentle, good-natured irony of Fontane's character portrayals is echoed in the early scenes of *Buddenbrooks*, especially in Mann's portrayal of some of the 'originals' in the wings. But as the story moves down the old century, from Johann the Elder to Jean and thence to Thomas, under whose management the firm attains its greatest prosperity and then plunges to its speedy decline, the irony becomes harsher and less forbearing – until at last it comes to envelop not merely individual characters and their amiable foibles, but the entire world in which their lives had once been so firmly anchored, all its commercial, social and emotional proprieties.

The substantial world the Buddenbrooks inhabit is real enough by any realistic standards. The novel opens with Frau Consul Buddenbrook as she sits 'with her mother-in-law on a straight white enamelled sofa with yellow cushions and a gilded lion's head', examining her daughter in the Catechism. And: 'I believe . . .', Tony begins her recital, looking round the 'landscape room' on the first floor of the Buddenbrooks' rambling old house in the Mengstrasse, with its heavy painted tapestries which were hung so that they stood away from the walls, 'I believe that God created me, together with all living creatures . . . and clothes and shoes, and meat and drink, hearth and home, wife and child, fields and cattle . . .' All of it, including old Johann Buddenbrook's burst of laughter while poking fun ('*sich mokieren zu können*') at the Catechism, could be Fontane's prose, it is 'the very age and body of the time, his form and pressure'.

With Fontane this prose of the perfect accommodation takes us all the way, to the very extremity of the human condition as he sees it. Dubslav von Stechlin is dying. The doctors haven't been much use and the – strictly illegal – herbal cures the village crone has prescribed 'against the congestion' haven't done much good either. But as he sits in his armchair near the French windows that give on to the verandah and the garden beyond, Dubslav is not alone. His regimental batman and faithful servant, '*der alte Engelke*', is with him, and so is a little girl, Agnes, grand-daughter of the village herbalist and daughter of, well . . . the novelist of decorum mentions Agnes's mother in Berlin but doesn't ever quite identify her father. Dubslav's is an old-fashioned death – the scene being wholly innocent of that catastrophic view which regards social experience as inauthentic and incapable of accommodating man *in extremis*. It is not only Engelke ('*alte Silberputzerseele*' Thomas Mann calls him in an essay of 1920) and the girl who are with Dubslav in his hour of need. He feels fear and apprehension, but not that notorious *Angst* beyond all meaning and possible comfort; he is not 'held out', as in a vice, 'into the Abyss of Nothing', as the fee-faw-fum of existentialism puts it. Even when Engelke leaves him for a while he is still comforted by the homely wisdom of a traditional tag (*'das Leben ist kurz, aber die Stunde ist lang'*) ('life is short, but the hour is long'), his mind still dwells among those certitudes which his illustrious fellow-countryman, old Immanuel Kant of Königsberg, had formulated (*'Ein ewig Gesetzliches vollzieht sich . . .'*) ('An eternal law is fulfilling itself . . .') and which, for the Stechlins at all events, are close to the comforts of religion itself.

The novelist too is with Dubslav to the end: gently intimating his own presence when the new day breaks (*'Es war wohl schon sieben – . . .'*) ('It must have been about seven . . .'), commenting approvingly on the child who does as Engelke suggests (*'Die Kleine trat auch leise durch die Balkontür . . .'*) ('The girl went quietly out through the balcony door . . .'), anticipating in his own voice (*'das Beste waren die Schneeglöckchen . . .'*) ('The snowdrops were the best . . .') Engelke's last words about the snowdrops Agnes has brought in from the garden (*'. . . un wihren ook woll de besten sinn'*) ('. . . and will probably be the best'), and avoiding all sentimentality by cropping his syntax to a bare brevity. A scene of death and anguish, to be sure, but it is fully encompassed by the incomparable charm of the social realist:[1]

Engelke ging, und Dubslav war wieder allein. Er fühlte, dass es zu Ende gehe. 'Das "Ich" ist nichts – damit muss man sich durchdringen. Ein ewig Gesetzliches vollzieht sich, weiter nichts, und dieser Vollzug, auch wenn er "Tod" heisst, darf uns nicht schrecken. In das Gesetzliche sich ruhig schicken, das macht den sittlichen Menschen und hebt ihn.'

Er hing dem noch so nach und freute sich, alle Furcht überwunden zu haben. Aber dann kamen doch wieder Anfälle von Angst, und er seufzte: 'Das Leben ist kurz, aber die Stunde ist lang.'

Es war eine schlimme Nacht. Alles blieb auf. Engelke lief hin und her, und Agnes sass in ihrem Bett und sah mit grossen Augen durch die halbgeöffnete Tür in das Zimmer des Kranken. Erst als schon der Tag graute, wurde durch das ganze Haus hin alles ruhiger; der Kranke nickte matt vor sich hin, und auch Agnes schlief ein.

Es war wohl schon sieben – die Parkbäume hinter dem Vorgarten lagen bereits in einem hellen Schein –, als Engelke zu dem Kinde herantrat und es weckte. 'Steih upp, Agnes.'

'Is he dod?'

'Nei. He slöppt en beten. Un ick glöw, et sitt em nich mihr so upp de Bost.'

'Ick grul mi so.'

'Dat brukst du nich. Un kann ook sinn, he slöppt sich wedder gesunn . . . Und nu, steih upp un bind di ook en Doog um'n Kopp. Et is noch en beten

*küll drut. Un denn geih in'n Goaren und plück em (wenn du wat finnst) en
beten Krokus oder wat et sünsten is.'*

*Die Kleine trat auch leise durch die Balkontür auf die Veranda hinaus und
ging auf das Rondell zu, um nach ein paar Blumen zu suchen. Sie fand auch
allerlei; das Beste waren Schneeglöckchen. Und nun ging sie, mit den Blumen
in der Hand, noch ein paarmal auf und ab und sah, wie die Sonne drüben
aufstieg. Sie fröstelte. Zugleich aber kam ihr ein Gefühl des Lebens. Dann
trat sie wieder in das Zimmer und ging auf den Stuhl zu, wo Dubslav sass.
Engelke, die Hände gefaltet, stand neben seinem Herrn.*

Das Kind trat heran und legte die Blumen dem Alten auf den Schoss.

'Dat sinn de ihrsten', sagte Engelke, 'un wihren ook woll de besten sinn.'*

Not two or three years but an era and a desolation lie between the

---

*Engelke went away and Dubslav was alone again. He felt that the end was
near. 'The Self is nothing – one must hold on to that. An eternal law is fulfilling
itself, that's all, and we mustn't be frightened of that fulfilment, even if its
name is Death. To submit to the law in peace and resignation is what makes
moral man and raises him up.'

He thought about this for a while and was glad at having overcome all apprehension. But then the attacks of fear returned and he sighed: 'Life is short,
but the hour is long.'

It was a bad night. Everyone stayed awake. Engelke rushed to and fro, and
Agnes sat in her bed and looked wide-eyed through the half-open door into
the sick man's room. It was only at daybreak that the whole house became more
peaceful; the invalid was nodding drowsily and Agnes fell asleep too.

It must have been about seven – the trees in the park beyond the front garden
were already in bright sunshine – when Engelke came to the child and woke
her. 'Get up Agnes.'

'Is he dead?'

'No. He's sleeping a bit. And I don't believe it's so heavy on his chest any
longer.'

'I'm so frightened.'

'You needn't be. And maybe he'll sleep until he's better . . . And now, get
up and put a scarf round your head. It's still a bit cold outside. And then go into
the garden and pick him a few crocuses if you can find any, or whatever there
is.'

The girl went quietly out through the balcony door on to the verandah, and
then towards the round flowerbed, to look for some flowers. She found quite
a few; the snowdrops were the best. And then, with the flowers in her hand,
she walked up and down for a while, watching the sun rising on the horizon.
She felt chilly. At the same time she was aware of a feeling of life. Then she
went back into the room and towards the chair on which Dubslav was
sitting. Engelke stood with folded hands near his master.

The child came up and laid the flowers on the old man's lap.

'Those are the first', said Engelke, 'and will probably be the best.'

death of Dubslav von Stechlin and the seizure of Thomas Buddenbrook
on his way home from his catastrophic visit to the dentist:[2]

*Und er ging langsam durch die Strassen, mechanisch Grüsse erwidernd, die
ihm dargebracht wurden, mit sinnenden und ungewissen Augen, als dächte er
darüber nach, wie ihm eigentlich zumute sei.*

*Er gelangte zur Fischergrube und begann das linke Trottoir hinunter-
zugehen. Nach zwanzig Schritten befiel ihn eine Übelkeit. Ich werde dort
drüben in die Schenke treten und einen Kognak trinken müssen, dachte er, und
beschritt den Fahrdamm. Als er etwa die Mitte desselben erreicht hatte, geschah
ihm folgendes. Es war genau, als würde sein Gehirn ergriffen und von einer
unwiderstehlichen Kraft mit wachsender, fürchterlich wachsender Geschwindig-
keit in grossen, kleineren und immer kleineren konzentrischen Kreisen herum-
geschwungen und schliesslich mit einer unmässigen, brutalen und erbarmungs-
losen Wucht gegen den steinharten Mittelpunkt dieser Kreise geschmettert . . . Er
vollführte eine halbe Drehung und schlug mit ausgestreckten Armen vornüber
auf das nasse Pflaster.*

*Da die Strasse stark abfiel, befand sich sein Oberkörper ziemlich viel
tiefer als seine Füsse. Er war aufs Gesicht gefallen, unter dem sofort eine
Blutlache sich auszubreiten begann. Sein Hut rollte ein Stück des Fahrdammes
hinunter. Sein Pelz war mit Kot und Schneewasser bespritzt. Seine Hände, in
den weissen Glacéhandschuhen, lagen ausgestreckt in einer Pfütze.*

*So lag er und so blieb er liegen, bis ein paar Leute herangekommen waren und
ihn umwandten.* ★

★ And he went slowly through the streets, mechanically answering the greet-
ings that were addressed to him, with a meditative and uncertain look in his
eyes as though he were pondering how he really felt.

He reached the Fischergrube and began to walk down the left-hand pavement. He had gone twenty paces when he was overcome by a feeling of nausea.
I shall have to go into that bar over there and drink a glass of brandy, he thought,
and stepped into the roadway. When he had about reached the middle of it,
this is what happened to him. It was exactly as though his brain were seized
and swung round with irresistible force at an increasing, terribly increasing
speed in large then smaller and smaller concentric circles, to be finally smashed
with tremendous, brutal, merciless force against the centre of the circles, that
was as hard as stone . . . He made a half-turn and fell face down, his arms out-
stretched, on to the wet cobbles.

As the street was on a steep slope, his body lay much lower than his feet. He
had fallen on his face, and a pool of blood immediately began to form under it.
His hat rolled a short distance down the roadway. His fur coat was bespattered
with mud and sludge. His hands, in their white kid gloves, lay stretched out in
a puddle.

So he lay, and remained lying there, until some people came up and turned
him over.

In its anonymity, desolation and solitude this is a death in the modern manner. Its description is as impersonal as the author can make it. He enters the dying man's mind as though it were the inside of a clock-work that has broken down. No firm belief sustains Thomas in his hour of need, no distinct self even: what is being described is not an individual consciousness, not this one man's fears and anguish, but a pattern of abstract shapes and mechanical reactions. The narrator's prose registers a case history: his place of observation and his choice of vocabulary are determined by a 'scientific' detachment and curiosity. There is a studied break in the narrative at the words '. . . this is what happened to him. It was exactly as if . . .' ('. . . *geschah ihm folgendes. Es war genau, als würde* . . .'). In much the same way, five chapters later, a long and fairly detailed account of the last illness of Thomas Budden-brook's son Hanno opens with the sentence, 'Now, a typhoid infec-tion proceeds in the following way: . . .' ('*Mit dem Typhus war es folgendermassen bestellt*: . . .'). In both instances – in Hanno's illness as in Thomas's collapse – the formal, pedantic break serves to combine the close view of the diagnostician with the distant view of the impersonal reporter. Only once, almost inadvertently, in the brief repetition of 'So he [Thomas] lay, and remained lying there, . . .' ('*So lag er und so blieb er liegen,* . . .'), is there some sign of narrative empathy, a hint of regret. For the rest, the emotion underlying the narrator's 'scientific' attitude is one of distaste. In earlier chapters the Senator's morbid care for his appearance was established as the desperate manoeuvre of his decaying will to keep the decline at bay. Now the physical details of the scene – the hat and fur-coat, the sullied white gloves – are all assembled to mock at that effort and to point to the utter indignity of Thomas Buddenbrook's collapse and eventual death.

The description of this modern death is 'exact': not merely by virtue of the naturalistic conceits employed or because it conveys what might be seen by a detached observer on the spot, but above all be-cause it marks the climactic completion of both aspects of the plot – the consummation of its events and ideas alike. Such a distinction between events and ideas (and hence their consummation) would make no sense in respect of Fontane's art – not because his novels are lacking in ideas, but because the ideas are wholly tied to and co-exten-sive with the events and cannot, without making nonsense of them, be detached from the events. Whereas it is precisely *this* question of what is the relationship between events and ideas – how ideas affect events – that *Buddenbrooks* is designed to answer; to answer, however, not abstractly and explicitly, but within the convention and with the resources of a realistic novel.

What distinguishes Thomas Buddenbrook from his forbears is his physical exhaustion and degeneration, and his loss of business acumen. Thus far, and with a wealth of circumstantial detail I can only hint at, all assembled to show the gradual nature of the process over three generations, the novel follows the traditional pattern of realistic literature. These are only partial causes of the decline, becoming effective through a slowly growing disillusionment with the whole business of living and caring, and meeting the ever more hostile challenges of a competitive mercantile society: this motivation too is enacted in the realistic mode. But there comes a moment when all the threads in the pattern of events are united in Thomas's consciousness, when the long-delayed awareness of the sheer pointlessness of his existence comes to him with the full force of an intellectual discovery: this moment, in the summer of his last year, constitutes the climax of the novel's 'intellectual plot' and the effective consummation of his will to live. The scene in the little garden house (Part 10, chapter 5), where Thomas finds a volume of philosophy which reconciles him to the idea of his death by arguing that his individual life will flow into the anonymous life-river of the great universal will beyond, does not in itself transgress the bounds of realism. The tired businessman does not suddenly turn into a philosophically-minded intellectual. The insight he attains during that evening is unsteady and vague, a flickering vision between daydream and sleep. (One is reminded of Gabriel's vision in the last story of Joyce's *Dubliners*.) And there will follow a few more months of routine living, including a holiday by the sea, before that visit to the dentist and the scene in the Fischergrube, when the alluring vision, by now almost forgotten, will have done its work. This delay is not (as some critics have suggested) a sign of faulty construction or narrative uncertainty. The pattern is repeated in *Der Zauberberg* (*The Magic Mountain*), where Hans Castorp's brief and unsteady insight into the mysteries of life (again in the form of a dream) is followed by several more years among the gay and scurrilous *morituri* of the tuberculosis sanatorium; in the *Joseph* tetralogy, where a dream discloses to Jaakob the knowledge of good and evil and the knowledge of his God on whom he will meditate and whom he will serve, more or less faithfully, throughout his long life; in *Dr Faustus*, where the moment of insight is the moment in which Adrian Leverkühn purchases his twenty-four years of creative life . . . All these delays, and the all-too-human modifications to which the central visions are subjected in the course of the delays, are determined by the requirements of realism – by its emphasis on the resistance of the real world to the force of ideas and the workings of consciousness itself. The moment in time when 'the idea' will do its work and the form in which it will attain reality are thus dictated by the shape of Thomas Mann's fiction; but the fiction in turn is designed to make the process of the realization of ideas plausible. The measure of the novelist's success lies in our inability to tell which came first.

Thomas Buddenbrook dies because he has ceased to will to live. The form of his dying – its desolateness and anonymity – is determined by the decay of his individual will. But it is only with the promise of that alluring vision of a Schopenhauerian[3] Nirvana beyond death (and realism) that his will-to-live abates. The story of the decline of the Buddenbrooks is thus counterpointed by another story: as their worldly and vital powers decline, so their consciousness grows. And consciousness, *in this situation*, is presented as the enemy of life, as a spirituality which exacts an understanding over and above the needs of practical life, an understanding of world and self at all costs – even at the cost of life itself.

2

If we now ask in what way Thomas Mann contributes to the 'modernity' of the novel, our first answer will be: by an increase in the consciousness portrayed and a corresponding increase in the consciousness of the portrayal. The philosophical epilogues by means of which Tolstoy sought to historicize and theoretically explain the events of *War and Peace* are here incorporated within the fictional structure itself. The story of the Buddenbrooks *is also* a criticism of the civilization that ended in August 1914: the mercantile ethos lacking in compassion, self-knowledge and a sense of values beyond its vital and business interests *versus* a spirituality lacking in vitality and at last contemptuous of life itself – these are the story's protagonists, and they are also among the causes of the European decline. But the 'intellectual plot' takes us one step further. The increased consciousness is portrayed not only as the mute and inglorious thing it is in Thomas. In his son Hanno it is turned into artistic creativity, and thus rendered morally suspect.

Even before *Buddenbrooks*, in several of his earliest stories, Thomas Mann had been fascinated by Nietzsche's etiology of the artist in an age of decadence. In this perspective the aesthetic attitude appears as a compensation of the sick and 'underprivileged' – Nietzsche's *Schlechtweggekommene* – a compensation for their inability to come to terms with the social world. Art, the product of this attitude, stands for a consciousness that is the enemy of life. Conversely, 'life', in the stories before and after *Buddenbrooks*, is seen by the artist-'heroes' as hardly more than the crude subject-matter of art. All these are fashionable themes of the *fin de siècle*.[4] What distinguishes Thomas Mann's work from the bulk of contemporary writers of novels and *Novellen*, the many *Künstlerromane* of the age, is the questioning, the ironical criticism to which he subjects the situation; and this in turn he is able to do because 'aestheticism' is, for him, always a matter of heightened consciousness. The early stories contain several variations on this theme. In some of them – 'Der kleine Herr Friedemann' and 'Bajazzo' (both 1897), 'Tristan' (1903) – the artistic disposition portrayed amounts to hardly more than a deprivation, a thing so lacking in vitality as to be quite uncreative. Then again it is shown at work in a genuine artist–'Tonio Kröger' (1903); Schiller in 'Schwere Stunde' ('Difficult Hour') (1905); Gustav von Aschenbach in 'Der Tod in Venedig' ('Death in Venice') (1912) – and the ensuing conflicts between the artistic disposition and life in its naïve and unquestioning forms, in all its unconsciousness, are explored though not necessarily resolved. Whereas in the fragmentary 'Felix Krull' (begun in 1909) and in the novel *Königliche Hoheit* (1909) the enmity between life and art is turned into a victory for art so complete that it makes life itself into an aesthetic phenomenon – but it does so in a world that offers no serious resistance to being moulded by the artistic disposition for its own aesthetic ends. (And this resolution of the conflict is triumphantly completed in the *Joseph* tetralogy, written between 1928 and 1943.)

The story of Hanno Buddenbrook's art still belongs to the stage of conflict and compensation. Young Hanno's miserable life at school, his difficult relationship with his father, his ill-health and sensitivity all contribute to a precocity that finds its 'natural' outlet in a musical gift evocative of an autoerotic indulgence. The boy's fantasies on the senatorial grand are a matter of subtle harmonies – hardly more than luscious chords and arpeggios – drenched in sentiment. All that holds them together is 'an entirely simple motif, a mere nothing, the fragment of a non-existent melody, a figure of a beat-and-a-half', a thing so slight and ephemeral that, once it was 'imperiously announced as the prime substance and beginning of all that was to come, it was impossible to make out what it really meant' (part 11, chapter 2).

Melody, in Schopenhauer's supremely illuminating exegesis of music, 'melody alone possesses a meaningful, purposeful coherence from beginning to end . . . In melody [we] recognize the highest stage of the objectivization of the Will, that is, the circumspect life and aspirations of man.'[5] But if now there is so little will left, so little of that 'objectivization' which once made up the solid world of the Buddenbrooks, what more could melody be, in Hanno's composition, than 'a mere nothing'? What his music expresses is the dark, inchoate sensuality of Hanno's puberty, it is the harbinger not of life but of a Wagnerian *Liebestod*. And with Hanno's death ('Now, a typhoid infection proceeds in the following way: . . .') the argument, the novel's 'intellectual plot', comes full circle in an excess of consciousness – artistic consciousness – over his life: an excess so radical that one can hardly speak of a conflict any more. Hanno's talent, his intelligence and his sensitiveness are all things almost without substance, the gifts not of life but of decadence. Just as the story of the earlier Buddenbrooks yielded an additional meaning as a criticism of the Wilhelminian civilization, so the story of Hanno yields an additional meaning as a criticism of that art of precocious, insubstantial feeling produced at the end of that civilization – a criticism, that is, of the alienation of art. Hanno's music does not validate the story of his forbears, it merely sounds the last chords of the generations' decline.

These, evidently, are conclusions which take *Buddenbrooks* beyond the realism which Fontane had made available to German literature in the last decades of the nineteenth century. But realism is not a static mode of writing. It is a matching and making,[6] in language, of the meeting ground between private cares and social world, and it changes as the object of the matching and the resources of the making change. With *Buddenbrooks* the resources change less than the object: the formal qualities of Thomas Mann's early work with their roots in the novels of Fontane are designed to hide the radical nature of the change. Through the rich décor of *bürgerlich* realism we glimpse an impenetrable solitude which, for Mann, constitutes the ground of the being of modern man.

The chief mode of literature in the new century (and not of literature only) is a weakening of the nexus between the private and social spheres, such as Fontane never knew; is the burgeoning of consciousness beyond the world of common indication, and thus the undermining of the realistic convention. To have given a critical account of this situation – to have enveloped the decline of realism in the subtle and complex web of realistic fiction – is the young Thomas Mann's distinctive achievement. Like Fontane's, Mann's fiction eschews all ideology, all simplifications of the human lot. In the modern world that Fontane never knew this is bound to be a strenuous achievement, based on scruples, qualifications, dissociations, refusals of commitment save to its own scrupulousness . . .: but this scrupulousness in turn is representative of the age at its best, of its heightened consciousness. Fontane's immortality, like Dickens's, derives from a fiction in which consciousness is wholly immersed in and absorbed by the fabric of the created world. In Thomas Mann's fiction, as in Gide's and Proust's and even Henry James's, consciousness moves into the centre. Mann's work will endure – as theirs will – as long as there are readers prepared to follow its exacting journey.

Notes

1 Chapter 42. Only a narrator who acknowledged his presence on the scene would use words like *wohl* and *auch*, or could repeat in his own voice something said by one of his characters.

2 Part 10, Chapter 7.

3 Erich Heller has shown how in the novel's 'intellectual plot' elements of Schopenhauer's philosophy blend with and are superseded by a vision of life derived from Nietzsche (whom the young Thomas Mann read before he read Schopenhauer); see Erich Heller, *The Ironic German: a Study of Thomas Mann* (London 1958), chapter II, 'Pessimism and Sensibility'.

4 Freud's *Psychopathology of Everyday Life* was first published in 1904; the pages of his early essays are filled with case-histories of *artistes manqués*.

5 A. Schopenhauer, *Die Welt als Wille und Vorstellung*, vol. I, book iii, para. 52.

6 The phrase, derived from E. H. Gombrich's *Art and Illusion* (London 1962), seems to me basic to any inquiry into realism. I have used it, as well as some arguments of the present essay, in my *On Realism* (London and Boston 1973).

SVEVO, JOYCE AND MODERNIST TIME

MICHAEL HOLLINGTON

I

IN Act IV of *The Cherry Orchard*, a characteristic Chekhovian non-event takes place: Lopahin goes through the motions of a half-hearted proposal to Varya, and it fizzles out. The little scene is placed near the end, where we would normally expect a major event. The characters in fact allow contingency, the trivial circumstances of the moment, to triumph – Varya the housewife fusses about looking for things, Lopahin the business-man worries about the train he must catch. Yet in two minutes' awkwardness about weather and thermometers, their futures are determined. The scene is interesting because it is demonstrably transitional, halfway between realism and Modernism. Behind it stands a scene in *Anna Karenina*, which Chekhov must have known, in which Koznyshev intends to propose to Varenka: he gets stuck, they talk about mushrooms, and that kills it. Ahead of it stands a scene in Svevo's *Confessions of Zeno*: the hero proposes, makes a wrong emphasis on the name of his prospective sister-in-law, and his chance is irrevocably gone. But there is a world of difference between the realist Tolstoy and the modernist Svevo: in place of the sharp moral criticism of Koznyshev's emotional deficiency – or Chekhov's more resigned awareness of inertia – there is in Svevo an amused ironical detachment.

'Non-events' are distinctive features in Modernist writing. If we think of events, from *The Three Sisters* to *Waiting for Godot*, it is remarkable how many of them never materialize. K.'s trial, in *The Trial*, never comes; nor does the 'great year' in Musil's *The Man Without Qualities*. At a lighter level, Hans Castorp's flirtation with Claudia Chaucat, in *The Magic Mountain*, never gets beyond exchanging x-ray negatives, and Bloom is barred from the sight of high-class underwear by intervening tramcars or people. More deeply, Stephen Dedalus's refusal to spend the night at Eccles Street frustrates our desire for a satisfactory conclusion to *Ulysses*. This absence of events reflects a contemporary sense of irony; it is also rooted in Modernist feelings about time. For the nineteenth-century novelist, time is the medium in which people grow, individually and collectively: hopes and ambitions come to fruition or are dismayed. Events mark the critical points of change. Individual development is regarded as of general human importance, and considered logical in form: laws of psychological cause and effect, of interaction between character and circumstantial environment, are in operation. So in *War and Peace* Natasha at the opera is the logical descendant of the girl who teases Boris Drubetskoy in the first chapter; chance may have brought her there, but her response to Kuragin obeys delicate laws of latent possibility in her character. None of these assumptions is shared by Modernist novelists. Even in the apparently conventional *Buddenbrooks*, Mann treats ironically the Consul's gilt-edged notebook in which he chronicles the family's developments: the significant events he records in the assumption that individual lives make coherent sense seem simply to betray a bourgeois self-importance. Three decades later, in Sartre's *Nausea*, the notion of coherent human growth in time is bourgeois bad faith, a piece of cowardice in the face of the surrounding contingency.

An essential influence in this shift was Bergson; we do not have to prove that Mann read him or Proust admired him to detect his importance for their art. He exposed fallacies in our way of thinking of time as if it could be apprehended 'spatially': events, he said, were imaginary spatial points in the uninterruptible, indistinguishable flow of time. In that scene I instanced in *The Cherry Orchard*, Varya remarks that the thermometer is broken; it is the precursor of many other moments – the thermometers of *The Magic Mountain*, the compass Ike McCaslin lays aside in *The Bear*, the tilted clock on the mantelpiece in *The Great Gatsby* – where conventional instruments of measurement become useless, and the implication is essentially in accord with Bergson. Criticism of Modernist writing has commented greatly on this matter,[1] though much of it misses the mark. Either the abstract philosophical dimension gets too much emphasis, so that, as Auerbach says in *Mimesis*, the critic ends up talking about ideas rather than literature; or else criticism concentrates very narrowly on the narrative technique, considering flashbacks, anticipations, repetitions, dislocations of time-sequence. The balance is best got in Frank Kermode's book *The Sense of an Ending*, which tries to combine a general sense of relevance with an acquaintance with the particular distinctive nature of literature. He takes literary form, especially in the arrangements of beginnings, middles, and ends, as a reflector of ideas about time and history. Because there is something irremediably temporal about literary form, he argues that Modernist writing does not forsake sequential arrangement entirely; rather it uses our normal temporal expectations, and then frustrates or complicates them. He thus takes up a position contrary to that critical orthodoxy which sees 'spatial form' as the norm of Modernist writing. This idea, most clearly promulgated by Joseph Frank in 1945, depends on the Imagist aesthetic in assuming that novels like *Ulysses* are designed as single, static images outside time, to be simultaneously apprehended.[2] In its cruder forms the idea tends to suggest that Modernism escaped the tyranny of logical sequence in order to embrace the tyranny of 'spatial form'. For me, the keynote of Modernism is liberation, an ironic distrust of all absolutes, including those of temporal or spatial form.

I therefore intend to follow Kermode rather than Frank in exploring these liberating ironies about time in the work of Svevo and Joyce, writers temperamentally very alike and with similar comic vision. At the personal level the relationship is well-known (Joyce encouraged Svevo, in Trieste, toward the writing of *The Confessions of Zeno* after a silence of several years, and Svevo's wife provided a model for Anna Livia Plurabelle in *Finnegans Wake*); but their literary affinities are relatively unexplored. At the technical level, they look very different: one obviously a major innovator and experimenter, the other apparently not. The affinity resides, I think, in the similarity of aim within their narrative techniques: the humorous celebration of the human advantages of a liberation from the enslaving temporal paradigms of experience. There is the evidence of a letter Joyce wrote to Svevo in 1924: praising *The Confessions of Zeno*, he declares 'there is no absence of wit in it', and expresses his interest in the novel's treatment of time.[3] It is the wit in the treatment of time by these two writers I want to compare, and as something very representative of a basic Modernist mood.

2

The confessions written by Zeno belong to a particular setting – Trieste, a provincial backwater, where profound social and political upheavals fall on a settled and unsuspecting bourgeoisie – and are given us in a particular tone, very distinctive, characteristically modern, a complexly situated, sceptically indeterminate irony, oscillating between compassion and melancholy. He writes them as part of a psychoanalytic cure: he has a lifelong preoccupation with finding health. 'Health', for Zeno, means above all pattern, order, coherence, exemplified for him by the gift, which he lacks, of getting musical rhythms right:

> Even the most undeveloped being, if he knows the difference between groups of three, four and six notes, can pass rhythmically and accurately from one to the other just as his eye can pass from one colour to another. But in my case, after I have been playing one of those rhythmic figures it clings to me . . . If I am to play the notes right I am compelled to beat time with my feet and head; but goodbye to ease, serenity and music! The music that is produced by a well-balanced physique is identical with the rhythm it creates and exploits; it is rhythm itself. When I can play music like that I shall be cured.

The musical metaphor, and its identification with an order of necessity transcending the surrounding incoherencies of contingency, has a familiar history in modern literature, from Proust to Sartre; likewise, in *The Confessions of Zeno*, a rival performs Bach's D Minor Chaconne to make the music seem, to the envious Zeno, 'unerring as fate'. Zeno hence turns to psychoanalysis to make his life like a Chaconne. It provides a causology, a logical model of personal development from birth, or even before it, and a psychopathology of everyday life that outrightly rejects the notion that any aspect of behaviour is accidental or sheerly phenomenal. But the cure goes wrong; the psychoanalyst, assuming that all behaviour is significant, allows Zeno to write anything about himself, in any order; and Zeno produces a document, the book itself, which is much more a journal than a psychoanalytic autobiography, and a text containing in itself dis- coveries and interpretations of experience which can exist independently of psychoanalysis, which becomes part of the object of observation. As a result disillusion sets in, and the journal form, as in modern fiction from *The Counterfeiters* to *Nausea*, becomes the expression of contingency unsubdued.

At one level, then, the book can be read as a satire against mechanistic psychology; but it is much more. The novel's modernity and its rare distinction rest in the superimposition of a number of patterns upon each other, each of which – and therefore none of which – is validated. We *are* invited to see the book from the psychoanalytic point of view, by a witty preface, written by the doctor, asking us to see Zeno's rejection of a cure as a classic case of resistance ('anyone familiar with psychoanalysis will know to what he should attribute my patient's hostility'). But we are also asked to see it from Zeno's point of view, with his presumption that muddle and chance form personality. And we can look at it from the traditional point of view of Providence, as a pattern in which Zeno's relationships do actually flourish and progress. In fact each pattern is relativized against the other; and the finest irony of all is that Zeno is cured in the process of writing his therapeutic confession – not by psychoanalysis but through the liberating stimulus of what he calls 'a psychical adventure'. If we look at Zeno's habitual approach to self-improvement, especially in its most hilarious manifestation, his lifelong attempt to stop smoking, we can see with particular vividness the principle on which the multiplicity of patterns in the book is based: any pattern fits, if you work hard enough at applying it. Zeno imposes patterns on time in order to stop smoking, perpetually setting himself a significant date for his last cigarette, but, like the apocalypticists who predict the millennium in *The Sense of an Ending*, he keeps revising his time-tables. He keeps a notebook to enter down his resolutions, and covers a roomful of walls with 'necessary' dates (9/9/99, 1/1/01, 3/6/12 and so on) until his landlord makes him re-paper them. Still the cigarette-duration continues unaffected by numerology, and Zeno's 'clerkly scepticism' leads him into experiments with random dates:

Some dates that I have put down in books or on the backs of favourite pictures arrest one's attention by their very inconsequence. For example, the third day of the second month of the year 1905 at six o'clock! It had its own rhythm, if you come to think of it, for each figure in turn contradicts the one that went before. Many events too, in fact all from the death of Pius XII to the birth of my son, I thought deserved to be celebrated by the customary iron resolution.

Zeno in fact discovers that all dates can be made equally significant, and that any pattern fits by some method of calculation or other; the system, as P. N. Furbank remarks,[4] is, we begin to realize, designed to enhance the enjoyment of every cigarette by making it the last. When Zeno later tries to give up something else – an extra-marital affair – according to a last kiss system, we begin to see that apocalyptic thinking is unequivocally the creature of the tyrannous id. Zeno tries to stiffen his will this time with a course in Bible reading (with the book of Revelation being inevitably prominent) but this only makes the rhythms of renewal more attractive. The affair ends only by chance.

But although Zeno's attempts at will do not alter, directly, the pattern of events, they do complicate them. Zeno's life has very syncopated temporal rhythms, highly irregular trajectories. That of his marriage is an example; it begins with a conscious determination to marry, and the choice of a father-in-law (a lot of 'events' in Modernist novels are deliberately like this, like the 'great year' in *The Man Without Qualities*). Svevo hints at a psychological interpretation of this, in Zeno's search for a father-substitute; but Zeno has his own more original pattern – the father-in-law's four daughters all have the initial 'A', and the union of A to Z would signify the concord of Alpha and Omega, Platonic transcendence, contingency conquered. He is not dismayed when the daughter he singles out, Ada, proves indifferent; always looking for negative versions of his plots, he decides that 'discords resolve themselves into harmonies'. But of course contingency intervenes to bend events. Zeno has a rival, Guido Speier, who plays the Chaconne and speaks pure Tuscan (a 'necessary' language, as compared with Zeno's 'contingent' bastard Triestine), and Zeno has little chance to further his prospects with Ada. Unexpectedly, in the favourable darkness provided by a séance, Zeno sees his chance, but grabs the wrong daughter and declares his love not to Ada but to Augusta. Now contingency, true to its nature, operates in his favour: the youngest daughter Anna screams out, and everyone but Zeno and Ada rush to her aid. The moment is propitious, but unfortunately Zeno's faulty rhythmic sense becomes dominant:

'Surely you must have understood!' I said. 'You couldn't have thought I wanted to make love to Augusta!'

I wanted to speak emphatically, but in my flurry I put my emphasis on the wrong place, and ended by pronouncing poor Augusta's name with a tone and gesture of contempt.

The result is that the proposal, like Lopahin's, awkwardly fizzles out; but the design can nonetheless still be completed and, fired by his enthusiasm for the letter A, Zeno proposes on the spot to the other daughters, and finally gains Augusta, whom he had liked least.

But ends in this novel proceed in strange fashion from beginnings and middles. Augusta turns out not to be ugly, but beautiful and desirable; the marriage is lastingly happy, and Augusta possesses that elusive health that Zeno perpetually seeks, and which consists not in imposing patterns of will on time, but in a joyous acceptance of the present, for her 'a tangible reality in which we could take shelter and be near together'. Zeno even loses his obsession with chronological sequence for a while, befriending a honeymoon guide who insists that the Romans used electricity. By contrast his rival Guido, who marries Ada, sinks into a morass of debt and failure. Gradually, in response to repeated vicissitudes, Zeno loses interest in 'necessary' forms, and begins to see life as an oscillation of rhythms, of intensity and inertia, with health as the almost non-existent and certainly only momentary point of balance. It is now Guido who looks for images of transcendence. During a night walk with Zeno, he is reminded of the eternal kiss not subject to time that the poet Zamboni saw in the moon. Zeno gently rebukes him: 'Of course one can't always be kissing here below. Besides, it is only the image of a kiss they have up there. Kissing is, above all, movement.' Guido replies with a dismal generalization – 'life is hard and unjust' – whereupon Zeno proceeds, in authentic random fashion, to a central insight:

One is often led to say things because of some chance association in the sound of the words, and directly one has spoken one begins to wonder if what one has said was worth the breath spent on it, and occasionally discovers that one has started a new idea. I said:
'Life is neither good nor bad; it is original.'

Zeno's discovery is of great importance in Modernist writing, representing a positive evaluation of the sense of uncertainty and relativity with which Modernism is preoccupied. Lukács, a critic hostile to Modernism, yet more illuminating than many of its admirers, regards the absence of perspective as a quintessential feature of the modern.[5] Perspective, he argues, issues from the standpoint of the end of affairs; it is, in the phrase that haunts *Ulysses*, a 'retrospective arrangement'. A relativistic novel like Svevo's, preoccupied with unpredictability, surprise, and discovery, has no end-perspective; it has the perspective from the middle that informs much Modernist writing – the exploratory rhythms of Lawrence's prose, for example: 'It seems to me as if a man, in his normal state, were like a palpitating leading-shoot of life, where the unknown, all unresolved, beats and pulses, containing the quick of all experience, as yet unrevealed, not singled out.'[6] It also helps explain the episodic structure of so many modern novels – *Women in Love*, for example, or *The Counterfeiters*, where, as Gide explains: 'every new chapter should pose new problems, serve as a new beginning, a new impulse, a new plunge ahead'.

In fact, *The Confessions of Zeno* is too intelligent and delicate a novel fully to endorse Zeno's discovery. Its surprises continue: Zeno's hard-won philosophy of movement becomes itself an obsession. So, late on in the novel, Zeno throws a bombshell into our conclusion-gathering responses: Zeno declares that the confessions are radically distorted by the 'correct' Italian in which they are written: 'Naturally it [my life] would take on quite a different aspect if I told it in our own dialect.' The reminder that all fictions inevitably lie comes a second time, when Zeno is suddenly transformed by the war into a successful businessman; this unexpected ending, he says, confers quite a different pattern on his autobiography, and he must rewrite it. Of course it does, and the pattern could go on changing until there were only one perspective – and therefore none – from which the life could be seen. The contemplation of how experience resists coherent temporal order certainly betrays, as Joyce said, 'no absence of wit'.

3

And nor, surely, does Joyce's *Ulysses*, the novel which has most fully supported modern views of spatial form, acquired that timeless mythical content which for many critics has seemed one of the great modern literary achievements. Most of these accounts give us a highly solemn version of the novel; the frequent assumption that the novel communicates profound truths – or could, once the allusions industry has completely decoded what is in it – frequently goes hand in hand with the belief that these truths concern correspondences between characters, symbols, and themes within the book and mythic counterparts without, transcending temporal distance, achieving coherent spatial order. Often images and allusions are lifted from context, often an ironic one, to join their *confrères* in space – a separation of theme from stylistic milieu which perhaps began when Stuart Gilbert relegated the comic dimension of the book to a secondary position: 'The greater the theme, the greater the parody.'[7] The seriousness of *Ulysses* would, to my mind, stand in sharper outline if that formula were simply reversed; and here the comparison with Svevo is tonic. *Ulysses* shares with Svevo's book a radically sceptical attitude to all absolutes. I take its version of Modernist relativity to be (as Ellmann and others have held) a humanistic 'wise passivity', its formal experimentation being the means of conveying the state of affairs where such an attitude makes sense. Like Svevo, Joyce is acutely conscious of *potential* significance; by flooding the day with an immense amount of experience and a very large number of lines of interpretation, he intends us to feel the comic arbitrariness of the patterns we are able to construct.

I presume, therefore, that the book's basic technique is associative, and that structure and pattern are built up in a way that is essentially the same as the way in which both Bloom's and Stephen's minds operate. As matter is accumulated in contingency and in consciousness, so it is in narrative, largely through verbal association, the staple diet of all the narrative voices of *Ulysses*. The novel provides, as one of the most important perspectives on the events of the day, an oceanic feeling in which the vastness of time and space dwarf any human individual whatsoever; this perspective obviously contains the possibility of limitless ironies concerning the trivialities which concern the characters, so that it is legitimate to see *Ulysses* – as Hugh Kenner does – as the culmination of Flaubertian indifference. But let us consider the particular preoccupations of the characters, taking them at face value. As with Zeno, they attempt a mental shaping of their experience of time. They are concerned with growing old, or growing up; they want to improve themselves, or alter course, to recover or restore or perpetuate some aspect of a past felt to be happier, more promising, or more energetic. Bloom has a variety of 'practical' projects to stave off old age: these include courses of exercises, masturbation, reading one's own obituary, or keeping ahead of the sun by perpetual journeying from East to West. For Molly the panacea for ageing is sex, and particularly the prospect of a young poet (the joke is that she thinks Stephen will be a 'clean young man', while we know he hasn't washed for ages). Correspondingly, both Bloom and Molly are nostalgic about their pasts; their thinking about time organizes it primarily in terms of the fall. In the past is a lost paradise, the present is fallen, in the future they hope to regain paradise. For Molly the lost paradise is Gibraltar, in particular the kiss with Mulvey: 'after that it's just the ordinary do it and think no more about it'. Bloom meditates on various states of 'forepassed happiness' – the halcyon days at school, the proposal to Molly on Howth promentory, the smell of lilacs at Mat Dillon's, the days at Lombard Street West. At least two events, one comic, one poignant, have the status of the fall for Bloom – masturbation twenty-two years previously on a high school excursion in the country (at the time of Stephen's birth!) and the suspension of full sexual relations with Molly, after the death of Rudy. The back-garden at Eccles Street also bears the same myth – the Whit-Monday bee that stung Bloom is the serpent of that paradise, to be regained with cowdung.

The paradise–fall–return pattern governs many readings of the novel. It makes the reader seek clues of a return to bliss; and we scrutinize Bloom's meeting with Stephen, the return to Eccles Street, and Bloom's unusual request for breakfast in bed for signs of significant improvement in this world, a Homeric return of Ulysses to Penelope's bed. Whether this enables us to read the novel in terms of mythical and symbolic elevation is another question. For Mircea Eliade, and a whole school of critics, this is the book's theme; it is 'saturated with nostalgia for the myth of eternal repetition and, in the last analysis, for the abolition of time'.[8] The events are cyclic, the analogues mythic: Bloom's wanderings like Odysseus, Christ, Parnell, Moses, Rip Van Winkle. In fact, if we look at the way in which these figures are introduced, we will surely be struck by the satiric inexactness of the supposed correspondences. Thus Bloom meditates at dusk on the links between now and seventeen years ago: 'June that was too I wooed. The year returns. History repeats itself.' Wooing at the present moment means masturbating at the sight of Gerty Macdowell, this compared with the prelapsarian bliss of wooing Molly at Mat Dillon's; the link is they both take place in June. A little further on, the first meeting in the garden at Mat Dillon's is itself thought of as a repetition of shadowy earlier meetings: 'Curious she an only child, I an only child. So it returns,' an interpretation to which Molly herself gives assent: 'the first night we ever met when I was living in Rehoboth Terrace we stood staring at one another for about ten minutes as if we met somewhere I suppose on account of my being jewess looking after my mother.' I think we are meant to laugh at the flimsiness of such theories of recurrence – as we are again at the parallel between Bloom and Parnell, wearily erected in the 'Eumaeus' episode, on the basis of supposed relationships between Bloom's sexual misdemeanours and Parnell's, between Molly and Kitty O'Shea, between the hostile forces facing Parnell on his return to Ireland and Bloom's sense of unfamiliarity on his return to Irishtown Street. The search for mythic 'eternal returns' is in fact so promiscuously pursued here that the appropriate comment is that delivered on the correspondence between Bloom's return home with Stephen and his earlier return home with a dog: 'not that the cases were either identical or the reverse.'

The similarities are surely *possibilities* deriving from the uses of association, which is the dominant method of the novel, prosecuted through puns, alliterations, homonyms, rhyming phrases, as well as events. The same is true of the Odyssean voyage parallels, which elaborate one potential among many, and elaborate both the idea of repetition and the idea of newness – as when in 'Nausikaa' Bloom's heroic materialism overcomes the attractiveness of return, to the prelapsarian past, in the episode: 'Returning not the same. Like kids your second visit to a house. The new I want.' The same is true of the apocalyptic pseudo-patterns that abound in *Ulysses* as they do in *The Confessions of Zeno*. Predictions and premonitions are plentiful: Alexander J. Dowie's proclamation of the coming of Elijah is echoed by other voices prophesying Home Rule for Ireland, disaster for England, new Jerusalems of various sorts, and significant forthcoming meetings and relationships. They are fed from indiscriminate sources: the supposed Jewish infiltration of England's economy, the Boer War, the clap of thunder, the eclipse due in September. 'God's time is 12.25,' says Dowie in the 'Circe' episode; in 'Oxen of the Sun,' Lynch speculates about a paradise of numerology, for 'both natality and mortality, as well as all other phenomena of evolution, tidal movements, lunar phases, blood temperatures, diseases in general . . . is subject to a law of numeration as yet unascertained'. But Bloom perhaps delivers the essential comment: 'One plus two plus six is seven. Do anything you like with figures juggling. Always find out this equal to that, symmetry under a cemetery wall.' The purpose of such juggling surely links with the chimera that pursues both Bloom and Stephen throughout the day: the idea of a mystical relationship between words and the things they signify. Language, for Stephen, is tainted by the fall: a Babel sets in in his description of the cocklepicker who is Eve after the expulsion: 'She trudges, schlepps, trains, drags, trascines her load.' Bloom later notes the redundancy of languages: '. . . there being more languages to start with than were absolutely necessary . . .' For Stephen's symbolist soul, this is a serious issue, for with the link between word and thing broken, language becomes matter, subject to time and history. But that situation too is part of the comic content. The author is a kind of super-tyrannical fate pursuing his characters with remorseless, ubiquitous motifs. 'Don't eat a beefsteak. If you do, the eyes of that cow will pursue you through all eternity,' ruminates Bloom, in a vegetarian mood; when we find that cow in the 'Circe' episode, it is Staggering Bob (after the drunkard Doran) proclaiming that it witnessed Bloom's fatal high school masturbation. On this basis, history can indeed be a nightmare from which we struggle to awake.

It is in this context that the 'wise passivity' of *Ulysses* operates; it is the appropriate attitude where so many patterns are pursued and held with such tenacity. Thomas Mann, who is a novelist of similar temper, perhaps provides the key:

Beautiful is resolution. But the really fruitful, the productive, and hence the artistic principle is that which we call reserve ... In the intellectual sphere we love it as irony ... guided as it is by the surmise that in great matters, matters of humanity, every decision may prove premature; that the real goal to reach is not decision, but harmony, accord. And harmony, in a matter of eternal contraries, may lie in infinity; yet that playful reserve called irony carries within itself, as the sustained note carries the resolution.

Like *The Confessions of Zeno*, *Ulysses* has perhaps no meta-language – such as myth – to offer; it rejects transcendent absolutes. It is thoroughly Modernist in its ironic, relativistic sense of the ways in which we shape our experience into meaningful temporal patterns, give it a manageable shape. Its vision is essentially comic, its aim to exorcise the enslaving structures language imposes upon experience.

Notes

1 On this general topic, see A. A. Mendilow, *Time and the Novel* (New York 1965).

2 Joseph Frank, 'Spatial Form in Modern Literature', reprinted in *The Widening Gyre* (New Brunswick, N. J. 1963).

3 See *Letters of James Joyce*, edited by Richard Ellmann (London 1966), vol. 3, p. 87.

4 P. N. Furbank, *Italo Svevo: The Man and the Writer* (London 1966).

5 Georg Lukács, *The Meaning of Contemporary Realism* (London 1962).

6 D. H. Lawrence, 'Study of Thomas Hardy', in *Phoenix* (London 1936), p. 424.

7 Stuart Gilbert, *James Joyce's 'Ulysses': a Study* (New York 1930).

8 Mircea Eliade, *The Myth of the Eternal Return* (New York 1954), p. 153.

THE JANUS-FACED NOVEL:
CONRAD, MUSIL, KAFKA, MANN

FRANZ KUNA

> 'Whatever is said, the same monotonous voice replies,
> and quivers up and down the walls until it is absorbed
> into the roof. "Boum" is the sound as far as the human
> alphabet can express it, or "bou-oum," or "ou-boum,"
> – utterly dull.'

> E. M. Forster, *A Passage to India* (1924)

I

IT has often been noted of *The Birth of Tragedy* (1871) that Nietzsche could discuss tragedy only in terms either of its origin (i.e. from the standpoint of the God Dionysus) or of its effects (i.e. from the standpoint of the spectator). Once he shifts to the works Aeschylus, Sophocles or Euripides had written, once he becomes a literary critic, the literary terms fail him and words like 'tragic' or 'dramatic' are no longer used. Tragedy is an epic myth or an epic effect; and his theory in the book needs really to be judged as a philosophy of man and his situation and of the nature of myth and ritual. Thus, as a systematic aesthetic theory, Nietzsche's book had only limited influence; but as a philosophy of life, a notion of myth and ritual, as 'a radical counter-doctrine ... to oppose the Christian libel on life'[1] it exercised the profoundest influence possible. Its ideas spread through the turn-of- the-century mind; its insights seem essential to the ideas of modern poets and novelists; and the dialectical scheme that Nietzsche offered seemed to become a blueprint, an aesthetic prototype, for nearly every major twentieth-century novel. When, in his preface to *What Maisie Knew* (1897), Henry James writes

No themes are so human as those that reflect for us, out of the con-fusion of life, the close connection of bliss and bale, of the things that

443

help with the things that hurt, so dangling before us for ever that bright hard metal, of so strange an alloy, one face of which is somebody's right and ease and the other somebody's pain and wrong

then he communicates to us a typically Nietzschean sense of the tragic base of life – the essence of what Nietzsche called 'the Janus face, at once Dionysiac and Apollonian, of the Aeschlyean Prometheus', and which he expressed in the following formula: 'Whatever exists is both just and unjust, and equally justified in both.' 'What a world!' Nietzsche adds, and it seems safe to say that that paradoxical world has been the world in depth of much modern art.

Henry James has more to say about his Maisie. He remarks: 'I lose myself, truly, . . . in noting what [Maisie] does by her "freshness" for appearances in themselves vulgar and empty enough. They become, as one deals with them, the stuff of poetry and tragedy and art.' It is striking that in discussing the art of this duplicitous world James uses the Nietzschean hierarchy; first comes poetry, then tragedy, which, being the highest form of art, is art itself. But what is even more striking is that the pursuit of this 'poetry and tragedy and art' became more and more expressed not in the dramatic context of tragedy, but in the epic context of the novel, as the twentieth century took over from the nineteenth. And it is indeed the modern novel which has dealt most willingly and most fully, at the greatest level of exploration and aesthetic satisfaction, with the kind of poetic and tragic phenomena that Nietzsche, Henry James, and many others were describing. It is the modern novel which has embodied most eagerly Nietzsche's formula of the 'Janus face' of modern man, who is doomed to exist tragically. The attempt to absorb and distil such a view of human existence has tended to make the modern novel itself Janus-faced and paradoxical, and to make many modern writers employ tragic, or tragic-comic, myths as the underlying patterns or plots in their work. This may be usefully illustrated by discussing examples chosen from the work of Conrad, Musil, Kafka and Mann.

2

Certain Nietzschean ideas, particularly those bearing on current attitudes towards unreason and anarchy, acted 'like a potent wine in the minds of a good many people'[2] and deeply affected the mood of the *fin de siècle*. If we strip his early philosophy of life, as *The Birth of Tragedy* expressed it, of all metaphysical extravagances, we arrive at a view of life as dark, blind and chaotic force – a destructive stream of passion tending to sweep away everything in its path, including man's rational cosmologies and the fossilized structure of civilization itself. In his commitment to the 'tragic view of life', Nietzsche was following Schopenhauer, but he arrived at exactly opposite conclusions. Schopenhauer emphasized the need to negate life, or the Will, because the Will was a terrible and absurd force; but the general drift of Nietzsche's thought was in fact towards its affirmation, because this 'ever-suffering and contradictory force' of which the figure of Dionysus stands as the supreme symbol, demonstrates its capacity for, and its constant need of, 'rapt vision and delightful illusion to redeem itself'. It needs, in fact, the 'Apollonian principle of individuation'. But as soon as Dionysus, 'the primordial one', has manifested himself concretely, the manifested world, which includes man, becomes aware of the illusory nature of its existence; it sees the Janus face.

For now in every exuberant joy there is heard an undertone of terror, or else a wistful lament over an irrecoverable loss. It is as though . . . a sentimental trait of nature were bemoaning the fact of her fragmentation, her decomposition into separate individuals.

Thus it is that in the Greek festivals, in Greek tragedy, and in music – which, like poetry, is a 'Dionysiac art' – one is brought face to face with a reality which is both earlier than appearance and beyond it. In our contemplation of those forces that threaten the individual with destruction, we are seized by both ecstasy and horror. There is generated a dual vision of life, 'the traumatically wounded vision of Dionysiac man'. Greek tragedy especially demonstrates to us this contradictory, dangerous and inexplicable quality of all existence; in it we may see the constant striking of the 'primordial one', the underlying Dionysiac essence of all things, to be at one and the same time 'destructively creative' (i.e. to form the temporal world of individuation and becoming, a process destructive of unity) and 'creatively destructive' (i.e. to devour the illusory universe of individuation, a process involving the recreation of unity).[3]

It is not hard to see why Nietzsche's paradoxical model of creation, of form and formlessness, optimism and tragic pessimism, should have appealed to the transitional sensibility of men at the turn of the century. Nor can we fail to see how his model could become the basis for a critique of culture and civilization as such. Belief in the satyr, the union of god and goat, the 'Dionysiac reveller' or the 'primary man', is belief in 'authentic man'. Forms of the Nietzschean hero populated the evolutionary thought of the period, and before him the cultured man dwindles to a false cartoon. On the other hand, belief in Socrates, in 'theoretical man', is belief in the great optimistic–rationalistic–utilitarian victory, in 'an Alexandrian utopia'; it is to miss the 'tragic vision' and be forgetful of a universal truth – namely, that all that is now called 'culture, education, civilization will one day have to appear before the incorruptible judge, Dionysus'.[4] Nietzsche fed the sense of confrontation with anarchistic forces; beneath the surface of modern life, dominated by knowledge and science, he discerned vital energies which were wild, primitive and completely merciless. At the appropriate hour, man, he proposed, would raise himself to titanic proportions and conquer his own civilization; the vital forces will be released in revenge, and produce a new barbarism. Promethean man will appear once more on the scene, carrying a single-minded vision to its inevitable and terrifying conclusion, and blotting out all distinctions between absolute idealism and absolute barbarism. In all of this, he proposed much that is in keeping with the themes and the very forms of modernistic art.

3

One of the most consistent writers in English in the Schopenhauerian–Nietzschean tradition is Joseph Conrad; from about 1897 onward that tradition provides the foundation on which all his major work is built. Perhaps the most distinctive treatment of what has generally become a major theme in modern literature is his *Heart of Darkness* (1902): 'the irreconcilable antagonism between egoism, the moving force of the world, and altruism, its essential morality'.[5] Without Marlow, the sceptical and contemplative narrator, the novel would probably be the most elaborate black-and-white picture in the history of literature.

On the one side we have Kurtz, the absolute idealist (and absolute barbarian), the romantic egoist, the self-styled lord of the jungle, the monstrous product of Europe who 'by the awakening of forgotten and brutal instincts, by the memory of gratified and monstrous passions' had been driven 'out to the edge of the forest, to the bush, towards the gleam of fires, the throb of drums, the drone of weird incantations', who had stretched 'his unlawful soul beyond the bounds of permitted aspirations'; Kurtz, the extremist of charismatic attraction, 'essentially a great musician' – one is reminded of Nietzsche's view of music as a Dionysian art – is 'a voice speaking from beyond the threshold of an eternal darkness', a titanic creature of sombre pride and ruthless power who lives and dies in the active knowledge of evil: 'The horror! The horror!' On the other side we have the members of the Eldorado Exploring Expedition, sordid profiteers and reckless exploiters, 'the dead cats of civilization'. And we have Europe, 'the dust-bin of progress', the doomed culture whose knowledge of life and commonplace assurance of safety is no more than an irritating pretence. The elaborate clusters of demonic and apocalyptic images sharply underline the dialectical structure of the book. But Marlow becomes the authoritative, if ambiguous, mediator between the two worlds. Whilst he is attracted by Kurtz – his originally vague interest in Africa turns into an active quest for Kurtz and what he represents – he does not lose his ability to see his hero as both an inspiration and a warning. As Lawrence Graver puts it: 'Just as all Europe contributed to the making of Kurtz, so in another sense did it contribute to the making of Marlow, the man who comes to the wilderness protected by certain defences against the darkness. These defences – courage, loyalty, and pragmatism – are tested and shown to be artificial props against a force that is clearly more natural. But Marlow accepts them as necessary and certainly preferable to no defences at all.'[6] Conrad's narrative provides an intriguing glimpse across the boundaries of conventional morality; it explores a territory beyond good and evil, and points with unrestrained frankness to the ecstasy and danger of living *On the Other Side*.[7]

Robert Musil too is concerned with examining the creative but otherwise undefinable force underlying all existence – to him a 'treasure glimmering in the darkness' (Maeterlinck), some kind of 'terrible beauty' (Yeats) – but, unlike Conrad, he considers the matter from a psychological and epistemological point of view. His novel *Young Törless* (1906) is a study of the kind of mental confusion that results from an awareness of what the protagonist calls 'the two faces' of things. To be more precise, it is a study of the limits of rationality. All things – events, people, and places – present themselves to Törless in a double-faced way; on the one hand they reveal to him the ordinary aspects of the everyday, on the other they face him with a dark, inexplicable, and horrible essence. In everything there is at once some insoluble enigma and some inexplicable kinship for which Törless can never quite produce any evidence. Things that induce a feeling of harmony and confidence at one moment, induce sheer fright and pure terror at the next. It is some time before Törless finds out – and then only after the most hair-raising experiences in the dark attic of the school – that this state of affairs derives as much from his own nature as it does from the phenomenal world. Such insight as is finally vouchsafed him has less to do with the nature of reality than it has with the ways of the human mind:

I wasn't wrong about Basini. I wasn't wrong when I couldn't turn my ear away from the faint trickling sound in the high wall or my eye from the silent, swirling dust going up in the beam of light from a lamp. No, I wasn't wrong when I talked about things having a second, secret life that nobody takes any notice of! I – I don't mean it literally – it's not that things are alive, it's not that Basini seemed to have two faces – it was more as if I had a sort of second sight and saw all this not with the eyes of reason. Just as I can feel an idea coming to life in my mind, in the same way I feel something alive in me when I look at things and stop thinking. There's something dark in me, deep under all my thoughts, something I can't measure out with thoughts, a sort of life that can't be expressed in words and which is my life, all the same . . .

He now knows that he will probably forever see things 'sometimes this way and sometimes that, sometimes with the eyes of reason, and sometimes with those other eyes . . . And I shan't ever try again to compare one with the other . . .' The narrator indicates that Törless subsequently becomes one of those aesthetics who find reassurance in giving allegiance to the law and settled public morals, since this absolves them from all coarse thoughts, from anything spiritually suspect. But the memory that there was a delicate and fragile envelope about each human being, that fevered dreams prowled threateningly round the soul, has lodged deep in Törless's consciousness. He cannot suppress his boredom whenever he is expected to show a personal interest in particular instances of the workings of the law and morality. His sole interest is in the development of his own incommensurable soul: 'the thing that is never there when we are writing minutes, building machines, going to the circus, or following any of the hundreds of other similar occupations'. Törless's dual vision of things is, arguably, Musil's own, leading him to a profoundly modern form of figurative language, to metaphors which are no longer figures of rhetoric but representative images, substitute concepts. But at the time of writing *Törless*, Musil had not yet adjusted his narrative technique to the demands of his characteristically modern vision; this came later, with *The Man Without Qualities*, and when he battled heroically to find some literary analogue to the relativism of Ernst Mach. The opening of Musil's long novel is a monument of ironic exposition, a testimony to the modern writer's belief that faith in reality, and any fictional representation of it, must spring from a profound scepticism about the efficacy of the method of approaching it.

Another writer who, with supreme sophistication and ingenuity, explored the paradoxes of human existence was Franz Kafka. For him life was balanced as on a razor-edge between a moral imperative, affirming the world we live in, and an irrepressible spiritual urge to transcend this world. It is often assumed that Kafka gave higher moral status to the latter, constructing a theodicy which awarded absolute value to the seekers of so-called religious truths. If anything, the opposite is true. One of Kafka's better known aphorisms declares: '*Im Kampf zwischen dir und der Welt sekundiere der Welt*' ('in the struggle between yourself and the world you must take the side of the world'). Moreover, stories like *Metamorphosis* and *The Hunger Artist* reveal an almost geometrical design, demonstrating that there are two sides to life which are of equal importance. Just as the slow deaths of Gregor Samsa and of the hunger-artist symbolize the human urge to transcend life, so, in the one case, the 'increasing vivacity' and the 'young body' of Gregor's sister and, in the other, the panther which replaces the hunger-artist in the cage symbolize the unrestrained commitment to the vitality, the energy and the sheer animal aspects of life. No hint is given as to which of the two constitutes the more positive commitment. Instead there is offered a parable about the dual nature of existence; and one's sense of paradox rather than one's (cruder) moral sense is appealed to. Another of Kafka's stories, *In the Penal Settlement*, explores the ambiguous forces inherent in social and political systems. An 'enlightened' explorer, conditioned by European ways of thought, is invited to witness an elaborate ritual of torture and purification enacted annually in the penal colony of an ancient régime. Whilst in the olden days the event used to be a significant festival in which everybody took part, it has now degenerated into the barely tolerated, isolated incident in a perverse judicial procedure. As it happens the explorer becomes a witness of the collapse of the ancient system and of the physical disintegration of its ingenious torture machine. But the story does not end on a note of triumph. 'Far from celebrating the defeat of the old order, the traveller slips hurriedly away from the island, as if in flight . . . The last section of the story, describing the visit to the grave of the Old Commandant and relating the prophecy that he will rise again to reassert his power in the colony, leaves the reader with a sense of foreboding.'[8] The Janus-faced nature of the observed social reality strikes the traveller – and the reader, who in true Kafka fashion has no choice but to adopt the protagonists' point of view – with almost magical intensity. One of Kafka's intentions, particularly obvious in *The Castle*, is indeed to portray generally dialectical relationships rather than allow his characters to arrive at one-sided views of reality, however 'workable'. In this way even the function of art itself becomes dual. It is symbolized, in Walter Sokel's words, by the *'Doppelgesicht Titorellis, der Januskopf der Kunst'* ('double face of Titorelli, the Janus head of art').[9] The painter Titorelli in *The Trial* is at once a formidable spokesman against Joseph K.'s attempts to achieve the highest possible freedom, and a spiritual guide to the very values he is trying to distract K. from. To put it more abstractly, art is a representation of two extremes – of practical living on the one hand, and of total commitment and fulfilment on the other. Each individual reader is left to find out for himself where exactly he stands on the scale between these two extremes. The invitation is not to judge whether one extreme is better than the other; still less to affect a compromise by taking an abstract view of things, as it might be 'in the light of reason'.

Ironist and perspectivist *par excellence* is however Thomas Mann, whose belief in the *'Januskopf der Kunst'* is self-evident. Most of his works, *Death in Venice* and *The Magic Mountain* in particular, are memorable designs in irony. But there may be a need to argue for a just assessment of the apparent break-down of all morals which some have claimed to detect in Mann's work. Does Mann's habit of portraying exhaustively the 'two faces' of things reveal a constructive sense of irony, or does it merely display a destructive tolerance of everything? Ronald Gray has argued the case for the latter, and accused Mann of working to a 'dual morality', deluding the reader rather than making him see through illusions. In the case of Mann's irony seemingly, 'it is not a matter of persuading the reader to perceive a genuine illusoriness in the world but of tricking him into thinking he does'.[10] The famous chapter 'Snow' in *The Magic Mountain*, considered by many to be one of the finest symbolic sequences in German literature, leaves Gray unimpressed, the 'bookish qualities' of this carefully arranged dream-vision 'seeming to have been evolved from the last paragraph of Nietzsche's *Birth of Tragedy* rather than from experience in either the life of reality or an imagined world'.[11] By way of defence, however, it has to be said, that, like all good modern art, Mann's novels and stories are not designed to appeal directly to our rational powers and to our instinctive need to pass moral judgement, but rather to our intelligence and our refined sense of the human paradox. Without these qualities we are likely to misread not only Mann's work but the larger part of truly modern literature.

The art of paradox and of ironic design is of course by no means exclusive to the authors I have considered. In *A Passage to India* (1924), E. M. Forster evokes for his Mrs Moore 'the twilight of the double vision', when the horror of the universe and its smallness are simultaneously visible, when 'we can neither ignore nor respect Infinity'. Such moments, both awesome and bleak, are as characteristic of James, Proust, Joyce, Virginia Woolf and of course Forster, as of the authors here discussed, whatever evident emotional and technical differences may otherwise exist among them. Directly or indirectly Nietzschean insights and models (and other nineteenth-century ones which Nietzsche helped to synthesize) have strangely determined the structure and metaphoric design of modern fiction. In Nietzsche's posthumous papers one finds the following sentence: 'There are no such things as facts, only interpretations.' Thus life for Nietzsche is composed of an infinite number of philosophic perspectives. In modern fiction Nietzsche's concept of innumerable intellectual perspectives appears in the form of innumerable existential possibilities. At the basis of all these possibilities lies Nietzsche's existential axiom of the 'Janus face of the Aeschylean Prometheus'. Or as Alfred Kubin put it in the concluding words of his novel *On the Other Side*: '*Der Demiurg ist ein Zwitter*' ('The demiurge is a hermaphrodite').

Notes

1 Friedrich Nietzsche, *The Birth of Tragedy and The Genealogy of Morals*, translated by Francis Golffing (New York 1956), p. 11.

2 Frederick Coplestone, *A History of Philosophy*, vol. vii (London 1963), p. 390.

3 Peter Heller, *Dialectics and Nihilism* (Amherst, Mass. 1966), p. 82.

4 Friedrich Nietzsche, *The Birth of Tragedy and The Genealogy of Morals*, translated by Francis Golffing (New York 1956), p. 120.

5 Lawrence Graver, *Conrad's Short Fiction* (London 1969), p. 45.

6 ibid., p. 87.

7 The title of Alfred Kubin's only novel, published in 1909 and translated into English in 1969.

8 J. M. S. Pasley, introduction to *Franz Kafka: Der Heizer, In der Strafkolonie, Der Bau* (Cambridge 1966). Mr Pasley also discusses Nietzsche's influences on Kafka.

9 Walter H. Sokel, *Franz Kafka – Tragik und Ironie* (Munich 1964), p. 363.

10 Ronald Gray, *The German Tradition in Literature* (Cambridge 1965), p. 155.

11 ibid., p. 164.

THE SYMBOLIST NOVEL:
HUYSMANS TO MALRAUX

MELVIN J. FRIEDMAN

I

WHEN the Symbolist poets declared an end to the notion of *genre tranché*, and opened the door to the cohabitation of prose and poetry in the same work, a new kind of novel came into being. The novels of James, Proust, Joyce, Conrad, Faulkner and Virginia Woolf are in some sense fictional inheritances from French Symbolist poetry. The new novel was less concerned than its predecessors with telling a story sequentially and delineating character vertically from birth to death; it was more willing to fragment narrative and to chop up experience into small blocks of time, connected through repeated images and symbols rather than exterior events. The Symbolist novel has less to do with an external reality, much more to do with other art-forms, than has its predecessor from Jane Austen through Turgenev and Maupassant. When we begin to discuss this type of fiction, words like 'pattern' and 'rhythm' must enter our vocabulary. These are in fact words E. M. Forster introduced into the eighth chapter of *Aspects of the Novel* in 1927; E. K. Brown went on to extend the critical potential of the second of them in his book *Rhythm in the Novel*.[1] Both of these commentators offer extended treatments of Proust's *À la recherche du temps perdu* (*Remembrance of Things Past*) (1913–27) to give an example of what 'rhythm' or what Brown calls 'expanding symbols' can accomplish in fiction. But they might in fact have gone back much earlier in French fiction, to the decade of the 1880s, to find the first concerted signs of this restlessness about the traditional novel and for early statements of the necessity for expanding its formal possibilities by Symbolist means. By this date, Zola was already defending the repetition in his Rougon-Macquart novels by connecting them with Wagnerian *leitmotifs*. More significantly, in 1884 J.-K. Huysmans published *À Rebours* (translated as *Against Nature*) and

453

appeared resolutely to abandon naturalistic for symbolistic practice. And in 1887, Dujardin – who was both a Symbolist poet and a confirmed Wagnerian – published *Les Lauriers sont coupés* (*We'll to the Woods No More*), a work one of whose significances is that Joyce announced some thirty years later that it was essential to the writing of *Ulysses*.

About the 'form' of Zola's Rougon-Macquart series or *À Rebours* there is nothing startlingly novel; both, in fact, are haunted by an omniscient storyteller who intrudes his presence at every turn. If *À Rebours* has claim to be the first Symbolist novel, this is for other reasons – especially because its eccentric and decadent hero, Des Esseintes, experiments with the possibilities of synaesthesia, refuses to live in the world with its 'waves of human mediocrity', and spends long hours fondling his volumes of Baudelaire and Mallarmé. Prose-poetry, characteristically enough, is Des Esseintes's favourite literary form: 'In short, the prose poem represented in Des Esseintes's eyes the dry juice, the osmazome of literature, the essential oil of art.' It most appropriately expresses the hermetic nature of his life, which is detached from the world: 'Des Esseintes shut himself up in his bedroom and stopped his ears against the sound of hammering outside . . .' But further *À Rebours* is a conspicuously *verbal* work. It was written by a man very much in love with language, who enjoyed indulging himself in rhetorical flourishes, who delighted in the sounds and contours of his words. *À Rebours* is really a novel *about* the Symbolist experience.

But *Les Lauriers sont coupés*, with its elliptical prose-poetry, offers the texture of Symbolism itself. As we examine *l'état d'âme* of its hero-monologuist, Daniel Prince, we do so through a chopped-up language offering an uninterrupted movement of consciousness. Daniel Prince's life, unlike Des Esseintes's walled-in existence and super-refined tastes, has a great deal to do with living in the world and indulging in its luxuries; we examine Prince's quite unspectacular mind for a six-hour period, from six p.m. until midnight on an April evening in Paris. Nothing very much happens to him during this time, though a particular refrain, '*le vin, l'amour et le tabac*' ('wine, love and tobacco') – Wagnerian in its insistence and recurrence – haunts his monologue, Prince's 'triple passion'. Prince enjoys a fugitive gastronomic bliss in the '*Café Oriental, restaurant*' before keeping his rendez-vous with Léa, the *amour* part of his refrain, who occupies most of his thoughts. He begins to despair somewhat of the chaste liaison he had been carrying on with her for an embarrassingly long time; he hopes to rectify matters later that evening, but the irresoluteness and flabbiness of his mind, which the novel represents, makes his failure predictable. *Les Lauriers sont coupés* is the record of Prince's monologue, the record of Prince's experience from his own mind, without interruptions by a third-person, intrusive narrator. It is really a novel about the interim between past and future experience and the way we accommodate to that 'hole' in time. Prince's mind reaches backwards and forwards from the corroding, in-between present, doting on past sensual joys and fondly anticipating the future. And, although Dujardin's Daniel Prince is distinctly more worldly than Huysmans's Des Esseintes, Mallarmé's Hérodiade, Laforgue's Hamlet, or Villiers de l'Isle-Adam's Axël, he has been nurtured on the same *paradis artificiels*; he suffers from the boredom and indecisiveness of the typical symbolist hero, even though his malaise is not quite as advanced as theirs is.

But the most interesting aspect of *Les Lauriers sont coupés* is Dujardin's discovery of a 'form' to express these symptoms. Dujardin, in a book he wrote more than forty years later, was to refer to that form as '*monologue intérieur*' and it was to become a familiar Modernist mode. It was to accommodate certain poetic and musical devices to the needs of the novel. The sameness of Prince's thoughts, the recurrence of certain haunting images, the repeated identifications of time and place, all instruments for separating the novel from an externally defined world or a familiar structure of cause and effect, aptly fit Forster's definition in *Aspects of the Novel* of 'easy rhythm': 'repetition plus variation'. There is nothing quite as elaborate and sophisticated as what Proust was to do with '*la petite phrase*', but Dujardin must be given enormous credit for suggesting a way of writing a novel which had less to do with the development of event and character than with the accumulation of image and symbolic device.

2

Dujardin's contemporary readers seemed unready for his experiments with psychological time and narrative point of view; accustomed to the complex devices of Baudelaire and Mallarmé, they were not apparently ready to acclaim similar liberties in fiction. However, his innovations were not to be forgotten. A decade after Dujardin's little novel, Henry James was to turn to his later manner, and Conrad was to begin his experiments with language and narration. But perhaps it was only in the years just before and during the First World War that novelists began to develop in ways parallel to Dujardin's experiments. In 1913 Proust published *Du Côté de Chez Swann* (*Swann's Way*), with its Wagner-type 'overture' and its musicological analogues. In 1915 Dorothy Richardson, in England, brought out the first volume of her *Pilgrimage* sequence, called *Pointed Roofs*; of this series May Sinclair was to say (the *Egoist*, April 1918): 'In this series there is no drama, no situation, no set scene. Nothing happens. It is just like life going on and on ..., neither is there any discernible beginning or middle or end.' Much the same could have been said about *Les Lauriers sont coupés*; and it could certainly be said of a developing kind of novel of which the central figures were James Joyce and Virginia Woolf.

Joyce published *A Portrait of the Artist as a Young Man* in 1916. And since 1914, he had been working on *Ulysses*, although it was not to appear as a book until 1922, in Paris. But these two works might well be said to be at the centre of the Modernist experience in fiction. It is clear that Symbolist practices in France – and to a lesser extent in Germany and England – towards the end of the nineteenth century made these books possible; it is also evident that Joyce's fiction had enormous impact on the novel of the next few decades in most of the literatures of western Europe. *Ulysses* especially has long been held in special reverence, partly for this reason: Leslie Fiedler said of it at the 1969 International James Joyce Symposium that '*Ulysses* was for my youth and has remained for my later years not a novel at all, but a conduct book, a guide to salvation through the mode of art, a kind of secular scripture.'[2] It is perhaps the most characteristic Symbolist novel, and we should look at its links backwards and forwards, with earlier and later writing. It clearly looks back to Symbolist poetry, especially in the early pages of the 'Scylla and Charybdis' chapter, where the allusions are specific. And we are never far from Des Esseintes's library, with its exotic gathering of difficult late nineteenth-century French texts, some of which tastes Stephen Dedalus shares.

Similarly Leopold Bloom has decided affinities with Dujardin's Daniel Prince. When he hums bits and pieces from *Don Giovanni* we are not far from Prince's refrain – '*le vin, l'amour et le tabac*' – and both threads run insistently through the characters' thoughts. Bloom and Prince both suffer keenly from unrequited sexual needs, memories and hopes, in something of the same comic way. Prince despairs of his chaste liaison with Léa; Bloom, compensating for his current unsatisfactory relations with Molly, carries on his pen-pal flirtation with Martha Clifford. The associations with Dujardin's book are particularly close in the 'Lestrygonians' chapter of *Ulysses*, where Bloom's sexual and culinary needs reach a crescendo; we watch his intense search for a 'moral pub' to satisfy his hunger for food, when it appears unlikely he can satisfy the other hunger, and his temporary haven at Davy Byrne's resembles that Daniel Prince found in the more exotic '*Café Oriental, restaurant*'. Bloom's Lestrygonian movements from one to two p.m. are a daytime equivalent of Prince's nocturnal wanderings; the settings are different, but the sensibilities not.

Ulysses is sometimes called a 'naturalist' novel; what is very clear, however, is that many features of it do look back to the Symbolist experience, and help centralize that experience for the modern novel. The novelist is persistently preoccupied with synaesthesia, for example: the 'Proteus' chapter, which opens up the intricacies of Stephen Dedalus's thought processes, has much to do with the confusion of sensory realms ('thought through my eyes') and the crossing of time and space, matters which greatly concerned Baudelaire, Mallarmé, Rimbaud, Valéry. And in broader formal terms and aesthetic presumptions the work is Symbolist. The often-made comparison with Proust is apt in many ways: in the concern with form realized through sequences of consciousness, in the relation between the characters and time, in the epic ambition of the devising, in the concern with the relationship between art and life. One area of note is the way in which musical preoccupations, so important to Symbolist thinking about language and form, link the two writers. Both Proust and Joyce – especially in 'Sirens' – have worked out literary formulae for introducing musical patterns into their work. Proust's Wagnerian overture serves somewhat the same purpose as those curious opening sounds which open that section of *Ulysses* which commentators generally agree has much to do with the arrangement of a fugue. In each case the compression of meaning is expanded and elaborated on in the work proper. Joyce has chosen to repeat the very words and sounds of his overture (like 'Imperthnthn thnthnthn') in the chapter which follows; Proust, of course, uses his motifs differently, much along the structural mode that Forster so exactly describes as 'repetition plus variation'. In both books, though, the musical reference points to a prime aspect of its form.[3]

Other comparisons may be made, but the point is, I think, clear: *Ulysses* benefits enormously from the literary climate which produced these earlier Symbolist novels and an immense amount of Symbolist poetry and prose poetry. What is also clear is that *Ulysses* radiated much further influence. If we now look beyond it, acknowledging its central position among Modernist works, we see an astonishing number of novels which were clearly written in its shadows. It directly inspired John Dos Passos's *Manhattan Transfer* (1925), Alfred Döblin's *Berlin Alexanderplatz* (1929), and Conrad Aiken's *Blue Voyage* (1927), and many ambitious novels of the city or the collage of modern consciousness from the late 1920s to the present are inconceivable without it. Jean Giraudoux's *Juliette au pays des hommes* (*Juliette in the Country of Men*) (1924) and William Carlos Williams's *The Great American Novel* (1923) tried gently to caricature some of its devices. Virginia Woolf may well have had the 'Wandering Rocks' chapter in mind when she wrote *Mrs Dalloway* (1925), and 'The Oxen of the Sun' section when she wrote *Orlando* (1928). The book's use of mythological parody, of stream-of-consciousness, of temporal concentration, of an urban setting, of an artistic hero and a Jewish one, all dominate the folklore of modern fiction. Many of the novels written by Jewish Americans, from Henry Roth's *Call It Sleep* (1934) to Saul Bellow's *Herzog* (1964), show close acquaintance with Joyce's devices, as if Joyce's Jewish hero and his urban preoccupation have made it a contribution to the Modernist Jewish tradition in fiction; hence perhaps Leslie Fiedler's comment that it was 'a conduct book, a guide to salvation through the mode of art . . .'. Certainly much of the lore of contemporary fiction, and our notions of artistic possibility, are very seriously shaped by Joyce's novel.

3

Ulysses is doubtless the high point of Symbolist achievement in fiction; all else seems to diminish when placed too near it. But I now wish to look closely at three novels which suggest the further evolution of Symbolist fiction – all published early in the decade of social protest in fiction, between 1930 and 1933, when there was said to be a reaction against Symbolist fiction, and yet much use of many of the impressionistic devices peculiar to the Symbolist novel of previous decades. In a sense, then, William Faulkner's *As I Lay Dying* (1930), Virginia Woolf's *The Waves* (1931), and André Malraux' *La Condition humaine* (*Man's Estate*) (1933) stand toward the end of Modernist practice, showing how formidably modern modes of image and symbol can reinforce character, yet suggesting that the basic symbolist form begins to yield to something else. The very bringing together of these three novels may itself seem odd; they are strikingly different in their settings and concerns. *As I Lay Dying* is entirely concerned with a burial procession in rural Mississippi, as seen successively through the monologues of members of the dead woman's family and of a variety of onlookers, and including a lengthy – seemingly post-mortem – monologue by the deceased herself. *The Waves* is a kind of *Bildungsroman* in six voices, or soliloquies, chronicling the genteel growing-up of three boys and three girls of very different temperaments. *La Condition humaine* is close to the sense of social and political protest of the 1930s as it describes – in violent and brutal terms – the unsuccessful attempt of Communist insurrectionists in Shanghai, in 1927, to undo Chiang Kai-shek. It is often cited as an example of the reaction *against* Symbolism in fiction, the return to social realism. Yet the links are there.

As I Lay Dying and *The Waves* proceed through monologue. We move from one mind to another with only minimal stage direction. Faulkner's presentational method in this novel is to print the name of his monologuist in bold type before we enter his mind: thus **VARDAMAN** would indicate to us that we are to be in the consciousness of the youngest of the Bundren family until another name appears in bold type. There is no room in the structure for Faulkner's own third-person manoeuvrings, though one does detect his rhetorical presence, especially in the sections given over to Darl. Virginia Woolf indicates the change from one mind to another with the intervention of 'said'. 'Said Louis' or 'said Jinny' has, in a certain sense, much the same effect as Faulkner's bold print. Mrs Woolf also uses italicized 'interchapters' which locate the position of the sun in the sky and the movement of the waves, a device also used in *To the Lighthouse* (1927) in another form, and partly serving to establish her own poetic presence in the novel.[4] We can say about these 'interchapters' what Hemingway said about his use of vignettes between the stories of *In Our Time* (1925): they 'give the picture of the whole between examining it in detail', and the two devices are in many respects very similar. By contrast, *La Condition humaine* uses very conventional devices, familiar to readers of eighteenth- and nineteenth-century fiction. It is a third-person novel which looks outward to external event and action, rather than inward toward consciousness. Yet there are certain techniques which keep on reminding us that Malraux's book belongs in the company in which I am placing it. Although *La Condition humaine* nervously makes us aware of the passage of time (almost every section starts with a precise temporal location, like 'March 21st 1927, 12:30 a.m.'), it does also have a spatial counter-movement. We frequently have a sense – as we do in the famous *comices agricoles* scene in Flaubert's *Madame Bovary*, or in the 'Wandering Rocks' chapter of *Ulysses* – of time having stopped, and of things existing side by side as in a painting. The immense amount of dialogue and the careful attention to scene further this illusion of simultaneity. Altogether the novel's hectic pace and staccato rhythm both advance it in time and offer a dense, chaotic sense of an over-crowded tableau. A French critic, R. M. Albérès, has likened *La Condition humaine* to a film, and spoken of its 'telegraphic' structure; Thierry Maulnier discovered in his 1954 dramatization of the novel how easily it became a play. If *La Condition humaine* resembles the conventional realistic fiction of the nineteenth century in its careful plotting and its linear development, it does have much more, finally, in common with the Symbolistic mode in fiction.

This is especially true of its use of symbol and metaphorical suggestion to delineate character; it is in this respect that it is closest to *As I Lay Dying* and *The Waves*. These three novels, more explicitly than any others that come readily to mind, use verbal devices and language peculiarities as precise measurements of character. We are accustomed to associating certain recurring phrases with Bloom and Stephen in *Ulysses*, though these have only limited application in explaining the fictional existence of these complex beings. But the single-dimensional characters of *La Condition humaine*, *As I Lay Dying* and *The Waves* do exist almost entirely in terms of clusters of images and verbal patterns, and these are the central features in their identification and a primary part of their Modernist mode.

This is very clear in *As I Lay Dying*, the first of the three novels to be published. Part of Faulkner's most experimental phase, it was nonetheless for a long time considered a breathing spell Faulkner permitted himself after the arduous labours of *The Sound and the Fury* (1929); and there is much in it to suggest a softening, and a rendering more accessible, of the complicated techniques Faulkner explored in that novel. Here, for example, Faulkner, concerned with the movement and the formation of consciousness in his primary characters, seems careful to connect most of the members of his Bundren family with a different symbol – we associate Vardaman with a fish, Jewel with a horse, Cash with a coffin, Anse with a set of false teeth, etc., and at each mention of the symbol the character, in a somewhat Wagnerian way, comes immediately to mind. In most of Vardaman's monologues we find the recurrent sentence: 'My mother is a fish.' The obsession haunts his juvenile thoughts; and it is at the centre of a mind which renders most experience in metaphorical terms. Many of Vardaman's impressions are indeed turned into the kind of poetry we associate with primitive sensibilities ('The hill goes off into the sky. Then the sun comes up from behind the hill and the mules and the wagon and pa walk on the sun. You cannot watch them, walking slow on the sun'). Jewel is far less verbal, less devoted to words, than his younger brother, and Faulkner gives him only one brief monologue; we discover his fixation with the horse from the other characters. In one of Vardaman's monologues, the child's mind is seen wandering freely over this poetic terrain:

> But my mother is a fish. Vernon seen it. He was there.
> 'Jewel's mother is a horse,' Darl said.
> 'Then mine can be a fish, can't it, Darl?' I said.
> Jewel is my brother.
> 'Then mine will have to be a horse, too,' I said.

Cash, who works with tools, and whose masterpiece is his mother's coffin, soliloquizes in the language of carpentry; his first monologue indeed has a series of brief sections, numbered one to thirteen, with the precision of a draughtsman's blueprints. Dewey Dell's *idée fixe* is about arranging an abortion for herself. The only members of the Bundren family not characterized by these obsessive symbols are Addie and Darl.

Addie – whose dying and burial the novel, at one level, is all about – has but one monologue, and it is singularly concerned with the futility of words: 'That was when I learned that words are no good; that words don't ever fit even what they are trying to say at.' Words, for her, are 'just a shape to fill a lack . . .'. This crucially-placed monologue – everything in the novel seems to build up to it and fall away from it – suggests that *As I Lay Dying* is as much about language and its limitations as it is about a mock-burial procession in rural Mississippi. As for Darl's many monologues (he has more than any other character), these often seem little more than verbal exercises in which Faulkner indulges his clear penchant for rhetoric. We are often amazed that Darl's mentality can manage phrasing like: 'It is as though the space between us were time: an irrevocable quality' or 'those mammalian ludicrosities which are the horizons and the valleys of the earth'. But we also experience here the same futility about words that concerned Addie: and Darl finally goes mad, intoxicated with language. In some ways he is another Des Esseintes, set in another world: he is the theoretician of *As I Lay Dying*, and seems to oversee the obsessions of the other members of the family and also direct the movement of the novel.

The comparable figure in *The Waves* is Bernard, whose artist's vocabulary favours words like 'form' and 'pattern' and clearly serves preoccupations of the author. Early in the novel, Bernard decides on his role: 'I must make phrases and phrases and so interpose something hard between myself and the stare of housemaids, the stare of clocks, staring faces, indifferent faces . . .' He is insistently a teller of stories, a not uncommon figure in modern fiction from Gide to Huxley, and Neville aptly notes: 'We are all phrases in Bernard's story, things he writes down in his notebook under A or under B.' Bernard does finally grow up, and despairs of words ('I have done with phrases'), ending, indeed, with the solution we are often told is

favoured by our post-modern artists: 'How much better is silence
...' And, as the Bundrens move in and out of Darl's controlling
'focus of narration', so do Virginia Woolf's other five monologuists –
Neville, Louis, Jinny, Rhoda, Susan – move in and out of Bernard's.
They are rendered largely through poetic turns and recurring phrases:
we think of Neville when 'that wild hunting song, Percival's music'
appears; Louis is characterized by his special symbol, the chained
beast stamping on the shore. The motifs offer a distinctive language of
characterization, but, as in Faulkner, the problem of the futility of
language is also involved. It is not only Bernard who is concerned:
Neville, who is preoccupied with Percival, reflects: 'Not the words –
but what are words? . . . I shall be a clinger to the outsides of words all
my life.' And when Percival's death is reported midway through the
novel, Neville reiterates that conviction as he holds on to three letters
received from his friend. The dead Percival has the same charismatic
presence as Addie in *As I Lay Dying*; though, again, he is a passive
agent, present only in the thoughts of other characters, he helps to
realize – to pattern – the structure of the book. Characters are intricately related to an insistent pattern of language and image which
helps to create form, the 'expansion' rather than 'completion' that
Forster sees as the emancipation of the modern novel.

In both books, then, there is an intricate, insistent pattern of
character, language and image which helps to create form, and so to
achieve that quality of 'expansion' or 'opening out', rather than of
completion, that E. M. Forster saw as essential to the modern novel
which would be more than a story.[5] The most obvious example in
his own work of the Symbolist novel is his *A Passage to India* (1924),
with its complex structure of imagery and verbal theme; but it is
also very much a social and political novel, and shows that the
Symbolist novel need not be only a work of sensibility and consciousness. *La Condition humaine* is of course even more a political and
documentary novel, but is not that alone. When he was reviewing
the American translation for *The New Republic* (4 July 1934), Malcolm
Cowley made a crucial observation about it: 'It is a novel written
sympathetically about Communists by a man whose own mentality
has strong traces of Fascism ... and a novel about proletarian heroes
in which the technique is that developed by the Symbolists of the
Ivory Tower.' Oddly, few subsequent commentators have taken up

Cowley's suggestion about Malraux's Symbolist inheritance, concentrating rather on his curiously protean politics. But the debt is there: most visibly, in his device for asserting and distinguishing the uniqueness of his characters. Faulkner and Virginia Woolf use symbols and turns of phrase as *leitmotifs*: Malraux uses peculiarities of speech, and several of his characters show curious speech habits or addictions to certain verbal patterns, leading to structural modes of repetition, aligned with speculation about language. Clappique, the Falstaffian mythomaniac, stutters and draws out the syllables of the longer words he speaks ('gi-gan-tes-que', 'é-per-due-ment'). Katow, one of the bravest of the insurrectionists, keeps repeating the word *'absolument'* – Malraux comments: ' *"Absolument"* passait dans toutes les langues que parlait Katow' ('"Absolutely" fitted all the languages Katow spoke') – and speaks in staccato fashion, swallowing certain vowels (*'d'mmage'* for *'dommage'*, etc.). Valérie, the financier Ferral's mistress, speaks in aphorisms; Tchen, the lonely terrorist who dies suicidally, throwing himself under Chiang Kai-shek's car, has difficulty with the French *'on'* (he says *'nong'*, *'distractiong'*). And these speech peculiarities are not simply characterizing devices for novelistic convenience; they suggest a frustration about language, already patent in Addie and Darl, Bernard and Neville, in *As I Lay Dying* and *The Waves*, as well as conveying the psychological configurations of his people.

Malraux also, like other modern novelists drawing on the Symbolist mode, tends to depend on the significant repetition of certain objects or situations. There is, for example, an extraordinarily high degree of attention to cats (which always seemed to charm Symbolist poets, from Baudelaire and Verlaine to Eliot): Ferral loves cats, Tchen dreams of a cat's shadow on the ground, and an alley cat relieves the solitariness of the opening scene of the book, when Tchen commits his first murder. Malraux's repeating and balancing of scenes can be observed in the two moments in which candy figures prominently. After he commits the murder, Tchen enters a shop filled with other insurrectionists; during the episode, Katow munches some sugar candies which Tchen desperately craves and feels the right to (*'Maintenant qu'il avait tué, il avait le droit d'avoir envie de n'importe quoi'*) ('Now that he had killed, he had the right to crave anything at all'). In the seventh and last section of the novel, by which time most of the insurrectionists have either been killed or have fled Shanghai, we see a gathering of the French financial establishment in Paris, with Ferral uncomfortably present; a box of caramels is passed round, and Ferral alone refuses. The two scenes are ironically juxtaposed: in the first, the situation is one of urgency, desperation, based on Tchen's need; in the second, the situation is one of calm, contentment, self-assurance, and is based on Ferral's refusal of the sweets.[6]

As I Lay Dying and *The Waves* are essentially forms of the lyrical novel; *La Condition humaine* is a political and social work, and yet in it there is much of the Symbolist inheritance in evidence, in forms decidedly analogous to those used by Faulkner and Virginia Woolf, and with a similar concern for the notion that the novel be a realizable whole rather than a contingently documentary form. None of these books has, of course, the hieroglyphic density of *Ulysses*, the intensity of its mysteries. But they do represent the further evolution, and perhaps in some respects the decline, of that tradition in the novel we associate with Symbolist poetry and theory and with Modernism. The problem of maintaining the ideal of 'art' in modern fiction has clearly been a considerable one; these three books, by virtue of their endeavour and the unease about language they also contain, are explorations of the possibilities and the difficulties. The problems about fiction they point to still persist for writers today.

Notes

1 E. M. Forster, *Aspects of the Novel* (London 1927), is a now classic work. E. K. Brown draws on it for his *Rhythm in the Novel* (Toronto 1950), an admirable study of Symbolist method in fiction. Also see William York Tindall, *The Literary Symbol* (New York 1955).

2 Leslie Fiedler, 'Bloom on Joyce; or, Jokey for Jacob', *Journal of Modern Literature*, vol. I, no. 1 (1970), pp. 19–29.

3 For a useful discussion of the significance of these developments, see Leon Edel, *The Psychological Novel: 1900–1950* (New York and London 1955). See also Richard Ellmann's excellent *Ulysses on the Liffey* (London 1972).

4 The best discussion of this aspect of Virginia Woolf is in David Daiches, *Virginia Woolf* (Norfolk, Conn. 1942), and *The Novel and the Modern World* (rev. ed., Cambridge 1960). In the equivalent dis-

cussion of Faulkner, the best discussion is in Olga Vickery, *The Novels of William Faulkner: A Critical Interpretation* (Baton Rouge, La. 1959).

5 For further discussion of these developments in English fiction, see Alan Friedman, *The Turn of the Novel* (New York and London 1966).

6 For a more extended discussion of Malraux along these lines, see my 'Some Notes on the Technique of *Man's Fate*', in Melvin J. Friedman and John B. Vickery (eds.), *The Shaken Realist: Essays in Modern Literature in Honor of Frederick J. Hoffman* (Baton Rouge, La. 1970), pp. 128–43. See also W. M. Frohock's *André Malraux and the Tragic Imagination* (Stanford 1952). Also useful is Denis Boak's *André Malraux* (New York 1968).

THE CITY OF RUSSIAN MODERNIST FICTION

DONALD FANGER

I

PRE-EMINENT in music, painting, ballet and cinema, Russian Modernism was hardly less vigorous in literature. But for us to speak of the accomplishment in poetry, fiction, and literary theory involves a descent into confusion and obscurity. The reasons are clear enough. Music, painting, ballet, cinema use an international language; they can find not only their audiences, but also their critics, interpreters, and eventually their historians through the normal operation of aesthetic Darwinism – if not in the homeland, then elsewhere. Hence our international familiarity with Stravinsky, Chagall, Kandinsky, Eisenstein, and other great Russian names of the modern visual and musical arts in recent decades. But in literature such transitions are harder, the mediation of domestic publisher and critic is more crucial, and contact can be more easily blocked. 'Difficult' works need time to discover and reach their ideal readers; those readers are themselves links in a cooperative process of accumulated knowledge and insight. Nor can translators simply move the enterprise to more favourable soil: where the medium is so integral to the message, much will be lost in the transfer. Even to salvage what is salvageable needs a translator who is also a sophisticated critic and a resourceful annotator – qualities which, again, depend on access to the work of others. Imagine the situation of Joyce today if, ten years after *Ulysses* was published, not only the dissemination of his books, but all public discussion of them and him, had been banned. Yet this is very nearly the situation of Russian Modernist prose today in the Soviet Union. Where critics can ask about western writing, 'What was Modernism?' – meaning 'What does Modernism now seem to us to have been?' – they must ask the question differently about Russian writing. We must ask: what will Russian Modernism seem to have been when it has been collected, studied, restored to its rightful public, or rather to the heirs of that public?

An assessment of Russian Modernism is thus both overdue and premature; but we can outline the phenomenon historically and survey, in fiction, some of its fruits. By the end of the 1880s, the first great age of Russian fiction was over, and its major practitioners – Gogol, Dostoyevsky, Turgenev, Goncharov, Tolstoy – either dead or silent. The assumptions that had guided their art, and public understanding of their art, now came inevitably into question. Chekhov was proceeding, in Gorky's phrase, to 'kill' realism by exploiting its extremest tendencies – an operation which others saw as the discovery of a new realm of artistic vision. Thus the leading Symbolist theoretician, Andrei Biely, could find 'the dynamite of authentic symbolism' in Chekhov's narrative vision, with each work comprising not the disposable agency of a message, but a self-justifying verbal creation. Dispensing with plot, Chekhov's stories worked by implication: some, like 'The Huntsman' or 'The Student', approached the condition of poetry. And the 'Modernist' period in Russia, the period from the early 1890s to about 1930, was supremely a great age of poetry, in which the Schools of Symbolism, Acmeism, Futurism, Imaginism, and dozens of smaller groups flourished, all marked by a new interest in the word as such. Gogol – recently regarded as the father of Russian realism – was rediscovered as the first Russian Symbolist, to become the most potent native influence on the experimental prose of the new century. Dostoyevsky and Leskov also found new appreciation as adoptive ancestors, providers of a usable past.

All this rediscovery was largely the work of the Symbolists – whose unprecedented concern with technique was to be extended by the work of the Formalist critics. The Russian writer, whose moral responsibility to the people had appeared central through most of the nineteenth century, became in the twentieth an artist: formerly sincere and direct, he was now artful and crafty. Most of the major poets experimented with prose forms – Biely, Briusov, Sologub, Pasternak, Khlebnikov, Kuzmin, Mandelstam – and experiments of hardly less radical a nature came from practitioners of prose such as Remizov, Babel, Olesha, Zamyatin and Pilniak. If the line between poetry and prose was being blurred, so was the distinction between literary and non-literary prose; witness the hybrid productions of

V. V. Rozanov and Victor Shklovsky. All these deserve chapters in the unwritten history of modern Russian prose – along with more recent figures like Abram Tertz (Andrei Siniavsky), whose work marks a recrudescence of experiment with the fantastic and the grotesque. But a simple catalogue of experiment, even if it were practicable here, would of necessity be parochial. Something of the various and significant achievement of Modernist fiction, however, may be represented in a triad of writers whose works, comparable in virtuosity and importance, are available in English versions and linked by a common theme – St Petersburg, the imperial capital and epicentre of the shocks that were transforming the cultural landscape of Russia.

2

The first is Andrei Biely (1880–1934). Poet, theoretician and propagandist of Symbolism, critic, prosodist, editor, memoirist, Biely was an enormously prolific writer. Brilliant and erratic, he provided a unique twentieth-century variant of the professional man of letters in Russia, perfecting a prose which (as Zamiatin observed) was no more common Russian than Joyce's was common English – a personal idiom, rather, which he made the vehicle of a luminously eccentric vision. Most of his fiction treats the conventions of the novel with iconoclastic freedom. The prose itself is frequently rhythmical, a near-musical orchestration of motifs and sound textures. In the preface to his last published novel he claimed that only considerations of space had prevented the work from having been set properly, in poetic lines. His masterpiece – 'one of the four great masterpieces of twentieth-century prose', according to Nabokov – is *Petersburg* (1913, 1916; revised in 1922; and published as *St Petersburg* in the sole English translation). It has been called a Cubist novel, and the label is apt as an indication of the way its several levels behave: for seeming – which is exploited both as theme and as effect – is so handled as to make it hard to be certain at any given moment which levels are primary and which subordinate, which metaphorical and which 'real' in the special terms of the narration.

The plot is that of a political thriller, paced by the ticking of a time-bomb which Nikolai Apollonovich Ableukhov, a sometime student and half-hearted revolutionary, has agreed to plant in the house of his father, the redoubtable Senator Apollon Apollonovich Ableukhov. The cast of pseudonymous characters includes double agents, terrorists and secret policemen, bohemians and society people; the tempo is Dostoyevskian, as are many of the squalid indoor settings. But the street scenes are Gogolian, one of the sub-plots is Tolstoyan, and a series of ubiquitous Pushkinian motifs condenses into a central scene which is a reprise of the tragic crux of *The Bronze Horseman*, staged in terms that recall the confrontation of Ivan Karamazov with his devil. The element of literary pastiche is thus strong. And it serves, along with a host of musical, poetic, legendary, and historical associations, to add an anomalous dignity, a kind of bizarre portentousness, to the cartoon-like banalities of the story and the disconcerting flippancies of the protean narrative voice. Biely's bag of tricks, in other words, is drawn from the work of his predecessors in the century-old Petersburg tradition, and so functions thematically. Motivation – in the broadest sense – works not to make the story humanly plausible but rather to make it symbolically coherent and expressionistically valid.

So the Senator, 'a dry and wholly insignificant figure' in everyday terms, figures throughout the first half of the book in his official capacity – where, as Biely presents him, he is 'a point of energy-stimulating power', 'a force in the Newtonian sense' (which, we are reminded, is 'an occult force'). As he sits at his desk, his bald head emits lightning-bolts that flash across Russia. 'His consciousness was separate from his personality: his personality, indeed, seemed to the Senator to be merely a skull-box, and like a hollow, emptied case.' Throughout the book, narrative emphasis is on the quasi-literal presentation of abstractions. If the Senator wields power, power will be shown in this sort of way. By the same token, if the urban masses are said to be faceless and anonymous, then Biely will describe them as a 'headless polypod' and a stream of shadows. 'The streets of Petersburg,' he declares, 'possess one indubitable quality: they transform the figures of passers-by into shadows.' Pedestrians intersect 'columns of conversation' – which are represented on the page. As in Gogol and Dostoyevsky, the city itself is characteristically misty, obscure, grey;[1] only the waning imperial presence provides a symbolic contrast through touches of brilliant colour that signal another temporal dimension:

> An enormous red sun was fleeing over the Neva: and the buildings of Petersburg seemed to have dwindled away, transformed into ethereal, mist-permeated amethyst lace; the windows reflected the fiery golden glow; the tall spires flashed rubies; and fiery flares invaded the recesses and the projections and set the caryatids and the cornices of brick balconies ablaze . . . And – the past glowed there.

But colour, beauty, symmetry are only vestigial remnants. For the present is chaos – moving toward an end, filled with apocalyptic figures. In a dream, the Senator's son is visited by an ancient Turanian, who makes it clear that the principle of revolution represented by the son and the principle of reactionary order represented by the father amount in the end to the same thing: 'a Mongolian affair' – which is to say, the end of Europeanism (the St Petersburg period). Only the means are different: one is destructive violence, the other paralysis. And when the Bronze Horseman himself visits the hallucinating terrorist Dudkin (who calls himself 'the quintessence of revolution'), symbolizing the final onset of madness and moving him to murder, the larger sense of a cycle completed enters again:

> The bronze giant had been galloping through ages of time and, reaching the present moment, had completed a cycle; ages had sped by; Nicholas I had ascended to the throne; and, after him, the Alexanders; and Alexander Ivanovich Dudkin, himself a shadow, had restlessly overcome the ages day after day, year after year, roaming up and down the Petersburg prospects – awake and in dream. The clanging thunder of metal had pursued him and all the others, shattering their life . . .
>
> These blows would make fragments of Lippanchenko [the double agent whom Dudkin will go to murder after this visit, his triumphant gesture parodying that of the Horseman himself], pulverise the attic [in which Dudkin lives], destroy Petersburg; and Ableukhov's bald head would likewise be broken.

The whole novel is indeed a ring of hauntings. The elements, subdued by Peter the Great in founding his city, are bursting their restraints – in the form of revolution, madness, ambiguity, malproportion, rumour, uncertain identity. Peter himself is evoked in the guise of the Flying Dutchman and in the image of his equestrian statue, literally (the key characters are constantly passing it) and figuratively (as refracted through Pushkin's poem). The Devil, disguised as a Persian, visits Dudkin – and the sense of his disquisition on Petersburg has a validity quite independent of the fact that he is a vision. Christ makes a series of ambiguous appearances – in one case he seems actually to be a secret policeman – indicating at least a yearning for him on the part of several characters he approaches.

And all this is irreducibly *real*, Biely insists, in the only way that matters. Hauntings and hallucinations acquire objective existence; just like the Red Domino in the novel which, once it had appeared in a newspaper column, 'unravelled into a series of events which had never occurred (but which were able) to threaten (the general) tranquillity'. In this disturbed world, fictions are facts. And within the novel, the concentric levels of consciousness lose their confusing relativity as they take up existence in the reader's mind. For this reason, Biely can afford to call attention to the artifice of his entire creation – and so he ends his first chapter with a section entitled 'You Will Never Forget Him!':

In this chapter we have seen Senator Ableukhov: we have seen as well the senator's idle thoughts in the form of the senator's house, in the form of the senator's son, who also carried in his head his own idle thoughts; we have seen, finally, still another idle shadow – that of the stranger.

This shadow arose accidentally in the consciousness of Senator Ableukhov, and received its ephemeral existence there; but Apollon Apollonovich's consciousness is a shadowy consciousness, because he too is the possessor of an ephemeral existence, and a product of the author's fantasy; a useless, idle, cerebral game.

Cerebral play is only a mask; beneath that mask is taking place the invasion of various forces into the brain; and though Apollon Apollonovich may have been created out of our brain, he will nevertheless manage to produce fear with that other staggering existence of his which attacks in the night.

The attributes of this existence have been bestowed on Apollon Apollonovich and . . . on his cerebral play.

Once his brain has begun to play with the mysterious stranger, that stranger exists, really *is*: he will not disappear from the Petersburg prospects so long as the senator exists with thoughts of that kind, because even a thought in a consciousness possesses its own existence.

May our stranger, then, be a real stranger! And may the two shadows of my stranger be real shadows!

And they will follow, those shadows, on the heels of the stranger, as the stranger himself will follow hard on the senator. And that ancient senator will pursue you, too, reader, in his black carriage. He will! And henceforth you shall never, never forget him!

A central aim of Biely's creative fantasy is clearly to exploit and extend the already surreal character of the city as it came to him in the Pushkin–Gogol–Dostoyevsky tradition, a tradition which itself had grown through a kind of atmospheric accretion: St Petersburg was already fictionally the spectral place where particular kinds of abnormality flourished – where a statue hounded a nameless little man through madness to death; where chance led a sober officer through temptation to the same end – madness and death; where the devil himself lighted the street-lamps along the main artery 'to show everything in an unreal guise'; where a nose absconded to lead a brief life of its own as a higher official; where delirium (and western ideas) led a poor student to transgress against the principles of human life itself, and to meet the agent of his redemption in the form of a religious prostitute. Fate as Nemesis, implicit in so many of these stories, rules the city, guiding its victims and mocking their pretensions to free will. *Petersburg* acknowledges this inheritance, by invoking its several styles, by including its key images, and by deepening its nightmare atmosphere. But it does all this to make a historical point. The thematic focus is the revolution of 1905 – not so much its events as its mood, feel and *sense*.[2] The revolution figures as background music, while the author presents the circulation of false rumours about the Red Domino as 'a key to the events of 1905'. And even if the fullest explanation of this 'key' may lie in the lore of anthroposophy, the varieties of inauthenticity in the book are clearly not just signs that the times are out of joint, but symbols of the impending apocalypse which is explicitly invoked by the narrator, and figured to his three main characters in dreams. These dreams, in their overlappings, seem to confirm each other; hence the suggestion that they are visitations from the same cosmic level. All are important, but Dudkin's carry a quite special importance – not only do they connect most directly with the St Petersburg tradition (Biely calls him a new Evgeny, underlining the way he re-enacts the fate of Pushkin's hapless victim in his poem *The Bronze Horseman*), but they invade even his waking consciousness, and claim him totally in the end. Dudkin, moreover, in describing his dreams, articulates and generalizes what is implicit elsewhere.

In the three nightmares he has each night, he hears 'an absurd and wholly senseless word' – *enfranshish* – through which 'he wrestles with some unknown power'. Aware that this means some disease is attacking him, he remarks: 'Do you think I alone suffer from this? You, Nikolai Apollonovich, are also ill. *Nearly everybody is sick* ... These days I meet this brain disorder, this elusive provocation, everywhere.' Like Dostoyevsky's underground man, he is merely the extremest manifestation of a general trend. So he admits to being a provocateur himself – 'but only in the name of a great idea, or, rather, of a new trend of thought' – which he recognizes as 'a common thirst for death'.

Testimony is abundant, within the literature of the time and outside it, that such a fascination with death was a key feature of the period. Suicides, literary and actual, were reaching epidemic proportions; murder and madness, treated with a mixture of horror and flippancy, dominated poetry and fiction to such an extent that the critic Kornei Chukovsky (in an article entitled 'The Jolly Graveyard') characterized the current scene as 'a kind of metaphysical potpourri of Offenbach' (*metafizičeskaja offenbaxovščina*). Though literature, he noted, continued to discusss the 'most enormous questions', it did so with a bizarre tinge of levity, and a strange tendency to jumble together 'several styles, several epochs and several genres in a single work'. This pathos of decadence was later to be defined as 'the sensation, at once oppressive and exalting, of being the last in a series'. Vaguer in *Petersburg*, it nonetheless pervades the book. Near its climax, when Dudkin is discussing the meaning of his hallucinations, he sets forth the rationale of the novel by calling them 'symbolic sensations' and remarking, 'Of course, *a modernist would call this the sensation of the abyss, and search for an image corresponding to the symbolic sensation.*' The atmosphere of *Petersburg* is that sensation; the whole book represents Biely's 'search for an image'.[3]

Given all this, we can appreciate one final feature of the novel which has not, to my knowledge, received critical attention. I have in mind the growing presence in the last third of the book of *normal* psychology, through the belated introduction of biographical background which gives a new perspective to the experiences of Apollon Apollonovich and his son, Nikolai. The Senator falls from power at the moment (in the masquerade scene) when his son's treachery invades his consciousness. The result: 'Against the flaming background of the burning Russian Empire – instead of a gold-braided personage – one beheld a poor hemorrhoidal old man, unkempt, unshaven, perspiring in a dressing-gown!' Now his domestic situation, present and past, comes to the fore. The narration itself subsides – and for the first time – into quasi-realistic depiction. The Senator's runaway wife returns; he accepts her; and even the shadowy son is shown 'unable to resist her': 'Falling on his knees before her, he embraced her; he pressed against her knees; and he broke into feverish sobs – no one knew why. His broad shoulders shook (in the last few years he had not experienced an affectionate caress) – "Mama, mama!" He wept.' We are, in short, back in the world of 'normalcy'. These characters have left the roles and setting in which they have had their special existence, suggesting that a cosmic storm has passed, and with it the rationale for all the queer symbolistic images and narrative devices. This movement away from the trappings of Symbolism, however, is itself symbolic: the passing of the world of *Petersburg* is the passing of the politico-cultural St Petersburg which had existed for two centuries and sustained the myth since Pushkin's time.

The year after *Petersburg* appeared in book form, events had already confirmed Biely's basic intuition, and so vindicated his strategy, which was to use components of the myth he had inherited to convey the 'symbolic sensations' of 1905, themselves heavy with the sense of an ending. In his success, Biely furnished an exemplary demonstration of the relation which another poet of another 'unreal city' was to posit between tradition and the individual talent.

3

Amid the dislocations of 1917 and after, in the shadow of a continuing poetic efflorescence, the most serious prose tentatives took the form of stories, sketches, fragments. In these shorter forms two remarkable writers, Osip Mandelstam and Evgeny Zamyatin, produced two memorable epilogues to Biely's epitaph – at a time when St Petersburg itself had already been renamed Petrograd and was soon to become Leningrad.

Mandelstam, who was born in 1891 and died in a Siberian prison camp in 1938, is increasingly recognized as one of the major poets of his time, despite a long ban on any substantial edition of his works in the Soviet Union. And Anna Akhmatova, shortly before her death, reported literary youth in that country to be 'wild' about his prose (a selection of which is now available in English, elegantly translated and annotated by Clarence Brown). This prose, unlike anything else in Russian before or since, bears witness to the author's conviction that the revolution marked not only the end of a cultural era but of the forms associated with that era. The preconditions for traditional fiction seemed gone; the individual was dwarfed by social forces (Mandelstam had no use for Biely's occultism). As for the artist, even before his personal survival came into question, the survival of his enterprise had already done so. 'Social distinctions and class oppositions,' he wrote in 1921, 'pale before the present division of people into friends and enemies of the word.' 'A new heroic era has opened in the life of the word. The word is flesh and bread. It shares the fate of bread and flesh: suffering.' At its deepest level, this is the subject of Mandelstam's prose.

The Egyptian Stamp (1928) is the writer's quasi-Surrealistic (in the sense of apparently random) shoring of fragments against the ruins of a vanishing St Petersburg. Where Biely's novel was freighted with dramatic anticipation, Mandelstam's brief narrative – which defies classification – is permeated with terror. 'It is terrifying,' he writes, 'to think that our life is a tale without a plot or hero, made up out of desolation and glass, out of the feverish babble of constant digression, out of the delirium of the Petersburg influenza.' The heroism of his word lies in its successful embodiment and transcendence of this terror, in the achieved equivalence of life and tale.

Set in the Kerensky summer of 1917 'when the lemonade government was sitting', the sketchy narrative deals with one Parnok, the traditional 'little man' in the Pushkin–Gogol–Dostoyevsky line,[4] seen now as 'a lemon seed thrown into a crevice in the granite of Petersburg, [to] be drunk with black Turkish coffee by the winged night that is approaching'. 'Lord!' the narrator exclaims at one point, 'Do not make me like Parnok! Give me the strength to distinguish myself from him . . . For I, too, am sustained by Petersburg alone . . .' Parnok, it will be seen, is at once the author's creation and his alter-ego, a participant in shadowy actions and an object among others in Mandelstam's feverish meditation – lyrical, sardonic, anguished – on the related themes of Russian literature, St Petersburg culture, memory (strikingly figured as 'a sick Jewish girl who steals away in the night from her parents' house to the Nicholas Station thinking that perhaps someone will turn up to carry her off'), and survival. Each of these themes is present in all of the others, and the intricated form itself, loose ends and all, shapes the poetic message. Mandelstam writes near the end:

Destroy your manuscript, but save whatever you have inscribed in the margin out of boredom, out of helplessness, and, as it were, in a dream. These secondary and involuntary creations of your fantasy will not be lost in the world but will take their places behind shadowy music stands, like third violins at the Mariinskij Theater, and out of gratitude to their author strike up the overture to *Leonora* or the *Egmont* of Beethoven.

A desperate gamble, based on a faith that time has confirmed.

Summary is not only inadequate to the thematic complexity of this poet's prose, it quite ignores the excerptable felicities on every page. Thus, like the 'luxurious rattle of a *droshky*' which 'evaporates in the silence' in chapter 5, it must be considered 'suspect as the prayer of a cuirassier'. The prose of Evgeny Zamyatin, by contrast, though more voluminous and various, is easier to characterize, because of its author's principled commitment to innovation, a theory of permanent revolution in the arts. His essay, 'On Literature, Revolution and Entropy' (1924), argues forcefully for heretics as 'the only (bitter-tasting) remedy for the entropy of human thought'. 'The formal characteristic of live literature,' in his view, 'is the same as its inner characteristic: the negation of truth, that is, the negation of what everyone knows and what I knew up to this moment. Live literature leaves the canonical rails, leaves the broad highway.' The best art of his time (including his own) he labelled 'Neo-Realism' or 'Synthetism', a kind of latter-day Impressionism:

The old, slow, creaking descriptions are a thing of the past; today the rule is brevity – but every word must be supercharged, high-voltage. We must compress into a single second what was held before in a sixty-second minute. And hence, syntax becomes elliptic, volatile; the complex pyramids of periods are dismantled stone by stone into independent sentences. When you are moving fast, the canonized, the customary eludes the eye: hence the unusual, often startling symbolism and vocabulary. The image is sharp, synthetic, with a single salient feature . . . The custom-hallowed lexicon has been invaded by provincialisms, neologisms, science, mathematics, technology.

Zamyatin's own work exhibits all these characteristics. Serving a less complex sensibility than Mandelstam's, it is analogous in technique and conception to such masterly graphic work as that of the painter and portraitist, Yurii Annenkov.

'The Cave', for example (written in 1920, published in 1922), presents a picture of the elemental struggle for life in wintry civil-war St Petersburg. 'Glaciers, mammoths, wastes. Black nocturnal cliffs, somehow resembling houses; in the cliffs caves. And no one knows who trumpets at night on the stony path between the cliffs, who blows up white snow-dust, sniffing out the path.' So the story opens, establishing the atmosphere and the 'matrix of metaphor'. As the conditions of existence have reverted to those of prehistoric man, the universe itself has shrunk to the dimensions of the 'bedroom-cave'. 'And in the centre of this universe – its god, the short-legged, rusty-red, squat, greedy cave god: the cast-iron stove.' To propitiate this god and stay alive, the intellectual Martin Martinych feeds it firewood stolen from his neighbours, books, papers. In vain. His only act of kindness can be to give his sick and suppliant wife the poison he wishes to take himself. This tragic vignette, made strange and awesome by the image-weaving of the exposition, represents a last artistic comment on the nature and destiny of St Petersburg, through a panorama of icy extinction.

4

In one way or another, the greatest achievements of Russian Modernist prose – in which these St Petersburg-oriented examples have a leading place – tend to be dominated by a sense of historical time, reflecting an obsessive awareness and often an anguished ambivalence toward the burden of the past. This can be seen in the better-known, brilliant miniatures of Isaac Babel and Olesha, as well as in the persona of Victor Shklovsky's writing (e.g., *Zoo*, and *A Sentimental Journey*). And it informs much of the work of Nabokov, so saturated with the pathos of space–time exile. Evidencing a subtlety and a scale rivalling Biely's in *Petersburg*, Nabokov's last novel to be written in Russian, *The Gift* (1937–8), treats traditional Russian culture; the author himself notes 'the participation of . . . many Russian muses within the orchestration of the novel', and identifies the heroine of his book as 'not Zina but Russian Literature'. The same might almost be said of his more recent work, *Ada* (1969), mined as it is with significant literary allusion.

In Russia itself, the Modernist movement was to be arbitrarily arrested at the beginning of the 1930s, before its energy was spent, its public formed, or the extent of its realizable promise made manifest; and the official Soviet view still portrays it as the dangerous bourgeois adversary to a democratic and realistic literature. Boris Pasternak, who had provided an extraordinary specimen of a uniquely new narrative style in 'The Childhood of Luvers' (1915), renounced such writing as affected when, near the end of his life, he undertook his major prose work, *Doctor Zhivago*. For the purposes of that novel simplicity and accessibility were deemed more desirable qualities, and a similar preference has evidently guided the development of Solzhenitsyn, whose work reaches back to touch and renew the realistic tradition of the nineteenth century. On the other hand, the *Fantastic Stories* of Abram Tertz (Andrei Siniavsky) and his remarkable essay 'On Socialist Realism' with its advocacy of a 'phantasmogoric art', though unpublished in the Soviet Union, do testify to some subterranean survival. Only the coming of a genuine thaw will allow the assembling of the heritage and the possibility of responsible historical assessment. Meanwhile, the publication abroad of banned Russian texts (Biely's prose and Zamyatin's, Mandelstam's and Pasternak's and Khlebnikov's complete works – all are in print only in the West), along with a slowly growing body of translations, bears out the hopeful symbolism of Mikhail Bulgakov's phrase, 'Manuscripts don't burn!', preserving and enlarging a rich and vital literary inheritance.

Notes

1 Biely was always particularly sensitive to colour symbolism. In 1909 he wrote: 'We live in a twilight world, neither light nor dark – a grey half-darkness.' And in his later book on Gogol (1934) he comments on the colour spectrum of his own *Petersburg* and finds that 'it corresponds to the tragicomedy of . . . darkness'.

2 Cf. Biely's remark in his article, '*Symbolism*', 'The life around us is a pale reflection of the struggle of vital human forces with fate. Symbolism deepens either the darkness, or the light: it transforms possibilities into realities [*podlinnosti*]: it confers existence on them.'

3 Cf. his *Cup of Snowstorms* (*Kubok metelej*): 'I have tried as accurately as possible to depict certain experiences which, so to speak constitute the background of ordinary life and are, in essence, not susceptible of incarnation in images.'

4 Parnok himself is twice called 'an Egyptian stamp' without explanation; Professor Omry Ronen, however, has recently suggested one, based on philatelic history. In 1902 and again in 1906, an Egyptian stamp was issued bearing the image of the Sphinx and designed to frustrate anyone who tried to erase the cancellation marks or steam uncancelled stamps off envelopes for re-use: In the face of any such attempt the printed surface of the stamp, Sphinx and all, would disappear. The symbolic applications to Mandelstam's prose hardly need elaboration.

THE LANGUAGE OF MODERNIST FICTION:
METAPHOR AND METONYMY

DAVID LODGE

I

My aim here is to see what generalizations we might make about the language of modern fiction. Let me suggest that modern fiction – using modern in its qualitative, as well as its merely chronological, significance – is fiction displaying some or all of the following features. First, it is experimental or innovatory in form, exhibiting marked deviations from existing modes of discourse, literary and non-literary. Next, it is much concerned with consciousness, and also with the subconscious or unconscious workings of the human mind. Hence the structure of external 'objective' events essential to narrative art in traditional poetics is diminished in scope and scale, or presented selectively and obliquely, in order to make room for introspection, analysis, reflection and reverie. Frequently, therefore, a modern novel has no real 'beginning', since it plunges us into a flowing stream of experience with which we gradually familiarize ourselves by a process of inference and association; its ending is usually 'open' or ambiguous, leaving the reader in doubt as to the characters' final destiny. By way of compensation for the weakening of narrative structure and unity, other modes of aesthetic ordering become more prominent – such as allusion to or imitation of literary models, or mythical archetypes; or repetition-with-variation of motifs, images, symbols, a technique often called 'rhythm', *'leitmotif'*, or 'spatial form'. Lastly, modern fiction eschews the straight chronological ordering of its material, and the use of a reliable, omniscient and intrusive narrator. It employs, instead, either a single, limited point of view, or multiple viewpoints, all more or less limited and fallible; and it tends toward a complex or fluid handling of time, involving much cross-reference back and forward across the temporal span of the action.

If we now summon up the names of those English-language novelists whom orthodox literary history tells us are 'moderns', we will find that some – James Joyce, Virginia Woolf, Gertrude Stein – exhibit nearly all these qualities, while others exhibit only some, or exhibit them in modified form: either because – like Henry James and Joseph Conrad – they belong to an early phase of Modernism and retain some of the conventions and assumptions of traditional fiction, or because – like D. H. Lawrence and Ernest Hemingway – they disagreed with certain Modernist aims and assumptions, or – like E. M. Forster or Ford Madox Ford – for a combination of those reasons. Nonetheless these writers are linked by a family resemblance that distinguishes them from other novelists of the same period who were *not* distinctively Modernist. But is it possible to formulate any generalization about the language of a set of stylists so self-conscious, and so idiosyncratic? The task is daunting; but let us be clear what it is. I am not concerned with 'style', meaning the use of language peculiar to a single individual or work, nor with the state of English at large in the modern period – not concerned, then, with either *parole* or *langue* (to invoke the categories of Saussure). I am concerned with literary language as it has interested Continental structuralist critics influenced by Saussure – with what Roland Barthes calls *écriture*, or 'mode of writing'.[1] And I propose to draw on the work of the linguistician Roman Jakobson, one of the most distinguished figures in this intellectual tradition; beginning first by indicating the nature of his theory concerning metaphor and metonymy and then considering its explanatory power when applied to the language of 'modern' fiction.

2

Jakobson begins his classic paper 'Two Aspects of Language and Two Types of Aphasic Disturbances'[2] by stating that language, like other systems of signs, has a twofold character. Speech (and writing) involves two operations: 'a selection of certain linguistic units and their combination into linguistic units of a higher degree of complexity'. Selection implies the possibility of substitution, and the perception of similarity, and is therefore the means by which metaphor is generated.

Metonymy (the figure which names an attribute, adjunct, cause or effect of the thing meant instead of the thing itself) and the closely associated figure of synecdoche (part standing for whole, or whole for part) belong to the combinative axis of language, since they operate with terms that are contiguous in the language and in reality. A simple example (mine, not Jakobson's): in the sentence, 'A hundred keels ploughed the waves', *keels* is a synecdoche meaning *ships*, derived from the contiguity of ships and keels, and *ploughed* is a metaphor derived from a perceived similarity between the movements of ships and ploughs.

Traditional rhetoric has usually associated metaphor and metonymy under the general heading of tropes and figures. Jakobson opposes them, and one of his main reasons for doing so is their manifestation in two distinctive types of aphasia, or severe speech disability. Aphasics who have difficulty in *selecting* the right linguistic units tend to use metonymic expressions, while those who are unable to *combine* linguistic units tend to use metaphorical expressions. 'In normal verbal behaviour,' Jakobson says, 'both processes are continually operative, but . . . under the influence of a cultural pattern, personality and verbal style, preference is given to one of the two processes over the other.' In the development of any discourse, one topic leads to another either through their similarity or through their contiguity, and on this basis Jakobson categorizes a wide range of artistic and cultural phenomena as either 'Metaphoric' or 'Metonymic'. Heroic epics tend toward metonymy; Russian lyrical songs toward metaphor. Drama is basically metaphoric, film a basically metonymic art – but, within the art of film, the technique of dissolves, jump-cuts and montage is metaphoric, while that of close-up, which represents the whole by the part, is synecdochic. In Freudian interpretation of dreams, 'condensation' and 'displacement' refer to metonymic aspects of the dream-work, and 'identification' and 'symbolism' to the metaphoric. In painting, Cubism is metonymic, Surrealism metaphoric. But, for our purpose, Jakobson's most interesting observation is that prose, 'which is forwarded essentially by contiguity', tends toward metonymy – while poetry, which, in its metrical structure and use of rhyme, stresses similarity, tends toward the metaphoric pole. He also suggests that Realistic writing is metonymic, and Romantic and Symbolist writing metaphoric. Hence the traditional novel – which is both realistic and written in prose – is essentially metonymic: 'Following the pattern of contiguous relationships,' he says, 'the realistic author metonymically digresses from the plot to the atmosphere and from the characters to the setting in space and time. He is fond of synecdochic details.'

Now, since modern fiction is generally regarded as having a Symbolist bias and as being in reaction *against* traditional realism, we should expect to find it tending toward the metaphoric pole of Jakobson's scheme. Intuition suggests this is true. No doubt a statistical analysis would reveal a higher incidence of metaphor in the work of James, Conrad, Forster and Ford than in Wells, Galsworthy, Bennett, Gissing. Indeed the very titles of their novels are an indication: the Edwardian realists, like the Victorians before them, tended to use the names of places or persons for titles (*Kipps, New Grub Street, Anna of the Five Towns, The Forsyte Saga*), while the moderns tended to favour metaphorical or quasi-metaphorical titles (*Heart of Darkness, The Wings of the Dove, A Passage to India, The Rainbow, Parade's End, To the Lighthouse, Ulysses, Finnegans Wake*). Joyce's *Finnegans Wake* (1939) indeed seems to fit the theory perfectly, since it is entirely based on the principle of similarity and substitution: structurally and thematically, in that every event is a re-enactment or a premonition of several other events in the history of the race, and verbally, in the use of a synthetic language based on the pun, which is a form of metaphor. But *Finnegans Wake* is at the extremity of modern fiction; and indeed suggests that, because the novel is inherently a metonymic form, to force it *completely* to the metaphoric pole entails its dissolution as a novel. What makes *Finnegans Wake* 'unreadable' for many people is actually not the expression of multiple similarities through the pun, but the lack of logical or narrative continuity in the combination of puns. And this in turn suggests that there may be modernistic uses of metonymic as well as metaphoric modes. This is the hypothesis I want to examine in a number of Modernist works.

3

A useful text to examine is *Ulysses* (1922), where, indeed, the two 'streams-of-consciousness' that constitute the linguistic staple –

Stephen's and Bloom's – may be said to tend toward the metaphoric and metonymic poles respectively. This is Stephen, catching sight of Mrs McCabe, a midwife, in the 'Proteus' episode:

> One of her sisterhood lugged me squealing into life. Creation from nothing. What has she got in the bag? A misbirth with a trailing navel-cord, hushed in ruddy wool. The cords of all link back, strandentwining cable of all flesh. That is why mystic monks. Will you be as gods? Gaze in your omphalos. Hello. Kinch here. Put me on to Edenville. Aleph, alpha: nought, nought, one.
>
> Spouse and helpmate of Adam Kadmon: Heva, naked Eve. She had no navel. Gaze. Belly without blemish, bulging big, a buckler of taut vellum, no, whiteheaped corn, orient and immortal, standing from everlasting to everlasting.

The significant thing is not merely the presence of specific metaphors ('cable of all flesh', 'buckler', etc.) but the fact that the interior mono-logue *proceeds* by perceived similarities and substitutions. The perception of an analogy between a telephone cable and the umbilical cord leads Stephen's thoughts comically from midwife to Genesis, from his own birth to that of the race. And drawn in are other simi-larities and contrasts: the cords round the habits of monks, which are symbols of chastity and, when linked, of community in the mystical body of Christ; the navels contemplated by oriental mystics; the images from the *Iliad, Song of Songs*, Thomas Traherne. This, now, is Bloom, looking at his neighbour's servant girl, served before him in the pork butcher's:

> A kidney oozed bloodgouts on to the willowpatterned dish: the last. He stood by the nextdoor girl at the counter. Would she buy it too, calling the items from a slip in her hand. Chapped: washing soda. And a pound and a half of Denny's sausages. His eyes rested on her vigorous hips. Woods his name is. Wife is oldish. New blood. No followers allowed. Strong pair of arms. Whacking a carpet on the clothes line. She does whack it, by George. The way her crooked skirt swings at each whack.
>
> The ferreteyed porkbutcher folded the sausages he had snipped off with bloody fingers, sausagepink. Sound meat there like a stallfed heifer.

Bloom's perception of the girl is strikingly synecdochic: he sees her in terms of chapped hands, vigorous hips, strong arms, and skirt: parts standing for the whole. His thought *proceeds* by associating items that are contiguous rather than, as Stephen, similar: the girl is linked with her master, the master with the mistress, the age of the mistress with the youth of the girl, and so on. In the second paragraph, with *ferreteyed, sausagepink*, etc., we appear to have reverted to metaphor; but these are *weak* metaphors, and are so precisely because they depend on contiguity and context. Thus the physical juxtaposition of the butcher's fingers and the sausages he handles provides the ready-made metaphor *sausagepink*; the butcher is compared with animals; and it is because the two terms of the comparison, the tenor and vehicle, are not widely separated that the metaphors are weak.[3]

The structure of *Ulysses* is metaphorical, being based on similarity and substitution (the parallel between modern Dublin and the *Odyssey* and the many other parallels subsequently superimposed). But it is clear that this is compatible with extensive and deliberate exploitation of metonymy; and that the basically metonymic writing through which Bloom's consciousness is rendered is no less 'modern' than the metaphoric rendering of Stephen's consciousness. The interesting conclusion follows that modern fiction may be characterized by an extreme or mannered drive toward the metonymic pole of language to which the novel naturally inclines, as well as by a drive toward the metaphoric pole from which it is naturally remote.

4

Another clear example of this double tendency is Gertrude Stein, a central figure in Modernist experimentation with language. Her writing went through distinct phases we can associate with the metonymic and metaphoric poles. This is from her early long novel *The Making of Americans* (1906–8):

It happens very often that a man has it in him, that a man does some-thing, that he does it very often that he does many things, when he is a young man when he is an old man, when he is an older man. One of such of these kind of them had a little boy and this one, the little boy wanted to make a collection of Butterflies and beetles and it was all exciting to him and it was all arranged then and then the father said to the son you are certain that this is not a cruel thing that you are wanting to be doing, killing things to make collections of them and the son was very disturbed then . . .

And so on. In 'The Gradual Making of *The Making of Americans*', Gertrude Stein observed that her 'sentences grew longer and longer', though of course they are artificially extended by absence of conventional punctuation.[4] This too she noted in 'Poetry and Grammar':[5]

> When I first began writing, I felt that writing should go on, I still do feel that it should go on but when I first began writing I was completely possessed by the necessity that writing should go on and if writing should go on what had colons and semi-colons to do with it, what had commas to do with it.

This both states and illustrates Jakobson's dictum that prose is naturally forwarded by contiguity; indeed it seems that Gertrude Stein was at this time deliberately and programmatically cultivating a kind of writing corresponding to the Similarity Disorder, or Selection Deficiency, type of aphasia of which Jakobson speaks. This type of aphasic has great difficulty in naming things; shown a pencil, he is likely to define it metonymically by reference to its use ('to write'), and in his speech main clauses disappear before subordinate clauses, subjects are dropped, while 'the words with an inherent reference to the context, like pronouns and pronomial adverbs, words serving merely to construct the context, such as connectives and auxiliaries, are particularly prone to survive'. Compare Stein in 'Poetry and Grammar':

> A noun is the name of anything, why after a thing is named write about it. A name is adequate or it is not. If it is adequate then why go on calling it, if it is not then calling it by its name does no good ... Verbs and adverbs are more interesting. In the first place they have one very nice quality and that is they can be so mistaken ... Then comes the thing that can of all things be most mistaken and they are prepositions ... I like prepositions best of all ... When I was writing those long sentences of *The Making of Americans*, verbs active present verbs with long dependent adverbial clauses became a passion with me. I have told you that I recognize verbs and adverbs aided by prepositions and conjunctions with pronouns as possessing the whole of the active life of writing.

What she was after was to make 'a whole present of something that it had taken a great deal of time to find out' – that is, to capture the living quality of a character or experience she had long observed or brooded over without giving the impression of *remembering* it. It was a technique of repetition, though she denied that it *was* repetition, and compared her method to the (metonymic) art of film, because 'each time the emphasis is different just as the cinema has each time a slightly different thing to make it all be moving'.

A little later, however, Gertrude Stein's methods changed, though a continuity of aim persisted. She began to write 'very short things and in doing very short things I resolutely realized nouns and decided not to get around them but to meet them, to handle in short to refuse them by using them and in that way my real acquaintance with poetry was begun'. She is here talking about her 'still-life' studies of objects,[6] collected in the 1911 volume *Tender Buttons*, of which this is an example:

APPLE

Apple plum, carpet steak, seed clam, coloured wine, calm seen, cold cream, best shake, potato, potato and no gold work with pet, a green seen is called bake and change sweet is bready, a little piece a little piece please.

A little piece please. Cane again to the presupposed and ready eucalyptus tree, count out sherry and ripe plates and little corners of a kind of ham. This is use.

She described her method as one of 'looking at anything until something that was not the name of that thing but was in a way that actual thing would come to be written'. In short, the technique was one of selection and substitution in Jakobson's sense, but the perception of similarities on which this operation depends was entirely private, and the result therefore inscrutable. Furthermore, the contextual relationships which should link the substitutions together into a chain are entirely neglected. The result is a writing resembling the speech of aphasics suffering from Jakobson's second disorder, Contiguity Disorder or Contextual Deficiency, where 'syntactical rules organizing words into a higher unit are lost' and sentences degenerate into 'a mere "word-heap"'. Superficially, the result is a writing resembling that of the Dadaists and the later exponents of randomness like William Burroughs, with his 'cut-up' method, developments Gertrude Stein might be held to have anticipated. However, where their aim is to affront human rationality, and/or to demonstrate the capacity of nature to generate its own meanings without human interpretation, hers is not. She still maintains the traditional stance of the artist, as one who by the exercise of a special gift or craft is seeking to bring her medium into closer and closer relation with her perceptions.

Hers is, indeed, an aesthetic of realization, a pursuit of the thing itself: 'I had to feel anything and everything that for me was existing so intensely that I could put it down in writing as a thing in itself without at all necessarily using its name.' This is essentially the Symbolist poetic – expounded by Mallarmé in terms of evocation and suggestion, by Pound in terms of the 'image', by Eliot in terms of the 'objective correlative'. All poets – and Gertrude Stein herself noted: '. . . and here was the question if in poetry one could lose the noun as I had really and truly lost it in prose would there be any difference between poetry and prose.' The answer must be no: apart from typographical layout, the sections of *Tender Buttons* are indistinguishable from Symbolist or Surrealist lyric poems. Prose, as Jakobson says, is forwarded essentially by contiguity, and narrative is inseparable from the combinative axis of language; to neglect this side of language completely removes the writer from the realm of prose fiction – and in Stein's case from the realm of meaningful communication, to an extent rare in Modernism. For even Joyce in *Finnegans Wake*, or, later, Samuel Beckett in 'Ping' (1967), though they exemplify many of the features of writing pushed far toward the metaphoric pole (e.g. the disappearance of grammatically functional words, conjunctions, prepositions, pronouns, articles), still preserve through word-order a tenuous narrative and logical continuity. However, the point I want to stress about Stein's work is this: though *The Making of Americans* and *Tender Buttons* tend toward the opposite poles of metonymy and metaphor, they are both recognizably 'modern' and both pursue the same general artistic aim – to render that elusive quality, 'existence'. Her use of repetition with slight variation in her earlier, metonymic prose has the effect of converting the dynamic into the static, the temporal into the spatial; this is entirely consistent with the aim of metaphor-oriented Symbolist and Imagist verse, or Pound's definition of the 'image' itself, which 'presents an intellectual and emotional complex in an instant of time'. This instantaneousness is necessarily an illusion, given the sequential character of language; but it is an illusion easier to achieve in poetry than prose. Stein showed how prose might achieve similar effects.

David Lodge

This was largely the basis of her influence on subsequent writers, like Hemingway, who saw that the artful use of repetition-with-slight-variation, both lexical and grammatical, combined happily with an imitation of casual vernacular speech; it was thus possible to be a realist *and* a Modernist. The opening paragraph of his story, 'In Another Country', is a representative example of how he applied to the American vernacular an elaborate and hidden verbal craft, so that the magical incantatory quality of Symbolist poetry is given without losing the effect of sincerity, of authentically observed experience. The story begins:

> In the fall the war was always there, but we did not go to it any more. It was cold in the fall in Milan and the dark came very early. Then the electric lights came on, and it was pleasant along the streets looking in the windows. There was much game hanging outside the shops, and the snow powdered in the fur of the foxes and the wind blew their tails. The deer hung stiff and heavy and empty, and small birds blew in the wind and the wind turned their feathers. It was a cold fall and the wind came down from the mountains.

On the surface, the passage develops along a line of 'contiguous' relationships; as Jakobson says, the realistic writer 'metonymically digresses from the plot to the atmosphere and from the characters to the setting in space and time'. And much of the presentation is synecdochic: Milan is conveyed by its shops, the shops by the game shops, the game by certain animals, the animals by certain parts of their bodies. But there is another system of relationships also at work in their passage: certain words, grammatical structures and rhythmic patterns are repeated, to the opposite effect, drawing attention to similarities rather than contiguities, keeping particular words and concepts echoing in our minds even as our eyes move forward to register new details. Particularly one responds to the recurrence of the words 'fall', 'cold', and 'wind', repeated several times before they are clustered in the last sentence. That sentence has a finality and resonance not easy to account for logically, but it functions as it does, surely, because it clinches a network of association between the weather and the emotions of the wounded soldiers, making the simple manner seem not naïve but exact. The carefully arranged words of the opening sentence indicate, and the story goes on to make explicit, the fact that the war is always with the soldiers, in their minds and in their wounds.

The war is in the mountains; the wind comes down from the mountains; 'cold' and 'fall' are both obviously connected with violent death; and in the context of these reverberating repetitions, the synecdochic details about the game function as symbols of death and destruction, even though there is nothing figurative about the manner of their description, as there is no pathetic fallacy in the description of the weather. In this way an essentially metonymic style is made to serve the purposes of metaphor.

Another modern novelist who uses repetition to give a basically metonymic style the kind of effect usually associated with metaphorical writing is D. H. Lawrence – though in his writing, of course, there is vastly more overt metaphor than in Hemingway. Here is a fairly representative passage from *Women in Love* (1921), just after Gudrun and Ursula have witnessed Gerald Crich ruthlessly controlling his horse, panic-stricken by the passing of a colliery train:

> The man [the gatekeeper] went in to drink his can of tea, the girls went on down the lane, that was deep in soft black dust. Gudrun was as if numbed in her mind by the sense of the indomitable soft weight of the man, bearing down into the living body of the horse: the strong, indomitable thighs of the blond man clenching the palpitating body of the mare into pure control; a sort of soft white magnetic domination from the loins and thighs and calves, enclosing and encompassing the mare heavily into unutterable subordination, soft-blood-subordination, terrible.

In this short, two-sentence paragraph there is a remarkable degree of repetition – lexical repetition ('soft', 'indomitable', 'man', 'body', 'thighs', 'mare', 'subordination') and syntactical repetition or parallelism, especially in the extraordinary expansions of the second sentence. Of special note is the behaviour of the most often repeated word 'soft'. In the first sentence, 'soft black dust' is a straightforward adjectival use; but 'soft weight', in the next, is more unusual, a kind of synaesthetic expression. It *could* be a literal description (some things are heavy and soft, others heavy and hard) but it doesn't seem particularly appropriate to Gerald in the circumstances. One cannot help feeling that the word in 'soft weight' has been suggested by the earlier use in 'soft black dust'; and that makes a certain metaphorical sense, since Gerald, the colliery owner, is linked with the black dust that covers the countryside, and the chapter is called 'Coal-Dust'. A kind of equation results – Gerald:mare as colliery:countryside. The next use of 'soft' ('a sort of soft white magnetic domination') is explicitly metaphoric and linked not just by repetition but also by inversion ('white' for 'black'). Throughout the book Gerald is associated with white as well as black: in his fair physique, and the 'soft white' snow in which he meets his death. Finally in 'soft-blood-subordination' we have another mysteriously metaphorical expression, of almost impenetrable meaning. Perhaps the nearest one can get to it is that the entire passage seems a premonition of the ultimately destructive sexual relationship that will develop between Gerald and Gudrun. Here Gudrun sees in his domination of the mare a type of sexual possession which both appals and fascinates her; and the language which seems oddly used of a man controlling a mare becomes more intelligible when applied to a man making love to a woman – or, more exactly, when applied to a woman's imagining what it would be like to be made love to by a certain kind of man.

Turning on Gudrun's perception of a similarity between herself and the mare, and an emotional substitution of herself for the mare, the entire passage seems metaphorical; yet Lawrence's prose is of the metonymic type, and advances, apparently, by contiguity, each clause or phrase typically taking its impetus from an item in the preceding clause or phrase. What we know of Lawrence's methods of composition supports this view: to revise his work, he had to write it all out again from the beginning, unlike Joyce, whose revision was a process of innumerable insertions and substitutions. The repeated words in the above paragraph have the effect of maintaining the metonymic continuity and the rhythmical flow of the writing, knitting the phrases together on the pattern 'A aB bC cD . . .'. Most of these words do not change in meaning; but 'soft' does, as I have shown, and it so directs our attention, almost subliminally, to the possibilities of a metaphoric meaning beneath the metonymic surface.

5

I have been arguing here that, while it seems true that Modernist fiction belongs to the metaphoric mode in Jakobson's scheme, this is perfectly compatible with the retention and exploitation of metonymic writing on an extensive scale. This is so for two reasons: first, that prose fiction is inherently metonymic, and cannot be displaced towards the metaphoric pole without turning into poetry, and, secondly, that metonymic techniques can be manipulated to serve or support the purposes of metaphorical writing. Much the same conclusion is reached by Gerard Genette in a perceptive essay on Marcel Proust: 'without metaphor, Proust says, more or less, no true memories: we add for him and for all; without metonymy, no linking of memories, no story, no novel'.[7]

The 'deep structure' of *Remembrance of Things Past* (1913–27) is, like the deep structure of *Ulysses*, essentially metaphoric: the action of involuntary memory, which is the prime moving force behind the narrative, is a linking of experiences on the basis of their similarity (an irregularity in the paving-stones of Paris, for instance, recalling to Marcel the floor of the baptistery of St Mark's in Venice) not their contiguity. But, says Genette, if the initial trigger-mechanism of memory is metaphoric, the expansion and exploration of any given memory is essentially metonymic, because of Proust's characteristic tendency towards 'assimilation by proximity . . . the projection of analogical affinity upon relationships of contiguity', and vice versa. Genette's first illustration of this interpenetration of metaphor and metonymy in Proust is a comparison of two descriptions of church steeples. In the first, from *Swann's Way*, the narrator contemplates the plain of Méséglise:

> *Sur la droite, on apercevait par delà les blés les deux clochers ciselés et rustiques de Saint-André-des-Champs, eux-mêmes effilés, écailleux, imbriqués d'alvéoles, guillochés, jaunissants et grumeleux, comme deux épis.**

In the second passage, from *Sodom and Gomorrah*, Marcel, at Balbec, evokes the church of St Mars-le-Vêtu thus:

> *Saint-Mars, dont, par ces temps ardents où on ne pensait qu'au bain, les deux antiques clochers d'un rose saumon, aux tuiles en losange, légèrement infléchis et comme palpitants, avaient l'air de vieux poissons aigus, imbriqués*

---

* 'On the right one saw, beyond the corn fields, the two carved and rustic steeples of St André-des-Champs, themselves tapering, scaly, honeycombed, symmetrically patterned as though by an engraving tool, yellowing and rough-textured like two ears of corn.'

d'écailles, moussus et roux, qui, sans avoir l'air de bouger, s'élevaient dans une eau transparente et bleue.*

Genette points out that the two pairs of steeples are clearly very similar in appearance, but that the basic analogies in each passage are quite different. Why does Proust compare the steeples in the first passage to ears of corn and those in the second passage to fish? Clearly because of the context of each perception – the cornfields of Méséglise and the sea and bathing of Balbec, respectively. As Genette observes, *resemblance* in an analogy mattered less to Proust than its *authenticity*, 'its fidelity to relations of spatio-temporal proximity'. The same could be said, I think, of novelists as different from Proust and from each other as Joyce and Lawrence. Such handling of analogy seems to follow inevitably from the modern novelist's concern with consciousness and the subconscious and the unconscious.

If an essentially metaphorical mode of writing can utilize metonymy in this way, it follows that the basically metonymic mode of traditional realism can make extensive use of metaphor. To investigate the handling of analogy characteristic of this kind of fiction is beyond the scope of this essay, but it is certainly different from Modernist writing's use of analogy. In the first of the two passages quoted from Proust, the key-image of the ear of corn is delayed by, or encrusted with, other subsidiary images drawn from different sources; and in the second passage the key image of the fish is developed with such elaboration as almost to overwhelm the literal subject. The effect of polyvalency, or synaesthesia, with its contingent demands upon the reader's concentration and responsiveness, is deeply characteristic of the modern literary imagination and contrasts with the use of analogy by traditionally realistic novelists, who usually maintain a clear distinction between what is actually 'there' and what is merely illustrative. Modernism questions such simple positivist distinctions. As James Ramsay realizes at the end of Virginia Woolf's *To the Lighthouse* (1927), in a passage which very clearly contrasts the metonymic with the metaphoric vision, 'nothing was simply one thing'. It comes

*'St Mars, whose two antique, salmon-pink steeples, covered with lozenge-shaped tiles slightly curved and seemingly palpitating, looked, in this scorching weather when one thought only of bathing, like pointed fish of great age that, covered with overlapping scales, mossy and russet, without appearing to move, rose in blue and transparent water.'

at the point when the adult James at last approaches the Lighthouse which had seemed such a magical object to his child's vision:

> The Lighthouse was then a silvery, misty-looking tower with a yellow eye that opened suddenly and softly in the evening. Now – James looked at the Lighthouse. He could see the white-washed rocks; the tower, stark and straight; he could see that it was barred with black and white; he could see windows in it; he could even see washing spread on the rocks to dry. So that was the Lighthouse, was it?
>
> No, the other was also the Lighthouse. For nothing was simply one thing. The other was the Lighthouse too. It was sometimes hardly to be seen across the bay. In the evening one looked up and saw the eye opening and shutting and the light seemed to reach them in that airy sunny garden where they sat.

That is perhaps the central assertion of the modern novel – nothing is simply one thing: it is an assertion for which metaphor is the natural means of expression.

Notes

1 'A language and a style are objects: a mode of writing is a function: it is the relationship between creation and society, the literary language transformed by its social finality, form considered as a human institution and thus linked to the great crises of history.' Roland Barthes, *Writing Degree Zero* (London 1963), p. 3.

2 Roman Jakobson, 'Two Aspects of Language and Two Types of Aphasic Disturbances', in Roman Jakobson and Morris Halle, *Fundamentals of Language* (The Hague 1956), pp. 55–82.

3 'It is an essential feature of a metaphor that there must be a certain distance between tenor and vehicle. Their similarity must be accompanied by a feeling of disparity; they must belong to different spheres of thought.' Stephen Ullmann, *Style in the French Novel* (Cambridge 1957), p. 214.

4 Unconventional punctuation is, in fact, one of the most obvious and universal signs of Modernism in prose fiction. Consider, for example, Joyce's use of an introductory dash to indicate direct speech, and the elimination of pointing from Molly Bloom's soliloquy; Henry James's often-parodied use of commas to enable the insertion of qualifications and parentheses in an unconventional order ('Almost the first thing, strangely enough, that, about an hour later, Strether

found himself doing . . .') and his rarer experiments in the opposite direction, omitting commas between adjectives strung together (e.g. Mme de Vionnet in *The Ambassadors* is 'bright gentle shy happy wonderful'); Ford Madox Ford's extravagant use of dots in rendering the stream-of-consciousness in *Parade's End*; the lower case title of Hemingway's most Modernist work, *in our time* (1925), and the studied avoidance of quotation marks or italics in his most celebrated sentence (from *A Farewell To Arms*), 'I was always embarrassed by the words sacred, glorious, and sacrifice and the expression in vain.' In *Lord Jim*, Conrad puts quotation marks around free *indirect* speech to convey the sense of Marlow reporting what Jim reported to him; and Auerbach observes in his analysis of a passage from Virginia Woolf's *To the Lighthouse* (in *Mimesis*) that words enclosed in inverted commas are not for certain spoken aloud, while words that are certainly spoken aloud are often left without inverted commas.

5 Gertrude Stein, *Look at me Now and Here I am: Writings and Lectures, 1909–45*, edited by Patricia Meyerowitz (Harmondsworth 1971). All the following quotations from Gertrude Stein are drawn from this source.

6 Sometimes described as 'Cubist' in technique, these pieces are in fact closer to Surrealist art, Surrealism being metaphoric and Cubism metonymic in Jakobson's scheme. The metaphorical title, *Tender Buttons*, recalls the soft treatment of hard objects in the painting of Salvador Dali.

7 'Metonymie chez Proust, ou la naissance du Recit', *Poetique*, vol. 2 (1970), pp. 156–73. The article came to my attention after I had written the first version of my own essay. The translations from Genette and Proust are my own.

SEVEN

Modernist Drama

ANY ordered account of Modernist drama depends ultimately on the identification or hypostatization of 'sets': the recognition of areas of shared or related assumption, of overlapping intent, of common antagonisms. Though the constituent names may vary, the form of the question is standard: What, if anything, is it that (let us say) Ibsen and Maeterlinck, Schnitzler and Claudel, Wilde and Lorca, Chekhov and Yeats, Hofmannsthal and Eliot, Pirandello and Synge have in common? Or Strindberg and Wedekind, Hauptmann and Jarry, Apollinaire and Kaiser, Marinetti and Mayakovsky, Brecht and the Dadaists?

The best replies do not necessarily order things most tidily. The more sensitive the criteria, the less comprehensive the groupings: a few paired names; at best a small cluster or two. Conversely, the more inclusive the categories, the weaker the group cohesion – a cohesion often either merely negative (like a common hostility to late-nineteenth-century naturalism) or so generalized as to lack any real discriminatory significance. Indeed, the search for 'sets' in Modernist drama that combine comprehensiveness with firm containment is sadly unrewarding. Declared allegiance on the part of individual dramatists to announced policy is rare, though when it *is* found it is generally strident. Even tacit acquiescence in the pursuit of common objectives is unusual. Criticism learns to be content with those aggregations or complexes or even domino-chains of preoccupations that distantly link dramatists together, often at several removes. Individual persuasions, convictions, beliefs, loyalties and admirations are discovered forming elaborate associational patterns; the component parts cohere not in obedience to some central containing force that holds them within well-defined boundaries but rather as loose lattices of relationships. Certain rough categories – like the 'intimate theatre', the 'problematic theatre', the 'drama of illusion' of the following pages – sometimes help, but as practical working devices chiefly; beyond them lie formidable – and, one suspects, in this present context unrewarding – complexities.

MODERNIST DRAMA: ORIGINS AND PATTERNS

JOHN FLETCHER AND JAMES MCFARLANE

I

WHEN Eric Bentley looked for the beginning of the 'modern movement' in the drama, he found it in the eighties and nineties: in those years when Henri Becque wrote his two great plays *Les Corbeaux* (*The Vultures*) (1882) and *La Parisienne* (*Woman of Paris*) (1885); when Ibsen's *Ghosts* (1881) established its author as a distinctively European dramatist; and when André Antoine founded the Théâtre Libre expressly for the performance of naturalist plays. The success of the new theatre movement of the nineties, Bentley claimed, was the success of naturalism: 'The little theatres in European capitals where the new plays were shown nearly all came into existence for the production of Naturalistic plays. The drama became a fighting issue.'[1]

Two coordinates – the one substantive and thematic, the other formal and linguistic – help to pinpoint the origins of European Modernist drama. On the one hand, there was the compulsive attention the eighties and the nineties gave to the problematic and the contemporary; on the other, there was the restless exploration of the resources of prose as a dramatic medium. Both things point unwaveringly back to Ibsen. 'The most important event in the history of modern drama,' it has been confidently (and, in approximate phrases, repeatedly) claimed, 'was Ibsen's abandonment of verse after *Peer Gynt* in order to write prose plays about contemporary problems.'[2] 'Problems', though of defining importance, were however not first in order of significance. The discovery of new potential in dramatic language, the extension of the concept of 'poetry' to embrace much linguistic territory that was previously neglected or even despised – whilst a much less conspicuous event in its own day than the debating of problems in the theatre – was in its long-term effect a factor of much more seminal influence.

Within a few years of completing *Peer Gynt* (1867), Ibsen had eagerly responded to those challenging and hortatory phrases of Georg Brandes in 1871: 'What shows a literature to be a living thing today is the fact of its subjecting problems to debate.' In becoming an unusually attentive and sensitive observer of the European scene, he set an example which many other dramatists attempted to follow without either having his innate talent for it or occupying a similar central yet detached situation. Resident in a number of different parts of Europe during his twenty-seven years of voluntary exile from Norway, Ibsen was a fascinated witness of many of the larger political events and social changes of the age: the Dano–Prussian and Franco–Prussian wars, the Paris Commune, the growing power of Germany, the unification of Italy, the spread of industrialization, the proliferation of capitalism, the emergence of the European political left-wing, the growth of communications, the changing standards of morals, the new preoccupation with the ways of the unconscious mind. Sometimes, in Rome or Dresden or Munich, he experienced these things at first hand on his own nerves and senses; sometimes, by virtue of his very foreignness, he found himself supremely equipped to play the detached observer.

For long years, his achievement remained in large measure domestic to Scandinavia; but in the nineties, when he himself had passed his sixtieth birthday, he burst upon the European scene with all the fury of a storm which had slowly been gathering force. Not only did this represent a theatrical occasion unique in its intensity and force, but it also marked a cultural event unprecedentedly European in its impact. When the choice of the new wave of 'independent theatres' fell upon *Ghosts* as that work which both best served their theatrical aspirations and at the same time most evidently expressed the spirit of the age, they succeeded in transforming Ibsen from a dramatic author of modest Scandinavian dimensions into one of imposing European proportions. By their productions of this play between 1889 and 1891, the Freie Bühne of Berlin, the Théâtre Libre of Paris and the Independent Theatre of London created what is probably the first example ever of a phenomenon which in recent years has grown increasingly common: the concerted launching in a whole range of the cultural capitals of Europe of a single literary or dramatic work. From then until the end of his life, the publication of a new Ibsen play was a distinctly European event. To take but one example: *Hedda Gabler*, published in Scandinavia in 1890, had, by 1892, been translated and published in Germany (three times), in Russia (three times), in England and America (twice), in France and in the Netherlands, and by 1895 had further been translated into Italian, Spanish and Polish; moreover, within a year of its composition, it had been played in Munich, Berlin, Helsinki, Stockholm, Copenhagen, Christiania, Rotterdam, London and Paris, and in the following year in St Petersburg and in Rome. Never before had a dramatic author so dominated the European theatre or so monopolized public debate.

The 'problem' element which so preoccupied Ibsen's contemporaries was, in one sense, very much a thing of its own day – Ibsen himself never tired of insisting that everything he had written was the result of direct personal experience, of something 'lived through'. Viewed in this limited way, his work quite properly takes its place (as Oswald Spengler observed in his *Untergang des Abendlandes (Decline of the West)*) in a cyclic phase of the European mind that began with Schopenhauer and ended with Shaw, and which included Proudhon and Comte, Hebbel and Feuerbach, Marx and Engels, Wagner and Nietzsche, Darwin and John Stuart Mill. Even today the Ibsenist problems still impinge, still have 'relevance', still have the power to disturb: the role of women in society (*A Doll's House*); the conflict across the generation gap (*The Master Builder*); the clash between individual liberty and institutionalized authority (*Rosmersholm*); the menace of pollution in a world of material and commercial values (*An Enemy of the People*).

Alongside the polemics that so excited and engrossed the public and filled the leader columns of the day, however, was the complementary attention to what Ibsen himself called 'the far more difficult art' of prose. After *Peer Gynt* – a work of which it has been provocatively said that it is 'the first, and so far the finest, of those plays that make it possible to speak of modern drama in the way we find it natural to speak of modern poetry or fiction'[3] – Ibsen gave himself strenuously and unremittingly to the task of exploiting the resources of language in ways never before attempted or even suspected. The detection and the communication of subtleties and profundities below the surface of what might seem nothing more than the commonplaces of everyday speech opened up new and important possibilities in drama. In his own quest for the most precise 'individualization' of character (as he termed it), Ibsen was even reported to have claimed that 'the dialogue of a play ought to have a different timbre if it was meant to be spoken in the morning from what it would be at night'. As the sweep of Ibsen's authorship took him from the social to the visionary, from the polemical to the psychological, from the naturalistic to the symbolic, from the demonstrative to the evocative, it stimulated among many of Europe's writers a new and intense awareness of what dramatic language (and not merely prose alone) might be made to 'say'.

Beyond the public stridencies of the 'problems under debate' there was thus another Ibsen: the writer's writer, the dramatist's dramatist. The admiring phrases of those who were themselves exceptionally sensitive practitioners of *language* – Hofmannsthal, Henry James, Chekhov and Maeterlinck in the nineties, James Joyce and Pirandello and Rilke later – were largely prompted by this more formal and technical and non-polemical quality of Ibsen's work. Fascinated by the subtle undertones of Ibsen's dramatic dialogue (mysteriously surviving even in translation), they detect a second unspoken reality behind the surface of things, a '*dialogue du second degré*' (Maeterlinck); or remark how 'at some chance expression the mind is tortured with some question, and in a flash long reaches of life are opened up in vista' (Joyce); or hearken to characters who 'think about thinking, feel about feeling, and practice autopsychology' (Hofmannsthal); or see in Ibsen's changing authorship 'an ever more desperate search for visible correlations of the *inwardly* seen' (Rilke). The line that runs from Ibsen's last works via the recognitions of his contemporaries to the larger abstraction of Cocteau's concept of '*poésie du théâtre*' is clear.

The dual nature of Ibsen's achievement anticipated and in some measure determined the two-ply development of European drama within the succeeding Modernist generation. On the one hand, there were what Brecht called 'the great attempts to give the problems of the age a theatrical structure', a class in which one might expect to find, alongside Ibsen, the names of (say) Gorky, Hauptmann, Shaw, Wedekind, Kaiser and O'Neill. (Even further sub-divisions within this class occasionally attract Ibsenist definition, as when Wedekind characterized himself as a kind of Gyntian Ibsenist, in contrast to Hauptmann who – he asserted – was Brandian). Within this tradition, and whatever the 'theatrical structure' adopted, the prime commitment is to truth, to an objective and inter-personal truth which must be fearlessly recognized and boldly declared. To see with a clear vision, to define the problems, to break free of convention, to proclaim in their own often very idiosyncratic way the truth, however unexpected or unpalatable – these were *their* imperatives of the modern spirit. Demonstrative, declarative, expressive, often ironical, occasionally absurdist, the line embraces the late-naturalistic drama of Germany, the work of Shaw in England, the early absurdists in France, Italian and Russian Futurism, the Expressionist drama at large, much of Dada and Surrealism, and individual elements in Brecht. Complementing them, and orientated more towards things structural and technical and linguistic, are those dramatists for whom the intimate, the oblique, the implied, the elusive, the subdued, the symbolic are of the essence: Maeterlinck, Hofmannsthal, Chekhov, Yeats, Lorca.

2

If, of modern drama, Ibsen is the origin and impetus, Strindberg is its astonishing prefiguration. Where Ibsen made penetration, broke through in unexpected directions and took himself and those who responded to him into new and previously unexplored territories of dramatic experience, Strindberg by a kind of visionary enactment anticipated the then still indeterminate future of Modernist drama. During Modernism's formative years, the creative careers of the two men ran in echelon, overlapping significantly in the nineties. For Ibsen, the years from 1877 to the end of the century marked a line of thrust that ran from the naturalistic breakthrough of *Pillars of Society* to the terminal symbolism of *When We Dead Awaken* (1899). Roughly parallel but distant from it by about ten years, the line of Strindberg's authorship ran from his naturalistic plays of the late eighties (notably *The Father* and *Miss Julie*) to the chamber plays of the first decade of the new century, and the first disturbing intimations of the coming Expressionist and Surrealist revolutions in drama.

Although Strindberg's was an essentially solitary spirit, his life and work seem against all expectation to constitute an essence, a reduction, a concentrate of an age that transcends even his own lifetime. Behind all the sensationalism of his career, the three achingly unsuccessful marriages, the total nervous breakdown in his forties, the stridency of his hates, the extreme subjectivity of his art, he was possessed of an extraordinary delicacy of mind and sensitivity of spirit that made of him a unique *sensor* of the shifts and movements that were pending in the sensibilities of the age. By the sheer universality of his genius, he invites comparison with Leonardo and Goethe. By stages radical, iconoclastic, sceptic, mystic, devout, he ranged intellectually and emotionally over an astonishingly broad spectrum of human endeavour. Few areas of human consciousness or social concern, of political moment or religious inquiry escaped the attention of his restlessly exploring mind, 'a mind on horseback' as one of his acquaintances once put it. His personal 'inferno' crisis rehearsed with uncanny prescience many of the neuroses of the twentieth-century mind. Conscious, like the student in the *Ghost Sonata*, of having 'been born into a bankrupt world' and familiar with the dimensions of hell from the history of his own mental anguish, he emerges as a private, intimate, prophetic embodiment of a *malaise* that is wholly and recognizably 'modern'.

The range and variety of his dramatic authorship is no less great: 'Byronic poetic plays, Naturalistic tragedies, Boulevard comedies, Maeterlinckian fairy plays, Shakespearean chronicles, Expressionistic dream plays, and chamber works in sonata form'.[4] That he was in addition a prolific novelist, essayist, critic, historian and letter-writer is also part of the record. Though his declared hostility to Ibsen was complete, the pattern of his earlier dramatic authorship – from the historical preoccupations of *Master Olof* (1872) to the naturalistic works of the late eighties and early nineties – might nevertheless almost seem like some act of unconscious mimicry of the Norwegian. Ultimately, however, it is the 'post-Inferno' work that gives the most impressive evidence of Strindberg's audacious experimentalism. These are the plays in which he returns to the historical and naturalistic modes he had attempted earlier; but now Swedenborg has replaced Nietzsche as the dominant influence, and the author is moved by a new complexity of intent, though the profound variety and diversity of style never fails to receive the stamp of his own personal and unifying vision. The year 1899 alone saw the composition of four historical dramas, a genre he was to find curiously amenable to the expression of his new and mystic conception of the nature of God and

Man; and the naturalism (or he preferred to call it, the neo-naturalism) of *Crimes and Crimes* (1899), *Easter* (1900) and (supremely) *The Dance of Death* (1901) lent itself to the creation of an intense, airless, existentialist realism which many have since compared with Sartre's interiors. It was however particularly with the anticipatory Expressionism of *To Damascus* (1898-1904) and *The Great Highway* (1909), the Neo-Romanticism of *The Crown Bride* (1902) and *Swanwhite* (1902), and the incipient Surrealism of *A Dream Play* (1902) and of *The Ghost Sonata* (1907) that Strindberg contributed most influentially to the European drama of the twentieth century.

3

As a teasing complexity superimposed upon these general patterns, Modernism – for the first time in the history of drama – raises in acute fashion the issue of meta-theatre, a concept which Lionel Abel has defined as resting on two basic postulates: (1) the world is a stage; and (2) life is a dream.[5] Neither of these two notions originated in the late nineteenth century, of course: 'Life is a dream' is a literal translation of the title of a play by Calderón, *La Vida es sueño* (1635); and 'the world's a stage' (or *theatrum mundi*) was a cliché long before Shakespeare and other Renaissance dramatists took it up. Elizabeth Burns derives the metaphor of *theatrum mundi* from the idea that God was the sole spectator of man's actions on the stage of life: 'In the early religious theatre,' she writes, 'the spectator was given a God's eye view of human destiny, acted out in the Miracle and Morality plays. But in the secular theatre man became the spectator of man, however slight his identification with the dramatic characters might be.'[6] Modernism's response to these two Renaissance concepts was to exalt them above the ethical plane they occupied in the post-medieval synthesis – a sphere in which disquisitions on the transitoriness of life and the shallowness of human endeavour held pride of place, a context where men and women are seen as mere actors, making their exits and their entrances on the stage of life (*As You Like It*) and mouthing tales 'full of sound and fury signifying nothing' (*Macbeth*) – and to transfer things to the realm of aesthetics, where the real was placed against the illusory, the mask set beside the face, the stage opposed to the auditorium, and where, above all, the smile was juxtaposed with the tear to produce that characteristically Modernist phenomenon, the grimace of tragicomedy. Tragicomedy – something both 'deeper and grimmer', in Shaw's estimate, than tragedy[7] – is in fact the Modernist mode *par excellence*. A seeming tentativeness compounds with a confidence and an assurance – a knowingness, indeed, which for the first time implicates the spectator in the very structure of the drama – to lend identification to the Modernist aesthetic, from *The Wild Duck* to *Waiting for Godot*. Hjalmar's 'nobility' in the presence of death is a form of spectacle which we, like Dr Relling, know to be a sham, because within a year he will be offering maudlin eloquence upon young Hedvig's suicide. It is also the spectacle of those clownish intellectuals in their down-at-heel togs playing histrionically to the gallery as they fill in the empty time waiting for Godot. In both cases the tone is ambiguous: Hjalmar's situation is heart-breaking, and Estragon's is desperate; but the manner in which these situations are presented is sufficient to make them risible. The end of Beckett's play, which has throughout balanced existential anguish against bowler-hatted slapstick straight out of Laurel and Hardy, offers the ultimate in this mode. Two men have just botched an attempt at suicide: their rope has snapped. Unfortunately the rope that was supposed to hang them also serves as the belt holding up Estragon's trousers. At one of the most sombre moments in the history of drama in this century – at a time when all hope, even of easeful death, has evaporated – the victim's trousers concertina around his ankles. 'Pull on your trousers', his comrade tells him. But this is not the whole joke. Because Estragon, in fine music-hall style, gets it all wrong. 'You want me to pull off my trousers?' he asks with comic oafishness. Astonishingly, we are within minutes only of the final curtain, of the unbearable poignancy of that last silence ('Let's go' – *They do not move*) with which the play ends.

That Ibsen and Beckett represent the poles of Modernism, in time and in spirit, is precisely the difficulty. How to define an aesthetic which needs to embrace two such disparate figures, two giants (in their very different ways) of modern dramaturgy? In this protean world of theatre, the issues are even more complex than in the sister genres of the novel and the lyric, where matters are already difficult enough. In poetry, Symbolism and Post-Symbolism admittedly pre-

sent discontinuities, but none so radical as those which attend the
publication within a few years of each other of plays as different as
Hedda Gabler (1890), *Ubu Roi* (1896) and *To Damascus* (1898); whilst in
the novel it is possible, as we have seen, to discern a general aesthetic
metamorphosis which basically takes the form of narrative involution.
No such single direction can be mapped out for the theatre. Rather,
the problem is one of resolving, within some acceptable aesthetic of
modern drama, a range of divergent, even contradictory, tendencies.

4

Certain indicators trace this 'meta-theatrical' aspect of Modernism.
With some exaggeration, one might label Modernist dramaturgy 'the
aesthetics of silence'. Never before had the fragmentary, the low-key,
the inarticulate, even the incoherent and the frankly non-verbal
tendencies of theatrical intercourse been so audaciously developed. It
was, of course, not unknown in earlier plays for characters to fall
silent, aghast, amazed or terrified; but such moments remained theatrical, belonged to the context of the play, did not comment upon it.
The silences in Strindberg, in Pinter or in Beckett are justified within
the play, but they also serve as a reflection upon it: in Beckett's case
quite explicitly so. 'This is deadly,' Hamm comments to the audience
in *Endgame* when he (and we) have been exasperated by a particularly
tedious piece of 'time-wasting' business from Clov. Or in *Godot*, after
the dialogue has once again run into the sand, the characters sigh, and
wait for someone to start things off once more. Bored and clumsy as
an office-boy taking sherry with the boss, Estragon breaks the silence
first, through the straightforward device of simply drawing attention
to it:[8]

ESTRAGON: In the meantime nothing happens.
POZZO: You find it tedious?
ESTRAGON: Somewhat.
POZZO: (*to Vladimir*). And you, sir?
VLADIMIR: I've been better entertained.
  Silence

In spite of this tendency to lapse into wordlessness, Beckett's plays are
very literate. The speakers know their classics, and quote from them

liberally (Estragon from Shelley's 'To the Moon', Winnie – with a fine sense of irony – from *Romeo and Juliet*, while Hamm sardonically distorts Baudelaire's sublime '*Tu réclamais le Soir; il descend; le voici*' ('You demand the evening; it falls; here it is') as his own evening draws in). The inarticulacy, in other words, is in the medium as much as in the message.

It is different with Pinter, who has always countered journalistic clichés about his work with the statement that he is not concerned with the so-called impossibility of communication, but with the fear of it; people take refuge in evasions rather than run the risk of having to articulate what is really bothering them. Silence or digression are after all a much safer refuge than discursive and explicit statements. The *locus classicus* of this is the seemingly astounding irrelevance of Aston's description in *The Caretaker* of his inability to drink Guinness from a thick mug, whereas what really troubles him is the haunting fear of another mental breakdown and of undergoing further electro-shock treatment. In Ionesco, likewise, language serves rather to mask than to reveal tensions and conflicts: *The Lesson* is a perfect exposition of how to conceal fantasies of rape and murder under a comically parodic form of academic discourse. But the veiling of erotic tensions under language which bears little surface relation to them was certainly not invented by Ionesco: Ibsen does it superbly in *Hedda Gabler* and *Little Eyolf*, and so does Strindberg in *Miss Julie*. Likewise Pinter is not the first playwright to show characters evading a realization of their plight: Chekhov's Gayev takes refuge from his embarrassments in *The Cherry Orchard* by imagining himself at billiards, 'potting into the corner pocket' or 'cannoning off the cushions'. The spectacle of language breaking down, the explosion of the hysteria underlying the polite banalities of social intercourse, and violence resulting from quite trivial provocations: all this forms the basis of Chekhov's drama just as it does of Pinter's. There is a difference in setting, of course: the estates of the declining nobility in pre-revolutionary Russia are a far cry from the seedy bed-and-breakfasts or the chi-chi converted farm-houses in which Pinter's characters tear each other apart, from *The Birthday Party* (1958) to *Old Times* (1971); but both are authentic locales of their respective periods. Long after the last derelict Victorian pile has disappeared under the developer's bulldozer as irrevocably as Ranyevskaia's cherry orchard under the axe, Pinter's people, like Chekhov's, will still be probing the resources of speech to find loopholes through which to escape from their truths, signalling messages of hostility and repression at each other either by irrelevant language ('I understood you were an experienced first-class professional interior and exterior decorator . . . You mean you wouldn't know how to fit teal-blue, copper and parchment linoleum squares and have those colours re-echoed in the walls? . . . You're a bloody imposter, mate!'), or by non-verbal means, as when Mick smashes the Buddha against the gas stove in *The Caretaker*.

5

Within this characteristically Modernist concept of meta-theatre, the role of the 'life is a dream' motif is of unifying importance. Central to Pirandello's theatre, of course, is the ambiguous interrelation of the 'fictive' and the 'real', which nevertheless derives from Strindberg's *Dream Play* (1901), a work of profound and revolutionary originality. This in its turn leads on to one of the most perfect works thrown up in the post-1950 renascence of Modernism, Arthur Adamov's *Professor Taranne* (1951), in which an eminent academic finds himself accused of an ever more serious list of offences, from lack of courtesy towards colleagues and students, to plagiarizing the work of another scholar, and finally to indecent exposure. It is impossible, within the play itself, to be sure whether or not the professor is the victim of a concerted campaign of defamation and distortion, or is genuinely guilty of the alleged offences. When told the contents of the Belgian vice-chancellor's letter explaining why he is not being invited to lecture again, Professor Taranne starts slowly to take his clothes off as the curtain falls; whereupon the audience is unsure if he is conforming to the nightmare or confirming its truth. The power of the work arises from the fact that its ambiguity remains entire. Is Taranne's dignity a mask for paranoia and deviant behaviour? Or is the whole thing simply a bad dream? What is the reality, and what the illusion? These are questions Modernism is adept at posing, undermining our categories and destroying our confidence in familiar things. Such as a middle-class flat: a safe enough place, one might have thought, until Ionesco in *Amédée* peoples it with a growing cadaver and covers the carpet in mushrooms; or until Pinter, in *The Room*, makes it the scene of Aeschylean ritual murder and blinding. Life and art are interfused. When tragedies are enacted in the drawing-room, when – as in *The Homecoming* by Harold Pinter – Iphigenia is sacrificed in North London, or when *The Taming of the Shrew* is sardonically rewritten as *Who's Afraid of Virginia Woolf*, there is a return by another route to that essential tragicomedy which is so inseparable from Modernism.

6

The dimensions and the perimeter of theatrical space are also subjected by Modernist drama to radical revision: sometimes the dividing line falls somewhere across the middle, sometimes it encircles the playhouse altogether. Pre-Modernist drama fostered the illusion that the audience was eavesdropping, that a fourth wall had fallen away unbeknown to the characters, and that the spectators were looking straight in. Ibsen frequently exploits this device: *The Wild Duck* begins in the most conventional manner imaginable, with the family servant explaining to the hired waiter the situation from which the drama is to spring – a simple artifice whereby the audience is 'put in the picture' and the action meaningfully started. But once this awkward but essential phase is past, the play is performed in a sense as if the audience were not watching; indeed, it needs to be so performed if the tension is to be effectively generated. The actors need to concentrate hard on the situation; any hint of a gesture to the gallery would destroy the illusion. Yet it is precisely this illusion – the illusion of realist drama, symbolized by a darkened and hushed auditorium opposite a brightly-lit and busy stage – which one of the greatest modern dramatists, Bertolt Brecht, sought to abolish. Not that he demanded removing the footlights and making the stage and the auditorium continuous. On the contrary, to do that would have been to create another illusion, just as totalitarian, that the world within the theatre walls is a real world, the only genuine world. This illusion, as we shall see, is fostered by the other tendency in Modernism: that fathered by Antonin Artaud.

The Brechtian rejection of theatrical illusion marks one of the truly original innovations in the entire history of drama. Brecht's purpose was didactic and political; but his innovation opened the way to much else that is vital in contemporary theatre, not least the works of Samuel Beckett, which self-consciously play 'across' the footlights. In *Waiting for Godot* the emptiness of the auditorium is humorously commented upon by the actor/characters; in *Endgame*, Hamm (like the 'ham actor' he is) plays to the stalls, and when Clov asks what keeps him there, he replies, truthfully enough, 'the dialogue'; and in *Happy Days* Winnie 'begins her day' like an old pro limbering up for another canter through the familiar material. Likewise Ionesco never wearies of reminding the audience that they are sitting in a playhouse, watching a game with rules which can be modified but still need to be respected; in such discussion Ionesco is not above puckishly referring to himself by name.

The other tendency – of a world in a room – is hymnic where the one above is ironic; it aims to be frenzied where the first pretends to a control of the anarchistic impulse. Here the greatest exponent is undoubtedly Jean Genet. By insisting that at every performance of *The Blacks* at least one white person must sit in the audience (or failing that, a dummy), Genet underlines the aggressive and even orgiastic nature of the work. This tendency has become fashionable in recent years with such remarkable manifestations of the Artaud spirit as Peter Weiss's *Marat/Sade*, which the director Peter Brook in the introduction to the English translation declared to have been 'designed to crack the spectator on the jaw, then douse him with ice-cold water, then force him to assess intelligently what has happened to him, then give him a kick in the balls . . .' The violence and crudity of this manifesto was more than matched by what was enacted under its aegis in the playhouse. Similarly extreme outbursts of controlled delirium have come to be associated with 'free' actors' groups like La Mama and the Living Theatre, which exalt irrationality and the flouting of social and cultural taboos, and repudiate 'good acting' which they see as a moribund 'professionalism'. Apart from the risk that in such a devaluation 'control over the audience, inherent in the ritual base and the conventional tradition, may be lost', there is the undoubted fact that such attempts to 'substitute theatrical experience for experience in the outside world' become a new form of ancient didacticism, a twist on 'all the world a stage', which simply becomes reformulated as 'the stage a whole world in itself'.[9] But however much one may deplore this tendency and see the dangers which the indiscriminate pursuit of unreason in the theatre may lead to, it is clear that it represents a genuine strain in the Modernist tradition and one which is perhaps, at least at the present time, the dominant one.

7

Other features – ritual and fairy-tale, mask and dance, stylization and formalization, relativity and flux – derive essentially from the more major elements considered in this section; some of them may also be observed operating in parallel in other performing arts in this century: the ballet, the cinema or, more recently, television. In the film, particularly, we see reflected nearly all the disjunctions affecting stage drama, in characterization, dialogue, and plotting. A great film-director like Ingmar Bergman owes a real debt to Strindberg, but equally a playwright like Pinter can learn from the art of a cinéast of genius like Hitchcock.[10] Ken Russell's screen version of *The Devils* outdid in violence the stage play by John Whiting based on the same historical events, but its catalyst was nonetheless theatrical: Peter Brook's Theatre of Cruelty, itself based on the theories of Antonin Artaud. Since theatre and cinema are subject to the same *Zeitgeist*, such congruences are hardly surprising; and indeed some people (like Marguerite Duras) operate quite happily in either medium. And from cinema itself some practitioners (like Truffaut and Bogdanovich) have shifted into metacinema. The same forces – pushing the medium progressively into an ever greater awareness of itself, and involving the spectator more intimately in its evolution – operate universally, fanning out widely beyond the frontiers of drama as traditionally understood. This is the most telling reason why, in the theatre, Modernism is more truly represented by Strindberg rather than Brieux, Wedekind rather than Hauptmann, and Yeats rather than Shaw.

Notes

1 Eric Bentley, *The Modern Theatre* (London 1948), p. 6.

2 Kenneth Muir, 'Verse and Prose', in *Contemporary Theatre*, Stratford upon Avon Studies no. 4 (London 1962), p. 97.

3 Ronald Gaskell, *Drama and Reality* (London 1972), p. 37.

4 Robert Brustein, *The Theatre of Revolt* (London 1965), p. 87.

5 Lionel Abel, *Metatheatre: A New View of Dramatic Form* (New York 1963), p. 105.

6 Elizabeth Burns, *Theatricality: A Study of Convention in the Theatre and in Social Life* (London 1972), p. 143.

7 Quoted in Karl S. Guthke, *Modern Tragicomedy: An Investigation into the Nature of the Genre* (New York 1966), p. 107.

8 Samuel Beckett, *Waiting for Godot*, Act I.

9 See Elizabeth Burns, *Theatricality: A Study of Convention in the Theatre and in Social Life* (London 1972), pp. 182, 227.

10 See John Fletcher, 'Bergman and Strindberg', and Alan Brody, 'The Gift of Realism: Hitchcock and Pinter', in *Journal of Modern Literature*, vol. III, no. 2 (April 1973), pp. 173–90 and pp. 149–72 respectively.

INTIMATE THEATRE: MAETERLINCK TO STRINDBERG

JAMES MCFARLANE

'THEY last a second, a minute,' wrote Knut Hamsun in 1890 of the nature of those impressions he sought to urge upon the attention of contemporary writers. 'They come and go like a moving winking light. But they have impressed their mark, deposited some kind of impression, before they vanished.'[1] The momentary, the fleeting, the transitory – those faint and insubstantial but significant signs that seemed to offer some new insight into life's meaning – these were the things the post-naturalist writer, his sensibilities refined to the utmost, was exhorted to capture and record. Aestheticism of almost Kierke-gaardian rigour claimed ever more adherents: men for whom sensations, impressions, responses were so much more the stuff of life than convictions, commitments, obligations. Some, like Maeterlinck and Hofmannsthal, sped across the nineties like bright falling stars before seeming to burn out after a brief decade of splendid brilliance, not merely by their authorship representing the new spirit but by their careers also uncannily exemplifying it.

I

Disablingly limited in comparison with Ibsen, much more narrowly focused than Strindberg, and with none of Chekhov's lithe subtleties, Maeterlinck nevertheless drew the attention of the age as none other. All Europe, seemingly, at the *fin du siècle* was ready to pay heed and homage to him. Strindberg, who translated into Swedish long excerpts from *Le Trésor des Humbles* (*The Treasure of the Humble*) (1896), de-clared himself unequivocally a 'disciple' of Maeterlinck; and *Crown-bride, Swanwhite* and *A Dream Play* are all deeply in debt to him. Chekhov, as his letters to Suvorin make abundantly clear, read Maeterlinck in 1895 with undisguised admiration and urged the in-clusion of his work in the repertoire of the recently established St

Petersburg Little Theatre: '[His plays] are strange and remarkable things, but they create an overpowering impression; and if I possessed a theatre I should most certainly perform *Les Aveugles* [*The Sightless*].' Gerhart Hauptmann's 'German fairy tale' *Die versunkene Glocke* (*The Sunken Bell*) (1896) shows strong affinities; Bjørnson's admiration stimulated him to try his own hand at 'symbolist' drama, though without conspicuous success. Hofmannsthal found himself in close rapport, especially in the matter of the secret significance of 'the everyday'. Dauthendey translated him into German and tried to make of his dramas the means of introducing 'intimate theatre' to Berlin at the turn of the century. Sibelius was moved to compose incidental music to some of the plays. The Irish dramatic movement made positive response: Yeats's own dramatic techniques bore the marks of influence, and Synge's admiration was generous. (*The Well of the Saints* is often compared with *Les Aveugles*.)

Maeterlinck was fortunate – indeed, as a Belgian, doubly fortunate – in having the collaboration of Lugné-Poë's Théâtre de l'Oeuvre in Paris, a company which was not only quick to give performances of his *Pelléas et Mélisande, L'Intruse* (*The Intruder*), *L'Intérieur* (*Interior*) and (after the turn of the century) *Monna Vanna*, but also took the initiative in staging other European dramatists whose work was considered complementary to that of Maeterlinck: Ibsen, Bjørnson, Strindberg, Hauptmann, D'Annunzio, Echegaray and (somewhat later) Claudel.

Early in his authorship, Maeterlinck became convinced that conventional poetic diction was ill-suited for the communication of those deeply-felt but indeterminate inner feelings to which the age was becoming increasingly devoted. Dramatic eloquence of any kind, even in prose, was to him thoroughly suspect. The mere attempt to contain such feelings in words was to do violence to them; the act of formulation was in itself an imposition, giving a hard-edge conceptual outline to feelings and emotional responses too fluid to tolerate it. Communication in the theatre, it was declared, was a matter not of definition but of revelation and betrayal: a hinting, a suggesting, a guessing. *La Princesse Maleine,* written originally in quite elevated and eloquent verse, was re-cast by Maeterlinck in deliberately hesitant prose. Sentences were left unfinished; thoughts inconsequential:[2]

On peut affirmer que le poème se rapproche de la beauté et d'une vérité supérieure, dans la mesure où il élimine les paroles qui expliquent les actes pour les remplacer par des paroles qui expliquent non pas ce qu'on appelle 'un état d'âme', mais je ne sais quels efforts insaisissables et incessants des âmes vers leur beauté et vers leur vérité.★

. Despite the superficial kinship with naturalistic dialogue – whose stumblings and stammerings, grunts and sighs and sustained silences had already declared war on conventional dramatic eloquence – the emphasis was different. Whereas naturalism strove above all for sheer verisimilitude, for a truth to life that would establish the dramatist's credentials as a fearless and unbiassed observer of life's actualities, the new art discovered unsuspected harmonics of meaning. Johannes Schlaf, himself a naturalistic dramatist, commented shrewdly on this new quality:[3]

It is closely connected with what Maeterlinck has written about silence. This second unspoken dialogue, which in effect for our poet is the real one, is faciliated by various devices: by pauses, by gestures and other such indirect means. It is however mainly the result of the spoken word itself . . . a dialogue of unprecedented triviality, of the flat banality of everyday speech which, by virtue of this second inner dialogue, is given an indefinable magic.

This indeed was the quality which Maeterlinck had himself recognized in John Ford's 'profoundly discreet' art (as he called it), whose characters at their most tragic moments say no more than two or three simple words – 'a thin coating of ice on which we remain for an instant looking into the abyss below'.[4] And it points straight down the years to the art of Pinter who, in his programme notes to *The Room* and *The Dumb Waiter* in 1960, argued strongly that

a character on stage who can present no convincing argument or information as to his past experience, his present behaviour or his aspirations nor give a complete analysis of his motives is as legitimate and as worthy of attention as one who, alarmingly, can do all these things. The more acute the experience, the less articulate its expression.

Quiet, low-keyed yet intense, Maeterlinck's art gave itself wholly to the exploration of those mysteries lying half-hidden below the

★One may state that the more the poem eliminates those words explaining the actions and replaces them with words explaining not what is called 'a state of mind' but those inexplicable, ineffable and ceaseless efforts of minds towards their beauty and their truth, the closer it will get to a superior form of truth and beauty.

surface of existence, of those meanings inhabiting the silence and the darkness, of those inscrutable and intangible realities of the inner life. He had learnt from Novalis that whereas at one level of personality even the most horrendous of crimes might leave one largely unmoved, at another part of the soul one 'could nevertheless be shaken to one's very depths by an exchange of looks, by an unexpressed thought, by a moment of silence'. He found further confirmation of this in Emerson's sense of 'the secret grandeur' that inhabits every life no matter how lowly, and the belief that no moment is 'without the profoundest miracles, the most ineffable meanings'. From such convictions (which also reach back to Wordsworth and to Adalbert Stifter) he derived his sense of 'everyday tragedy' ('*le tragédie quotidien*'). Man is profoundly mistaken, he insists in *Le Trésor des Humbles*, if he attaches significance only to moments of high passion:

I have come to think that an old man sitting in his armchair, merely waiting in the lamplight, listening unmoved to all the eternal laws that prevail about his house, responding intuitively to the silence of the doors and the windows and the subdued voice of the light, submitting to the being of his soul and his destiny, inclining slightly his head, ignorant of the fact that all the worldly powers enter and survey the room like attentive servants . . . I am persuaded that in reality this motionless old man lives a much deeper, much more human and much broader life than the lover who strangles his mistress, the army officer who wins a victory, or 'the husband who avenges his honour'.

The perceptive eye of the dramatist sees the seemingly innocuous surface of life as a complex tissue of signs, symbols and indices. Precision of observation and sensitivity of recording retained their importance as under naturalism; a certain scientificism of vision, a distinct documentary quality persisted from the old into the new. Only now the drama showed affinity rather with the emergent psychological sciences than with the natural sciences, offering case histories rather than observers' reports. Ordinariness, it was increasingly recognized, had its own very evident psychopathology; and both the dramatist's and the audience's sensibilities had to be attuned to the betrayal values of life's minutiae. In close association with this was a mystic sense of the essential inter-relatedness of all things, an infinite wealth of correspondences. Again, for Maeterlinck, the inspiration came from Novalis who, seeing nothing as isolated, was 'the astonished teacher of the mysterious relations that exist among all things ... He senses strange coincidences and astounding analogies – obscure, trembling, fugitive, shy – which fade before they can be apprehended.'[5]

Not unexpectedly, this was a dramatic credo which in practice frequently resulted in a heavily symbolical, often cryptic and on occasion unbearably portentous kind of drama. Commonplace events which might in some other context have had simple naturalistic explanations – the scythe sharpened outside in the garden, the stopped clock, the lamp that failed, the cry of a child – come almost by routine to invite deep and alarming significance. Life becomes full of omens, warnings, signs; the mind is required to keep constant and anxious watch; and the air grows tense with the menace of familiar things.

2

In the early years of the nineties, Chekhov turned away from drama and appeared to be wholly absorbed in his fiction. His plays of the late eighties – *Ivanov* (1887) and *The Wood Demon* (1889) – had not achieved conspicuous success. The later dramatic masterpieces – *The Seagull* (1895), *Uncle Vanya* (1897), *Three Sisters* (1900–1901) and *The Cherry Orchard* (1903–4) – were still to be written. But he nevertheless continued to brood on problems of dramatic composition, especially those bearing on the communication of unspoken thought which (it is reported) he hoped to solve by combining a basic realism with a controlled use of symbols.

How far he was guided in his thinking by what he read during these years of his contemporaries elsewhere in Europe – in particular Ibsen and Maeterlinck – can only be conjectural. Some not wholly flattering remarks he passed about Ibsen reveal at least a measure of familiarity – comments, the unsympathetic nature of which contrasts strangely with his later admission, in a letter to Alexander Vishnevski in 1903, that Ibsen was of course his favourite author. His admiration for Maeterlinck was altogether more evident (see above, p. 515), and it is clear that many of the Belgian's ideas found a ready response in his mind. Certainly, Chekhov's maturer dramatic practice is compounded of elements, many of which are directly reminiscent of what was happening elsewhere in European drama: the attention given to individual states of mind, the complex and ambiguous tensions between conscious control and unconscious urge; the preoccupation with the trivia of existence, the small change of everyday life, as indices of events that were occurring at deeper levels of consciousness; the increasing fragmentation of character *à la Strindberg*; the emphasis on the random, the casual, the contingent as the surest way of achieving an authenticity of reality; the elimination of unnatural heroics; and the introduction of pervasive 'symbols' like the seagull and the cherry orchard – on the analogy, it is often argued, of Ibsen's wild duck – as a device for deepening and enriching the dramatic meaning.

The Chekhovian mode, distinctive as that of no other dramatist of the age, tends to leave orthodox critical terminology uneasy: 'psychological naturalism' and 'realistic symbolism', two of the commoner attempts to label his work, are equally unhappy. There is general recognition that his unique achievement lies in the skill with which he creates an atmosphere or a mood, an individual state of mind or a society's state of being. 'The action [of *The Seagull*]', wrote Suvorin, 'takes place behind the scenes rather than on stage, as though the author was interested only in showing how the characters reacted to events, to reveal their natures.' Behind the façade, below the surface, within the *persona*, submerged, suppressed – this is where and how the significant action takes place. Overt incident merely provokes to introspection and self-betrayal; and the medium of self-betrayal is the commonplace, the inconsequential, the seemingly perfunctory. For him, dramatic action is essentially a 'continuum, interruptible or terminable only by drastic melodramatic intervention. One remembers the triumph with which – of his last play, *The Cherry Orchard* – he reported: 'There's not a single pistol-shot in the whole play.' It is as though the relentless grip exerted on the lives of his characters by yearning, frustration, boredom, disillusion or guilt could only be prised open by the force of sensation. Captives of private thoughts and desires, Chekhov's individuals talk past each other, filling the emptiness of the air with speech – complaints, reproaches, catchwords, regrets – while their thoughts endlessly circle round their own secret obsessions. Thrown by family or social circumstance into close proximity, nevertheless in essence they remain estranged; in their muted lives, tedium forms a very focus of attention, and passivity becomes a way of life.

The orchestration of its parts rather than the form and structure of the whole is what gives a Chekhov drama its distinctive quality. Mood and atmosphere are made to serve a *structural* purpose, providing the cohesive force that holds together the constituent dramatic elements: words, silence, movement, gesture, tempo, lighting and all the other non-verbal components that make their eloquent contribution to his dramas. The right intensity, the right amplification, the right timbre was crucial. The cast of *Three Sisters* at the Moscow Arts Theatre were astonished to discover that Chekhov seemed less concerned about how they spoke their lines than about the precise sound of the church bells ringing the alarm off-stage in Act III: 'On every convenient occasion he would come up to one or other of us,' Stanislavsky later reported, 'and try by the use of his hands, by rhythm and gesticulation to impress on us the mood evoked by this soul-searing provincial fire alarm.'[6] (From which report it appears that, for Chekhov, the non-verbal must supplement, might even supplant, the verbal in total communication.) The hoot of an owl, the tapping of a night watchman, a faintly heard song, the strike of an axe on a tree, and – uniquely haunting – the sad distant sound of the breaking string that ends *The Cherry Orchard*, all were made to contribute to the mood, the all-important '*nastroenie*', of the play.

In contrast to Maeterlinck whose importance lies more in his immediate influence on the drama of the day than in any intrinsic quality, Chekhov meant less to his contemporaries in drama than his present stature might lead one to suppose. But later generations have listened much more attentively; and more than one voice is ready today to claim him as an important source of 'absurdist' drama, and to assert affinities with Beckett, Ionesco, Adamov, Albee and Pinter.

3

Within this general displacement of emphasis from the direct to the oblique, from the cumulative to the selective, from the demonstrative to the suggestive, Vienna had its own distinctive contribution to make.

In kind, if not strictly in time, the dramas of Arthur Schnitzler occupy an intermediate stage between the old and the new. Decadence, or naturalism in decay, is the description often applied to those of his dramas written in the nineties: particularly *Anatol* (1893), *Liebelei* (*Playing with Love*) (1895), *Der grüne Kakadu* (*The Green Cockatoo*) (1899) and *Reigen* (*Merry-go-round*) (written in 1897 and published in 1900). His stance is that of one who, quietly amused or gently cynical, holds himself somewhat apart from the society of the day to interpret the outer signs in terms of inner tensions. Social comment of a kind is everywhere evident in his work, but it is never brutal or acerbic. Protest, satirical assault, denunciation – these were not Schnitzler's *métier*. '*Böser Dinge hübsche Formel*' ('nice formula for nasty things'), to use the phrase Hofmannsthal used of his work, was the best – or the worst – he could offer, as he coolly observed; and – as befitted one whose profession was medicine – he skilfully diagnosed the nervous maladies of the age, the unrelenting pursuit of pleasure, the insistent eroticism, the defiantly rococo quality of life in a declining culture, and the anxiety to keep at bay even the faintest threat of disenchantment. Sceptical, sensual, anti-doctrinaire, he was completely at home in that Viennese tradition which knows how to turn the most sober or terrifying of insights into an elegant witticism; and always there was at work a wry and confident sensitivity, a responsiveness to significant and revealing detail, and an exquisite sense of human frailty.

Hofmannsthal's gifts were of a different order. Despite his early and profound admiration for Ibsen's dramatic art (which found expression in his essay 'Die Menschen in Ibsens Dramen' ('The People in Ibsen's dramas') of 1891), and despite his increasing adoption as the decade progressed of many of Maeterlinck's ideas, he was never moved by the example of either to compose his earliest dramas in prose. In *Gestern* (*Yesterday*) (1892) written when he was still only eighteen, in *Der Tod des Tizian* (*The Death of Titian*) (1892) and, supremely, in *Der Tor und der Tod* (*The Fool and Death*) (1893), his work was dominated by an astonishing and precocious *lyric* talent. His characters, highly strung and resonant instruments full of a great yearning for self-understanding, willing prey to perversion, endlessly racked by doubt and obsessed with the problem of life's meaning, were all wondrously articulate. Not for them the hesitant and stumbling phrases of Maeterlinkean speech; their utterances are pure lyricism, dramatically orchestrated.

For Claudio, the languid, sophisticated young hero of *Der Tor und der Tod*, life is something that is lived at the Kierkegaardian 'aesthetic stage'; the sanctity of impressions is the supreme concern; morals are the stuff of play. Reality leaves him untouched, unmoved, except at the level of *frisson*; like the young man in Ibsen's poem 'On the Heights' (who enjoys the aesthetic spectacle of his mother's cottage burning down, and shades his eyes with his hands 'to get the perspective right'), Claudio sees life as a passing show; he is unmoved by it except at the shallowest level until Death himself comes to compel him to an awareness of what his past actions have meant. Some phrases that Hofmannsthal used some three years later, in his 'In memoriam Raoul Richter', suggest that this *'tragédie-proverbe'* contained a good measure of self-portraiture, of 'autopsychology': 'I had within me a threefold yearning: for the innocence of youth; for the middle of life; and for the achievements of old age. Would that I might have been in all of them at once – yet I only stood by the side of the road.'

Life, as one of his later characters puts it, is nothing but a 'play of shadows'. Nevertheless it is as though an instrument of such sensitivity that it can respond to and interpret these faint and shadowy promptings needs protection from the impact of sterner reality, otherwise it shatters. Only by keeping the mainstream of life at a distance, only by standing *'seitwärts am Wege'*, was Hofmannsthal able to record and articulate the delicacies, the exquisite subtleties, the trembling nuances that the nineties gave its attention to. In *Der weisse Fächer (The White Fan)* (1897), Fortunio broods on his adventure in phrases which could well have been written by Maeterlinck, and which surely define the limited area of reality that the Symbolist imagination of the nineties was more and more confined to:

This adventure is almost nothing, yet it leaves me confused. One must beware, for 'almost nothing' is the very stuff of existence: words, a raised eyebrow, a lowered eyebrow, an encounter at the crossroads, one face that resembles another, three memories that fuse together, the scent of flowers on the wind, a dream that was believed forgotten . . . there is nothing else.

With the passing of this stage, Hofmannsthal was still inclined to see art deriving more from art itself than from life. He turned to the re-creation of antique drama in modern form, to opera libretti for Richard Strauss; and when the rest of German drama turned to occupy itself almost wholly with the ecstatic stridencies of Expressionism, Hofmannsthal gave his aristocratic attention to medieval allegory, to adaptations of Molière, to light comedy in the manner of Goldoni, and to reinterpretations of Calderon.

4

Strindberg would not accept that he was a Symbolist. When pressed, he allowed that he might reasonably be called a 'neo-naturalist'. The term administers a timely corrective. It is fatally easy to assume that, with the years, Strindberg simply 'outgrew' naturalism. As early as 1890, voices in many parts of Europe had proclaimed that naturalism was dead, *überwunden*, vanquished; and when the contemporary eye was caught by those startlingly novel and experimental works which Strindberg wrote about the turn of the century – the mythic explorations of *To Damascus*, the audacious fluidity of *A Dream Play*, and the fairly-tale fantasy of *Crownbride* and *Swanwhite* – the natural response was to pencil in a linear path of development which Strindberg's later work was confidently expected to follow, and to plot the later chamber plays as an extrapolation taking Strindberg ever further away from the outdated and outmoded naturalism of his earlier years.

Yet one has only to compare the phrases Strindberg used in later life to define his concept of 'intimate theatre' with the declarations of his Preface to *Miss Julie* of close on twenty years before to see how appropriate is the description 'neo-naturalist' in his own case. With the advantages of hindsight, it is clear how this Preface, whilst arguing strongly for naturalism by name, was nevertheless by its insistence on the random, the fragmentary and the contingent anticipating a great deal of what was to come. As he wrote to Adolf Paul in January 1907, what he was seeking in his mature art was that kind of play which was 'intimate in form; a simple theme considered in depth; few characters; wide perspectives; something freely imaginative but taken from observation, experience, all carefully studied'. Though this is far from representing some simple regression to the kind of naturalism he pursued in the eighties, it nevertheless betrays a characteristic uneasiness on Strindberg's part – even at moments of high stress, imaginative vision, fantastic speculation – ever to be far distant from life's realities, from 'observation', from 'experience'. But, in the years up to 1907, it was compounded with the new convictions and the new perspectives that his own 'Inferno crisis' had given him: the faith in an assertive *inner* reality, the sense of the illogical's inner logic, and the recognition of the supremacy of those forces (both within and without the individual) which are not wholly under conscious control.

Although he was now aware as never before of the anguish, the flux, the doubts and uncertainties attaching to the new vision of reality with which his crisis had left him, his last works are in no sense a simple retreat into himself. Admittedly dreams continued to fascinate and preoccupy him. In *To Damascus* (which, with its unnamed characters having the status neither of types nor individuals but acting rather as indices of mental and emotional states), as well as in *A Dream Play*, Strindberg reached out after 'the disconnected but seemingly logical form of a dream':

Anything can happen; everything is possible and probable. Time and space do not exist; against an unimportant background of reality, the imagination spins and weaves new patterns: a blend of memories, experiences, free ideas, absurdities, improvizations. The characters split, double, multiply; they evaporate, crystallize, scatter and converge. But a single consciousness holds dominion over them all; that of the dreamer.

It was not merely that these phrases outlined a most audacious strategy; they also urged a mode of dramatic communication which the new century was quick to recognize as peculiarly apt to its condition, and which within a few years the theatres of Expressionism and of Surrealism were to exploit to the full. *To Damascus* was an eloquent declaration that science had nothing to do with faith, and that when confronted by the deeper mysteries of life rationality is helpless. Transformations, the merging of one thing into another, came to dominate Strindberg's thinking, much as they did for the Rilke of the *Sonnets to Orpheus* some twenty years later. Dreams offered a means for giving form to apparent randomness – mixing, transforming, dissolving. They provided multiple identities, self-projection in infinite variety, and the opportunity for the clarification of a distorted reality. The associative truth of dreams and their inherent logicality (which, when distanced by time and wakefulness, tend to appear absurdly inconsequential) quite overwhelmed him and broke through the flimsy membrane that divided life and art.

Yet when he addressed himself to his chamber plays, Strindberg showed no inclination to surrender his control over reality as completely as one does in a dream. Some yielding he was ready to agree to – to inspiration, ecstasy, intoxication. But there were distinct limits:

> Sometimes I think of myself as a medium: everything comes so easily, half unconsciously, with just a little bit of planning and calculation . . . But it doesn't come to order, and it doesn't come to please *me*.

Control there undoubtedly is, even if on occasion only of an unconscious kind; but the development is of theme and mood, rather than of anything as firmly outlined as plot. The desire is to get behind the façade, beneath the surface; to strip man and woman naked in order to reveal the blemished reality; to expose the flawed thought processes behind the words. *The Storm*, muted in its evocation of the mood of late summer (and, in this, greatly reminiscent of Maeterlinck), moves through from the tempestuousness of an early storm to the quietude that lies beyond, linking the year's seasonal progressions with man's passage through the ages of life, and relating nature's landscape to the inner terrain of the soul.

In *The Burnt House*, where the exposed ruins of the house lay bare the past history of things, the symbolism is even more overt; and there are still residual elements of an earlier design – from the days when the play bore the provisional title of *The World Weaver* – where the insistence is that each thread of life is and must necessarily be ignorant of its part in the grand design until the final thread is woven and the pattern completed. The peak of allusiveness is finally achieved in *The Ghost Sonata*: 'It is a world of allusion,' Strindberg declared, 'where people talk in semi-tones, in muted voices, and one is ashamed of being human.' Nothingness – as in Chekhov, in Hofmannsthal – lies at the centre of it; silence is its mode; disbelief in what the other says is the motivating force.

Two things coalesce in these plays. On the one hand, there was the encouragement Strindberg drew from the analogy with chamber music in its relationship to the fully orchestrated piece. He is eager to make the comparison, to call his late plays his 'last sonatas', to introduce the terminology of coda, cadenza, and the notion of ritardando, and to indicate the counterpointing that relates the various elements in the drama: the set, the lights, the movement and the words. And on the other hand there was his enduring dislike of the staged, the bombastic, the strident and the portentous in the theatre. He set himself to command the subdued, the simply subtle, the delicately modulated; to invite a reading between the lines and a listening between the words; to load the interstices – the pauses, the silences, the breaks – with profound significance. The figures in the plays, poised between the substantiality of 'characters' and the abstraction of personified concepts, become the differentiated images of a tormented humanity. These above all were the plays that prompted Eugene O'Neill to declare in 1924 that 'Strindberg was the precurser of all modernity in our present theatre . . . the most modern of moderns'.

Notes

1 Knut Hamsun in an essay, 'Fra det ubevidste Sjæleliv' ('From the Unconscious Life of the Mind'), in *Samtiden* (1890), pp. 325ff.

2 Quoted in J. Chiari, *Landmarks of Contemporary Drama* (London 1965), p. 83.

3 Johannes Schlaf, *Maurice Maeterlinck* (Berlin 1906), p. 31.

4 Maeterlinck, introduction to his *Annabella*, a translation of John Ford's *'Tis Pity She's a Whore*.

5 Maeterlinck, introduction to *Les Disciples à Saïs et les Fragments de Novalis* (1895).

6 See *The Oxford Chekhov*, edited by Ronald Hingley, vol. 3 (London 1964), p. 315.

MODERNIST DRAMA: WEDEKIND
TO BRECHT

MARTIN ESSLIN

I

IN the hard-fought struggle for naturalism in the theatre, Germany undoubtedly was the main battleground. It was in Germany that the great masters of the movement, Ibsen and Strindberg, received their first international recognition: as early as 1886 *Ghosts* was performed by the Meininger company (albeit almost behind closed doors) but at the beginning of 1887 the play received a public and triumphantly successful performance at the Berlin Residenztheater. Strindberg's *The Father* was performed by Otto Brahm's Freie Bühne, which became the focal point for the propagation of Modernist drama, in October 1890, *Miss Julie* in April 1892. Georg Brandes, the great Danish critic, had prepared the ground for the breakthrough of naturalism in Germany: he had lived in Berlin from 1877 to 1883.

Germany's own naturalistic drama emerged in 1889 with Gerhart Hauptmann's *Vor Sonnenaufgang* (*Before Sunrise*) a gloomy Ibsenite play about the ravages of hereditary alcoholism. Hauptmann's decisive success, however, was *Die Weber* (*The Weavers*) (first performed by the Freie Bühne in February 1893), a play without an individual hero in which a whole class, the down-trodden weavers of Silesia, was the protagonist. It is remarkable that the *reaction* against this meticulously thorough, photographic reproduction of external reality in naturalistic drama was almost simultaneous with its first emergence. For Frank Wedekind's (1864–1918) *Frühlings Erwachen* (*Spring's Awakening*) had appeared in book form in Zürich in 1891 even before the first performance of *Die Weber*. Admittedly, Wedekind's play was considered far too obscene to be performed: it did not reach the stage till fifteen years later, in November 1906.

Wedekind's rejection of naturalism was based on his contempt for the small-mindedness of the naturalists, the narrowness of their political and social aims and the pettiness of their concern with the reproduction of external detail. 'When realism has outlived itself', says one of the characters in Wedekind's satirical comedy *Die Junge Welt* (*The Young World*), 'its representatives will earn their living as secret policemen.' Wedekind despised the respectable, social-democratic reformism of a man like Gerhart Hauptmann who tried to improve society without attacking its true basis, bourgeois morality. He saw himself as far more destructive, far less healthy and wholesome, but for that very reason far more *modern*, than Hauptmann, against whom he also bore a personal grudge, because Hauptmann had used some details about Wedekind's family background, which he had told him in strict confidence, as the basis of his play *Das Friedensfest* (*The Coming of Peace*) (1890).

In one of his sketchbooks Wedekind drew up a whole table of contrasting traits which marked Wedekind and Hauptmann as opposing archetypes: if Hauptmann was an altruist, Wedekind saw himself as an *egoist*; if Hauptmann belonged to the day-time, Wedekind felt himself as part of the *night*; if Hauptmann was an artist, Wedekind wanted to be a *thinker*; if Hauptmann belonged to the country Wedekind saw himself as part of the modern *city*; if Hauptmann corresponded to the character of Ibsen's Brand, Wedekind was *Peer Gynt*; if Hauptmann made himself out as an 'ethical being, who, however, achieves a brilliant career as a *grandseigneur*', Wedekind considered himself 'a practical man, who has to fight every step of his way'; and if Hauptmann was 'charming, but insincere, with insincerity, his pleasure in the beauty of empty words, spoiling his whole activity', Wedekind characterized himself as 'genuine, though loathsome'.

There is much truth in Wedekind's assessment. For Hauptmann, who outlived Wedekind by more than twenty-five years and died, after the Second World War in 1946, a chastened and disillusioned classicist, had – on the most charitable interpretation – at least allowed himself to be exploited by the Nazi régime as a propaganda asset, while Wedekind, who died in the last months of the First World War, has exercised a more decisive and more lasting influence and can, today, be seen as the far more daring, the more advanced, the more truly *modern* playwright.

Both Hauptmann and Wedekind had to transcend the phase of meticulously accurate external realism, just as Ibsen and Strindberg themselves had to pass beyond it, Ibsen into symbolism, Strindberg into heightened dream visions. Because, as Wedekind had so acutely observed, Hauptmann took pleasure in the beauty of empty words and laid undue stress on charm, because at the core of his sensibility there was a soft centre of sentimentality, Hauptmann transcended external realism by falling back into a sugary neo-romanticism. Hauptmann's *Hannele* (first performed in 1893; later re-named *Hanneles Himmelfahrt*) marks the point of transition; it also offers a most illuminating point of comparison with Wedekind's *Frühlings Erwachen* (*Spring's Awakening*), a play which also deals with the problems of children, and also progresses from purely naturalistic scenes towards an inner, dream-reality.

In Hannele we witness the death of a poor proletarian child in a workhouse. As Hannele lies dying she sees the heavenly hosts while the teacher she loves appears as the Saviour himself and leads her, delivering a speech in flowery verse, into the realms of eternal bliss, while an angelic choir sings a lullabye. It is a highly effective scene, but utterly sentimental. In *Spring's Awakening*, the schoolboy hero, Melchior Gabor, who has fathered an illegitimate child on a fourteen-year old girl and has indirectly killed her, because her parents took her to an abortionist, wants to commit suicide. In the cemetery his friend Moritz Stiefel, who killed himself because he could not face failure in his exams, emerges from his grave, carrying his head under his arm and invites Melchior to join him in death. A masked gentleman (whom Wedekind himself used to play) appears and pleads the case of life; and in the end Melchior decides that he will live.

Whereas in Hauptmann's play, therefore, the dream element is brought in to turn the tragedy of the child's death into comforting mush, in Wedekind's play the fantastic element is introduced to heighten the grotesque horror of the situation, even though, in the end, life conquers. So Hauptmann wallows in a sugary death, while Wedekind opts for an astringent, bitter and grotesque confrontation with the need to go on living.

In their subsequent development Hauptmann gradually receded into a pre-naturalist romanticism and eventually classicism, while Wedekind resolutely advanced towards an increasingly revolutionary and forward-looking attitude.

The significance of naturalism in the development of Modernism in drama lay with its adoption of the scientific attitude by postulating that, ultimately, *truth* was the highest value, and that beauty without truth was a contradiction in terms. The description of external surfaces *could* however, only be the first phase, for it soon became obvious that outward appearances could never be the whole truth. In the novel this led to the introspective method of the internal monologue, to Henry James's subjective narrator. In drama the consequences were Ibsen's use of symbols, Strindberg's dream plays, Chekhov's use of surface dialogue to point towards the hidden reality of the unspoken sub-text behind it – and Wedekind's resort to the heightened realism of grotesquely caricatured characters and situations. *Realism* remained the objective of all these efforts and experiments, but a realism *more* real, more profoundly *true* than that of merely external reality.

In Wedekind's case, his determination to reach a deeper layer of truth by grotesque caricature and black humour went hand in hand with the opening up of hitherto taboo subject matter. *Spring's Awakening* set a precedent by including a scene in a lavatory, into which one of the schoolboys consigns the picture postcards of nudes from the local museum which have formed the basis of his masturbation fantasies. (In 1900 Arthur Schnitzler (1862–1931) even put the sex act itself on the stage, in his brilliantly sardonic exploration of the social element in sex, *Der Reigen* (*The Round Dance*; later to become world-famous in the highly distorted and over-sugary film *La Ronde*). The book of the play circulated, but it did not reach the stage till 1920 – and then it became the subject of prosecution.)

Unlike Strindberg (whose second wife, Frida Uhl, bore Wedekind an illegitimate son – in 1897 – shortly after her marriage had come to grief; so strangely are personal antagonisms and attractions intertwined with the great controversies of literary history!) Wedekind was anything but a misogynist: he was a pioneer of sexual freedom, for men as well as for women, and played in Germany in the first two decades of this century the part which D. H. Lawrence assumed in Britain in the third and fourth. For Wedekind the separation of the spiritual from the carnal side of life was the ultimate heresy. For him the flesh had its own spirit, there was nothing indecent in nature; he saw sexuality as an elementary force, as powerful as the tides or the current of mountain streams, a force which man must tame, to be able to control it and use it to increase his happiness. But if this was to happen, Wedekind argued, then it must be made possible to discuss this force of nature as openly and objectively as any other natural phenomenon could be studied and talked about. *Spring's Awakening* is a powerful plea for the sexual education of children; and the two Lulu plays (written originally as one five-act play in 1892–4; later divided into two separate plays *Erdgeist* (*Spirit of the Earth*) and *Die Büchse der Pandora* (*Pandora's Box*) because there was no chance of getting the last two acts, involving lesbianism and prostitution onto the stage, so that Wedekind rounded off the first part into a self-contained play) which are usually regarded as portraying an evil *femme fatale* who is the death of all the men in her life, in fact make the opposite point: Lulu is a completely *natural* woman who spontaneously follows her sexual impulses; she has no evil intentions: the men in her life merely come to grief because of the irrational demands of conventional morality and respectability, which decrees that woman should be her husband's property and dooms any man whose wife cannot be wholly faithful to him to disgrace, ridicule and suicide. Lulu is a character of pristine *innocence*; it is society which is sick.

The influence of Wedekind's ideas about sexuality was immense. When he died Brecht, then twenty years old, called him 'with Tolstoy and Strindberg one of the great educators of the new Europe'.

But Wedekind's influence was not merely ideological. It was equally, and perhaps even more, decisive, on the technique of dramatic writing.

Because he despised the meticulous pedantry of naturalism and because he was essentially an ideologue, a fighter for his ideas, and because he used the methods of a satirist, a cartoonist, Wedekind was one of the main influences which moved dramatic writing away from the *Impressionism* of naturalistic drama which built up its effects from a multitude of minute details, a veritable *pointillisme* of theatrical technique. The mainstream continuation of naturalism, the symbolism of Maeterlinck, the late Ibsen; or the neo-romanticism of the later Hauptmann and Hofmannsthal also relied on subtle atmospheric effects; in Britain this tendency was represented by the drawings of Beardsley or plays like Wilde's *Salome*. Wedekind rejected the subtle half-tones of this *art nouveau* of atmospheres and moods. He opted for bold, direct effects. It is no coincidence that it is Wedekind who forms the first link between the tradition of German cabaret and the legitimate stage.

In 1901 the *Elf Scharfrichter* (*Eleven Executioners*) cabaret opened in Munich, the creation of a group of advanced writers and painters – the collaboration of painters and poets is one of the outstanding characteristics in the formation of these new trends – and it was here that Wedekind sang his own songs to the guitar. The cabaretistic element – the short sketch in bold strokes which aims at producing a heightened, compressed form of comment on social reality – is an important stylistic component of Wedekind's plays. Here impressionism gives way to the primacy of the *ideas* to be expressed – *expressionism*. It is, however, interesting that Wedekind refrained from using cabaretistic songs in his plays; it was Brecht who – very much under the influence of Wedekind – took that logical next step. On the other hand Wedekind liked using the imagery of the *circus* in his drama: the prologue to the Lulu plays, for example, is spoken by a trainer of wild animals who introduces Lulu as a dangerous snake.

All these endeavours must be seen as attempts to realize the original programme of the naturalists in a more far-reaching, more radical, more revolutionary manner. If the naturalists wanted truth, reality unvarnished and unadorned, then clearly the mere representation of surface detail would not do. The playwright had to get *behind* the mere surface of outward appearances, behind the polite small talk over coffee-cups which naturalism inevitably produced. On the other hand, the impulse to portray life as it really is led to a number of important discoveries which made stage dialogue more naturalistic than Ibsen, Zola or the early Hauptmann had ever thought of. It was Chekhov who realized that in dialogue what is not said explicitly, and hardly even hinted at by implication, very often is the decisive dramatic ingredient: in the last act of *The Cherry Orchard* Lopakhin's failure to declare his love for Varya is expressed indirectly under a surface of trivial dialogue about galoshes which have been mislaid. Wedekind on the other hand made another discovery which has had equally far-reaching consequences: he saw that people very often do not listen to each other, and that therefore in real life there is often no dialogue at all – merely monologues running on parallel lines. Again and again, in Wedekind's plays, we find such cross-cut monologues often with highly dramatic effect: for the audience the tension in seeing two characters talk to each other who are not communicating becomes almost unbearable: for they, the audience, realize what the characters are unable to see, namely that opportunities of establishing a relationship, of solving a problem are being tragically missed.

At the end of the first act of *Der Marquis von Keith* (*The Marquis of Keith*) (1900), the Marquis, who is in fact an impostor and floater of bogus companies, has been asked by his childhood friend Scholz to introduce him to the sensual delights of Munich; the Marquis's common law wife Molly, on the other hand, is trying to persuade him to abandon his dangerous career and to come and live snugly with her parents in the provincial safety of small-town Bückeburg. The dialogue which provides the first act curtain runs as follows:

MOLLY: So you are not coming to Bückeburg?
The MARQUIS: I'd like to know how we can make a sensualist out of *him*! [Scholz].

Here non-communicating dialogue achieves a striking effect of dramatic irony.

Wedekind himself must be seen in the context of an older tradition: the wild, revolutionary radicals of the *Sturm und Drang* (Storm and Stress) movement of the last quarter of the eighteenth century; the proto-realists of the early nineteenth century, notably Georg Büchner (1813–37) whose three astonishingly modern plays only reached the stage at the turn of the twentieth century; and Christian Dietrich Grabbe (1801–36) another wild and unhappy genius; and above all the revolutionary influence of the writings of Friedrich Nietzsche, whose attack on bourgeois morality and its Christian basis formed the starting point for Wedekind's attempts to formulate a new sexual morality. There can be no doubt that, quite apart from Wedekind's own influence, these were some of the basic sources of the movement which has become known as German Expressionism, although to this day there is still considerable doubt whether such a movement can actually be said to have existed.

The term Expressionism itself was coined in France in 1901 – by the painter Hervé who used it to describe artists like van Gogh, Cézanne, Matisse and Gauguin. In Germany it was first applied to poetry around 1910. By 1913 one of its early theoreticians characterized it as a movement distinguished by a striving for 'concentration, conciseness, impact, firmly structured form and the rhetoric of strong passion'. And the same critic, Leonore Ripke-Kühn, added: 'Gone are the days of half-tones and subtle nuances, of scintillating highlights in word, sound or colour, of tender abandon and all-embracing mingling of moods ... I believe we are again going to get some dramatists.'

This is the same impulse which drove a writer like Wedekind to reject naturalism and the subtle half-tones and neo-romantic poetical moods of the Symbolist movement which continued it. But the stance of the Expressionists was infinitely more radical than Wedekind's. Many of them – and it must be emphasized that the label 'Expressionist' has been applied to a wide variety of very different writers – completely rejected any preoccupation with outside reality. As another leading critic and theoretician of Expressionism, Kurt Pinthus, put it: 'in art the process of realization does not proceed from the outside to the inside, but from the inside outwards; the point is: inner reality must be helped to realize itself through the means of the spirit'. Wedekind's use of concretized inner realities, like the masked gentleman in the last scene of *Spring's Awakening*, certainly was an example of this tendency; but even more powerful was the influence of the late Strindberg, whose trilogy *To Damascus* (1898–1904) provided a model for the Expressionist type of play, often conceived as a human being's quest for spiritual regeneration through a series of stages on his upward path. For once the writer had decided to make his play the outward projection of an inner reality (which could only be the writer's own personal – and therefore egocentric – inner world) all drama of necessity reduced itself to *monodrama*, in which all other characters became either projections of the main character's own personality (hence Expressionist drama is full of *Doppelgänger* figures, characters which are merely aspects of the hero's personality which have split off and have taken on an independent existence) or mere ciphers seen from the outside, 'feeds' for the central character's musings with himself. The archetypal Expressionist play thus becomes a *Stationendrama* (a *passion* play in the sense that each scene corresponds to one of the stations of the cross on a road to redemption or to calvary). Having abandoned a concern for outward reality, the writers concerned lost interest in the individual characteristics of the people in their plays: the hero became simply the 'I' of the author, an undefined young man battling his way to self-realization, while the people he encountered on his way dwindled into 'A Man', 'The Father', 'The Mother', 'The Friend', 'The Girl', 'The Prostitute' (a favourite figure on this road to self-knowledge among Expressionist playwrights), etc.

In a monodrama there can be no real dialogue; hence Expressionist drama tends towards the self-declaratory statement. The hero faces the audience and *proclaims* his suffering and his aspirations. And because there can be no half-tones in an art striving for the maximum in intensity and expressiveness, these self-declaratory statements assume the character of *exclamations*. Expressionist drama of this particular type (which is the one which immediately springs to mind when Expressionism in the theatre is mentioned) is therefore a theatre of *cries*, a theatre of ecstasy, or at least frenzied intensity.

The style of the writing reflects this tendency: it is often exclamatory to the point where coherent statements tend to disappear. In Walter Hasenclever's (1890–1940) play *Die Menschen (Human Beings)* (1918) we find for example the following complete scene in a restaurant:

OLD WAITER: (*reads the paper*) Murder
THE GUEST (*lecherously*): The legs?
OLD WAITER: The head's missing
THE GUEST: One Beer!
ALEXANDER (*enters with the sack through the curtain*)
THE GUEST: Sex Crime?
OLD WAITER: Reward
THE GUEST: The Bill!
OLD WAITER: One roast beef
THE GUEST: A man?
OLD WAITER: 3.90
THE GUEST: (*exit*)
ALEXANDER: Human beings!
OLD WAITER: Alexander!
ALEXANDER: Where am I?
OLD WAITER: Missing

This, admittedly, is an extreme case, bordering on self-parody: there is hardly one more extended speech in the whole play. But this extreme case does illustrate one of Expressionism's predominant traits. Another, corresponding trait, however, is extreme wordiness, long speeches, in prose and verse, and often of an exasperating abstractness. Yet even in these long speeches the striving for a maximum of intensity leads to a cramped, over-emphatic and jerky style which is the hallmark of German Expressionist theatre. It is exceedingly difficult to render this effect in English – one of the reasons why German Expressionist drama has had so little impact in the English-speaking world. But it may be worth while giving an example – from one of the very best of these plays, *Die Bürger von Calais* (*The Burghers of Calais*) (1914) by Georg Kaiser (1878–1945). The play tells the story of the siege of Calais by King Edward III of England in 1346. The town cannot defend itself, the English king is determined to punish it for betraying its allegiance, total destruction seems inevitable. Yet the King relents: if six of the town's citizens are willing to die, he will spare the rest. The leading citizens heroically vie with each other for the honour of sacrificing their lives: seven volunteer, only six are needed. The decision at the end is: the last to arrive at the appointed hour when they are to go to their death, can go scot-free. Six arrive, the seventh, Eustache de Saint-Pierres, is still missing. Should he, who was thought the noblest of them all, have lost his nerve? At this moment his old, blind father appears with his son's corpse. Eustache de Saint-Pierres has killed himself to spare the others the pain of deciding who should escape death. Eustache's father addresses the remaining six burghers as follows:

Seek your deed – your deed seeks you: you are called! – The door is open – now the wave of your deed is rolling out. Does it carry you – do you carry it? Who cries out his own name – who grabs fame for himself? Who is the doer of this new deed? Are you heaping praise upon yourselves – does this desire stir within you? – The new deed does not know you! The rolling wave of your deed buries you. Who are you still? Where do you glide with your arms – hands? – The wave rises up – propped up by you – billowing over you. Who throws himself above it – and destroys its smooth sphere? Who devastates the work that has been accomplished? Who hurtles himself higher and rages at the whole? Who separates limb from limb and disturbs perfection? Who shares the task which is laid upon all? Is your finger more than the hand, your thigh more than your body? – The body seeks the service of all the limbs – the hands of one body create your work. Through you rolls your work – you are the road and the wayfarers upon the road. Something and nothing – in the greatest and in the smallest – in the smallest the most important. With your weakness a part of all – strong and mighty in the sweep of unity! (*His words echo across the market place. Visionary, vivid*) Step out – into the light – from this night. An august clarity has arisen – the darkness is dispersed. From all the depths the conclusion is a lightness seven times silvery – the enormous day of days lies out there! (*Stretching one hand across the bier*) He announced it – and lauded it – and awaited in gay exuberance the bell that would toll to a feast – then he raised the cup in his steadfast hands from the table and drank upon calm lips the juice which burned him . . . I come from that night – and shall go into no other night. My eyes are open – I shall not close them again. My blind eyes are good not to lose it again: – I have seen the new man – in this night he has been born! Why should it still be difficult – to go? Does not already at my side roar the surging stream of the new arrivals? Billows there not emotion, which acts – in me – beyond me – where is an end to it? Into a creative upsurge I am set – I live – I step from today into tomorrow – indefatigable in all – imperishable in all – (*he turns, the boy carefully leads him off right, his steps re-echo through the street*).

Adequate translation of such a passage is well-nigh impossible. Yet it must be said that the original is certainly as opaque, as stilted and as over-emphatic as the translation, if anything more so, as the very spirit of English is far too soberly practical ever to be capable of containing the compressed passion – *pathos* in the German sense – of Kaiser's writing. Yet all that this long speech states is: that Eustache has demonstrated that unity and self-sacrifice are the foundation of true strength and that in such self-sacrifice the *new man* has been born. The *new man* is the central, key concept of Expressionist drama. Again and again the Expressionist playwrights made their heroes call upon this new man. Hence, in Germany at the time, one spoke of the whole movement is that of the '*Oh Mensch*' drama.

There is a sense of urgency, of impatience behind all the over-emphasis, the excessive intensity of these plays. And no wonder: it was a movement of young people who became aware of themselves and the world in a period of impending war, were then engulfed in the horrors of that most horrible of all wars, and emerged – those of them who had not perished in the trenches, as many of them did – into the new horrors of defeat, abortive revolution and post-war misery and materialism. The first truly Expressionist play to be publicly performed was probably Oskar Kokoschka's *Sphinx und Strohmann* (*The Sphinx and the Straw Man*); Kokoschka's fellow-students in the Vienna College of Applied Art acted it out in 1907 – a weird, symbol-laden allegory of masked marionettes, an Expressionist painting come to life. But the main upsurge of Expressionist drama only began in 1910; and by 1924 the movement had spent itself.

Urgency and impatience lie behind the wildly truncated sentences of the explosive outcries of Hasenclever's *Die Menschen* just as much as behind the ecstatic rhetoric of Kaiser's *Burghers of Calais*. The *new man* had to be created in a hurry, at once! And he had to emerge against the opposition of the old man, the father. Essentially German Expressionist drama revolves round the father/son conflict.

Reinhard Johannes Sorge's (1892–1916) play *Der Bettler* (*The Beggar*), written in 1910, when the author was eighteen years old, is the first full-length Expressionist play. It deals with a young poet who is trying to find himself, to become the new man, and who in the course of his journey from one station of his calvary to the next, kills both his parents – not because he hates them, but because he *pities* them for being old, fossilized and irredeemable. Sorge was killed in the war, in 1916, at the age of twenty-four. His play was first performed in December 1917.

Arnolt Bronnen's (1895–1959) play *Vatermord* (*Parricide*) (1920) is equally typical of this archetypal theme of Expressionism. Here a tyrannical father is tormenting his young son; he, in turn lusts after the mother, who half repels, half seduces him. The play ends in a scene of characteristically over-compressed and over-intense action. The mother is about to seduce the son; as she stands naked before him the father bursts into the room, there is a struggle in the course of which the son stabs the father with a knife. As the father lies dead in a pool of blood, the mother says:

FRAU FESSEL: Come to me oh oh ohh come to me.

WALTER: I am fed up with you/I am fed up with everything/Go bury your husband you are old/But I am young/I don't know you/I am free/

No-one in front of me no-one beside me no-one above me the father dead/Heaven I am jumping up to you I fly/Everything presses

trembles groans laments is compelled upwards swells surges explodes
flies is compelled upwards compelled upwards

I

am in bloom

(The unorthodox punctuation is the author's; and, of course, part of
the personal style he was developing.)

The violence of these plays is overwhelming; and yet it is allied with
a radical – one is tempted to say – ultra-violent pacifism. It has been
said that the extremism of the Expressionists foreshadowed the extreme
violence of the Nazi régime and its concentration camps and mass
murders. And there is certainly a grain of truth in this observation.
Bronnen himself, at the time he wrote *Vatermord* Brecht's closest
friend and constant companion, and of the radical left, became a
supporter of the Hitler régime: after the war he reconverted himself
to Communism and died in East Germany. Another Expressionist
dramatist Hanns Johst (1890–) became the head of the Nazi writers'
organization; other Expressionists remained committed to the extreme
left.

All the violence, ecstasy, urgency and impatience of the Expressionist generation adds up to a truly touching naïvety (very reminiscent in many ways of the equally pure, violent, naïve and touching
manifestations of the counter-culture of the period of the Vietnam
war and the 1968 Paris student riots). An example which, I think, is
typical and can best convey the flavour of this child-like belief in the
power of simple ideas like the unity of mankind is Ludwig Rubiner's
(1881–1920) drama *Die Gewaltlosen* (*The Non-violent Ones*) (written
1917–18, first performed 1920).

One of the heroes of the play, Klotz, the leader of a revolutionary
movement confronts the governor of the prison who interrogates him:

THE GOVERNOR: . . . I tell you: abandon your activity.

KLOTZ: No, Governor.

THE GOVERNOR: Do not believe that your defiance arouses respect in
me. There is no point in it.

KLOTZ: No, there would be no point in it. But it is not meant to impress, nor is it defiance.

THE GOVERNOR: What, then, is it?

KLOTZ: It is my faith.

THE GOVERNOR: Your faith? But do you not see that it has led you
astray?

KLOTZ: No.

THE GOVERNOR: All fanatics are like this. They have their faith, and the other person has none, or a false one.

KLOTZ: I know; Governor, you too are a human being.

There follows a discussion about power: Klotz asks the Governor whether he really wants to hurt other human beings.

KLOTZ: ... you must know: I am free. Here in prison. You are not free. You have everything to lose, I nothing. I am the one who can offer you a gift.

THE GOVERNOR: You? A gift?

KLOTZ: The gift of a human being: freedom.

THE GOVERNOR: Yes, with words!

KLOTZ: If you want it, with deeds! – Do you want it?

THE GOVERNOR: What?

KLOTZ: The ultimate.

THE GOVERNOR: And?

KLOTZ: Come with me?

THE GOVERNOR: Look around you. All this is me. The whole house is me. This lamp burns through me. The guards' steps outside, which you are hearing, happen through me. If it were not for me, all this would be emptiness. These walls sway. Everything crumbles in a moment and in its place there is a heap of rubble, on which children and dogs play.

KLOTZ: Say the word: no longer a prison; instead a heap of rubble on which children and dogs play. Through you. Miraculous day!

THE GOVERNOR: But I must not.

KLOTZ: Then leave me here and go alone.

THE GOVERNOR: Here are my hands, as empty as they is my life. I need nothing. I am alone. Solitary. The other who comes after me will leave everything as before and my leap will have been for myself alone.

KLOTZ: Ah, one man only, who makes the leap; a single one who becomes wholly aware that he is a human being: and you have destroyed all the power in the world. You would be invincible, a seed flying through the air, invisible, omnipresent, through all the walls, and after that all the power in the world would fall apart like a rotten shack in the damp air. You are Man. You are: all of us. And only he who would dare, unaware, to take your place and continue to make the wheels of power creak on, only he would be alone. Terrible would he be among the new human beings, hollow, doomed to a certain crash into deadly oblivion, like a rotten telegraph pole blown down by the wind. Power lies behind you. You are free. You know that you are free! Come!

THE GOVERNOR: My power? This bunch of keys here on the table is my power. This is the key to my flat. This the key to my desk. And this to my room. And this is the key to my decisions. Here they are. Take them. I give them to you. With these little pieces of forged iron you command the world.

KLOTZ: Take the keys back. I do not want them. I do not need them. I do not command.

THE GOVERNOR: You stand so far from me, that I cannot even stretch out my arms towards you. This floor is a jagged mountain-range. Can I still save myself?

KLOTZ: You are saved, you are beyond death. Now go.

THE GOVERNOR: I am free, I know it. But where am I to go?

KLOTZ: To the human beings.

THE GOVERNOR: Who are they? I am a human being, you are a human being. Is it not presumption to go? I was born and created into this world, in which I have lived. If I go with you, is that not a lie? I command armies and win battles. Tomorrow the sun will rise, and I shall command armies of human beings, and human beings will allow themselves to be commanded by me! Does anything change? Power remains. I know too much about human beings. I am alone. I am no brother.

KLOTZ: No, you are no longer alone. Nobody is alone. Each of us is a giant, a burning sun in space; it shines mild and small into a sick-room, and only there someone becomes aware of it. Ah, I feel it, power is dead within you; but you are still trembling before that knowledge? Oh stretch out your hand for the first time, not to command but to help. Turn your head, for the first time, not to judge, but to lead. You have been born out of millions of generations into the light, to be a human being, fluttering in the wind, wholly among human beings...

At last the Governor is won over.

THE GOVERNOR: Where? Where?

KLOTZ: Into our Empire [*In unser Reich*]. With you we shall build the new earth. Brother! We are waiting for you.

THE GOVERNOR: You are waiting for me?

KLOTZ: Yes. In freedom, in love, in community: to free all mankind! Cast off your servitude, be free – free! A human being, which you really are! Push the fear from you! Help mankind! You – our brother!

THE GOVERNOR: To be a human being. – Brother. – I go with you!

Only by quoting a scene like this at some length (and in the original it is very much longer) can one give a flavour of the atmosphere, the 'feel' of the Expressionist generation, of that truly tragic mixture of purity, of idealism, of naïve simplicity, of poetry and empty rhetoric. It is touching that a radical idealist like Ludwig Rubiner should really have believed that abstract speeches about mankind would, in a few minutes, turn a prison governor into the leader of a revolution and make him hand over the keys of the prison to one of its inmates. But it is also frightening: for, inevitably, the disillusionment on contact with reality, when a real revolution really took place, and developed along totally different lines, was bound to have the most far-reaching consequences. It was this disillusionment which turned into violence and totalitarianism, of the right and of the left. The terminology of 'our *Reich*'; of freedom and brotherhood remained the same, but it became allied to brutal *realpolitik*; and it was the impatience, the pressure of urgency which characterized all the Expressionists that converted itself into the short-cuts of the most extreme measures, like the extermination of whole groups of human beings who were felt to be unclean or evil.

It must also be said, that, artistically, on the whole, German Expressionist drama was a failure. Perhaps it was the impatience of the writers which kept them from developing their talents, which induced them to remain in an area of grandiloquent rhetoric, schematic characterization, careless plotting. It is above all, however, the *language* of these playwrights which disappoints. And it is through their language, after all, that the Expressionists aspired to be *modern*. Newfangled their language certainly appeared: with its strange inversions, omitted definite articles, contortions of syntax, concentration, explosiveness, accumulation of adjectives, its incessant string of climaxes. But – with very few exceptions – the passage of time has shown up all these devices as mere trickery which served to conceal a profound *lack of originality*, of genuine poetic or linguistic invention. The long speeches in plays by writers like Toller or Hasenclever now seem no more than leading articles shouted at the top of the speaker's voice. Sorge's or Bronnen's assaults against the older generation have become positively comic. And, indeed, one of the Expressionists' great short-comings (very much in contrast to their model, Wedekind) is their monumental lack of a sense of humour. When Hasenclever announced that he had decided to write comedies, this amounted to and was received as no less than his renunciation of Expressionism.

Very few of the Expressionists are still performed: it is, perhaps, more than a coincidence that the only one among them whose plays are still popular on the German stage is the one who stood nearest to Wedekind in keeping in close touch with social reality and in having a sense of humour: Carl Sternheim (1878–1942), the author of a cycle of six plays under the generic title *From the heroic life of the Bourgeoisie* (*Aus dem bürgerlichen Heldenleben*). The first of these *Die Hose* (*The Knickers*) (1909–10) is the most famous: Theobald Maske is a small civil servant whose rise to fortune is founded on an incident in which his wife disgraced herself by losing her knickers in public during a royal procession. A number of bystanders have been so in-flamed by witnessing this truly 'unspeakable' event that they try to meet and win the favours of Frau Maske by becoming lodgers in her house. It is through exploiting these lodgers – who do not succeed in their objective – that Maske achieves his social advancement. The respectable bourgeois, in other words, is no better than a pimp. Two other plays of the cycle deal with the further fortunes of Maske and his family: *Der Snob* (1913) and *1913* (written in 1913–14).

These and the remaining three plays in the cycle – *Das Fossil* (*The Fossil*), *Die Kassette* (*The Strongbox*, probably Sternheim's most popular play today) and *Bürger Schippel* – are well constructed, witty and amusing. But they too suffer from a linguistic handicap: their clipped, inverted style frequently contradicts the naturalness of the situations, which, after all derive their impact, from the accuracy and acuteness of the observations on which their social satire is based. By omitting the definite article, by using highly artificial sentence structures Sternheim seems to be asserting his status as an original, a reformer of language, a major intellectual dramatist, as though he feared that without these devices his plays might be taken to be no more than conventional social satire.

If Sternheim is the most frequently performed of the Expressionists in the contemporary theatre, the most talented and interesting writer among them was undoubtedly Georg Kaiser (1878–1945), a playwright of immense inventiveness. Kaiser's plots are often brilliantly original, tautly constructed and full of suspense. Yet Kaiser's linguistic perversity is such that even his best works are rarely performed today. His search for compression led him – as in the lengthy passage from *The Burghers of Calais* quoted above – into obscurity and – even worse – over-intensity which to our present-day sensibility appears as no more than bombast. In reading Kaiser's splendidly conceived plots one often longs for an adaptor who might be able to translate the dialogue into more acceptable language.

Kaiser was very prolific: the recent collected but far from comprehensive edition of his works contains no less that forty-two completed plays. His subject matter ranges from Greek mythology (*Europa*), Celtic legend (*König Hahnrei* (*King Cuckold*), the story of Tristan and Iseult seen from King Mark's point of view), medieval history (*The Burghers of Calais, Gilles und Jeanne* (*St Joan and Gilles de Rais*)), biblical themes (*Die jüdische Witwe* (*The Story of Judith*)), eighteenth-century Paris (*Der Brand im Opernhaus* (*Fire at the Opera*)), ancient Athens (*Der gerettete Alkibiades* (*Alcibiades Saved*) – how Greek philosophy arose from a thorn in Socrates' foot) to contemporary social satire and serious philosophical exploration of the problems of wealth and power. Best known among these – and one of the few of Kaiser's works to get performed in the English-speaking world – is *Von Morgens bis Mitternacht* (*From Morning to Midnight*) a typical *Stationendrama* which shows a little bank cashier who is tempted to embezzle a large sum of money from his bank and vainly tries to find satisfaction from his wealth until, after a series of episodes, he shoots himself.

Most impressive, however, and also most characteristic of Kaiser as an Expressionist is the trilogy *Die Koralle* (*The Coral*) (1917), *Gas* (1918) and *Gas, Part II* (1919–20). The first play tells the story of an immensely rich industrialist, the Milliardaire, whose motivation in acquiring his wealth has been his flight from the horrors of the poverty of his childhood. The Milliardaire has a secretary who is his exact double (he was chosen for that reason, so that he could relieve his master at boring official functions). When the Milliardaire learns that this secretary looks back on a blissfully happy childhood he kills him so as to be able to assume his personality and acquire his happy past.

When he is condemned to death for the murder of himself, he goes to his execution happy in the knowledge that he now has a happy youth to look back on. The coral of the title is the sign of identity by which the Milliardaire and his secretary could be told apart. Having acquired that coral the Milliardaire has acquired the symbol of a happy life. When the clergyman who assists him in the death cell holds up the cross, the Milliardaire clutches the coral as an alternative and more potent consolation.

In the second part of the trilogy, *Gas*, the Milliardaire's son, whom revulsion against his father's wealth has made a socialist, has given the factory to the workers. But the workers, who now own all this wealth, have become so greedy that they neglect safety, and the whole factory explodes. The Milliardaire's son now decides that the factory should disappear; in its place he wants to build a garden city. But the workers, led by a materialist technician, demand the rebuilding of the factory, even if that means that there will be other destructive explosions in the future.

In *Gas, Part II* the factory has been rebuilt and enlarged; it now works for the armaments industry. A world war is in progress between blue and yellow armies. The Milliardaire's great-grandson is the 'new man' of this play: he calls upon the workers, who have become slaves of the production process, to go on strike. But the yellow armies occupy the works and force the workers to resume their labours. The chief technician of the factory, 'the great engineer', has invented a new deadly poison gas: with this, he tells the workers, they can regain their old power. But the Milliardaire's socialist grandson calls upon them to abandon work altogether and evokes the green garden city utopia of his forebear. In the confrontation between the utopian dreamer and the practical technician, it is the latter who seems to have the sounder case; he wants to use the workers' power for their own good. The utopian socialist, in his defeat, however, breaks the poison gas container and destroys everything.

There can be no doubt that, in its basic conception, Kaiser's trilogy would still be topical half a century after it was written. But the perversity of its language and the schematism of its characters militate against it. His acute intelligence earned Georg Kaiser the sobriquet '*Der Denkspieler*' ('the player with thought'). Yet one frequently feels that his plays are no more than brilliant first drafts of the works he could have written had he not also been beset by the characteristic vice of the Expressionists, impatience.

None of the other German Expressionist playwrights can approach Kaiser or Sternheim in importance or achievement. The one who came nearest to finding a measure of recognition in the English-speaking world was Ernst Toller (1893–1939), who had a number of his plays translated into English in the early thirties, after he had become a refugee from Hitler; yet he reached no more than a decent mediocrity. His personality and career were more interesting than his writing: he played an important part in the short-lived Bavarian Communist régime in 1919 and spent a considerable amount of time in prison after its suppression, aroused much sympathy when he became a refugee, had one of his late, no longer Expressionist, anti-Nazi plays, *Pastor Hall*, filmed in England and committed suicide in New York in 1939.

Ernst Barlach (1870–1938) a sculptor of genius, also expressed his sense of doom and mystical belief in the need for a confrontation between God and Man in a number of strange, haunting plays in which the landscape of the East German lowlands appears closely akin to that of the Russian steppes. Fritz von Unruh (1885–1971), the scion of a famous military family, served as an officer in the First World War and became an ardent pacifist. His two most important plays *Ein Geschlecht (A Family)* (written 1915–16, first performed 1918) and *Platz (The Place)* (1917–20) are verse dramas of great intensity: in the first play the children revolt against the mother who has borne them into a world of strife; she dies with a vision of a new world of peace before her. In the second play the youngest son abandons his efforts to create a new form of society, because he realizes that violence can not transform man himself; the play ends with his declaration of his belief in the power of love. It is significant that there is a certain amount of controversy among critics and interpreters of this latter play whether it was meant in earnest, or is, in fact a parody of the worst excesses of Expressionism. Another Expressionist who dealt with the theme of war was Reinhard Goering (1887–1936) whose play *Seeschlacht (Naval Battle)* (1917) shows the seven members of the crew of a gun turret in a warship during the battle which ends with their annihilation. Alfred Brust (1891–1934) wrote plays as broodingly

East European as Barlach, but remains always on the border of the unintentionally comic. Franz Werfel (1890–1945) was undoubtedly one of the most gifted writers active in the Expressionist vein; his 'magic trilogy' *Der Spiegelmensch* (*Mirrored Man*) (1920) is a vast verse drama about man's quest for his true self: the existential ego divides itself from the ego of make-believe, and this, the mirror-self, becomes a kind of Mephistophelian evil influence on the road through the three worlds: of the spirit of eros and of the mirror-values, glory and power. The disappearance of the false, make-believe, mirror-self marks the emergence of the new, mature, spiritual man. Werfel, who was also one of the leading poets of Expressionism, soon abandoned it and became a vastly successful best-selling novelist, playwright and Catholic convert. He died at Beverly Hills, having achieved fame as the author of the novel from which the film *The Song of Bernadette* was made, and of the Broadway hit *Jakubowsky and the Colonel*. Werfel, like Kafka, came from Prague. His countryman Paul Kornfeld (1889–1942) who died in a Nazi extermination camp in Poland wrote a number of plays in the Expressionist vein, before he too took up a more realistic style. He was also one of the movement's most lucid theoreticians. His most important play *Die Verführung* (*The Seduction*) (written 1913) embodies his rejection of psychological motivation by taking a motiveless murder as its starting point. The hero is condemned to death, but his purity leads the authorities to allow him to escape; at first he refuses, but eventually a young girl seduces him into the world and life; the girl's brother, however, is outraged and poisons the hero.

Here too, talented though the writing undoubtedly is, the over-intensity of the emotions and the language to which it gives rise, result in old-fashioned melodramatic bombast. If the symbolism and neo-romanticism of the playwrights who had previously reacted against naturalism led to what must be regarded as a return to an earlier, pre-Modernist style, most of the products of the Expressionist drama of the period between 1910 and 1924 can now be seen in a similar light: behind all the radical ideology, the pacifism, the extremism and the violence of these plays there lay little more than the over-emotional, supercharged melodrama of previous epochs in which loud-voiced periwig-pated fellows tore passions to tatters.

In the best work of Sternheim and some of the most viable plays of

Kaiser it is the element of the grotesque which has best survived the passage of time. There can be little doubt that it is this element which had the greatest potential for the development of a really modern style. One of the most interesting figures on the fringe of the Expressionist movement was Heinrich Lautensack (1881–1919) a Bavarian playwright who appeared with Wedekind in the Munich cabaret *Die Elf Scharfrichter* and who wrote some very funny and irreverent grotesquely caricatured comedies about the intimate life of the Catholic clergy, such as *Die Pfarrhauskomödie* (*The Parsonage Comedy*) (1911). Lautensack who was mentally unbalanced had acquired a considerable sum of money by writing film scripts. When Wedekind died, he invested this capital in engaging half a dozen cameramen who were posted along the route of the funeral procession to make a record of Wedekind's last journey. 'When the last words had been spoken at the graveside he rushed forward, threw his hands in the air with a tragic gesture and exclaimed: "Frank Wedekind – your unworthy pupil Lautensack!" At this the soil gave way under his feet and he slid into the grave. Poor Lautensack died soon afterwards of paralysis.' Among the crowd at Wedekind's graveside on that 12 March 1918 was Bertolt Brecht who regarded Wedekind as his master.

Yet before we can deal with Brecht, whose work is a unique synthesis of a number of other influences beside that of Wedekind and the German Expressionist playwrights, we must consider some of these other trends, which, of course, all have a good deal in common as they all sprang from the common roots of the intellectual and artistic climate of Europe at the turn of the century.

2

In France as in Germany the first and most important reaction against naturalist drama was the symbolism of playwrights like Maurice Maeterlinck (1862–1949) with its heavy emphasis on half-tones of mood and atmosphere. But, as in Germany, there was also an almost simultaneous parallel reaction which stressed the grotesque, and aimed at a maximum of directness. The first appearance of this tendency on the stage was undoubtedly the memorable première of

Ubu Roi (King Ubu) by Alfred Jarry (1873–1907) at the Théâtre de l'Oeuvre on 10 December 1896.

Jarry, one in the line of French *poètes maudits* from Villon to Charles Cros, Corbière, Rimbaud and Verlaine, an eccentric who haunted the cafés of the left bank and died young from over-indulgence in absinthe, fiercely rejected all subtleties of mood and atmosphere: he was out to shock a bourgeois audience by confronting them with a monstrously exaggerated image of their own greed, a horrid caricature of their own competitive lives. *Ubu Roi*, and the other Ubuesque plays which followed it, is a wild parody of a Shakespearian history: the hero is a monstrously fat puppet-like figure who is determined to make himself King of Poland and to this end indulges in wholesale murder and deceit. W. B. Yeats who was present at the first performance of *Ubu Roi* was deeply shocked, and not only by the opening line, *Merdre!* which had immediately unleashed a storm of protest. 'The players', he reported in *The Trembling of the Veil*, 'are supposed to be dolls, toys, marionettes, and now they are all hopping like wooden frogs, and I can see for myself that the chief personage, who is some kind of King, carries for a sceptre a brush of the kind that we use to clean a closet.' As in Germany the connection between the literary Post-Impressionists and the Post-Impressionist painters was close. Jarry was a fervent admirer of the Douanier Rousseau (who in turn wrote two delightfully outrageous plays, as childlike and naïve as his paintings) and it is significant that the scenery for *Ubu Roi* which, in the style of a child's painting, represented several contradictory venues simultaneously – indoors and outdoors, tropical and arctic landscapes – was designed by Jarry with the active cooperation of painters like Vuillard, Bonnard, Sérusier and Toulouse-Lautrec. No wonder that Yeats' verdict was '. . . after all our subtle colour and nervous rhythm, after the faint mixed tints of Conder, what more is possible? After us the Savage God.'

So violently hostile was the reaction of the public to *Ubu Roi* that Jarry's experiment remained an almost isolated instance of Post-Symbolist drama in France. Its direct successor, Guillaume Apollinaire's *'drame surréaliste'*, *Les Mamelles de Tirésias (The Breasts of Tiresias)* reached the stage more than twenty years after Ubu, on 24 June 1917, although Apollinaire claimed that most of it had been written as far back as 1903. Apollinaire, the chief propagandist and theoretician of the Cubist school of painters, coined the term *surrealist* for this play:

> . . . I have coined the adjective 'surrealist' which does not mean symbolical . . . but rather well defines a tendency of art that, if it is no newer than anything else under the sun, has at least never been utilized to form an artistic or literary creed. The idealism of the dramatists who succeeded Victor Hugo sought likeness to nature in a conventional local colour that corresponds to the *trompe-l'oeil* naturalism of drawing room comedy . . . To attempt if not a renewal of the theatre, at least a personal effort, I thought one should return to nature itself, but without imitating her in the manner of a photographer. When man wanted to imitate the action of walking he invented the wheel, which does not resemble a leg. He thus used Surrealism without knowing it . . .

Surrealism for Apollinaire thus meant, as for the Expressionists, truth to nature at a deeper and more expressive level than that of the mere reproduction of surfaces. *Les Mamelles de Tirésias* is a wild extravaganza which hardly lives up to the theoretical pretensions of its author. The main character, Thérèse, changes sex and turns into Tiresias, her breasts floating upwards as toy balloons. And all this happens to further Apollinaire's obsession that the ravages of the war must be compensated by a strenuous effort to repopulate France. Thus Tiresias, in the play, produces no less than forty thousand and forty-nine children.

From the movement represented by Jarry and Apollinaire, by the Post-Impressionist and Cubist painters, sprang a number of the *avant-garde* trends which dominated European art and literature throughout the twenties and thirties right down to the present day: Surrealism, Dadaism, Futurism.

It is significant that the founder of the Italian Futurist movement, Filippo Tommaso Marinetti (1876–1944), spent his formative years in Paris and wrote his first poetry and plays in French. His somewhat Ubuesque drama *Le Roi Bombance*, which portrays a war between the fat and the lean, and ends with the revolutionary victory of the lean over the fat, written in 1905, was performed at the Théâtre de l'Oeuvre on 1 April 1909. While Marinetti's fairly voluminous dramatic output never made a lasting impact on the stage, his theories and manifestos have continued to exercise a profound, though often 'overlooked, influence. His first Futurist Manifesto about the theatre, dated 'Milan, 29 September 1913' starts with the statement:

We are profoundly bored with the contemporary theatre (verse, prose and musical) because it fluctuates stupidly between historical reconstruction and photographic reproductions of our daily life: a pedantic, slow, analytical and diluted theatre, worthy at best of the age of the paraffin lamp.

FUTURISM EXTOLS THE VARIETY THEATRE

because: 1. The Variety Theatre, born as we are, from the age of Electricity, fortunately has no tradition of any kind, neither masters, nor dogmas, and is nourished from the fast-moving actuality of our lives. 2. The Variety Theatre is absolutely practical, for it aims at entertaining and amusing its public with effects of comedy, erotic excitement and imaginative shock . . .

There follow seventeen further reasons why the Variety Theatre (or Music Hall) is the model of Futurist drama: among these we find its utilization of the then still-new cinema, its conciseness, its inventiveness, its speed, its contempt for old-fashioned ideas of romantic love, its contempt for anything solemn, sacred, serious and sublime, its insistence on physical fitness and daring (Marinetti later became one of the chief supporters of Fascism).

Two years later there followed a second *Manifesto* on the Futurist theatre, dated January/February 1915 and signed by Marinetti, Emilio Settimelli (1891–1954) and Bruno Corra (born 1892) in which they call for a 'synthetic futurist theatre'. Here the emphasis is on brevity, speed and conciseness – in a spirit similar to the impatience and feeling of urgency of the German Expressionists. 'It is stupid to write a hundred pages when one would be sufficient.' Logic and verisimilitude are equally denounced. Instead the demand is for our 'ULTRAMODERN CEREBRAL CONCEPT OF ART ACCORDING TO WHICH NO LOGIC, NO TRADITION, NO AESTHETICS, NO TECHNIQUES . . . SHOULD BE IMPOSED UPON THE GENIUS OF THE ARTIST WHOSE SOLE PREOCCUPATION MUST BE WITH THE CREATION OF SYNTHETIC EXPRESSIONS OF CEREBRAL ENERGY WHICH HAVE ABSOLUTE NOVELTY VALUE . . .' Here too the parallel with the ideas of the German Expressionists is very striking.

Unlike the German Expressionists, however, the Italian Futurists produced few plays of lasting value, perhaps because, following their principles, their best work consisted in ultra-short sketches, which they called 'syntheses' and which amounted to no more than a few lines, at best a page or two. Marinetti himself produced a number of more substantial works: in *Poupées électriques* (*Electric Dolls*) (1909) he used, in accordance with his belief in technological means, mechanical puppets to express the inner life of characters which appeared split in two; while in *Simultaneità* (1915) he showed two different worlds – lower and upper-class – simultaneously on a divided stage, until in the end the upper-class world invades the other side and sweeps their possessions under the table.

Yet, however little Italian Futurism produced in the theatre of its own country, its long-term influence was deep and world-wide.

Strangely enough the first immediate impact of Futurism made itself felt in Russia where, as early as October 1913 a group of painters and poets, among them Casimir Malevich (1878–1935), one of the originators of abstract painting, and Vladimir Mayakovsky (1893–1930) the leading poet of the Russian Revolution, organized an evening of readings and recitations of Futurist poetry. Significantly enough the Russian group, although directly under the impression of Marinetti's manifestos, called itself the 'cubo-futurists', a sign how closely Cubism and Futurism seemed allied in their eyes.

The first theatrical manifestation of the Russian Cubo-Futurists was the performance of Mayakovsky's play *Vladimir Mayakovsky* at the St Petersburg Luna Park on 2 December 1913. The title of the play was to have been *The railway*, then *The revolt of objects* and thirdly *Tragedy*. It was under this title that the play was submitted to the censor; he passed it, but in issuing his permit mixed up the title and the author, so that the licence was for a tragedy called *Vladimir Mayakovsky*. To get that changed would have involved a repetition of the tedious bureaucratic procedure, so Mayakovsky decided to stick to the new title. Ironically, the title the censor had bestowed on the play was probably the most appropriate that could have been found. For the play shows Mayakovsky himself (he also played the part in the performance) surrounded by a number of strange characters somewhere in a modern city. There are echoes of Oedipus in the play, parodies of works by the Russian Symbolists, notably Alexander Blok, and it ends with Mayakovsky, Oedipus-like, taking the city's guilt upon himself. All the characters in the play are – as in so many German Expressionist works – emanations of the author. As the great critic and theoretician of Russian formalism, Victor Shklovsky put it

In the tragedy *Vladimir Mayakovsky* the poet is completely alone. People walk around him, but they are not three-dimensional. They are ... painted posters ... The poet has divided himself on the open stage, he holds himself in his hand like a card-player his cards. This is Mayakovsky: Ace, King, Queen, Knave. The play is about love. It is lost.

Mayakovsky's later plays, *Mysterium Buffo* (1918), *The Bedbug* (1928–9) and *The Bathhouse* (1929–30) are more accessible than his first play: they are more openly grotesque and satirical, but nevertheless inspired by the same impulse as his early Cubo-Futurist work, and certainly among the most successful examples of Futurist-inspired drama, closely akin to the best in German Expressionism.

Mayakovsky's *Vladimir Mayakovsky* was essentially a *monodrama*. Another important champion of Modernism in Russia at the same period, who experimented with monodrama and wrote a book on it, was Nikolay Nikolayevich Evreinov (1879–1953), a director and playwright of immense inventiveness and talent who exercised a considerable influence on the great Russian directors of his time, notably Meyerhold and Tairov. Evreinov's theory of monodrama clearly has much in common with the work of the Expressionists in Germany. Among his many plays one of the most interesting and significant in the light of subsequent developments is the short sketch *V Kulisakh Dushy (Behind the Scenes of the Soul)* (1912) in which the action takes place inside the body of the only character, a man called Ivanov, who is on the point of having to decide whether to stay with his wife or to run away with a nightclub singer. Ivanov's emotional self urges the cause of the seductive tart, his rational self dangles the madonna-like image of his wife, the mother of his child, before him. In the end the two conflicting parts of the self strangle each other; at this moment an immense gash opens in the heart which has been beating in the background (we have been watching the inner conflict happening on Ivanov's diaphragm, the place where the ancient Greeks placed the soul) – Ivanov has shot himself. At this moment a third character, dressed in travelling clothes, who has been sleeping in the background, rises and takes up his suitcase – while a railway porter is heard calling 'All change!'. This is the immortal part of Mr Ivanov who will now have to move elsewhere. This little play anticipates the theatre of inner reality of a much later era and foreshadows much of Ionesco and Beckett (notably *Endgame*).

The most immediate and most widely felt impact of the Russian *avant-garde*, however, came through the Russian Ballet of Diaghilev and the work of his designers and musicians.

Nor must it be forgotten that a good deal of the inspiration for the further development of Modernist movements in Western Europe came from other parts of Eastern Europe. In Romania the founders of the review *Symbolul* (*The Symbol*) which began publication in 1912 included Tristan Tzara and Marcel Janco, who were among the creators of Dadaism. And the poet who wrote under the name of Urmuz, in real life a respectable magistrate named Demetresco (1883–1923) can be regarded as a precursor of Surrealism and is recognized as one of his chief inspirations by Eugène Ionesco.

In Poland the reaction against Symbolism, whose main representative in the field of drama had been Stanislaw Wyspianski (1869–1907), was embodied in the work of the brilliant painter and playwright Stanislaw Ignacy Witkiewicz (1885–1939), who also called himself Witkacy; a man of many parts who had served with the Russian Imperial Guard and accompanied the anthropologist Malinowski, who was a close friend of his, on expeditions to the South Seas, Witkiewicz painted in a style akin to that of the Expressionists, but also foreshadowing much of present-day psychedelic painting – he experimented with taking drugs – and wrote grotesquely dream-like dramas that anticipate much of the Theatre of the Absurd of the fifties and sixties; he is acknowledged by the present-day Polish *avant-garde* as their model and master.

The First World War acted as a catalyst to many of these tendencies by bringing painters and writers from many parts of an embattled Europe together in the neutral haven of Switzerland. It was in Zürich that the Dadaist movement crystallized on 2 February 1916 with the formation of the Cabaret Voltaire in premises in the old town right opposite the house inhabited by another important exile, Lenin. Here the Rumanians Tzara (1896–1963) and Janco (1895–) collaborated with German pacifists like Hugo Ball (1885–1948) and Hans Arp, the sculptor and poet (1887–1966), and performed plays like Oskar Kokoschka's *Sphinx and Strawman* – a connecting link between the early Expressionist movement and Dada. The first and only number of their periodical, also called 'Cabaret Voltaire', contained contributions from Apollinaire, Picasso, Kandinsky, Marinetti and Modigliani. The aims of the Dadaist were simple enough: the destruction of the bourgeois concept of art as a sacred and solemn ritual. The emphasis was on the grotesque, the nonsensical, the shocking: the cramped and starry-eyed idealism of the German Expressionists was as alien to the Dadaists as the pompous traditionalism of the Académie Française.

After the war Paris and Berlin became the centres of continuing activity. In Paris Dada gave theatrical manifestations (one could not call them plays or performances) in 1920 and 1921 during which sketches by Tzara, Soupault, Ribemont-Dessaignes, Aragon, Benjamin Péret, André Breton and others were staged at the same Théâtre de l'Œuvre which, a quarter-century before, had witnessed the scandal of the first night of *Ubu Roi*.

The French Dadaist movement itself produced little of lasting value in drama. Nor did the Surrealist movement, which emerged from it, with the exception perhaps of Roger Vitrac's (1899–1952) plays of which *Victor ou Les Enfants au Pouvoir (Victor or Power to the Children)* (1924) still holds the stage. Yet another Surrealist, Antonin Artaud (1896–1948), who wrote few plays of lasting significance, became the theoretician of a new total theatre in which movement, inarticulate sound and the sheer magic of the stage would reduce language to its proper and no longer dominant position. This concept of a Theatre of Cruelty (the cruelty here stands for the seriousness with which the performance is to affect and transform the spectator rather than merely titillate him) has become one of the dominant influences on the theatre of the sixties and seventies, on great directors like Peter Brook and Jerzy Grotowski.

The German Dadaists who returned from Zürich to Berlin and Munich after the end of the First World War were less playful, more decisively political than the French movement (although that too sympathized with the Russian Revolution and Communism). A link between the French and the German groups and also with the Expressionists was formed by Yvan Goll (1891–1950) a poet bilingual in

French and German – he came from Alsace-Lorraine – who had also spent some of the war years in Switzerland where he met Arp and other Dadaists. A follower of Jarry and Apollinaire, Goll, like Marinetti, was deeply influenced by the cinema. He published two plays under the joint title *Überdramen* (super – i.e. surreal – plays) in which he used film and mechanized actors. In another play *Methusalem* one of the characters appears split into three distinct sections of his ego. The resemblances with Marinetti as well as Evreinov are thus quite evident. The published version of *Methusalem* (1922) is preceded by a preface from Georg Kaiser and contains designs by George Grosz, who, together with John Heartfield, was responsible for designing the stage performance (Königsberg, 1922). Grosz and Heartfield were among the leaders of the Berlin Dadaists.

The exuberant Dadaist antics of the Berlin group (Grosz, Heartfield, Arp, Huelsenbeck, Ball, Mehring) were too destructive to last. Heartfield – one of the inventors of photomontage – and his brother Wieland Herzfelde became the founders of a publishing house, Malik-Verlag, which developed into a centre for the publication of deeply committed left-wing material, notably the products of the new literature of Soviet Russia.

Brecht was a close friend of the Herzfelde brothers and of George Grosz. In the light of subsequent strenuous efforts by the followers of the official Soviet line about socialist realism, it may appear difficult to realize the close connection between Communist tendencies and *avant-garde*, formalistic, introspective, phantasy-inspired and futuristic movements like the abstract art of Malevich and Kandinsky, the Cubism of Picasso and Juan Gris, the wild exuberance of Kokoschka and the German Expressionists, the exaltation of a mixture of technology and warlike manliness by Futurists like Marinetti, the Constructivism of a Gabo or Lissitzky, Dadaism, Surrealism and, indeed, the anarchic nihilism of Brecht's early period. Nevertheless that connection is not only a historical fact; it is also due to a genuine organic relatedness of all these modernistic tendencies in literature, drama, painting, sculpture and, indeed, music (after all Brecht's closest collaborators among left-wing composers were Weill, a pupil of the Modernist Busoni and Hanns Eisler, a pupil of Schoenberg).

In the theatre Expressionism's greatest influence may well have been less in the achievement of the Expressionist playwrights than in the work of great directors like Leopold Jessner or Erwin Piscator, whose impact is still very much with us. The element of Expressionism in the work of Bertolt Brecht (1898–1956) lies as much in this practical side of staging – for Brecht was also a great director and wrote all his plays with the eyes and imagination of a practical man of the theatre – as in his writing. More important among the early influences on Brecht than that of Expressionism was certainly that of Wedekind (and his predecessors Büchner and Grabbe); the German cabaret; the popular theatre of the Munich beer-halls, as exemplified by Brecht's idol, the great beer-hall comedian Carl Valentin (1882–1948) whose humour was closely akin to that of the Theatre of the Absurd; the cruel grotesquerie of the more destructive side of Dadaism, the music hall and the sports arena, extolled as examples by Marinetti; and the revolutionary futurism of the plays of Mayakovsky as staged by Meyerhold. In Brecht all these various tendencies, which had produced interesting but flawed experiment in the theatre, at last found a triumphantly successful synthesis.

Brecht's work as a playwright falls roughly into three, at times overlapping periods: his early, pre-Marxist anarchically exuberant style (roughly 1918–28); his severely didactic period of Marxist *Lehrstücke* and more popular anti-Nazi propaganda (1928–38); and his mature style of large-scale parable plays (1938–48). In the last eight years of his life Brecht concentrated on production rather than playwriting.

At the start of his career Brecht was under the influence of Expressionism, but, at the same time, already reacting against it. His first completed play *Baal* (1918) was written as an answer, and indeed, a parody, of an Expressionist play, Hanns Johst's bombastic biographical drama about the drunken early-nineteenth-century precursor of Expressionism, the playwright Grabbe. In one of the versions of *Baal* Brecht inserted quotations from the more ridiculously extreme Expressionist poetry; and the hero of the play, the anti-social poet Baal, is clearly intended to parody the ludicrously egocentric hero of the typical Expressionist *Oh-Mensch* drama, just as the construction – a sequence of short scenes in the picaresque story of Baal's life – reproduces the Expressionist *Stationendrama*. All this may be parody – and yet, with the true ambivalence of a real poet, Brecht has also infused a great deal of genuine feeling, even a degree of autobiographical self-identification, between himself and Baal, into the character of the wild bohemian whose destructiveness is merely an expression of his mystic belief that life has to be accepted in all its beauty *and* horror.

Another, perhaps the most important, of Brecht's early plays *Im Dickicht der Städte* (*In the Jungle of the Cities*) (1923) also has many of the hallmarks of the Expressionist theatre, notably in the exuberance of its language, but it also reflects some of the ideas of the Futurists – drama as a sporting contest, the rejection of psychology – and anticipates, in its insistence on a *motiveless action*, a sequence of logically inexplicable events, much of Surrealist and Absurdist drama. There can be little doubt that close contact with the Dadaist circle and its ideas played its part in shaping this play.

What distinguishes Brecht from his contemporaries who pursued similar ideas, however, is the fact that he was able to find a way out of the dead end of destructiveness for its own sake or the somewhat infantile playfulness which characterized many of the Dadaists and Surrealists without, at the same time, falling victim to the empty and bombastic idealism of the Expressionists. Like many of his contemporaries he reacted against both these tendencies by a return to sober objectivity, the *Neue Sachlichkeit* (New Objectivity) of the midtwenties which found one of its chief expressions in the applied art of the Bauhaus; but unlike many of his contemporaries he also managed to anchor this new attitude in a practical creed, Marxism. For Brecht Marxism was, and always remained – often in contradiction to the evidence of brutal facts – an ideology of pacifism and human friendliness and cooperation.

The best plays of his didactic period, however, also mirror some of the lessons learned from the Expressionists: the masterpiece of this didactic style *Die Massnahme* (*The Measures Taken*) (1930) uses the Expressionist technique of presenting a highly schematized action with nameless types rather than fully developed characters. What is missing is merely the windy rhetoric and cheap sentiment with which an equally committed Expressionist like Toller might have approached the subject.

In his mature period, in the years of his exile in Scandinavia and later the United States, Brecht achieved a brilliant synthesis between the anarchic exuberance of his first, and the austerity of his didactic style. The great parable plays, *Mother Courage*, *The Life of Galilei*, *The*

Good Woman of Setzuan, Puntila, The Caucasian Chalk Circle, have enough human detail to lift them above the stark schematism of Expressionist drama; yet they are conceived as more than merely anecdotal accounts of the lives of particular people: they are parables designed to teach and to illustrate basic problems of human behaviour. These great plays freely use Expressionist and other techniques derived from the Modernist *avant-garde* of the first quarter of the century, but fuse them all into a wholly satisfying stylistic unity. It is ironical that, in Stalin's time and for quite a long period after that, official Soviet opinion condemned Brecht for using masks, introducing surreal effects and grotesque exaggerations which strongly reminded them of the Futurism of Meyerhold and Mayakovsky they had so brutally condemned.

Seen from today's vantage point the work of Brecht and his followers as well as that of the Absurdists, who finally fulfilled the aims which the Dadaists and Surrealists had vainly struggled to attain in the theatre, can be regarded as the twin culminations of the revolt against naturalism; both trends, ultimately, amount to a resolute rejection of stage illusion. Brecht's concern was with means and ways of representing *contemporary reality* in the theatre: he felt that a rigid photographic reproduction of the external lives of individuals simply could not do justice to the complexity of the innumerable social, economic and political factors which determine life in a highly structured, over-organized society. That is why he agreed with Piscator, who illustrated his plays with documentary films, projections of statistical information and excerpts from newspapers. Eventually he found his own solution in the stylistically more unified and artistically more satisfying form of the parable play, which does not conceal its didactic purpose and makes it quite clear that its whole action is no more than a demonstration of general truths by actors who do not even have to pretend that they imagine themselves to be identical with the characters they portray; Brecht wanted his actors to be able to step outside their roles and even to show to the audience that they disapproved of the actions of the characters they were embodying. Very similarly Marinetti, who extolled the music hall where the performers always remain themselves, the Dadaists, who appeared as themselves, the Surrealists, who projected their dreams and nightmares, and playwrights like Ionesco or Beckett, who tend to portray an inner, dream-reality with the techniques of the music hall, also treat the stage quite openly as a stage instead of pretending that it is the real world seen through a missing fourth wall.

This, however, is simply the position as it existed before the naturalists developed their demand for a strictly realistic theatre.

The movement which began with Wedekind and culminated in Brecht and the Absurdists, although it sailed under the flag of an extreme Modernism, can thus be seen, ultimately, as an attempt to return to the age-old tradition of theatre in which naturalism was merely one brief episode.

NEO-MODERNIST DRAMA:
YEATS AND PIRANDELLO

JAMES MCFARLANE

I

IN 1917, Apollinaire instructed the theatre public to prepare itself for innovation. *'On tente ici d'infuser un esprit nouveau au théâtre'* ('One is trying here to infuse a new spirit into the theatre'), he announced in the prologue to *Les Mamelles de Tirésias* (*The Breasts of Tiresias*) (a play on which he had been engaged for some fourteen years); and he went on to outline a set of proposals which were meant to inaugurate a wholly new departure, a distinctly fresh start. His personal concept of theatre was one of a number of separate and distinct and yet mutually reinforcing assaults in these years on the prevailing dramatic tradition – assaults which, when taken together, have encouraged many critics to identify in these years a distinctively second-stage Modernism, a 'Neo-Modernism', in twentieth-century European drama.

From what in the *detail* of its change was a dauntingly complex development, two main strands can be separated out. The first was the desire to liberate the contemporary theatre from its continuing naturalistic constraints – physical (the 'missing fourth wall') as well as ideological (the 'slice of life') – by the introduction of new methods of staging and the encouragement of freer intercourse with other art forms. The second was the emergence of a deeply and destructively *ironic* attitude to naturalistic reality, a determination to replace the illusionistic counterfeiting of reality by the recognition of the profounder reality of illusion. Of the first of these developments, Yeats (following Apollinaire) is the supreme representative; of the second, Pirandello. They find common ground in their obsessive preoccupation with *masks*.

2

Two specific areas were marked down by Apollinaire for contemptuous repudiation: one was the form and arrangement of the contemporary theatre, *'une scène ancienne'* ('an ancient theatre') as he called it dismissively; the other was the 'centuries-old pessimism' that hung over the plays which this form of theatre engendered. He wanted the theatre to be an arena of uninhibited and voluptuous joy, in which the arts and the techniques of music hall, circus and ballet should contribute towards a new and twentieth-century form of *Gesamtkunstwerk*. He envisaged a multi-purpose, multi-media theatre which would triumphantly inaugurate

> *Le grand déploiement de notre art moderne*
> *Mariant souvent sans lien apparent comme dans la vie*
> *Les sons les gestes les couleurs les cris les bruits*
> *La musique la danse l'acrobatie la poésie la peinture*
> *Les choeurs les actions et les décors multiples . . .**

Within this new diversification lay a rich promise. In the view of Francis Fergusson, the most interesting writers for the stage between 1918 and 1939 – among whom he includes Yeats, Eliot, Cocteau, Obey and Lorca – find in these new sources the opportunity for a completely fresh start: 'The influences of the Moscow Art Theatre, the Ballet, and the Music Hall, combine to produce a new conception of the theatrical medium. Not only nineteenth-century naturalism, but most European drama back through the seventeenth century, is explicitly rejected in favour of medieval farce, Greek tragedy, peasant rituals and entertainments.'[1] Yeats's deep-rooted impatience with the constraints of naturalism found in these and related things a new source of strength. Taking his cue from Ezra Pound, and finding seminal inspiration in the Japanese *Noh* plays, he 'invented' (as he claimed) a new form of drama in his *Plays for Dancers* (though he was quick to acknowledge that this newness was in a sense age-old): 'My blunder,' he wrote in 1916, 'has been that I did not discover in my youth that my theatre must be the ancient theatre that can be

*'The grand deployment of our modern art – merging, without apparent connections as in life, sounds, gestures, colours, cries, noises, music, dancing, acrobatics, poetry, painting, choruses, actions, and multiple *décor*.'

made by unrolling a carpet or marking out a place with a stick, or setting a screen against the wall.'[2]

Over the first twenty years or so of his dramatic authorship – from *The Countess Cathleen* of 1892 to the publication in 1911 of his *Plays for an Irish Theatre* – there was little of distinction (or even, apart from the dedicated Irishness of the works, of distinctiveness) to mark Yeats out among his European Symbolist contemporaries. Implacably anti-naturalistic, and unremittingly hostile to the angular problematics of Ibsen and Shaw, he hated *A Doll's House*: 'What was it but Carolus Duran, Bastien-Lepage, Huxley and Tyndall all over again? I resented being invited to admire dialogue so close to modern educated speech that music and style were impossible ... As time passed Ibsen became in my eyes the chosen author of very clever young journalists who, condemned to their treadmill of abstraction, hated music and style. . .' He stood aghast at the sheer energy of *Arms and the Man*, which seemed to him to offer only 'inorganic, logical straightness and not the crooked road of life'.[3] He denied that drama had any business with reason or proof or the onward march of an argument, and asked that it should come flooding over us like some great tide, 'the drowner of dykes, the confounder of understanding'. It must turn its back on all things 'that can be codified for ready understanding'; its way was to move us 'by setting us to reverie by allowing us almost to the intensity of trance'; the spectator must feel his mind expand convulsively, or 'spread out slowly like some moon-brightened image-crowded sea'.[4] To set drama to work pleading the National Cause, or insisting on the Ten Commandments, or discussing abstractions or the immediate circumstances of life or the things of the brain only was an abuse; the theatre should be the home of 'mysterious art doing its work by suggesting, not by direct statement, but by complexity of rhythm, colour and gesture'.

For him, as for Maeterlinck and Strindberg, the fairy tale exerted a deep fascination; from it he fashioned a mode of drama both delicate and powerful. In *The Countess Cathleen* he turned, not for the last time, to Irish medieval legend; and although the atmosphere of the setting in cottage and castle – the portentous calls of animals and birds, the obtrusive omens – give the impression of being derivatively Maeterlinckean, it is doubtful whether at this early stage in his authorship Yeats was in any way familiar with Maeterlinck's work, though that familiarity grew swiftly, both from the theatre and from the printed page, as the decade progressed. A sense of quiet brooding and of intense longing, the simple profundities and the eloquence of silence create for these early dramatic works a world of Maeter-linckean outline; it is peopled by characters greatly preoccupied with their search for the one scene, the one adventure, the one picture which is the image of their secret lives. Intensity, simplicity, quietude are their goals, yearning as they do for 'that far household where the undying gods await all those whose souls have become simple as flame, whose bodies have become quiet as an agate lamp'.[5]

His hostility to the use in drama of the pallid phrases of 'modern educated speech' was matched by a faith in the poetic resources of Irish peasant speech; his own (and, following his encouragement, Synge's) use of the rhythms and images of spoken peasant language was the first of a number of attempts over the following years else-where in Europe to do something comparable – the supreme example being of course Lorca, but including also some of the earlier works of Pirandello. Yeats came very soon to recognize also that the achievement was not merely the replenishment of the sources of dramatic language but the articulation of values and views which would otherwise have remained unexpressed, the opening up of new and previously unplumbed 'deeps of the mind'. When in 1919 he reflected on what he and his fellows had achieved by their endeavours, he defined it as 'the first doing of something for which the world is ripe, something that will be done all over the world and done more and more perfectly: the making articulate of all the dumb classes each with its own knowledge of the world . . .'[6]

To give assent to Edmund Wilson's much-quoted paradox that Yeats's greatest contribution to the theatre was not his own plays but those of Synge (whom, in 1896, he discovered stagnating in Paris and induced to return to Ireland) is to focus attention too exclusively on the plays of his Abbey Theatre period and to neglect the very great seminal significance of the later dramas from 1916 onwards. For, as Eliot rightly remarked, Yeats only found his right and final dramatic form in the *Four Plays for Dancers* and other plays of his later years. Two things combined to give them their distinctive character. On the one hand there was the fact – which Yeats would surely be the first to give assent to – that his was a mind of promiscuous habits: 'I have always sought,' he admitted, with considerable understatement, 'to bring my mind close to the mind of Indian and Japanese poets, old women in Connaught, mediums in Soho.' A roll-call of those who at one time or another had held his attention would have to include – alongside those with more obviously literary connections such as Blake and Shelley, Maeterlinck and Villiers de l'Isle Adam and the French Symbolists – the names of thinkers and mystics and works from Plotinus and Boehme and Swedenborg and the Kabbalah, to Mme Blavatsky and the Theophists, Rabindranath Tagore and the Japanese *Noh* plays. From the complex chemistry of these elements were produced Yeats's mature views on the proper role of drama. As one critic has put it: 'The forms of Irish myth, the ideas and cosmology of Buddhism, and the dramaturgy of *Noh* would restore drama to its original sources and theatre to its only valid function, the evocation of a sacred presence.'[7]

The other realization was more formal. The mature Yeats, like the mature Strindberg before him, came to recognize that the sheer bigness of the contemporary theatre inhibited genuine drama. He found that the theatre with its mass audience was not giving him a sympathetic hearing; he felt himself 'sitting behind the wrong people'; he realized he was beginning to shrink away from the forbidding elaborateness of organization, the man-management side, the daily rehearsals. Like Strindberg, he then gave himself to the creation of *intimate* theatre, to the composition of chamber plays, with few props and no stage machinery, communicating not to a mass audience but to a small and discriminating group. He 'invented a form of drama, distinguished, indirect, and symbolic and having no need of mob or Press to pay its way' – to use his own words.[8]

The over-riding concern was to achieve a distanced intimacy: to counterbalance this new intimacy of setting with a new and organic separating strangeness. This strangeness was entirely different from the 'bodily distance' which the mechanicalness and noise of the contemporary theatre created; it was to be achieved by 'human means', by ritual, stylization, the formalization of the dance, by abstractive transposition into music, by the de-personalizations of the mask – the creation not of artificial worlds of elaborate sets and of reproduction reality, but of a distanced world with its own inherent authenticity:[9]

All imaginative art remains at a distance and this distance once chosen must be firmly held against a pushing world. Verse, ritual, music and dance . . . must help in keeping the door . . . The arts which interest me, while seeming to separate from the world and us a group of figures, images, symbols, enable us to pass for a few moments into a deep of the mind that had hitherto been too subtle for our habitation.

The innovatory significance of these later highly formalized dramas, sustained as they were by 'verse, ritual, music and dance', the imaginative use of masks and the consequent diminution in the importance of 'character' – a complex term in Yeats – did not win immediate critical recognition. But they can now be seen to have played a decisive part in creating conditions where 'poetic drama' – a term quick to take on a 'distinctly effete and pejorative meaning'[10] – was once again possible in Europe; and to have inaugurated the intensive exploration of a number of elements in drama that had long suffered neglect. The later theatrical tradition of *Waiting for Godot* and *Fin de parti* – it is argued – can be seen to have its origins in *At the Hawk's Well*, *The Cat and the Moon* and *The Herne's Egg*.[11]

3

The naturalistic belief, associated supremely with Henry James, that the one merit on which all others 'helplessly and submissively depend' is the writer's capacity to produce the 'illusion of life' met its greatest challenge in Pirandello. In his case, however, it was not an attack from without, such as one finds in the direct hostility of Apollinaire, Yeats and Eliot, but a reduction from within, a spinning convoluting assault that turned on – and turned in upon – itself to find, deep down within, the sources of decay. It led not to simple repudiation but to the discovery of the inner contradiction to which all mimesis is exposed: that the imitation of reality is not immediately distinguishable from the imitation of an imitation, and that spuriousness has a genuine and enduring reality which is not often recognized.

Fascinated by the interpenetration of appearance and reality, of object and reflected image, of face and mask, Pirandello achieved in his pitiless honesty a kind of second-degree naturalism, the sophistication of which announces itself in the title he gave the ten-volume edition of his collected dramas: *Maschere nude* (*Naked masks*). It proclaims the paradox that man is only able truly to be himself when wearing the mask, for only then does he feel free to discard pretence. In a very real sense, the naked face *is* the mask; and, conversely, only the wearing of the mask allows genuine revelation.

That which is recognizably and plausibly real – the essence of conventional naturalism – becomes at this new level the palpably false; but at the same time, the 'new' reality is still only illusorily real, still only meta-illusion. *Six Characters in Search of an Author* (1921) – like many of his other dramatic explorations of reality and illusion, especially *Right You Are, If You Think You Are* (1922) and *Henry IV* (1922) – first violates our willingness to suspend belief, then at once offers restitution under new terms of reference. Pretence of any kind – and his plays examine countless manifestations of it: impersonation, deception, disguise, masquerade, the 'antic disposition' – is always both a pretended reality and a real pretence, relative to the (indeterminate) standpoint of the observer. In essence, it is between these two poles – the lying nature of appearance and the truth of the lie – that Pirandello's dramas oscillate.

There are moments when Pirandello is discovered, as in *Six Characters*, removing *two* 'fourth walls' where orthodox naturalism would be content to remove one: the first is the wall lying in the plane of the proscenium arch, the other is that 'front of the house' that separates the fictive life of the theatre as a whole from the everyday life outside. The stage is set as a stage-set; the theatre becomes theatre; and two levels of existence coalesce. The 'illusory reality' of the one order of existence yields to the 'real illusion' of the next, *gedichtete Wahrheit* to *wahre Dichtung*. The audience is granted not only a spectacle (in the Aristotelian sense) but the spectacle of a spectacle; the action reaches out to encompass itself; a new and extra dimension is introduced to give not so much a play *within* a play as a play *beyond* a play.

The problem of identity, of the nature of the self, is followed through rigorously to its *illogical* conclusion. As the Father in *Six Characters* points out, a fictional figure has an enduring life of its own, has a permanence and stability that comes from a specific and unchanging text; this is what gives identity, makes the invented character 'a somebody', whilst a real-life person may well be 'a nobody'.

He puts it to the Manager: 'Don't you feel the ground sink beneath your feet as you reflect that this "you" which you feel today, all this present reality of yours, is destined to seem mere illusion to you tomorrow?' Always the emphasis is on the mutability, the essential discontinuity of the individual ego. Man's nature, as much in its social manifestations as in its psychological, is an elusive and unstable and even illusory thing. No fixed coordinates are at hand by which to measure identity; the naturalistic faith in a determinism of natural (inherited) or contrived (environmental) forces is rejected. Certainty about one's role or purpose in life is unattainable.

Truth is indeterminate; all accounts conflict. Ponza's explanation, in *Right You Are, If You Think You Are*, of the triangular relationship between himself, his wife and his mother-in-law – a not wholly plausible account that imputes insanity to others and confesses to personal duplicity – is completely at odds with the equally unconvincing account given by the mother-in-law. Truth hangs concealed and suspended within a web of pretence, deception, illusion, allegation, imputation, delusion and madness. When, towards the end of the play, the one person appears who might be in a position to sort out the contradictions in the two accounts – the wife, Signora Ponza – she is heavily (and symbolically) veiled; she declines to give the lie to either of the accounts, and affirms both. 'For my own part,' she insists, 'I am what people think I am.'

In *Henry IV*, Pirandello crosses and re-crosses a very tortuous stretch of frontier between appearance and reality, sanity and insanity, the guileless and the feigned. Twenty years before the play begins, the hero allowed himself an innocent and wholly voluntary act of pretence: he attended a masquerade dressed as the Emperor Henry IV. Thrown from his horse and injuring his brain, he is condemned in his derangement to continue the pretence. But now the masquerade is an imposed and involuntary one. When after some years his sanity returns, he nevertheless sees continuing advantage in 'playing the lunatic'; and in his feigned madness, he once again appears to regain control of things. Finally, however, in a moment of anger he stabs and kills one of his visitors, and sheer self-preservation requires that he continue the pretence. Not only must he go on *seeming* to be unbalanced, but by his act of murder he has perhaps become 'in reality' unbalanced, even to himself who knows so much more than the mere outside observer. Superimposed upon this (in itself) complex action is a further highly wrought overlay of allusions and cross-references between the twentieth-century Henry on the one hand and the historical Emperor Henry IV on the other, between the modern Matilda and the earlier Marchioness of Tuscany, and between the two social and political situations. The result is a virtuoso piece of dramatic writing, and quintessentially Pirandello.

Everything in Pirandello's world is in flux; all is relative. What is 'reality' there but (as Leone Gala puts it, in *The Rules of the Game*) 'a ceaseless flow of perpetual newness which reason breaks down into so many static and homogeneous particles'? (In later life, Pirandello was in the habit of declaring that his contribution to modern drama had been to 'turn reason into passion'.) There is no fixed point from which to start making calculations. Words are among the least reliable of things. The Father, in *Six Characters*, notes that any idea we may have of enjoying a shared meaning in words is sheer delusion: 'We think we understand each other, but we never really do understand.' Communication between individuals is in any real sense impossible; and in this melancholy insight the individual sees even more clearly his essential isolation.

It has taken much time to see just how deep and pervasive Pirandello's influence on twentieth-century drama has been, and indeed continues to be. He has been hailed as 'the most seminal dramatist of our time',[12] and the Einstein of the drama,[13] responsible for an entire revolution in man's attitude to the world. Connections are established between his work and the anti-illusionist theatre of Brecht, of Thornton Wilder, of Peter Weiss. He is seen straddling the cross-over point of two distinct dramatic traditions, completing the 'process of Romantic internalizing begun by Ibsen and Strindberg',[14] and anticipating and provoking some of the most significant advances in later European drama: by his agony over the nature of existence, he anticipates Sartre and Camus; by his insight into the disintegration of personality, Beckett; by his assault on received ideas, Ionesco; by his exploration of the conflicts of reality and appearance, O'Neill; and by his probing of the relationship between self and persona, actor and character, face and mask, the work of Anouilh, Giraudoux and Genet.

James McFarlane

Notes

1 Francis Ferguson, 'James's Idea of Dramatic Form', *Kenyon Review*, vol. V (1943), pp. 506–7.

2 Yeats, Notes to his *Four Plays for Dancers* (1921).

3 Yeats, *Autobiographies* (London 1955), p. 279 and p. 283.

4 Yeats, 'The Tragic Theatre', in *Essays and Introductions* (London 1961), p. 245.

5 Yeats, 'The Philosophy of Shelley's Poetry' (1900), in *Essays and Introductions* (London 1961), p. 95.

6 Yeats, 'A People's Theatre', in *Plays and Controversies* (London 1923), p. 206.

7 Thomas Parkinson, 'The Later Plays of W. B. Yeats', in *Modern Drama: Essays in Criticism*, edited by T. Bogard and W. I. Oliver (New York 1965), pp. 388–9.

8 Yeats, 'Certain Noble Plays of Japan', in *Essays and Introductions* (London 1961), p. 221.

9 ibid., pp. 224–5.

10 J. Chiari, *Landmarks of Contemporary Drama* (London 1965), p. 81.

11 Thomas Parkinson, 'The Later Plays of W. B. Yeats', in *Modern Drama: Essays in Criticism*, edited by T. Bogard and W. I. Oliver (New York 1965), p. 392.

12 Robert Brustein, *The Theatre of Revolt* (London 1965), p. 316.

13 Martin Esslin, *Reflections: Essays on Modern Theatre* (New York 1971), p. 47.

14 Robert Brustein, *The Theatre of Revolt* (London 1965), p. 316.

Chronology of Events

COMPILED BY JAMES MCFARLANE
IN COLLABORATION WITH ROBIN YOUNG

KEY

Ang British, American, English-language
Fre   France, French-language
Ger Germany, Austria, German-language and Netherlands
Lat   Spain, Italy, Latin Europe
Nor Scandinavia and Northern Europe
Sla   Russia, Eastern Europe, Slavonic countries

The author's date of birth is given in brackets, except in the case
of works published posthumously when the date of death is
given, shown 'd'.

1890

Ang   Frazer (1854) *The Golden Bough* (2 vols;
           12 vols 1911–15)
       James, H. (1843) *The Tragic Muse*
       James, W. (1842) *Principles of
           Psychology*
       Whistler (1834) *The Gentle Art of
           making Enemies*

William Morris founds
    Kelmscott Press
Free elementary
    education established
    in England
Founding of Rhymers'
    Club
Sherman Anti-Trust
    Law

Fre   Claudel (1868) *Tête d'Or*
       Maeterlinck (1862) *Les Aveugles*
       Villiers de l'Isle Adam (d. 1889) *Axël*
       Zola (1840) *La Bête humaine*

Ger   Bahr (1863) *Zur Kritik der Moderne*
       George (1868) *Hymnen*
       Holz (1863) and Schlaf (1862) *Die
           Familie Selicke*
       Langbehn (1851) *Rembrandt als
           Erzieher*

Fall of Bismarck,
    succeeded by
    Caprivi; repeal of
    Socialist Law
Freie Volksbühne
    established in Berlin
Van Gogh dies

Lat

Nor   Hamsun (1859) *Hunger*
       Ibsen (1828) *Hedda Gabler*
       Strindberg (1849) *By the Open Sea*

Sla   Tolstoy (1828) *Kreutzer Sonata*

1891

Ang   Gissing (1857) *New Grub Street*
Hardy (1840) *Tess of the D'Urbervilles*
Howells (1837) *Criticism and Fiction*
Kipling (1865) *The Light that Failed*
Moore (1852) *Impressions and Opinions*
Morris (1834) *Poems by the Way*
Pinero (1855) *The Times, Lady Bountiful, The Profligate*
Shaw (1856) *The Quintessence of Ibsenism*
Whitman (1819) *Good Bye, My Fancy*
Wilde (1854) *Picture of Dorian Gray*

The Saga Library begun, edited by Morris and Magnusson
The Chase Act regulates copyright in the United States
The Independent Theatre established in London

Fre   Barrès (1862) *Le Jardin de Bérénice* (3 vols., 1888–91)
Gide (1869) *Les Cahiers d'André Walter*
Huysmans (1848) *Là-Bas*
Mallarmé (1842) *Pages*
Verhaeren (1855) *Les Flambeaux noirs*
Verlaine (1844) *Bonheur*

Gauguin travels to Tahiti
Rimbaud dies

Ger   Bahr (1863) *Die Überwindung des Naturalismus*
Dehmel (1863) *Erlösungen*
George (1868) *Pilgerfahrten*
Hofmannsthal (1874) *Gestern*
Holz (1863) *Die Kunst, ihr Wesen und ihre Gesetze*
Wedekind (1864) *Frühlings Erwachen*

Lat

Nor   Garborg (1851) *Weary Men*
Lagerlöf (1858) *Gösta Berling's Saga*

Sla

1892

Ang	Bosanquet (1848) *History of Aesthetic*	Tennyson dies
	Kipling (1865) *Barrack Room Ballads*	Whitman dies
	Pinero (1855) *Cabinet Minister, Hobby Horse*	
	Shaw (1856) *Mrs Warren's Profession*	
	Swinburne (1837) *The Sisters*	
	Zangwill (1864) *Children of the Ghetto*	
Fre	Claudel (1868) *La Ville*	Renan dies
	Gide (1869) *Traité du Narcisse*	
	Maeterlinck (1862) *Pelléas et Mélisande*	
Ger	Fontane (1819) *Unwiederbringlich*	*Blätter für die Kunst*
	George (1868) *Algabal*	begins publication
	Haeckel (1834) *Der Monismus*	Munch exhibition at
	Hauptmann (1862) *Die Weber*	Verein Berliner
	Hofmannsthal (1874) *Der Tod des Tizian*	Künstler shut down
		Munich *Sezession*
Lat	D'Annunzio (1863) *L'Innocente, Giovanni Episcopo*	
	Svevo (1861) *Una Vita*	
Nor	Hamsun (1859) *Mysteries*	
	Hansson (1860) *Materialism in Literature, Young Ofeg's Ditties*	
	Ibsen (1828) *The Master Builder*	
	Jørgensen (1866) *Moods*	
	Strindberg (1849) *The Bond*	
Sla		

Chronology of Events

1893

Ang   Bradley (1846) *Appearance and Reality*
      Gissing (1857) *The Old Woman*
      James (1843) *The Private Life*
      Pater (1839) *Plato and Platonism*
      Patmore (1823) *Religio Poetae*
      Pinero (1855) *Dandy Dick, Sweet
        Lavender*
      Thompson (1859) *Poems* (included
        'Hound of Heaven')
      Wilde (1854) *Salome* (published in
        French in Paris)
      Yeats (1865) *Celtic Twilight*

Fre	Gide (1869) *Tentative amoureuse, Voyage d'Urien* Hérédia (1842) *Les Trophées* Mallarmé (1842) *Vers et Proses* Verhaeren (1855) *Campagnes hallucinées*	Maupassant dies Taine dies Lugné-Pöe's Théâtre de l'Oeuvre founded
Ger	Dehmel (1863) *Aber die Liebe* Fontane (1819) *Frau Jenny Treibel* Halbe (1865) *Jugend* Hauptmann (1862) *Der Biberpelz, Hanneles Himmelfahrt* Hofmannsthal (1874) *Der Tor und der Tod* Przybyszewski (1868) *Totenmesse* Schnitzler (1862) *Anatol*	Van Gogh retrospective exhibition in Amsterdam
Lat		Verdi (1813) *Falstaff*
Nor	Jørgensen (1866) *The Tree of Life* Obstfelder (1866) *Poems*	Jørgensen and others found periodical the *Tower* Munch (1863) *The Cry*
Sla		

1894

Ang	Gissing (1857) *In the Year of Jubilee*	Pater dies
	Grossmith, G. (1847) and W. (1854)	*Yellow Book* launched
	The Diary of a Nobody	Gladstone finally
	Kipling (1865) *Jungle Book*	resigns
	'Mark Twain' (1835) *The Tragedy of*	
	Pudd'nhead Wilson	
	Moore (1852) *Esther Waters*	
	Pinero (1855) *The Weaker Sex, The*	
	Schoolmistress	
	Swinburne (1837) *Astrophal and Other*	
	Poems	
	Webb, S. (1859) and B. (1858) *History*	
	of Trade Unionism	
	Wilde (1854) *A Woman of No Importance,*	
	Salome (translated by Lord Alfred	
	Douglas, illustrated by Beardsley)	
	Yeats (1865) *Land of Heart's Desire*	
Fre	Jarry (1873) *Les Minutes de Sable*	Dreyfus trial (1894–9)
	mémorial	begins in Paris
	Maeterlinck (1862) *Intérieur*	
Ger	Mombert (1872) *Tag und Nacht*	
	Rilke (1875) *Leben und Lieder*	
	Steiner (1861) *Philosophie der Freiheit*	
Lat		
Nor	Fröding (1860) *New Poems*	
	Hamsun (1859) *Pan*	
	Ibsen (1828) *Little Eyolf*	
Sla	Chekhov (1860) *In the Twilight*	Alexander III of
		Russia dies; Nicholas
		II succeeds

1895

Ang	Conrad (1857) *Almayer's Folly*	Translation of Beowulf
	Crane (1871) *The Red Badge of Courage*	by William Morris
	Gissing (1857) *Eve's Ransom, Paying Guests, Sleeping Fires*	
	Hardy (1840) *Jude the Obscure*	
	James (1843) *The Reprobate*	
	Meredith (1828) *The Amazing Marriage*	
	Moore (1852) *Celibates*	
	Pinero (1855) *The Notorious Mrs Ebbsmith, The Second Mrs Tanqueray, The Amazons*	
	Symons (1865) *London Nights*	
	Yeats (1865) *Poems*	
Fre	Gide (1869) *Paludes*	Dumas *fils* dies
	Huysmans (1848) *En route*	Cézanne exhibition in Paris
	Ibels (1872) *Les Cités futures*	
	Valéry (1871) *Introduction à la méthode de Léonard de Vinci*	Lumière brothers invent cinematograph
	Verhaeren (1855) *Les Villes tentaculaires*	
	Verlaine (1844) *Confessions*	
Ger	Fontane (1819) *Effi Briest*	Periodicals *Pan* and *Simplizissimus* founded
	George (1868) *Die Bücher der Hirten- und Preisgedichte*	
	Hofmannsthal (1874) *Alkestis*	Engels dies
	Schnitzler (1862) *Liebelei*	Röntgen discovers X-rays
	Wedekind (1864) *Der Erdgeist*	Kiel Canal opened
Lat		Marconi invents wireless telegraphy
Nor	Brandes (1842) *William Shakespeare*	
	Hansson (1860) *The Journey Home*	
Sla	Merezhkovsky (1865) *Christ and Anti-Christ* (1895–1905)	

1896

Ang	Conrad (1857) *An Outcast of the Islands*	William Morris dies
	Housman (1859) *A Shropshire Lad*	*Daily Mail* launched
	James (1843) *The Other House*	Periodical *Savoy*
	Pinero (1855) *Benefit of the Doubt*	founded by Symons
Fre	Bergson (1859) *Matière et mémoire*	Verlaine dies
	Jarry (1873) *Ubu Roi*	
	Maeterlinck (1862) *Le Trésor des*	
	Humbles	
	Proust (1871) *Les Plaisirs et les jours*	
	Renard (1864) *Histoires Naturelles*	
	Valéry (1871) *La soirée avec M. Teste*	
	Verhaeren (1855) *Les Heures claires*	
Ger	Dehmel (1863) *Weib und Welt*	Periodical *Die Jugend*
	Fontane (1819) *Die Poggenpuhls*	founded
	Hauptmann (1862) *Florian Geyer,*	
	Die versunkene Glocke	
	Hofmannsthal (1874) *Der Kaiser und die*	
	Hexe	
	Rilke (1875) *Larenopfer*	
Lat		Puccini (1858) *La*
		Bohème
Nor	Bjørnson (1832) *Beyond Our Powers II*	
	Fröding (1860) *Splashes and Rags*	
Sla	Chekhov (1860) *The Seagull*	
	Tolstoy (1828) *The Power of Darkness*	

1897

Ang	Conrad (1857) *Nigger of the Narcissus*	Queen Victoria's
	Gissing (1857) *The Whirlpool*	Diamond Jubilee
	Hardy (1840) *The Well-Beloved*	J. J. Thompson
	James (1843) *What Maisie Knew, The Spoils of Poynton*	discovers the electron
	Ker (1855) *Epic and Romance*	*Yellow Book* ceases
	Kipling (1865) *Captains Courageous*	publication
	Meredith (1828) *Essay on Comedy*	Goldfields discovered
	Wells (1866) *Invisible Man*	in Klondyke
	Yeats (1865) *Secret Rose, Tables of the Law, Adoration of the Magi*	

Fre	Gide (1869) *Les Nourritures terrestres*	Matisse (1869) *La*
	Mallarmé (1842) *Divagations, Un Coup de Dés*	*Desserte*
	Péguy (1872) *Jeanne d'Arc*	
	Rostand (1868) *Cyrano de Bergerac*	

Ger	George (1868) *Das Jahr der Seele*	Vienna *Sezession*
	Hofmannsthal (1874) *Das Kleine Welttheater, Reitergeschichte*	Burckhardt dies
	Przybyszewski (1868) *Satanskinder*	Brahms dies
	Rilke (1875) *Traumgekrönt*	

Lat	D'Annunzio (1863) *Trionfo della Morte*

Nor	Heidenstam (1859) *King Charles' men*
	Strindberg (1849) *Inferno*

Sla	Chekhov (1860) *Uncle Vanya*
	Tolstoy (1828) *Resurrection*

1898

Ang	Gissing (1857) *Human Odds and Ends, The Town Traveller*	Gladstone dies
	Hardy (1840) *Wessex Poems*	
	James (1843) *In the Cage, The Two Magics*	
	Shaw (1856) *Plays Pleasant and Unpleasant, The Perfect Wagnerite*	
	Wells (1866) *War of the Worlds*	
	Wilde (1856) *Ballad of Reading Gaol*	
Fre	Huysmans (1848) *La Cathédrale*	Rodin (1841) *Balzac*
	Péguy (1873) *Marcel*	Curies discover radium
	Verhaeren (1855) *Les Aubes*	Mallarmé dies
Ger	Fontane (d. 1898) *Der Stechlin*	C. F. Meyer dies
	Holz (1863) *Phantasus*	Fontane dies
	Mann, T. (1875) *Der kleine Herr Friedemann*	Bismarck dies
	Nietzsche (1844) *Gedichte*	
	Rilke (1875) *Advent*	
Lat	D'Annunzio (1863) *La città morta*	
	Svevo (1861) *Senilità*	
Nor	Bang (1857) *The White House*	
	Bjørnson (1832) *Paul Lange and Tora Parsberg*	
	Hamsun (1859) *Victoria*	
	Jensen (1873) *Stories of Himmerland* (3 vols., 1898–1910)	
	Jørgensen (1866) *Poems 1894–98*	
	Strindberg (1849) *To Damascus I and II, Legends*	
Sla	Tolstoy (1828) *What is Art?*	Founding of Moscow Arts Theatre

1899

Ang Dowson (1867) *Decorations*   Beginning of Boer
    Ellis, Havelock (1859) *Studies in*   War
      Psychology of Sex I
    Gissing (1857) *Crown of Life*
    James, H. (1843) *The Awkward Age*
    James, W. (1842) *Talks on Psychology*
    Kipling (1865) *Stalky & Co.*
    Pinero (1855) *Trelawney of the Wells*
    Symons (1865) *The Symbolist Movement*
      in Literature
    Wilde (1856) *An Ideal Husband, The*
      Importance of being Earnest
      (performed 1895)
    Yeats (1865) *The Wind among the Reeds,*
      Poems

Fre Jarry (1873) *L'Amour absolu*   Second trial and pardon
    Moréas (1856) *Les Stances*   of Dreyfus
    Verhaeren (1855) *Les Visages de la vie*   Monet (1840) *Rouen*
      Cathedral

Ger Chamberlain (1855) *Die Grundlagen*   *Die Fackel* (edited by
      des neunzehnten Jahrhunderts   Karl Kraus) founded
      (English translation 1911)
    Freud (1856) *Traumdeutung* (dated
      1900)
    George (1868) *Der Teppich des Lebens*
    Haeckel (1834) *Die Welträtsel*
    Hauptmann (1862) *Fuhrmann Henschel*
    Hofmannsthal (1874) *Die Hochzeit der*
      Sobeide, Das Bergwerk zu Falun
    Holz (1863) *Revolution der Lyrik*
    Rilke (1875) *Mir zur Feier*
    Schnitzler (1862) *Der grüne Kakadu*

Lat

Nor Ibsen (1828) *When We Dead Awaken*
    Strindberg (1849) *Crimes and Crimes,*
      Gustav Vasa

Sla

1900

Ang	Conrad (1857) *Lord Jim*	Stephen Crane dies
	Dreiser (1871) *Sister Carrie*	Ruskin dies
	James (1843) *The Soft Side*	Wilde dies
	Pinero (1855) *Gay Lord Quex*	British Labour Party
	Saintsbury (1845) *A History of Criticism*	founded
	Shaw (1856) *Three Plays for Puritans*	
	Wells (1866) *Love and Mr Lewisham*	
	Yeats (1865) *Shadowy Waters*	
Fre	Bergson (1859) *Le rire*	Péguy founds *Cahiers de la quinzaine*
	Claudel (1868) *Connaissance de l'Est* (1895–1900)	Gauguin (1866) *Noa-Noa*
	Jarry (1873) *Ubu enchaîné*	
	Renard (1864) *Poil de Carotte*	
	Verhaeren (1855) *Le Cloître*	
Ger	Husserl (1859) *Logische Untersuchungen*	Nietzsche dies
	Kassner (1873) *Die Mystik, die Künstler und das Leben*	Cabaret Überbrettl founded
	Mach (1838) *Analyse der Empfindungen*	Planck's Quantum theory
	Mann, T. (1875) *Buddenbrooks* (imprint 1901)	Berlin *Sezession*
	Nietzsche (d. 1900) *Ecce Homo*	
	Rilke (1875) *Geschichten vom lieben Gott*	
	Schnitzler (1862) *Reigen*	
	Spitteler (1845) *Olympischer Frühling* (1900–1905)	
Lat	D'Annunzio (1863) *Il Fuoco*	
Nor	Obstfelder (1866) *A Priest's Diary*	
	Strindberg (1849) *Easter*	
Sla		

1901

Ang	Butler (1835) *Erewhon Revisited*	Queen Victoria dies;
	Gissing (1857) *By the Ionian Sea*	Edward VII succeeds
	Hardy (1840) *Poems of the Past and Present*	McKinley assassinated; Th. Roosevelt
	James (1843) *The Sacred Fount*	succeeds
	Kipling (1865) *Kim*	First wireless
	Moore (1852) *Sister Teresa*	communication
	Wells (1866) *First Men in the Moon*	between Europe and
	Yeats (1865) *Poems*	America
Fre	Maeterlinck (1862) *La Vie des Abeilles*	Sully Prudhomme awarded first Nobel Prize for literature
Ger	George (1868) *Fibel*	Planck's law of
	Nietzsche (d. 1900) *Nietzsche contra Wagner*	radiation
	Schnitzler (1862) *Leutnant Gustl*	
	Wedekind (1864) *Der Marquis von Keith* (periodical publication 1900)	
Lat		Picasso's 'blue period' begins
Nor	Strindberg (1849) *The Dance of Death*	
Sla	Chekhov (1860) *Three Sisters*	

1902

Ang	Bennett (1867) *Anna of the Five Towns* Conrad (1857) *Heart of Darkness* James, H. (1843) *The Wings of the Dove* James, W. (1842) *Varieties of Religious Experience* Kipling (1865) *Just So Stories* Yeats (1865) *Cathleen Ni Houlihan*	Boer War ends Granville–Barker takes over Royal Court Theatre
Fre	Gide (1869) *L'Immoraliste* Jarry (1873) *Le Surmâle* Marinetti (1876) *La Conquête des Étoiles* Verhaeren (1855) *Les Forces tumultueuses*	Zola dies
Ger	Hauptmann (1862) *Der arme Heinrich* Hofmannsthal (1874) *Ein Brief* (the 'Lord Chandos letter') Huch (1864) *Ausbreitung und Verfall der Romantik* Rilke (1875) *Das Buch der Bilder*	Stadler and Schickele found periodical *Der Stürmer* Nobel Prize to T. Mommsen Warburg Library begun (transferred 1933 from Hamburg to London)
Lat	Croce (1866) *L'Estetica*	
Nor	Strindberg (1849) *A Dream Play*	
Sla	Bely (1880) *The Dramatic Symphony* (first of four 'symphonies' 1902–8) Gorky (1868) *The Lower Depths, The Smug Citizen, Three of them*	

1903

Ang	Butler (d. 1902) *The Way of all Flesh*	Gissing dies
	Conrad (1857) *Typhoon*	Spencer dies
	Dewey (1859) *Studies in Logical Theory*	Whistler dies
	Gissing (d. 1903) *The Private Papers of Henry Ryecroft*	*Daily Mirror* launched
	James (1843) *The Ambassadors, The Better Sort*	First flight by Wright brothers
	Moore, G. E. (1873) *Principia Ethica*	
	Russell (1872) *Principles of Mathematics*	
	Shaw (1856) *Man and Superman*	
	Yeats (1865) *Ideas of Good and Evil, Where there is Nothing*	
Fre	Gide (1869) *Prétextes*	Gauguin dies
	Huysmans (1848) *L'Oblat*	
Ger	Dehmel (1863) *Zwei Menschen*	
	Hauptmann (1862) *Rose Bernd*	
	Hofmannsthal (1874) *Elektra*	
	Mann, T. (1875) *Tonio Kröger, Tristan*	
	Rilke (1874) *August Rodin*	
	Weininger (1880) *Geschlecht und Charakter*	
Lat		
Nor		Nobel Prize to Bjørnson
Sla	Bely (1880) *Gold in Azure*	Socialist movement splits into Bolsheviks and Mensheviks

1904

Ang   Barrie (1860) *Peter Pan*   *Entente cordiale* between
      Conrad (1857) *Nostromo*   Britain and France
      de la Mare (1873) *Henry Brocken*
      Hardy (1840) *The Dynasts I* (II 1906,
        III 1908)
      James (1843) *The Golden Bowl*
      Veblen (1857) *The Theory of Business
        Enterprise*
      Wells (1866) *The Food of the Gods*
      Yeats (1865) *The King's Threshold, The
        Hour Glass*

Fre   Gourmont (1858) *Promenades*   Mistral shares Nobel
      littéraires (to 1928)   Prize
      Marinetti (1876) *Destruction: Poésies
        lyriques*
      Rolland (1866) *Jean Christophe* (1904–
        12)

Ger   Freud (1856) *Zur Psychopathologie des*   Die Brücke group of
      Alltagslebens   artists formed in
      Hesse (1877) *Peter Camenzind*   Dresden
      Steiner (1861) *Theosophie*
      Wedekind (1864) *Die Büchse der
        Pandora*

Lat   D'Annunzio (1863) *La Figlia di Jorio*   Echegaray shares Nobel
           Prize

Nor   Strindberg (1849) *To Damascus III,
      Gothic Rooms, Black Flags*

Sla   Bely (1880) *Ashes*
      Blok (1880) *Verses about the Lady
        Beautiful*
      Chekhov (1860) *The Cherry Orchard*

1905

Ang Forster (1879) *Where Angels Fear to
        Tread*
     Shaw (1856) *Major Barbara*
     Synge (1871) *The Shadow of the Glen,
        Riders to the Sea, The Well of the
        Saints*
     Wells (1866) *A Modern Utopia, Kipps*
     Wharton, E. (1862) *The House of Mirth*
     Wilde (d. 1900) *De Profundis*

Liberal Cabinet formed
   in Britain
Sinn Fein founded in
   Dublin

Fre Claudel (1868) *Partage de Midi*
     Huysmans (1848) *Les Foules de Lourdes*
     Verhaeren (1855) *Les Heures d'après-midi*

Beginning of Fauvism
   in art, led by
   Matisse
Separation of Church
   and State in France

Ger Dilthey (1833) *Das Erlebnis und die
        Dichtung*
     Hesse (1877) *Unterm Rad*
     Hofmannsthal (1874) *Das gerettete
        Venedig*
     Mach (1838) *Erkenntnis und Irrtum*
     Mann, H. (1871) *Professor Unrat*
     Morgenstern (1871) *Galgenlieder*
     Rilke (1875) *Das Stundenbuch*

Einstein's special theory
   of relativity
Max Reinhardt takes
   over Deutsches
   Theater in Berlin

Lat Unamuno (1864) *Vida de Don Quijote y
        Sancha*

Marinetti founds
   periodical *Poesia*

Nor Brandes (1842) *Autobiography* (3 vols.,
        1905–8)

Norway gains
   independence from
   Sweden

Sla

Abortive revolution in
   Russia
Nobel Prize to H.
   Sienkiewicz

1906

Ang	Conrad (1857) *Mirror of the Sea*
	de la Mare (1873) *Poems*
	Galsworthy (1867) *The Man of Property*
	Kipling (1865) *Puck of Pook's Hill*
	Pinero (1855) *His House in Order*
	Sinclair (1878) *The Jungle*
		Movement for
		  Women's Suffrage
		  becomes active

Fre	Verhaeren (1855) *La Multiple Splendeur*	Cézanne dies Fauvism develops

Ger	Ernst, P. (1866) *Der Weg zur Form*
	Hauptmann (1862) *Und Pippa tanzt*
	Musil (1880) *Die Verwirrungen des
	  Zöglings Törless*
	Rilke (1875) *Die Weise vom Leben und
	  Tod des Cornetts Christoph Rilke*	

Lat		Nobel Prize to Carducci
Nor	Bjørnson (1832) *Mary* Hamsun (1859) *Under the Autumn Star* Lagerlöf (1858) *The Wonderful Adventures of Nils*	Ibsen dies
Sla		General strike in Russia

1907

Ang	Conrad (1857) *The Secret Agent*	Nobel Prize to Kipling
	Forster (1879) *The Longest Journey*	
	Gosse (1849) *Father and Son*	
	James, W. (1842) *Pragmatism*	
	Joyce (1882) *Chamber Music*	
	Shaw (1856) *John Bull's Other Island*	
	Synge (1871) *Playboy of the Western World*	
	Yeats (1865) *Deirdre*	
Fre	Bergson (1859) *L'Évolution créatrice*	
	Gide (1869) *Le Retour de l'enfant prodigue*	
Ger	George (1868) *Der siebente Ring*	
	Rilke (1875) *Neue Gedichte I*	
Lat		
Nor	Hamsun (1859) *Benoni*	Grieg dies
	Strindberg (1849) *The Ghost Sonata,*	
	Storm Weather, The Pelican	
Sla	Gorky (1868) *Mother*	

1908

Ang	Bennett (1867) *The Old Wives' Tale*	Asquith prime
	Davies (1871) *Autobiography of a Super-Tramp*	minister, Old age pensions in Britain
	Forster (1879) *A Room with a View*	F. M. Hueffer founds
	Sinclair (1878) *The Metropolis, The Moneychangers*	*English Review*
	Stein G. (1874) *Three Lives*	
	Synge (1871) *The Tinker's Wedding*	
	Wells (1866) *The War in the Air*	
	Yeats (1865) *Collected Works I and II*	
Fre	Romains (1885) *La Vie unanime*	Cubism begins with
	Sorel (1847) *Reflexions sur la violence* (originally published as articles in 1906)	Picasso and Braque
Ger	Hauptmann (1862) *Kaiser Karls Geisel*	First big Matisse
	Holz (1863) *Sonnenfinsternis*	exhibition in Berlin
	Rilke (1875) *Neue Gedichte II*	Nobel prize to R. C.
	Schnitzler (1862) *Der Weg ins Freie*	Eucken
	Worringer (1881) *Abstraktion und Einfühlung*	Mahler (1860) *Das Lied von der Erde*
		Webern (1883) *Passacaglia*
Lat	Pirandello (1867) *Umorismo*	
Nor	Hamsun (1869) *Rosa*	
	Strindberg (1849) *Open Letters to the Intimate Theatre*	
Sla	Bely (1880) *Urn*	
	Gorky (1868) *The Confession*	
	Lunacharsky (1875) *Faust and the City*	

1909

Ang	Barker (1877) *The Voysey Inheritance* James, W. (1842) *A Pluralist Universe* Pound (1885) *Personae and Exultations* Synge (d. 1909) *Poems and Translations* Wells (1866) *Tono Bungay*	Synge dies Swinburne dies Meredith dies

Fre	Bergson (1859) *Matière et Mémoire*
	Gide (1869) *La porte étroite*
	Maeterlinck (1862) *L'Oiseau bleu*
	Marinetti (1876) *Manifeste du futurisme*
		Gide and others found
		  *Nouvelle Revue
		  française*
		Blériot flies the English
		  Channel

Ger	Mann, T. (1875) *Königliche Hoheit*
	Rilke (1875) *Requiem*
		Der Neue Club
		  founded in Berlin
		Schoenberg (1874)
		  Erwartung

Lat		
Nor	Bjørnson (1832) *When the New Wine blooms* Hamsun (1859) *With Muted Strings* Strindberg (1849) *The Great Highway* Undset (1882) *Gunnar's Daughter*	Nobel Prize to Lagerlöf
Sla		

1910

Ang	Bennett (1867) *Clayhanger*
	Forster (1879) *Howards End*
	James (1843) *The Finer Grain*
	Russell (1872) and Whitehead (1861)
	    Principia Mathematica I
	Wells (1866) *The History of Mr Polly*
	Yeats (1865) *Poems II*
		Edward VII dies;
		   George V succeeds
		William James dies
		Mark Twain dies
		London's first
		   Post-Impressionist
		   exhibition

Fre	Péguy (1873) *Le Mystère de la charité de
	    Jeanne d'Arc*
	Verhaeren (1855) *Les Rythmes
	    souverains*	

Ger	Freud (1856) *Über Psychoanalyse*
	Hauptmann (1862) *Die Ratten*
	Hofmannsthal (1874) *Christinas
	    Heimreise*
	Rilke (1875) *Malte Laurids Brigge*
	Wedekind (1864) *Schloss Wetterstein*
		Herwarth Walden
		   founds periodical
		   Der Sturm
		Neopathetisches
		   Cabaret begins in
		   Berlin
		Nobel Prize to Paul
		   Heyse

Lat		
Nor	Hamsun (1869) *In the Grip of Life*	Bjørnson dies

Sla	Bely (1880) *Symbolism, The Silver Dove*	Russian manifesto
		   *Concerning beautiful
		   Clarity* (= Acmeism)
		   appears
		Tolstoy dies
		Stravinsky (1882) *The
		   Fire Bird*

1911

Ang	Beerbohm (1872) *Zuleika Dobson*	Copyright extended to fifty years from author's death
	Brooke, R. (1887) *Poems*	
	Conrad (1857) *Under Western Eyes*	
	Dreiser (1871) *Jennie Gerhardt*	Parliament Act
	James (1843) *The Outcry*	Rutherford's nuclear theory of the atom
	Lawrence, D. H. (1885) *The White Peacock*	
	Pound (1885) *Canzoni*	J. M. Murry *et al* found *Rhythm* (later the *Blue Review*)
	Shaw (1856) *The Doctor's Dilemma, Getting Married, The Showing-up of Blanco Posnet*	
	Synge (d. 1909) *Deirdre of the Sorrows*	
	Webb, S. (1859) and B. (1858) *Poverty*	
Fre	Claudel (1868) *L'Otage*	Nobel Prize to Maeterlinck
	Colette (1873) *La Vagabonde*	
	Jarry (d. 1907) *Les Gestes et Opinions du Docteur Faustroll*	
	Péguy (1873) *Le Porche du mystère de la deuxième vertu*	
	Saint-John-Perse (1887) *Les Éloges*	
	Verhaeren (1855) *Les Heures du soir*	
Ger	Heym (1887) *Der ewige Tag*	Der Blaue Reiter group of artists formed in Munich
	Hofmannsthal (1874) *Jedermann, Der Rosenkavalier*	
	Kaiser (1878) *Die jüdische Witwe*	Pfemfert founds periodical *Die Aktion*
	Musil (1880) *Vereinigungen*	
	Vaihinger (1852) *Die Philosophie des Als Ob*	Mahler dies
Lat		
Nor	Hamsun (1859) *Look back on Happiness*	Amundsen reaches South Pole
	Undset (1882) *Jenny*	
Sla		

1912

Ang	Conrad (1857) *'Twixt Land and Sea*	*Poetry* (Chicago) begins
	de la Mare (1873) *The Listeners and other poems*	*Georgian Poetry* begins
	Lawrence D. H. (1885) *The Trespasser*	
	Pound (1885) *Ripostes*	
	Wells (1866) *Marriage*	
Fre	Claudel (1868) *L'annonce faite à Marie*	Futurist exhibition in
	Péguy (1873) *Le Mystère des Saints Innocents*	Paris
	Verhaeren (1855) *Hélène de Sparte*	
Ger	Barlach (1870) *Der tote Tag*	Sturm Gallery opened:
	Benn (1886) *Morgue*	*Der Blaue Reiter*
	Heym (1887) *Umbra vitae, Der Dieb*	exhibition of Italian
	Hofmannsthal (1874) *Ariadne auf Naxos*	Futurists
	Kafka (1883) *Betrachtung* (earlier editions in 1908, 1910)	Nobel Prize to Hauptmann
	Kandinsky (1886) *Über das Geistige in der Kunst*	
	Sorge (1892) *Der Bettler*	
	Werfel (1890) *Der Weltfreund*	
Lat		
Nor		Strindberg dies
Sla	Bely (1880) *Petersburg*	Russian Futurist manifesto

1913

Ang	de la Mare (1873) *Peacock Pie* Flecker (1884) *The Golden Journey to Samarkand* Frost (1875) *A Boy's Will* Lawrence, D. H. (1885) *Sons and Lovers, Love Poems* Stein, G. (1874) *Portrait of Mabel Dodge at Villa Caronio*	Woodrow Wilson president of U.S.A.
Fre	Apollinaire (1880) *Alcools, Les Peintres cubistes* Fournier (1886) *Le Grand Meaulnes* Péguy (1873) *Eve* Proust (1871) *Du côté de chez Swann* Romains (1885) *Odes et Prières*	
Ger	Dehmel (1863) *Schöne wilde Welt* Freud (1856) *Totem und Tabu* Husserl (1859) *Phänomenologie* Kafka (1883) *Der Heizer, Das Urteil* Mann, T. (1875) *Der Tod in Venedig* Stramm (1874) *Sancta Susanna* Trakl (1887) *Gedichte*	Einstein's General Theory of Relativity
Lat	Unamuno (1864) *Del sentimiento trágico de la vida*	
Nor	Hamsun (1869) *Children of the Age*	Bohr's discovery of the atom structure
Sla	Blok (1880) *The Rose and the Cross* Gorky (1868) *My Childhood* Mandelstam (1892) *Stone*	Stravinsky (1882) *The Rite of Spring*

1914

Ang   Conrad (1857) *Chance*
       Frost (1875) *North of Boston*
       Joyce (1882) *Dubliners*
       Lawrence D. H. (1885) *The Prussian
         Officer, The Widowing of Mrs
         Holroyd*
       Pound (ed.) (1885) *Des Imagistes*
       Shaw (1856) *Misalliance, Fanny's First
         Play, The Dark Lady of the Sonnets*
       Yeats (1865) *Responsibilities*

Wyndham Lewis
founds Vorticist
movement;
periodical *Blast*
begins publication
Egoist begins
First World War
begins

Fre   Gide (1869) *Les Caves du Vatican*

Ger   George (1868) *Der Stern des Bundes*
       Hasenclever (1890) *Der Sohn*
       Hesse (1877) *Rosshalde*
       Kaiser (1878) *Die Bürger von Calais*
       Mann, H. (1871) *Der Untertan*
       Stramm (1874) *Die Haidebraut*

Periodical *Der Kondor*
begins publication

Lat   Campana (1885) *Canti orfici*
       Unamuno (1864) *Niebla*

Nor   Lagerkvist (1891) *Motifs*

Sla

1915

| Ang | Brooke (d. 1915) *1914 and other poems* | Lusitania sinks |

Ang   Brooke (d. 1915) *1914 and other poems*   Lusitania sinks
Conrad (1857) *Victory*
Dreiser (1871) *The Genius*
Ford (1873) *The Good Soldier*
Lawrence, D. H. (1885) *The Rainbow*
Masters (1869) *Spoon River Anthology*
Pound (1885) *Cathay*
Sitwell, E. (1887) *The Mother*
Stein (1874) *Tender Buttons*
Woolf, V. (1882) *The Voyage Out*

Fre   Nobel Prize to R.
Rolland

Ger   Edschmid (1890) *Die sechs Mündungen*
Hesse (1877) *Knulp*
Kafka (1883) *Die Verwandlung*
Stadler (d. 1914) *Der Aufbruch*
Trakl (1887) *Sebastian im Traum*

Lat

Nor   Hamsun (1869) *Segelfoss Town*

Sla   Yesenin (1895) *Rejoicing*

1916

Ang	Graves (1895) *Over the Brazier*	Henry James dies
	Joyce (1882) *Portrait of the Artist as a Young Man*	
	Lawrence, D. H. (1885) *Amores, Twilight in Italy*	
	Pound (1885) *Lustra*	
	Sandburg (1878) *Chicago Poems*	
	Shaw (1856) *Androcles and the Lion, Overruled, Pygmalion*	
	Wells (1866) *Mr Britling sees it through*	
	Yeats (1865) *Reveries over Childhood and Youth*	
Fre	Apollinaire (1880) *Le poète assassiné*	
	Barbusse (1873) *Le Feu*	
Ger	Bahr (1863) *Expressionismus*	Dada launched in Zürich with Cabaret Voltaire
	Benn (1886) *Gehirne*	
	Edschmid (1890) *Das rasende Leben*	
	Jung (1875) *Psychologie des Unbewussten*	
	Kaiser (1878) *Von Morgens bis Mitternachts*	
Lat	Jiminez (1881) *Diario de un poeta recién casado*	
	Pirandello (1867) *Il Barretto a sonagli*	
	Ungaretti (1888) *Il Porto Sepolto*	
Nor	Jørgensen (1886) *An Autobiography* (6 vols., 1916–19)	Nobel Prize to Heidenstam
	Lagerkvist (1891) *Anguish*	
Sla		

1917

Ang	Douglas (1868) *South Wind*	T. E. Hulme dies
	Eliot (1888) *Prufrock*	Edward Thomas dies
	Graves (1895) *Fairies and Fusiliers*	U.S.A. enters the war
	Lawrence, D. H. (1885) *Look! We have Come Through*	
	Thomas (d. 1917) *Poems*	
	Yeats (1865) *The Wild Swans at Coole*	
Fre	Apollinaire (1880) *Les Mamelles de Tirésias* (performance)	
	Duhamel (1884) *La vie des Martyrs*	
	Valéry (1871) *La Jeune Parque*	
Ger	Benn (1886) *Fleisch*	
	Edschmid (1890) *Timur*	
Lat	Pirandello (1867) *Così è, se vi pare, Il Piacere dell'onesta*	
Nor	Hamsun (1869) *Growth of the Soil*	Nobel Prize shared by
	Lagerkvist (1891) *The Last Man*	Gjellerup and
	Undset (1882) *Images in a Mirror*	Pontoppidan
Sla	Pasternak (1890) *Life My Sister*	Bolshevik Revolution

1918

Ang	Hopkins (d. 1889) *Poems*	Rutherford splits the
	Joyce (1882) *Exiles*	atom
	Lawrence, D. H. (1885) *New Poems*	Wilfred Owen dies
	Lewis, W. (1884) *Tarr*	First World War ends
	Sitwell, E. (1887) *Clown's Houses*	
	Stein (1874) *Mary, he giggled*	
	Strachey, L. (1880) *Eminent Victorians*	
	Yeats (1865) *Per amica silentia lunae*	
Fre	Apollinaire (1880) *Calligrammes*	Debussy dies
	Giraudoux (1882) *Simon le pathétique*	
	Proust (1871) *A l'ombre des jeunes filles en fleurs*	
Ger	Barlach (1870) *Der arme Vetter*	Revolutionary
	Edschmid (1890) *Über den Expressionismus in der Literatur*	movement begins in Germany
	Hauptmann (1862) *Der Ketzer von Soana*	First Dada evening in Berlin
	Kaiser (1878) *Gas I*	
	Mann, T. (1875) *Betrachtungen eines Unpolitischen*	
	Spengler (1880) *Der Untergang des Abendlandes I*	
Lat	Pirandello (1867) *Il ginco delle Parti*	
Nor	Duun (1876) *The People of Juvik* (6 vols., 1918–23)	
Sla	Blok (1880) *The Twelve*	
	Mayakovsky (1893) *Mystery Bouffe*	
	Yesenin (1895) *Comrade Inonia*	

1919

Ang	Anderson (1876) *Winesburg, Ohio*	First Atlantic flight
	Conrad (1857) *The Arrow of Gold*	Treaty of Versailles
	Dreiser (1871) *The Twelve Men*	
	Keynes (1883) *The Economic Consequences of the Peace*	
	O'Neill (1888) *The Moon of the Caribbees and six other plays*	
	Shaw (1856) *Heartbreak House, Great Catherine*	
	Wells (1866) *Outline of History*	
	Woolf, V. (1882) *Night and Day*	
	Yeats (1865) *The Cutting of an Agate, Two Plays for Dancers*	
Fre	Gide (1869) *La Symphonie pastorale*	Breton and others found periodical *Littérature*
	Superveille (1884) *Poèmes*	Renoir dies
Ger	Hesse (1877) *Demian*	The Bauhaus founded in Weimar
	Hofmannsthal (1874) *Die Frau ohne Schatten*	Nobel Prize to Spitteler
	Kafka (1883) *Ein Landarzt, In der Strafkolonie*	Break-up of Austrian Empire
	Kraus (1874) *Die letzten Tage der Menschheit*	
	Stramm (d. 1915) *Tropfblut*	
Lat	Ungaretti (1888) *Allegria di naufragi*	
Nor		
Sla		

1920

Ang	Conrad (1857) *The Rescue*	Prohibition in U.S.A.
	de la Mare (1873) *Poems 1901–18*	First meeting of League
	Eliot (1888) *The Sacred Wood*	of Nations
	Fry (1866) *Vision and Design*	
	Galsworthy (1869) *In Chancery, The Skin Game*	
	Graves (1895) *Country Sentiment*	
	Lawrence, D. H. (1885) *The Lost Girl, Touch and Go*	
	Lewis, S. (1885) *Main Street*	
	O'Neill (1888) *Beyond the Horizon*	
	Owen (d. 1918) *Poems*	
	Pound (1885) *Umbra, Hugh Selwyn Mauberley*	
	Weston (1850) *From Ritual to Romance*	
	Yeats (1865) *Michael Robartes and the Dancer*	
Fre	Apollinaire (1880) *La Femme Assise*	Dada Festival in Paris
	Montherlant (1896) *La Relève du Matin*	
	Proust (1871) *Le coté de Guermantes*	
	Valéry (1871) *Le Cimetière Marin, Odes, Album des vers anciens*	
Ger	Barlach (1870) *Die echten Sedemunds*	Dada exhibition in
	Edschmid (1890) *Die doppelköpfige Nymphe*	Cologne shut by the police
	Kaiser (1878) *Gas II*	
Lat	Unamuno (1864) *Tres novelas ejemplares y un prologo*	
Nor	Hamsun (1869) *The Women at the Pump*	Nobel Prize to
	Undset (1882) *Kristin Lavransdatter* (3 vols., 1920–22)	Hamsun
Sla	Bely (1880) *The First Meeting*	

1921

Ang	Huxley, A. (1894) *Crome Yellow* Lawrence, D. H. (1885) *Women in Love,* *Tortoises, Sea and Sardinia* Lubbock (1879) *The Craft of Fiction* Mencken (1880) *Prejudices* O'Neill (1888) *The Emperor Jones* Shaw (1856) *Back to Methuselah* Woolf, V. (1882) *Monday or Tuesday* Yeats (1865) *Four Plays for Dancers*	Irish Independence

Fre	Breton (1896) *Les Champs magnétiques*
	Giraudoux (1882) *Suzanne et le*
	    Pacifique
	Proust (1871) *Sodome et Gomorrhe*
	    (4 vols., 1921–3)
		Nobel Prize to Anatole
		    France
		Trial of Barrès

Ger	Hofmannsthal (1874) *Der Schwierige* Musil (1880) *Die Schwärmer*	
Lat	Pirandello (1867) *Sei personaggi in* *cerca d'autore* Unamuno (1864) *La tia Tula*	
Nor		
Sla	Capek (1890) *R.U.R., The Insect Play* Yesenin (1895) *The Confession of a* *Hooligan*	

1922

Ang	Cummings (1894) *The Enormous Room*	
	Eliot (1888) *The Waste Land*	
	Flecker (d. 1915) *Hassan*	
	Galsworthy (1867) *The Forsyte Saga* (as one work)	
	Garnett (1892) *Lady into Fox*	
	Joyce (1882) *Ulysses* (published in Paris)	
	Lawrence, D. H. (1885) *Aaron's Rod, Fantasia of the Unconscious, The Ladybird*	
	Lewis, S. (1885) *Babbitt*	
	O'Neill (1888) *Anna Christie*	
	Sitwell, E. (1887) *Façade*	
	Woolf, V. (1882) *Jacob's Room*	
	Yeats (1865) *Later Poems*	
Fre	Bergson (1859) *Durée et simultanéité*	Proust dies
	Colette (1873) *La Maison de Claudine*	
	Valéry (1871) *Charmes*	
Ger	Barlach (1870) *Der Findling*	
	Brecht (1898) *Baal, Trommeln in der Nacht*	
	Hesse (1877) *Siddharta*	
	Hofmannsthal (1874) *Das Salzburger grosse Welttheater*	
	Spengler (1888) *Der Untergang des Abendlandes II*	
	Wittgenstein (1889) *Tractatus Logico–Philosophicus*	
Lat	Pirandello (1867) *Enrico IV*	Mussolini's march on Rome Nobel Prize to Benavente y Martinez
Nor		
Sla	Mandelstam (1891) *Tristia*	

1923

Ang	Conrad (1857) *The Rover*	Nobel Prize to Yeats
	Forster (1879) *Pharos and Pharillon*	
	Frost (1875) *New Hampshire*	
	Huxley (1894) *Antic Hay*	
	Lawrence, D. H. (1885) *Birds, Beasts and Flowers, Kangaroo, Studies in Classic American Literature*	
	Santayana (1863) *Scepticism and Animal Faith*	
Fre	Cocteau (1889) *Thomas l'imposteur*	
	Mauriac (1885) *Génitrix*	
	Proust (d. 1922) *La prisonnière*	
Ger	Mann, T. (1875) *Bekenntnisse des Hochstaplers Felix Krull* (fragment)	German inflationary crisis
	Moeller van den Bruck (1876) *Das dritte Reich*	
	Musil (1880) *Vinzenz und die Freundin bedeutender Männer*	
	Rilke (1875) *Duineser Elegien, Sonette an Orpheus*	
Lat	Svevo (1861) *La coscienza di Zeno*	
Nor	Hamsun (1869) *Chapter the Last*	
Sla		U.S.S.R. established

1924

Ang	Forster (1879) *A Passage to India*	First short-lived Labour
	Hemingway (1898) *In Our Time*	Government in
	Hulme (d. 1917) *Speculations*	Britain under
	Lawrence, D. H. (1885) *England, my*	Macdonald
	England	Conrad dies
	Melville (d. 1891) *Billy Budd*	
	Shaw (1856) *St Joan*	

Fre Breton (1896) *Manifeste du surréalisme:*   Review *La Révolution*
     Poisson soluble   *surréaliste* founded
     Cocteau (1891) *Poésie 1916–23*   A. France dies
     Éluard (1895) *Mourir de ne pas mourir*
     Valéry (1871) *Variété*

Ger Barlach (1870) *Die Sündflut*   Stabilization of the
     Benn (1886) *Schutt*   German mark
     Brecht (1898) *Im Dickicht der Städte*   Kafka dies
     Kafka (d. 1924) *Ein Hungerkünstler*
     Mann, T. (1875) *Der Zauberberg*
     Musil (1880) *Drei Frauen*

Lat

Nor

Sla Yesenin (1895) *Tavern Moscow*   Lenin dies
     Nobel Prize to W.
     Reymont

1925

Ang	Dickinson, Emily (d. 1886) *Complete Poems*	Nobel Prize to Shaw
	Dos Passos (1896) *Manhattan Transfer*	
	Dreiser (1871) *An American Tragedy*	
	Eliot (1888) *Poems 1905–25*	
	Fitzgerald (1896) *The Great Gatsby*	
	Hardy (1840) *Collected Poems*	
	Powys, T. F. (1875) *Mr Tasker's Gods*	
	Woolf, V. (1882) *The Common Reader, Mrs Dalloway*	
	Yeats (1865) *A Vision*	
Fre	Montherlant (1896) *Les Olympiques*	
	Proust (d. 1922) *Albertine disparue*	
	Supervielle (1884) *Gravitations*	
Ger	Hitler (1889) *Mein Kampf*	Neue Sachlichkeit exhibition
	Hofmannsthal (1874) *Der Turm* (first version)	
	Kafka (d. 1924) *Der Prozess*	
Lat	Montale (1896) *Ossi di Seppia*	
Nor	Lagerkvist (1891) *A Guest in the Real World*	
	Undset (1882) *The Master of Hestviken* (4 vols., 1925–7)	
Sla	Yesenin (d. 1925) *Soviet Russia, Persian Sketches*	

1926

Ang   Conrad (d. 1924) *Last Essays*   General strike in
       Faulkner (1897) *Soldiers' Pay*   Britain
       Fitzgerald, Scott (1896) *All the Sad
          Young Men*
       Hemingway (1898) *The Sun also Rises*
       Lawrence, D. H. (1885) *The Plumed
          Serpent*
       Lawrence, T. E. (1888) *Seven Pillars of
          Wisdom*
       O'Casey (1884) *The Plough and the
          Stars*
       Pound (1885) *Personae*
       Wells (1866) *The World of William
          Clissold*

Fre   Claudel (1868) *Feuilles de Saints*
       Cocteau (1892) *Rappel à l'ordre*
       Colette (1873) *Sous le Soleil de Satan*
       Gide (1869) *Si le grain ne meurt, Les
          Faux-monnayeurs*
       Giraudoux (1882) *Bella*
       Maurois (1881) *Meïpe, Bernard Quesnay*
       Proust (1871) *Thérèse Desqueyroux*

Ger   Barlach (1870) *Der blaue Boll*
       Kafka (d. 1924) *Das Schloss*

Lat   Nobel Prize to Deladda

Nor   Lagerkvist (1891) *Songs of the Heart*

Slà

1927

Ang	Forster (1879) *Aspects of the Novel*	Lindbergh flies
	Hemingway (1898) *Men without Women*	Atlantic solo
	Joyce (1882) *Pomes Penyeach*	
	Lawrence, D. H. (1885) *Mornings in Mexico*	
	Lewis, Sinclair (1885) *Elmer Gantry*	
	O'Neill (1888) *Marco Millions*	
	Wilder (1897) *Bridge of San Luis Rey*	
	Woolf, V. (1882) *To the Lighthouse*	
	Yeats (1865) *October Blast*	
Fre	Benda (1867) *La Trahison des clercs*	Nobel Prize to Bergson
	Maurois (1881) *Disraeli*	
Ger	Benn (1886) *Gesammelte Gedichte*	
	Brecht (1898) *Hauspostille*	
	Hesse (1877) *Der Steppenwolf*	
	Kafka (d. 1924) *Amerika*	
Lat		
Nor	Hamsun (1859) *Vagabonds*	
Sla		

1928

Ang	Eliot (1888) *For Lancelot Andrewes*	Women in Britain
	Forster (1879) *The Eternal Moment*	enfranchised
	Huxley (1894) *Point Counter Point*	
	Joyce (1882) *Anna Livia Plurabelle*	
	Lawrence, D. H. (1885) *Lady Chatterley's Lover, The Woman Who Rode Away, Collected Poems*	
	Lewis, W. (1884) *The Childermass*	
	O'Casey (1884) *The Silver Tassie*	
	O'Neill (1888) *Strange Interlude*	
	Powys, T. F. (1875) *Mr Weston's Good Wine*	
	Woolf, V. (1882) *Orlando*	
	Yeats (1865) *The Tower*	
Fre	Giraudoux (1882) *Siegfried*	
	Malraux (1901) *Les Conquérants*	
Ger	Binding (1867) *Erlebtes Leben*	
	George (1868) *Das neue Reich*	
	Hauptmann (1862) *Wanda*	
	Remarque (1898) *Im Westen nichts Neues*	
Lat		
Nor		Nobel Prize to Undset
Sla		

1929

Ang	Compton-Burnett (1892) *Brothers and Sisters*	Wall Street crash
	Eliot (1888) *Dante*	
	Faulkner (1897) *The Sound and the Fury*	
	Graves (1895) *Goodbye to All That*	
	Hemingway (1898) *A Farewell to Arms*	
	Lawrence, D. H. (1885) *Pansies*	
	Lewis, Sinclair (1885) *Dodsworth*	
	Wolfe, T. (1900) *Look Homeward, Angel*	
	Woolf, V. (1882) *A Room of One's Own*	
	Yeats (1865) *The Winding Stair*	
Fre	Claudel (1868) *Le Soulier de Satin*	
	Cocteau (1868) *Les Enfants terribles*	
	Colette (1873) *La Joie*	
Ger	Döblin (1878) *Berlin Alexanderplatz*	Hofmannsthal dies
		Nobel Prize to T. Mann
Lat		
Nor		
Sla		

1930

Ang Auden (1907) *Poems*
Dos Passos (1896) *The 42nd Parallel*
Eliot (1888) *Ash Wednesday*
Empson (1906) *Seven Types of Ambiguity*
Faulkner (1897) *As I Lay Dying*
Lawrence, D. H. (d. 1930) *The Virgin and the Gypsy*
Lewis, W. (1884) *The Apes of God*
Shaw (1856) *The Apple Cart*

D. H. Lawrence dies
Nobel Prize to Sinclair Lewis

Fre Cocteau (1892) *La Voix humaine*
Giono (1895) *Regain*
Giraudoux (1882) *Amphitryon*

Ger Freud (1856) *Das Unbehagen in der Kultur*
Hesse (1877) *Narziss und Goldmund*
Musil (1880) *Der Mann ohne Eigenschaften I*

Lat

Nor Hamsun (1859) *August*

Sla

Brief Biographies

THE nature of the following entries has been largely determined by considerations of space. The number of entries is arbitrarily set at a hundred; the *average* entry is fixed at a hundred words. Those who seek somewhat fuller information, including titles and dates of English translations, and bibliographical details of collected works, editions and of secondary literature, are referred to *The Penguin Companion to Literature*, vols. 1–3.

APOLLINAIRE, Guillaume (pseud. for Wilhelm de Kostrowitzky), 1880–1918, French poet, playwright, critic, and one of the most influential 'cultural impresarios' of the early years of the century, played a defining role in the establishment of Cubism, was boldly and vigorously experimental in his own poetry (*Alcools*, 1913) and took his place in the very forefront of the European *avant-garde*. His 'surrealistic' play *Les Mamelles de Tirésias* (published 1918) was his attempt to give imaginative form to the 'new spirit' of the years; *L'esprit nouveau et les poètes* defined the theoretical basis.

BAHR, Hermann, 1863–1934, Austrian critic, dramatist and prose writer, whose sensitivity to the new directions and shifts in literature has left its record in a number of Modernism's key publications: *Zur Kritik der Moderne* (1890) and *Die Überwindung des Naturalismus* (1891) in its early days, and *Expressionismus* (1916) for the generation of the First World War.

BANG, Herman Joachim, 1857–1912, Danish novelist, turned to writing after failing as an actor. His novels *Generations without Hope* (1880) and *Tine* (1889) reflect his morbidly sensitive, highly introspective nature. Sympathy for the downtrodden of all kinds, the lonely, the rejected, together with a deep distrust of sexuality pervade his work.

BARLACH, Ernst, 1870–1938, German playwright, novelist and sculptor, combines in his work – sculptural as well as literary – qualities which are sometimes mystical, often ecstatic, occasionally allegorical and even grotesquely Gothic. His first drama *Der tote Tag* explores the tension between maternal and paternal forces – a tension which in different guises can also be detected in many of his subsequent dramas: *Der arme Vetter* (1918), *Die echten Sedemunds* (1920), *Der Findling* (1922), *Der blaue Boll* (1926) and *Die Sündflut* (1924).

BENN, Gottfried, 1886–1956, German poet whose first volume of verse drew heavily for its imagery upon its author's medical training and experience. From an initial adherence to Expressionism he moved – via the poems of *Fleisch* (1917) and *Schutt* (1924) – to a greater sobriety and objectivity of style, which serves to heighten the horror of much of what he reports. His later output includes many essays and works of criticism.

BERGSON, Henri, 1859–1941, French philosopher and Nobel Prize-winner for Literature in 1927, was one of the most formidable intellects to be deployed against the deterministic, rationalistic and over-intellectualized patterns of thought of the nineteenth century. His voice is most distinctively heard in *Essai sur les données immédiates de la conscience* (1889), in *Matière et mémoire* (1896), and – most influentially – in *L'évolution créatrice* (1907), where man's creative spirit is defined in terms of an *élan vitale* which is fluid, mobile and intuitive. Only by the recognition and acknowledgement of forces of this order can man free himself from the fatalistic and mechanistic determinants to which the nineteenth century paid such homage. Bergson's ideas exercised an influence on twentieth-century European literature second only to Nietzsche's.

BIELY (or BELY), Andrey (pseud. for Boris Nikolayevich Bugayev), 1880–1934, Russian poet, novelist and critic, was one of the chief architects of Russian Symbolism in the years before the First World War: as lyric poet, with the volumes *Zoloto v lazuri* (1904), *Pepel* (1909) and *Urna* (1909); as author of the two novels *Serebryany golub'* (1910) and *Petersburg* (1913); and as collaborator on the journal *Vesy* (1904–9). His (largely reminiscent) *Vospominaniya o Bloke* (1922) helps to fill out the Symbolist record. His sense of affinity with Gogol, and the example he set for his contemporaries Zamyatin and Pil'nyak are factors that help to define his central position.

BLOK, Aleksandr Aleksandrovich, 1880–1921, Russian poet and the determining spirit of Russian Symbolism (see his essay 'On the Present State of Russian Symbolism', 1910) wrote his earliest poetry – ethereal, mystical, impassioned – in the years at the turn of the century. Later the mood was more frenzied, assertive, apocalyptic, ironic. His poem *Dvenadtsat'* (1918) is full of revolutionary fervour; *Skify*, written the same year, has its origins similarly in the political situation. Nevertheless at the deepest level, his poems are always profoundly personal, revealingly 'confessional'.

BRECHT, Bertolt, 1898–1956, German poet and playwright, made his debut with a dramatic technique at once modishly expressionistic and experimentally realistic: *Baal* (1922) and *Trommeln in der Nacht* (1922) both examine private rather than social values within a disturbingly new dramatic idiom. In the twenties, *Im Dickicht der Städte* (1923-7) and *Mann ist Mann* (1927) carry the exploration forward with techniques that strangely anticipate Ionesco and Beckett and the Absurdists. It was with the satirical *Dreigroschenoper* (1929) however that Brecht first began to achieve an international reputation. Thereafter, as his work progressively revealed an explicitly Marxist intent, he elaborated his ideas of 'epic theatre', a concept which attempted, by the employment of various *Verfremdungseffekte*, to impose a necessary emotional detachment on the audience. After 1933, his life was unsettled: fleeing from Nazism in 1933, he turned for refuge first to Scandinavia, then to Russia, and finally arrived in the U.S.A. where he took up residence in 1941. Returning after the war to Europe, he lived first in Switzerland and then (from 1949) in East Berlin. In the period 1937-45 he wrote what are perhaps the greatest of his dramatic works: *Leben des Galilei*, *Mutter Courage*, *Der gute Mensch von Sezuan*, and *Der kaukasische Kreidekreis*. His declared purpose as a playwright was to identify the chief problems of the age and give them appropriate dramatic form.

BRETON, André, 1896–1966, French poet and member of the Dada group, was one of the founders and chief theoreticians of Surrealism. His initial *Manifeste du surréalisme* of 1924 – it was followed after long intervals by two supplementary manifestos of 1930 and 1942 – sets out the fundamental ideas and beliefs of the movement. His *Le surréalisme et la peinture* (1928) is a further elaboration of selected aspects.

CHEKHOV, Anton Pavlovich, (1860–1904), Russian playwright and short story writer, wrote much fiction in his early twenties. After 1886 his artistry became more discriminating; his first works for the stage (dramatic sketches and the full-length play *Ivanov*, 1887) evinced a naturalistic style quickened by a sharp, satirical, occasionally grotesque humour. *The Seagull* (1896) uses the techniques – and some of the mannerisms – of symbolic drama, but already blends them with the uncanny, almost surreal naturalism of the last plays: *Uncle Vanya* (1897), *Three Sisters* (1901), *The Cherry Orchard* (1904). In these plays are shown the minor provincial nobility, charming, melancholy and resigned, in the seemingly endless moment before their annihilation.

CLAUDEL, Paul, 1868–1955, French dramatist and poet, drew inspiration and confidence from his Roman Catholic faith to be able to assert – in a series of (frequently re-modelled and re-written) plays from the early *Tête d'or* (1890) and *La Ville* (1893) through to the technically audacious *Le soulier de satin* (1928-9) – a unity and coherence in all the world's multiplicity. Uninhibitedly anti-rationalistic (as befitted a convinced Bergsonian) in his beliefs, uncompromising in both the matter and the manner of his assertions, he revelled in the dissent he invited. In his poetry, and especially in his highly personal prose poetry, he moved easily and confidently into metaphysics.

COCTEAU, Jean, 1889–1963, French poet, dramatist, novelist, critic and cultural virtuoso, was at home in an astonishing range of literary, visual, musical, filmic and performing arts, and enjoyed close association with many of their distinguished practitioners of the day, among them Apollinaire, Picasso and Dufy, Diaghilev and (in music) 'Le groupe des Six'. This versatility, the sheer fecundity of his creative inspiration is what gives distinctiveness in the first place to his achievement, rather than any towering individual excellence in the works – though the merit of the dramas *Les mariés de la Tour Eiffel* (1921), *Orphée* (1926) and *La machine infernale* (1934), and of the novels *Le grand écart* (1923), *Thomas l'Imposteur* (1923) and *Les enfants terribles* (1929) is high.

CONRAD, Joseph, (pseud. for Teodor Jozef Konrad Korzeniowski) 1857–1924, Polish-born master-mariner who settled in England to produce, in English, some of the most important of early-twentieth-century fiction. His achievement – centred in *Lord Jim* (1900), *Heart of Darkness* (1902), *Nostromo* (1904), *The Secret Agent* (1907), *Under Western Eyes* (1911) and *The Shadow Line* (1917) – lies in relating an ironic, existential vision of exposure to an impressionistic mode of rendering experience. Conrad's world is nihilistic, nightmarish, arbitrary; his central figures are men on the point of test, threatened by a secret or alternative self, or a void at the centre of their values – often redeemed by an elected act of courage or commitment. This ambiguous world comes to us through an ambiguous technique: mixing an intense realization of particular occasions with an elaborate, often a-chronological or otherwise deceptive, narrative presentation, most familiarly through the pieced-together insights of his surrogate narrator Marlow. Usually, in experience and form, Conrad finally reasserts a precarious order, a return from the dark places to the light.

D'ANNUNZIO, Gabriele, 1863–1938, Italian poet, dramatist and novelist, found inspiration for his earliest poems (*Primo vere*, 1879, and *Canto novo*, 1882) in Carducci, and confirmation for his uncompromising view of life in Nietzsche, whom he read between 1892 and 1894. The following decade – to which also belonged his relationship with the actress Eleonore Duse – saw the creation of some of his most accomplished works: the novel *Il Trionfo della Morte* (1894), the dramas *Francesca da Rimini* (1901) and *La Figlia di Jorio* (1904), and certain of the poems of *Le Laudi*. Barbaric and often cruel in its immediacy, erotic and brutal in its emphasis on the physical, his work marks an untiring quest for sensation.

DEHMEL, Richard, 1863–1920, German poet, broke violently with conventional form in his lyrics of the nineties: *Erlösungen* (1891), *Aber die Liebe* (1893) and *Weib und Welt* (1896). His appeal was for greater freedom of thought and behaviour, especially in respect of man's sexual nature. His verse romance, *Zwei Menschen* (1903), combines a feeble plot with an often startling power of expression.

DOS PASSOS, John, 1896–1970, American novelist, was an ambulance man in the First World War, and produced two war novels before writing *Manhattan Transfer* (1925) – which crosses expressionistic techniques from Bely and Zamyatin, tactics from American naturalism, and filmic methods of cross-cutting and rapid impressionism to generate the pluralism, indifference and mechanical force of New York City life. The techniques expand into the trilogy *U.S.A.*, consisting of *The 42nd Parallel* (1930), *1919* (1932) and *The Big Money* (1936); this uses four basic modes – the 'Camera Eye' glimpses; newsreels and newspaper collages; factual biographies of leading Americans; and several fictional stories about individuals – to build up a massive portrait, historically factual, anarchistically critical, of the U.S.A. from 1900 to the Depression. Later his work tended to lose both political bite and technical rigour.

EDSCHMID, Kasimir (pseud. for Eduard Schmidt), 1890–1966, German novelist, essayist and critic, sustains a reputation today more as an apologist of Expressionism than as an independently creative writer: particularly by his *Über den Expressionismus* (1919) and – retrospectively – *Frühe Manifeste. Epochen des Expressionismus* (1959) and *Lebendiger Expressionismus* (1961).

ELIOT, T(homas) S(tearns), 1888–1965, American-born poet, critic and dramatist who became perhaps *the* key figure in English-language poetic Modernism, settled in London in 1915. In 1917 came the ironic, symbolist-influenced, neo-metaphysical poems of *Prufrock and Other Observations*; in 1920 *The Sacred Wood*, essays which began an extended process of recasting critical norms and the sense of significant tradition behind modern poetry and culture. *The Waste Land* (1922), that polyglot anti-epic of modern sterility and hinted redemption, compounded from fragments, reduced to greater intensity by the editing of his mentor Pound, established his centrality and pervasive influence. *Sweeney Agonistes* (1926–7) began his experiments in verse-drama, to develop in *Murder in the Cathedral* (1935), *The Confidential Clerk* (1954), etc. Eliot became a British citizen and an Anglo-Catholic, the turning point being *Ash Wednesday* (1930). The core of his later work is *The Four Quartets* (1943), personal, speculative, religious poems in which earlier images of social and sexual sterility transform into precarious richness.

ERNST, Paul, 1866–1933, German dramatist, prose writer and critic, turned away from an early adherence to Marxism and naturalism and formulated a 'neo-classical' view of modern literature: a belief in absolute values, unchanging principles, and rigorous formal concepts. *Der Weg zur Form* (1906), a collection of studies in the theory of tragedy and the *Novelle*, is in many respects an anticipation of Wyndham Lewis and T. E. Hulme.

FAULKNER, William, 1897–1962, American novelist, storywriter, was born in the Southern state of Mississippi, in the imaginary Yoknapatawpha County of which most of his novels from his third book, *Sartoris* (1929), are set. His fourth, *The Sound and the Fury* (1929) – which has four narrators, the first an idiot with limited capacity to establish chronicity, order, significance – begins a sequence of elaborate technical experiments running through the thirties. His central achievement is in *As I Lay Dying* (1930), a mythical, grotesque novel about a funeral journey; *Light in August* (1932), paralleling a bleak story of lynching and prejudice with another of pregnancy and endurance; *Absalom, Absalom!* (1936), an experimental plantation novel. His experiments with time-shift, stream-of-consciousness, intersecting narratives, are partly conditioned by his sense of Southern history itself, a history of doom with glimpsed epiphanies of redemption; but also his concern with the way art itself mediates history and form, time and timelessness.

FONTANE, Theodor, 1819–98, German novelist, turned from journalism to fiction writing relatively late in life. *Vor dem Sturm* (1878) is set in the Napoleonic period; subsequently he turned to contemporary Prussia. He offers sensitive, acutely observed portraits of an individual's fall from grace, either through social evils (*Irrungen, Wirrungen*, 1888), weakness of character (*Unwiederbringlich*, 1892) or the pressure of changing social values (*Effi Briest*, 1895). Naturalism here acquires an unexampled terseness and precision: yet between the richness of human sympathy and the ultimate refusal to make moral judgements, there is a strange disjunction which gives the later novels, and especially *Der Stechlin* (1898) their strangely modern, 'suspended' quality.

FORSTER, E(dward) M(organ), 1879–1971, English novelist and essayist, explores in his early novels – *Where Angels Fear to Tread* (1905) and *A Room with a View* (1908) – the tensions between conformity and freedom, between the well-bred sterility of England and the warmth and violence of Italy. In *The Longest Journey* (1907) suburban gentility confronts the instinctive life of the earth. It is on the complex masterpieces of his maturity, however, *Howards End* (1910) and *A Passage to India* (1924), that Forster's reputation must rest. Both explore the reactions of a doomed class to an incomprehensible future. *Howards End* turns on the violent death of the clerk who has disturbed the social order; *A Passage to India* ends with the symbolic separation of England and India, divided by history, by experience, by the earth itself. Despite a weakness for melodramatic climaxes, Forster's writing is never strident or aggressive.

FREUD, Sigmund, 1856–1939, psychiatrist, founder of psychoanalysis and one of the seminal influences on the literature of Europe in this century. From his early collaborative inquiries into abnormal states of mind, the results of which were published as *Studien über Hysterie* (1895), his clinical studies led him to propound an entirely new concept of mind, its life and ways, its structure and development. *Die Traumdeutung* (1899), *Zur Psychopathologie des Alltaglebens* (1904) and *Totem und Tabu* (1912–13), along with the later *Das Unbehagen in der Kultur* (1930) went to re-form the ideas of an epoch, not merely in the specialist fields of psychiatry and psychology, but also in the very widest of social contexts. And in consequence he became, in Auden's phrase, 'a whole climate of opinion'.

GEORGE, Stefan, 1868–1933, German poet, was sustained throughout his creative career by a quest for formal excellence; to this he brought an impressively wide familiarity with European literature (studied, more often than not, in the original languages), a trained sensitivity to linguistic values, and an unconquerable sense of the poet's mission as prophet and priest. The course of his poetry from the earlier *Hymnen* (1890), *Pilgerfahrten* (1891) and *Algabal* (1892), through the middle years of *Das Jahr der Seele* (1897), *Der siebente Ring* (1907) and *Der Stern des Bundes* (1913), to the wearily oracular *Das neue Reich* of his later years was from the bejewelled to the chiselled, from the Symbolist to the mystic and esoteric (the George 'circle'), and ultimately to the portentously superficial. His journal *Blätter für die Kunst* (1890–1919) documents some of Modernism's central features.

GIDE, André, 1869–1951, French novelist, critic and prolific diarist and correspondent, in the mid-nineties repudiated (yet without ever being able wholly to detach himself from) the puritanical standards of his strict Protestant upbringing, together with many other of the prevailing literary and social conventions. In their place he commended an amalgam of pagan, Nietzschean, hedonistic modes of conduct – a complex exhortation that lies at the heart of his novel *Les nourritures terrestres* (1897), and which directly or obliquely surfaces in much of his subsequent fiction: *L'immoraliste* (1902), *La porte étroite* (1909), and supremely in *Les Faux-monnayeurs* (1926), a work of formidable technical complexity. His autobiography *Si le grain ne meurt* (1926) and his *Journal 1885–1949* (1953) are endlessly revealing, both of himself and of his age.

GORKY, Maksim (pseud. for Aleksey Mikhaylovich Peshkov), 1868–1936, Russian novelist and dramatist, widely regarded as the father of modern Soviet literature, began his literary career in the early nineties with a succession of short stories of great power and poignancy, including *Makar Chudra* (1892) and *Chelkash* (1895), which then led on to his first novel *Foma Gordeyev* (1899), a kind of Russian *Buddenbrooks*. A highly successful production in 1902 of *The Lower Depths* at the Moscow Arts Theatre consolidated his already considerable reputation in Russia and the West. Revolutionary activities brought him into disfavour with the authorities; after the events of 1905, he was forced into exile, first briefly to America, then to Capri. To this period his novel *Mother* (1907) belongs. In 1913 he returned to Russia where he was resident eight years, active in support of the coming revolution, critical of its realities once achieved. Abroad again between 1921 and 1931, ostensibly for his health, he returned to Russia for the last five years of his life to play the role of cultural elder-statesman. His work, though greatly uneven in quality, often deficient in imaginative insight, unhappily didactic in places, is nevertheless formidably if crudely powerful and shows deep rapport with its age.

HAMSUN, Knut, 1859–1952, Norwegian novelist, poet and dramatist, left school early, worked as shoemaker's apprentice, wrote some early bad fiction. After two visits to America in the eighties, he returned to Europe; his novels of the nineties – particularly *Hunger* (1890), the complex *Mysteries* (1892), and *Pan* (1894) and *Victoria* (1898) – explore with sensitive precision the reaction of isolated individuals to the menaces of their environment. Of his later novels, some – *Under the Autumn Star* (1906), *Growth of the Soil* (1917), *Vagabonds* (1927) – develop his strangely tangential and ambivalent relationship with the Norwegian pastoral tradition; others – *Children of the Age* (1913), *Segelfoss Town* (1915) – are more satirical in intent. He was a consummate prose stylist.

HAUPTMANN, Gerhart, 1862–1946, German dramatist, novelist and poet, after establishing himself in 1889 with his drama *Vor Sonnenaufgang* virtually at a stroke as the leading dramatist of German naturalism and further consolidating a growing international reputation with *Die Weber* in 1892, then moved progressively and eclectically away from an undifferentiated naturalism to permit elements of romanticism, fantasy, mysticism and Hellenic classicism to assert themselves to a greater or lesser degree in his work: in *Hanneles Himmelfahrt* (1893), in the hilarious *Der Biberpelz* (1893), in the fey *Die versunkene Glocke* (1896), alongside the starker *Fuhrmann Henschel* (1898) and *Rose Bernd* (1903). The novels *Der Narr in Christo Emanuel Quint* (1910) and *Der Ketzer von Soana* (1918) add further substance to the denial of simple naturalism as the basis of his art.

HEIDEGGER, Martin, 1889–   , German philosopher, developed (mainly from his reading of Kierkegaard) his own individual philosophy of (atheistic) existentialism, though personally repudiating the classification of existentialist. In *Sein und Zeit* (1927) he pursued his concern to determine the '*Sein des Seienden*'; and in an endeavour to analyse what he termed '*Dasein*', the peculiar condition of the being and existence of man, became probably the most influential German philosopher in the period following the end of the twenties.

HEMINGWAY, Ernest, 1898–1961, American novelist, storywriter, wounded as an ambulance man in the First World War, lived as an expatriate in Paris in the twenties. His wound became the metaphor of modernistic initiation in *The Sun Also Rises* (1926), an expatriate novel about bohemians living on a reduced, post-war moral economy, *In Our Time* (1925), and *Men Without Women* (1927), stories about sleepless men living at the limits of pain, action, or experience. Brief, lucid, unadjectival sentences carrying a substratum of symbolic weight and moral innuendo, together with a supporting life-style of 'grace under pressure' in a world of action and existential encounter characterize his work. *A Farewell to Arms* (1929) intensified the tragic aspect of his vision; *To Have and Have Not* (1937) and *For Whom the Bell Tolls* (1940), set in the Spanish Civil War, the social and political aspects. A big game hunter, fisherman, war correspondent, Hemingway was a desperate man of action, finally of suicide.

HESSE, Hermann, 1877–1962, German novelist and poet, attempted alternately to placate and escape from his pietistic background. Earlier novels, like *Peter Camenzind* (1904), explore the theme of the artist's youth; but not until *Demian* (1919) and *Siddhartha* (1922) did Hesse find a theme and style of his own. Their 'oriental' mysticism found, and still finds, an immediate response as interpretations of youthful idealism and revolt. *Steppenwolf* (1927) explored the theme of world-embracing mysticism as a solution to mental suffering, and this novel has an intensity of style and an ingenuity of form not to be found in his later books *Narziss und Goldmund* (1930) or the monumental, all-too-monumental *Das Glasperlenspiel*.

HEYM, Georg, 1887–1912, died young, drowned in a skating accident. The world of his poems – *Der ewige Tag* (1911), *Umbra vitae* (post-humously in 1912) – is one of visionary horror; demons of war and disease rise in cities bleak as deserts; and the square impersonality of the poetic form exactly reflects the inhumanity both of society itself and of the means of its destruction.

HOFMANNSTHAL, Hugo von, 1874–1929, Austrian poet, dramatist and essayist, testified in his early exquisitely wrought lyrics to his sense of the essential inter-relatedness of all things in a world threatened by growing fragmentation; at the same time, his lyric dramas of these years – *Gestern* (1891), *Der Tod des Tizian* (1892), *Der Tor und der Tod* (1893) – bemoaned the inability of the modern sophisticated mind to achieve authentic living or to establish such relationships. At the turn of the century, a crisis of faith in the power of language to encompass reality provoked *Ein Brief* (1902), the so-called 'Chandos letter' – one of Modernism's key documents. Underlying most of his later work – as festival dramatist(*Jedermann*, 1911; *Das grosse Salzburger Welttheater*, 1922), as opera librettist (*Der Rosenkavalier*, 1911; *Ariadne auf Naxos*, 1912; *Die Frau ohne Schatten*, 1919), and as perceptive and prolific essayist – is a profound faith in the strength and unity of the European cultural tradition. The two dramas of the twenties, *Der Schwierige* (1921) and *Der Turm* (1925), mark the peaks of his mature achievement.

HOLZ, Arno, 1863–1929, German poet, dramatist and critic, is most readily remembered for his theory of Naturalism ('Art = Nature—x') and for his exposition of this formula in *Die Kunst: ihr Wesen und ihre Gesetze* (1891), together with the early works associated with this: the *Novellen* of *Papa Hamlet* (1889) and the drama *Die Familie Selicke* (both written in collaboration with Johannes Schlaf). Critical opinion may yet come to believe, however, that his more lasting achievement was in his experiments – with inner rhyme, with elaborate rhythmic patterns and with complex verse structures based on the notion of a 'central axis' – in the field of the lyric, especially in *Phantasus* (1898). *Die Revolution der Lyrik* (1899) sets out the theoretical basis.

HUYSMANS, Joris-Karl, 1848–1907, French novelist, opened up a deeply flanking movement out of orthodox naturalism with his novels *À rebours* (1884), whose hero Des Esseintes with his ultra-refined sensibilities, his ambiguous standards of conduct, his responsiveness to the mystical came to personify the new emergent 'decadence' of the age, and *Là-bas* (1891), whose hero Durtal moves in his religious experience via the occult to Roman Catholicism. Huysmans also wrote perceptive criticism of Impressionist art in *L'art moderne* (1883) and in *Certains* (1889).

IBSEN, Henrik, 1828–1906, Norwegian dramatist, by abandoning verse as his dramatic medium after *Brand* (1866) and *Peer Gynt* (1867) and addressing himself to 'the far more difficult art of prose', stimulated a new development in European drama which is still vigorous today, a century later: the search for new dramatic eloquences in seemingly ordinary language. As Ibsen then progressed from the more socially weighted problems of *A Doll's House* (1879) and *Ghosts* (1881), to those of individual human and sexual relationships in *Rosmersholm* (1886) and *Hedda Gabler* (1890), to his last explorations of individual obsession and frustration in *John Gabriel Borkman* (1896) and *When We Dead Awaken* (1899), he highlighted a range of concerns, both thematic and technical, which have greatly preoccupied succeeding generations of dramatists.

JAMES, Henry, 1843–1916, American novelist and critic, had a European–American education and settled in England in 1876. Though a self-confessed realist, inheriting the European social tradition from George Eliot, Balzac and Flaubert, his career gradually evolves toward that symbolistic mode, concern with consciousness as the source of all perception, and introverted technical curiosity one associates with Modernism. His early novels, from *Roderick Hudson* (1876) to *The Portrait of a Lady* (1881), are international explorations of the apprehensive, curious learner encountering experience, seeking to realize life. In the 1880s, with *The Princess Casamassima* (1886), etc., his novels grew more massively social. But subsequent work reverts toward a new concern with consciousness: the learner is now not a character but the active narrator himself, making life as he makes form, or else an articulately artistic consciousness, like Strether's (*The Ambassadors*, 1903). His brother William, the psychologist, spoke of the 'stream' of consciousness; Henry's later books, where acts and movements of perception are central, make it not a free flow but an active reflector – very like the artist at his work.

JARRY, Alfred, 1873–1907, French dramatist, poet and novelist, achieved with his bitterly farcical *Ubu Roi* in 1896 what his contemporaries grudgingly admitted to be a *succès de scandale* and which since has been acknowledged as the start of a line that led via the Surrealists to the present-day Theatre of the Absurd. He followed it with *Ubu enchaîné* (1900). As Jarry himself asserted: '*L'absurde exerce l'esprit et fait travailler la mémoire*' ('The absurd exercises the mind, and makes the memory work').

JENSEN, Johannes Vilhelm, 1873–1950, Danish novelist, poet and essayist, soon came to repudiate the 'decadence' of his own early work and that of his contemporaries – an attack which carried over into his own fiction in the novel *The Fall of the King* (1901) – and then succeeded with the tales of *Himmerland tales* (1898–1910) in giving a new twentieth-century voice to the traditional art of regional fiction. His central and not altogether preposterous work is the six-volume novel cycle *The long journey* (1908–22) in which a sustained Darwinism binds many disparate elements of science, mythology, folk-lore and history with astonishing virtuosity into an account of the descent of man from prehistory to historical times. His poems, collected in *Poems* (1952) are altogether more modest, both in their range and in their achievement.

JIMÉNEZ, Juan Ramón, 1881–1958, Spanish poet, documented the turning point of his own career – and, by extension of the wider development of Modernist Spanish poetry – with his *Diario de un poeta recién casado* in 1917: from the impressionistically decorative *Almas de violeta* (1900) and the rich elaborations of *Baladas de primavera* (1910) to the spare and powerful simplicities, the *poesia desnuda*, of the collections of the post-*Diario* years, especially *Eternidades* (1918) and *Piedra y cielo* (1919). He was awarded the Nobel Prize in 1956.

JØRGENSEN, Johannes, 1866–1937, Danish poet, shifted with the changing mood of the age from an early Brandes-inspired radicalism to the new romanticism of the nineties. The sensitive poems of *Moods* (1892) and of *Poems 1894–1898*, though essentially Danish, are very much in the international Symbolist mode; and the periodical he edited in 1893–4, *The Tower*, served as a focal point for the new ideas in Scandinavia. Following his conversion in 1896 to Roman Catholicism, and particularly after settling permanently in Assisi in 1913, he devoted himself in large measure to hagiography. His own autobiography is usefully informative about the Scandinavian *fin de siècle*.

JOYCE, James, 1882–1941, novelist, story-teller, was born in Dublin, which city provides the naturalistic roots for all his fiction – the entrapping environment of the stories in *Dubliners* (1914); the point of flight for Stephen Dedalus in *A Portrait of the Artist as a Young Man* (1916); the urban setting for the Bloomsday of *Ulysses* (Paris, 1922); the hometown of the publican who is the human figure at the centre of the verbal web of *Finnegans Wake* (1939). Joyce's entire enterprise in Modernist aesthetics starts from this naturalistic base, transcending it more massively in each new work: through epiphanies of form and illumination, through the mythical counterpointing of *Ulysses*, the linguistically generated multivalent codes of the *Wake*. A vast linguistic, scholastic, and formal enterprise, Joyce's evolving experiment was also a voyage, to Paris, Trieste, Zürich, Paris again and then, when World War disturbed him a second time, Zürich again, where he died. The European disorder of the century does not figure directly in Joyce's work, but it is an émigré art of linguistic pluralism, a modern semiology which both releases the word and rigorously defines its modern potential; hence Joyce's persistent appeal to Post-Modernist writers.

JUNG, Carl Gustav, 1875–1961, Swiss psychiatrist and psychologist and for a number of years one of Freud's closest collaborators, broke clear in 1913 to pursue his own line: analytical psychology. Doubtful about the total and overriding importance Freud attached to the 'libido', and persuaded that man's basic drive was to achieve a surer balance – the essence of 'individuation' – between the conscious and the un-conscious parts of his mind, he advocated (notably in *Wandlungen und Symbole der Libido* (1912), *Psychologische Typen* (1921) and *Die Beziehungen zwischen dem Ich und dem Unbewussten* (1928)) adoption of a new set of concepts, the yield from which would clarify many of the more bewildering areas of religion, art history, mythology and symbolism in general. His notion of the 'collective unconscious' was in support of his view that the human psyche was only in part *individually* determined, and that part was an interpersonally shared experience of 'archetypal' phenomena.

JÜNGER, Ernst, 1895–   , German novelist and essayist, knew war and its ways as the central reality of his earlier life, and took it as the supreme concern of his art; in the first instance as a much-decorated front-line officer in the First World War, and subsequently (in the twenties) as the author of *In Stahlgewittern* (1920), *Das Wäldchen 125* (1925) and *Feuer und Blut* (1926). The strangely visionary effects of violence, the heightened awarenesses that danger brings are some of the areas his fiction of these years explores. His later fiction, preeminently the allegorical *Auf den Marmorklippen* (1939) and *Heliopolis* (1949) admit a greater contemplative element.

KAFKA, Franz, 1883–1924, Austrian novelist, whose lesser pieces published during his life-time – e.g. *Die Verwandlung* (1916), *Das Urteil* (1916), *In der Strafkolonie* (1919) – were little known, and whose major and posthumously published novels – *Der Prozess* (1925), *Das Schloss* (1926) and *Amerika* (1927) – would have been destroyed in manuscript if his wishes had been respected, achieved belated recognition, especially in the years following the Second World War, as one of the greatest of European novelists. His work documents with patient and anguished lucidity the modern individual's endeavours to penetrate life's purposes, to elucidate the mysteries of existence, in a world in which indefinable but implacable forces confront the aspirations of the self.

KAISER, Georg, 1878–1945, German playwright, enjoys his reputation as Expressionism's leading dramatist as much for the sheer fecundity of his creative imagination – he wrote no fewer than seventy-four dramas in all – and for his immense technical inventiveness as for the intrinsic literary or theatrical merit of his work. *Die Bürger von Calais* (1914), *Von Morgens bis Mitternachts* (1916), and *Gas I* and *Gas II* (1918–20), with their emphasis on typified characters, stridency of dialogue, stylized theatrical effects and social 'relevance', are the works which best and most typically represent his achievement.

KARLFELDT, Erik Axel, 1864–1931, Swedish poet and (posthumously, in 1931) Nobel Prize winner, found a rich source of simple poetic power in regionalism. *Fridolin's songs* (1898) and *Fridolin's villa* (1901) take inspiration from peasant speech, from rural practices and traditions, and from the changing moods of nature as observed, often with a primitive's eye, in his native province of Dalarna. His final collection, *Harvest horn* (1927) invites comparison with Yeats.

KRAUS, Karl, 1874–1936, Austrian poet, dramatist and satirist, produced virtually single-handedly, as editor and as main contributor, over a period of thirty-seven years the Viennese periodical *Die Fackel*, in its own day an influential instrument of astringent social and cultural criticism (especially in matters of language and linguistic usage and the dangers to the human spirit of a debasement in communication standards), and uniquely important now as a historical document in its own right and as a repository of source material. His huge 'drama' *Die letzten Tage der Menschheit* (1919) documents the tensions of the years of the First World War.

LAFORGUE, Jules, 1860–1887, French poet, whose ironic and individual talent in (especially) the use of *vers libre* impressed and influenced T. S. Eliot, and who through Eliot won acceptance as an innovatory force of seminal importance in Modernist poetry. In his brief career, he published only two collections of verse: *Les complaintes* (1885) and *L'imitation de Notre Dame la Lune* (1886).

LAGERKVIST, Pär, 1891–1974, Swedish poet, novelist and playwright, is preoccupied with the tension between inhuman evil and human frailty. The early poems of *Anguish* (1916) and the expressionist plays *The Difficult Hour* (1918) and *The Secret of Heaven* (1919) cry out at the world's inhumanity. For him, evil is a more impressive presence than good: the bland religiosity of *The Songs of the Heart* (1926) and the Christian novels from *Barabbas* (1950) onwards, is less convincing than the study of evil in *The Hangman* (1933), *The Dwarf* (1944), and the wonderfully evocative *Evil Tales* (1924).

LAWRENCE, D(avid) H(erbert), 1885–1930, English novelist, poet and playwright, allowed the tensions of his childhood – between passion and reason, between nature and civilization – to form the basis of his earlier novels: *The White Peacock* (1911), *Sons and Lovers* (1913), and *The Rainbow* (1915). From *The Lost Girl* (1920) and *Women in Love* (1920) onwards, the novels become harsher, the subject matter more complex and more dubious. In *Aaron's Rod* (1922) and *Kangaroo* (1923) an obsession with the darker side of sexuality combines with an appeal to some overpowering masculine force which will dominate and ful-fil the 'power-soul in a man'. *The Plumed Serpent* (1926) develops this idea almost beyond the point of self-parody. His last novel, *Lady Chatterley's Lover* (1928; complete English edition, 1961) returns to the world of the earlier novels. Of his work in other genres, the stories and poems are sometimes raw and unfinished, sometimes wonder-fully sharp and evocative of a specific situation or atmosphere – qualities especially notable in his travel books *Mornings in Mexico* and *Etruscan Places*.

LEWIS, Wyndham, 1884–1957, Canadian-born painter, novelist, critic, studied art in Paris before becoming the central force in Vorticism in London in 1914. He founded *Blast* (two issues, 1914–15), with Pound and others; his energy-centred painting – part-adaptation, part-refutation of Futurism – and hard prose satire were crucial to the movement. Lewis promoted an exteriorized, satirical Modernism, purged of romanticism or interiorized psychological overtones. His novel *Tarr* (1918), a comedy of machines, a Bergsonian performance, exemplifies the method in prose, while *The Apes of God* (1930) attacks soft bohemianism with hard technique and tough satire, as Lewis was now doing in his critical books. The trilogy *The Childer-mass* (1928–55) is a massively grotesque effort, meriting serious atten-tion, at exploring the human condition as it awaits entrance into 'Heaven'.

LORCA, Frederico Garcia, 1898–1936, Spanish poet and playwright, alternates in his poetry between sunlight and scented darkness, be-tween sensuous laziness and cruelty, between sexuality and repression. His mature plays, especially *Bodas de Sangre* (1933) and *Yerma* (1934) evoke a passionate (usually feminine) sexuality frustrated by conven-tion or circumstance, and blend lyrical, almost surrealist expressive-ness of language with inexorably tragic action. In his last play, *La casa de Bernada Alba* (1936), the language is more subdued, the action swifter and more stark.

MAETERLINCK, Maurice, 1862–1949, Belgian dramatist, poet and essayist exerted an influence upon contemporaneous European drama-tists – especially Chekhov, Strindberg and Yeats – wholly disproportionate to his own modest posthumous reputation. His Symbolist dramas of the *fin de siècle* – beginning with *La Princesse Maleine* (1889) and including *L'intruse* (1890), *Les aveugles* (1890), *Pelléas et Mélisande* (1892) and *L'intérieur* (1894) – with their brooding lyricism, their sense of fatality, and their exploitation (sometimes deft and moving, sometimes heavily portentous) of the techniques of oblique communication contributed influentially to the establishment of a new dramatic mode in Europe. Many of his ideas found more direct expression in his essays, for example *Le trésor des humbles* (1896) and *La vie des abeilles* (1901).

MALLARMÉ, Stephane, 1842–98, French poet, sought an ideal world beyond the realities of the everyday, a purity and an essence accessible only to the supreme concentration, a new and untarnished context for the word, and a profundity of meaning expressible only by the most exquisite linguistic (and typographical) innovations. His early *L'après-midi d'un faune* (1876) was known in its day to few; the *Poésies complètes* (1887), *Pages* (1891) and *Vers et prose* (1893), though not easily penetrable, had a uniquely great influence on the development of European poetry. In the event, however, the *Grand Oeuvre* he strove for eluded him.

MANDELSTAM, Osip Emil'evich, 1891–1938(?), Russian poet, was (in company with Akhmatova) among the leading spirits of the 'Acmeist' group, after the formation of the 'Poets' Guild' in 1911. The poems of his first published volume, *Kamen'* (1913), reflect his and the group's concern for 'beautiful clarity', precision, concrete imagery and disciplined utterance. The harmonics of his later collections *Tristia* (1922) and *Shum Vremeni* (1925) are however richer and subtler.

MANN, Thomas, 1875–1955, German novelist, gathered together in his own distinctive and ironic style impulses from Goethe, Schopenhauer, Nietzsche, Wagner, and from the great nineteenth-century French, Scandinavian and Russian novelists. *Buddenbrooks* (1900) consolidated a decade of more limited endeavour in shorter fiction; and between this and his next large-scale novel, *Der Zauberberg* (1924), came a probing succession of shorter narrative works – *Tonio Kröger* (1903), *Tristan* (1903), *Königliche Hoheit* (1909) and *Der Tod in Venedig* (1911) – in which Mann's coolly monumental style is richly orchestrated. In exile from Nazi Germany, he addressed himself in the period 1937– 44 to the tetralogy *Joseph und seine Brüder*, before putting out post-war a more explicitly symbolic analysis of Germany's and Europe's dilemma in *Dr Faustus* (1947). The shorter novels of his later life – *Lotte in Weimar* and *Der Erwählte* (1951) – offer further comment on the ambiguous poise of life's contradictions; whilst the comic *Felix Krull* (1954), in which he once more took up a motif from his earlier years, carries a proposal that culture, and perhaps even all life itself, is no more than some complex duplicity.

MARINETTI, Filippo Tommaso, 1876–1944, Italian novelist and poet (though often preferring to write in French than in Italian), and 'literary activist' who made his mark as the founder of Futurism in Italy at the end of the first decade of the twentieth century – a movement which repudiated the past, venerated the machine, 'liberated the word' from grammatical and syntactical order, pursued all that could be called dynamic, welcomed the coming of Fascism, and hailed war as the world's one salvation ('*la guerre seule hygiene du monde*'). His novel *Mafarka le futuriste* (1909) marks the term's invention.

MAYAKOVSKY, Vladimir Vladimirovich, 1893–1930, Russian poet and dramatist and a leading figure in Russian Futurism, dominated the post-Revolution period in literature. A political activist in his early years, a literary activist after 1917 (e.g. as founder and editor of the periodical *LEF* in 1923), he unhesitatingly put literature at the service of the Revolution. His main concern was for a new literary order, his instrument the 'depoetized' word, his intention shock, and his ultimate objective the replacement of the delicate refinement of the Symbolists by a determinedly abrasive impact on the mind of the ordinary man. From the early *Vladimir Mayakovsky* (a highly subjective piece in conception, execution and performance in 1913) to the now internationally known satires *The Bedbug* (1928) and *The Bath-house* (1929), his work for and in the theatre sustained his basic convictions. He committed suicide in 1930.

MEREZHKOVSKII, Dmitriy Sergeyevich, 1865–1941, Russian novelist, poet and critic, helped – more by erudite theory and criticism (e.g. *O prichinakh upadka i o novykh techeniyakh sovremonnoy literatury*, 1893) than by creative example – to initiate a Symbolist movement in Russia. His critical revaluations of the great nineteenth-century Russian writers provoked a measure of fruitful debate. After the Revolution, as an émigré in Paris, he devoted most of his somewhat limited literary talent to anti-Bolshevist polemic.

MUSIL, Robert, 1880–1942, Austrian novelist, is frequently classed – and ranked – with Proust and Joyce, essentially by virtue of the complex subtleties of observation and the virtuoso stylistic achievements of his one major work: the three-volume *Der Mann ohne Eigenschaften* (1930–43, revised 1952). This explores inexhaustibly one year in the life of an introspective intellectual within the context of a decaying Austrian society shortly before the outbreak of the First

World War. His shorter fiction – *Die Verwirrungen des Zöglings Törless* (1906) and *Drei Frauen* (1924) – and the essays of *Nachlass zu Lebzeiten* (1936) idiosyncratically reinforce the central achievement.

NABOKOV, Vladimir, 1899–   , is now usually associated with current Post-Modernism; in fact his roots, associations and literary evolution are in a tradition arising from Russian and European Symbolism. Born in St Petersburg, to an eminent Russian family dispossessed and exiled by the Bolshevik Revolution, he became an émigré in England, Germany, and France. In 1923 he published two books of poetry, in 1926 the novel *Mashenka*. Then followed a multilingual activity in fiction, poetry, drama, essays, translations, in the Modernist émigré tradition. In 1941 he moved to America, beginning a fresh career as an English-language writer and stylist, winning high reputation with *Lolita* (1955). Behind all his work from first to last runs a Symbolist notion of a lost linguistic and social order. Memory, form, and erotic desire afford brief butterfly glimpses of it; games, puzzles, doubles, mirrors and translation itself hint at revelation and harmony behind chaos. Recent translations of earlier works have made this evolution clearer, and established the distinction and the consistency of his long *œuvre*.

NIETZSCHE, Friedrich, 1844–1900, German philosopher and poet, welcomed the term 'aristocratic radicalism' (proposed in the first instance by Georg Brandes) as that which most appropriately defined his maturer ideas of the eighties: the proposition that 'God is dead'; the myth of the Eternal Recurrence; the emergence of the Superman; and the coming inevitability of the 'transvaluation of all values'. From his early examination of the origins of poetry and tragedy in *Die Geburt der Tragödie* (1872), through the cultural pessimism of a series of works – *Menschliches Allzumenschliches* (1878–80), *Morgenröte* (1881), *Die fröhliche Wissenschaft* (1882) – of the late seventies and early eighties, he moved to the formulation of ideas which had (and continue to have) the profoundest influence on Western thought and literature: *Also sprach Zarathustra* (1883–92), *Jenseits von Gute und Böse* (1886), *Zur Geneologie der Moral* (1887), *Die Götzendämmerung* (1889) and the uncoordinated fragments which were intended to form a systematic exposition of his most advanced thinking under the title of 'Der Wille zur Macht'.

OBSTFELDER, Sigbjørn, 1866–1900, Norwegian poet, playwright and prose writer of a peculiarly delicate yet strangely limited distinction. His work is – for Scandinavia – uniquely characteristic of (as well as contained wholly within) the nineties: *Poems* (1893), which create for their author the image of one who 'had surely come to the wrong planet' (as a line from one of his best-known poems puts it); a number of plays and dramatic fragments; the short novel *The Cross* (1896); and the evocative though unfinished *A Priest's Diary* (1900). He died young, without – as Rilke said of him – having given his work the full measure of his tormented and generous soul; it is widely believed he served as the model for Rilke's Malte Laurids Brigge.

O'CASEY, Sean, 1880–1964, Irish dramatist, was born into a Dublin Protestant family. He won his reputation at the Abbey Theatre with a group of plays – *The Shadow of a Gunman* (1923), *Juno and the Paycock* (1924) and *The Plough and the Stars* (1926) – set in the Dublin slums during the Troubles and the Civil War, using naturalistic techniques to generate lyricism, comedy and tragedy. Trouble with Irish censorship encouraged his exile in England. Later work, like *The Silver Tassie* (1928), used much more Expressionist techniques, here for an anti-war theme, in *The Bishop's Bonfire* (1955) for anti-clerical purposes.

O'NEILL, Eugene, 1888–1953, was the American dramatist who, by tireless experiment and stage versatility, put American theatre on a serious modern footing. Essentially a man of the theatre, O'Neill usually employed rather than utterly comprehended the techniques of naturalism and Expressionism that are found in the extraordinary range of his plays; but his over-riding concern with underlying, Nietzschean force and his sense of tragic inexorability turned his stage into elaborate spectacle and deep, tense psycho-drama. Early work with the Provincetown Players developed into popular success with *Beyond the Horizon* (1918) and *Anna Christie* (1920). He turned to themes of brutality and atavism (*The Emperor Jones*, 1920; *The Hairy Ape*, 1921) using the stage expressionistically, clearly indebted to European practices, though with a sense of innately American conflicts, like that between the Puritan and the rebellious energies in *Desire Under the Elms* (1924). Greek tragedy gave him the structure for the trilogy *Mourning Becomes Electra* (1930), though here O'Neill makes melodramatic rather than psychological his variant on Aeschylus. But with *Long Day's Journey Into Night* (1940: produced 1956) the psychological family tragedy he was reaching for finally realizes itself, partly because of the obvious autobiographical intensity of the work.

PASTERNAK. Boris Leonidovich, 1890–1960, Russian poet and novelist, accepted formative influences from the Symbolists and the Futurists before fashioning his own individual lyric style – most notably in, for example, *Sestra moya zhizn'* (1922) and *Temy i variatsii* (1923). These he followed with two epic poems of revolutionary inspiration, *Devyat'sot pyatyi god* (1927) and *Leitenant Shmidt* (1927), and in 1932 by a further collection of lyric verse *Vtoroe Rozhdenie*. Later – and in part because official disfavour made it difficult for him to publish any original work – he turned to translation, especially of Shakespeare, in which he produced distinguished work. His novel *Doctor Zhivago* (1957) – beyond question his greatest work – seems to belong to an altogether different context.

PÉGUY, Charles, 1873–1914, French poet and essayist, founded and edited the *Cahiers de la Quinzaine* (1900–1914), in the pages of which many of the writers of the day first found a way into print. Modishly unfashionable in matters of faith and patriotism, eloquent as a spokesman for the heroic, and a skilful innovator (often whilst still employing the most traditional of technical devices) in his verse, he became something of a cult figure – a development to which the manner of his death on the battlefield at Marne contributed. Romain Rolland wrote his biography in 1944.

PIRANDELLO, Luigi, 1867–1936, Italian dramatist and novelist, operated on that indeterminate boundary between sanity and madness, between truth and illusion, where certainty is unattainable, personality multiple, reality indefinable and faith incommunicable. His works show an obsession with the nature of identity, with the irreconcilable contradictions of modern life, and with the inadequacy of formal rational thinking. His dramas – collected under the eloquent title of 'Naked masks' – include *Così è, se vi pare* (1918), *Sei personaggi in cerca d'autore* (1921), and *Enrico IV* (1922).

POUND, Ezra, 1885–1974, American poet and critic, was born in Hailey, Idaho, and studied comparative literature before coming to London in 1908 to become the key figure in Anglo-American Modernist literary politics. In the process of inventing Imagism and Vorticism, his own work shifted out of a cosmopolitan medievalism into a hard technique of superpositioning. His poetics, which he urged massively, favoured short poems; but he had already begun *The Cantos*, and this he recast in the *avant-garde* atmosphere of 1920s Paris. In 1924 he moved to Rapallo, and his growing fiscal-cultural concerns led him to see Mussolini as an economic saviour; after the Second World War he was arrested as a traitor and confined in a mental hospital. The massive, eclectic *Cantos*, in many volumes, distil this personal experience, his economic concerns, and the great critical-cultural history he had always pursued to see how society generates art. Pound's work is vast and coherent, a continuous enterprise in artistic revolution, conducted through verse, critical texts, polemic and action, much of it in support of the artistic advancement of others.

PROUST, Marcel, 1871–1922, French novelist, began as early as the mid-1890s preparatory work for the novel that came to fill his life and its waking hours: *À la recherche du temps perdu*. When still in his thirties he privately established for himself the theoretical basis for his future novel with *Contre Sainte-Beuve* (published 1954), a claim that the art of the novelist should be directed to revealing the author-hero's past and hidden self; and from the same years, *Jean Santeil* (published 1952) contains much that can now be recognized as preliminary for the later novel. From an early life and career much given to the social round of Paris, he turned recluse in 1907; and in the cork-lined insulation of his room he wrote, between 1909 and 1912, a first draft of *À la recherche*, later re-writing and compulsively expanding it. The first volume of what was ultimately nine appeared in 1913 to only muted acclaim; the second volume in 1919 won the Prix Goncourt; and the remaining volumes followed, some after his death and thus not fully revised, in the years up to 1927. Predominantly autobiographical in inspiration, intricately wrought in its narrative detail, with a deftly but firmly controlled complexity of structure, the novel turns in upon itself in search of the meaning that informs the rich totality of individual life.

PRZYBYSZEWSKI, Stanislaw, 1868–1927, Polish novelist, dramatist and essayist, whose German-language works contributed influentially and provocatively to the European *fin de siècle* and who then after 1898, in Cracow, became one of the leaders of the 'Young Poland' movement. Taking inspiration on the one hand from Nietzsche and on the other from Chopin, and in obedience to a belief that sexuality was humanity's supreme driving force, he advocated the exposure in literature of '*die nackte Seele*' ('the naked soul'). His very real impact on European literature was probably more through his personality and his presence than through his works: among them, *Totenmesse* (1893), *Satanskinder* (1897), and his volumes of reminisence and autobiography of later years.

RICHARDSON, Dorothy, 1873–1957, English novelist, a recognized innovator in modern fiction for her 13-volume novel *Pilgrimage* (1915–38). Here she attempts to produce 'a feminine equivalent of the current masculine realism', in which 'contemplated reality' has 'its own say'; the result is a use of interior monologue techniques which is antecedent to, though less successful than, the technical achievements of Virginia Woolf and Joyce.

RILKE, Rainer Maria, 1875–1926, Austrian poet and uniquely sensitive interpreter of the consciousness of the modern age. Solitary, 'the Santa Claus of loneliness' (as W. H. Auden called him), rootlessly self-contained, endlessly fastidious in his art as in his life, he held the world, its people and its things at the distance of an arm's length the better to subject them (and the *Weltinnenraum* that lies beyond) to the intense and unremitting scrutiny of his vision. The lyric poetry of his early and middle years – the *Erste Gedichte* (written 1899–1904, published 1913), *Das Stundenbuch* (1905) and the two volumes of his *Neue Gedichte* (1907–8) – traces an intellectual path that runs from the speculative and mystical to a concern for the greater concreteness of *Dinge* (things) which are nevertheless experienced as an extension of individual being. His prose – *Geschichten vom lieben Gott* (1900), *Die Weise vom Leben und Tod des Cornetts Christoph Rilke* (1906) and, supremely and hauntingly, *Die Aufzeichnungen des Malte Laurids Brigge* (1910) – echoes this displacement in a different register, in language that is always tending towards the condition of verse. His towering, overwhelming poetic achievement came shortly before his death like the release of some great containment: *Die Sonette an Orpheus* (1923) and the *Duineser Elegien* (1923), in which he explores with fervent dispassion his visionary sense of the nature of being and meaning.

ROLLAND, Romain, 1866–1944, French novelist, playwright and scholar, began as a musicologist and art historian before turning to imaginative literature: his '*roman fleuve*' *Jean-Christophe* first began to appear serially in Péguy's *Cahiers de la Quinzaine* in 1904, when he was thirty-eight, and continued through to 1912. His volume of pacifist essays *Au-dessus de la mêlée*, published from Switzerland in 1915, helped to bring him the award of the Nobel Prize later that same year. His post-war novels, including *L'âme enchantée* (1922–33) are worthy; his plays dispensable; his biographical studies of men of genius (including Beethoven, Michelangelo, Tolstoy and Gandhi) impressive.

SCHNITZLER, Arthur, 1862–1931, Austrian dramatist and novelist, uniquely captured the decadent mood of Vienna at the *fin de siècle*. Sex, cynicism, melancholy, wit, frustration, disillusion, sophistication provide the ingredients for many of his most characteristic works: *Anatol* (1893); *Liebelei* (1896); *Der grüne Kakadu* (1899); *Reigen* (1900).

SHAW, George Bernard, 1856–1950, Irish dramatist, novelist and critic, drafted his own specifications for the design of a modern dramatist by reference to Ibsen (*The Quintessence of Ibsenism*, 1891) and then set out to meet them himself by his own early plays: *Widowers' Houses* (1892), *Arms and the Man* (1894) and *Candida* (1894). Unashamedly polemical, and holding drama to be primarily a vehicle for discussion, an instrument for social change, he applied his sharp and subversive wit – in, for example, *Man and Superman* (1901), *Pygmalion* (1912), *Heartbreak House* (1913–16), *Back to Methuselah* (1921) and *St Joan* (1923) – to the task of making a theatrical performance the occasion for the conversion of minds.

SILLANPÄÄ, Frans Eemil, 1888–1964, Finnish novelist and short story writer, Nobel Prize-winner in 1939, shows distinct affinities with Maeterlinck, with Hamsun, and (in a limited sense) with D. H. Lawrence. He is concerned with the more obviously elemental aspects of human nature, with the primitive qualities of peasant life, with the fundamental motivation of men and women. His first novel *Elämä ja aurinko* (1916) won immediate though geographically limited critical acclaim; his wider reputation derives chiefly from the 'meek heritage' of *Hurskas kurjuus* (1919), and from the internationally acclaimed *Nuorena nukkunut* (1931), translated as *Fallen Asleep While Young*.

SÖDERBERG, Hjalmar, 1869–1941, Swedish novelist, had his roots in the turbulent Scandinavian literature of the eighties, his links being especially with Georg Brandes and with the early Strindberg. The partially autobiographical *Martin Birck's Youth* (1901), followed by the elegantly evocative *Doctor Glas* (1905), established him as a sensitive analyst of the modern condition. In his prose style he shows a close affinity with Anatole France, as well as with his fellow Scandinavians Herman Bang and J. P. Jacobsen. In later life, his convictions took him first in the direction of anti-Christianity, and then later towards anti-Nazism.

SÖDERGRAN, Edith, 1892–1923, Finland–Swedish poet, is both the first great Modernist poet of Scandinavia (Lagerkvist's early verse seems adolescent and derivative in comparison) and a writer who could turn the new styles of her Russian and German contemporaries into an original personal language, combining the ecstatic intensity of free verse with a logical rigour of expression. In her poems written in Swedish – *Poems* (1916), *September Lyre* (1918), *The Rose-Altar* (1919), *The Shadow of the Future* (1920) – her spirit 'discovers its shell'. Discipline and passion characterize her last poems, collected in *The Land that does not exist* (1923).

STADLER, Ernst, 1883–1914, German poet, was killed in action. The tone of his first collection *Praeludium* (1904) is one of luxurious melancholy, in the manner of Hofmannsthal and George. He did not publish again until the last years of his life (in the periodicals *Die Aktion* and *Das Aufbruch*). These later poems are differently attuned, and use all the resources of free verse with a percussive aggression in which the new Germany of factories and railway-bridges is evoked in a panic frenzy of disjointed images.

STEIN, Gertrude, 1874–1946, American novelist and prose-poet, studied psychology and automatic writing with William James before moving to Paris in 1903. Here, collecting paintings, she became the friend of Picasso, Matisse, etc., and sought a verbal equivalent. If her *Three Lives* (1909) is influenced by James and Flaubert, *The Making of Americans* (written pre-war, published 1925) is an attempt at a Cubist space–time continuum. Her methods are synchronic, a-logical, dependent on repetition and accumulating verbal motif. Lexical simplicity generates complexity by patterned reformation, a mode clearest in character in some of her verbal portraits, which have direct Cubist analogies. By 1920s she was established, at 27 rue de Fleurus, as the guru of the new expatriate generation, and her lexicon was picked up by many in various forms (Sherwood Anderson, Hemingway, for example). But Tzara and others attacked her for falsifying essential Modernist principles, and for her underlying simplicity.

STEVENS, Wallace, 1879–1955, American poet, an executive with an insurance company, produced his major *œuvre* in his spare time. He began writing at the time of the Modernist revival in American poetry, around 1912, but did not produce a volume until *Harmonium* in 1923. His work has obvious Symbolist origins, but proceeds in a pure, logical development, a poetry of the modern poetic act itself, seeking to create a significant fiction in a post-religious, post-pantheistic world. Many of the key-phrases of Modernism – the rage for order, the supreme fiction – are Stevens's terms, tactically and rigorously pursued through a career in which every poem is a special occasion for perception, a relation of perceiver and perceived. His prose speculations about the modern imagination are collected in *The Necessary Angel* (1951).

STRINDBERG, Johan August, 1849–1912, Swedish dramatist, novelist, poet and prolific correspondent, was an obsessed and restless genius, boldly experimental, unbelievably fecund. His life and authorship fall into two divisions, separated by the nervous breakdown, his 'Inferno crisis', of 1895–7. His earlier dramas are historical (e.g. *Master Olof*, 1878) and realistic (*The Father*, 1887; *Miss Julie*, 1888; *The Stronger*, 1889); post-Inferno, they are again historical or (more importantly) expressionistic: *To Damascus* (1898–1904); *A Dream Play* (1902); *The Ghost Sonata* (1907). Throughout his life, he was preoccupied by the problems of guilt, sin, the occult, abnormal mental states, and the relationship between the sexes.

SUPERVIELLE, Jules, 1884–1960, French poet, novelist and playwright, brought to his lyrics (in which certain distinctive Latin American overtones are audible) a deft and sensitive though *epigonenhaft* post-Symbolist talent. His concern for the human predicament – in, for example, *Gravitations* (1925) as in most of the volumes of verse that followed – is real, delicately expressed, sweetly sad, and undisturbing.

SVEVO, Italo (pseud. for Ettore Schmitz), 1861–1928, Jewish-Italian novelist born in Trieste under the Austro-Hungarian empire. His writing falls into two stages. Two ironic novels about marginal, maladjusted heroes in the declining bourgeois world of Trieste, *Una vita* (1892) and *Senilita* (1898) appeared in the nineties, with little success. In 1906 Svevo met Joyce, who encouraged him: this produced more writing, including short stories and his best-known novel, *La conscienza di Zeno* (1923), an even more ironic study of a listless bourgeois in psychoanalysis. Svevo's heroes, like Musil's, are men without qualities, vaguely aspiring to love and cultural achievement, yet with a self-diminishing, self-persecuting psychology that Svevo exactly catches, to produce tense comedies with tragic overtones, stories of culturally conditioned self-delusion and self-defeat.

TRAKL, Georg, 1887–1914, Austrian poet, committed suicide whilst working as a medical orderly on the Eastern Front. His verse – *Gedichte* (1913), *Sebastian im Traum* (which appeared after his death in 1915) – is limited in range but profoundly suggestive in tone; for all the neo-Romantic gloom of the subject matter, his work presents an abstract design of symbols and colours, musical not only in its euphony but in its capacity to evoke a response from the unconscious. As in Austrian music and painting of the same period, the exaggerated gestures of late Romanticism are already in the process of becoming formal, abstract, modern.

TZARA, Tristan, 1896–1963, French poet, founded the Dada movement in 1916 in Zürich (see *Sept Manifestes dada*, 1920), and then four years later settled in Paris where his ideas, through the intermediacy of Breton and Aragon, helped to provoke the emergence of Surrealism. Audacious linguistic experimentation, the repudiation of merely rational order in thought and word, and a predilection for the brutal and the chaotic characterize his middle work, especially *L'homme approximatif* (1931). His late work is unexpectedly disciplined.

UNAMUNO, Miguel de, 1864–1936, Spanish writer and thinker, found deep but productive intellectual anguish in the problem – fundamental, he felt, to all existence – of how to reconcile man's irrational, subconscious, intuitive drives and longings with the impositions of scientific, rational, logical and analytical thinking. His

Amor y pedagogia (1902), an early exploration of this problem, was in part stimulated by his reading of Kierkegaard, William James and Bergson; a more deeply pondered and more widely influential analysis is offered in his *Del sentimiento trágico de la vida* (1913) and *La agonia del Christianismo* (1924). The same existential concerns also lie at the heart of his novels (pre-eminently *Niebla*, 1914) and his other creative work in the drama and the short story.

VALÉRY, Paul, 1871–1945, French poet and critic, as a young man established an initial reputation as an analytical and reflective prose writer – particularly through his *Introduction à la méthode de Leonard de Vinci* (1895) and *La soirée avec Monsieur Teste* (1896) – and as the author of occasional poems in the literary journals of that decade. Not until he himself was in his forties did he turn, dedicatedly and seriously, to the writing of poetry: 1917 saw the completion and publication of *La jeune parque*, which won immediate acknowledgement as a major poetic achievement; this was followed in 1921 by *Charmes*, a collection which included the great 'Le cimetière marin'. His astonishing range of intellectual interests – not wholly recognized for the impressive thing it was until the posthumous publication of the twenty-nine volumes of his *Cahiers 1894–1945* – pervades all his poetry like an essence.

VERHAEREN, Emile, 1855–1916, Belgian poet, whose *vers libres* with their exuberant and declarative forcefulness, their grammatical abrasiveness, their homage to energy and their faith in the brotherhood of man have drawn comparison with Walt Whitman, moved on from a fairly orthodox eighties naturalism to a more symbolistically orientated style – in *Les Campagnes hallucinées* (1893), *Les villages illusoires* (1895) and *Les villes tentaculaires* (1895). *Les rythmes souverains* (1910) reflects something of his later preoccupation with industrialization, its grandeur and its servitude.

VERLAINE, Paul, 1844–1896, French *poète maudit*, moved progressively away from the Parnassian mode of the early *Poèmes saturniens* (1866) and *Fêtes galantes* (1869) in the direction of the new and personal style – oblique, impressionistic, intensely musical, metrically experimental – of the *Romances sans paroles* (1874). A two year prison sentence (1873–5) for an attempt on the life of Rimbaud (who had deeply disturbingly entered his life) induced a religious crisis, a return to Catholicism, and – not unrelatedly – the re-introduction in *Sagesse* (1881) and his later work of a more traditional discipline into his poetry, both in content and form. His later work following *Jadis et naguère* traces a graph of declining quality.

WEDEKIND, Frank, 1864–1918, German dramatist, was also an actor and cabaret artist. His *Frühlings Erwachen* (1891) inaugurated a career of literary exploration into the sexual and erotic drives within the individual and society. *Erdgeist* (1895) and *Die Büchse der Pandora* (1904) – often collectively identified as the 'Lulu tragedies' – follow the progress of a primitive soul through the corrupting environment of modern civilization. His preface to a volume of short stories in 1905, 'Über die Erotik', outlines his philosophy of life and art.

WILDE, Oscar, 1854–1900, Irish-born poet, critic, novelist, dramatist, and apostle of decadence. *Poems* appeared in 1881, but his best achievements belong to the 1890s, which he dominated. His involvement with the international movement is best seen, not in the familiar stage comedies (*The Importance of Being Earnest* (1895), etc.), but in the decadent novel *The Picture of Dorian Gray* (1891) about hedonism and art, and the play *Salome*, produced in Berlin by Max Reinhardt in 1903.

WILLIAMS, William Carlos, 1883–1963, American poet, novelist and playwright, was a doctor in Rutherford, N.J. An early friend of Ezra Pound's, and influenced deeply by Imagism, he nonetheless insisted on an experimental mode that was natively American, free both of European internationalism and of pessimism. His work is a tight, controlled celebration, of people, of things, dependent on precise acts of perception controlled by exact speech rhythms: 'No ideas but in things'. His lifetime of verse and prose experiment, concentrated in *Kora in Hell* (1920), *Spring and All* (1923), *Paterson* (4 vols., 1946–58), *Collected Later Poems* (1950), and *Pictures from Breughel* (1962), influenced many subsequent American poets and helped establish a distinctly American experimental tradition.

WOOLF, Virginia, 1882–1941, English novelist and critic, was committed to the Modernist–aesthetic preoccupations of Bloomsbury by her kinship with Clive Bell, friendship with Roger Fry and marriage to Leonard Woolf well before she began writing fiction. Her first novel, *The Voyage Out*, appeared in 1915; but her major experimental work starts with *Jacob's Room* (1922) and centres in *Mrs Dalloway* (1925), *To the Lighthouse* (1927) and *The Waves* (1931). These novels, explicitly anti-materialistic, concerned with 'the atoms as they fall', depend on elaborate transactions of consciousness among characters and with the author, a complex use of symbolism, an exact aesthetic sense, and a strong sense of the female imagination as a creative order of feeling, compared with the rational harshness of mind often associated in her work with the male. Mrs Woolf's can seem in some respects a domesticated Modernism, but it contains shrill undertones of disturbance and terror, dark insights undoubtedly related to her suicide in 1941.

YEATS, William Butler, 1865-1939, Irish poet and playwright, wrote early poetry – *The Wanderings of Oisin* (1889), *The Wind Among the Reeds* (1899) – heavy with the atmosphere of the *fin de siècle*. In his collections – *Responsibilities* (1914), *The Wild Swans at Coole* (1919), *Michael Robartes and the Dancer* (1921), *The Tower* (1928), *The Winding Stair* (1933), *Last Poems* (published 1939) – the interplay of bitter nostalgia for youth with a neo-Platonist philosophy and a (highly eccentric) brand of spiritualism give the poetry a unique richness of suggestion. The ideas contained in them are frequently bizarre (see *A Vision*, 1926), but the passion and precision which he brings to their expression in verse gives them a dignity which their sources lack. Yeats's plays, though secondary to the poetry, have a special fascination; they range from the Romantic fuzziness of *The Countess Cathleen* (1892) to the bleak Expressionism of *At the Hawk's Well* (1917) and *Purgatory* (1939) and the grotesque farce of *The Player Queen* (1917) and *The Herne's Egg* (1938).

YESENIN, Sergey, 1895-1925, Russian poet, helped to form the Imaginist group of poets in 1919. Coming from simple peasant origins, he first turned in his pre-Revolution days to the writing of artless poems about the simple life. In the twenties, disillusioned by the new régime, his sense of alienation led him to seek satisfaction in urgent travel, in a hectic, rootless life-style, in alcohol, and in conduct which he took a defiant pride in calling 'hooliganism'. His more confessional poems of these years are deeply moving. For some years he was married to the dancer Isadore Duncan. In 1925 he committed suicide.

ZAMYATIN, Yevgeniy Ivanovich, 1884-1939, Russian novelist and critic, whose view of social and cultural change as consisting essentially of a succession of 'heresies', and whose conviction – expressed both in his own creative practice and in his criticism (e.g. *O literature, revolyutsii, entropii*, 1924) – that art needs to resist the threat to its own nature and independence that political pressure always brings, prompted him in 1921 to form the group of Russian writers known as the Serapion Brothers, inspired by these and similar views. His best-known novels – *My* (1920), a work in the prophetic Wellsian–Huxleyan–Orwellian tradition, and *Rasskaz o samom glavnom* (1924) – belong to the period before his falling into official Soviet disfavour and his voluntary exile to Paris in 1931.

Bibliography

THIS is a *general* bibliography listing main works of historical significance and also of studies of that significance, and showing trends, movements, intellectual tendencies, and the range and internationality of research and debate. Its organization, parallel to the structure of the book, thus covers, in order, literature on: (1) general works on Modernism; (2) intellectual, social and historical background: European life, thought and culture, 1890–1930; (3) the nations of Modernism; (4) the movements of Modernism; (5) poetry; (6) the novel; and (7) drama. A full bibliography of Modernism would be massive: we have selected major and central works, many of which will themselves lead readers to more detailed bibliographical references. Imaginative works by, and studies of, single authors are not included: references to these will be found in the articles themselves, the brief biographies, and the useful entries in the *Penguin Companion to Literature*, vols. 1–3. For space reasons, articles in periodicals must be omitted.

I. GENERAL WORKS ON MODERNISM

RENE ALBÉRÈS, *L'aventure intellectuelle du XXe siècle: panorama des littératures européennes, 1900–1963* (Paris 1963).

A. ALVAREZ, *Beyond All This Fiddle: Essays, 1955–1967* (London 1968).

W. H. AUDEN, *The Dyer's Hand and Other Essays* (London 1962).

ROLAND BARTHES, *Le Degré Zéro de l'écriture* (Paris 1964), translated as *Writing Degree Zero* (London 1967).

JACQUES BARZUN, *Classic, Romantic, and Modern* (London 1962).

W. BENJAMIN, *Über Literatur* (Frankfurt 1969).

— *Illuminationen* (Frankfurt 1969), translated as *Illuminations* (London 1970).

BERNARD BERGONZI (ed.), *Innovations: Essays on Art and Ideas* (London 1968).

R. P. BLACKMUR, *Anni Mirabiles, 1921–1925: Reason in the Madness of Letters* (Washington D.C. 1956).

C. M. BOWRA, *The Background of Modern Poetry* (Oxford 1946).

— *The Heritage of Symbolism* (London 1943).

JOSEPH CHIARI, *The Aesthetics of Modernism* (London 1970).

CYRIL CONNOLLY, *The Modern Movement: One Hundred Key Books from England, France, and America, 1880–1950* (London 1965).

ANTHONY CRONIN, *A Question of Modernity* (London 1966).

DENIS DONOGHUE, *The Ordinary Universe: Soundings in Modern Literature* (New York 1968).

RICHARD ELLMANN, *Golden Codgers: Biographical Speculations* (New York and London 1973).

— *Eminent Domain: Yeats Among Wilde, Joyce, Pound, Eliot and Auden* (London 1968).

RICHARD ELLMANN and CHARLES FEIDELSON, JR (eds.), *The Modern Tradition: Backgrounds of Modern Literature* (New York and London 1965).

W. EMRICH, *Protest und Verheissung* (Frankfurt 1960).

WALDO FRANK, *The Widening Gyre: Crisis and Mastery in Modern Literature* (New Brunswick, N.J. 1963).

G. S. FRASER, *The Modern Writer and his World* (London 1964).

MELVIN FRIEDMAN, *Stream of Consciousness: A Study in Literary Method* (New Haven, Conn. 1955).

NORTHROP FRYE, *The Modern Century* (Toronto 1968).

WILLIAM GAUNT, *The March of the Moderns* (London 1949).

CHARLES I. GLICKSBERG, *Tragic Vision in Twentieth-Century Literature* (Carbondale, Ill. 1963).

CESAR GRANA, *Bohemian Versus Bourgeois* (later titled *Modernity and its Discontents*) (New York 1964).

HARVEY GROSS, *The Contrived Corridor: History and Fatality in Modern Literature* (Ann Arbor 1971).

GEOFFREY HARTMAN, *Beyond Formalism: Literary Essays, 1958–1970* (New Haven 1970).

IHAB HASSAN, *The Dismemberment of Orpheus: Toward a Postmodern Literature* (New York 1971).

— *The Literature of Silence: Henry Miller and Samuel Beckett* (New York 1967).

— *Paracriticisms: Seven Speculations of the Times* (Urbana and London 1975).

HELMUT HEISSENBÜTTEL, *Zur Tradition der Moderne: Aufsätze und Anmerkungen, 1964–1971* (Neuwied 1972).

ERICH HELLER, *The Disinherited Mind* (Cambridge 1952, Harmondsworth 1961).

WALTER HILSBECHER, *Wie modern ist eine Literatur: Aufsätze* (Munich 1965).

FREDERICK J. HOFFMAN, CHARLES ALLEN, and CAROLYN F. ULRICH, *The Little Magazine: A History and Bibliography* (Princeton 1947).

Bibliography

FREDERICK J. HOFFMAN, *The Mortal No: Death and the Modern Imagination* (Princeton 1964).

HANS EGON HOLTHUSEN, et al., *Avantgarde: Geschichte und Krise einer Idee* (Munich 1966).

GRAHAM HOUGH, *Image and Experience: Studies in a Literary Revolution* (London 1960).

IRVING HOWE, *The Decline of the New* (New York 1970).

IRVING HOWE (ed.), *The Idea of the Modern in Literature and the Arts* (New York 1967). (Paperback edition: *Literary Modernism* (Greenwich, Conn. 1967).)

J. ISAACS, *An Assessment of Twentieth Century Literature* (London 1951).

DAVID JONES, *Epoch and Artist* (London 1959).

LOUIS KAMPF, *On Modernism: Prospects for Literature and Freedom* (Boston, Mass. 1967).

HUGH KENNER, *Gnomon: Essays on Contemporary Literature* (New York 1958).

FRANK KERMODE, *Continuities* (London 1968).

— *Modern Essays* (London 1971).

— *Puzzles and Epiphanies: Essays and Reviews, 1958–1961* (London 1963).

— *The Sense of an Ending* (London and New York 1966).

W. KILLY (ed.), *Das 20. Jahrhundert, 1880–1933* (Munich 1963).

LEO KOFLER, *Zur Theorie der modern Literatur: der Avantgardismus in sooziologisches Sicht* (Neuwied 1962).

MURRAY KREIGER, *The Tragic Vision* (New York 1960).

HELMUT KREUZER, *Die Boheme: Beiträge zu ihrer Beschreibung* (Stuttgart 1968).

JOSEPH WOOD KRUTCH, *The Measure of Man: On Freedom, Human Values, Survival, and the Modern Temper* (Indianapolis 1953).

JOHN LEHMANN, *New Writing in Europe* (London 1940).

HARRY LEVIN, *Refractions: Essays in Comparative Literature* (New York and London 1966).

S. LUBLINSKI, *Die Bilanz der Moderne* (Berlin 1901).

— *Der Ausgang der Moderne* (Berlin 1909).

GEORG LUKÁCS, *Zur Gegenwartsbedeutung des kritischen Realismus* (1958), translated as *The Meaning of Contemporary Realism* (London 1963).

— *Studies in Contemporary Realism* (London 1972).

GERHARD MASUR, *Propheten von gestern: zur europäischen Kultur, 1890–1914* (Frankfurt 1965), translated as *Prophets of Yesterday* (London 1963).

HANS MAYER (ed.), *Deutsche Literaturkritik im 20. Jahrhundert* (Stuttgart 1965).

Bibliography

A. MOELLER VAN DEN BRUCK, *Die Moderne Literatur in Gruppen- und Einzeldarstellungen* (Berlin 1899–1902).

JOSE ORTEGA Y GASSET, *The Dehumanization of Art and Other Essays* (London 1972).

— *The Modern Theme* (London 1931).

JOHN OLIVER PERRY (ed.), *Backgrounds to Modern Literature* (San Francisco 1968).

RENATO POGGIOLI, *The Theory of the Avant Garde* (London 1968).

GEORGES POULET, *Études sur le temps humaine*, vols I–IV (Edinburgh and Paris 1949–64), part translated as *Studies in Human Time* (Baltimore 1956) and *The Interior Distance* (Baltimore 1959).

HERBERT READ, *Art Now* (London, 1933; revised edition 1960).

— *Collected Essays* (2nd edition) (London 1962).

HERBERT READ (ed.), *The Modern Movement in English Architecture, Painting and Sculpture* (London 1934).

HAROLD ROSENBERG, *The Tradition of the New* (London 1962).

NATHAN SCOTT, *Negative Capability: Studies in the New Literature and the Religious Situation* (New Haven, Conn. 1969).

SUSAN SONTAG, *Against Interpretation and Other Essays* (New York 1966).

STEPHEN SPENDER, *The Struggle of the Modern* (London 1963).

GEORGE STEINER, *Extraterritorial* (London 1972).

— *Language and Silence: Essays 1958–1966* (London 1967).

WYLIE SYPHER, *Four Stages of Renaissance Style: Transformations in Art and Literature* (New York 1955).

— *Literature and Technology: The Alien Vision* (New York 1968).

— *Loss of the Self in Modern Art and Literature* (New York 1962).

— *Rococo in Cubism in Art and Literature* (New York 1960).

LIONEL TRILLING, *The Opposing Self: Nine Essays in Criticism* (London 1955, New York 1955).

— *A Gathering of Fugitives: Critical Essays* (London 1957, Boston 1956).

— *The Liberal Imagination: Essays on Literature and Society* (London 1951, New York 1950).

— *Beyond Culture: Essays on Literature and Learning* (London 1966).

— *Sincerity and Authenticity* (London 1972).

— *Mind in the Modern World* (New York 1973).

JOHN WEIGHTMAN, *The Concept of the Avant-Garde* (London 1973).

B. VON WEISE, *Deutsche Dichter der Moderne* (2nd enlarged edition) (Berlin 1969).

RÉNE WELLEK, *A History of Modern Criticism 1750–1950: vol. 4, The Later Nineteenth Century* (New Haven 1955).

EDMUND WILSON, *Axel's Castle: A Study in the Imaginative Literature of 1870–1930* (New York 1931).

Bibliography

2. INTELLECTUAL, SOCIAL AND HISTORICAL BACKGROUND:
EUROPEAN LIFE, THOUGHT AND CULTURE, 1890–1930

H. D. AIKEN, *et al.*, (eds.), *Philosophy in the Twentieth Century* (4 vols.) (New York 1962).

RAYMOND ARON, *Main Currents in Sociological Thought* (London 1965–8).

HANS ARP, *On My Way: Poetry and Essays, 1921–1947* (New York 1948).

A. J. AYER, *Language, Truth and Logic* (London 1936).

WILLIAM BARRETT, *Irrational Man: A Study in Existential Philosophy* (London 1961).

JACQUES BARZUN, *Darwin, Marx, Wagner* (Boston 1941).

HENRI BERGSON, *Essai sur les données immédiates de la conscience* (Paris 1889), translated as *Time and Free Will* (London 1910).

— *L'évolution créatrice* (Paris 1907), translated as *Creative Evolution* (London 1910).

H. J. BLACKHAM, *Six Existentialist Thinkers* (London 1952).

F. H. BRADLEY, *Appearance and Reality* (London 1893).

CRANE BRINTON, *The Shaping of the Modern Mind* (New York 1953).

MARCEL BRION, *L'Art Abstrait* (Paris 1956).

J. A. C. BROWN, *Freud and the Post-Freudians* (New York 1961).

NORMAN O. BROWN, *Life Against Death* (New York and London 1959).

LYMAN E. BRYSON (ed.), *Man's Knowledge of the Modern World* (New York 1960).

ALBERT CAMUS, *L'homme revolté* (Paris, 1951), translated as *The Rebel* (London 1960).

C. B. COX and A. E. DYSON (eds.), *The Twentieth Century Mind* (3 vols.) (London 1972).

P. DEMETZ, *Marx, Engels und die Dichter* (Stuttgart 1959).

HERBERT DINGLE (ed.), *A Century of Science* (London 1951).

SERGEI EISENSTEIN, *Film Form: Essays in Film Theory* (New York 1957).

T. S. ELIOT, *Notes Towards the Definition of Culture* (London 1949).

MAX ERNST, *Beyond Painting* (New York 1948).

J. C. FLUGEL, *A Hundred Years of Psychology 1833–1933* (London 1948).

SIR J. G. FRAZER, *The Golden Bough* (London 1923, reprinted 1963).

SIGMUND FREUD, *Das Unbehagen in der Kultur* (Vienna 1930), translated as *Civilization and Its Discontents* (London 1930).

ERICH FROMM, *The Fear of Freedom* (London 1945).

ROGER FRY, *Vision and Design* (London 1923).

H. GOLLWITZER, *Europe in the Age of Imperialism* (London 1969).

E. H. GOMBRICH, *Art and Illusion* (London 1962).

WERNER HAFTMANN, *Painting in the Twentieth Century* (revised edition) (London 1965).

ARNOLD HAUSER, *Sozialgeschichte der Kunst und Literatur* (Munich 1953), translated as *The Social History of Art* (4 vols.) (London 1962).

A. E. HEATH (ed.), *Scientific Thought in the Twentieth Century* (London 1951).

WERNER HEISENBERG, *The Physicist's Conception of Nature* (London 1955–8).

B. HOFFMANN, *The Strange Story of the Quantum* (revised edition) (London 1965).

F. J. HOFFMAN, *Freudianism and the Literary Mind* (Baton Rouge, La. 1957).

J. T. HOWARD and J. LYONS, *Modern Music* (New York 1966).

H. STUART HUGHES, *Consciousness and Society: The Reorientation of European Social Thought 1890–1930* (London 1967).

T. E. HULME, *Speculations* (London and New York 1924).

G. B. DE HUSZAR (ed.), *The Intellectuals: A Controversial Portrait* (Glencoe, Ill. 1960).

S. E. HYMAN, *The Tangled Bank: Darwin, Marx, Frazer, and Freud* (New York 1962).

WILLIAM JAMES, *Principles of Psychology* (New York 1890).

C. G. JUNG, *Seelenprobleme der Gegenwart* (Zürich 1931), translated as *Modern Man in Search of a Soul* (London 1953).

WALTER A. KAUFMAN (ed.), *Religion from Tolstoy to Camus* (New York 1961).

— *Existentialism from Dostoevsky to Sartre* (New York 1956).

PAUL KLEE, *On Modern Art* (London, 1948).

J. LANGBEHN, *Rembrandt als Erzieher* (Leipzig 1890).

SUSANNE LANGER, *Philosophy in a New Key* (Cambridge, Mass. 1942).

G. LICHTHEIM, *Marxism* (London, 1961).

LEO LOWENTHAL, *Literature and the Image of Man* (Boston, Mass. 1957).

G. LUKÁCS, *Die Zerstörung der Vernunft* (Berlin 1954).

KARL MANNHEIM, *Ideologie und Utopie* (Bonn 1929), translated as *Ideology and Utopia* (London 1936).

HERBERT MARCUSE, *Eros and Civilization: A Philosophical Inquiry Into Freud* (Boston, Mass. 1955).

MARSHALL MCLUHAN, *The Gutenberg Galaxy* (Toronto 1965).

HANS MEYERHOFF (ed.), *The Philosophy of History in Our Time* (New York 1959).

Bibliography

LEWIS MUMFORD, *The Myth of the Machine: Technics and Human Development* (New York 1968).

BENJAMIN NELSON (ed.), *Freud and the Twentieth Century* (New York 1957).

FRIEDRICH NIETZSCHE, *Also sprach Zarathustra* (Chemnitz 1883–91), translated as *Thus Spoke Zarathustra* (London 1961).

E. NOLTE, *The Three Faces of Fascism* (London 1965).

MAX NORDAU, *Entartung* (Berlin 1892), translated as *Degeneration* (London 1895).

JOSE ORTEGA Y GASSET, *La rebelión de las Masas* (Madrid 1930), translated as *The Revolt of the Masses* (London 1932).

AMADÉE OZENFANT, *The Foundations of Modern Art* (New York 1931).

J. A. PASSMORE, *A Hundred Years of Philosophy* (London 1957).

ALAN PRYCE-JONES (ed.), *A New Outline of Modern Knowledge* (London 1956).

HERBERT READ, *A Concise History of Modern Painting* (London 1960).

PHILIP REIFF, *The Triumph of the Therapeutic* (London 1966).

PAUL ROTHA, *The Film Till Now* (London 1949).

BERTRAND RUSSELL, *The Scientific Outlook* (London 1931).

GILBERT RYLE, *The Concept of Mind* (London 1949).

SALLIE SEARS and GEORGIANA LORD (eds.), *The Discontinuous Universe* (New York and London 1972).

GEORGES SOREL, *Réflexions sur la violence* (Paris 1908), translated as *Reflections on Violence* (London 1912).

P. A. SOROKIN, *Social Philosophies in an Age of Crisis* (Boston, Mass. 1950).

OSWALD SPENGLER, *Untergang des Abendlandes* (2 vols.) (Munich 1918–22), translated as *The Decline of the West* (London 1926–9).

F. STERN, *The Politics of Cultural Despair* (Berkeley 1961).

PAUL TILLICH, *The Courage to Be* (New Haven 1952).

FERDINAND TONNIES, *Gemeinschaft und Gesellschaft* (Leipzig 1887), translated as *Community and Association* (London 1955).

LIONEL TRILLING, *Freud and the Crisis of our Culture* (New York 1955).

LEON TROTSKY, *Literature and Revolution* (New York 1925).

BARBARA TUCHMAN, *The Proud Tower: 1870–1914* (New York 1966).

HANS VAIHINGER, *Die Philosophie des Als Ob* (Berlin 1911), translated as *The Philosophy of 'As If'* (New York 1952).

MORTON WHITE (ed.), *The Age of Analysis* (New York 1960).

ALFRED NORTH WHITEHEAD, *Science and the Modern World* (Cambridge 1926).

GEORGE WOODCOCK, *Anarchism* (London 1963).

3. THE NATIONS OF MODERNISM

Germany

M. ARENDT et al., *Geschichte der Stadt Berlin* (Berlin 1937).

J. BAB, *Die Berliner Bohème* (Berlin 1905).

MICHAEL BALFOUR, *The Kaiser and His Times* (London 1964).

L. BERGSTRASSER, *Geschichte der politischen Parteien in Deutschland* (Mannheim 1926).

RALF DAHRENDORF, *Gesellschaft und Demokratie in Deutschland* (Munich 1965).

RONALD GRAY, *The German Tradition in Literature 1871–1945* (Cambridge 1965).

R. HAMANN and J. HERMAND, *Deutsche Kunst und Kultur von der Gründerzeit bis zum Expressionismus* (4 vols.) (Berlin 1959–67).

MICHAEL HAMBURGER, *From Prophecy to Exorcism* (London 1965).

G. L. MOSSE, *The Crisis of German Ideology* (New York 1964).

ROY PASCAL, *From Naturalism to Expressionism: German Literature and Society 1880–1918* (London 1973).

G. RITTER, *Die Arbeiterbewegung in Wilhelminischen Reich* (Berlin 1959).

A. ROSENBERG, *Die Enstehung der deutschen Republik, 1871–1918* (Berlin 1928).

H. ROTHFELS (ed.), *Berlin in Vergangenheit und Gegenwart* (Tübingen 1961).

R. H. SAMUEL and R. H. THOMAS, *Education and Society in Modern Germany* (London 1949).

Austro-Hungary

M. BROD, *Der Prager Kreis* (Stuttgart 1966).

A. JANIK and S. TOULMIN, *Wittgenstein's Vienna* (London 1973).

R. KRALIK, *Geschichte der Stadt Wien* (Vienna 1926).

A. J. P. TAYLOR, *The Hapsburg Monarchy* (London 1955).

Scandinavia

M. S. ALLWOOD, *Twentieth Century Scandinavian Poetry* (Helsinki and Oslo 1950).

H. BEYER, *A History of Norwegian Literature* (New York 1956).

— *Nietzsche og Norden* (2 vols.) (Bergen 1958–9).

H. BORLAND, *Nietzsche's Influence on Swedish Literature* (Gothenburg 1956).

E. BREDSDORFF et al., *Introduction to Scandinavian Literature* (Cambridge 1951).

Bibliography

B. W. DOWNS, *Modern Norwegian Literature, 1860–1918* (Cambridge 1966).

A. GUSTAFSON, *A History of Swedish Literature* (Minneapolis 1961).

— *Six Scandinavian Novelists* (Princeton 1940).

J. W. MCFARLANE, *Ibsen and the Temper of Norwegian Literature* (London 1960).

P. M. MITCHELL, *A History of Danish Literature* (Copenhagen 1957).

Great Britain

MALCOLM BRADBURY, *The Social Context of Modern English Literature* (Oxford 1971).

DAVID DAICHES, *The Present Age in British Literature* (Bloomington, Ind. 1969).

R. C. ENSOR, *England: 1870–1914* (Oxford 1936).

BORIS FORD (ed.), *The Pelican Guide to English Literature, Volume 7: The Modern Age* (Harmondsworth 1961).

ROGER FRY, *Reflections on British Painting* (London 1934).

HOLBROOK JACKSON, *The Eighteen-Nineties* (London 1931).

C. L. MOWAT, *Great Britain Since 1914* (London 1970).

V. DE SOLA PINTO, *Crisis in English Poetry: 1880–1914* (London 1951).

ENID STARKIE, *From Gautier to Eliot: The Influence of France in English Literature, 1851–1939* (London 1962).

C. K. STEAD, *The New Poetic: Yeats to Eliot* (London 1964).

A. J. P. TAYLOR, *English History, 1914–1945* (Oxford 1965).

WILLIAM YORK TINDALL, *Forces in Modern British Literature, 1885–1956* (New York 1956).

RAYMOND WILLIAMS, *Culture and Society: 1780–1950* (London 1959).

France

E. CAHM, *Politics and Society in Contemporary France* (London 1972).

D. CAUTE, *Communism and the French Intellectuals* (London 1964).

K. CORNELL, *The Post-Symbolist Period: French Poetic Currents, 1900–1920* (New Haven 1958).

J. CRUICKSHANK (ed.), *French Literature and its Background, Volume 6: The 20th Century* (London 1970).

MICHAEL CURTIS, *Three against the Republic: Sorel, Barrès and Maurras* (Princeton 1959).

E. R. CURTIUS, *The Civilization of France* (London 1932).

M. DÉCAUDIN, *La crise des valeurs symbolistes* (Toulouse 1960).

H. DUBIEF, *Le syndicalisme révolutionnaire* (Paris 1969).

N. GREEN, *From Versailles to Vichy* (New York 1970).

S. HOFFMANN et al., *France: Change and Tradition* (London 1963).

H. STUART HUGHES, *The Obstructed Path* (New York 1966).

D. JOHNSON, *France and the Dreyfus Affair* (London 1966).

F. F. RIDLEY, *Revolutionary Syndicalism in France* (Cambridge 1970).

R. RUDROFF, *Belle Époque* (London 1972).

A. SALMON, *Souvenirs sans fin* (3 vols.) (Paris 1955–61).

PAUL SÉRVANT, *Le Romantisme fasciste* (Paris 1959).

E. WEBER, *Action Française* (Stanford 1962).

— *The Nationalist Revival in France* (Berkeley 1959).

T. ZELDIN, *France 1848–1945: Vol. 1* (London 1973).

Italy

E. CECCHI and M. SAPEGNO (eds.), *Storia della letteratura italiana, Vol.IX, Il novecento* (Milan 1969).

F. CHABOD, *A History of Italian Fascism* (London 1963).

B. CROCE, *La Letteratura della nuova Italia* (6 vols.) (Bari 1947).

E. FALQUI. *Novecento letterario italiano* (4 vols.) (Florence 1970).

— *Il futurismo e il Novecentismo* (Turin 1958).

D. FERNANDEZ, *Il romanzo italiano e la crisi della coscienza moderna* (Milan 1960).

A. GALLETTI, *Il novecento* (Milan 1961).

D. MACK SMITH, *Italy: A Modern History* (Ann Arbor 1959).

C. MARZORATI (ed.), *Letteratura italiana, Le correnti*, Vol. II, and *I contemporanei* (3 vols.) (Rome 1956).

S. PACIFICI, *A Guide to Contemporary Italian Literature* (Cleveland and New York 1962).

— *The Modern Italian Novel* (Carbondale, Ill. 1967).

A. RHODES, *The Poet as Superman* (London 1959).

Russia

VERA ALEXANDROVA, *A History of Soviet Literature: 1917–1964* (New York 1964).

N. BERDYAEV, *The Russian Idea* (London 1947).

C. M. BOWRA (ed.), *A Book of Russian Verse* (London 1943).

— *A Second Book of Russian Verse* (London 1948).

E. J. BROWN, *Russian Literature Since the Revolution* (London 1969).

BABETTE DEUTSCH and A. YARMOLINSKY (eds.), *Modern Russian Poetry: An Anthology* (London 1923).

C. GRAY, *The Great Experiment: Russian Art, 1863–1922* (London 1962).

MAX HAYWARD and LEOPOLD LABEDZ (eds.), *Literature and Revolution in Soviet Russia: 1917–1962* (London 1963).

ALEXANDER KAUN, *Soviet Poets and Poetry* (Berkeley 1943, reprinted 1968).

Bibliography

ROBERT LORD, *Russian and Soviet Literature: An Introduction* (London 1972).

VLADIMIR MARKOV and MERRILL SPARKS (eds.), *Modern Russian Poetry* (London 1966).

P. MILIUKOV, *Outlines of Russian Culture* (Philadelphia 1942).

D. S. MIRSKY, *Contemporary Russian Literature: 1881–1925* (London 1925).

HELEN MUCHNIC, *From Gorky to Pasternak: Six Modern Russian Writers* (London 1963).

RENATO POGGIOLI, *The Phoenix and the Spider* (Cambridge, Mass. 1957).

— *The Poets of Russia: 1890–1930* (Cambridge, Mass. 1960).

M. RAEFF (ed.), *Russian Intellectual History, Volumes 2 and 3* (New York 1960).

ERNEST J. SIMMONS, *An Outline of Modern Russian Literature: 1880–1940* (New York 1944, reprinted 1971).

MARC SLONIM, *From Chekhov to the Revolution: Russian Literature, 1900–1917* (New York 1962).

— *Modern Russian Literature from Chekhov to the Present* (New York 1953).

L. I. STRAKHOVSKY, *Craftsmen of the Word: Three Poets of Modern Russia* (Westport, Conn. 1969).

G. P. STRUVE, *Russian Literature under Lenin and Stalin: 1917–1953* (Norman, Okla. 1971).

BORIS THOMSON, *The Premature Revolution: Russian Literature and Society, 1917–1946* (London 1972).

V. ZAVALISHIN, *Early Soviet Writers* (New York 1958).

United States

FREDERICK L. ALLEN, *The Big Change: America Transforms Itself, 1900–1950* (New York 1952).

JOSEPH WARREN BEACH, *American Fiction: 1920–1940* (New York 1941).

RUDI BLESH, *Modern Art U.S.A.: Men, Rebellion, Conquest, 1900–1956* (New York 1956).

LOUISE BOGAN, *Achievement in American Poetry: 1900–1950* (Chicago 1951).

JOHN W. CHASE, *Years of the Modern: An American Appraisal* (New York 1949).

MALCOLM COWLEY (ed.), *After the Genteel Tradition* (New York 1937, revised edition 1964).

Bibliography

BERNARD DUFFEY, *The Chicago Renaissance in American Letters* (Greenwood, Conn. 1954).

ERIC F. GOLDMAN, *Rendezvous with Destiny: A History of Modern American Reform* (New York 1952).

HORACE GREGORY and MARYA ZATURENSKA, *A History of American Poetry: 1900–1940* (New York 1946).

OSCAR HANDLIN, *The American People in the Twentieth Century* (Cambridge, Mass. 1954).

RICHARD HOFSTADTER, *The Age of Reform: From Bryan to F.D.R.* (New York 1955).

CHRISTOPHER LASCH, *The New Radicalism in America, 1899–1963* (New York 1965).

MAX LERNER, *America as a Civilization: Life and Thought in the United States Today* (New York 1957).

JAY MARTIN, *Harvests of Change: American Literature 1865–1914* (Englewood Cliffs, N.J. 1967).

HENRY F. MAY, *The End of American Innocence: 1912–1917* (New York 1959).

FRANCIS NEWTON, *The Jazz Scene* (London 1959).

SONIA RAIZISS, *La poesie américaine 'moderniste', 1910–1940* (Paris 1948).

BARBARA ROSE, *American Art Since 1900: A Critical History* (London 1967).

ARTHUR M. SCHLESINGER, *The Rise of Modern America: 1865–1951* (New York 1951).

GORDON O. TAYLOR, *The Passages of Thought: Psychological Representation in the American Novel, 1820–1900* (New York 1969).

WILLARD THORP, *American Writing in the Twentieth Century* (Cambridge, Mass. 1960).

CAROLINE F. WARE, *Greenwich Village, 1920–1930* (New York 1935).

RAY B. WEST, *The Short Story in America, 1900–1950* (Chicago 1952).

EDMUND WILSON, *American Earthquake: A Documentary of the Twenties and Thirties* (New York 1958).

— *The Shores of Light: A Literary Chronicle of the Twenties and Thirties* (New York 1952).

MORTON D. ZABEL (ed.), *Literary Opinion in America* (revised edition) (2 vols.) (New York 1951).

Bibliography

4. THE MOVEMENTS OF MODERNISM

There are various useful series on movements, in English, French, German, etc. The most useful English series is the 'Critical Idiom' series, titles from which are listed below; this series is emphatically literary, where others are often concerned with the fine arts.

The Transition from Naturalism

ERIC AUERBACH, *Mimesis: The Representation of Reality in Western Literature* (Princeton 1953).

H. BAHR, *Die Überwindung des Naturalismus* (Berlin 1891, reprinted Stuttgart 1968).

GEORGE M. BECKER (ed.), *Documents of Modern Literary Realism* (Princeton, N.J. 1963).

CHARLES BEUCHAT, *Histoire du naturalisme français* (2 vols.) (Paris 1949).

HASKELL M. BLOCK, *Naturalistic Triptych: The Fictive and the Real in Zola, Mann, and Dreiser* (New York, 1970).

FERDINAND BRUNETIÈRE, *Le Roman naturaliste* (Paris 1896).

PIERRE COGNY, *Le Naturalisme* (Paris 1963).

LILIAN R. FURST and PETER SKRINE, *Naturalism* (London 1971).

RICHARD HAMANN and JOST HERMAND, *Naturalismus* (Berlin 1959).

S. HOEFERT, *Das Drama des Naturalismus* (Stuttgart 1968).

W. LINDEN (ed.), *Naturalismus* (Leipzig 1936).

GEORG LUKÁCS, *Studies in European Realism* (London 1950).

— *Probleme des Realismus* (Berlin 1955).

P. MARTINO, *Le Naturalisme français* (Paris 1969).

ERICH RUPRECHT (ed.), *Literarische Manifeste des Naturalismus, 1880-92* (Stuttgart 1962).

G. B. SHAW, *The Quintessence of Ibsenism* (London 1922).

AUGUST STRINDBERG, 'Preface to *Miss Julie*: A Naturalistic Manifesto', in *Plays* (Chicago 1955).

ROLAND STROMBERG (ed.), *Realism, Naturalism and Symbolism: Modes of Thought and Expression in Europe, 1848-1914* (London 1968).

VIKTOR VINOGRADOV, *Evolutsia russkovo naturalisma: Gogol i Dostoevskii* (Leningrad 1929).

CHARLES C. WALCUTT, *American Literary Naturalism: A Divided Stream* (Minneapolis, Minn. 1956).

EMILE ZOLA, *Le Roman expérimental* (Paris 1880).

Symbolism, Impressionism, Decadence

MARIO AMAYA, *Art Nouveau* (London 1966).

ANNA BALAKIAN, *The Symbolist Movement* (New York 1967).

Bibliography

A. BARRÉ, *Le Symbolisme* (Paris 1912).

ANGELO BERTOCCI, *From Symbolism to Baudelaire* (Carbondale, Ill. 1964).

C. M. BOWRA, *The Heritage of Symbolism* (London 1943).

A. E. CARTER, *The Idea of Decadence in French Literature, 1830–1900* (Toronto 1958).

CHARLES CHADWICK, *Symbolism* (London 1971).

JOSEPH CHIARI, *Symbolism from Poe to Mallarmé* (New York and London 1956).

KENNETH CORNELL, *The Symbolist Movement* (New Haven, Conn. 1951).

G. DONCHIN, *The Influence of French Symbolism on Russian Poetry* (The Hague 1959).

EDWARD ENGELBERG, *The Symbolist Poem* (New York 1967).

WILLIAM GAUNT, *The Aesthetic Adventure* (London 1945).

HARVEY GROSS, *Sound and Form in Modern Poetry* (Ann Arbor 1964).

R. V. JOHNSON, *Aestheticism* (London 1969).

FRANK KERMODE, *Romantic Image* (London 1957).

DOROTHY KNOWLES, *La réaction idéaliste au théâtre* (Paris 1934).

JAMES L. KUGEL, *Techniques of Strangeness in Symbolist Poetry* (New Haven and London 1971).

JAMES R. LAWLER, *The Language of French Symbolism* (Princeton, N.J. 1970).

A. G. LEHMANN, *The Symbolist Aesthetic in France 1885–1895* (Oxford 1950).

SVEN LOEVGREN, *The Genesis of Modernism: Seurat, Gaugin, Van Gogh and French Symbolism of the 1880s* (Bloomington, Ind. and London 1971).

EDWARD LUCIE-SMITH, *Symbolist Art* (London 1972).

STEPHANE MALLARMÉ, *Selected Prose Poems, Essays, and Letters* (Baltimore 1956).

G. MICHAUD, *Message Poétique du Symbolisme* (3 vols.) (Paris 1947).

JOHN MILNER, *Symbolists and Decadents* (London 1971).

RUTH MOSER, *L'Impressionnisme français* (Geneva, 1952).

PHOEBE POOL, *Impressionism* (London 1967).

MARCEL RAYMOND, *De Baudelaire au Surréalisme* (Paris, 1952), translated as *From Baudelaire to Surrealism* (London 1957).

E. RAYNAUD, *La Mêlée symboliste* (3 vols.) (Paris 1918, 1920, 1922).

JOHN REWALD, *Post-Impressionism from Van Gogh to Gaugin* (New York 1956).

ERICH RUPRECHT and DIETER BÄNSCH, *Literarische Manifeste der Jahrhundertwende 1890–1910* (Stuttgart 1970).

Bibliography

KONRAD SWART, *The Sense of Decadence in 19th Century France* (The Hague 1964).

ARTHUR SYMONS, *The Symbolist Movement in Literature* (London 1899).

RENÉ TAUPIN, *L'Influence du Symbolisme français sur la poésie Americaine* (Paris 1929).

RUTH Z. TEMPLE, *The Critic's Alchemy: A Study of the Introduction of French Symbolism into England* (New York 1953).

PAUL VALÉRY, *The Art of Poetry* (Bollingen Series, Volume VII) (New York 1958).

EMILE VERHAEREN, *Sensations* (Paris, 1927).

JAMES D. WEST, *Russian Symbolism* (London 1970).

PHILIP WHEELWRIGHT, *The Burning Fountain: A Study in the Language of Symbolism* (Bloomington, Ind. 1968).

Fauvism, Cubism, Post-Impressionism

GUILLAUME APOLLINAIRE, *Les peintres cubistes* (Paris 1913), translated as *The Cubist Painters* (New York 1944).

ALFRED H. BARR, JR., *Cubism and Abstract Art* (New York 1936).

GEORGES DUTHUIT, *Les Fauves* (Geneva 1949), translated as *The Fauvist Painters* (New York 1950).

CHRISTOPHER GRAY, *Cubist Aesthetic Theories* (Baltimore 1961).

A. HASKELL, *Ballet Russe: The Age of Diaghilev* (London 1968).

GEORGE LEMAITRE, *From Cubism to Surrealism in French Literature* (Cambridge, Mass. 1941).

WILHELM WORRINGER, *Abstraktion und Einfühlung* (Munich 1908), translated as *Abstraction and Empathy* (London 1953).

Imagism and Vorticism

STANLEY K. COFFMAN, *Imagism: A Chapter in the History of Modern Poetry* (Norman, Okla. 1951).

J. B. HARMER, *Victory in Limbo: Imagism 1907–1917* (London 1975).

GLENN HUGHES, *Imagism and the Imagists: A Study in Modern Poetry* (Stanford 1931).

PETER JONES (ed.), *Imagist Poetry* (Harmondsworth 1972).

HUGH KENNER, *The Pound Era* (London 1972).

AMY LOWELL, *Tendencies in Modern American Poetry* (Boston and New York 1917).

EZRA POUND (ed.), *Des Imagistes* (London and New York 1914).

ROBERT H. ROSS, *The Georgian Revolt: 1910–1922* (Carbondale Ill. 1965).

A. KINGSLEY WEATHERHEAD, *The Edge of the Image* (Seattle 1967).

WILLIAM C. WEES, *Vorticism and the English Avant-Garde* (Manchester 1972).

Bibliography

Futurism

UMBRIO APOLLONIO (ed.), *Futurist Manifestos* (London 1973).

CHRISTA BAUMGARTN (ed.), *Geschichte des Futurismus* (Hamburg 1966).

PAR BERGMAN, *Modernolatria et Simultaneità* (Uppsala 1962).

F. CECCHINI and G. GABELLI (eds.), *Italia nuova: pagine di trent'anni di storia contemporanea, 1918–1948* (Rocca San Casciano 1962).

D. CHYZHEVSKYI, *Anfänge des Russischen Futurismus* (Wiesbaden 1963).

R. T. CLOUGH, *Futurism: The Story of a Modern Art Movement* (New York 1961).

M. D. GAMBILLO and T. FIORI (eds.), *Archivi del Futurismo* (Rome 1958).

MICHAEL KIRBY, *Futurist Performance: With Manifestos and Playscripts* (New York 1971).

L. DE MARIA, (ed.), *Opere di F. T. Marinetti* (Verona 1968).

V. MARKOV, *Russian Futurism: A History* (London 1968).

MARIANNE W. MARTIN, *Futurist Art and Theory, 1909–1915* (Oxford 1968).

LEON ROBEL (ed.), *Manifestes Futuristes Russes* (Paris 1971).

JANE RYE, *Futurism* (London 1972).

JOSHUA C. TAYLOR, *Futurism* (New York 1961).

MARIO VERDONE, *Cinema e Letteratura del Futurismo* (Rome 1968).

— *Teatro Italiano d'avanguardia: drammi e sintesi futuriste* (Rome 1970).

Expressionism

A. ARNOLD, *Die Literatur des Expressionismus* (Stuttgart 1966).

C. E. DAHLSTROM, *Strindberg's Dramatic Expressionism* (New York 1965).

WOLF-DIETER DUBE, *The Expressionists* (London 1972).

C. EDSCHMID, *Frühe Manifeste: Epochen des Expressionismus* (Darmstadt 1960).

LOTTE E. EISNER, *The Haunted Screen: Expressionism in the German Cinema* (London 1969).

PAUL FECHTER, *Der Expressionismus* (Munich 1920).

H. FRIEDMANN and O. MANN (eds.), *Expressionismus: Gestalten Einer Literarischen Bewegung* (Heidelberg 1956).

MICHAEL HAMBURGER and CHRISTOPHER MIDDLETON (eds.), *Modern German Poetry, 1910–1960* (London 1962).

RICHARD HUELSENBECK, *En avant Dada* (Hanover, 1920).

E. VON KAHLER, *Untergang und Übergang* (Munich 1920).

ALFRED R. MEYER, *Das Maer von der Musa Expressionistica* (Dusseldorf 1948).

BERNARD S. MYERS, *Expressionism: A Generation in Revolt* (London 1963).

— *The German Expressionists* (New York 1957).

Bibliography

W. PAULSEN, *Expressionismus und Aktivismus* (Leipzig 1935).

P. PORTNER (ed.), *Literatur-Revolution, 1910–1925: Dokumente* (Neuwied-am-Rhein 1961).

P. RAABE (ed.), *Expressionismus: Der Kampf um eine literarische Bewegung* (Munich 1965).

PAUL RAABE and KARL LUDWIG SCHNEIDER, *Expressionismus* (Freiburg 1965).

M. RAGA, *L'Expressionisme* (Lausanne 1966).

W. ROTHE, *Expressionismus als Literatur* (Bern 1969).

W. ROTHE (ed.), *Der Aktivismus, 1915–20* (Munich 1969).

G. RUHLE, *Theater für die Republik, 1917–1933* (Frankfurt 1967).

R. SAMUEL and R. HINTON THOMAS, *Expressionism in German Life, Literature and the Theatre* (Cambridge 1939).

WALTER H. SOKEL, *The Writer in Extremis: Expressionism in 20th Century German Literature* (Stanford 1959).

CARL STERNHEIM, *Die Deutsche Revolution* (Berlin 1919).

ULRICH WEISSTEIN ed.), *Expressionism as an International Literary Phenomenon* (Paris and Budapest 1973).

FRANK WHITFORD, *Expressionism* (London 1970).

JOHN WILLETT, *Expressionism* (London 1970).

Dada and Surrealism

FERDINAND ALQUIÉ (ed.), *Entretiens sur le Surréalisme* (Paris 1968).

— *Philosophy of Surrealism* (Ann Arbor 1965).

ANON, *Cinquant' Anni a Dada, Dada in Italia, 1961–1966* (Milan 1966).

ANNA BALAKIAN, *The Literary Origins of Surrealism* (London 1947).

— *Surrealism* (New York 1959).

ALFRED H. BARR, JR., *Fantastic Art, Dada, Surrealism* (New York 1936).

ROBERT BENAYOUN, *Erotique du surréalisme* (Paris 1965).

C. W. E. BIGSBY, *Dada and Surrealism* (London 1972).

ANDRÉ BRETON, *Manifestes du surréalisme* (Paris 1924, 1930, 1942, 1962), translated as *Manifestoes of Surrealism* (Ann Arbor 1969).

ROGER CARDINAL and ROBERT SHORT, *Surrealism: Permanent Revelation* (London 1970).

MICHEL CARROUGES, *André Breton et les donnés fondamentales du surréalisme* (Paris 1967).

MARY ANN CAWS, *The Poetry of Dada and Surrealism* (Princeton, N. J. 1970).

WALLACE FOWLIE, *Age of Surrealism* (London 1957).

HERBERT S. GERSHMAN, *A Bibliography of the Surrealist Revolution in France* (Ann Arbor 1969).

GEORGES HUGNET, *L'Aventure Dada 1916–22* (Paris 1957).

MARCEL JEAN, *The History of Surrealist Painting* (London 1959).

ADO KYROU, *Le Surréalisme au cinéma* (Paris 1963).

LUCY R. LIPPARD (ed.), *Dadas on Art* (Englewood Cliffs 1971).

— *Surrealists on Art* (Englewood Cliffs 1971).

J. H. MATTHEWS, *An Introduction to Surrealism* (Philadelphia 1965).

— *Surrealism and the Novel* (Ann Arbor 1966).

J. H. MATTHEWS (ed.), *An Anthology of French Surrealist Poetry* (London 1966).

ROBERT MOTHERWELL (ed.), *Dada Poets and Painters: An Anthology* (New York 1951).

MAURICE NADEAU, *Histoire du surréalisme, suivie de Documents surréalistes* (Paris 1964), translated as *History of Surrealism* (London 1968).

PAUL C. RAY, *The Surrealist Movement in England* (Ithaca 1971).

HERBERT READ (ed.), *Surrealism* (London 1936, 1971).

HANS RICHTER, *Dada, Art and Anti-Art* (Cologne 1964, London 1965).

WILLIAM S. RUBIN, *Dada, Surrealism and their Heritage* (New York 1968).

PETER SCHIFFERLI (ed.), *Das war Dada: Dichtungen und Dokumente* (Munich 1963).

TRISTAN TZARA, *Lampisteries: précedées des sept manifestes dada* (Paris 1963).

WILLY VERKAUF (ed.), *Dada: Monograph of a Movement* (New York 1957).

PATRICK WALDBERG, *Surrealism* (London 1965).

5. POETRY

DONALD M. ALLEN (ed.), *The New American Poetry* (New York 1960).

A. ALVAREZ, *The Shaping Spirit* (London 1961).

K. A. BATTERBY, *Rilke and France: A Study in Poetic Development* (London 1966).

S. BERNARD, *Le poème en prose de Baudelaire jusqu'à nos jours* (Paris 1959).

R. P. BLACKMUR, *Form and Value in Modern Poetry* (New York 1952).

— *Language as Gesture: Essays in Poetry* (London 1961).

MAUD BODKIN, *Archetypal Patterns in Poetry* (London 1934).

C. M. BOWRA, *The Creative Experiment* (London 1949).

CLEANTH BROOKS, *Modern Poetry and the Tradition* (Chapel Hill, N.C. 1939).

GERALD F. BRUNS, *Modern Poetry and the Idea of Language: A Critical and Historical Study* (New Haven 1974).

DAVID DAICHES, *Poetry and the Modern World: A Study of Poetry in England, 1900–1939* (Chicago 1940).

DONALD DAVIE, *Articulate Energy* (New York 1958).

Bibliography

L. S. DEMBO, *Conceptions of Reality in Modern American Poetry* (Berkeley 1966).

G. DONCHIN, *The Influence of French Symbolism on Russian Poetry* (The Hague 1959).

ELIZABETH DREW and JOHN SWEENEY, *Directions in Modern Poetry* (New York 1940).

LILLIAN FEDER, *Ancient Myth in Modern Poetry* (Princeton 1972).

G. S. FRASER, *Vision and Rhetoric: Studies in Modern Poetry* (London 1959).

HUGO FRIEDRICH, *The Structure of Modern Poetry: From the Mid-Nineteenth to the Mid-Twentieth Century* (Evanston, Ill., 1974).

ROBERT GRAVES and LAURA RIDING, *A Survey of Modernist Poetry* (London 1927, New York 1969).

MICHAEL HAMBURGER, *The Truth of Poetry: Tensions in Modern Poetry from Baudelaire to the 1960s* (London 1969, New York 1970).

GEOFFREY HARTMAN, *The Unmediated Vision: An Interpretation of Wordsworth, Hopkins, Rilke, and Valery* (New York 1966).

J. F. HEATH-STUBBS and DAVID WRIGHT (eds.), *The Faber Book of Twentieth Century Verse* (London 1853).

ERICH HELLER, *The Hazard of Modern Poetry* (Cambridge 1953).

J. ISAACS, *The Background of Modern Poetry* (London 1951).

FRANK KERMODE, *Romantic Image* (London 1957, New York 1958).

W. KILLY, *Elemente der Lyrik* (Munich 1972).

F. R. LEAVIS, *New Bearings in English Poetry* (London 1932).

AMY LOWELL, *Tendencies in Modern American Poetry* (Boston and New York 1917).

EDWARD LUCIE-SMITH (ed.), *Primer of Experimental Poetry: 1870–1922* (London 1971).

LOUIS MACNIECE, *Modern Poetry: A Personal Essay* (Oxford 1938).

OLEG MASLENIKOV, *The Frenzied Poets: Andrey Biely and the Russian Symbolists* (Berkeley 1952).

D. J. MOSSOP, *Pure Poetry: Studies in French Poetic Theory and Practice, 1746–1945* (Oxford 1971).

WILLIAM VAN O'CONNOR, *Sense and Sensibility in Modern Poetry* (Chicago 1956).

OCTAVIO PAZ, *Children of the Mire: Modern Poetry from Romanticism to the Avant-Garde* (Cambridge, Mass. 1974).

EZRA POUND, *Literary Essays* (London 1954).

HERBERT READ, *Form in Modern Poetry* (London 1957).

— *The True Voice of Feeling* (London 1968).

JAMES REEVES (ed.), *Georgian Poetry* (London 1962).

JEAN-PIERRE RICHARD, *Onze études sur la poésie moderne* (Paris 1964).

D. S. SAVAGE, *The Personal Principle: Studies in Modern Poetry* (London 1944).

JAMES SCULLEY (ed.), *Modern Poets on Modern Poetry* (London 1966).

PRISCILLA W. SHAW, *Rilke, Valéry and Yeats: The Domain of the Self* (New Brunswick 1964).

MONROE K. SPEARS, *Dionysus and the City: Modernism in Twentieth Century Poetry* (New York and London 1970).

YVOR WINTERS, *On Modern Poets* (New York 1959).

6. THE NOVEL

WALTER ALLEN, *Tradition and Dream: The English and American Novel from the Twenties* (London 1964).

HELMUT ARNTZEN, *Der moderne deutsche Roman: Voraussetzungen, Strukturen, Gehalte* (Heidelberg 1962).

JOSEPH WARREN BEACH, *The Twentieth Century Novel: Studies in Technique* (New York 1932).

MORRIS BEJA, *Epiphany in the Modern Novel* (London 1971).

MAURICE BOUCHER, *Le roman allemand (1914–1933) et la crise de l'esprit* (Paris 1961).

MALCOLM BRADBURY, *Possibilities: Essays on the State of the Novel* (London 1973).

GERMAINE BREE and MARGARET O. GUITON, *Age of Fiction: The French Novel from Gide to Camus* (New Brunswick 1957).

J. G. BRENNAN, *Three Philosophical Novelists: James Joyce, André Gide, Thomas Mann* (New York 1964).

VICTOR H. BROMBERT, *The Intellectual Hero: Studies in the French Novel, 1880–1955* (London 1962).

JOHN CRUICKSHANK (ed.), *The Novelist as Philosopher: Studies in French Fiction, 1935–1960* (London 1962).

DAVID DAICHES, *The Novel and the Modern World* (revised edition) (Cambridge 1960).

LEON EDEL, *The Psychological Novel: 1900–1950* (London 1961).

EDWARD ENGLEBERG, *The Unknown Distance: From Consciousness to Conscience, Goethe to Camus* (Cambridge, Mass. 1972).

SHERMAN H. EOFF, *The Modern Spanish Novel* (New York 1961).

DOMINIQUE FERNANDEZ, *Le roman italien et la crise de la conscience moderne* (Paris 1958).

RALPH FREEDMAN, *The Lyrical Novel: Studies in Hermann Hesse, André Gide, and Virginia Woolf* (Princeton 1963).

ALAN J. FRIEDMAN, *The Turn of the Novel* (New York and London 1966).

MELVIN J. FRIEDMAN, *Stream of Consciousness: A Study in Literary Method* (London 1955).

MELVIN J. FRIEDMAN and JOHN B. VICKERY (eds.), *The Shaken Realist: Essays in Modern Literature* (Baton Rouge, La. 1970).

WILLIAM C. FRIERSON, *The English Novel in Transition: 1885–1940* (Norman, Okla. 1942).

ROLF GEISSLER (ed.), *Möglichkeiten des modernen deutschen Romans* (Frankfurt-am-Main 1962).

RENÉ GIRARD, *Deceit, Desire and the Novel* (Baltimore, 1965).

JOHN HALPERIN (ed.), *The Theory of the Novel: New Essays* (New York 1974).

J. E. HARDY, *Man in the Modern Novel* (Seattle and London 1964).

W. J. HARVEY, *Character and the Novel* (London 1965).

FREDERICK J. HOFFMAN, *The Modern Novel in America: 1900–1950* (Chicago 1951).

IRVING HOWE, *Politics and the Novel* (London 1961).

ROBERT HUMPHREY, *Stream of Consciousness in the Modern Novel* (Berkeley 1954).

HENRY JAMES, *The Art of the Novel* (edited by R. P. Blackmur) (New York 1934).

GABRIEL JOSIPOVICI, *The World and the Book: A Study of Modern Fiction* (London 1971).

F. R. KARL and M. MALAGANER, *A Reader's Guide to Great Twentieth Century English Novels* (London 1959).

WOLFGANG KAYSER, *Das Groteske: Seine Gestaltung in Malerei und Dictung* (Oldenburg 1957), translated as *The Grotesque in Art and Literature* (Bloomington, Ind. 1963).

MURRAY KRIEGER, *The Tragic Vision: Variations on a Theme in Literary Interpretation* (New York 1960).

RENÉ LALOU, *Le roman français depuis 1900* (Paris 1960).

F. R. LEAVIS, *The Great Tradition* (London 1948).

R. W. B. LEWIS, *The Picaresque Saint: Representative Figures in Contemporary Fiction* (Philadelphia 1959, London 1960).

A. WALTON LITZ (ed.), *Modern American Fiction: Essays in Criticism* (New York and London 1963).

DAVID LODGE, *Language of Fiction* (London 1966).

PERCY LUBBOCK, *The Craft of Fiction* (London 1921).

CLAUDE-EDMONDE MAGNY, *L'Age du Roman Américain* (Paris 1948).

A. A. MENDILOW, *Time and the Novel* (London 1952).

HANS MEYERHOFF, *Time in Literature* (Berkeley 1955).

HERBERT J. MULLER, *Modern Fiction: A Study of Values* (New York and London 1937).

WILLIAM VAN O'CONNOR (ed.), *Forms of Modern Fiction* (Bloomington, Ind. 1948).

DONAT O'DONNELL (Conor Cruise O'Brien), *Maria Cross: Imaginative Patterns in a Group of Modern Catholic Writers* (London 1954).

SEAN O'FAOLAIN, *The Vanishing Hero: Studies in the Novelists of the Twenties* (London 1956).

ROY PASCAL, *The German Novel* (Manchester 1965).

HENRI PEYRE, *The Contemporary French Novel* (New York 1955).

GILBERT PHELPS, *The Russian Novel in English Fiction* (London 1956).

PHILIP RAHV, *Literature and the Sixth Sense* (London 1970).

NATALIE SARRAUTE, *L'ère du soupçon: Essais sur le roman* (Paris 1956), translated as *The Age of Suspicion* (New York 1963).

MARK SCHORER (ed.), *Modern British Fiction* (New York and London 1961)

PHILIP STEVICK (ed.), *The Theory of the Novel* (New York 1967).

PATRICK SWINDEN, *Unofficial Selves: Character in the Novel from Dickens to the Present Day* (London 1973).

MARTIN TURNELL, *The Novel in France* (London 1951).

KARL D. UITTI, *The Concept of Self in the Symbolist Novel* (The Hague 1961).

STEPHEN ULLMAN, *Style in the French Novel* (New York 1957).

H. M. WAIDSON, *The Modern German Novel* (London 1959).

PAUL WEST, *The Modern Novel* (London 1963).

RAY B. WEST and R. W. STALLMAN, *The Art of Modern Fiction* (New York 1949).

JOHN J. WHITE, *Mythology in the Modern Novel: A Study of Prefigurative Techniques* (Princeton N.J. 1971).

RAYMOND WILLIAMS, *The English Novel from Dickens to Lawrence* (London 1970).

MORTON D. ZABEL, *Craft and Character: Texts, Method, and Vocation in Modern Fiction* (New York and London 1957).

7. DRAMA

HERMANN BAHR, *Wiener Theater, 1892–98* (Berlin 1899).

ERIC BENTLEY, *The Playwright as Thinker* (New York 1946).

— *The Modern Theatre* (London 1948).

— *In Search of Theatre* (New York 1952).

GÖSTA BERGMAN, *The Breakthrough of the Modern Theatre 1870–1925* (London 1973).

TRAVIS BOGARD and WILLIAM OLIVER (eds.), *Modern Drama: Essays in Criticism* (New York 1965).

M. BRADSHAW (ed.), *Soviet Theatres: 1917–1941* (New York 1954).

ROBERT BRUSTEIN, *The Theatre of Revolt* (New York 1964).

HUNTLEY CARTER, *The New Spirit in the European Theatre: 1914–1924* (London 1925).

— *The New Spirit in the Russian Theatre: 1917–1928* (London 1929).

J. CHIARI, *The Contemporary French Theatre* (London 1958).

— *Landmarks of Contemporary Drama* (London 1965).

RICHARD N. COE et al., *Aspects of Drama and the Theatre* (Sydney 1965).

M. CORVIN, *Le théâtre nouveau en France* (Paris 1963).

E. GORDON CRAIG, *On the Art of the Theatre* (London 1929).

B. DIEBOLD, *Anarchie im Drama* (Frankfurt 1921).

DENIS DONOGHUE, *The Third Voice: Modern British and American Verse Drama* (Princeton 1958).

UNA ELLIS-FERMOR, *The Frontiers of Drama* (London 1945).

MARTIN ESSLIN, *The Theatre of the Absurd* (London 1962).

— *Reflections: Essays on Modern Theatre* (New York 1971).

PAUL FECHTER, *Das europäische Drama* (Mannheim 1957).

FRANCIS FERGUSSON, *The Idea of a Theater* (Princeton 1949).

H. F. GARTEN, *Modern German Drama* (London 1959).

RONALD GASKELL, *Drama and Reality: The European Theatre since Ibsen* (London 1972).

D. I. GROSSVOGEL, *Twentieth Century French Drama* (New York 1961).

J. GUICHARNAUD, *Modern French Theatre* (Yale 1961).

ANDRÉ VAN GYSEGHEM, *Theatre in Soviet Russia* (London 1943).

PHYLLIS HARTNOLL (ed.), *The Oxford Companion to the Theatre* (London 1951).

WOLFGANG KAYSER, *Das sprachliche Kunstwerk* (Bern 1948).

A. KERR, *Die Welt im Drama* (5 vols.) (Berlin 1917).

VOLKER KLOTZ, *Offene und Geschlossene Form im Drama* (Munich 1960).

JOSEPH WOOD KRUTCH, *Modernism in Modern Drama: A Definition and an Estimate* (Cornell 1967).

R. LALOU, *Le Théâtre en France depuis 1900* (Paris 1961).

M. LAMM, *Modern Drama* (London 1952).

ALLARDYCE NICOLL, *The Theory of Drama* (London 1931).

— *World Drama from Aeschylus to Anouilh* (London 1949).

JOHN OSBORNE, *The Naturalist Drama in Germany* (Manchester 1971).

RONALD PEACOCK, *The Art of Drama* (London 1957).

ROBERT PETSCH, *Wesen und Formen des Dramas* (Halle 1945).

L. PIRANDELLO, *L'Umorismo* (Florence 1920).

G. SERREAU, *Histoire du 'nouveau théâtre'* (Paris 1966).

C. STANISLAVSKY, *Stanislavsky on the Art of the Stage* (London 1950).

PETER SZONDI, *Theorie des modernen Dramas* (Frankfurt-am-Main 1959).

RAYMOND WILLIAMS, *Drama from Ibsen to Brecht* (London 1969).

— *Modern Tragedy* (London 1966).

Index

This Index includes all references to people – authors, critics, artists etc. – and their works. It does not include places, movements or groups (for which the Contents list should provide an adequate guide) or references to the Chronology of Events. Page references in **bold type** indicate Brief Biographies.

Aaron's Rod (Lawrence), 33

Abel, Lionel, 505

'Above the Dock' (Hulme), 234

Abstraction and Empathy (Worringer), 63

Action Française, 166, 176, 234, 240

Adamov, Arthur, 509, 520

Adams, Henry, 51, 160

Adler, Friedrich, 129

Aiken, Conrad, 458

Akhmatova, Anna, 476

Aktion, Die (German magazine), 204, 275, 281–5, 387–8

Alain-Fournier (Henri-Alban Fournier), 65

À la recherche du temps perdu (*Remembrance of Things Past*) (Proust), 401–5, 453, 493

'A l'Automobile de Course' (Marinetti), 244, 260

Albee, Edward, 520

Albérès, R. M., 460

Aldington, Richard, 186, 229–30, 232–3, 236

A l'Échelle humaine (Blum), 169

Alexis, Paul, 43

Allen, Charles, 204

Altenberg, Peter, 125

Alvarez, A., 32, 46

Ambassadors, The (James), 185, 396

Amédée (Ionesco), 509

America (Kafka), 132

America's Coming of Age (Brooks), 157

Anatol (Schnitzler), 127, 521

Anderson, Margaret, 153

Anderson, Sherwood, 153–4, 159

Andrian-Werburg, Leopold von, 125

Anna Christie (O'Neill), 33

Anna Karenina (Tolstoy), 430

Annenkov, Yurii, 478

Anouilh, Jean, 569

Anti-tradition futuriste, L' (*Futurist Anti-tradition*) (Apollinaire), 237, 249

Antoine, André, 499

Antonioni, Michelangelo, 328

Apollinaire, Guillaume, 29, 65, 162–3, 165, 167–71, 176, 237, 243, 249, 298, 304, 549–50, 555–6, 561–2, 566, **613**

Appia, Adolphe, 65

Aragon, Louis, 203, 299–301, 304, 307, 555

Archipenko, Alexander, 63

À Rebours (Huysmans), 453–6

Aristotle, 312, 356

Armory Show, 157

Arms and the Man (Shaw), 563

Arnauld, Céline, 300

Arnold, Matthew, 31, 40, 178

Arp, Hans, 63, 286, 295, 297–8, 300, 332, 554, 556

Artaud, Antonin, 305, 510–12, 555

Art of the Commune, The (Russian journal), 267
As I Lay Dying (Faulkner), 459–65
Aspects of the Novel (Forster), 407, 453, 455
Auden, W. H., 101, 317, 319, 340
Auernheimer, Roaul, 125
Au Jardin de l'Infante (Samain), 216
Ausgang der Moderne, Der (Lublinski), 39
Austen, Jane, 20, 453
Aveugles, Les (Maeterlinck), 515
Awkward Age, The (James), 397
Axel's Castle (Wilson), 31, 206

Baader, Johannes, 296
Baal (Brecht), 33, 557
Baargeld, Johannes, 297
Bab, Julius, 117
Babbitt, Irving, 240
Babel, Isaac, 468, 479
Bach, J. S., 405, 410
Bahr, Hermann, 39, 43, 122, 125, **613**
Bajazzo, Der (Mann), 121, 426
Ball, Hugo, 286, 294–6, 298, 300, 332, 554, 556
Balla, Giacomo, 231, 245, 251, 255–6
Balzac, Honoré de, 99
Bang, Herman Joachim, **613**
Banquet Years: The Arts in France, 1885–1918 (Shattuck), 68, 102
Banville, Theodor de, 315
Barbey d'Aurévilly, Jules, 116, 213, 350, 357
Barlach, Ernst, 546–7, **613**
Baron, Jacques, 305
Barrès, Maurice, 165–6, 234, 304
Barth, John, 394, 412
Barthelme, Donald, 35
Barthes, Roland, 20, 89, 91, 269, 327, 482
Bartok, Bela, 64
Baudelaire, Charles, 30, 31, 36, 68, 97, 99–101, 136, 210–11, 214–18, 313–14, 319–20, 326, 330, 337–44, 353, 357–9, 454, 456–7, 464, 508

Bauhaus, Das, 63–4, 146, 279, 558
Baumgardt, David, 282
Beardsley, Aubrey, 185, 531
Beaujour, Michel, 308
Becher, Johannes, 288, 389–90
Beckett, Samuel, 34–5, 101, 412–13, 489, 506–7, 511, 520, 554, 559, 569
Becque, Henri, 499
Beerbohm, Max, 185
Beer-Hoffmann, Richard, 125
Behind the Scenes of the Soul (Evreinov), 553
Behrens, Peter, 64
Beiträge zur Analyse der Empfindungen (Mach), 129
Bellmer, Hans, 303, 307
Bellow, Saul, 458
Bely, Andrei, *see* Biely, Andrei
Benn, Gottfried, 86–7, 320, 326, 383–5, 390, **614**
Bennett, Arnold, 173, 175, 178, 484
Benois, Alexander, 146–7
Bentley, Eric, 499
Berdyaev, N. A., 140–41, 143, 146
Berg, Alban, 64, 124
Berg, Leo, 39, 109, 113
Bergman, Ingmar, 512
Bergson, Henri, 82, 176, 187, 228, 235–6, 431, **614**
Berlin Alexanderplatz (Döblin), 100, 458
Berlin: das Ende einer Zeit in Dramen (Holz), 105, 118
Bernheim, Hippolyte, 156
Bertrand, Aloysius, 351, 353
Bettler, Der (Sorge), 538
Biely, Andrei, 99–100, 468–76, 479, **614**
Bierbaum, Otto Julius, 106
Bilanz der Moderne, Die (Lublinski), 39, 78
Billroth, Theodor, 120
Birthday Party, The (Pinter), 508
Bjørnson, Bjørnstjerne, 42, 108–9, 115–16, 515
Blackmur, R. P., 45

Blacks, The (Genet), 511

Blake, William, 32, 175, 319, 341, 347, 565

Blass, Ernst, 282

Blast, 65, 187, 203, 237, 249

Blaue Reiter group, 63, 157, 284

Blavatsky, Mme, 565

Blendung, Die (Canetti), 91, 100

Blok, Alexander, 144, 149, 317, 552, **614**

Bloom, Harold, 47

Blow-up (Antonioni), 328

Blum, Léon, 169

Boccioni, Umberto, 231, 245, 255–6, 261, 266

Böcklin, Arnold, 116

Bogdanovich, Peter, 512

Bohemian Versus Bourgeois (Graña), 194

Bölsche, Wilhelm, 108–9, 114

Bomberg, David, 238

Bon, Gustav le, 67

Bonnard, Pierre, 549

Borges, Jorges Luis, 34, 35, 394, 412

Bourget, Paul, 43, 71, 77, 116, 196, 418

Bourne, Randolphe, 157

Bousquet, Jöe, 305

Bowra, Maurice, 31, 169

Brahm, Otto, 110–12, 527

Brahms, Johannes, 120

Brancusi, Constantin, 63, 157

Brandes, Georg, 37, 38, 42–3, 79, 116, 201, 500, 527

Braque, Georges, 29, 63, 157, 274

Brecht, Bertolt, 33, 101, 239, 267, 315, 349, 502–3, 510, 531–2, 539, 548, 556–60, 569, **614–15**

Breton, André, 29, 193, 203, 246, 299–304, 306–8, 326, 329, 555, **615**

Bridge, The (Hart Crane), 100, 159, 345–6

Brieux, Eugène, 512

Briggs, Asa, 180

Brik, Osip, 267

Briusov, 468

Broch, Hermann, 124, 126, 129, 131

Brod, Max, 131, 286

Bronnen, Arnolt, 538–9, 542

'Bronze Horseman, The' (Pushkin), 340, 470, 473

Brook, Peter, 511–12, 555

Brooke, Rupert, 180, 388

Brooks, Van Wyck, 157–8

Broom (Paris magazine), 204

Brown, E. K., 453

Browning, Robert, 176, 178

Brücke, Die, group, 63

Bruno, Giordano, 87

Brust, Alfred, 546

Büchner, Georg, 42, 533, 557

Buckle, H. T., 74

Buddenbrooks (Mann), 406, 416–19, 422–8, 431

Bulgakov, Mikhail, 479

Bulgakov, S. N., 139–40, 142

Bunuel, Luis, 304–5

Bürger von Calais, Die (Kaiser), 536, 538, 544

Burlyuk, David, 259, 264

Burnt House, The (Strindberg), 525

Burroughs, William, 35, 488–9

Butler, Samuel, 178

Buzzi, P., 244

Byron, George Gordon, Lord, 144

Cabaret Voltaire (in Zürich), 294–5, 554–5

'Café Griensteidl' (in Vienna), 125–6, 200

Cage, John, 35

Calderón de la Barca, Pedro, 505, 523

Campbell, Joseph, 233

Camus, Albert, 32, 132, 413, 569

Canetti, Elias, 91–2, 100

Cannell, Skipwith, 232–3

Carducci, Giosué, 243

Caretaker, The (Pinter), 508–9

Carli, 250, 252–4

Carrà, Carlo, 231, 245, 255–6, 261

Catullus, 22

Cavacchioli, 244

Caves du Vatican, Les (Gide), 163

Cézanne, Paul, 63–4, 274, 533

Chagall, Marc, 63, 146, 467

Champs Magnétiques, Les (Breton and
    Soupault), 300

Chants de Maldoror, Les
    (Lautréamont), 301, 358

Chapbook, The (Chicago magazine),
    153

Char, René, 305

Charcot, J. M., 77

Chekhov, Anton, 65, 148, 430, 468,
    502–3, 508–9, 514, 518–20, 525,
    530, 532, **615**

Cherry Orchard, The (Chekhov), 430,
    508, 518, 519–20

Chirico, Giorgio de, 63

Chiti, 251, 256

Chopin, Frédéric-François, 117

Chukovsky, Kornei, 474

'City of Dreadful Night, The'
    (Thomson), 343–4

Claudel, Paul, 65, 319, 353, 364, 515,
    615–16

'Cloud in Trousers' (Mayakovsky),
    259, 262, 347

Clough, A. H., 22, 343

Cocteau, Jean, 267, 502, 562, **616**

Coin du Table, Le (Fantin-Latour),
    315

Coleridge, Samuel Taylor, 370

'Comedian as the Letter C, The'
    (Stevens), 159

Comte, Auguste, 74, 501

Condition humaine, La (Malraux), 413,
    459–60, 463–5

'Confession dedaigneuse' (Breton),
    304, 329

Confessions of a Young Man (Moore),
    175

Confessions of Zeno (Svevo), 430,
    433–7, 439, 441–2

Connolly, Cyril, 31, 32, 37, 322

Conrad, Joseph, 22, 29, 41, 65,
    99–100, 172–3, 177, 182, 185,

398–401, 441, 446–7, 453, 456,
    482, 484, **616**

Conrad, M. G., 42, 110

Conradi, Hermann, 38, 109, 115

Coppée, F. E. J., 315

Corbière, Tristan, 100, 176, 549

Corra, Bruno, 250–51, 256, 551

Countess Cathleen, The (Yeats), 563–4

Cournos, John, 232

Cowley, Malcolm, 463

Craft, Robert, 64

Craig, Gordon, 65

Crane, Hart, 46, 100, 151, 156, 158,
    337–8, 345–7

Crane, Stephen, 99, 100, 159, 177, 229

'Crepuscule du Soir' (Baudelaire),
    341

Crevel, René, 301–2, 304–5

Crise de vers (Mallarmé), 207, 209

Criterion, The (London review), 204,
    346

Crownbride (Strindberg), 505, 514,
    523

Cubist Painters, The (Apollinaire), 237

Cummings, E. E., 31, 158–9

Curtius, Ernst Robert, 168

Cusa, Nicholas of, 87

'Cygne, Le' (Baudelaire), 340–42

Dada (magazine), 203

Dali, Salvador, 303, 305, 307

Dance of Death, The (Strindberg), 505

'Dandy, Le' (Baudelaire), 211

D'Annunzio, Gabriele, 243, 515,
    616–17

Dante, Alighieri, 147, 236

Darwin, Charles, 27, 38, 73, 501

Daudet, Alphonse, 42

Dauthendey, Max, 106, 107–8, 117,
    221, 515

Davidson, John, 184, 218, 343–4

Davie, Donald, 228, 240

Davies, W. H., 388

'Dawn Whiteness, The' (Campbell),
    233

Debussy, Claude, 31, 64, 162, 165

De Descriptione Temporum (Lewis), 20

Defence of Poetry (Shelley), 194

Degas, Edgar, 219, 222, 263, 380

Dehmel, Richard, 106, 115, 118, **617**

Dehumanization of Art, The (Ortega y Gasset), 27, 410

Dell, Floyd, 156

Demian (Hesse), 86

Demoiselles d'Avignon, Les (Picasso), 58, 62, 163

Demokrat, Der (German journal), 283

Demos (Gissing), 181

Derain, André, 63

Dermée, Paul, 300

Descartes, René, 144, 169, 380

Descent of Man, The (Darwin), 73

Desnos, Robert, 302, 305, 307

Destruction of Grammar – Wireless Imagination – Free Words (Marinetti), 247–8

Deutscher Werkbund, 64

Devil's Doll, The (Gippius), 138

Diaghilev, Serge, 65, 146, 162, 231, 554

Dial, The (American review), 153, 156, 204

'Dichter greift in die Politik, Der' (Rubiner), 280

Dickens, Charles, 97, 99, 178, 181, 343, 428

Döblin, Alfred, 100, 458

Dobuzhinskii, 146

Doctor Zhivago (Pasternak), 134, 149, 479

Dodge, Mabel, 156

Doktor Faustus (Mann), 406, 425

Doll's House, A (Ibsen), 111, 501, 563

Dominguez, 307

Donne, John, 22, 30, 176, 323

Donoghue, Denis, 159

Doolittle, Hilda, 176–7, 186, 192, 228–9, 232–3, 236

Dos Passos, John, 46, 99–100, 159, 255, 458, **617**

Dostoyevsky, Fedor, 68, 97, 99–100, 109, 128, 131, 136, 140, 265, 340, 468, 470, 473–4, 476

Douglas, Lord Alfred, 218

Douglas, Norman, 186

Dowson, Ernest, 178, 184, 214–16

Drachmann, Holger, 42, 115, 118

Dream Play, A (Strindberg), 85, 505, 509, 514, 523–4

Dreiser, Theodore, 99, 151, 153, 156

Dubliners (Joyce), 424

Duchamp, Marcel, 63, 294, 299

Du Côté de Chez Swann (Proust), 456, 493

Dufy, Raoul, 274

Duhamel, Georges, 211

Dühring, Eugen, 39

Duineser Elegien (Rilke), 33, 87, 205, 319, 323, 327, 331, 335, 364

Dujardin, Edouard, 222, 355, 454–7

Duncan, Isadora, 65

Duras, Marguerite, 512

'Durch' (in Berlin), 38, 105, 109

Durkheim, Emile, 67

Easter, (Strindberg), 505

Echegaray, José, 515

Edschmid, Kasimir, 274–6, 278, **617**

'Effects of Music upon a Company of People' (Pound), 232

Egoist, The (London review), 187, 204, 232, 456

Egyptian Stamp, The (Mandelstam), 476

Ehrenstein, Albert, 284, 286, 387

'Eiffel Tower Restaurant' (in London), 186, 229, 239

Einstein, Albert, 66, 569

Einzige und sein Eigentum, Der (Stirner), 76

Eisenstein, Sergei, 467

Eisler, Hanns, 556

'Elf scharfrichter' (in Munich), 532, 548

Eliade, Mircea, 439

Eliot, George, 178

Eliot, T. S., 26, 29, 31–3, 48, 50, 83, 90–91, 97, 99–100, 140, 154–5, 158–9, 173, 175–77, 184, 186–7, 212, 228–9, 232, 234, 236, 239–40, 254, 270, 313, 315–16, 319–20, 322–4, 326, 330, 337, 339, 342–7, 359, 364–6, 390, 418, 464, 489, 562, 564, 566, **617-18**
'Elis' (Trakl), 362
Ellis, Havelock, 185
Ellmann, Richard, 32–3, 185, 438
Éluard, Paul, 300, 302–4, 307–8
Emerson, Ralph W., 346
Endgame (Beckett), 507, 511, 554
Enemy of the People, An (Ibsen), 111, 501
English Review, The, 185
Enormous Room, The (Cummings), 159
Ensor, James, 63
Epstein, Jacob, 238
Ernst, Max, 297, 303, 306–8, 411
Ernst, Paul, 105, 108–9, 115, **618**
Essai de psychologie contemporaine (Bourget), 196
Essai sur les données immédiates de la conscience (Bergson), 82
Étranger, L' (Camus), 413
Étude sur le zoo-magnetisme (Liébéault), 77
Evreinov, Nikolay Nikolayevich, 553–4, 556
Existence du symbolisme (Valéry), 211
'Exorcism by laughter' (Khlebnikov), 264
'Extraordinary Adventure which befell Vladimir Mayakovsky in a Summer Cottage, An' (Mayakovsky), 266
Extra-Territorial (Steiner), 101

Faber Book of Modern Verse, The (Roberts), 38
fackel, Die (Kraus), 125
Fantasia (Disney), 244, 252
Fantin-Latour, Henri, 315
Father, The (Strindberg), 503, 527

Faulkner, William, 29, 31, 159, 413, 453, 459–65, **618**
'Fauves, Les', painters, 244
Faux-monnayeurs, Les (Gide), 409–10, 434, 437
Fechter, Paul, 275–6
Feidelson, Charles, 32
Fels, Friedrich Michael, 197–8
Fenêtres, Les (Baudelaire), 338
Fergusson, Francis, 562
Fêtes galantes (Verlaine), 213
Fiedler, Leslie, 456, 458
Fifteen Years of Russian Futurism (Kruchonykh), 272
Finnegans Wake (Joyce), 405, 412, 432, 484, 489
Fire Bird, The (Stravinsky), 64
Fischer, Richard, 387
Fitzgerald, F. Scott, 51, 159
Flake, Otto, 275, 385
Flaubert, Gustave, 21, 31, 36, 42, 68, 89, 143, 187, 192, 240, 396, 418, 460
Fletcher, John Gould, 176, 233, 238
Flint, Frank Stewart, 176, 186, 228–33, 239
Florensky, P., 139
Florian Geyer (Hauptmann), 106
Flucht aus der Zeit, Die (Tzara), 295
Fogazzaro, Antonio, 243
Fontane, Theodor, 416, 418–21, 423, 427–8, **618**
Ford, Ford Madox, 154, 174, 177–8, 183, 185–6, 192, 229, 232–3, 482, 484, 516
Form in Gothic (Worringer), 63
Forster, E. M., 49, 178, 185, 407, 443, 451, 453, 455, 458, 463, 482, 484, **618-19**
'For the Marriage of Faustus and Helen' (Crane), 345–6
Four Quartets (Eliot), 319
Fowles, John, 412
France, Anatole, 165
François de champi (Sand), 403
Frank, Joseph, 432
Frank, Leonhard, 286

Index

Frank, Waldo, 157

Fraser, G. S., 22

Frazer, Sir James, 41

Freie Bühne theatre group in Berlin, 111–12, 500, 527

Freie Bühne für das moderne Leben, after 1894 *Neue deutsche Rundschau* (German periodical), 39, 106, 116

Freud, Sigmund, 27, 37, 41, 66–7, 85, 120, 126, 128–9, 154, 269, 317–18, **619**

Freytag, Gustav, 109

Friedensfest, Das (Hauptmann), 528

Frost, Robert, 177, 229

Frühlings Erwachen (Wedekind), 527, 529–31, 534

Fry, Roger, 176, 231

Furbank, P. N., 435

Futurist Aesthetics (Soffici), 250

Futurist Life (film), 251

Futurist Manifesto (Marinetti), 243–6

Futurist Synthetic Theatre (Marinetti, Corra, Settimelli), 250, 551

Gabo, Naum, 63, 146, 556

Gallén, Axel, 116

Gallienne, Richard le, 181, 184, 218

Galsworthy, John, 22, 175, 484

Game of Chess, The (Pound), 236

Garborg, Arne, 43, 115–16

Garnier, Tony, 63

Gaspard de la nuit (Bertrand), 351

Gas trilogy (Kaiser), 544–5

Gaudier-Brzeska, Henri, 187, 237–8

Gauguin, Paul, 20, 533

Gautier, Théophile, 210, 236

Geburt der Tragödie aus dem Geiste der Musik, Die (Nietzsche), 443, 445, 451

Geibel, Emanuel, 109

'Geländer' (Arp), 332

Genet, Jean, 511, 569

Genette, Gerard, 493–4

'Genteel Tradition in American Philosophy, The' (Santayana), 157

Geometric and Mechanical Splendour and Numerical Sensitivity (Marinetti), 248

George, Stefan, 14, 65, 315–17, 320, 383, **619**

Georgian Poetry anthologies (Marsh), 187, 231

Gershman, Herbert S., 301

Gesellschaft, Die (German periodical), 38, 110

Gewaltlosen, Die (Rubiner), 289, 539–42

Ghosts (Ibsen), 110, 499–500, 527

Ghost Sonate, The (Strindberg), 504–5, 525

Ghuttmann, Simon, 282

Giacometti, Alberto, 295, 305

Gide, André, 29, 31–3, 65, 163, 165, 171, 404, 409–10, 428, 437, **619–20**

Ginna, 250–51

Gippius, Zinaida, 137–8

Giraudoux, Jean, 458, 569

Gissing, George, 99, 178, 180–81, 343, 484

Goering, Reinhard, 546

Goethe, Johann Wolfgang von, 32, 87, 131, 321, 418, 504

Gogh, Vincent van, 20, 221, 274, 533

Gogol, N. V., 468, 470, 473, 476

Golden Bowl, The (James), 185

Golden Fleece (Russian journal), 146

Goldoni, Carlo, 523

Goldring, Douglas, 187

Goldsmith, Oliver, 365

Goll, Yvan, 326, 389, 555–6

Goncharov, I. A., 468

Goncharova, Nathalie, 146, 259, 261

Goncourt, Edmond and Jules de, 402

Gorky, Maxim, 148–9, 468, 502

Gourmont, Remy de, 176–7

Grabar', 146

Grabbe, Christian Friedrich, 533, 557

Gracq, Julien, 303

Graña, Cesar, 194

Grand Meaulnes, Les (Alain-
Fournier), 65
Grass, Günther, 394
Graver, Lawrence, 447
Graves, Robert, 31, 366
Gray, Ronald, 451
Great Gatsby, The (Fitzgerald), 159,
431
Grillparzer, Franz, 131
Gris, Juan, 63, 556
'Grodek' (Trakl), 387
Gropius, Walter, 64
Grossen der modernen Literatur, Die
(Dühring), 39
Grosz, Georges, 296, 556
Grotowski, Jerzy, 555
Guérin, Maurice de, 350, 352

Haas, Willy, 130
Hadwiger, Victor, 130
Halbe, Max, 106, 108, 115
Hamsun, Knut, 43, 81, 100, 116,
196, 514, **620**
Handke, Peter, 131
'Hands' (Symons), 214
Hanneles Himmelfahrt
(Hauptmann), 529
Hansson, Ola, 43, 106, 114–17
Happy Days (Beckett), 511
Hardy, Thomas, 174, 178, 185–7,
388
Harland, Henry, 177, 185
Harmsworth, Alfred, 60
Hart, Heinrich, 107–9, 114
Hart, Julius, 101, 107, 109, 113–14,
385
Harte, Bret, 42
Hartley, Marsden, 157
Hartman, Geoffrey, 47
Hartmann, Eduard von, 76
Hasenclever, Walter, 286, 288, 535,
538, 542–3
Hassan, Ihab, 35
Hauptmann, Gerhart, 105, 108–9,
111, 502, 512, 515, 527–8, 531–2,
620–21

Hauser, Arnold, 86–7, 206
Hausmann, Raoul, 296, 334
Haussmann, Baron, 339–40
Heartfield, John, 296, 556
Heart of Darkness (Conrad), 173, 182,
446
Heather (Pound), 236–7
Hebbel, Friedrich, 501
Hedda Gabler (Ibsen), 196, 500–501,
507–8
Hegel, Georg Wilhelm Friedrich,
87–8
Heiberg, Gunnar, 115
Heidegger, Martin, 327, **621**
Heine, Heinrich, 144, 360
Heisenberg, Werner, 27, 84
Heller, Leo, 130
Hemingway, Ernest, 31, 101, 159,
413, 460, 482, 490–91, **621**
Henckell, Karl, 38, 109, 115
Henley, W. E., 218
Hennings, Emmy, 286, 295
'Henrik Ibsen und das
Germanenthum in der modernen
Literatur' (Berg), 113
Henry IV (Pirandello), 567–9
Heraclitus, 87
'Herbsttag' (Rilke), 317
Herder, Johann Gottfried, 131
Hervé, Julien Auguste, 163, 166, 170,
274, 533
Herwig, Franz, 390
Herzfelde, Wieland, 296–7, 556
Herzl, Theodor, 125
Hesse, Hermann, 29, 34, 65, 86,
88–9, 100, **621**
Heym, Georg, 277, 281–2, 286,
383–5, 390, **622**
Heyse, Paul, 107, 109
Hiller, Kurt, 274–5, 277, 279–80,
282–3
Hirsch, Jakob, 389
Hitchcock, Alfred, 512
Hitler, Adolf, 36, 539, 546
Hobson, J. A., 67
Hoddis, Jakob van, 282–3, 383–4

Hoffman, Frederick J., 204
Hoffmann, Camill, 129–30
Hofmannsthal, Hugo von, 49, 71–2,
   83–4, 120, 122, 125–8, 197, 317,
   324–5, 330, 354, 356, 372, 383,
   502–3, 514–15, 521–3, 525, 531,
   622
Hölderlin, Friedrich, 323
Holz, Arno, 38, 105–6, 108–9,
   115–16, 118, 201, 224, 359, **622**
Homage to Sextus Propertius
   (Pound), 154, 159
Homecoming, The (Pinter), 510
Homer, 246, 318
Hoover, Herbert, 180
Hopkins, Gerard Manley, 346
Hose, Die (Sternheim), 543
Hough, Graham, 31, 32, 37, 45, 228
How are Verses Made? (Mayakovsky),
   260, 262, 267
Howe, Irving, 29
Howells, William Dean, 151
How to Read (Pound), 211
Hueffer, Ford Madox, *see* Ford,
   Ford Madox
Huelsenbeck, Richard, 286–8,
   294–6, 298, 300, 556
Hughes, Glenn, 233
Hughes, H. Stuart, 44, 83, 128
Hugh Selwyn Mauberley (Pound),
   100, 159, 172–3, 177, 182, 184, 323,
   330
Hugo, Victor, 350, 550
Hulme, T. E., 176, 178, 185–6,
   188, 228–30, 232–8, 356
Hume, David, 323, 369
Hunger (Hamsun), 100
Hunger-artist (Kafka), 132, 332, 449
Huret, Jules, 43
Huxley, Aldous, 31
Huysmans, J. K., 31, 116, 175,
   453–5, **622**
*Hypnotisme, suggestion, psycho-
   thérapie* (Bernheim), 77

Ibsen, Henrik, 37, 42–4, 46, 68, 80

   108–13, 115–16, 127, 136, 166, 187,
   499–503, 506, 510, 514–15, 518–19,
   521, 527–8, 530, 532, 563, 569, **623**
Illuminations, Les (Rimbaud), 301,
   353
Image, Selwyn, 184
Imagistes, Des, anthology (ed.
   Pound), 230, 232
Im Dickicht der Städte (Brecht), 558
Imperialism (Hobson), 67
'Impressionisten' (Rilke), 223
Impressions and Opinions (Moore),
   175
In Darkest London and the Way Out
   (Booth), 180
Independent Theatre, The (in
   London), 500
In der Strafkolonie (Kafka), 131, 450
Innovations (ed. Bergonzi), 34–5
Intérieur, L' (Maeterlinck), 195, 515
In the American Grain (Williams), 159
'Invitation au voyage, L' '
   (Baudelaire), 357–8
Ionesco, Eugène, 508–11, 520, 554,
   559, 569
Italia Futurista, L' (review), 251–2
Ivanov, Viacheslav, 146

Jackson, Holbrook, 38, 182–3
Jacob, Max, 298
Jacobsen, Jens Peter, 42, 116
Jacob's Room (Woolf), 33
Jakobson, Roman, 268–72, 482–92
James, Henry, 26, 29, 31, 65, 100,
   151, 155, 172–3, 175, 177, 179, 181,
   185–6, 196, 396–7, 401, 411, 428,
   443–4, 451, 453, 456, 482, 484, 502,
   530, 566, **623**
James, William, 196–7
Janco, Marcel, 286, 295, 554
Jarry, Alfred, 299, 549–550, 556, **623**
Jaures, A. M. J. J., 166, 170
Jawlensky, Alexei von, 63
Jedermann (Hofmannsthal), 127
Jensen, Johannes Vilhelm, **623–4**
Jentzsch, Robert, 282

Jessner, Leopold, 557
'Jet d'Eau, Le' (Apollinaire), 170
Jiménez, Juan Ramón, 624
Johnson, Lionel, 184
Johnson, Samuel, 97
Johst, Hanns, 539, 557
Jones, Robert Edmond, 156
Jørgensen, Johannes, 624
Joseph tetralogy (Mann), 406, 424, 426
'Journey to Berlin' (Julius Hart), 101
Joyce, James, 26, 29, 31–4, 44, 65, 83, 86, 97, 101, 159, 175, 178, 187–8, 232–4, 269, 295, 318, 403–7, 409, 424, 432, 437–42, 451, 453–4, 456–60, 467, 469, 482, 484, 489, 492, 494, 502, 624–5
Jude the Obscure (Hardy), 174
Jung, C. G., 318, 322, 625
Jung, Franz, 275
Jünger, Ernst, 625
Jungle, The (Sinclair), 154
'jüngste deutsche Literaturströmung und das Prinzip der Moderne, Die' (Wolff), 38

Kafka, Franz, 29, 32, 65, 120–21, 126, 131, 286, 328, 332, 361, 444, 449–50, 625
Kahn, George, 243
Kahn, Gustave, 246, 354, 359, 363
Kaiser, Georg, 279, 289, 502, 536–8, 543–6, 548, 556, 626
Kamenskii, Vassily, 136, 264
Kandinsky, Wassily, 63, 146, 157, 237, 278, 298, 467, 555–6
Kangaroo (Lawrence), 33
Kant, Immanuel, 123, 420
Karlfeldt, Erik Axel, 626
Kenner, Hugh, 228, 439
Kermesse (Lewis), 231
Kermode, Frank, 26, 32, 34–5, 37, 46, 51, 82, 128, 228, 432
Khlebnikov, Velemir, 259, 264–6, 268–72, 468, 479
Kierkegaard, Sóren, 43, 68, 87–8, 131

Kipling, Rudyard, 152
Kisch, Egon Erwin, 130
Klee, Paul, 48, 63
Kleist, Heinrich von, 131
Klemm, Wilhelm, 387
Klimt, Gustav, 124
Klopstock, F. G., 359
Koffka, Fritz, 282
Koht, Halvdan, 111
Kokoschka, Oskar, 63, 124, 284, 538, 555–6
Komisarshefsky, Fedor, 65
Kondor, Der, anthology (ed. Hiller), 275
Kornfeld, Paul, 130, 286, 547
Kraus, Karl, 37, 121, 125, 626
Kritische Waffengänge, 108–9
Krohg, Christian, 118
Kronegger, M. E., 225
Kruchonikh, 145, 259, 264–6, 268, 272
Kubin, Alfred, 452
Kunst: Ihr Wesen und ihre Gesetze, Die (Holz), 114
Kurtz, Rudolf, 276
Küster, Konrad, 109
Kuzmin, 468

Lacerba (Italian periodical), 248, 250
Lady from the Sea, The (Ibsen), 111
Laforgue, Jules, 176, 184, 211–13, 339, 245, 351, 359, 365, 455, 626
Lagarkvist, Pär, 626
Landmarks (*vekhovtsy* symposium), 141
Lane, John, 184
Langbaum, Robert, 47
Langbehn, Julius, 113
Larionov, Michel, 146, 259
Lasker-Schüler, Else, 279
Lasserre, Pierre, 228
Lauriers sont coupés, Les (Dujardin), 222, 454–6
Lautensack, Heinrich, 548
Lautréamont, Comte de, 31, 301, 351–2, 358

Index

Lawrence, D. H., 31–3, 46, 51, 65, 101, 139, 159, 174, 176, 178, 186–7, 229, 233, 249, 263, 318, 437, 482, 491–2, 494, 530, **626–7**

Lawrence, Frieda, 46, 176

Leavis, F. R., 228

LEF (Russian *Left Front of Art* journal), 272

Léger, Fernand, 63

Legrand, Gérard, 307

Leiris, Michel, 305

Lenin, Nikolai, 61, 147–8, 164, 171, 295, 554

Leonhard, Rudolf, 389

Leppin, Paul, 129

Lermontov, M. Y., 144

Leskov, N. S., 468

Lesson, The (Ionesco), 508

Leutnant Gustl (Schnitzler), 124, 126

Levin, Harry, 33

Lévi-Strauss, Claude, 271

Lewis, C. S., 20

Lewis, Sinclair, 154, 159

Lewis, Wyndham, 65, 175–7, 185, 187–8, 193, 203, 231–2, 236–8, 243, 248–9, **627**

Leybold, Hans, 385–6

Lichtenstein, Alfred, 383–4

Lidforss, Bengt, 118

Liébeault, A. A., 77

Liebelei (Schnitzler), 126, 521

Liebknecht, Karl, 284, 288

Limbour, Georges, 305

Lindau, Paul, 109

Lindeman, Hermann, 388

Lindsay, Vachel, 154–5

Lissitskii, El, 145, 556

Littérature (French magazine), 203, 293, 299–300, 302

Little Review (American magazine), 153, 156, 203

Locke, John, 148

Loewenson, Erwin, 279, 282–3

Lombroso, Cesare, 77

London Nights (Symons), 215

Loos, Adolf, 64, 122

Lorca, Garcia, 29, 315, 318, 326, 330, 390, 503, 562, 564, **627**

Lotz, Ernst Wilhelm, 384–6

Lovejoy, A. O., 23

Lowell, Amy, 228–9, 232–3, 362–3

Lowry, Malcolm, 413

Lublinski, Samuel, 39, 78

Lugné-Poë, A. M., 515

Lukács, Georg, 23, 437

Luxemburg, Rosa, 284, 288

Mach, Ernst, 84, 122, 125, 129, 449

Mackay, John Henry, 76, 109, 115, 118

MacLeish, Archibald, 159

Maeterlinck, Maurice, 43, 166, 195–7, 447, 502–3, 514–18, 520–22, 525, 531, 548, 563, 565, **627–8**

Mafarka le Futuriste (Marinetti), 244–5

Maggie (Crane), 100

Magritte, René, 303

Mahler, Gustav, 142

Mailer, Norman, 414

Maillart, Robert, 63

Main Street (Lewis), 159

Making of the Americans, The (Stein), 486–7, 489

Malevich, Kasimir, 63, 145, 261, 266, 552, 556

Mallarmé, Stéphane, 29, 31, 175–6, 207–10, 212–14, 220, 223–5, 235, 262–3, 315–16, 319–20, 329, 359–60, 371, 454–7, 489, **628**

Malraux, André, 21, 31, 316, 413, 459–60, 463–5

Malte Laurids Brigge (Rilke), 115

Mamelles de Tirésias, Les (Apollinaire), 550, 561

Mandelstam, Osip, 468, 475–9, **628**

Manhattan Transfer (Dos Passos), 100, 458

Mann, Thomas, 26, 29, 32–3, 65, 101, 121, 332, 335, 372, 404, 406–7, 416–19, 422–8, 431, 441, 444, 450–51, **628–9**

Mann ohne Eigenschaften, Der (Musil), 121, 404, 410, 430, 435, 449
Mansfield, Katherine, 177, 187
Marat/Sade (Weiss), 511
Marc, Franz, 63
Marcuse, Herbert, 279
Marholm, Laura, 106
Marienhof, 207
Marinetti, Filippo Tommaso, 176, 193, 203, 231, 243–57, 260, 263, 265–71, 298, 550–52, 555–7, 559, **629**
Maritain, Jacques, 380
Marquet, Albert, 63
Marquis von Keith, Der (Wedekind), 533
Marsh, Edward, 186–7, 231
Marx, Karl, 27, 142, 501
Marxism and the Philosophy of Language (Voloshinov), 269
Masses, The (American magazine), 156
Massnahme, Die (Brecht), 558
Masson, André, 305, 307
Masters, Edgar Lee, 153–4
Mathews, Elkin, 184
Matisse, Henri, 29, 63, 156, 167, 185, 533
Mauclair, Camille, 360
Maugham, W. Somerset, 175, 181
Maulnier, Thierry, 460
Maupassant, Guy de, 453
Maurier, George du, 175
Maurras, Charles, 166–7
Maximus Poems (Olson), 160
Mayakovsky, Vladimir, 100, 145, 259–64, 266–7, 270–72, 337–8, 347, 552, 557, 559, **629**
Mehring, Franz, 556
Meier-Graefe, Julius, 106
Mencken, H. L., 157
Men of the Modern Breakthrough (Brandes), 37
Menschen, Die (Hasenclever), 535, 538
Menschheitsdämmerung (ed. Pinthus), 391

Meredith, George, 38
Merezhkovskii, Dimitri, 137–8, 140, **629**
Mesens, E. L. T., 306
Metamorphosis (Kafka), 131–2, 449
Metaphysical Poets, The (Eliot), 323
Methusalem (Goll), 556
Meurer, Kurt Erich, 288
Meyer, Alfred Richard, 281, 283
Meyerhold, V. E. 553, 557, 559
Meyrink, Gustav, 130
Mies van der Rohe, Ludwig, 64
Mill, John Staurt, 42, 501
Millay, Edna St Vincent, 156
Miller, J. Hillis, 47
Mimesis (Auerbach), 431
Minskii, 137
Miro, Joan, 305, 307
Miss Julie (Strindberg), 47, 80–81, 503, 508, 523, 527
'Modern Art' (Hulme), 238
Moderne Architektur (Wagner), 122
Moderne Dichtercharaktere (ed. Arendt), 38
'Modernisms' (Kermode), 34
Modern Love (Meredith), 38
Modern Movement, The (Connolly) 31
Modern Tradition, The (Ellmann and Feidelson), 22, 32
Modigliani, Amedeo, 63, 555
Moeller, Philip, 156
Moeller van der Bruck, Arthur, 127
Mondrian, Piet, 63
Monet, Claude, 218, 222–4
Monro, Harold, 187, 231
Monroe, Harriet, 154, 230, 232
Montale, Eugenio, 315
Monticelli, A., 219
Moore, George, 101, 175, 177, 214, 220
Moore, G. E. 176
Moore, Marianne, 31, 158, 229, 240
Moréas, Jean, 166, 208
Morgue (Benn), 384
Morisot, Berthe, 222
Morris, William, 182

Morrison, Arthur, 181
Moscow Arts Theatre, 65, 520, 562
Moscow Linguistic Circle, 268, 271
Mrs Dalloway (Woolf), 100, 408, 458
Mumford, Lewis, 157
Munch, Edvard, 63, 115, 118
Murdoch, Iris, 394, 412
Murger, Henri, 194
Murry, John Middleton, 186
Musil, Robert, 29, 120–21, 126, 129, 132, 403, 410, 430, 444, 447–9, 629–30
Musique et les lettres, La (Mallarmé), 210
Mussolini, Benito, 254
Muthesius, Herrmann, 64

Nabokov, Vladimir, 35, 101, 392, 412, 469, 479, 630
Nausée, La (Sartre), 100, 413, 431, 434
Naville, Pierre, 305
Neopathetische Cabarets (in Berlin), 283–4
Neruda, Pablo, 315
Neue Club, Der (in Berlin), 279, 281–2
Neue Gedichte (Rilke), 219–20, 225, 323, 331
Neue Rundschau, Die (German review), 204
Nevinson, C. R. W., 238, 248
New Age, The (English Journal), 185–6
New Critics, The, 271
Newest Russian Poetry, The (Jakobson), 268
New Grub Street (Gissing), 343
News from Nowhere (Morris), 182
Nietzsche, Friedrich, 25, 30, 41–3, 46, 68, 77–9, 107, 115–17, 122, 125, 132, 136, 259, 279, 378, 426, 443–7, 451–2, 501, 504, 533, 630
Nijinsky, Vaslov, 65
Nolde, Emil (Emil Hansen), 63
Nordau, Max, 42

Norris, Frank, 154
Notes from Underground (Dostoyevsky), 100
Notes sur la technique poétique (Duhamel and Vildrac), 212
Nouvelle Revue Française, La, 204
Novalis (Friedrich von Hardenberg), 517
Novyi Lef (*New LEF* Russian journal), 272

Obey, André, 562
Obstfelder, Sigbjrn, 115, 630–31
O'Casey, Sean, 631
Offenbach, Jacques, 187, 474
Of Human Bondage (Maugham), 175
'Of Modern Poetry' (Stevenson), 372
Old Times (Pinter), 508
Olescha, Yury, 468, 479
Olson, Charles, 160, 241
O'Neill, Eugene, 33, 46, 156, 502, 526, 569, 631
'On the Modern Element in Literature' (Arnold), 40
'On the Modern Element in Modern Literature' (Trilling), 40
On the Origin of Species by Means of Natural Selection (Darwin), 73, 178
On the Origins of the Decline of Russian Literature and on New Currents in It (Merezhkovskii), 137
Orage, A. R., 186
Ordeal of Mark Twain, The (Brooks), 158
Origin of Species (Darwin), 73, 178
Ortega y Gasset, J., 26, 27, 28, 83, 263, 396–7, 410
Otten, Karl, 284, 389
Owen, Wilfred, 387–8

Paalen, 307
Palazzeschi, Aldo, 250
Pan (German magazine), 106, 203
Papini, Giovanni, 250
Parade (Cocteau, Picasso, Satie), 267
Pareto, Wilfredo, 67

Parole in Libertà (Marinetti), 246, 265–6

Parry, Albert, 156

Pascoli, Giovanni, 243

Passage to India, A (Forster), 443, 451, 463

Pasternak, Boris, 134, 260, 317, 468, 479, **631–2**

Pater, Walter, 30, 175–6, 215, 237, 370

Paterson (Williams), 100, 159, 160

Pavlova, Anna, 65

Pavolini, 255

Paz, Octavio, 303

Peckham, Morse, 47

Peer Gynt (Ibsen), 499, 501, 528

Péguy, Charles, 165, **632**

People of the Abyss, The (London), 181

Péret, Benjamin, 300, 303–4, 555

Perret, Gustave, 63

Petroushka (Stravinsky), 64

Pevsner, Antoine, 63, 146

Pfemfert, Franz, 280, 283–4, 388

Philosophie des Unbewussten, Die (von Hartmann), 76

Picabia, Francis, 157, 294, 296, 299–300, 302, 304

Picasso, Pablo, 20, 29, 32, 58, 62–3, 157, 163, 165, 167, 238, 267, 274, 555–6

Picture of Dorian Gray, The (Wilde), 175

Pillars of Society (Ibsen), 110, 503

Pilniak, Boris, 468

Pinter, Harold, 507–10, 512, 516, 520

Pinthus, Kurt, 275, 279, 285, 534

Piper, R., and Co. Verlag, 63

Pirandello, Luigi, 29, 502, 509, 561, 564, 566–9, **632**

Piscator, Erwin, 388–9, 557, 559

Pissarro, Camille, 222

Platz (von Unruh), 546

Plays Unpleasant (Shaw), 181

Poe, Edgar Allan, 116, 319–20, 347

Poesia (Italian Journa l),243

'Poet and the City, The' (Auden), 340

Poetry (Chicago magazine), 153–4, 204, 230, 232

Poetry and Grammar (Stein), 487–8

Poetry Bookshop (in London), 187

Poetry of Ezra Pound, The (Kenner), 228

Poetry Review (English Magazine), 187, 231–2

Poggioli, Renato, 193

Pope, Alexander, 97

Portrait of the Artist as a Young Man, A (Joyce), 101, 405, 456

'POST modern ISM' (Hassan), 35

Pound, Ezra, 29, 31–33, 46, 48, 65, 97, 100–101, 154–6, 158–9, 172–4, 176–8, 182, 184–8, 192–3, 204, 211–12, 225, 228–41, 254, 265, 272, 320, 323, 327, 330, 356, 359, 363, 366, 489, 562, **632**

Poupées électriques (Marinetti), 552

Prévert, Jacques, 305

Princess Casamassima, The (James), 100, 172, 181

Princesse Maleine, La (Maeterlinck), 515

Principles of Psychology (James), 197

Principles of Psychology (Spencer), 75

Professor Bernhardi (Schnitzler), 126

Professor Taranne (Adamov), 509

Proust, Marcel, 29, 31–3, 65, 159, 165, 171, 213, 220, 224, 372, 401–4, 406, 428, 431, 433, 451, 453, 455–8, 493–4, **633**

Prozess, Der (Kafka), 131, 430, 450

'Prufrock' (Eliot), 154, 339, 343, 345, 347

Przybyszewski, Stanislaw, 106, 108, 116–18, 196, **633**

Psychology of Crowds (le Bon), 67

Pushkin, A. S., 144, 265, 268, 340, 342, 347, 472–3, 476

Quasimodo, Salvatore, 315

Queneau, Raymond, 305

Racine, Jean, 314, 341
Rahv, Philip, 80
Ravel, Maurice, 64
Read, Herbert, 20, 228
Redon, Odilon, 157
Reed, John, 156
Reflections on Violence (Sorel), 67
Reigen (*La Ronde* in film version)
  (Schnitzler), 124, 521, 530
Reinhardt, Max, 65
Rembrandt als Erzieher (Langbehn),
  113, 115
Remizov, Aleksey, 468
Renan, Ernest, 42
Renoir, Pierre Auguste, 222–4
Rhymers' Club (in London), 184,
  200
Rhymes to be Traded for Bread
  (Lindsay), 154
Rhys, Ernest, 184
Rhythm (English magazine, later the
  Blue Review), 186
Ribemont-Dessaignes, Georges, 300,
  555
Richards, I. A., 268
Richardson, Dorothy, 178, 456, 633
Richepin, Jean, 116
Richter, Hans, 295
Riding, Laura, 366
Right You Are, If You Think So
  (Pirandello), 567–8
Rilke, Rainer Maria, 29, 32–3, 65, 72,
  87, 90, 115, 120, 125, 130, 219, 220,
  223–5, 239, 315–20, 323–4, 329,
  331, 364, 371–2, 374–9, 383, 502,
  524, 633–4
Rimbaud, Arthur, 21, 184, 223–4,
  240, 301, 314–15, 319, 321–2,
  330–31, 353–7, 457, 549
Ripke-Kühn, Leonore, 534
Ripostes (Pound), 230
Robbe-Grillet, Alain, 32, 413
Roberts, Michael, 38
Robinson, Edwin Arlington, 153
Rodchenko, Alexander, 63
Rodenbach, Georges, 197

Rodin, Auguste, 239, 371
Rohe, Ludwig Mies van der, 64
Roi Bombance, Le (Marinetti), 550
Rolland, Romain, 164, 295, 634
Roma Futurista (magazine), 252
Romains, Jules, 230, 232
Roman expérimental, Le (Zola), 30
'Romanticism and Classicism'
  (Hulme), 238
Roman Tsarevich (Gippius), 138
Ronsard, Pierre de, 22
Room, The (Pinter), 510, 516
Rosenberg, Harold, 34–5, 159
Rosenberg, Isaac, 388
Rosmersholm (Ibsen), 111, 501
Ross, Robert, 186
Roth, Henry, 458
Rouault, Georges, 63
Rousseau, Henri, 'le Douanier', 157,
  236
Rousseau, Jean-Jacques, 144, 148,
  342, 549
Rowohlt, Ernst, 285
Rozanov, Vasilii, 138–9, 469
Rubiner, Ludwig, 280, 286, 289, 539,
  542
Rules of the Game, The (Pirandello),
  569
Ruskin, John, 127, 176, 228
Russell, Ken, 512
Russolo, 245, 255–6

Sacre du Printemps (Stravinsky), 64,
  124, 162–3, 165, 167, 265
Sadleir, Michael, 186–7
Sainte-Beuve, Auguste, 350
St Petersburg (Biely), 100, 469–75,
  479
Saison en Enfer (Rimbaud), 319
Salomé (Wilde), 101, 531
Salus, Hugo, 129
Samain, Albert, 216
Sand, George, 403
Sandburg, Carl, 152–4, 229
Sanouillet, Michel, 301
Santayana, George, 80, 157

Sartre, Jean-Paul, 32, 100, 413–14, 431, 433, 505, 569

Saussure, Ferdinand de, 482

Savonarola, 147–8

Savoy (English Magazine), 185

Scheerbart, Paul, 118

Scheffler, Karl, 274

Schelling, Friedrich von, 87

Schickele, René, 286

Schiele, Egon, 124

Schlaf, Johannes, 108–9, 115, 201, 516

Schlenther, Paul, 110–11

Schloss, Das (Kafka), 131, 450

Schnitzler, Arthur, 120, 124–6, 128, 131, 521, 530, **634**

Schoenberg, Arnold, 29, 37, 64, 123, 405, 556

Schopenhauer, Arthur, 122, 132, 427, 445, 501

Schorer, Mark, 401

Schreyer, Lothar, 285

'Schrifttum als geistiger Raum der Nation, Das' (Hofmannsthal), 128

Schulze-Maizier, Friedrich, 281

Schwitters, Kurt, 297–8

Scott, Walter, 20

Scott-James, R. A., 186

Seagull, The (Chekhov), 518–19

Secession (Paris magazine), 204

Secret Agent, The (Conrad), 100, 172, 182, 400

Seeschlacht (Goering), 546

(Sélavy, Rose), 307

Sense of an Ending, The (Kermode), 51, 432, 434

Serner, Walter, 295

Serres Chaudes (Maeterlinck), 197

Sérusier, Paul, 549

Servaes, Franz, 105–6, 111

Settimelli, Emilio, 250–52, 254–6, 551

Severini, Gino, 157, 245, 255

Severyanin, Igor, 267

sexuelle Problem in der modernen Literatur, Das (Berg), 39

Shakespeare, William, 265, 313, 505

Shattuck, Roger, 68, 102

Shaw, George Bernard, 14, 44, 125, 175, 177, 181, 185–6, 501–3, 506, 512, 563, **634–5**

Shelley, Percy Bysshe, 83, 194, 312, 508, 565

Shershenevich, 267

Shkolvsky, Victor, 269, 469, 479, 553

Sibelius, Jean, 116, 515

Sillanpää, Frans Eemil, **635**

Simon, Claude, 412, 414

Simultaneità (Marinetti), 552

Sinclair, May, 456

Sinclair, Upton, 154

Sisley, Alfred, 223

Sister Carrie (Dreiser), 151–2

'Situation der deutschen Dichtung, Die' (Edschmid), 276

Sitwell, Edith, 31

Six Characters in Search of an Author (Pirandello), 567–9

Slap in the Face of Public Taste manifesto (Mayakovsky, Khlebnikov, Kruchonykh, Burlyuk), 259, 264–5

Slodki, Marcel, 295

Smithers, Leonard, 185

Social History of Art, The (Hauser), 206

Social Statics (Spencer), 75

Society for Psychical Research, 75

Socrates, 378, 446

Söderberg, Hjalmar, **635**

Södergran, Edith, **635**

Sodome et Gomorrhe (Proust), 33, 493

Soffici, Ardengo, 250

Sokel, Walter, 450

Sologub, Fedor, 468

Soloviev, V. S., 139–40, 144

Solzhenitsyn, Alexander, 479

Some Imagist Poets, anthologies (ed. Lowell), 233

Sonette an Orpheus, Die (Rilke), 33, 87, 324, 331, 524

Index

Sonnenschein, Hugo, 387

Sons and Lovers (Lawrence), 101

Sontag, Susan, 377

Sorel, Georges, 67, 82, 163, 170, 228

Sorge, Reinhold, 538, 542

Sound and the Fury, The (Faulkner), 159, 461

Soupault, Philippe, 203, 299–301, 305, 555

Soutine, Chaim, 63

Sozialaristokraten, Die (Holz), 105, 118

Spark, Muriel, 394, 412

Spencer, Herbert, 75

Spender, Stephen, 24, 32, 240, 314

Spengler, Oswald, 345, 501

Spenser, Edmund, 22

Spiegelmensch, Der (Werfel), 547

Spielhagen, Friedrich, 109

Spirit of Romance, The (Pound), 158

Spleen de Paris, Le (Baudelaire), 353, 357

Stadler, Ernst, 279, 384–5, **635–6**

Stanislavsky, Konstantin, S., 65, 520

Stechlin, Der (Fontane), 416–17, 419–22

Stein, Gertrude, 23, 34, 65, 102, 154, 156, 162, 482, 486–9, **636**

Steiner, George, 37, 101

'Stella Maris' (Symons), 215

Stendhal (Henri Beyle), 99, 137

Steppenwolf (Hesse), 100

Stern, J. P., 126

Sterne, Laurence, 30

Sternheim, Carl, 326, 543, 546–7

Stevens, Wallace, 25, 29, 151–2, 155, 158–60, 229, 239–40, 371–9, **636**

Stieglitz, Alfred, 156–7

Stifter, Adalbert, 517

Stirner, Max, 76, 116

Storm, The (Strindberg), 525

Strachey, Lytton, 178

Stramm, August, 284–5, 298, 387–8, 390

Strauss, Richard, 127, 523

Stravinsky, Igor, 29, 64, 124, 162, 165, 169, 171, 265, 467

Strindberg, August, 29, 37, 42–4, 47, 49, 65, 79, 81, 88, 103, 116–18, 131, 196, 199, 503–5, 507, 509, 512, 514–15, 519, 523–32, 534, 563, 565, 569, **636**

Strong, Josiah, 98

Structural Anthropology (Lévi-Strauss), 271

Struggle of the Modern, The (Spender), 24

Studien zur Kritik der Moderne (Bahr), 43, 122

Studies on Hysteria (Freud and Breuer), 66, 126

Sturm, Der (German magazine), 204, 276, 281–5

Sturrock. John, 413

suggestion, De la (Bernheim), 77

Supervielle, Jules, **637**

'Surgi de la croupe et du bond' (Mallarmé), 209–10

Svevo, Italo (Ettore Schmitz), 29, 100, 430, 432–8, **637**

Swanwhite (Strindberg), 505, 514, 523

Swedenborg, Emanuel, 504, 565

Symbolist Movement in Literature, The (Symons), 175, 184

Symons, Arthur, 175–6, 178, 184, 213–15, 217, 219, 221, 225, 235

Synge, J. M., 515, 564

Synthetic Philosophy (Spencer), 75

Sypher, Wylie, 195, 199

Taeuber, Sophie, 295

Tagore, Rabindranath, 154, 565

Taine, Hippolyte, 74, 77

Tanguy, Yves, 305, 307

Tarr (Wyndham Lewis), 175

Tatlin, Vladimir, 63, 70, 145

Technical Manifesto of Literature, The (Marinetti), 245–6, 248

Tender Buttons (Stein), 488–9

Tennyson, Alfred Lord, 22

'Ten O'clock' (Whistler), 237

Index

Tertz, Abram (Andrei Siniavsky), 469, 479

Thackeray, William Makepeace, 178

Théâtre de l'Œuvre (in Paris), 515, 549–50, 555

Théâtre Libre (in Paris), 499–500

Théorie de la Littérature (Todorov), 271

Theory of the Avant Garde, The (Poggioli), 193

'Thirty Bob a Week' (Davidson), 343

Thomas, Dylan, 239

Thomas, Edward, 388

Thomson, James, 343–4, 347

Three Sisters (Chekhov) 430, 518, 520

Tieck, Ludwig, 40, 350

Tinguely, Jean, 35

Tocqueville, Alexis de, 142

To Damascus (Strindberg), 85, 88, 505, 507, 523–4, 534

Tod in Venedig, Der (Mann), 407, 426, 451

Toller, Ernst, 289, 542, 546, 558

Tolstoy, Leo, 42, 109, 116, 148, 166, 418, 430, 468, 531

Tomashevsky, Boris, 266

Tonio Kröger (Mann), 404, 426

Tonnies, Ferdinand, 98

Tono-Bungay (Wells), 172–3, 180

Tor und der Tod, Der (Hofmannsthal), 127, 521–2

To the Lighthouse (Woolf), 25, 408, 460, 494–5

Toulouse-Lautrec, Henri de, 156, 549

'Tradition and the Individual Talent' (Eliot), 158

Trakl, Georg, 282, 286, 317, 362, 383, 387, 390, **637**

Traumdeutung, Die (Freud), 67, 85, 126, 128, 317

Trebitsch, Siegfried, 125

Trembling of the Veil, The (Yeats), 184, 549

Trésor des Humbles, Le (Maeterlinck), 514, 517

Trevelyan, G. M., 19

Trilby (du Maurier), 175

Trilling, Lionel, 22, 30, 40–41

Trotsky, Leon, 261–2

Trubetskoi, Sergei, 140

Truffaut, François, 512

Tucholsky, Kurt, 388

Turgenev, I. S., 108–9, 453, 468

Twain, Mark, 158

'Twelve, The' (Blok), 144

'Two Aspects of Language and Two Types of Aphasic Disturbances' (Jakobson), 482

Tzara, Tristan, 164, 193, 203, 286, 294–6, 298–305, 554–5, **637**

'Über das Geistige in der Kunst' (Kandinsky), 63, 237

'Über den dichterischen Expressionismus' (Edschmid), 276

'Über die dichterische deutsche Jugend' (Edschmid), 276

Übermensch in der modernen Literatur, Der (Berg), 39

Ubu Roi (Jarry), 507, 549, 555

Uhl, Frida, 530

Ulrich, Carolyn, 204

Ultra Violett (Dauthendey), 221

Ulysses (Joyce), 26, 33, 50, 87, 124, 184, 203, 205, 403, 405–6, 409, 431–2, 437–42, 454, 456–61, 465, 467, 484–6, 493

Umbra Vitae (Heym), 383, 390

Unamuno, Miguel de, **637–8**

Uncle Vanya (Chekhov), 518

Under Western Eyes (Conrad), 65, 398

Undset, Sigrid, 14

Unger, Erich, 282

Unruh, Fritz von, 289, 546

Upward, Allen, 232

Urmuz (Demetresco), 554

Urteil, Das (Kafka), 131

Urzidil, Johannes, 129

U.S.A. (Dos Passos), 159, 255

Utrillo, Maurice, 63

Vaché, Jacques, 299–300
Valéry, Paul, 29, 31–3, 65, 163, 171,
 175–6, 207, 211–12, 217, 315, 320,
 371–5, 377–8, 380, 457, **638**
Van nu en straks (Dutch magazine),
 203
Variety Theatre, The (Marinetti
 manifesto), 551
Vases Communicants, Les (Breton),
 303
Vatermord (Bronnen), 538–9
Veblen, Thorstein, 67
Verführung, Die (Kornfeld), 547
Verga, Giovanni, 243
Verhaeren, Émile, 219, 243, 347, 364,
 638
Verlaine, Paul, 136, 184–5, 214–19,
 223, 225, 315, 320, 360, 464, 549,
 638
Ver Sacrum (Austrian magazine), 120,
 122, 203
'Verstehen der Kunst, Das' (Walden),
 280
Verwirrungen des Zöglings Törless, Die
 (Musil), 448
Vico, Giambattista, 32
Victory over the Sun (Kruchonykh),
 266–7
'vierge, le vivace et le bel aujourd'hui,
 Le' (Mallarmé), 210
Vie Unanime, La (Romains), 232
Vigeland, Gustav, 115
Vildrac, Charles, 211, 231
Ville Tentaculaire (Verhaeren), 347
Villiers de L'Isle-Adam, P. H., 31,
 455, 565
Villon, François, 22, 30, 549
Virgil, 22
Vitrac, Roger, 305, 555
Vladimir Mayakovsky: A Tragedy
 (Mayakovsky), 266, 552–3
Vlaminck, Maurice de, 63
voix de silence, Les (Malraux), 21
Voloshinov, V. N., 269

'Von der jüngsten Literatur'
 (Flake), 275
Von Morgens bis Mitternachs (Kaiser),
 544
Vonnegut, Kurt, 412
Vor Sonnenaufgang (Hauptmann),
 111, 527
Vuillard, Édouard, 549

Wadsworth, Edward, 238
Wagner, Otto, 122
Wahrmund, Ludwig, 121
Waiting for Godot (Beckett), 430,
 506–7, 511, 566
Walden, Herwarth, 279–80, 284
Wallas, Graham, 67
War and Peace (Tolstoy), 418, 425,
 431
Washington Square (James), 155
Wassermann, Armin, 282
Waste Land, The (Eliot), 33, 46, 89–91,
 100, 124, 158–9, 173, 182, 184, 205,
 320, 324, 326, 330, 337, 339, 341–2,
 345–7
Watteau, (Jean) Antoine, 213
Waves, The (Woolf), 72, 408, 459–63,
 465
Weaver, Harriet Shaw, 188, 232
Weber, Die (Hauptmann), 527
Weber, Max, 67
Webern, Anton von, 64, 124
Wedekin, Frank, 29, 115, 295, 502,
 512, 527–34, 543, 548, 557, 560,
 638–9
Weg ins Freie, Der (Schnitzler), 126
Weill, Kurt, 556
Weiss, Peter, 511, 569
Weisse Fächer, Der (Hofmannsthal),
 522
Weissen Blätter, Die (Swiss periodical),
 286
Wells, H. G., 172–3, 180, 411, 484
Werfel, Franz, 130, 285–6, 288–9,
 417, 547
What Maisie Knew (James),
 443–4

Index

Whistler, James Abbott McNeill, 174, 181, 237

Whitehead, Alfred North, 24

Whitman, Walt, 42, 243, 346, 360

Wild Duck, The (Ibsen), 111, 506, 510

Wilde, Oscar, 101, 174–5, 177, 220–21, 225, 352, 531, **639**

Wilder, Thornton, 569

Wille, Bruno, 108–9, 114, 118

Williams, Raymond, 99

Williams, William Carlos, 46, 100, 155, 158–60, 187, 229, 232–3, 239–41, 364, 458, **639**

Wilson, Angus, 414

Wilson, Edmund, 31, 206, 564

Wine of the Puritans, The (Brooks), 157

Winesburg, Ohio (Anderson), 101, 159

Witkiewicz, Stanislaw Ignacy, 554

Wittgenstein, Ludwig, 37

Wolff, Eugen, 38, 41–2, 109–10

Wolff, Kurt, 275, 285

Wolzogen, Ernst von, 106

Women in Love (Lawrence), 437, 491–2

Woolf, Virginia, 25, 31, 33, 51, 72, 100, 178, 401, 408–9, 451, 453, 456, 458–65, 482, 494, **639**

Wordsworth, William, 32, 323, 338, 350, 517

World of Art (Russian journal), 146

Worringer, Wilhelm, 63, 176, 228, 237, 274

Wyspianski, Stanislaw, 554

Yeats, W. B., 26, 31–3, 49, 65, 128, 154, 160, 173, 175, 177, 184–5, 229, 235, 239, 315–16, 318–19 321, 324, 326, 330–31, 447, 503, 512, 515, 549, 561–6, **640**

Yellow Book (London magazine), 153, 175, 185, 203

Yesenin, Sergey, **640**

Zamyatin, Evgeny, 347, 468–9, 475, 477–9, **640**

Zang Tumb Tumb (Marinetti), 246–8

Zauberberg, Der (Mann), 124, 406–7, 424, 430–31, 451

Zech, Paul, 288

Zeit, Die (Vienna weekly review), 125

Zola, Émile, 30, 42–3, 99, 105, 109–10, 116, 174, 181, 192–3, 220, 243, 418, 453–4, 532

'Zone' (Apollinaire), 163

Zuckmayer, Carl, 284

Zukofsky, Louis, 241

'Zum schwarzen Ferkel' (in Berlin), 44, 117–18, 200

'Zur jüngsten Dichtung' (Pinthus), 275

Zur Kritik der Moderne (Bahr), 39, 43

Zur Psychologie des Individuums (Przybyszewski), 117

Zweig, Stefan, 123, 125

MORE ABOUT PENGUINS
AND PELICANS

Penguinews, which appears every month, contains details of all the new books issued by Penguins as they are published. It is supplemented by the Penguin stocklist, which includes around 5,000 titles.

A specimen copy of *Penguinews* will be sent to you free on request. Please write to Dept EP, Penguin Books Ltd, Harmondsworth, Middlesex, for your copy.

In the U.S.A.: For a complete list of books available from Penguins in the United States write to Dept CS, Penguin Books, 625 Madison Avenue, New York, New York 10022.

In Canada: For a complete list of books available from Penguins in Canada write to Penguin Books Canada Ltd, 2801 John Street, Markham, Ontario L3R 1B4.

In Australia: For a complete list of books available from Penguins in Australia write to the Marketing Department, Penguin Books Australia Ltd, P.O. Box 257, Ringwood, Victoria 3134.

FICTION AND THE READING PUBLIC
Q. D. Leavis

'Mrs Leavis's astringent essay on the use and abuse of the novel as a mode of literary expression does not suffer from any uncertainty of thought or statement . . . my first comment on this admirably urged and scholarly work must be in praise of its passionate sincerity' – *Sunday Times*, 17 April 1932

THE COMMON PURSUIT
F. R. Leavis

' "The common pursuit of true judgement": that is how the critic should see his business and what it should be for him. His perceptions and judgements are his, or they are nothing; but, whether or not he has consciously addressed himself to cooperative labour, they are inevitably collaborative. Collaboration may take the form of disagreement; and one is grateful to the critic whom one has found worth disagreeing with.'

Categorical, uncompromising and deeply committed to his task, the tone is unmistakably Dr Leavis's, the most controversial critic of our time.

PRINT AND THE PEOPLE
Edited by Louis James

This is a unique collection of popular literature published in England between Peterloo and the Great Exhibition. Ranging from 'Varney, the Vampyre' and 'The Frisky Girls of London' to 'Beware of the Pope!' and exhortations to temperance, a large part of the material is reproduced in facsimile to give an even better idea of what the working classes were reading and concerned with. The resulting volume combines the interests of literature, history, printing, the sociology of communications, and the sheer vitality and variety of the life of the people at a time of radical change.